Standards, Principles, and Techniques in Quantity Food Production
Fourth Edition

STANDARDS, PRINCIPLES, AND TECHNIQUES IN

Quantity Food Production

FOURTH EDITION

Lendal H. Kotschevar, Ph.D.

Distinguished Professor
Florida International University
Tamiami Trail
Miami, Florida

 VAN NOSTRAND REINHOLD
_____*New York*

Printed in the United States of America

Designed by AUTOSPEC Design Systems

Van Nostrand Reinhold
115 Fifth Avenue
New York, New York 10003
Chapman and Hall
2-6 Boundary Row
London, SE1 8HN, England

Thomas Nelson Australia
102 Dodds Street
South Melbourne 3205, Victoria, Australia

Nelson Canada
1120 Birchmount Road
Scarborough, Ontario M1K 5G4, Canada

16 15 14 13 12 11 10 9 8 7 6 5 4

Library of Congress Cataloging in Publication Data

Kotschevar, Lendal Henry, 1908–
    Standards, principles, and techniques in quantity
food production.

    Bibliography: p.
    Includes index.
    1. Quantity cookery. I. Title. II. Title: Quantity
food production.
TX820.K585   1988   641.5'7   88-5473
ISBN 0-442-25662-0

Contents

Preface to the Fourth Edition

In its fourth edition, *Standards, Principles, and Techniques in Quantity Food Production* still retains its basic emphasis on the *what*, *why*, and *how* of producing good foods in quantity. All chapters have been completely updated and rewritten because quantity food production has changed so much since the third edition. In its fourth edition, *Quantity Food Production* also reflects our further growth in the use of things such as bakery mixes; convenience foods; high speed, automatic computer-operated equipment; more fruits and vegetables and vegetables slightly under-cooked to retain color, flavor, and texture; and salar bars together with a higher interest in health and fitness foods. It also recognizes the need to blend our growing knowledge in the science of food with the culinary art of the chef and the fact that more and more foodservice workers are not just experience-trained, but now couple such training with academically gained knowledge to obtain job competency.

Though we now purchase foods in a highly processed or ready-to-use state as puff paste, ice cream, bakery goods, food bases, instants, pre-cooked meats and entrées, waffles, and a host of others, this book still emphasizes the basics. This is because to know food quality and when an item meets an established standard, one has to know what the food should be. Knowing how a food is prepared and what the result should be are ways to meet desired standards. Experience has shown that acceptance of lesser quality products does not spell success in winning patron approval. Furthermore, much food is still produced from scratch, and many operations that do use new products blend them in with foods produced by conventional methods. In many instances food can only be produced the conventional way. Also, patrons today often prefer more "natural" foods and try to avoid the more highly processed.

The author is deeply grateful for the wide acceptance of *Quantity Food Production* over the past twenty-five years and hopes that the book will continue to be of value as a text to the educational field and as a resource reference to the foodservice industry.

Miami, Florida   LENDAL H. KOTSCHEVAR, PH.D.
January 1988

Preface to the Third Edition

Quantity Food Production has had wide acceptance from its first publication in 1964. In this short period, however, enough changes have occurred to require a third edition. A *completely* revised work has had to be produced.

While this new text still emphasizes the basic production of food from the standpoint of techniques, standards, and principles, it is set now against a backdrop of new systems and a wide variety of new foods coming onto the market. For those who wished a simpler work, technical material is now presented in chapters that can be skipped or kept as desired. New systems and new equipment are explained. Service needs have been emphasized. A chapter on nutrition has been added which, while rudimentary, gives essential information needed to observe good dietary practices in producing food. Safety and sanitation have been updated and the chapter on work simplification rewritten. Because of the increasing emphasis on new systems with new procedures for processing, handling, and preparing foods, a separate chapter has been added covering some of the basic concepts needed to understand the use of heat and energy in these new systems and in the use of these new foods. Many technical tables formerly in the appendix are in this chapter. The book looks forward also to the time when we may be converting to the metric system by including information whereby quantities and measurements from our cumbersome system may be converted to this much more logical one. To give proper updating, new illustrations have been added but many of the old ones have been retained since they so vividly portray essential standards, techniques, or principles. The use of many new foods as they modify food production has been mentioned. Conciseness has been sought and a shorter book with more in it has been the result. The book is not a rudimentary one but is designed to develop competency to enter the foodservice industry at a fairly high level.

The author wishes to thank the many users of this book who took the time to indicate their views and needs for a third edition. He is also thankful for the assistance of the many professional individuals and his students who made this book possible, especially Mr. and Mrs. Jack Ryan, who did so much in editing to give a happy book.

Honolulu, Hawaii   LENDAL H. KOTSCHEVAR, PH.D.
February 1973

Preface to the First and Second Editions

This book is written to state some of the standards, principles, and techniques required to produce food in quantity. It is not a recipe book but one that attempts to give the *what, why,* and *how* behind the use of recipes. It is written for managers and supervisors who must bear the responsibility for food production and for students who must learn how to bear this responsibility. It is intended as a working manual. Management will find the illustrations and explanations helpful not only to itself but also as a training guide for workers. The main emphasis of this book is on standards and how they are achieved. While the young manager close to food production will find this book helpful in his immediate problems of administration, he will find it continually useful as he rises in management responsibilities and becomes less and less involved in the actual production of food, for it should remain a constant source of reference in food production.

The operation of a quantity food kitchen cannot be learned, however, from a book. For this knowledge, the student must work with foods, see actual reactions in large quantity cooking, and learn to use food production equipment by operating it. Menu planning, scheduling of employees, ordering and storing of foods, preparation, service, and the application of management principles must be related to actual conditions. The dynamic flow of food production under the stress of meeting a meal deadline can only be learned when work situations are real and not hypothetical.

As a text, this material should be related to lectures, demonstrations, and actual work experiences. Many of the illustrations found in this book have been duplicated in color on film strips along with recordings which explain the principles and techniques illustrated on the strips. It is hoped that the visual and oral joining of textual materials, along with lectures, demonstrations, and laboratory experiences, will vastly improve learning and interest as well as allow students to study more on their own.

While many people have assisted in the production of this book, special thanks are due to Mr. Michael Palmer, Research Chef of Proctor and Gamble, and Mr. Stan Rosswurm, Field Baker for Pillsbury Company, for their assistance in making many of the illustrations in the chapters on cakes and breads.

This book is dedicated to my students who have inspired and encouraged me to write it.

Seeley Lake, Montana   LENDAL H. KOTSCHEVAR, PH.D.
June 1963

Standards, Principles, and Techniques in Quantity Food Production
Fourth Edition

PART

I

Management in Quantity Food Production

CHAPTER 1

Planning Food Production

Outline

I. The Industry and Its Management
II. The Aim of This Text
III. Understanding Quantity Food Production
IV. Convenience Foods and Food Production
V. Quantity Food Production Methods
VI. Food Production Organizations
VII. Menu Planning
   A. Menu Makeup
   B. Making Menu Selections
   C. Menu Pricing
   D. Menu Analysis
   E. Menu Forecasting
VIII. The Standardized Recipe
IX. Portion Costing
   A. Portion Cost from Purchase Price
   B. Yield Tests
   C. Recipe Costing
X. Recipe Development
   A. Taste Panels
   B. Flavor
   C. Changing Recipe Yields
   D. Using the New Recipe
XI. The Production Department in the Foodservice Organization
XII. The Computer
   A. The Menu
   B. The Recipe
   C. Other Computer Jobs
XIII. Scheduling

Goals

1. To introduce the subject of quantity food production and to present the aims of this text.
2. To indicate how standards, principles, and techniques in quantity food production are used by management, supervisors, and workers.

3. To list various methods of quantity food production used by foodservices and to cover basic personnel organization in quantity food production.
4. To detail basic points in menu planning and to relate these to quantity food production.
5. To discuss the standardized recipe, portion costing, and recipe development.
6. To show how the quantity food production department relates to other departments in a foodservice organization.
7. To summarize computer applications in quantity food production.
8. To point out how scheduling for quantity food production is managed.

THE INDUSTRY AND ITS MANAGEMENT

The foodservice industry is the United States' fifth largest industry, registering over $200 billion a year in sales and contributing 6 percent of the country's gross national product. For a number of years after World War II, the foodservice industry grew at the rate of 9 to 11 percent per year; although the rate of increase has since slowed, the annual growth is still appreciable. The foodservice industry is also the nation's biggest employer, comprising about 700,000 units of such diverse kinds as restaurants, drive-ins, hotels, nurseries, hospitals, clubs, and railroads.

Such a massive industry needs highly competent management that is well-versed in handling the many facets of operation. Foodservice produces, merchandises, and serves, and managerial competence is needed in all three areas. Foodservice is a people-oriented business, and the success of an enterprise often depends on how well management directs and leads people. Workers and staff must be selected not only for their professional competence, but for their ability to blend into a unified operation that reaches its goals. Management that lacks organizational and staffing ability can cause failure. Merchandising ability is essential in both commercial and noncommercial operations. Hospitals, schools, and other institutions find they no longer have built-in systems that guarantee patrons, and so must "merchandise" to get them. With even small units doing over $1 million a year in sales, competence in financing is needed. Menu planning must be a practiced art in which selling is achieved, patrons are satisfied, and costs and other factors are controlled. Expertise is also essential in purchasing, labor scheduling, forecasting, preparation, and service. Good management adequately balances all these areas so that the operation does not founder in the sea of necessary activities.

At one time managers gained their competence through experience—learning on the job and often rising through the ranks from pot washer to boss. That the industry was successful and grew as it did attests to the value of such management training, but today's more sophisticated competition, larger businesses, increasingly complex technology, and more dynamic situations call for management professionals who have been educated for managing. Schools now teach management, finance, accounting, computer applications, and food production. Graduates of these programs continue to emerge and are beginning to influence the industry. Middle-management and supervisory personnel are also coming from training programs; workers likewise now receive formal training to augment the traditional method of learning on the job.

THE AIM OF THIS TEXT

This text covers a single (but extremely important) facet of competence in foodservice operation: food production. It seeks to teach not by means of recipe and actual practice—although these are very important adjuncts to complete learning—but by stating the standards, principles, and techniques required in quantity food production. It also covers such essentials of planning as estimating quantities, establishing purchase requirements, planning menus, using recipes, and controlling quantities and qualities. Sanitation, nutrition, work methods, and equipment are discussed, as well.

Chemistry, physics, and some other sciences are best learned when the more academic information is coupled with actual laboratory experience. Food production is no different. Besides learning about standards, principles, and techniques, students need the opportunity to participate in practical laboratory experiences that demonstrate the academic concepts. Reinforcement by audiovisual means is desirable, too. Bringing the textual material into view by example induces *real* learning: the evidence is there. To understand how a quantity food kitchen operates, the student should work in quantity production, see actual reactions, and operate real equipment. Tasks of menu planning, scheduling, food ordering, storage, preparation, service, and applying management principles must be related to actual conditions. The dynamic flow of food production under the stress of meeting a meal deadline is only learned when work situations are real and not hypothetical.

UNDERSTANDING QUANTITY FOOD PRODUCTION

Before getting further into our subject, perhaps we should try to define the term *quantity food production*. Some say it signifies the preparation of twenty-five or more orders—but a single broiled steak or an order of scrambled eggs can be an instance of it. Others say it refers to any effort to supply food to people who are away from home—but this would then include Thanksgiving dinner at grandma's or serving guests in our homes. When we speak of *quantity food production*, we think of an organization of professional workers using special equipment and facilities to produce food for the consumption of others. This organization is quite complex and requires specialized knowledge such as menu planning, merchandising, and selling. Therefore, quantity food production is perhaps more distinguished by the organization and mode of operation that attend it than by any other factor.

To understand food production, we need to know what is to be produced (standard), what knowledge we must apply to get the desired result (principle), and how to go about doing it (technique). Historically, much learning in our field was done by doing, but this involved only partial learning. If something went wrong, the person producing the item did not know why or how to correct it. If the result was a broken egg custard, what was the cause—too much heat? too much liquid? inadequate preparation? poor material quality? Knowing the principle often gives an immediate answer. For example, evidence of a hard, rubbery curd separated out in a liquid indicates that heat was the problem; to correct the problem, techniques might have to be varied or ingredients changed. Knowledge of the standard is also desirable. We need to know the quality of product needed to produce the correct product. Without knowing the standard, we might be satisfied with a broken custard that is relatively hard to eat and has an eggy flavor. Poor standards often yield poor food and dissatisfied patrons. Ignorance of the appropriate standard leaves us shooting in the dark at a target not seen. While we can learn by using only a recipe, we learn better by knowing the *what, why,* and *how* behind the recipe.

Management, supervisors, and workers make different use of their knowledge of standards, principles, and techniques. Management is interested mainly in standards. When patrons are not satisfied, it needs to know enough about standards to understand the basis for patron comments and criticisms. Management must establish the standard and must know when it is met and when it is not. When a standard is not met, management needs to know enough about principles and techniques to discuss the problem with supervisors and workers and come up with solutions. If management is not knowledgeable in these three areas, it loses control over the production section and relegates itself to front-of-the-house management only.

Supervisors act as liaisons between workers and management and must interpret management's desires to workers. Thus, they must have an accurate knowledge of standards in order to indicate to workers what is wanted and when it is achieved. Mastery of principles and techniques is important because supervisors need to know when workers have done something right and when they have done it incorrectly. When problems arise, the supervisor must know the proper principles and techniques to use to obtain a desirable solution. Correcting a curdled soup involves knowing what principle or technique was violated. Supervisors must instruct workers on what is to be done and how it is to be done. They are resource people whom workers rely upon to know the correct standard, principle, or technique.

Workers need to know the principles and techniques required to produce the right standard. *Fold* and *stir* are two quite different techniques. If a recipe says fold and the worker stirs, the product may fail. Principles must be known so as to produce the right techniques. While in a sense workers simply do, they must know why, what, and how they are to do in order to perform adequately.

Thus, to have adequate food production, *all* personnel must know *what* is wanted, *how* to get it, and *what* to do to get it—which translates into a knowledge of standards, principles, and techniques.

CONVENIENCE FOODS AND FOOD PRODUCTION

Some people think that our need to know food production has considerably lessened because so much food is purchased in a ready-to-serve state. This is not true. Many operations still do a lot of basic food production, using only a small amount of what we call convenience food. And even in operations where large amounts of these foods are purchased, we need to know quantity food production in order to evaluate them for quality and price. It could easily be that more, not less, knowledge is needed when such foods are used. Their handling, serving, and merchandising often are based on how we use foods from scratch. Without special treatment, many convenience foods would become the same thing others serve. To make them different, we should know how to turn them into products with the mark of the operation—and we have to know what the convenience food consists of before we can make it into an original. Many convenience foods require some intermediate treatment because they are not entirely ready for use. Cake mixes, for example, need mixing, panning, and baking. Only the beginning steps are eliminated; the rest must follow.

It is extremely important that standards be known. Otherwise, our standards may gradually adapt to a lower and inferior product because we get used to it. People can drink a poor instant coffee for so long that, when good coffee is served, they do not like it because their taste for coffee has shifted to the other product. Convenience foods have their place, but a sound knowledge of quantity food production puts them in their proper niche and enhances their value to an operation.

QUANTITY FOOD PRODUCTION METHODS

The usual method of quantity food production is to purchase items fairly close to their natural state, without benefit of much processing, and turn these into servable menu items. Many years ago this meant keeping a herd of cattle for milk, cream, and butter or raising grain for flour or growing grapes for wine. Gradually we have reduced the amount of preparation that occurs on the premises, letting much of it be done elsewhere.

There is no prominent line of demarcation between normal and convenience foods. A convenience food is one close to its servable state, allowing the labor that would normally be required to bring it to this state to be used elsewhere. What is a convenience food in one era becomes a natural product later. Milk, flour, and wine are to us natural foods, but in the form we use them they were once considered convenience foods. No one thinks of ice cream as a convenience product, but it was once. Some time ago, prepared frozen potato strips were called a convenience food; today they are like ice cream—a normal product. Within living memory, first canned foods and then frozen foods have undergone this metamorphosis. Some foodservice operations strongly affirm that they make all products from scratch, and yet if we were to walk through their kitchen spaces we would likely see many items that qualify as convenience foods.

Convenience foods make it possible to operate a foodservice without a kitchen. Ready-to-serve food is received, plated, and then rewarmed at the service area in a microwave. Machines exist that hold plated foods refrigerated and at a preset time turn into heating units, leaving the food ready to serve at a specified time. Product quality and variety, however, limit the use of foods in this manner.

The cook-chill method of production has many advocates. Foods are prepared in large batches, and then packaged while still hot (to reduce microorganism contamination) and stored under refrigeration. Shelf-life can be up to 60 days for such products. The method has the labor-saving benefits of separating the tasks food production and service and of allowing large batch preparation, which provides substantially greater yields for marginally higher preparation and cleanup efforts. Many cooked foods handle well this way. The cook-chill method enables them to retain a fresher flavor, reduces preparation time, and is less expensive than cooking and freezing. Both methods require strong moisture- and vapor-proof wraps from which all air is removed when the product is sealed inside. Items preserved in some liquid or sauce (especially frozen items) have better quality than those bagged dry.

At one time, considerable food production seemed likely to take the form of central commissary manufacture, in which foods are prepared in a servable or near-servable state so that a minimum of labor is needed. Advantages in cost and standardization could also be realized: small independent kitchens need not have been built; mass production reduced per-unit labor; and greater standardization was possible. But problems in product quality, the fact that savings were not as great as had been thought, and dangers of food poisoning and food deterioration have dampened the original enthusiasm. As a result, many large commissaries have closed or had their production curtailed. Today the trend is toward leaving more of the final part of food preparation to the satellite operation, with the central commissary doing the basic work. Such commissaries also act as transfer points for many goods received from wholesalers and others.

FOOD PRODUCTION ORGANIZATIONS

While the personnel organization of a food production operation varies with need and with operation type, simple structures are preferable. Location of the foodservice department in the overall organization is also important. If it is too far down the chain of command, the department functions less effectively than it does when placed near the top.

The foodservice may be managed by the owner, a food and beverage manager, a manager, a dietitian, or some other person. A chef, supervisor, or food production manager is usually in direct charge of production. Supervisors and workers complete the staff. Figures 1-1, 1-2, 1-3, and 1-4 show some of these organizations.

The classical (continental) staff has a *Chef de cuisine* (executive chef) in charge, a *sous chef* (under chef) under the executive chef, and department heads (*chefs des parties*) in charge of various sections, such as a *chef de saucier* (head of sauces) and a *chef de rôtisseur* (head of roasting). Assistant cooks (*commis*) work under them. An *aboyeur* (announcer) calls orders to the cooks, reducing confusion in the kitchen and ensuring that the right section gets the order. A checker checks orders, prices them, and sees that the proper foods go out as ordered on the check. In some cases, the checker acts as cashier also. A chef steward purchases food and supplies, oversees storage spaces, laundry, china, and silverware, and may work with the executive chef in menu planning. Working chefs manage but

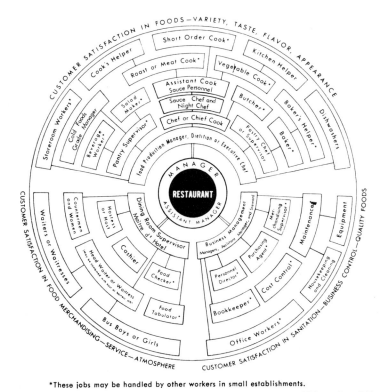

*These jobs may be handled by other workers in small establishments.

Figure 1-1. General schematic drawing of restaurant organization. Although a different organization is required for each kind of foodservice operation, this chart from the National Restaurant Association is applicable to many different ones.

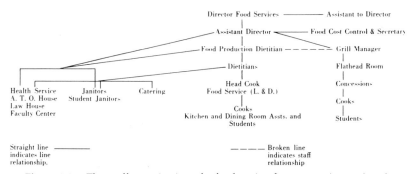

Figure 1-2. The staff organization of a foodservice department in a university.

also participate in cooking—an arrangement that often meets the needs of small organizations.

Food production managers may act in place of chefs. Head cooks are in charge of specific food sections, where they supervise assistants and workers. Small kitchens may be run by a single head cook, with assistants in charge of different sections.

In many hotels and other operations, a food and beverage manager is in charge of the foodservice department. This person may be assisted by a chef, with a typical or nontypical organization of cooks, assistants, and workers. Sometimes a catering manager is retained to handle special

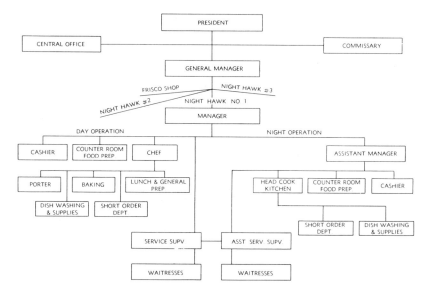

THE NIGHT HAWK

Figure 1-3. Organization of the Night Hawk restaurants of Austin, Texas. Notice that this is a chain group, with only the organization of Night Hawk #1 being shown in detail. (*Courtesy Harry Aiken*)

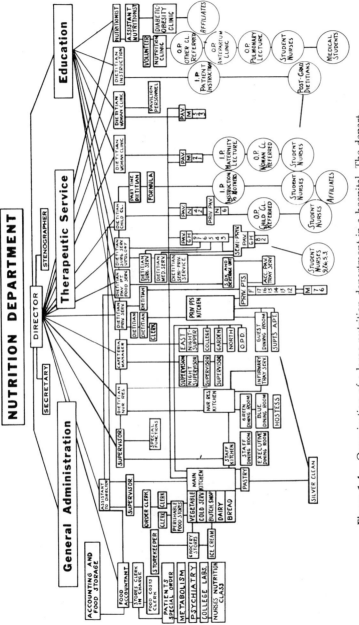

Figure 1-4. Organization of a large nutrition department in a hospital. The department has a general administration section where food production occurs, a therapeutic service where most dietary matters are handled, and an education section where instruction is given.

affairs. Often the food and beverage manager supervises a small accounting unit and even a purchasing department. The food and beverage manager works closely with the sales department because it books all business for the foodservice department.

In many organizations, the foodservice department is a service unit of the overall enterprise, such as the dietary department in a hospital, the foodservice of a hotel, or the foodservice on board ship or at a racetrack. In other situations, it functions as the sole unit, as in the case of a freestanding restaurant. In the first instance, the foodservices work with other departments and often depend on them for services or supplies—receiving materials through the purchasing department, service from the engineering department, laundry from laundry services, and so on. In a freestanding unit, many of these services are performed by the foodservice itself or are obtained from other independent enterprises.

Food preparation is much the same regardless of the kind of organization. A chocolate cake comes from the same balanced recipe that all use, and poached eggs vary little from one organization to another. Standards and principles are essentially constant throughout the industry; any variation can usually be traced to techniques.

MENU PLANNING

The menu authorizes production of meal items, just as a production order in a factory sets in motion a series of planning, procurement, and manufacturing functions that culminate in a finished product. Menus should state what is to be produced; the kitchen staff also need to know when to produce it, how much of it to produce, and what recipe to use. It can also serve as a sort of production schedule if it incorporates additional information (discussed later).

There are numerous kinds of menus. An *à la carte* menu offers items priced singly; a *table d'hôte* menu prices foods together as a unit, often as a meal. A *du jour* menu lists the dishes being offered on that day only. A cycle menu is one that repeats menu items; perhaps it runs for ten days before repeating the whole sequence. A California menu is one that offers various foods, enabling a patron to get breakfast at dinner time or dinner at breakfast time; snacks and other partial meal items are featured. Such a menu is seldom changed except when the whole menu is completely redone for a new period. A limited menu is one that offers a limited number of foods. This is often seen in a drive-in or other operation that serves only a few specialized foods. A common variety of menu is the special menu, such as a chuck wagon breakfast menu where steaks, hotcakes, hash browns, fried eggs, and other foods are featured. A brunch menu presents a breakfast-lunch combination. In some cases it describes an elaborate buffet offering of many foods, including salads and desserts. Champagne brunches are popular on Sundays. Still other special menus, such as a children's menu or an early bird menu, may offer lower prices and perhaps smaller portions to those who eat at nonpeak patronage times. A catering or sales department keeps many different menus on hand for special occasions such as wedding breakfasts, wedding dinners, cocktail receptions, banquets, and speaker luncheons. The person planning such a menu must know a lot about the kind of food and beverages needed, as well as about any special arrangements required.

MENU MAKEUP

Menus can take many forms. Hospital menus are usually printed on special colored paper—each color indicating a menu for a certain diet; thus, a menu for diabetic patients or low-calorie meals may be printed on light green paper, while a menu for a low-sodium diet is printed on tan paper. Dinner menus in a fine restaurant may be placed in highly decorated and firm board covers. Others may be cut into special shapes and have special decorations on them. The usual hardpaper backing for the printing, called *tag, bristol,* or *cover stock,* is at least 0.006 inch thick and is used for menus that are handled repeatedly for a period. Typically the backing is covered with plastic to reduce soiling. Menus can also be printed on ordinary paper, but these are used only once or for a single day; sometimes such a paper menu is placed on a tag cover or is used for clip-ons (see fig. 1-5).

The typeface should be clear and sharp—for example, Bodoni or Garamond. Menu items are usually written in 10- or 11-point type, and headings are written in 18-point (there are 72 points per inch). Descriptions of items are usually written in type smaller than 10-point. Italic, script, and other fancy kinds of type are hard to read. For emphasis, bold (heavyprint) type may be used so that the boldfaced words stand out from the regular-weight type.

The following rules are helpful in writing menus:

1. Capitalize all words except articles, prepositions, and descriptive material. Capitalize the first word in descriptions and all proper names.
2. Offer foods in the order in which they are eaten in a meal or course. Group foods logically together.
3. Consider symmetry and form in setting up the menu, utilizing space, print, and other factors to promote rapid comprehension.
4. Give main course or meal items the most prominent placement. Accompaniments, in small print, should follow or be placed directly below items:

   Prospector's Stew with Parsley Dumplings. $4.75
   with selection of salad, roll, and beverage

5. Place prices near items; do not run them far to the left.
6. Do not list condiments, butter, cream, sugar, and so on, unless they are special or unless you wish to remind those in production or service that they are to be served.

DINNER

Served from 5:00 P.M. to 9:00 P.M. ONLY

ENTREES

*All entrees are served with salad, vegetables and potato
or rice and roll and butter.*

FRESH SEAFOOD SPECIALTIES OF THE DAY .... ask waiter

SCAMPI with SHALLOTS and PERNOD 15.25

NEW YORK STEAK...16.95

FILET MIGNON 18.95

BROILED LOBSTER TAIL 19.95

10 OZ. PRIME RIB 14.95

LAMB CURRY 15.95

ROAST CHICKEN 13.95

RACK OF LAMB, (for two) 38.00

BROILED CHICKEN BREAST 11.50
With herbs and mushrooms.

BEVERAGES

FRESH BREWED ICED TEA... 1.00

HOTTLE OF COFFEE, TEA or DECAF. 1.25

DESSERTS

GOURMET CAKES 3.75

ICE CREAM or SHERBET 3.00

CHOCOLATE MOUSSE... 3.25

APPLE PIE.. 3.25

Figure 1-5. One page of an attractive California-type menu. This menu provides lots of space to set items off and uses easy-to-read kinds and sizes of type. (*Courtesy Menu Man*)

7. Use accurate descriptions. Do not use foreign words or phrases or other materials patrons do not understand.
8. Specialties, sandwiches, and other items may be listed in separate groups on the menu.
9. Do not arrange items by order of price.
10. Items stand out when they appear first or last in a column, are placed in a special box, are set out alone in space, or are positioned in the menu center or to the left side. Items management does not want to sell but has to offer can be hidden by being indented among other items.

Recommendation 7 is of considerable importance. Some states and localities have accuracy-in-menu or truth-in-menu regulations, and fines can be imposed in situations where a menu offers an item that is not delivered. Thus, it is illegal to soak pork in milk and offer it as veal, to offer deep-fried fish chunks as deep-fried scallops, to call an item fresh when it was frozen, or to call it home-made when it is not.

A menu's main purpose is to communicate, and care must be taken to make the menu easily comprehensible. Overcrowding is a common transgression. A menu should be about 60 to 65 percent type; the rest should be space setting off the type. Allow margins, rather than running type completely to the edges.

MAKING MENU SELECTIONS

The selection of items for a menu is often constrained by considerations such as suiting items to patron's wants, facility limitations, availability of the item, cost, and even workers' abilities and duties.

Patrons should heavily influence the selection offered, and items must meet patrons' budgets, tastes, and (in some cases) needs. The kind of operation, the meal, and the occasion are often factors underlying what patrons feel they should pay for food. A fastfood operation must have moderate prices, while a deluxe restaurant can have much higher ones; consequently, different items can be served in each. Patrons do not go to a drive-in expecting to order beef Wellington. Different foods must be priced differently: a steak must be priced differently from a hamburger, and if patrons do not want to pay as much as must be charged for a steak, it should not be put on the menu. Patrons expect to pay a different price for breakfast, lunch, or dinner; again, items must be suited to price. The occasion also affects what is offered. A wedding dinner has different selections from an alumni banquet for a football homecoming. In some cases, the patrons' special needs must be met. Hospitals have to limit certain items; elementary schools must meet Type A meal regulations; athletes at a training table need a lot of good, filling food.

The menu planner must also select items that the facility can produce. Equipment must be considered. If there is no broiler, the menu cannot offer broiled items; and if the facility lacks a bakery, the menu cannot easily offer home-made breads and desserts.

Menu planners must watch carefully to see that what is selected as a menu item is available. It is not wise to offer a fresh raspberry shortcake if the market does not normally stock fresh raspberries. Sometimes a menu may place after an item a qualification such as "Maine Lobster (market availability)" or "Melon (in season)." Or, the menu might state, "Each day Chef X selects three of the finest vegetables offered on the market for our patrons. Please ask your server what these are and select the ones you desire." This enables the operation to select daily the best produce on the market.

Cost is always a constraint—not only in cost of the item, but in cost of labor. Menu planners often set up cost lists so that they can limit items within the range that can be paid and still suit menu item pricing.

The ability of workers to produce or serve an item is also a limiting factor. Beef Wellington cannot be offered if no worker is available who can make it. Crêpes Suzette cannot be offered if no waiter is employed who has the finesse to prepare and serve these from the cart (*guéridon*) at the tableside.

Menus should offer a variety of foods that might please patrons. Entrées should be selected from beef, pork, ham, poultry, fish, seafood, and perhaps vegetable or casserole dishes. Soups should be varied among clear broth, heavy clear soups, cream soups, and purees. Other menu offerings should be similarly varied so that patrons will find something they want. Menu planners also take care to achieve variation in color, flavor, form, texture, and temperature. Patrons of different sexes, ages, and ethnic backgrounds often want different foods. Braised pork and sauerkraut might please a Wisconsin person of German background, but not an Orthodox Jewish one. Descriptions of menu items should be simple and should use language that patrons can readily understand.

MENU PRICING

Menus must be priced to cover budgeted costs for the nonprofit operation and costs plus profit for the profit-oriented one. This is done in various ways. Some operations charge what the traffic will bear; if this is done, the price should cover costs and other factors. Others price according to competition: a price may be set and shaded up or down in response to the competition's price. Sometimes tradition sets a price. This occurs when a price becomes so customary that the item has to be priced at this or not sold. For example, the 5¢ cup of coffee was so traditional after World War II that, when the cost of coffee went up (and labor with it), operators had a terrible time in raising the price. Patrons resisted the price rise because they had become so accustomed to paying the nickel price. Some operations have just one price which may or may not reflect all the costs. This happens in Las Vegas where a showroom has one price for a dinner with show; the price may cover costs of food and labor but does not cover the show cost entirely, the difference being made up by the "pit" or gambling area. A dinner dance may offer a menu with selections at one price because the cost of the food is only a small portion of the entire costs, and differences can be absorbed. A doughnut shop may offer all of its doughnuts and coffee at one price, since the cost of one selection differs little from that of any other selection. Some few operations are able to price according to what the market will bear. Thus, the price is set at what the customer will pay for the menu item.

The most common way of pricing is to base menu price on food cost. A desired ratio of material cost of the menu item to menu price is established—say, 38 percent. Then, for example, if the food cost is $1.70, 38 percent is divided into it to arrive at a selling price, which in this case would be $4.50 ($1.70/0.38 = $4.47). Another way of reaching the same result is to convert the material-cost-to-menu-price ratio into a markup factor. Thus, given a cost-to-price ratio of 38 percent, 38 would be divided into 100 to get a markup factor (namely, 100/38 = 2.63). Then this figure is used to multiply the dollar food cost ($1.70 × 2.63 = $4.47). If management wanted a food cost of 40 percent, the factor would be 2.5 (100/40), and this would be used to multiply dollar food cost to give the menu price ($1.70 × 2.5 = $4.25). Pricing on the basis of food cost alone has its limitations, but it has worked well enough to bring success to many foodservices and thus has stood the test of time.

MENU ANALYSIS

Menus can be analyzed in various ways to ascertain their suitability and value. One of the simplest and most common ways is to make a subjective evaluation. A series of characteristics of good menus are identified, and the menu is scored on a scale of, say, 1 to 10 on how well it meets each criterion. Thus, one may ask such questions as, "Does the menu contain enough good gross profit items?" and "Does the menu state clearly and precisely what each menu item is?" Each factor is then scored, and a total score is obtained as a means of assessing the menu.

Another simple method is to make a menu tally to see how many items of each kind are being sold. This may be expressed as a percentage or as a raw count. The percentage approach can be termed a *popularity index*. Thus, if a menu tally or count reveals that 10 items of a particular type are sold, out of 120 items sold in the overall group, the percentage sold is 8.3 percent and the popularity index is 8.3. Sometimes a tally is made of the number of items each server sells; this procedure, called a *productivity report*, is performed more to check how well servers sell than to analyze the menu. Often menu tallies, popularity indexes, and productivity reports are calculated by computer.

A *menu factor analysis* compares the actual popularity index to what management considers the expected index. It is thus a ratio. If the actual index is 8.3 but management expects it to be 12, the menu factor is 0.70 (8.3/12). Menu factor analysis can be extended to compare ratios for dollar sales, for food cost, and for gross profit, widening the range of study of factors that influence a menu's profitability and sales appeal. A factor greater than 1 is desirable; a factor under 1 shows that an item is not doing as well as was expected. The reverse is true for food cost: under 1 is good, and over 1 is not good.

The Hurst method of scoring* is another method of analyzing food cost, gross profit, sales volume, and dollar volume. It allows menu scores to be compared, thus giving information on what some menu changes might contribute to patron appeal or profit. Break-even point analysis can also be used to analyze a menu.

Several matrix methods of menu analysis have been devised. Miller's method finds an average food cost and an average volume in sales for menu items, and then compares individual menu items' performance against the average. Kasavana and Smith's method is called *menu engineering* and follows Miller's method closely, using volume and gross profit as its matrix criteria. The volume average, however, is calculated on a slightly different basis from the one used in Miller's method. Pavesic developed a matrix analysis system that uses an average food cost percentage and a weighted gross profit. In general, these four methods all yield about the same results.

Hayes and Huffman have developed a system for analyzing menus called *goal-value analysis*. It follows to some extent the matrix methods just described, but it develops a much more sophisticated system of analysis.

MENU FORECASTING

After a menu has been planned, a forecast of demand must be made to give production an estimate of how much food is needed. Poor forecasting increases costs, wastes supplies, and leads to poorer-quality food. Carry-over food may not be usable or may work into poorer-quality items that have to be sold at a lower price than the original food goes for.

The time of the forecast is important. Some foodservices, such as those in the army and in elementary schools, make forecasts six months or more in advance so that bids can be let and proper arrangements made to have the food on hand when needed. Hospitals collect menus from patients one day in advance so that they can make up a forecast tally shortly before production. Some restaurants make forecasts two or three days in advance of production. A few operations make no forecasts; they keep enough on hand and keep supplies flowing to meet the demand.

Some operations can anticipate fairly well how many people are to be served. Institutions such as prisons, where the patronage is fixed, know the serving count well in advance. More variation is found in other foodservices, but patterns of patronage do exist that can be used to predict

---

* A complete description of this and the other methods mentioned in the remainder of this section is beyond the scope of this text. See *Kotschevar, L., *Management by Menu*, Chicago: NIFI (1986) for a detailed explanation of menu factor analysis and the Hurst method of scoring. See also Miller, J., *Menu Pricing and Strategy*, 2d ed., New York: Van Nostrand Reinhold (1987); Kasavana, M., and Smith, D., *Menu Engineering*, Okemos, MI: Hospitality Publishers (1982); Pavesic, D., "Prime Numbers: Finding Your Menu's Strengths," *Cornell Quarterly* (Nov. 1985) 25(3):64–69; Hayes, D., and Huffman, L., "Menu Analysis: a Better Way," *Cornell Quarterly* (Nov. 1985) 25(4):71–77.

business fairly accurately. Facilities keep records and can look back to see what patronage was at specific times. Most operations experience a rather rhythmic ebb and flow of patronage. Some dinner houses expect low counts on Monday and Tuesday nights, with a gradual picking up to very busy nights on Friday and Saturday.

Forecasting is most difficult when a foodservice depends on walk-in business. Perhaps there is a rhythmic pattern, but it can be suddenly thrown into disarray when a blizzard hits the area and everyone stays home. Or an event may bring in a much larger crowd than expected, with far more patrons to be served. Where reservations for a guaranteed number are made, knowing how much to prepare is no problem.

Foodservices in Florida know that patronage drops off in the summer, but then a gradual rise begins in October that swells to a climax in the winter months before falling off again as spring comes. Weather conditions can make forecasting difficult. When it is stormy and rainy, a downtown restaurant that depends on office workers who walk in may find itself with a low count. A big convention in a convention hall nearby can signal a patronage rise. During the National Restaurant Convention in Chicago, many operations open their doors even on their normally closed day because they know there will be an unusually high demand for their services.

Special promotions affect patronage. A Kentucky Fried Chicken outlet that offers buckets of fried chicken at a special price can be expected to increase sales by a third or more. Early Bird dinner menus bring in a larger crowd when patronage is usually down.

Long-term trends should be considered in making long-range forecasts. The desire among foodservice patrons for more fruits, vegetables, chicken, and fish, and for fewer fats and other high-calorie or high-cholesterol items should be noted. Many steak and roast beef houses have added other items to their menus to suit these changing tastes. The number of patrons selecting red meats is less today than it was in the past.

Forecasting should tie in with financial planning and general economic conditions. A downturn in the economy may call for a revision of forecasts. If many foodservices had known that the hard winter of 1985–86 was going to reduce business so drastically, many would have been saved financial losses. Birthrates and population trends have meaning. Population shifts also are important. It pays to take note of predictions of reliable economists, of associations such as the National Restaurant Association, and of others.

THE STANDARDIZED RECIPE

A menu authorizes production, while a recipe controls it. No factory makes a product until blueprints, purchase specifications, labor, equipment, materials, and methods are established in detail. These are to a factory what the recipe is to the production department. *A standardized recipe produces a known quantity of food of desired quality* (see figs. 1-6 and 1-7). It increases management control and reduces human failure by standardizing production.

An operation should maintain three files of standardized recipes: a master file, a production supervisor's file, and a file of recipes in production sections of the kitchen. Encasing the recipes in plastic reduces soiling. A device to hold the recipe so that workers do not have to handle it saves time.

The lower the employee's level of skill, the more information a recipe must contain. A standardized recipe usually includes the following data:

1. Name of the food item and its file code
2. Total quantity and number of portions of a specific size obtained
3. Ingredients by weight, measure, and (sometimes) count
4. Procedures and times for combining ingredients
5. Cooking or baking times and temperatures
6. Panning information
7. Cost information
8. Standard of quality expected
9. Total time for producing the recipe

Recipe names should be brief, descriptive, and immediately recognizable. Different-colored cards help identify groups of foods. For example, light green cards may be used for salads, light blue for cakes and cookies, and so on. The total quantities produced should be expressed in terms related to portion size; thus, stating a yield as "26 lb or 192 portions—scale each 18 × 26 in. pan 6½ lb each" ties in with a portioning instruction to "cut each pan 6 × 8 for approximately 3 × 3 in. squares (2 oz each)." State portions in quantities AS (as served) using count, size, weight, volume, or portioning tool used; for example, "Portion: No. 12 scoop rounded." The following guidelines may be helpful in establishing format:

1. Use large print or extra spacing for emphasis or special directions. Do not crowd. Use lines to isolate groups of ingredients that are handled together in procedures.
2. Use 5 × 8-in. or 6 × 8-in. cards.
3. Place the title at top center and the filing or index code at top right.
4. List the portion size below the title on the right-hand side.
5. List the total yield and portions opposite the portion size on the left-hand side.
6. In procedures, state the work to be done in advance first.
7. On the left-hand side, list the ingredients in order of use; on the right-hand side, list procedures for handling the ingredients. Between these, list weights and measures. If a count is used, indicate it beneath these or beside the measure in parentheses. Do not use abbreviations in methods. Number procedures in sequence, arranging them opposite the ingredients used.

WORK SHEET FOR RECIPE STANDARDIZATION

RECIPE FOR (Name of Item)_____WORK ORDER NO._____

TESTED BY_____ DATE_____APPROVED BY_____DATE____ _____

COSTED BY_____DATE_____CHECKED BY_____DATE_____.

PRODUCTION RECIPE PREPARED BY_____DATE_____FIRST SERVED (date)_____ ___

FOOD INGREDIENTS USED	WEIGHT AND/OR MEASURE For (Portions) (number) (Gallons) ( ) (other)	A/P or E/P	PRO-CEDURE No. (See back of this sheet for detailed procedure)	UNIT A/P	COST PER UNIT A/P	COST OF QUANTITY OF INGREDIENT USED IN THIS RECIPE
			TOTAL COST OF FOOD USED			

FOOD PRODUCTION RECAPITULATION

YIELD: Weight and/or Measure____Lbs_ _ __oz,_____(Gallons) PORTIONS: No._____ Size:_____ _
(No.) (Unit)

PANS: No. Counter pans (size:___"x___ "x___") ___Wt/pan___lbs___Oz No. Portions/pan_____ ___

COST: Portion $_____Selling Price/Portion $_____Food Cost Percent (Cost/Portion) _____ ___%
(Selling Price)

LABOR COST RECAPITULATION

OPERATION	TIME (min.)	EMPLOYEE (Class No.)	RATE (Hr.)	LABOR COST
ASSEMBLY OF MATERIALS AND EQUIPMENT REQUIRED				
PRE-PREPARATION OF FOODS (Washing, peeling, cutting, etc.				
FINAL PREPARATION OF FOODS (Mixing, cooking, baking, etc.				
GARNITURE AND/OR PORTIONING				
SERVICE				
DEAD TIME (Watching and waiting)				
TOTAL DIRECT TIME AND LABOR COST		XXXXXXXXXXXX		
OVERHEAD AND MANAGEMENT (%)				
TOTAL LABOR COST OF RECIPE				

LABOR COST/PORTION $_____LABOR COST: PERCENTAGE (Labor Cost/Portion)_____%
(Selling Price)

FOOD PLUS LABOR COSTS/PORTION $_____FOOD PLUS LABOR COSTS: PERCENT_____%

RECIPE REVIEW DATE_____

Figure 1-6. Practical form for recording data in recipe costing or development. (*Courtesy Dr. Jack Welch*)

BECHAMEL SAUCE   O. SAUCES No. 14

INGREDIENTS	WEIGHTS	MEASURES	PORTIONS	METHOD
YIELD: 2 Gallons or 100 Portions				EACH PORTION: 1/4 Cup
Stock, white		1 1/2 gal		1. Cook together 20 minutes. Strain. There should be 4 quarts of liquid.
Onion, sliced	2 oz	1/4 cup		
Carrots, chopped	1/2 lb	1 1/2 cups		
Bay leaves		2 leaves		
Butter, melted	1 lb	2 cups		2. Blend butter and flour. Stir into strained stock.
Flour, sifted	1 lb	4 cups		
Milk, hot		1 gal		3. Add hot milk, salt, and pepper. Stir and cook until thick and blended.
Salt	1/2 oz	1 tbsp		
Pepper		1 tsp		
Pepper, red		few grains		

NOTE: 1. For a yellow sauce, stir the sauce into beaten yolks of 16 eggs.
       2. Serve with meat croquettes.

Figure 1-7. Standardized recipe following the form developed by the author for use in the Navy Recipe Service.

8. An extra blank column can be included for changing weights and measures.
9. Put panning instructions at the recipe bottom. List pan sizes and the quantity of ingredients put into each, state the portioning needed (such as marking crusts), and so on.
10. Put notes or variations on the recipe bottom, numbered when more than one is to be identified.
11. Write abbreviations for weights and measures in the singular, such as 4 qt, 5 oz, except that *cups* can be written out and made plural if more than one is indicated.
12. Do not put periods after abbreviations except inches (in.) and number (No.), capitalizing the latter.
13. Write *t* and *T*, respectively, for *teaspoon* and *tablespoon*.
14. Use "8 to 10 min" or "8 × 10 in."—not "8–10."
15. Write "No. 10 can" or "No. 2 can" instead of "#10" or "#2."
16. For emphasis, capitalize rather than underlining.
17. Put all substitutions for ingredients and consequent changes in notes.
18. Capitalize *AP, EP,* and *AS* as abbreviations for *as purchased, edible portion,* and *as served,* respectively.
19. Use for shell eggs: "Eggs, whole   1 lb   1 pt
                                          (10 eggs)."
20. State quantities of milk in the form in which it is used; if water is used, identify the amount of water required to bring the milk to a proper liquid state. For example:

         Milk, liquid, whole   8 1/4 lb   1 gal
                             or
         Milk, dry, instant nonfat   1 lb   2 1/4 qt
         Water, tap   7 1/2 lb   3 1/2 qt
                             or

Milk, evaporated	$2\frac{3}{4}$ lb	$5\frac{1}{2}$ c
Water, tap	$5\frac{3}{4}$ lb	$11\frac{1}{2}$ c

21. Do not continue a recipe on the back of the card; use a new card. Use bottom space or the reverse side for instructions on garnishing, serving, holding time, storing, and so on, or for a picture of the item.

PORTION COSTING

AP stands for *as purchased; EP* is an abbreviation for *edible portion;* and *AS* is short for *as served*. These symbols are used often in quantity food work. AP would refer to Irish potatoes purchased in a 100-lb bag; EP would refer to the same potatoes pared and ready to cook. AS would characterize the potatoes after cooking. In most portion costing, we are primarily concerned with the AS cost, but at times we may want to know the EP cost (such as the cost of a 10-oz strip steak ready to cook) or even the AP price (which is often what is quoted on the market).

PORTION COST FROM PURCHASE PRICE

It is not difficult to calculate a portion cost for items that are purchased by portion, such as a 7-oz pork chop costing $0.65. The task becomes only a bit more complicated if we purchase a cake for $8 and cut it into sixteen portions. It becomes substantially more complex if we purchase a case of six No. 10 cans of string beans costing $24 (meaning that each can costs $4). Suppose that, after draining the juice, we find that the drained weight of a can is 70 oz. If a 3-oz portion constitutes a standard serving, the can gives twenty-three portions (70 oz/3 oz = 23), and the portion cost is 17.4¢ ($4/23 portions = 17.4¢).

An even more difficult calculation is needed when preparation, cooking, or other losses occur. If fresh string beans cost 64¢ per lb AP, and 12 percent of the beans (by weight) is lost in eliminating ends, strings, and so on, and 6 percent of the remaining weight is lost in cooking, the per-pound cost AS is best computed in two steps:

$$64¢/(100\% - 12\%) = 72.7¢ \text{ (EP cost per lb)}$$

$$72.7¢/(100\% - 6\%) = 77.3¢ \text{ (AS cost per lb)}$$

A 3-oz portion would then cost $77.3¢/16 oz = 4.8¢ per oz × 3 oz (for one portion) = 14.4¢.

In comparing the cost of fresh string beans with canned string beans, we must also take labor costs into consideration. It takes 14 minutes of labor at $5.40 per hour (9¢ per minute) to open a No. 10 can and prepare 70 oz of string beans AS. In contrast, we need 84.5 oz AP of fresh string beans to get 70 oz AS, given a 12 percent preparation loss and a 6 percent cooking loss (70 oz AS/(100% − 12%) = 79.5 oz EP, and 79.5 oz EP/(100% − 6%) = 84.5 oz AP). It takes the same worker 42 minutes to prepare and cook these beans. Hence, the labor cost of preparing and cooking 70 oz AS of fresh string beans is $3.78 (42 min × 9¢ = $3.78), or 5.4¢ per oz ($3.78/70 oz = 5.4¢), or 16.2¢ per 3-oz portion. Adding this to the portion cost of fresh beans (14.4¢) sums to 30.6¢ per 3-oz portion. Canned beans labor cost is 14 min × 9¢ = $1.26, and $1.26/70 oz gives 1.8¢ per oz or 5.4¢ labor cost for a 3-oz portion; this, added to 17.4¢, gives 22.8¢ per 3-oz portion. Thus, fresh string beans cost 7.8¢ more per portion.

YIELD TESTS

Portion cost calculations become most challenging when an operation purchases items AP and various preparation, cooking, and other losses occur before the AS stage is reached. Often a yield test is done to obtain the desired information. This method involves preparing an item from AP to EP or AS and calculating the yield and the values as the test proceeds. Weight and cost figures are compiled. Table 1-1 shows a series of yield tests in which final cost for an 8-oz portion AS is obtained for roast ribs of beef. Starting with a No. 102 forequarter at $1.28 per lb, the final cost is $4.27 AS per lb or $2.14 for an 8-oz serving ($4.27/2). In Test I a No. 103 full rib is obtained, which in Test II yields a 22.8-lb No. 109 oven-ready rib valued at $2.29 per lb; this, when roasted, in Test III yields 16 lb at $4.05 per lb. When portioned, 15.2 lbs of roasted rib are obtained, values at $4.27 per 8-oz serving. Test V is a check on this $2.14 value. It comes out at $2.16 per serving—close enough. Note that to simplify the test, no butchering cost was included, which would be necessary under actual conditions.

RECIPE COSTING

Many portion costs are obtained after costing out the recipe. It is usual in recipe costing to add 2 percent to total ingredient cost to pay for salt, pepper, other seasonings, pan greasing, and so on. We shall take as our example a simple recipe costed out for shrimp Newburg. Ingredient costs are as follows:

Rice, long grain, polished	$0.16/lb
Half and half	1.34/qt
Sherry, dry, cooking	3.00/.750 ml
Shrimp, cooked	6.00/lb
Butter	1.80/lb
Egg yolks	3.00/lb
Cream, heavy, whipping	4.00/qt
Flour, pastry	0.16/lb

The recipe is as follows:

SHRIMP NEWBURG   Portions: 25 portions; ¾ c Newburg over ¾ c rice

Rice	2 lb	6 c	1. Cook rice; blanch and keep warm.
Flour	4 oz	1 c	2. Make a roux of the flour and butter.
Butter	6 oz	¾ c	Add the half and half and cook to

Half and Half	2½ qt	
Sherry	250 ml	1 c
Egg yolks	8 oz	1 c
Shrimp	3 lb	

thicken. Add the sherry. Then take about 2 c of the sauce and blend well with the yolks; add this mixture to the hot sauce, mixing vigorously while adding.

3. Add the shrimp and heat well. Add the heavy cream; heat well but do not boil.

4. Dish up ¾ c rice and cover with ¾ c of shrimp Newburg.

TABLE 1-1. Yield test of beef forequarter to 8-oz portion of roast beef

YIELD TEST I NO. 103 FULL (PRIMAL) RIB (38 LB) FROM NO. 102 FOREQUARTER (200 LB)

	Lb	%	Value/lb	Total value
No. 102 Forequarter	200	100	$1.28*	$256.00
No. 132 Triangle	162	81	$1.18*	$191.16
No. 103 Rib	38	19	$1.71	64.84
	200	100		$256.00

YIELD TEST II NO. 109 OVEN-READY RIB (22.8 LB) FROM NO. 103 FULL RIB (38 LB)

No. 103 Full Rib	38	100	$1.71	$64.84
No. 123 Trimmed Short Ribs	3.3	9	$1.20*	$ 3.96
No. 135 Diced Beef	5.0	13	$1.40*	$ 7.00
No. 109 O-R Rib	22.8	60	$2.29	52.22
Cube steak	0.7	2	$1.80*	1.26
Fat	3.0	8	$0.08*	0.24
Bones	3.3	9	$0.05*	0.16
	38.1	100		$64.84

YIELD TEST III NO. 109 O-R RIB (22.8 LB) TO ROASTED RIB (70% YIELD OR 16 LB)

No. 109 Roasted Rib	16	100	$4.05	$64.84

YIELD TEST IV NO. 109 ROASTED RIB (16 LB) PORTIONED (95% YIELD OR 15.2 LB)

No. 109 Rib portioned	15.2	100	$4.27	$64.84

YIELD TEST V PORTION COST OF NO. 109 RIB (8-OZ AS)

15.2 lb × 16 oz = 243 oz/8-oz portion = 30 portions $64.84/30 portions = 2.16 per portion

* These prices are based on market-quoted prices at the time of the test.

NOTE: The above tests do not include butchering labor, which would have to be done under actual operating conditions.

The total recipe cost is calculated as follows:

Rice	2 lb @ 16¢/lb	$ 0.32
Flour	¼ lb @ 16¢/lb	0.04
Butter	6 oz @ $1.80/lb	0.67
Half and half	2½ qt @ $1.34/qt	3.35
Sherry	250 ml @ $3/750 ml	1.00
Egg yolks	½ lb @ $3/lb	1.50
Shrimp	3 lb @ $6/lb	18.00
Cream, heavy	¼ qt @ $4/qt	1.00
		$25.88
Plus 2% for miscellaneous seasonings		0.52
Total recipe cost		$26.40

$26.40/25 portions = $1.03 per portion

If the desired food cost is 33.3 percent, a portion should sell for about $3.10 ($1.03/.333 = $3.09).

Some foodservice operators use a factor instead of a percentage to calculate selling price. The factor is obtained by dividing desired food cost into 100 percent and using this factor as a multiplier of dollar food cost. For example, by dividing the desired food cost of 33.3 percent into 100 percent, we get a factor of 3, and 3 × $1.03 = $3.09.

RECIPE DEVELOPMENT

Keep a file of new recipe ideas that seem practical and desirable for development and testing. New recipes or revisions of old recipes are always needed. New foods, improved ingredients, and new equipment often necessitate recipe changes. Cost requirements make it desirable to review recipes frequently for update and possible savings. Progress and efficiency are achieved by instituting a good recipe development program. This is as essential to the success of a foodservice as the development of a new model car is to the success of an automobile manufacturer.

Recipe development is a highly specialized task. Careful study of the recipe is needed before testing. Certain well-defined ratios must be maintained among ingredients for successful products; if necessary, adjust these. Visualize the item as it goes through production. Are all procedures and their sequence correct? Can work be simplified? Consider quality factors. A good flavor sense is needed to detect subtle flavors that are true and pleasing. A taster should not only be able to remember flavors during a test but also be able to carry them in memory in order to compare them with other flavors later. A good knowledge of patrons' likes and dislikes is also needed. Too frequently the items produced represent what the chef, manager, or someone else in authority likes but few others do.

Tables 3-3 through 3-11 in chapter 3 contain helpful information on converting and rounding off weights and measures.

After checking the recipe, write it up in the smallest quantity that gives a good estimate of appearance, flavor, texture, yield, and portion size. Then test and evaluate. Be extremely critical. Slight imbalances may seem unimportant, but in a larger quantity they may be critical. Make comments and suggest changes in detail. Retest repeatedly until the product is satisfactory.

TASTE PANELS

Panel tasting is recommended for evaluating item acceptability. Select panel members who possess good food standards, can taste well, and know something about quantity food and its service. Nonsmokers usually have better taste acuity but, if an otherwise desirable judge does not smoke for 2 hours before a test, his or her taste is usually good. Colds, emotional disturbances, fatigue, and other factors may cause a loss of taste, so all panel members may not be expert at every test. Methods for ascertaining such a loss can be found in the literature. Allow members who fail to pass preliminary tests to taste anyway; then eliminate their judgments without informing them that they failed, to enable them to retain their confidence. Use judges of different ages and sexes. Elderly people may retain good taste sense, and this coupled with experience makes them good judges. Use score sheets listing the factors to be judged. In addition to quality factors, judge adequacy of portion and acceptability with patrons (see fig. 1-8). Judge in a quiet room with good natural light or light that is normal for the conditions under which the food is consumed.

Consuming food any time within 2 hours before a test dulls the palate; consequently, 11:30 A.M. and 4:30 P.M. are times when individuals possess best taste acuity. Alcohol dulls the palate. Because flavors are not as prominent in cold foods as in hot ones, the former must be more highly seasoned than the latter. Flavor judgment is not only a matter of sense acuity but also a matter of experience.

FLAVOR

Anyone working with foods needs to be sensitive to flavor, which is composed of taste and odor. Most of our taste sensations come from the tongue, mouth, and throat, the tongue being the main sensory organ. Fragrances or odors from food travel through the back nasal passages and are picked up by our olfactory (smell) senses. We then combine the two sensations to arrive at flavor. Temperature, stickiness, crumbliness, fuzziness, visual appearance, and other sensory factors can affect our sense of flavor. If odor is cut off, we cannot tell the difference between a carrot, a turnip, and a potato, since the texture and taste of all three are the same. We distinguish these in final form by smell. If the color of a food or its texture is off, we may reject it. Milk colored blue, for example, may be refused; and some who do drink it may get nauseated.

We receive taste sensations—sensations of sweetness, saltiness, sourness, and bitterness—from tiny papillae on the tongue and in other

Type of Vegetable————————————— Judge————————————————————————

Date————————————————————————

	Maximum Score	Score
Exterior Appearance	20	

Regular, unbroken, even-shaped pieces
Correct size
Good color, bright, even, clear, fresh; not dull, pale,
   or muddy
Proper moistness; not dry, watery, or shriveled

Interior

   Texture: tender, slightly crisp, very crisp, mushy,   30
      stringy, tough, woody, hard
   Good color

Palatability   45

   Flavor: pleasant, true, not lacking in flavor, raw,or
   strong; well-seasoned, not burned
   Temperature proper

Portion

   Adequacy of portion   5
   Attractiveness of serving   ———
                             100

Figure 1-8. Score sheet form for judging vegetables.

mouth or throat areas (see fig. 1-9). We taste bitter items in the back of the tongue. Most sour-sensing papillae are back on the sides of the tongue, but in front of the bitter-sensing ones. Salty sensations arise in front of the sour ones on either side of the tongue. Sweet tastes come largely from the front of the tongue. A normal adult has about 10,000 taste papillae on the tongue. Children have more and consequently have a more delicate sense of taste. They have considerably more sweet-sensing papillae and thus like sweets better than most adults do. We are not the best tasters in the animal kingdom. A pig has about 15,000 taste papillae on its tongue, and a cow has about 35,000. Some papillae are not stimulated by only one taste but can sense two or even four.

Several thousand years ago, the Greek philosopher Democritus said that taste and odor come from tiny fractions of food that are given off by it. He was right: molecules of food set up sensations, which we detect as taste, odor, or flavor. Our taste papillae receive no sensations from dry food; the substance must be moist. Salt gives off very active taste fractions, so we can taste salt quickly at very low levels. Bitter substances are less active: while we taste salt in about a third of a second, we taste bitterness in approximately a full second. Because molecules move at a slower pace when they are cold, cold foods must be seasoned more than

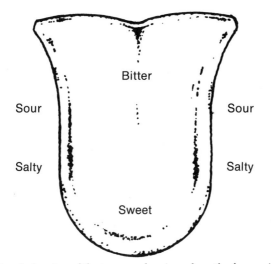

Figure 1-9. Rough drawing of the tongue, showing where the four major taste sensations occur.

hot ones. Less sugar is needed in hot tea than in iced tea to give the same level of sweetness.

Our odor perception is far more complicated than our sense of taste. Attempts to classify the thousands of odors that exist have not been wholly successful. Fragrance molecules in the air stimulate the odor-sensing mechanisms, and the sensation is transferred to the brain where it is combined with taste sensations to produce a sensation of flavor. Often if we lose our sense of smell—for example, when we get a cold and our nose gets stuffed up—we lose over half our taste of food. Again, children have a better sense of smell than older people. Some elderly people lose almost all their sense of smell and thus their perception of flavor.

One taste can modify others. Thus, salt may be used to subdue sweetness, bitterness, or tartness, smoothing them out. A bit of sugar added to a sauce can smooth out and blend the flavors. The Chinese give great emphasis in their cooking to flavor blends and balances; frequently they blend all four tastes in one dish to achieve what they want in flavor. Flavors should be true; that is, a product should taste the way that customers expect it to. False flavors, on the other hand, are not typical of a product and may cause customers to reject it. Because flavor is one of the primary bases on which patrons judge food, we must pay a lot of attention to it in quantity food production.

CHANGING RECIPE YIELDS

To change a recipe yield, convert all weights to ounces. If possible, restate all ingredients formerly given by count or volume in ounces; if this is not feasible, establish a factor for the change and multiply by this. The following chart indicates how ingredients in a recipe would be raised from 50 portions to 250:

COCONUT DROP COOKIES

Ingredients	Column				
	(1)	*(2)*	*(3)*	*(4)*	*(5)*
Milk, condensed	$1\frac{1}{2}$ c	17 oz	85 oz	$7\frac{1}{2}$ c	15 c
Coconut, shredded	1 lb	16 oz	80 oz	5 lb	10 lb
Vanilla	1 T	$\frac{1}{2}$ oz	$2\frac{1}{2}$ oz	$\frac{1}{3}$ c	$\frac{2}{3}$ c
Nuts, chopped	8 oz	8 oz	40 oz	$2\frac{1}{2}$ lb	5 lb

Column 1 gives the recipe weight or measure. Column 2 shows the corresponding ounce conversion, while column 3 gives the ounce weights after they are increased fivefold. Column 4 shows the reconversion to original values at the increased size. Corrections for variations in weights or measures are made here so that these remain even and are stated in meaningful values. If the cookies were to be scaled at 1 oz instead of $\frac{1}{2}$ oz, the recipe would be doubled; column 5 shows the resulting change in quantities. Testing should be performed to check yield and product quality. Today it is easy to increase the yield of a recipe if it is in the computer and multiplication programing has been established. Increasing a recipe by computer is called an *explosion*.

USING THE NEW RECIPE

Before using a new recipe, go over essential points with the worker who is to make the product. If necessary, set up a work sheet to obtain needed data. Enlist the cooperation of the worker, explaining aims and giving him or her responsibility and credit for doing a critical task. Work through department heads, too. They should be close to the program, and their ideas should receive careful consideration. Introduce new recipe products at employee meetings so that employees can judge and comment on them.

THE PRODUCTION DEPARTMENT IN THE FOODSERVICE ORGANIZATION

Preparation of food by the production department is only one of a series of steps that occur in bringing food to patrons. Once the menu is written and a forecast made, the quantity of ingredients that must either be purchased or be on inventory is known. Purchasing means receiving and (often) storing, and storage means inventory and eventual withdrawal by requisition. Pre-preparation may be necessary—for example filleting fish, cutting up meats, peeling or otherwise readying vegetables for preparation. Actual food production then occurs, followed by additional steps such as transporting, holding for service, and serving. The last step after service is cleanup and put-away. And this cycle is repeated again and again.

Auxiliary functions must also occur. The series of steps just outlined requires record keeping and financial accounting. Purchasing originates purchase orders, which in turn require delivery slips, invoices, a receiving report, and other documents. Storage raises the need for inventorying and requisitioning, for accounting purposes. Frequently the storage function alerts the purchasing department of needs that must be satisfied in order to meet production requirements. Based on the menu and on data from the sales department and forecasting, a work schedule for production is planned. Often such diverse production records must be maintained as amounts produced, a red meat usage record (recording how many expensive items such as steaks or lobsters are ordered and prepared by production), delivery amounts (the amounts and value of foods sent to various dining areas or locations), and special reports such as yields from recipes and drained weight data. Another whole series of records and accountability factors may arise in service. Checks are issued to servers, who must acknowledge their numbers. Check transfers—for example, when a patron in the bar asks that the bar check be transferred to and consolidated with the dining room check—must be recorded. Orders must be placed with production, and special records may be used for this purpose. Cashiers must collect and be accountable for cash. Management often wants information on the number of people a server serves in a given period, plus the number of various entrées sold and the dollar sales of the server.

Other data may be required, but this is enough to indicate how food production functions in the middle of a series of interconnected functions and how a vast amount of record keeping and accountability is required. Food production is not simply a matter of producing food; it is also vitally concerned with record keeping and accountability.

THE COMPUTER

Use of the computer has simplified and extended record keeping in foodservices. Production departments can make extensive use of the computer's ability to compile and furnish information. Indeed, the computer has to some extent changed the nature of record keeping and accountability procedures in that department.

THE MENU

Computers can plan menus. They can be told to set up a standard form, with appetizers, soups, sandwiches, and other food groups. They can make selections that satisfy a required variety of types, and they can arrange for special foods to appear on the menu on certain days. They can group certain foods together so that, for example, if roast ribs of beef are listed on the menu, the accompaniments of Yorkshire pudding and horseradish sauce immediately follow. Computers can also price items. They can be told not to plan too many of one kind of food. For instance, they may be programmed to recognize that an offering of tomato soup, spaghetti with tomato sauce, and a baked tomato in the same meal is too heavy on the tomatoes; if so, they will automatically reject the baked tomato and select, say, stuffed zucchini instead. Computers can be ordered to plan menus and menu items within specific cost restraints, too. In any case, computers can be overridden by management. Computers are not independent decision makers; they are slaves that respond accurately to their masters' orders.

To plan a menu, a computer needs to be provided with a file of menu items from which to select. If the computer is to cost out items (or recipes), it must have access to a file of ingredients and their costs. If the menu is to prepare a forecast, it needs to be given a file of data telling it how to indicate the quantities needed. The computer also must be programmed to utilize the data and to output the proper information.

THE RECIPE

Computers often have a recipe file in which recipes for almost all prepared items in the menu item file are listed. With such a file, it is possible to have the computer "explode" (increase the number of portions produced by) a recipe. Thus, if a recipe is for twenty-five portions but fifty-two are desired, the computer will identify the amount of each ingredient needed and its cost to produce this increased number of portions. It stands to reason that, if a computer can explode or increase a recipe, it can also decrease one.

OTHER COMPUTER JOBS

Today, all of the methods of menu analysis discussed earlier in this chapter can be handled by the computer. Thus, management can quickly obtain vital information on menu performance without having to do a lot of time-consuming and costly compilation. The computer can also generate precost information that allows management to review expected results and make desirable changes. With a forecast on hand and all recipe costs in place, the computer need only multiply out each item cost, compile a total, and then compare this with the revenue total gained through the price file on items sold. Other information is also available to management and to other departments, such as purchase information and needs based on menu items and on the forecast amounts.

A computer can print out purchase orders, keep inventory, and indicate to purchasing when orders must be placed to bring stock up to desired levels. It can compile the daily food cost and labor cost report, and it can handle receiving reports, keeping track of what goes into storage (and on inventory) and what goes directly to the production department for immediate use (and is to be recorded as a cost). It can deduct requisitions from inventory and carry these also as costs. It can also aid in labor scheduling.

The computer's greatest value to foodservices is in the service area, where it can be tied in with the cash register so that all cash records, order placements, and so on are recorded. The computer can also transfer orders to the bar or kitchen, once the order is placed with the cashier. A printout machine in the kitchen or bar can notify those areas of orders placed. A hand-held device is also available that enables a server to record patrons' orders as they are given at the table. The device automatically sends the orders to the computer, which in turn records the orders in the cash register and on the printout machine in the bar or kitchen.

Students working in food production today should be given the opportunity to see how computers affect the process of food production planning, control, and accountability. They make such acquaintance an actual laboratory and learning experience, conducted in conjunction with quantity food production work.

SCHEDULING

A *work schedule* shows the hours or shifts when workers are to be working. In contrast, a *production schedule* gives details about the work to be done, such as the following:

1. Period covered
2. Work to be done
3. Who does the work
4. Amount to produce
5. Recipe to use (usually by name and number)
6. Portion size
7. Meal or completion time
8. Run-out time
9. Comments
10. Slack-time assignments

It is possible to combine the information given on the work and production schedules. Figures 1-10 through 1-12 show different schedules. Sometimes *time management schedules* are used; these indicate exactly what a worker is to be doing at a specific time. The time management schedule ties in with the work schedule and is most effective when a worker repeats tasks each day.

Good scheduling saves labor, increases productivity, and gives management tighter control over what workers do. It should ensure that workers are on the job when work is to be done and are not there when there is no work to do. To accomplish this, the schedule planner must know the length of time and the amount of labor needed to do various jobs. Establishing work standards can increase the planner's accuracy in predicting job needs. Sometimes production and work schedules are tied in with a *labor budget* that contains information such as period covered, preparer, employee, employee classification and pay rate, number of hours of work per day, total hours and cost for employees, and overall time and dollars used. This is then compared with the actual figures, and the planner must justify differences. Figure 1-13 shows a basic labor budget.

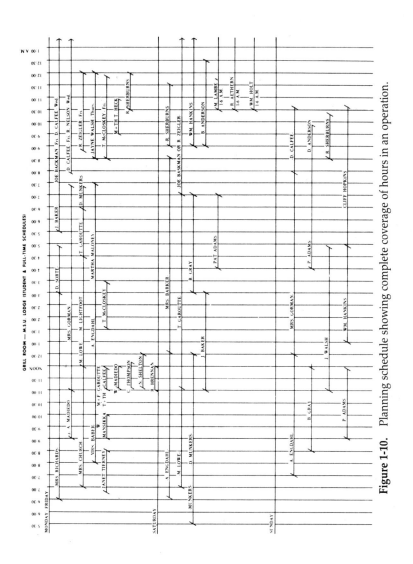

Figure 1-10. Planning schedule showing complete coverage of hours in an operation.

NEIMAN MARCUS
Food Production Schedule

DEPT._____

MONDAY	TUESDAY	WEDNESDAY	THURSDAY	FRIDAY	SATURDAY
ZODIAC					
LITTLE DIPPER					
PRESTON CENTER AND HASKELL					
SPECIAL ORDERS					

Form No. 908

Figure 1-11. Menu planning form used by Helen Corbitt at Neiman-Marcus. Every day of operation and various dining services are covered.

WORK SHEET

Food Quantities

BREAKFAST	Total Prepared Weight or Count	Carry Over or Run Out Time	Total Used Weight or Count	Meal Count
LUNCH				
DINNER				
Bread				
Butter				
Milk				
Cream				
Coffee				

Figure 1-12. Typical production schedule work sheet. Many other work sheets include space for indicating who is to prepare various items, the date, the meal, the recipe to use, the time required for completion, and so on. This work sheet can be filed away for use in future planning.

WEEKLY LABOR SCHEDULE AND FORECAST

WEEK BEGINNING ____________

DEPARTMENT ____________

PREPARED BY ____________

(USE SEPARATE SHEET FOR SUMMARY) (REPORT DUE IN AUDITING—4 P.M. THURSDAY PRECEDING WEEK)

EMPLOYEE'S NAME	Classification	Rate	Monday			Tuesday			Wednesday			Thursday			Friday			Saturday			Sunday			Totals	
			From / To	hrs.	COST	From / To	hrs.	COST	From / To	hrs	COST	From / To	hrs.	COST	From / To	hrs.	COST	From / To	hrs.	COST	From / To	hrs.	COST	HRS.	COST
TOTAL FORECAST																									
ACTUAL																									

Figure 1-13. A basic labor budget.

Chapter Review

1. Answer True or False:
      _____ A good time to have a taste panel test a product is about 11:30 A.M.
      _____ The best print size to use for individual menu items on a menu is 18-point.
      _____ A work schedule indicates when workers are to be on the job, and a production schedule details work to be done.
      _____ Flavor is a combination of taste and aroma.
      _____ A person's sense of taste never varies.
2. What is a *recipe explosion?*
3. Calculate the selling price from the following data: desired food cost is 30 percent, and food cost is $3.00.
4. Match each item listed with the proper description:

California	Chef steward
À la carte	*Aboyeur*
Convenience	Cook-chill method
Chef du partie	Executive chef
Du jour	*Table d'hote*
Cycle	

      _____ The individual who calls orders out in the kitchen.
      _____ The name of a menu that repeats itself.
      _____ The head cook of a section.
      _____ Separates food production from service by preparing food and refrigerating it for future use.
      _____ The name of foodservice items that are purchased in a nearly servable state.
      _____ The chief of the kitchen.
      _____ Means "of the day."
      _____ Foods sold in a group at a set price.
      _____ A menu that allows patrons to get any kind of food or meal at almost any time of the day.
      _____ Foods sold individually.
      _____ The individual who purchases food and supplies, is in charge of the storage area, and may help plan the menu.
5. A menu count shows that 36 of 108 entrée orders are for steak. What is this entrée's popularity index? If management expects steaks to account for 35 percent of all entrée orders, what is the menu factor? Is actual performance good or bad?

CHAPTER 2

Health and Safety

Outline

I. **Introduction**
II. **Nutrition**
    A. Increasing Nutritional Awareness
    B. Nutritional Responsibility
    C. Principles of Nutrition
        1. Energy Suppliers
        2. Vitamins
        3. Minerals
        4. Water
        5. Fiber (Roughage)
    D. Food Concerns
        1. The Adequate Diet
            a. The RDA
            b. The Basic Four Plan
            c. The Exchange Food Plan
        2. Weight Control
        3. Additives
            a. Protecting Our Food
        4. Natural Foods
        5. Sodium
        6. Fats and Cholesterol
        7. The High-energy Diet
III. **Sanitation and Safety**
    A. Sanitation
        1. Principles
            a. Bacteria, Viruses, and Parasites
            b. Poisons
            c. Food Deterioration
        2. Cleaning and Sanitation
    B. Safety

Goals

1. To call attention to the growing nutritional awareness and nutritional concern in this country, and to indicate the responsibilities of the foodservice industry in meeting nutritional demands of the public.
2. To identify some of the basic nutrients, and to give their source in foods and their function in the body.
3. To indicate what an adequate diet is and how we can calculate it.
4. To discuss some of the major nutritional concerns of the public today.

5. To list some of the basic facts about food poisoning, food poisons, and food deterioration.
6. To cover some of the basic principles of cleaning and sanitation.
7. To summarize some principles relating to safety in foodservice work.

INTRODUCTION

An underlying obligation of quantity food production is that it meet high standards in protecting the health and safety of those who eat the food. To achieve this, proper planning of the menu is needed, followed by the purchase of foods that contain the requisite nutrients, and then by careful handling, preparation, and serving so that a maximum quantity of nutrients are preserved. Procedures for sanitation should be observed scrupulously so that the healthfulness and safeness of the food are safeguarded in this area. Both nutrition and sanitation are of great importance in achieving good food production. A failure in either can prevent an operation from reaching its goals.

Nutrition and sanitation are complex subjects that are covered as separate courses in many foodservice programs. This text covers only major points, to give individuals who are not knowledgeable in this area some background before we move on to consider quantity food production itself.

NUTRITION

If one out of every four meals is consumed outside the home, the industry serving those meals is responsible for 25 percent of the nutrition in this country. This is a heavy responsibility, and failure to discharge it properly could have serious adverse consequences on our national health, economy, and social welfare.

INCREASING NUTRITIONAL AWARENESS

The relationship between good health and adequate nutrition is recognized today by most people in this country. Our lifespan and our enjoyment of life are strongly influenced by what we eat. Seven of our biggest killers are diet-related. Surveys by the Gallup Poll indicate that people are concerned about their diets, want foods that promote health, and are changing their dietary patterns to consume more healthful foods. Food selections in foodservices have changed to lower-calorie and less rich offerings. Fish, veal, chicken, and other light, white meat are now selected instead of red meat in many cases. Fresh fruits and vegetables are popular. Patrons want foods higher in fiber, lower in cholesterol, and lower in saturated fat. Many want to reduce their sodium intake by consuming less salt. There is concern about food additives and about livestock and crops treated with chemicals to encourage or protect their growth. This public awareness of the impact of food on health is something to which the foodservice industry must respond in a satisfactory manner.

Our populace's concern about nutrition has been nurtured by increased educational opportunities. Elementary and secondary schools no longer teach nutrition exclusively as special courses, but instead give nutrition emphasis in many courses. Many students eat in the foodservice where a balanced menu is served, and students are often told of the benefits that can accrue from following such a dietary regimen. Colleges often have courses in nutrition for ordinary students as well as for those pursuing a career in nutrition or dietetics. Schools that teach foodservice management also offer special nutrition courses. If they do not include treatment of it, courses in quantity food production or menu planning do. Much nutritional information is also available in our communications media. Good coverage is given to any announcement of a new medical-diet-related discovery. Wide publicity was given the recommendations of the American Heart Association on reducing the intake of salt, saturated fats, and cholesterol. With greater awareness and knowledge on the part of the public, foodservices are being challenged to meet more stringent nutritional demands.

Our government has also been instrumental in promoting nutritional information. The school foodservice program under the U.S. Department of Agriculture (USDA) has given heavy emphasis to promoting an understanding of nutrition. The USDA and the Department of Health and Human Services have agencies that do much to disseminate nutritional information. In 1977, the Senate Select Committee on Nutrition and Human Needs published a list of recommendations entitled "Dietary Goals for the United States" that has given considerable impetus to efforts to increase public awareness of nutritional needs. The following goals were identified in the list:

1. To avoid overweight, consume only as much energy (calories) as is expended; if overweight, decrease energy intake and increase energy expenditure.
2. Increase the consumption of complex carbohydrates and "naturally occurring" sugars from about 28% of energy intake to about 48%.
3. Reduce the consumption of refined and processed sugars by about 45% to account for about 10% of total energy intake.
4. Reduce overall fat consumption from approximately 40% to about 30% of energy intake.
5. Reduce saturated fat consumption to account for about 10% of total energy intake; balance that with polyunsaturated and monounsaturated fats, which should account for about 10% of energy intake each.
6. Reduce cholesterol consumption to about 300 mg a day.
7. Limit the intake of sodium by reducing the intake of salt to about 5 grams a day.

To meet these goals, the following changes in food selection and preparation are suggested:

1. Increase consumption of fruits, vegetables, and whole grains.
2. Decrease the intake of sugars and foods containing large amounts of sugar (whether refined, corn sugar, syrups, molasses, or honey.)

3. Decrease the consumption of foods high in fat, and substitute some saturated fat with polyunsaturated fat.
4. Increase consumption of poultry and fish while decreasing consumption of meats relatively high in saturated fat.
5. Except for young children, substitute nonfat milk and low-fat milk products for whole milk and whole milk products.
6. Decrease consumption of butterfat, eggs, and other high-cholesterol sources. However, the egg is still recognized as a good source of protein for certain population groups.
7. Decrease consumption of salt and foods high in salt content.
8. Try to balance total energy intake with the following percentage intakes of
    10% saturated fats
    10% polyunsaturated fats
    10% monounsaturated fats
    12% protein
    48% complex carbohydrates and naturally occurring sugars
    10% refined sugars.

This same committee also came close to recommending to Congress that foodservices be required to list the nutrient value of all foods offered on menus. The move was defeated, but only after the foodservice industry and others came out strongly against it. Had it been put into effect, foodservices would have had to become much more knowledgeable in the area of nutrition.

The foodservice industry needs to become better informed on nutrition. Menu planners need to know dietary basics in order to offer foods that meet patrons' dietary expectations. The right foods, proper preparation, and effective menu presentation also require some knowledge about nutrition. Nutritious foods cannot be served if foods of poor nutritional quality are purchased. Thus, wise selection of what is purchased is a prerequisite of good nutrition. Serious nutrient loss often occurs in handling and preparing foods. A knowledge of how to prevent this is essential. Those who come in contact with patrons also need to be informed in nutrition so they can talk intelligently to patrons about menu offerings and indicate which foods might be suitable for an individual patron's needs. Nutritional concern is in the mainstream of American thinking, and our industry needs to be well-informed in nutrition if it is to keep pace with popular thinking.

The foodservice industry has been criticized by authorities for not being sufficiently attentive to the demands of patrons in dietary matters. Critics say that the foods offered are too rich, that meals lack nutrients, and that menus often misinform. They inveigh against high-cholesterol and high-saturated-fat foods, overcooked vegetables, wilted salads, fat meats, oversalted food, and other factors that make for foods of low health value. Foods that are often presented as being low in calories sometimes are not. In a study of over sixty menus in Illinois that claimed to offer a low-calorie meal, only one met the requirement. A 4-oz hamburger patty, for example, is a poor component to select for a low-calorie lunch because it accounts for 485 calories by itself. Critics also say that the foodservice industry needs to learn how to plan better menus, paying more attention to the nutritional value of food and to the conservation of nutrients in handling, preparing, and serving food.

NUTRITIONAL RESPONSIBILITY

Opinions vary as to the level of responsibility that should be expected of foodservices in the area of nutrition. Little has been published on this question, so some clarification seems advisable.

The responsibility of a foodservice rests mainly on three factors: the degree of freedom patrons have in selecting where they eat; the degree of freedom patrons have in selecting foods; and the purpose or goals of the operation. If patrons are free to select where and what to eat, the major responsibility for selection of a balanced diet rests with the patron. The foodservice serving such patrons should offer foods of proper nutritional value and should ensure that the nutrients that ought to be in the foods are there. If the menu offers complete meals or is one from which complete meals can be selected, a balanced selection should be available. If the operation offers only partial meals—fastfood operations, for example, do—this requirement of balance does not exist. As the patrons' degree of freedom to decide where and what to eat diminishes, the foodservice's responsibility for nutrition increases. Inmates of a prison, because they eat nowhere else, should be served completely nutritious foods. The length of time a patron eats in the unit is also a factor. If the person's stay is a short one, it is less essential that strict standards of nutritional adequacy be met. If the stay is long, however, responsibility increases. In an operation run for profit, the efforts made to see that patrons select foods of adequate quality are usually minimal. Patrons would look upon an attempt to limit their freedom to eat what they want as a denial of their rights. In contrast, a foodservice such as a hospital or other health-related facility has an active responsibility to serve a controlled diet. Dietary departments in these operations exist specifically to serve such foods.

Most patrons should know what foods are healthful to eat. Where they have freedom of choice but do not select correctly, the responsibility lies with them and not with the foodservice. If a patron does not know (as might be the case with children or people who are mentally handicapped, senile, or ill) or cannot otherwise make a choice, the operation selecting the foods has full responsibility.

PRINCIPLES OF NUTRITION

We need a large number of nutrients to live. If any nutrient is missing or in low supply, our health does not prosper, and we can even die. We separate nutrients into five groups: carbohydrates, proteins, fats, vitamins, and minerals. While water and fiber are not nutrients, they also merit discussion because they are essential in the diet for proper health.

Energy Suppliers

Carbohydrates, fats, and proteins can be turned into calories or energy. Carbohydrates are used only for calories; if the body gets too many of them, they are converted into fat. Protein furnishes calories but is also used to build soft tissues, bones, teeth, and hair. In addition, it is used to produce blood, hormones, antibodies, and other bodily fluids. Protein makes up a part of vitamins, as well. Carbohydrates and proteins furnish 4 calories per gram; thus, an ounce of either yields 112 calories (4 × 28 grams). Fat is largely stored energy which the body can call on when it lacks carbohydrates or protein. Fat supplies 9 calories per gram, so an ounce of fat yields 252 calories. Alcohol, which supplies 7 calories per gram, is often considered closely related to carbohydrates, but it is metabolized in the body much as fat is. One ounce has 196 calories.

About 55 to 65 percent of the total calories a person needs each day should come from carbohydrates. They are found in cereals and grains, legumes, sugars, syrups, and other starchy foods. Bread is about 50 percent carbohydrate. Proteins are plentiful in all animal-based foods, such as meat, milk, fish, and poultry. Beef is about 18 percent protein; eggs, 12 percent; and bread, around 7 percent. Not all protein in food is of the same value to the body. Protein is composed of units called *amino acids*, and some proteins do not contain the amino acids the body cannot make. Animal proteins and soy beans are called *complete proteins* because they contain all the 8 or 9 essential amino acids that our body cannot synthesize. A complete protein can be produced by combining a food that contains one group of essential amino acids with another food (eaten at the same time) that contains the amino acids missing in the first. Thus, lentils and rice (major foods to the people of India), pinto beans and corn tortillas (Mexican food), and even our Boston baked beans and brown bread produce complete protein combinations. About 15 percent of our total calories should come from protein, 25 percent of which should be from animal sources or from complete protein combinations. Fats are found in fats and oils such as butter, salad oil, animal fat, nuts, and seeds. Avocados are a fruit that is high in fat. Only about 30 percent of our calories should come from fats, but we usually consume more, at the expense of other foods we need.

All substances burned in the body for energy are first turned into a carbohydrate or related product. Thus, the body removes a nitrogen fraction from protein to convert it into glucose, a simple sugar. Carbohydrates are also turned into glucose. Fats are oxidized and chemically altered until they become a substance that, like glucose, can then be converted into energy. We call this conversion of nutrients into energy in the body *metabolism*.

Fats in foods can be saturated, monounsaturated, or polyunsaturated. Saturated fats are usually hard, solid fats such as suet from beef, tallow from mutton, chocolate fat (cocoa butter), and coconut oil. Saturated fats already hold all the hydrogen atoms they can manage. A monounsaturated fat retains one spot where it can accept two hydrogen atoms.

Many vegetable oils or margarines made from them usually are good sources. A polyunsaturated fat can hold two or more additional hydrogen atoms. Safflower or fish oil are good sources of polyunsaturated fats. Table 2-1 lists the quantities of saturated and unsaturated fats in some fatty foods.

Saturated fats have been associated with heart and other arterial problems. If the blood is high in saturated fat, the cholesterol level is often high; if it is high in mono- or polyunsaturated fat, the cholesterol level is usually lower.

An unsaturated fat can be made into a saturated fat through a process called *hydrogenation* (adding hydrogen at the unsaturated spot). This process usually turns oils into solid fats so that they are firmer and can be used in margarine or other foods. It is therefore wise to check labels to see if the product has been hydrogenated, if saturated fats are to be avoided.

Fat needs to combine with some carbohydrate in order to be completely burned into energy. Any reducing diet should contain not less than 500 calories (125 grams) of carbohydrate for this reason. If insufficient carbohydrate is present, ketones and other acid products form, which can disturb the body's acid-base balance. A coma occurs, and death may follow. Diabetics who burn too much fat for energy can develop ketosis, a condition in which excessive ketones are accumulated in the body.

Vitamins

Vitamins are substances that in very small quantity carry out essential regulatory functions in the body. They seldom work alone, but most often team with other vitamins, hormones, enzymes, or minerals. Little benefit is gained by taking more vitamins than are needed; and harm can be done if an excess of some kinds is taken, especially an excess of the fat-soluble ones. Massive doses of vitamin A or vitamin D, for example, can be harmful, and deaths have been known to result from them. Massive doses of vitamin C might help the body resist the common cold and may give body cells stronger resistance to cancer, although some well-known authorities dispute this.

Vitamins perform vital functions in the body. As they were discovered, they were assigned alphabetical names because no one knew exactly what they were. When vitamin B was found not to be one but many vitamins—including thiamine (vitamin B_1) and riboflavin (vitamin B_2)—the use of chemical or other names came into being. Today, nutritionists call vitamins more by their chemical names than by their alphabetical ones. Some vitamins do not exist as vitamins in food; instead, the body changes substances in the food into vitamins—for example, β-carotene in carrots into vitamin A, and cholesterol in seafood into vitamin D. The essential amino acid, tryptophan, is converted into niacin, a B-vitamin.

An adequate supply of vitamins comes with having a varied diet rich in fruits and vegetables, meats or other animal foods, and cereals and grains (especially whole or enriched ones). Vitamins can be destroyed. Light

TABLE 2-1. Fat content of selected foods

	Total fat (%)	Saturated fat (%)	Monounsaturated fat (%)	Polyunsaturated fat (%)
DAIRY				
Cheese, cheddar	32.2	18	11	1
Cottage cheese	4.2	2	1	0
Cream cheese	37.7	21	12	1
Cream, half & half	11.7	6	4	0
Cream, coffee	20.6	11	7	1
Cream, whip, light	31.3	17	10	1
Cream, whip, heavy	37.6	21	12	1
Cream substitute	26.7	15	9	1
Ice cream	12.5	7	4	0
Milk, whole	3.7	2	1	0
Milk, 2% butterfat	2.0	1	1	0
Milk, evaporated	7.9	4	3	0
Milk, dry, whole	27.5	15	9	1
FATTY FOODS				
Butter	81.0	46	27	2
Chocolate, bitter	53.0	30	20	1
Lard	100.0	38	46	10
Margarine	81.0	18	17	14
Oil, corn	100.0	10	28	53
Oil, cottonseed	100.0	25	21	50
Oil, olive	100.0	11	76	7
Oil, peanut	100.0	18	47	29
Oil, safflower	100.0	8	15	72
Oil, sesame	100.0	14	38	42
Oil, soybean	100.0	15	20	52
Salad dressing, French	38.9	7	8	20
Salad dressing, mayonnaise	79.9	14	17	40
Salad dressing, plain	70.1	18	15	35
Shortening	100.0	43	41	11
FRUITS AND VEGETABLES				
Avocados, raw	17.0	3	8	2
Coconut, fresh	35.3	28	2	0
MEATS, ETC.				
Bacon, fried	52.0	17	25	5
Beef, choice	20.4	12	11	1
Chicken, raw	4.9	2	2	1
Eggs, whole	11.5	4	5	1
Lamb, choice	21.3	2	8	2
Pork, total	52.0	19	22	5
Pork, lean	10.5	4	4	1
Pork, fat only	83.7	30	35	8
Salmon, king	15.6	5	5	0
Turkey	14.7	4	6	8
Veal	12.0	6	5	0

destroys riboflavin; heat destroys thiamine, ascorbic acid, and some other vitamins. Water-soluble vitamins can easily be leached out of foods as a result of soaking, cooking in water, or other water-leaching circumstances. Some vitamins are destroyed by an alkaline reaction; adding baking soda to cooking water to keep vegetables green or to speed the cooking of legumes is harmful to these vitamins. Some, like vitamin C and vitamin A, can be oxidized. Table 2-2 lists the major vitamins, along with some of their sources and functions.

TABLE 2-2. Sources and functions of vitamins

Vitamin	Chemical name	Source and function
A	Retinol	Found in yellow and orange fruits and vegetables as a carotene, which the body changes into the vitamin found in eggs, butter, and liver; essential for good eyesight, skin, and mucous lining; resists infection; stimulates cell growth.
B-group		
B_1	Thiamine hydrochloride	Found in meats and in whole-grain or enriched cereals; needed for muscle action including heart; necessary for nerve functions including brain action; maintains good appetite, normal digestion, and gastrointestinal tone; required for growth, fertility, and lactation; essential for breakdown and use of carbohydrates in the body; cures beriberi.
B_2	Riboflavin	Found in leafy vegetables, some meats, milk, and cereals; helps maintain skin and nerves; helps eyes adapt to light; with pyridoxine, changes tryptophan, an amino acid, into niacin, a vitamin; essential for oxidation reactions in the body.
Niacin	Nicotinic acid	Found in organ meats, meats, peanuts, poultry, and cereals; if the diet has enough tryptophan in it, it will be changed into this vitamin; cures pellagra; works as a coenzyme to remove hydrogen fractions from substances so the body can use them; helps maintain skin and nervous system.
B_6	Pyridoxine	Widely distributed in plant and animal foods; muscle meats, liver, vegetables, and whole-grain cereals are the best sources; maintains skin; needed to prevent anemia; works as a coenzyme in many body reactions; lack of it causes convulsions.
Folid acid	Folacin	Widely found in green parts of plants; works as a coenzyme to further body reactions; helps in the use of amino acids; helps make choline, a vitamin; helps make purines and pyrimidines; works with vitamin B_{12} and vitamin C to prevent anemia.
B_{12}	Cyanocobalamin	Found in animal protein foods; mainly associated with the prevention of some anemias.
Pantothenic acid	Pantothenic acid	Plentiful in most animal and plant foods; functions as a coenzyme that must be present to metabolize fats and carbohydrates in the body.

continued

TABLE 2-2. Sources and functions of vitamins (*continued*)

Vitamin	Chemical name	Source and function
Biotin	Biotin	Found in organ meats, chicken, eggs, milk, most fresh vegetables, and some fruits; needed to metabolize fats, carbohydrates, and proteins in the body.
Choline	Choline	Found in brains, organ meats, eggs, yeast, wheat germ, milk products, beef, and vegetables; functions in protein and fat metabolism.
Myoinositol	Myoinositol	Found in organ meats, brains, whole-grain cereals, and yeast; probably works in metabolic functions.
C	Ascorbic acid	Citrus fruits, tomatoes, leafy vegetables, members of the cabbage family, tropical fruits, and potatoes contain significant amounts; essential for the formation of collagen, bone cartilage, and teeth matrix; keeps up the capillary blood vessels; needed for healing; prevents scurvy; related to the metabolism of some amino acids and other essential body functions; helps make some hormones; helps maintain bones and teeth.
D	Ergocalciferol or Choleciferol	Found in butter and milk products, fish and fish oils, and organ meats; added to milk products and margarines; prevents rickets; needed to make and maintain bones and teeth; helps keep up muscle tone; few foods contain vitamin D as such; ergosterol (D_2) or dehydrocholesterol (D_3) is converted into the vitamin by sunlight (ultraviolet rays).
E	Tocopherol	Plentiful in plant oils; acts as a physiological antioxidant inhibiting the oxidation of essential unsaturated fatty acids; not a fertility vitamin for human beings; some claims are made for its effectiveness against aging and cardiovascular problems, but scientific support for this is lacking; may help prevent damage from smog and other harmful gases in the atmosphere.
K	Menadione	Many vegetables contain this vitamin, especially leafy ones; required for blood clotting; may affect blood manufacture; can be made in the intestines.

Minerals

Minerals form body tissues such as muscles, bones, and teeth. They transfer electrical impulses, enabling nerve reactions to occur. Some are components of vitamins, as cobalt is of vitamin B_{12}. Sulfur is needed to form the protein substances in hair, skin, and nails. Iron is important for making blood. Iodine is in thyroxine, which regulates the speed at which metabolism occurs. Our muscles contract and relax because of minerals. They also maintain the proper acid–alkaline balance of the body. Just as in the case of vitamins, we must have a wide variety of food in our diet to obtain all the minerals we need. Milk or milk products, meat or its equivalent, fruits, vegetables, and cereals provide such variety.

Minerals are water-soluble, so they can be lost by foods during soaking, cooking in water, or other water-leaching processes. They are rather stable with respect to heat, oxidations, and other types of exposure. Often they are lost because of poor handling, such as paring potatoes or other items too deeply. Many minerals lie just under the skin of fruits and vegetables; leaving them unpeeled or only peeling them lightly can help retain more minerals. Table 2-3 lists the minerals essential to human health, with some of their sources and functions.

TABLE 2-3. Sources and functions of minerals

Mineral	Source and function
Iron	Good sources are egg yolk, dried beans and other legumes, nuts, enriched or whole grains, molasses, meats (especially organ meats), and some fruits and vegetables; helps prevent anemia by making hemoglobin (a part of blood that carries oxygen and nutrients around the body); because it is not well-absorbed, the diet must be high in it; women in their menstruation years need 18 mg or more per day; since milk is not a good source of it, babies should receive food that are good iron sources early in their infancy.
Iodine	Good sources are iodized salt, seafood and sea plants, and vegetables and fruits grown in soil having a good supply of iodine; it is used to make thyroxine, the hormone that regulates the speed of body metabolism; if it is lacking, the thyroid gland in the throat works overtime trying to produce it, and a goiter appears; if a women lacks iodine during pregnancy, a mentally deficient child may be born; iodine is also important in the manufacture of cholesterol.
Calcium	Milk and milk products, leafy green vegetables, shellfish, and egg yolk give good amounts; normally, adults should have two glasses of milk per day or the equivalent; calcium is needed to make teeth and bones; it is an important part of collagen and is important in blood coagulation, in muscle functioning, and in maintaining a proper acid–base balance; old people lose calcium from their bones and often have skeletal problems such as osteoporosis; the need for calcium is especially high in growing children, pregnant women, and nursing mothers.
Phosphorus	Good sources are meat, milk, poultry, fish, egg yolk, cereals, legumes, and nuts; it can work to help sway the body toward either an acid balance or a base balance; it works with calcium in the body to make teeth and bones; It is also an important part of the substances that develop energy; phospholipids are fatty substances joined with phosphorus, and a number are important for body functions. The genetic compounds DNA and RNA contain phosphorus, too.
Sodium	Many foods, including root vegetables, milk, and seafoods, contain it; we get most from table salt and from items such as baking soda, baking powder, and monosodium glutamate; about a third of our sodium comes from salt that we add, another third comes from what manufacturers add to food, and the final third exists naturally in the foods we eat; it is important in maintaining our fluid balance and our acid–base balance.
Chlorine	Good sources are chlorinated water or salt (sodium chloride); it is important in making hydrochloric acid for gastric juices, and it combines with many other substances to make essential compounds for the body.
Magnesium	Good sources are leafy green vegetables, nuts, soybeans, and snails; it is an activator of enzymes and peptidases, which work in the energy-making process and in building or breaking down body substances, it is active in muscular contraction and in nerve reactions; magnesium sulfate is a laxative.

continued

TABLE 2-3. Sources and functions of minerals (*continued*)

Mineral	Source and function
Potassium	Good sources are bran, brewer's yeast, cocoa, coffee, dried legumes, molasses, potatoes, spices, and tea; it helps maintain the body's osmotic pressure and acid–base balance; it promotes several important enzymatic processes and is important in muscular function.
Sulfur	No deficiency of sulfur has ever been observed; we get all we need from almost any group of foods, especially meats; it is a part of hard proteins, such as nails, hair, and skin.
Manganese	We seldom lack it, but best sources are dry tea, instant powdered coffee, cocoa powder, bran, shredded wheat, oatmeal, walnuts, peanut butter, canned pineapple, and whole wheat bread; it is important in energy creation and in some enzymatic actions; it helps form blood; in excess, it can act as a poison.
Copper	The ordinary diet contains enough, but best sources are cocoa powder, dry tea, beef and pork liver, pecans, walnuts, bran, and peanut butter; it is important in the formation of blood, melanin (the dark pigment found in hair and skin), and sheaths that surround the nerves.
Cobalt	We have little information about its presence in foods, but the ordinary diet containing meat and milk seems to give enough; it is not found in fruits and vegetables, so vegetarians who do not eat eggs, milk or milk products may lack it; it is an important part of vitamin B_{12}, which is needed to avoid pernicious anemia.
Molybdenum	Good sources are legumes, cereal grains, certain dark-green vegetables, liver, and kidney; it is active in some enzymatic actions and some catabolic processes.
Chromium	Best sources are cheddar cheese, dry beans, peanut butter, meat, whole grains, and brewer's yeast; it is important in helping the body handle glucose; chromium chloride administered to diabetics improves their glucose tolerance; it is also thought to be important in converting glucose to energy.
Selenium	Seafoods, fish, meat, eggs, milk, and whole-grain cereals are good sources; it is thought to be related to the antioxidant activities of vitamin E; an excess can cause dental problems in children.
Fluorine	Most people get their fluorine from drinking water, to which it is usually added in concentrations of about 1 part per million; it makes large strong dental crystals, especially when teeth are being formed; it helps maintain sound tooth health during life; it also helps make bones stronger and keeps them stronger during life; it can help reduce the incidence of osteoporosis.
Zinc	Its best source is flesh foods; it activates enzymes used to metabolize proteins and helps transfer carbon dioxide out of the body; it is an important part of insulin; it is also needed for sexual maturity in males, growth, a sense of taste, and wound healing; it assists thiamine in some of its reactions.

Water

About two-thirds of our body consists of water. Water forms an essential part of body cells and is a major part of blood, lymph, and other body fluids. It is the medium in which many important body reactions occur. It helps carry nutrients through the body and is essential in promoting good digestion. The evaporation of water when we sweat helps cool the body. Water is a lubricant that helps avoid friction between moving body parts, thus preventing fatigue.

The body obtains water from fluids and foods that are consumed and also from the production of energy. Carbon dioxide and water are formed in the production of energy, and the body uses this water for its needs. Salt and other minerals affect the amount of water the body carries. The body eliminates water in the urine, in the breath, by sweating, and in the feces. If the body does not have enough water, injury may result, especially to the kidneys. Excessive sweating can cause dehydration and an excessive loss of salt. The average individual should get the equivalent of six to eight glasses of water in fluids a day.

Fiber (Roughage)

Fruits, vegetables, nuts, legumes, and some other items contain a substance called *cellulose,** which human beings cannot digest. Cattle, horses, rabbits, and other animals have digestive systems that are able to break cellulose down into glucose or blood sugar. It is not a waste to human beings, however, because it gives bulk to the intestinal contents. We call this bulk *fiber* or *roughage*, and we know that it serves at least four valuable functions. First, it moves foods through the intestinal tract more quickly, thereby reducing the chance for constipation and hemorrhoids (the former by drawing water into the intestines, giving softer stools, the latter by reducing intestinal pressure) and reducing the chance of being affected by cancer-producing substances (by moving them out faster). Second, it reduces bacterial build-up by eliminating digestive wastes faster, thereby reducing the chance of diverticulosis. Muscle tone and health is improved, lessening the danger that the intestinal walls will bulge out and form pockets where masses of bacteria can form. Third, it gives a more even intake in the digestive tract of glucose, which is good for everyone but especially for diabetics. Fourth, it binds in fatty substances, reducing the amount of cholesterol absorbed by the body.

The presence of too much fiber reduces the amount of food that can be digested, and thus reduces the ability of the body to get enough nutrients. If food is moved too quickly through the digestive tract, absorption of nutrients is hampered. A heavy loss of water can also result from too much elimination, causing dehydration. Nutritionists think that adults need 6 to 30 grams per day of dietary fiber. This can come easily from whole grains, bran, nuts, fruit, vegetables, and legumes. A list of the fiber in some common foods is given in table A-9 in the appendix. Eating among other foods one canned peach, 1 oz of cornflakes, and two slices of whole-wheat toast for breakfast, a lettuce and tomato sandwich on white bread for lunch, and 4 oz of canned fruit cocktail, a portion of string beans, a boiled potato, and a piece of pumpkin pie for dinner yields 16.4 grams of dietary fiber.

---

* *Crude* fiber is the fiber that remains after food is treated in the laboratory with acids and alkalis. *Dietary* fiber is the actual amount of fiber in food as it goes through the digestive tract. Dietary fiber is approximately two to three times greater than crude fiber for the same food source. Most food labels today state fiber as dietary fiber.

FOOD CONCERNS

Americans today have a number of concerns about the food they eat. They are aware of the relationship between food and health and want food that promotes health and reduces the risk of disease. They want a diet that provides adequate nutritional balance. They are very weight-conscious and want calorie restrictions. They wonder about the safety and purity of our foods. Many seek to consume only natural or organic foods. Food additives and the loss of nutrients during processing are matters of concern. Better food protection is sought, and they want foods processed with less salt and fewer chemicals such as saccharin, nitrites, and even sugar.

These concerns of the public have been recognized by the foodservice industry. The use of sodium sulfite as a bleach and fruit and vegetable preservative has decreased. A number of foodservices now advertise foods fried in fats that are high in unsaturated particles. A few foodservices offer a menu completely directed to health foods, while others have sections of the menu set aside for it or offer selected "good-for-you" items. Because of the seriousness of these concerns and the need to heed them, they are briefly reviewed here.

The Adequate Diet

What an adequate diet is may be controversial, but all would agree that it involves food that is pleasing and satisfying to eat and promotes health, growth, and reproduction. Standards have been established based on our best scientific information; when followed, these seem to be satisfactory for most individuals. Various people, however, have different ideas on what constitutes an adequate diet. Many of these amount to fad diets—popular for a time, but destined to lost their credibility. Most such diets are of little value, and some are downright harmful or even fatal.

The RDA. Perhaps the most reliable and widely used standard for establishing an adequate diet is the RDA (Recommended Daily Allowances), established by the Food and Nutrition Board of the Academy of Sciences. It indicates the amount of certain nutrients needed per day by individuals at certain stages of life. (In some cases, the amount is not given because it is not known.) The amount set is based on an average need plus a safety factor, thus ensuring adequacy for most individuals. Table 2-4 lists these RDA amounts.

To ascertain the adequacy of a person's food intake, we simply tabulate the types and amount of all foods eaten, and then use a table of nutrient values to look up the specific amount of nutrients each food should contribute. We then compare the total for each specific nutrient with the RDA amount. Table 2-5 shows such a calculation for one breakfast.* We would need to do a similar calculation for the other foods consumed in the course of a day to make the complete comparison.

* Food values used in this chapter are taken from USDA, Research Bulletin No. 8, *Composition of Foods*. Washington, D.C.: U.S. Government Printing Office (1963).

TABLE 2-4. Recommended dietary allowances (RDA), 1980

Age (years)	Weight (kg)	Weight (lbs)	Height (cm)	Height (in)	Protein (g)	Vitamin A (RE)	Vitamin D (µg)	Vitamin E (mg)	Vitamin C (mg)	Thiamine (mg)	Riboflavin (mg)	Niacin (mg equiv.)	Vitamin B$_6$ (mg)	Folacin (µg)	Vitamin B$_{12}$ (µg)	Calcium (mg)	Phosphorus (mg)	Magnesium (mg)	Iron (mg)	Zinc (mg)	Iodine (µg)
INFANTS																					
0.0–0.5	6	13	60	24	kg × 2.2	420	10	3	35	0.3	0.4	6	0.3	30	0.5	360	240	50	10	3	40
0.5–1.0	9	20	71	28	kg × 2.0	400	10	4	35	0.5	0.6	8	0.6	45	1.5	540	360	70	15	5	50
CHILDREN																					
1–3	13	29	90	35	23	400	10	5	45	0.7	0.8	9	0.9	100	2.0	800	800	150	15	10	70
4–6	20	44	112	44	30	500	10	6	45	0.9	1.0	11	1.3	200	2.5	800	800	200	10	10	90
7–10	28	62	132	52	34	700	10	7	45	1.2	1.4	16	1.6	300	3.0	800	800	250	10	10	120
MALES																					
11–14	45	99	157	62	45	1,000	10	8	50	1.4	1.6	18	1.8	400	3.0	1,200	1,200	350	18	15	150
15–18	66	145	176	69	56	1,000	10	10	60	1.4	1.7	18	2.0	400	3.0	1,200	1,200	400	18	15	150
19–22	70	154	177	70	56	1,000	7.5	10	60	1.5	1.7	19	2.2	400	3.0	800	800	350	10	15	150
23–50	70	154	178	70	56	1,000	5	10	60	1.4	1.6	18	2.2	400	3.0	800	800	350	10	15	150
51+	70	154	178	70	56	1,000	5	10	60	1.2	1.4	16	2.2	400	3.0	800	800	350	10	15	150
FEMALES																					
11–14	46	101	157	62	46	800	10	8	50	1.1	1.3	15	1.8	400	3.0	1,200	1,200	300	18	15	150
15–18	55	120	163	64	46	800	10	8	60	1.1	1.3	14	2.0	400	3.0	1,200	1,200	300	18	15	150
19–22	55	120	163	64	44	800	7.5	8	60	1.1	1.3	14	2.0	400	3.0	800	800	300	18	15	150
23–50	55	120	163	64	44	800	5	8	60	1.0	1.2	13	2.0	400	3.0	800	800	300	18	15	150
51+	55	120	163	64	44	800	5	8	60	1.0	1.2	13	2.0	400	3.0	800	800	300	10	15	150
PREGNANT					+30	+200	+5	+2	+20	+0.4	+0.3	+2	+0.6	+400	+1.0	+400	+400	+150	*	+5	+25
LACTATING					+20	+400	+5	+3	+40	+0.5	+0.5	+5	+0.5	+100	+1.0	+400	+400	+150	*	+10	+50

* Supplemental iron is recommended (30 to 60 mg).
SOURCE: Reproduced from *Recommended Dietary Allowances*, 9th ed. (1980), with the permission of the National Academy of Sciences, Washington, D.C.

TABLE 2-5. Yields of selected nutrients for a breakfast

Food item	Calories	Carbohydrate (g)	Protein (g)	Fat (g)	Calcium (mg)	Phosphorus (mg)	Iron (mg)	Vitamin A (IU)	Thiamine (mg)	Riboflavin (mg)	Niacin (mg)	Ascorbic acid (mg)	Fiber (g)	Sodium (mg)
½ grapefruit	38	11	0.5	0	0	15	0.4	250	0.04	0.02	0.2	40	0.2	1
granulated sugar, tsp	13	4	0	0	0	0	0	0	0	0	0	0	0	0
bran flakes, 1 oz	80	29	3.0	1.8	24	250	2.2	0	0.07	0.05	3.5	0	2.0	125
½ c 3½% milk	45	6	4.5	4.5	144	95	0.1	175	0.03	0.20	0.1	1	0	50
shirred egg, with	80	0	6.0	6.0	27	100	1.1	260	0.05	0.15	0.1	0	0	5
2 T evap milk	42	3	2.0	2.5	80	11		100	0.02	0.11		0.5	0	6
½ oz cheddar cheese	60	4	4.5	4.5	106	110	0.1	185	0.01	0.06		0	0	110
slice whole w toast	65	14	1.0	1.0	24	75	0.8	0	0.09	0.03	0.8	0	1.8	60
coffee (no cream or sugar)	0	0	0	0	0	0	0	0	0	0	0	0	0	0
Totals	423	71.1	22.5	20.4	210	641	4.7	800	0.31	0.62	4.7	41.5	4.0	357
RDA for 21-yr-old male	2,900*	425*	56	128*	800	800	10	1,000	1.5	1.7	19	60	6*	2,200*

* Not an RDA recommendation but probably represents a normal average in diets today for this kind of individual.

The Basic Four Plan. A much simpler method for providing adequate food intake is the Basic Four Plan. This method is portion-oriented rather than nutrient-oriented. It lists portions of food in different food groups that should be consumed. Then, if a person eats these foods, the proper amount of nutrients is ensured. Table 2-6 indicates the plan. An intake of one good vitamin C food every day and one good vitamin A food every other day is recommended for everyone. It is also wise to see that a good source of iron is consumed frequently. Table 2-7 shows an example of one day's meals selected according to this plan.

The Exchange Food Plan. Another plan frequently used, especially for weight-reducing, diabetic, or other prescribed diets is the Exchange Food Plan. This was originally developed cooperatively by the American Diabetic Association and the American Dietetic Association for diabetic diets, but it has been extended to suit other dietary needs. It places foods into certain groups and allows selection of a prescribed number of any of these foods per day. Any food can be exchanged for another food in the group, as long as the prescribed number is not exceeded. This plan also makes it possible to calculate a person's total calorie, carbohydrate, protein, and fat intake for one day. It is expected that selecting foods from the various food groups that are established leads to an adequate intake of other nutrients. Table 2-8 indicates how a day's selections might be made to fit a required diet of not more than 150 grams of carbohydrate and 1,200 calories.

TABLE 2-6. The basic four dietary plan

SELECT:

from milk group	2 8-oz portions of milk or equivalent.*
from meat group	2 portions of 2- to 3-oz servings of beef, veal, pork, lamb, poultry, fish (without bone). Substitutions: 1 egg for 1 serving of the above; or 1 c cooked dry beans, peas, lentils, or other dry legumes; or 4 T peanut butter; or 2 to 3 oz tofu.
from vegetable–fruit group	½ c serving or one piece of fruit that is a good source of vitamin C, or 2 servings of a fair source; 1 serving of a dark green or deep yellow vegetable at least every other day for vitamin A; in addition, consume 2 or more servings of other vegetables or fruit, including potatoes, daily; thus, eat four portions in this group every day.
from cereal group	4 or more servings of bread. Substitutions for 1 serving of bread: 1-oz serving of ready-to-eat cereal, or ¾ c of cooked cereal such as oatmeal, grits, cornmeal, macaroni, rice, or noodles.

---

* The equivalent of 1 portion of whole 3½% milk in calcium yield would be: 1 1-oz slice of cheese, 1¼ c of cottage cheese, 1⅔ c cream cheese, 1 c skim or 2% milk, ½ c evaporated whole or skim milk, or 1½ c ice cream.

NOTE: The above selections will give about 1,200 calories per day. Select other foods such as salad dressings, butter, desserts, other foods named above, or others not named to obtain the total number of calories desired.

TABLE 2-7. One day's selection of foods meeting the basic four plan

Breakfast	Lunch	Dinner
6 oz orange juice	Large bowl cream of tomato	Grilled pork steak, 4 oz
¾ c oatmeal with ½ c whole	soup	Boiled potato with ½ c sauer-
milk	Toasted cheese sandwich	kraut
3-oz slice grilled ham	Coca-cola, 8 oz	Pear Waldorf salad
1 slice whole-wheat toast,		2 baking powder biscuits, 2
buttered		pats butter
Coffee (no cream or sugar)		Iced tea, lemon slice
		Apple betty

PLAN TABULATION:

Milk group:	¾ c milk, cream of tomato soup, cheese, and milk in the baking powder biscuits meet this requirement.
Meat group:	The ham and the pork steak more than meet the requirement.
Vegetable–fruit group:	Orange juice, tomatoes in the soup, sauerkraut, salad, and apple betty more than meet requirements for this group. Vitamin C needs are more than met with the orange juice, tomato soup, and sauerkraut. The diet needs a good source of vitamin A the next day, since this is lacking in the day's selections.
Cereal group:	The oatmeal, toast, sandwich with 2 slices of bread, 2 baking powder biscuits, and crumbs in the apple betty more than meets this requirement.

NOTE: This diet will approximate 1,800–1,900 calories for the day.

Weight Control

Undoubtedly the desire to reduce calories in order to lose weight is the public's major nutritional concern today. Americans are estimated to spend over $10 billion a year on trying to control their weight.

An overweight person is one who exceeds by 10 percent his or her normal weight, while an obese person exceeds normal weight by more than 20 percent. People who exceed their normal weight are more susceptible to heart problems, strokes, diabetes, and other health problems. Thus, the widespread concern about excess weight is based not only on a desire to be more attractive but also on a desire to have better health.

People usually reach their normal weight in their 20s; maintaining this weight throughout life is considered best for good health. One way to calculate what one should weigh is to use the following method:

Men: Multiply by 6 lb for every inch over 5 feet, and add to 106. Thus, a 5'11" man should weight 11 × 6 + 106 or 172 lb.
Women: Multiply by 5 lb for every inch over 5 feet, and add to 100. Thus, a 5'2" woman should weigh 2 × 5 + 100 or 110 lb.

It is common to add 5 lb for large frames and to deduct 5 lb for small frames.

To calculate the number of calories they need per day, men should multiply their normal weight by 18, and women should multiply theirs by 16. Thus, the man in the preceding example needs 3,096 calories, and

TABLE 2-8. Menu based on the food exchange plan

	Carbohydrate (g)	Calories
BREAKFAST		
½ grapefruit	10	40
Poached egg on		75
whole-wheat toast, with	15	70
with butter, 1 t		45
Milk, skim, 8 oz	12	80
Totals	37	310
LUNCH		
¼ c low-fat cottage cheese	12	80
Sliced tomatoes	5	25
6 saltines with	15	70
butter, 1 t		45
½ banana	10	40
Totals	42	260
DINNER		
Chicken fricassée (1 4-oz leg, no skin)		210
Dumpling	15	70
Harvard beets	10	40
Sliced cucumbers in vinegar	5	25
Plain roll	15	70
Strawberries, ¾ c	10	40
with light cream, 4 T		90
Skim milk	12	80
Totals	65	625
Totals for all day	144	1,195

This menu is based on a restriction to 150 grams of carbohydrate and 1,200 calories per day, using at least 2 meat exchanges, 2 fruit exchanges, 3 vegetable exchanges, 2 milk exchanges, and 4 cereal exchanges.

the woman needs 1,760 calories. For sedentary or semisedentary individuals, the calorie need is less; older people (perhaps over age 45) also need fewer calories.

When we use more calories than we take in, we usually burn fat. Eating 9 fewer calories than we expend takes off a gram of fat. Thus, if we want to lose 1 lb per week, we should consume about 4,000 fewer calories that week. (There are 454 grams in a pound, and 9 calories times 454 grams equals about 4,000 calories). There is also some water loss, but this is not immediately evident. If one goes on a low-salt diet, the tendency to hold this extra water is broken. The maximum amount of weight a normal person should lose per week is 1 or 2 lb.

Increasing activity through exercise or by other means increases caloric need, so it is usually recommended that any weight reduction program be accompanied by an exercise program. While the amount lost is not great—a person expends 150 calories per hour bicycling, 300 per hour swimming or playing tennis, and 400 per hour playing basketball or football—it all helps, and, if maintained, can make a significant contribution to weight loss.

People differ in their caloric needs. Body size and shape, level of activity, temperament, and stage of life are all factors. A large person needs more calories than a smaller one does. A lean, tall person needs more calories than a short, compact one does. A baby needs a lot of calories, and so does a growing teenager; when we reach 45, our metabolic rate slows and we need fewer calories. A pregnant woman needs more calories than she does normally.

A person can eat well and still lose weight: it is all a matter of proper food selection and preparation. Thus, one way to reduce calories is to avoid foods that are high in fat or alcohol (9 or 7 calories per gram, respectively) and instead to consume a lot of fruits and vegetables. Another way is to avoid junk or empty-calorie foods—foods that provide a lot of calories but few other nutrients, such as carbonated beverages and potato chips. By replacing high-calorie snacks with low-calorie ones, a person can reduce calorie intake. For example, 5 oz of chocolate provides 725 calories, but 5 oz of apple provides only 70 calories. Eating slowly produces a "filled up" feeling with a smaller amount of food. Many people go on reducing diets and do a good job of losing weight, only to gain it all back again. To lose weight and remain at a desired weight, a person usually must accept a permanent change in dietary pattern. Many people go on roller-coaster diet rides, instead—up and down, up and down, always going in circles and coming back to the same place.

It is important not only to select low-calorie foods, but also to see that proper food preparation occurs. Poached, boiled, broiled, or steamed foods are desirable because they contain no added fat. Sauces, salad dressings, and other items containing fat are reduced. Selecting a large amount of fruits and vegetables, without adding higher-calorie foods, is desirable. A lettuce and tomato salad with low-cal French dressing provides about 35 calories; using regular French dressing raises the number of calories to 50; using salad dressing raises it to 90; and using mayonnaise raises it to 125. Likewise, a plain, medium-size boiled potato provides 55 calories; mashing it, adding butter and milk, raises the number of calories to 100; turning it into hash browns raises the number to 175; french-frying it increases the number to 215; and pan-frying it raises the count to 230.

Table 2-9 presents various low-calorie meals that might be on a menu.

Additives

One of the major concerns of many is the safety and purity of our foods. Most of this concern revolves around the question of what additives are and what harm they do. Another significant issue involves how processing and other treatment of foods before the consumer gets them damage nutritional and other values.

An *additive* is a substance not consumed as a food itself but added to

TABLE 2-9. Representative low-calorie meals

Item	Calories	Item	Calories
BREAKFAST			
½ cantaloupe	60	Orange juice, 6 oz	85
Oatmeal ¾ c	90	Bran flakes, 1 oz (1 c)	105
½ cup skim milk	45	½ cup skim milk	45
Poached egg	80	Broiled ham, 3 oz	210
on toast, plain	70	Toasted English muffin, plain	85
Coffee, plain	0	Coffee, plain	0
Total calories	345	**Total calories**	530
LUNCH			
Salad Plate			
Cold boiled salmon (3 oz)	120	Fresh fruit salad, 8 oz	140
Cucumbers in vinegar ½ c	10	with low-cal Fr dressing	10
Sliced tomatoes, 1 medium	40	Open-face toasted cheese	
Relish sticks, 10	15	sandwich, 1 sl bread, 1 oz	
with 1 T cream cheese	30	American cheese	185
Hard roll, plain	85	Tea, plain	0
Chocolate iced milk, ½ c	35		
Tea, plain	0		
Total calories	335	**Total calories**	335
DINNER			
Apple juice cocktail	50	Fresh melon-ball cocktail, 4 oz	40
Poached chicken breast, 3 oz		Steamed flounder, 4 oz	
with 1 oz Mornay sauce	160	with lemon slice	200
Mashed potato, 4 oz	65	Boiled potato, parsleyed, 4 oz	55
Boiled green beans, 4 oz	25	Boiled zucchini, 4 oz	15
Lettuce salad, low-cal French		Spinach, mushroom, and bean	
dressing	15	sprout salad, low-cal French	
Hard whole-wheat roll	85	dressing	20
Butter, 1 pat	35	Hard whole-wheat roll	85
Pineapple sherbet, 4 oz	135	Butter, 1 pat	35
Skim milk, 8 oz	90	Fresh papaya, 4 oz	40
		Skim milk, 8 oz	90
Total calories	660	**Total calories**	580
Total day's calories	1,400	**Total day's calories**	1,445

food in order to serve some special purpose or to produce some special effect. Under these circumstances, the additive is intentionally introduced. We must also consider as additives some substances that get into food by accident or during growth, processing, storage, or marketing.

Additives can be harmful or beneficial. Some may be toxic; others can trigger allergic reactions; some are claimed to cause cancer or to have other harmful effects on health. But additives are in food to improve our food supply by enhancing the color, texture, or flavor of food. If we did not use them, we would not have the plentiful supply of good food we have today.

Additives help foods in many ways, including the following:

1. Some improve nutritional value, as when vitamins A and D are added to margarine or when vitamin C is added to a breakfast drink.
2. Sodium propionate retards mold formation in bread.
3. Potassium sorbate extends shelf life.
4. Salt, sugar or other substances preserve food.
5. Antioxidants prevent or retard food rancidity. Vitamins C and E add nutritional value also.
6. BHA (butylated hydroxy-anisole) and BHT (butylated hydroxy-thiazole) are effective fat antioxidants, and BHT is also thought to aid in preventing cancer.

The benefits additives provide must be weighed against the harm they are claimed to do. Sugar added to food helps preserve it and helps it retain color and texture. But sugar also adds calories without making a significant nutritional return, and it replaces other foods that possess better nutritional value. It tends to increase consumers weight, leaving them more susceptible to heart and other cardiovascular problems. Some people say sugar causes diabetes, although this is disputed; some evidence indicates that sugar can overwork the pancreas in making insulin and thereby do it harm. The correlation between sugar and tooth decay is well known.

Are artificial sweeteners good or bad? They improve flavor while adding no calories, but some critics say that items such as saccharin, cyclamates, and aspartame are not good. Some claims have been made that cyclamates and saccharin are carcinogenic, but this has never been proved in human beings. Cyclamates can no longer be used in the United States, and saccharin has also been removed from the approved list of food additives, although Congress intervened and allowed it to be used. (Canada has banned saccharin but allows the use of cyclamates.) Aspartame is condemned because it breaks down at low temperatures into methyl alcohol and other substances. Methyl alcohol can cause people to go blind, and some lawsuits have been filed claiming eye damage from the consumption of aspartame. In 1986, a law was introduced in Congress to ban the use of aspartame as a food additive; its most common use is as the sweetener Nutrasweet in carbonated beverages.

Sodium sulfite is used on foods such as potatoes and peaches to prevent them from developing a brownish tarnish. Restaurants have used it in water into which lettuce and other items are dipped to preserve their freshness and give them a bright appearance. But, sodium sulfite causes allergic reactions in some people, especially asthmatics. Thirteen deaths are known to have resulted from its use in a five-year period, and many severe reactions have also been reported. Because of this problem, the use of sodium sulfite on fresh fruits and vegetables has been banned; it is still allowed, however, on raw prepared potatoes and on some other foods. Where it is allowed in processed foods, it must be noted on the label if it is present in concentrations greater than 10 parts per million. The National Restaurant Association has asked its members not to use it and has reported that 97 percent of its members have complied with this request.

Sodium nitrite is a preservative used in cured meats to lessen the risk of the development of botulin, a dreaded toxin. It can, however, break down in the stomach into nitrosamine, a substance suspected of being carcinogenic. Eating a food containing vitamin C retards this breakdown. On the other hand, heat in cooking can aid in nitrosamine development, so it is advised that bacon not be fried crisp and that the fat drippings not be used (since this is where the product concentrates). Sodium nitrite has not been banned because there is no good, economical substitute for it.

Some additives are known to be harmful in large quantities but are considered safe in limited quantities. The government limits the amount allowed to a proportion below this safe level. Thus, the maximum allowable amount of sodium benzoate, a preservative, is $\frac{1}{10}$ of 1 percent of a food such as catsup. Similarly, the use of antibiotics as a dip for slaughtered chickens after evisceration is carefully controlled.

Some artificial colors are banned because they are suspected of being carcinogenic, notably red dye no. 2 (although Canada allows it). Tartrazine or yellow dye no. 5 may be removed from the government's approved additive list because it produces allergic reactions in some people, including respiratory problems, itching, and hives. Individuals allergic to aspirin are more apt to be affected by this dye. Tartrazine is used to color pastas, macaroni dinners, cheese, cake mixes, and some beverages. Annatto is another dye used to color cheese, butter, and other foods. Because it, too, is thought to have harmful effects on people, it is presently under attack in Congress and may be banned.

Some artificial flavoring substances are also questioned, notably monosodium glutamate (MSG). Some people claim that it is carcinogenic, but there is no proof of this. Some people do get an allergic reaction from it, commonly called the Chinese Restaurant Syndrome because MSG is often added to Chinese foods. MSG is a flavor enhancer used in many foods. It is an important product in food bases, soup bases, and dry and liquid soups.

Caffeine is a stimulant found naturally in tea, coffee, and chocolate. It is added to carbonated beverages and other foods. It increases respiratory and heart rates, raises blood pressure, and can influence hormone secretion. People with heart problems may be especially affected by it. Caffeine has been accused of helping to develop hyperactive children, but some experts doubt this. Older people are also susceptible to the effects of caffeine. Caffeine has been proved to cause sleeplessness: about an hour after some people drink coffee and go to sleep, it gives a "wake-up call," leaving the person sleepless for some time. A 12-oz bottle of caffeinated carbonated beverage contains about 50 mg of the stimulant. Medical authorities think that a normal individual can tolerate up to 200 mg per day. The response of foodservices to the concern of patrons about caffeine is evidenced by the increased availability of brewed decaffeinated coffee.

Irradiation is a way of preserving food by subjecting it to radiation after placing it in an air-tight seal. This procedure kills any bacteria present, but unfortunately the enzymes are not destroyed, as they are with heat; consequently, the enzymes continue to act, causing some foods to change. Bacon was once approved by the government as an irradiated product, but is no longer is. Recently, manufacturers have been required to note on the labels of all irradiated foods the fact that they have been irradiated. Irradiation does not make food radioactive because too little radiation is used. Many cereals can be irradiated to kill insect eggs; irradiated potatoes will not sprout; fruits and vegetables after irradiation have a longer shelf-life. Irradiation may be more widely used in the future, but only if it is proved completely safe and the public accepts it.

Some additives get into food unintentionally, often as residues from pesticides or other chemicals. Radioactive fallout, such as occurred in Europe after the Russian nuclear disaster, can appear in foods. Chemicals and other substances can enter food during processing or during other marketing procedures. The acid solvent used to extract caffeine from coffee becomes a residue. PBB (polybrominated biphenyl) and other contaminants can get into animal feed and thence into our food supply. Mercury, lead, and other heavy metals are harmful toxic substances. DDT is soluble in oils and fats and in this way can get into our food. Its use now is banned in many instances, so the danger from it has lessened. DDT can break down in the body into DDE, which is thought to be a carcinogen. It can also attack the central nervous system.

The body has a number of built-in mechanisms for getting rid of various undesirable substances; as long as the intake does not exceed a certain level, we can eliminate them without harm. Other items, however— such as the halogens, lead, and mercury—are not removed. Instead, they accumulate and finally reach a level at which they are toxic. The government has established levels of safety for some food products, and it works to prevent contamination of the others not always with success.

Some foods, such as poisonous mushrooms, contain natural toxic substances. Solanine in potatoes that turn green from sun exposure is a poison, but to be seriously threatened by it a person would have to eat 17 lb of such potatoes. Spinach and rhubarb contain oxalates; one serving of rhubarb contains 20 percent of what is considered a toxic dose. Fava beans contain a substance that causes anemia. Plants of the *Brassica* genus (cabbages, turnips, mustard greens, radishes, and rutabagas) contain a compound that encourages goiters. Some cereals, legumes, and fruits cause allergies. The oxalic acid in rhubarb, spinach, and some other items inhibits the absorption of calcium and iron in the intestines. Sassafras, chamomile, and some other items used for herbal teas contain harmful substances, and some may attack the liver. Hallucinogens that produce unreal sensory feelings are found in some herbal teas (jimsonweed), mushrooms, and spices (nutmeg and mace). Bananas, pineapples, tomatoes, avocados, and licorice can raise blood pressure. Maize, sorghum millet, some beans, cassava, and the seeds of apples, apricots, cherries, pears, plums, and prunes contain a powerful cyanide poison. In the tropics, where some populations eat large amounts of cassava, deaths from its over consumption are known. Some cheeses and wines contain a substance that constricts the blood vessels. Some fish are poisonous. The Japanese eat a highly poisonous puffer fish called *fugu*, but they know how to rid it of most of the poison. Eating the fish is sometimes face-tiously referred to as "Japanese roulette." In the summer months bi-valves can become contaminated with a red dinoflagellate called *red tide* that makes them poisonous. At such times, no bivalves in the area can be taken from the waters.

For the most part, the average person can go ahead and consume most of these foods without harm. The harmful substances they contain are present at levels that we can tolerate. It is rare for harm to be done by these foods, just as it is rare for intentionally introduced additives to be harmful at the levels the government sets for them. Life is always a risk. Water in excess can be toxic to the body and cause illness. Sometimes people become overconcerned about risks and exaggerate the danger. We need to be watchful and to ensure that our food supply is as safe as possible, but we should not push the panic button when some news report goes overboard and makes things sound far more dramatic and dangerous than they really are.

Protecting Our Food. A person may wonder why we allow our food to contain undesirable substances. We do have laws that are designed to give us safe food, but some say they are not strong enough, while others say they are too strong. There must always be some compromise when two opposing viewpoints exist and convincing proof of either position is lacking. Some people will always try to transgress or skirt the law, and regulatory authorities have difficulty in apprehending them. One of the problems is asserted to be underfunding: the Food and Drug Administra-tion (FDA) complains that it has only enough inspectors to inspect food manufacturers' premises. Moreover, there must be proof that a product is harmful before the government can do anything.

The Food, Drug, and Cosmetic Act requires that food be produced in a sanitary and safe manner; it also regulates additives that can be placed in foods. The Meat Act does the same for meats. These and other regula-tions have been set up in the past, and conditions have changed. Many new substances are available for use in our foods. It is difficult in the first place to keep them under control; then, too, as experience is gained and better detection becomes possible the laws fail to provide up-to-date guidance on how to proceed. Revision must occur as conditions change, but the wheels of government move slowly. Ralph Waldo Emerson once said that the government is usually sixty years behind the times, and not much has changed in this regard. We need more up-to-date laws, and we need a better definition (and enforcement) of what is harmful and what is not.

INGREDIENTS: WHEAT FLOUR, EGG
YOLKS, WHOLE EGGS.
ENRICHED WITH: B VITAMINS
(NIACIN, THIAMINE MONONI-
TRATE, RIBOFLAVIN) AND IRON
(FERROUS SULFATE).

Figure 2-1 List of ingredients for egg noodles. Ingredients must be listed by amount, from greatest to least.

The FDA has established a "generally recognized as safe" (GRAS) list of some 3,000 approved substances that can be added to food. Of these 3,000 substances, 30 are today being criticized as potentially harmful. Items are placed on the list only after extensive testing establishes that they are not harmful. The GRAS list is constantly under review. One of the factors in the Food, Drug, and Cosmetic Act that has spurred more FDA action against additives and has created more publicity is the Delaney amendment to the act, which says that any substance suspected of being carcinogenic must be removed from the list. Under this provision, various items have been removed from the approved list, including saccharin, cyclamates, and stibesterol. Some people claim that the amendment is not realistic and should be modified, but whether a change will occur is still questionable.

All noncommon food (which covers most food) that is packaged must include on its label the ingredients in the food, from greatest amount in the food to least. This tells consumers what is in the food—information that can be useful not only in assessing the dollar value of the food but also in determining what is being taken into the body. Some people have allergies and must avoid certain ingredients; such information is of vital interest to them. Figure 2-1 shows how ingredients are listed.

Another means by which labels can inform us is through nutritional labeling. Such labeling is voluntary except when (1) a nutritional claim is made, and (2) any nutrient is added. In nutritional labeling, the following information must appear:

Serving size	Protein per serving
Servings per container	Carbohydrates per serving
Calories per serving	Fat per serving

In addition, the percentage of the U.S. RDA* per serving must be given for:

Protein	Riboflavin
Vitamin A	Niacin
Vitamin C	Calcium
	Iron

* The U.S. RDA (recommended daily allowances) were established by the FDA for use in labeling nutrient values for infants, children, adults, and pregnant and lactating women. They differ from the RDA mentioned previously. Most values encountered on packages state values for an adult male. When a serving of food supplies less than 2 percent of a nutrient, the percentage is shown in one of two ways: as 0%; or as an asterisk (*), with the footnote: "Contains less than 2% of the U.S. RDA of this [or these] nutrients.[11]

If any of the following are added, the percentage of the U.S. RDA per serving must be listed (or may be listed, whether added or not):

Vitamin D	Vitamin B_6	Zinc
Vitamin E	Phosphorus	Copper
Vitamin B_1	Iodine	Biotin
Folacin	Magnesium	Pantothenic acid

The sodium contribution is stated in mg of sodium per serving and in mg per 100 grams. If cholesterol is listed, it must also be stated in these amounts.

Nutrition labeling gives consumers the opportunity to compare nutrient values and quality and the relative cost of foods similar in nutrient values. Figures 2-2 and 2-3 show different examples of nutritional labeling. Analysis of the information given in these and other labels can uncover many helpful facts.

Our food laws represent a compromise between different viewpoints, with adjustments being made slowly as proof of the need for them is generated. In any case, we can be sure that our food supply is one of the safest and best of any in the world.

Natural Foods

The term *natural* might suggest that the concern here is that foods should not be imitation or synthetic. It does mean that, but it also carries addi-

NUTRITION INFORMATION

SERVING SIZE: 5 LEVEL TABLESPOONS (22.7 GRAMS) RECONSTITUTED TO ONE 8 FL. OZ. GLASS.
SERVINGS PER CARTON: 80

	PER SERVING (8 FL. OZ.)	PER QUART
CALORIES:	80	320
PROTEIN:	8 GRAMS	32 GRAMS
CARBOHYDRATES:	12 GRAMS	48 GRAMS
FAT:	*	*
SODIUM:	125 MG	500 MG
PERCENTAGE OF U.S. RECOMMENDED DAILY ALLOWANCES (U.S. RDA):		
PROTEIN	20%	80%
VITAMIN A	10%	40%
VITAMIN C	2%	8%
THIAMINE	6%	25%
RIBOFLAVIN	25%	100%
NIACIN	**	4%
CALCIUM	30%	120%
IRON	**	**
VITAMIN D	25%	100%
VITAMIN B_6	4%	15%
VITAMIN B_{12}	20%	80%
PHOSPHORUS	25%	100%
MAGNESIUM	6%	25%
PANTOTHENIC ACID	8%	30%

*CONTAINS LESS THAN 1 GRAM.
**CONTAINS LESS THAN 2% OF THE U.S. RDA OF THESE NUTRIENTS.
INGREDIENTS: MILK, VITAMIN A, VITAMIN D_3.

Figure 2-2 Label providing nutritional information for a box of nonfat dry milk.

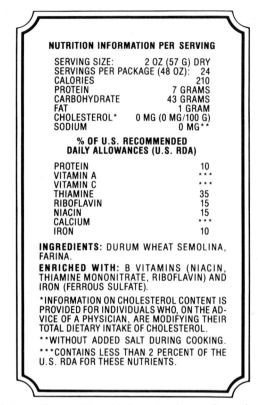

NUTRITION INFORMATION PER SERVING

SERVING SIZE:	2 OZ (57 G) DRY
SERVINGS PER PACKAGE (48 OZ):	24
CALORIES	210
PROTEIN	7 GRAMS
CARBOHYDRATE	43 GRAMS
FAT	1 GRAM
CHOLESTEROL*	0 MG (0 MG/100 G)
SODIUM	0 MG**

**% OF U.S. RECOMMENDED
DAILY ALLOWANCES (U.S. RDA)**

PROTEIN	10
VITAMIN A	***
VITAMIN C	***
THIAMINE	35
RIBOFLAVIN	15
NIACIN	15
CALCIUM	***
IRON	10

INGREDIENTS: DURUM WHEAT SEMOLINA, FARINA.

ENRICHED WITH: B VITAMINS (NIACIN, THIAMINE MONONITRATE, RIBOFLAVIN) AND IRON (FERROUS SULFATE).

*INFORMATION ON CHOLESTEROL CONTENT IS PROVIDED FOR INDIVIDUALS WHO, ON THE ADVICE OF A PHYSICIAN, ARE MODIFYING THEIR TOTAL DIETARY INTAKE OF CHOLESTEROL.

**WITHOUT ADDED SALT DURING COOKING.

***CONTAINS LESS THAN 2 PERCENT OF THE U.S. RDA FOR THESE NUTRIENTS.

Figure 2-3 Label providing nutritional information for a package of spaghetti noodles.

tional meaning. Another word often used in place of it is *organic,* and this gives a clue to the larger meaning. The full meaning might be "a food altered as little as possible from its natural state." If it is grown in soil, only natural fertilizers should be used; no chemical ones are allowed, and the food must not be treated during growth with any chemical pesticide or substances that aids its growth. If it is of animal origin, the animal's diet should not include drugs, hormones, or other additives. Eggs should be produced naturally by allowing hens to run freely with roosters. Foods called *natural* should not lose a significant amount of their nutrients in processing or marketing. They should contain no additives. Organic foods include unbleached whole-grain flours, naturally sunripened fruits, and unpasteurized milk. Natural vitamins must come from natural foods and not be laboratory-made.

Some advocates of natural foods have carried their beliefs to extremes and introduced odd diets, some of them harmful to health. Normal foods of the type served in most foodservice operations are unacceptable to them; if such a person is a patron, the foodservice is almost sure not to please. Some foodservice groups have sought to capture this market with considerable success, but the market remains a small, highly select one. A much larger number of patrons have taken the middle road of favoring natural foods and must be reckoned with.

Undoubtedly the natural food movement has had beneficial effects: it has led to increased consumption of fruits, vegetables, whole grains, and other healthful foods. But some of the theory on which the natural food program has been built is flawed. For example, there is no evidence that the body can distinguish between a nutrient from a fruit or vegetable grown in naturally fertilized soil and a nutrient from one grown in chemically fertilized soil. Many foods protected by pesticides or other substances are actually better from the standpoint of nutrition and other quality factors than foods left to struggle for survival without such substances. Most of these chemicals easily wash away and leave no residue. Some of the diets introduced have been strange, and odd theories about diet, drugs, and health have appeared—some of them not good.

Overuse of various preparations sold in natural food stores is also a matter of concern. High intakes of some vitamins, minerals, and other substances are recommended, and some of these could be harmful. As noted earlier, a number of what we feel are natural foods—even water—can be harmful. In small amounts, very harmful additives can be beneficial. The iodine in salt is a health factor, but alone in larger amounts it can be a strong poison. Cobalt, selenium, and some other minerals are harmful in too great an amount. Thus, while eating natural foods may be thought to guarantee health, it does not. It all depends on what the food is, what nutrients it contains, and how well these nutrients meet our need. As yet, we know of no program that guarantees better nutrition than the ones outlined previously. Carefully selecting natural foods within these programs will certainly lead to no worse nutrition than would be achieved by following any other dietary program.

Sodium

Sodium is a necessary mineral that helps keep a proper balance between fluids outside and inside cells and helps maintain a proper acid–base balance. It also plays a role in the transmission of nerve impulses and in the relaxation of muscles after contraction. The absorption of glucose is facilitated by sodium as well.

A safe level of sodium for some people is about 1.1 to 3.3 grams per day. Most of us take in about 2.3 to 7 grams per day, but some people who eat a lot of salty foods get between 30 and 40 grams per day. About 1 gram per day is all an adult needs. We get most of our sodium from salt, which is about 40 percent sodium. On the average, a third of our sodium comes from the salt we add to our food, another third from sodium that is added to food we buy (baking soda, baking powder, monosodium glutamate) and the final third from naturally occurring sodium in foods. Milk contains 140 mg per glass; beets, carrots, and other root vegetables are good sources; and animal flesh foods and eggs are, too. A teaspoon of salt weighs 3 grams, which yields 1.2 grams of sodium. The American

Heart Association recommends an intake of 1 teaspoon or 3 grams per day. If a person loses a lot of water through sweating, diarrhea, vomiting, or otherwise, more salt is needed—a gram (or a third of a teaspoon) per quart of water consumed.

Some people think we train ourselves to consume too much salt. Because of this, no salt is added now to infant or baby foods. School food-services also have been told to reduce the amount of salt added to food.

Sodium is thought to increase blood pressure. Some people can consume considerable salt without being harmed; others are very adversely affected. It is thought that individuals inherit their susceptibility.

Since 1984, food that carries nutritional labeling must disclose the sodium content per serving of the food. It can also be voluntarily listed, even though nutritional labeling is not used. If the label says "sodium free," the food contains less than 5 mg/serving; if it says the sodium content is "very low," it is less than 35 mg/serving; if the content is 140 mg/serving or less, the label can say "low"; if the label says "reduced," the food per serving contains at least 75 percent less sodium than it normally would have. Labels may also state "no added salt," "unsalted," or "no salt added" if no salt is added to the food.

Fats and Cholesterol

Diseases of the heart and arterial system (atherosclerosis) are associated with high fat and cholesterol levels in the bloodstream. Fats and oils are triglycerides—three fatty acids attached to a glycerine radical. When they are plentiful in the blood stream, cholesterol is also plentiful. This is especially true when the fats are saturated. As was noted previously, unsaturated fats can be made into saturated ones by hydrogenation. Normally, the harder a fat is at room temperature, the greater is its degree of saturation. Animal fats tend to contain more saturated particles than plant fats (oils) do, but coconut oil and chocolate do not follow this rule: they are fairly saturated. The recommendation that we reduce our consumption of fats—especially saturated ones—is made in "Dietary Goals for the United States."

Cholesterol is a fatty substance essential to the body. It is a constituent of bile (a digestive fluid), sex hormones, other hormones, vitamin D, and brain and nerve cells. A desirable level is 130 to 190 mg per 100 ml of blood. The adult body uses about 900 mg a day, 600 mg of which usually comes from our food and the rest of which is made in the body. Table 2-10 identifies the cholesterol content of various foods.

Cholesterol accumulates as a waxy plaque that forms deposits in artery walls, causing them to thicken and become less flexible. Because the artery cannot expand, the heart must pump harder, which can cause an aneurysm and eventually a bursting of the artery. So much plaque can be deposited that the artery becomes plugged and a stroke or heart attack occurs. The same result can occur when an artery's clear flow space grows so narrowed that a blood clot can get caught. If this happens in the

TABLE 2-10. Cholesterol content of selected foods

Item	Cholesterol in 100 g edible portion (mg)	Cholesterol in edible portion of 1 lb, as purchased (mg)	Refuse from item, as purchased (%)
Beef, raw:			
with bone............................	70	270	15
without bone.........................	70	320	0
Brains, raw............................	>2,000	>9,000	0
Butter	250	1,135	0
Caviar or fish roe	>300	>1,300	0
Cheese:			
cheddar.............................	100	455	0
cottage, creamed......................	15	70	0
cream...............................	120	545	0
other (25% to 30% fat).................	85	385	0
Cheese spread.........................	65	295	0
Chicken, flesh only, raw	60		0
Crab:			
in shell	125	270	52
meat only...........................	125	565	0
Egg, whole............................	550	2,200	12
Egg white.............................	0	0	0
Egg yolk:			
fresh	1,500	6,800	0
frozen	1,280	5,800	0
dried	2,950	13,380	0
Fish:			
steak	70	265	16
fillet...............................	70	320	0
Heart, raw............................	150	680	0
Ice cream	45	205	0
Kidney, raw...........................	375	1,700	0
Lamb, raw:			
with bone...........................	70	265	16
without bone.........................	70	320	0
Lard and other animal fat	95	430	0
Liver, raw............................	300	1,360	0
Lobster:			
whole	200	235	74
meat only...........................	200	900	0
Margarine:			
all-vegetable fat......................	0	0	0
two-thirds animal fat, one-third			
vegetable fat	65	295	0
Milk:			
fluid, whole.........................	11	50	0
dried, whole	85	385	0
fluid, skim	3	15	0
Mutton:			
with bone...........................	65	250	16
without bone.........................	65	295	0
Oysters:			
in shell	>200	>90	90
meat only...........................	>200	>900	0

continued

TABLE 2-10. Cholesterol content of selected foods (*continued*)

Item	Cholesterol in 100 g edible portion (mg)	Cholesterol in edible portion of 1 lb, as purchased (mg)	Refuse from item, as purchased (%)
Pork:			
with bone..............................	70	260	18
without bone..........................	70	320	0
Shrimp:			
in shell	125	390	31
flesh only	125	565	0
Sweetbreads (thymus).....................	250	1,135	0
Veal:			
with bone..............................	90	320	21
without bone..........................	90	410	0

SOURCE: *Composition of Foods,* Agricultural Handbook No. 8, USDA (1963).

brain, a stroke occurs; if it happens in an artery adjacent to the heart, the result is a heart attack. Often high blood pressure is an indicator of undesirable plaque deposition. While no known dietary practice retards the formation of blood clots in the blood stream, aspirin is thought to retard their formation. Thus, one tablet every other day may be prescribed for individuals who are susceptible to atherosclerosis.

We do not know all we should about cholesterol and how it works in the body, and opinions differ about how best to treat it. Just consuming less fat and cholesterol in the diet at best reduces such intake by 5 to 10 percent. To make a substantial difference, a person must eat other foods that reduce cholesterol, exercise, have good emotional health, reduce stress, stop smoking, and often reduce calories and weight among other things to really reduce cholesterol levels. Table 2-11 lists foods, drugs, and activities that either increase or decrease cholesterol in the body. Avoiding items in the first list and emphasizing items in the second, along with reducing intake of cholesterol and saturated fat in the diet, can improve a person's cholesterol level markedly.

The presence in table 2-11 of some items listed as factors thought to increase or decrease cholesterol in the blood may call for explanation. Soft water often is softened by adding sodium; hard water contains magnesium. Petted and loved animals have lowered levels of cholesterol, showing the effect of love and lack of stress. The fibers of oats, legumes, and many fruits and vegetables lower cholesterol; wheat fiber and others do so to a lesser extent. Lecithin contains polyunsaturated fatty acids as a part of its structure and is thought to work as polyunsaturates do in removing cholesterol from the blood.

Heredity usually has decisive influence in deciding what a person's cholesterol level is. A person who comes from a family with a history of high blood pressure, high cholesterol level, strokes and heart problems is

TABLE 2-11. Some factors influencing cholesterol levels in the blood

Cholesterol increasers	Cholesterol decreasers
Increasing calories and weight	Decreasing calories and weight
Animal proteins	Increasing exercise and activity
Fats, especially saturated	Fat fish (salmon, mackerel, trout, whitefish, etc.)
Obesity	Legumes
Vitamin C and fluoride deficiency	Garlic
Diabetes	Hot pepper
Smoking	Alcohol (up to 4 oz a day)
Oral contraceptives for females	Glucose control in diabetics
Soft water	Hard water
Low-fiber diet	Good emotional health
Sucrose and fructose	Low stress in living
Marijuana	Ginseng
Alcohol (by adding calories)	Whole grains
Shellfish	Milks, especially soured ones such as like buttermilk and
Eggs	yogurt
	Lecithin

a high risk. Many people in such family trees find that reducing cholesterol in the diet does nothing to reduce the blood's cholesterol level.
What the diet eliminates, the body manufactures, keeping the level up
anyway. Males are usually a higher risk than females, up to about age 45;
then women after menopause become as high or even higher risks. Cholesterol levels gradually rise as people age. A person over 50 is at six times
the risk of having cholesterol-related health problems than a person under 20. Thus, the risk seems largely to depend on a person's heredity,
sex, and age.

Some individuals are also lucky in that their blood carries relatively
many high-density lipoproteins (HDL) and relatively few low-density
lipoproteins (LDL). A lipoprotein is a combination of a fat (lipid) and a
protein. If it is composed of a lot of fat and little protein, it is low-density;
if the opposite, it is high-density. LDL tend to favor the retention of
cholesterol in the blood stream, but HDL carry it away to the liver where
it is destroyed. Reducing weight, lessening the consumption of saturated
fats, increasing the consumption of unsaturated fats (cod liver oil, high in
polyunsaturates is very beneficial in amounts of 1 T a day), exercising
and eating finned fish increase HDL and lower LDL. Reducing the intake
of cholesterol-carrying foods may not be effective in reducing blood cholesterol, but drinking alcohol in moderation (the American Heart Association says the amount should not exceed 4 oz per day) has been shown to
raise HDL and reduce the risk of heart attacks.

A method of calculating a person's risk of developing some form of
atherosclerosis is presented in table 2-12.

The High-energy Diet

Many people want to have more energy. They feel run down and lack
vitality, so they consume special foods or take medicines or drugs that

TABLE 2-12. Atherosclerosis: what are your chances?

Factor	Small to greater risk				
Heredity (strokes or heart problems)	None (1)	1 relative over 60 (2)	2 relatives over 60 (3)	1 relative under 60 (4)	2 relatives under 60 (6)
Exercise (work and recreation)	Lot (1)	Moderate (2)	Somewhat sedentary(3)	Moderate sedentary (5)	Very sedentary (6)
Age (yrs)	1–20 (1)	21–30 (2)	31–40 (3)	41–50 (4)	51–65 (6)
Weight (over or under standard)	−6 lb or more (0)	+ or − 5 lb (1)	+6–20 lb (2)	+21–35 lb (4)	+36 lb up (6)
Tobacco	None use (0)	Cigar or pipe (1)	10 cigarettes a day or less (2)	20 or more cigarettes a day (4)	30 or more cigarettes a day (6)
Saturated fat (animal or solid)	None (1)	Very little (2)	Little (3)	Much (4)	Very much (6)

NOTE: To use, check the category to which you belong for each factor, and put down the amount shown in parentheses. Add these amounts and get a total. If your total is:

4 to 9   Your chances are remote
10 to 15   They are below average
16 to 20   You are an average risk
21 to 25   You are a moderate risk; needs some attention
26 to 30   Danger; watch out and take action
31 to 35   Big risk; take aggressive protective action

In using this risk table, also evaluate stress in your life, your emotional life and security, your blood pressure, and your bloodstream's cholesterol level. They can make a difference.)

SOURCE: U.S. Senate, Select Committee on Nutrition and Human Needs, *Diet Related to Killer Diseases II, Part 1. Cardiovascular Disease (Hearings)*. Washington, D.C.: Government Printing Office (1977).

perk up the body functions. Athletes who want to have greater energy reserves seek similar panaceas or even resort to using hormones. Some of these practices can be downright dangerous, and others are completely nonbeneficial. It is usually impossible to get the body to do more than it is capable of doing, but some people attempt to do this. A lack of vitality and energy can occur because of faulty food consumption, because of a lack of iron in the diet, or for other dietary reasons; medical examination and advice is the way to go on this, however—not self-treatment through diet. Normally, following the Basic Four Plan provides all the nutrients a person needs. By adding more high-calorie foods, the person can get the additional calories needed to produce extra energy. Often this is all it takes. The body is only capable of using a limited amount of minerals, vitamins, and energy-giving foods. Trying to add more is either wasteful or fattening.

The best energy food is a carbohydrate, preferably a complex one such as starch. From 50 to 60 percent of the total calorie needs of a normal adult should be met from this source. Taking glucose, fructose, other sugars, or protein mixes, does little to help and may not be as healthful as eating bread, cereals and other good carbohydrate foods. There must also be a proper intake of other foods. Various vitamins and minerals are tied up in energy production, and these must be present for good energy conversion. Thiamine, for example, is essential in the diet—especially in proper ratio to the calories burned.

The body can be trained to produce more energy and to maintain greater energy reserves. Athletes learn to do this, but it must be accompanied by good exercise and a strict dietary regimen.

Blood normally carries a certain amount of glucose or sugar that can be converted into energy quickly, but this quantity is limited. To get more glucose, the body must take carbohydrate, protein, or fat and convert it into glucose—a slow process. When we need quick energy, we can call on a substance called *glycogen*, a body starch that is fairly concentrated and readily converts into glucose and energy. Most of our glycogen reserves are in the liver, but an additional amount is usually stored in the body tissues. Our glycogen reserve is maintained by the liver, which takes excess glucose and—instead of turning it into fat—turns it into glycogen. Thus, after we make a high expenditure of energy, some or all of the extra calories we eat because we are hungrier than usual go into storage as glycogen.

Some years ago it was widely believed that, to build muscle and strength, a person should eat a lot of protein foods such as meat. Meat is muscle, and so (people reasoned) muscle made muscle. This is not true. An athlete doing heavy exercise requires only about 10 percent more protein per day than for normal needs, so 80 grams per day should be enough. Any excess is turned into glucose or fat. To build muscle, a person should eat plenty of carbohydrate to spare protein use and then exercise the muscles that are to be built. Exercise causes the muscle cells to enlarge and multiply. Special protein muscle-builders or other foods do little good.

To build up energy reserves, a person should eat a normal amount of carbohydrate while doing a lot of exercise and then reduce the amount of exercise but increase the quantity of carbohydrate. This can be repeated several times; each time, during the high-carbohydrate feeding period, the body increases its ability to store glycogen—not only in the liver, but also in the muscles (where it is quickly utilized). A more effective approach is to eat very little carbohydrate during the first period and then follow the second as outlined. This procedure sometimes leads to a bad reaction, however, altering the heart rate, causing sore and swollen muscles, and increasing weight.

It is also important to learn to breathe heavily and deeply and to develop the heart muscles by exercise. To create energy, the body needs oxygen, which good breathing and heart action can furnish; this promotion of both is sometimes called aerobic exercise. Lactic acid is a chemical product that often remains in the muscles after incomplete burning of glucose. This chemical can cause muscles to feel sore. With good aerobic conditions—brought about by a continued period of exercise—the body learns to get rid of this lactic acid, and soreness is avoided. Thus, a person who does little preparatory exercise and then runs a mile is apt to be sore the next day; but a person who is accustomed to running a mile feels no soreness afterward. It is important to reduce calorie intake when no exercise is being taken, so as to avoid weight gain.

The meal before an athletic event should be consumed far enough in advance to free the body of the need to carry on digestion while undertaking heavy exercise, since digestion can detract from the body's ability to create energy. The meal should be high in carbohydrates and can be in liquid form. Consuming plenty of fluids is also desirable. A 5 percent reduction in fluids in the body below the quantity needed for full functioning can reduce a person's ability to produce energy by 20 to 30 percent. Athletes are frequently called to the bench to rest and drink some liquid. The rest helps the body to reduce the amount of lactic acid present, and the fluid replaces fluid lost in sweating. Too much fluid however, deters energy production. The body can absorb only about 1 quart of liquid per hour. The efficacy of drinking special fluids that sellers claim can be absorbed by the body at a faster rate has not been proved. Water is about the best fluid a person can take. Alcohol acts as a diuretic and increases fluid loss so it should be avoided. Drinking one or two cups of coffee about a half hour before commencing an activity causes the liver to start breaking down fat, which then becomes available for energy.

A popular myth is that, if a person takes some sweet just before expending a large amount of energy, the blood receives an extra shot of glucose and the person can perform better. This procedure can actually decrease energy production by increasing the need for fluid. As has been noted, a heavy steak dinner might not be digested by the time the heavy exercise was to begin, and the body would then have not only to produce energy but to digest as well. Probably the best practice is to take some fluid—sweetened slightly, if desired—immediately before beginning the heavy exercise.

SANITATION AND SAFETY

Sanitation and safety are the joint responsibility of management and workers. Management must promote a clean and safe operation by ensuring that facilities, equipment, and materials meet sanitary and safety standards. It must design programs that meet these standards, and it must train and give leadership to workers to see that they are met. Workers must learn to do sanitation tasks, to work in an efficient and proper way, and to achieve proper sanitation and safety. Limiting precautions to steps required by law may not be enough: patrons may demand more, or problems may arise. High standards here are desirable.

SANITATION

Food should not only have a good taste and an attractive appearance, it should be nutritious, clean, and safe to eat. Patrons demand high standards, neatness, and order. A facility that offers a tidy parking lot, bright, sparkling windows, trim and neat landscaping, and a clean, inviting interior appeals to patrons. State codes for sanitation and safety are often based on the federal Foodservice Sanitation Ordinance and Code, which is administered by the U.S. Public Health Service. OSHA (Occupational Safety and Health Administration) sets many standards for safety. The National Sanitation Foundation and our own professional associations set standards, too.

Principles

Foods can become unsuitable for consumption through contamination by living organisms, chemicals, or spoilage. A good sanitation program eliminates or controls these, making foods safe to eat. Patrons also have a right to expect that the food they eat is clean and is not handled in any repugnant manner.

Bacteria, Viruses, and Parasites. Bacteria and viruses are present in the air and live in and on everything; some grow in food and can pose mild or serious health hazards. *Intoxicants* are organisms that develop toxins in food, which when consumed cause illness. Once the toxin is formed, the organism that produced it may be destroyed, without making the food any less harmful. *Infectants* are organisms that must be taken into the body before they can grow and develop harmful substances. When they are present in food, they may be destroyed by cooking; if this occurs, no harm results from the contamination. With an intoxicant, however, we can cook the food and destroy the organism but still be left with the dangerous toxin in the food.

Bacteria and viruses grow slowly at temperatures below 45°F and are destroyed at temperatures above 140°F; the danger zone is between these extremes. These organisms must have food and moisture to thrive. They grow well in most foods, except foods high in acid, high in salt, or low in moisture. They do especially well in combinations of protein and starch—broths, cream pies, chicken salad, and the like. Some require air; others do not. Knowing what favors this growth is important in promoting good sanitation control.

Bacteria are unicellular organisms that reproduce by transverse fission: they grow larger and larger until they split in two. The progression thus proceeds at a geometric rate of increase: 1, 2, 8, 16, 32, 64, 128, 256, 512, 1,024, 2,048, 4,096, 9,192, 18,384, . . . ; thus, the number of bacteria can reach the millions quickly. Time and temperature are factors in their growth. Usually food left standing for over 4 hours at room temperature can be considered dangerous. In general, the temperature range between room temperature and 110°F favors growth. Chilling or freezing arrests growth. Bacteria in frozen food gradually die, but the process is slow; diphtheria bacteria in raw oysters, for example, survive for over 3 months in the frozen state. Viruses are not destroyed by freezing but go into a suspended state.

Infectants such as scarlet fever, hepatitis, and tuberculosis can be present in food and cause serious illness in a few days or weeks. Others may cause only digestive upset. The most common infectious organisms in food are *Salmonella, Clostridium perfringens,* and *bacillary dysentery (Shigella).* Vomiting, cramps, headache, fever, and perhaps diarrhea may develop from these in a few hours.

The most common intoxicant is *Staphylococcus.* It develops a dangerous toxin in food in about 4 hours if conditions are right. The symptoms are about the same as indicated for the infectants just named. *Clostridium botulinum,* another intoxicant, produces a deadly poison that paralyzes the nervous system, causing violent and sudden death. A mere $\frac{1}{2}$ cup of the bacteria would be enough to destroy everyone on earth! Most deaths from it are the result of consuming tainted home-canned foods. While 20 minutes of boiling destroys this toxin, it is extremely foolish to rely on this procedure to render suspect foods safe. Any such food should be removed from storage and destroyed. A person should never taste any food that is suspected of being spoiled or of containing harmful substances. Doing so is like playing Russian roulette.

Parasites such as *Endamoeba histolytica,* trichinae, and tapeworm can infest food. Endomoeba is found in impure water, in the soil, on fruits or vegetables, or in other foods. The intestinal tracts of people and animals can be infested with it, and then the infestation can be transferred to others. Trichina are found most notably in pork but also can be in bear, rabbit, or other meat. They are nematode worms whose small larvae burrow into our muscles and cause trichinosis, a condition characterized by nausea, cramps, and diarrhea and then aching muscles, fever, and chest pain. Because pigs are sometimes infested with trichinae, pork should always be cooked until well done. Eggs of the tapeworm in raw meat are usually the source of its infection in the body. Table 2-13 summarizes various types of food poisoning and the factors involved in each type.

Poisons. Many elemental chemicals are poisonous, such as lead, antimony, and cadmium. Lead is a common substance in plumbing fixtures, paints, and some equipment. Antimony is sometimes used in enameled dishware and on the enameled bodies of equipment. Cadmium is also used in food utensils. Normally these metals must dissolve (usually through contact with an acid) in order to enter into and contaminate food. A combination of acid and copper can produce a poison, as well. Poisons are used in foodservices to destroy insects and animals. These should never be stored with or near food. One highly poisonous roach powder looks very much like dry milk and has been mistaken for it. Oxalic acid is an excellent bleach for wooden table tops and other surfaces but is poisonous. Some silver polishes contain cyanide, the substance put into medicine capsules that killed some people a few years ago. All poisonous substances should be kept away from foodservice areas; if allowed in the vicinity, they should be kept separate from everything else, be plainly labeled, be kept under locked storage, and be used only by those who know how to handle them safely and properly.

Food Deterioration. Foods spoil for many reasons. Enzymes in the food can bring about spoilage changes. Meats, fresh produce, and other nonpreserved foods can remain in storage too long and deteriorate from these enzymes. Bacteria, molds, and yeast can also spoil food.

Some of the same substances and organisms that spoil food can benefit it. Cheese and meat improve with aging because of the action of enzymes, but they can also spoil because of them. Bacteria are helpful in developing cheese. Yeast destroys food by causing fermentation, but the same fermentation in beer or bread is beneficial. Bacteria that produce lactic acid sour milk but are helpful in making sauerkraut, pickles, and other items. Molds are used to make such cheeses as Stilton and Roquefort.

We can never completely isolate ourselves from organisms that might harm us, so we must build up immunities against them while continuing to do everything possible to eradicate them from our environment. Some people are highly susceptible to even mild infections or toxic doses. At times such a person may not feel well, thinking the problem is a slight headache or cold when the real cause is a mild infection or toxic reaction. We need to avoid all infections and toxins, no matter how mild.

Spoilage can be controlled by using fresh foods as quickly as possible and by never letting spoilage agents attack food. Food purveyors should have clean operations, trucks, and personnel, and should handle only clean food. Meats should be inspected and passed. Seafoods should come from beds approved by the Public Health Service. Unpasteurized milk, egg products, and other foods that may carry harmful organisms should not be used. A constant watch must be kept to ensure that harmful food is not served.

TABLE 2-13. Summary of factors involved in food poisonings

Agent	Incubation period	Duration of illness	Symptoms
Staphylococcus aureus	2–4 hours.	24 to 36 hours.	Vomiting, cramps, abdominal pain, diarrhea, headache, nausea. Sometimes accompanied by fever.
Clostridium botulinum	18–36 hours. Shortest 4 hours. As long as 6 days.	70% die in 4–8 days.	Nervous symptoms: diplopia, weakness and paralysis of muscles. Inhibition of body secretions, inability to swallow, constipation.
Salmonella typhimurium, etc.	6–12 hours. As long as 72 hours.	1–3 days.	Nausea, vomiting, cramps, diarrhea, fever, headache, prostration.
Typhoid (*Eberthella typhosa*)	3–28 days.	3–4 months.	Continued fever, skin (rash) eruption, diarrhea, depression, prostration, enlargement of spleen.
Bacillary Dysentery (*Shigella*)	2–7 days.	Self-limited. Several weeks.	Acute febrile, bloody diarrhea, nausea, prostration.
Amoebic Dysentery (*Endamoeba hystolytica*)	10–14 days. Variable months.	Chronic.	Bloody diarrhea; abdominal pains; abscesses in liver, spleen, and intestines.
Fluoride	15 minutes to 1 hour.	Several hours.	Cold sweats, nausea, vomiting, cramps, desire to sleep (lachrymation).
Cadmium	15 minutes to ½ hour.	Several hours.	Nausea and violent vomiting.
Antimony	15 minutes to ½ hour.	Several hours.	
Cyanide			Cyanosis, mental confusion, glassy eyes.
Lead	Chronic.		Blue line on gums; cramps in stomach, bowels, and legs; constipation; wrist drop.
Trichinosis (*Trichinella spiralis*)	Primary: 24–72 hours. Secondary: 4–5 days.	As long as a year or more.	Pri: Nausea, vomiting, abdominal pain, diarrhea. Sec: Suborbital edema, chest pain, muscular pain, fever.
Wild Mushrooms: 1. Inedible (*Boletus*) 2. Poisonous (*Amanita*)	1. Several hours. 2. 6–14 hours.	1. 24 hours 2. 3–4 days (muscarine, death in 15 minutes).	1. Nausea, vomiting, cramps, diarrhea. 2. Sudden severe abdominal pain, intense thirst, nausea, retching, vomiting, contracted pupils, convulsions, delirium, coma.
Weil's Disease (*Leptospira icterohemorrhagica*)	5–7 days.	Several months.	Jaundice, muscular pain, fever, spleen and liver enlargement, constipation.

Foods implicated	Mode of transmission	Prevention
Under favorable conditions, toxin is formed in many foods: custards, chopped or comminuted foods (chicken salad, fish salad, meat salad), gravies, soups, hollandaise sauce, hash, etc.	Infections in food handlers; droplet infection from nose or throat.	Sanitation, sterilization, and refrigeration of perishable foods; careful food handling; health food handlers; heating to 190°F (toxin is heat-resistant).
Food kept under anaerobic conditions. Prefers protein foods but grows in all common foods (canned and improperly processed foods).	Soil- and dirt-contaminated foods. 1. Spores not killed in processing. 2. Toxin easily destroyed.	Autoclaving, under pressure, canned foods of pH over 4.0; for home-canned foods, boiling for 20 minutes after removal from can; use of antitoxin of proper type soon after attack, if infected.
Under favorable conditions, salads, milk, comminuted foods, custards, soups, gravies, sauces, meats, shellfish.	Fecal contamination of food; bathing in polluted water; shellfish from polluted water; diseased animals; carriers (ducks).	Good personal habits of food handlers; sufficient cooking and refrigeration of perishable foods; controlled shellfish production.
Shellfish, salads, raw vegetables, milk, milk products, water, soft cheese, fresh cheddar.	Carriers; sewage; polluted water supplies; contact (flies and rodents) through food; shellfish.	Sanitary water supplies; proper sewage disposal; control of known carriers; shellfish sanitation.
Milk, water, or any food may be vehicle.	Carriers; polluted water; milk; contact.	Good personal habits of food handlers; sanitary water supplies and sewage disposal; sanitary plumbing installations.
Water or food may be vehicle; raw vegetables.	Cyst in feces of carriers, through food or polluted water supplies.	Sanitary plumbing and water supplies; good personal habits of food handlers.
Accidental contamination of any food or drink by insecticides.	Insecticides.	Careful use of insecticides.
Acid food or drink.	Cadmium-plated vessels.	Prohibiting use of cadmium in manufacture or repair of food utensils.
Acid food or drink.	Pigments; chipped enamel-lined utensils.	Discarding chipped enameled pots and pans.
Accidental in any food or drink.	Silver polishes; fumigation.	Prohibiting use of silver polishes containing cyanides; close supervision of fumigators.
Water pipes, acid fruits in contact with lead vessels, beer, CO_2, water.	——	Prohibiting use of lead in any food plant for containers, container repair piping, or paint.
Pork and pork products.	Poorly cooked pork; improperly processed pork products.	Eliminating feeding of uncooked garbage to swine; enforcing proper processing of pork products; cooking all pork until well-done.
Mushrooms picked wild.	Eating wild mushrooms, not knowing identification.	Avoidance of wild mushrooms; use of cultivated commercial varieties.
Anything contaminated by the urine of rats infected with the disease.	By mouth or through skin.	Warfare against rats; sanitation; guarding foods against contamination; cooking; protection of skin.

SOURCE: *Sanitation Manual* published by the New York State Restaurant Association, from a table originally prepared by Joseph Schiftner, former supervising health inspector in charge of investigating food poisoning for the New York City Health Department.

Utensils, tools, and the environment must be clean. Harmful organisms thrive at room temperature: freezing or cooking foods stops their action; refrigeration retards it. Canned foods are sterilized in a sealed container and then are preserved in that state until the seal is broken. A food containing 5 percent salt resists deterioration, while a level of 10 percent salt acts as a preservative. Food containing more than 50 percent sugar keeps fairly well. Drying takes away moisture that spoilage agents need in order to grow. Pickling is another method of introducing acid and other preservatives to preserve a food. An acid reaction retards bacterial growth. Mayonnaise and cooked salad dressings are not dangerous foods by themselves, but when we mix them with other foods we reduce their acidity, making them potential havens for microorganisms. Meats wiped with a cloth that has been moistened in vinegar tend to resist bacteria because of the action of the vinegar's acetic acid. Curing retards deterioration: creosotes (from the smoke), salt, and nitrites are effective agents here.

Cleaning and Sanitation

Utensils and equipment can be sanitized by thorough washing with soap or a detergent to remove all soil, followed by wiping with a solution containing chlorine, iodine, or some other bactericide. Friction is a more effective agent in removing soil than are detergents or soaps; the two should be used in combination to remove soil. Then the soap or detergent should be rinsed off thoroughly.

Exposure to hot water spray or immersion in 180°F water for 10 seconds destroys most pathogens; exposure or immersion at 170°F for 30 seconds does the same thing. Chlorine or iodine—50 parts per million (ppm) of the former, or 25 ppm of the latter—in water at a temperature of 75°F, with 1 minute's immersion, destroys most pathogens. We usually start with 100 ppm of chlorine or 50 ppm of iodine to be sure we keep above these levels. Any one of the following amounts of disinfectant in 10 gallons of water gives desirable levels:

$4\frac{1}{4}$ T ($2\frac{1}{4}$ oz) of $5\frac{1}{2}$% sodium hypochlorite
$1\frac{1}{2}$ T ($\frac{3}{4}$ oz) of 12% sodium hypochlorite
$1\frac{1}{2}$ t ($\frac{1}{4}$ oz) 70% sodium hypochlorite
$\frac{1}{2}$ c (4 oz) iodine-type disinfectant

In a mechanical dishwasher's final rinse, we may introduce a wetting agent containing chlorine. A wetting agent in the final rinse gives water easier runoff, so items do not spot; items also dry faster. Air-drying is recommended; towel drying often reintroduces organisms.

We also use dips containing sanitizing agents for silverware. Even stronger sanitizing agents are used to sanitize floors. In hospitals, these may contain fairly strong bactericides. Proper use of these compounds is essential. Using more than recommended does not do a better job and may even destroy the benefit.

Detergents often contain chelating and sequestering agents, which are added to hold onto soil and keep it away from utensils once it is removed. *Chela* means claw, as on a crab or lobster; to *sequester* means to hide away. Thus, a chelating compound picks soil up and holds onto it, while a sequestering agent bars it from reuniting with the utensil. Detergents and soaps loosen soil, often by emulsifying or saponifying it. This allows water to get at soil and wet it. Detergents and soaps do 30 percent of the cleaning job; friction or "elbow grease" does the rest.

Good sanitation practices in handling and storage are also required. Items should be covered as much as possible; glasses and cups should be rack-inverted. Working or eating ends of silverware should be pointed down in containers.

Sanitation failures are 5 percent a failure of equipment and 95 percent human failure. Good personal hygiene is terribly important in reducing the incidence of food poisoning. One of the chief sources of food contamination is people. We harbor many organisms and spread them around. *Staphylococci* are in our nasal passages and throat, and when we sneeze or cough we spread them. They also are found in cuts, boils, acne, and any other place where pus may develop. *Salmonella* and other bacteria are in our intestinal tracts; if we fail to wash our hands after using the toilet, they can be the source of food poisoning. Our bodies and clothes should be as clean as we can keep them.

Steam is an excellent cleaner, and many operations use it to clean equipment. Garbage collection should occur frequently, and cans and areas where it is present should be kept scrupulously clean. The insides of poultry sometimes contain *Salmonella*, which can be transferred to food or equipment and cause food poisoning. Flies, roaches, mice, rats, and other vermin carry and spread disease. They should be kept away from the operation.

The time taken to train employees in how to clean and sanitize properly is well repaid in cleanliness and a healthful operation. Schedules for cleaning and proper procedures for doing it should be posted and followed. Daily checks of work areas, storage spaces, and other spaces should be made. Violations of good practices should not be permitted. The National Sanitation Foundation describes cleanliness as a way of life; in a foodservice, it is the only way.

The following rules should be observed in practicing good sanitation:

1. Keep cold foods cold (below 40°F) and hot foods hot (above 140°F).
2. Cook poultry to an internal temperature of 180°F, and pork to 170°F; use a meat thermometer.
3. Cool cooked food that is to be kept for future use as quickly as possible. Do not store it in large bulk, but spread it out, cover it, and refrigerate it. Never allow any potentially dangerous food to stand at room temperature for more than 4 hours. Store carry-over food immediately.
4. Defrost frozen foods under refrigeration.

5. Boil sauces, gravies, soups, and broths for several minutes, and serve at once.
6. Never taste any food from a bulging or leaking can. Never taste any food suspected of being contaminated. Throw it out.
7. Store refrigerated food so that air can circulate around it; do not store food near water or heating pipes. Never keep cleaning supplies, poisons, and other dangerous substances in areas where food is stored.
8. Cook all meats separate from their stuffing. Store such stuffings at shallow depths in covered pans.
9. Wash all poultry, fresh vegetables, and fresh fruits thoroughly.
10. Some molds may be toxic (not molds in some cheeses). Do not cut away mold and use the food. The mold tendrils can run deeply into food without there being evidence of them.
11. Keep yourself clean; work in a clean, orderly area.

SAFETY

Safety is freedom from danger. Foodservices have a high rate of accidents largely because hot foods are handled and many cutting tools are constantly in use. Accident statistics show that it is safer to work in a mine than in a foodservice!

Management should make frequent checks to ascertain that work areas are safe. Electrical, plumbing, and other services should be checked. All electrical equipment should be grounded. Mechanical equipment should be made safe to handle. Cutoff switches should be located close by the equipment. Guards should be placed over all areas where cutting occurs and all areas where moving gears or parts are found. Workers should be taught to work safely. Surprise factors are frequently the greatest cause of accidents, and a search should be made to identify and reduce these. Equipment should bear approval stamps of the American Gas Association (AGA) or Underwriters' Laboratories (UL). Equipment should be maintained properly: set up a maintenance schedule, and see it is followed. Finally, management should see that water, steam, and other turnoff locations are known by employees and are not locked up.

Workers should be trained to respond quickly to emergency situations and should go through drills for this purpose. Tours should be given, and the location and operation of emergency equipment should be explained and learned. It is essential that the location of a blanket be known in case someone catches fire. The location of the first-aid kit should also be known by all employees. First-aid procedures for cuts, burns, and electric shock should be understood. Workers should know how to protect themselves in time of emergency, how to get out of a dangerous area, and how to help others do the same. Management should see that all precautions are taken and should set up emergency plans for contingencies; then it should ensure that employees know them. If management fails to do this, it may regret it later.

There are three kinds of fire: (A) a fire from combustible material such as rags, paper, or wood; (B) a grease, gas, or petroleum fire; and (C) a fire caused by electricity. Each must be fought differently, and personnel should know how to respond to each. The fire-fighting equipment and techniques to use for each should be available and familiar to workers. Removing fire hazards, potential fuel, heat or electricity, and oxygen retards a fire. Water can put some fires out but can spread or worsen others. Removing combustible material, reducing heat, or cutting off oxygen helps to discourage any fire.

Good work habits can eliminate many accidents. Alertness and awareness of danger are important habits to develop. Learning how to work correctly is, too. Some people are accident-prone because they are careless, are not on guard, or do not realize that danger can be present. As individuals tire, accident rates rise. Workers should be taught how to handle cutting tools, how to take care of broken glass and how to work safely in other ways. All workers should be trained to wipe up spills immediately and to clean up work areas. To the experienced worker, safety is an inseparable part of learning. The inexperienced worker must also learn this—and the faster, the better.

Chapter Review

1. Describe the "Dietary Goals for the United States."
2. What are your opinions about the nutritional responsibility of
   a. a drive-in serving partial meals?
   b. a restaurant serving complete meals?
   c. a factory's foodservice serving workers?
   d. an orphanage's foodservice?
   e. a retirement home's foodservice?
   f. a hospital's dietary department?
3. What are the three energy suppliers in food, and how many calories does each supply per gram?
4. What is a saturated fat? a monounsaturated fat? a polyunsaturated fat? Which should be watched in the diet? Why? What is cholesterol, and why is it a problem in health?
5. What should your normal weight be, and what should your calorie intake be per day?
6. What is your opinion about the good or harm done by artificial sweeteners? sodium sulfite? sodium nitrite? caffeine? irradiation? sodium?
8. What is GRAS? What is nutritional labeling? What is the list of ingredients on a label?
9. What is the difference between *clean* and *sanitary*?
10. What are bacteria, viruses, and parasites, and how do they grow? What is the difference between the infectant and an intoxicant?
11. What are some of the agents that spoil food, and how can they be controlled?
12. How would you fight a grease fire?

CHAPTER 3

Temperatures and Equipment

Outline

I. **Introduction**
  1. How Heat Changes Food
  2. Fahrenheit and Celsius Scales
  3. Heat Movement and Action
  4. Specific Heat, Heat of Fusion, and Heat of Vaporization
  5. pH
  6. Metric Conversion

II. **Light Equipment**
  1. Hand Tools and Small Utensils
     a. Hand Tools
     b. Serving Tools
     c. Utility Items
     d. Pots and Pans
     e. Weighing and Portioning Equipment

III. **Heavy Equipment**
  1. Heating Equipment
     a. Direct-heating Equipment
     b. Food-handling Equipment
     c. Steam-cooking Equipment
     d. Beverage-making Equipment
     e. Miscellaneous Cooking Equipment
  2. Mechanical Equipment
     a. Cutting Equipment
     b. Mixers
     c. Refrigeration and Freezing Equipment
     d. Butchershop Equipment
     e. Bakery Equipment
     f. Dishwashers and Potwashers

Goals

1. To detail some basic facts about temperature and about how heat works in cooking food.
2. To show how heat is used for refrigeration, distillation, evaporation, humidifying, and other purposes in the kitchen.
3. To describe the makeup and operation of various tools and equipment used in quantity food work.

INTRODUCTION

Cooking can change food, making it more acceptable and digestible. We cook by boiling, steaming, broiling, frying, barbecueing, or roasting. Cooking changes the texture, color, form, and flavor of food; it also sanitizes food. To cook well, we must learn how to use and control heat.

We develop heat by friction, by chemical means, or by physical change. When the flow of electricity is slowed in an element, the friction develops heat. Dielectric heat results when electricity is directed into food and friction occurs just as in an element. When carbon or hydrogen combines with oxygen, the mixture burns and gives off heat; we call this *combustion*, and the point at which it starts is called *ignition* or *flash point*. Cooking oils and fats have flash points around 600°F—not much higher than the temperature to which we raise them in frying. When we explode an atomic bomb we create heat by physical change. The sun is a seething mass of material undergoing similar physical change, generating and emitting much energy in the form of electromagnetic energy or light. In 45 hours, we receive more energy from this source than is stored in all our reserves of natural gas, coal, and oil. The energy is turned into warmth, but the earth radiates a lot of it back into space.

HOW HEAT CHANGES FOOD

Starch in the presence of moisture is thickened by heat. This gelatinization (swelling or thickening) starts at about 150°F and ends at around 203°F. Proteins denaturate (lose moisture) at about 140°F and coagulate at around 160°F. We see this happen when an egg or steak cooks; the color changes and the protein firms up. We call such firming of protein *coagulation*. Some of the moisture lost in this process is evident in the drippings from the steak. The combination of heat plus moisture tenderizes meat by breaking down collagen, a white connective tissue. The combination of acid plus heat can break down starch, as happens in a lemon pie filling that thins if we cook it too much. Baking powder or soda when moistened and heated gives off carbon dioxide, which leavens cakes and some other pastries. Cellulose, pectins, and other fibrous products in fruits and vegetables are softened by heat and moisture.

We must control heat in cooking, or we will produce overcooked or undercooked food. A cream puff shell only rises well if we get rapid heat into it so that steam develops inside and puffs up the dough. In cooking bakery goods, we control heat in such a way that we get proper gelatinization of starch and coagulation of protein simultaneously with maximum expansion from the leavening agent. A sugar solution must be cooked to a certain temperature if it is to yield the right cake frosting.

FAHRENHEIT AND CELSIUS SCALES

Temperature is a relative measure of the level or intensity of heat; it does not indicate quantitatively how much heat there is. Fahrenheit and Celsius (centigrade) scales are used to measure the level of heat. One Fahr-

TABLE 3-1. Equivalent Fahrenheit and Celsius temperatures

°F	°C	°F	°C	°F	°C
0	−17.8	60	15.6	120	48.9
10	−12.2	65	18.3	150	65.6
15	−9.4	70	21.1	200	93.3
20	−6.7	75	23.9	212	100.0
32	0	80	26.7	250	121.1
35	1.7	85	29.4	300	148.9
40	4.4	90	32.2	350	176.7
45	7.2	95	35.0	400	204.4
50	10.0	100	37.8	450	232.2
55	12.8	110	43.3	500	260.0

RULE: Fahrenheit to Celsius: Subtract 32 from Fahrenheit degrees and multiply the remainder by $\frac{5}{9}$; product is Celsius degrees.
Celsius to Fahrenheit: Multiply Celsius degrees by $\frac{9}{5}$ and add 32; product is Fahrenheit degrees.

enheit degree equals $\frac{5}{9}$ of a Celsius degree and a Celsius degree is $\frac{9}{5}$ of a Fahrenheit degree. To convert from Celsius to Fahrenheit, we multiply the Celsius temperature by $\frac{9}{5}$ and add 32. To change Fahrenheit to Celsius, we subtract 32 from the Fahrenheit temperature and multiply by $\frac{5}{9}$. Thus, to change 75°C to Fahrenheit, we multiply 75 by $\frac{9}{5}$ and add 32 ($[75 \times \frac{9}{5}] + 32 = 167°F$). To change 182°F to Celsius, we substract 32 from 182 and multiply the result by $\frac{5}{9}$ ($[182 − 32] \times \frac{5}{9} = 83.3°C$). Table 3-1 shows some equivalent Fahrenheit and Celsius temperatures.

Heat causes many substances to expand in a set ratio to the level of heat. Mercury does this, as do some solid metals. This enables us to use them to make thermometers. Aluminum and brass expand differently, so if we bind them together one bends the other when the temperature rises. We can use this phenomena to make a meat thermometer. As the two metals inside the stem twist, they move a dial and thereby indicate the temperature. We make a candy thermometer by filling a small bulb with mercury. As the temperature rises, the mercury in the bulb expands and rises up a tiny column inside the thermometer.

HEAT MOVEMENT AND ACTION

Heat can be transferred by conduction, by convection, or by radiation. Conducted heat moves from one particle of matter to another. It moves quite fast in a copper rod; we can heat one end and soon we feel heat at the other end. It moves less quickly in liquids and even more slowly in gas. We often use tiny bubbles of enclosed air to prevent heat transfer, as we do when we use urethane or cork in refrigerator insulation. When we cover ice cream with egg foam in making a Baked Alaska, we are using the egg foam to insulate the ice cream from the heat while the meringue bakes.

Stainless steel is a very poor heat conductor; copper is excellent, and aluminum is good. We use aluminum and copper for pots and pans that must cook food. A stainless steel pan is a poor heat conductor, so we put copper on the bottom of the pan to capture and spread the heat out. We can also put a thin layer of aluminum or copper between two sheets of stainless steel to achieve the same result. Such "clad" stainless steel is used for pots and pans. If sodium-aluminum borosilicate is added to glass, the glass becomes a good heat conductor and does not shatter when a lot of heat strikes it.

Convection occurs when heated gas is moved around. A fan in a convection oven blows hot air around the oven. As a natural process, warm air rises and cold air falls, and this kind of convection is utilized in regular ovens where the heating source is located at the base of the oven chamber.

When charcoal or an electrical element glows with heat, it is emitting a lot of radiated heat. Radiated heat is transferred through space just as electromagnetic waves are. The infrared radiation leaps with the speed of light from one mass to another. Warm objects radiate heat to cooler ones. More heat is picked up by a rough, dark surface than by a bright, shiny one. Thus, the aluminum pans that contain some frozen foods come with black outside surfaces instead of shiny ones, in order to absorb heat better. We use bright shiny surfaces to radiate heat to places we want the heat.

Microwaves are a form of radiated energy; they have longer wave lengths than regular radiated heat (infrared) waves and are usually generated in a cathode-ray tube. These waves penetrate food, causing a friction called *kinetic action*, and this heats the food.

A flame is a dull red at 900° to 1,100°F, dark red at 1,100° to 1,500°F, bright red at 1,500° to 1,800°F, yellowish red at 1,800° to 2,200°F, and white at temperatures above 2,200°F. The sun's surface is 6,000°F but its interior is much hotter. If a gas flame is yellow, it is not operating properly. It should be a bluish-white. Some char-broilers have ceramic units that heat up almost to the intensity of white heat.

Temperature gauges the level or quality of heat; the actual quantity of heat is indicated by Btu (British thermal units) and calories. A Btu represents the amount of heat needed to raise a pound of water 1 Fahrenheit degree; a calorie represents the amount of heat needed to raise 1 cc of water 1 Celsius degree. When we speak of calories in relation to foods, we are actually referring to kilocalories, each of which is the equivalent of 1,000 regular calories.

Fuels give off different amounts of heat; thus, 1 lb of fuel oil yields 19,000 Btu; 1 lb of coal yields 14,000 Btu; 1 ft³ of natural gas yields 1,000 Btu; 1 ft³ of propane gas yields 3,200 Btu; and 1 kilowatt hour (kwh) of electricity yields 3,416 Btu. It takes approximately 1,150 Btu to cook the average meal. Not all the heat in fuel is captured in cooking. We lose it from equipment surfaces in exhausting fumes, or from the food itself. Gas, coal, and fuel oil lose more heat than electricity does, because about

40 percent is lost in exhausting fumes. Consequently, we must expend 1.6 times more gas Btu than electricity Btu to obtain the same amount of usable heat. To equal a kwh of electricity, 5,466 Btu of gas are needed (3,416 × 1.6 = 5,466).

If electricity sells for 8¢ per kwh, a competitive gas price would be $0.0000146 per Btu ($0.08/5,466 Btu = $0.0000146). Since 1 ft³ of gas contains 1,000 Btu, and since gas is sold in units of 100 ft³, the equivalent cost of gas would be $0.0000146 × [100 cuft × 1000 Btu] = $1.46 per 100 ft³. If gas were being sold at $1.75/100 ft³, the equivalent price per kwh of electricity would be [$1.75/100 ft³ × 1,000 Btu] × 3,416 Btu/kwh of electricity = $0.06.

SPECIFIC HEAT, HEAT OF FUSION, AND HEAT OF VAPORIZATION

Specific heat is the amount of heat required to raise the temperature of 1 gram of a particular substance by 1 Celsius degree. Water, at 1.0, is the standard. In contrast to water, fresh peas have a specific heat of 0.79; frozen peas, 0.42; fat, 0.5; copper, 0.092; aluminum, 0.22; and iron, 0.11. If we put 1 pound of water in an aluminum pan that weighs 1 pound, the water requires almost 5 times more heat to get to 212°F than does the aluminum pan (1.0/0.22 = 4.54). If we could capture all the heat and put it into the water, the pan, and 1 pound of fresh peas, it would take 426 Btu to get all three to 212°F ([212°F × 1.0] + [212°F × 0.22] + [212°F × 0.79] = 426.12.)

At absolute zero (−460°F), all molecular motion stops. As heat increases, so does molecular motion. Finally the motion becomes so great that a solid becomes a liquid, and then (at an even higher level of excitation) a gas. The internal molecular pull in solids is so great that, even though finely divided, they will not blend. Some combinations of liquids blend easily, but others, such as vinegar and oil, do not. In the case of vinegar and oil, each has a strong molecular pull that resists the pull of the other; if we add an emulsifier, however, this pull can be negated. Thus, when we make mayonnaise, the protein in the egg attracts both the vinegar and the oil, and as a result we get an emulsion or blend.

A solid must absorb heat to become a liquid, while a liquid must give off heat to become a solid. A gram of ice at 32°F requires 80 calories of heat to melt; thus, when a gram of ice at 32°F melts, it absorbs 80 calories. This heat is called the substance's *heat of fusion*. The slight thinning and shininess seen in fondant as it crystallizes is caused by the heat given off as the syrup solidifies. Liquids change to solids at different temperatures, olive oil at 40°F, ice cream at 24°F, alcohol at −146°F.

Heat is also needed to change a liquid into a gas, and heat is given off when a gas turns into a liquid. This heat is called *heat of vaporization*. The physical property liquids exhibit in picking up heat in order to turn into a gas and in giving it off when condensing back into a liquid is the basis for mechanical refrigeration. Freon or ammonia gas is forced by pressure to become a liquid in a condenser, where heat is given off. This liquid is then piped to an expansion chamber where it expands back into a gas, absorbing its needed heat of vaporization for this change of state from the refrigerator chamber and its contents (the food). The newly re-formed gas is then piped away to cooling tubes and recondensed in the condenser, after which the cycle is repeated. Freon requires 44 calories per gram to expand; ammonia requires 325.

It takes 80 calories per gram to evaporate water. This process must take heat from something in order to occur. Sweat evaporates on the body, cooling it; alcohol rubbed on the arm cools it by evaporating quickly. Boiling is an instance of fast evaporation: enough heat is entering the water to force evaporation. The water is actually leaping into the air (as water vapor) as additional heat is put into it. Not all liquids boil at the same temperature. Because of this, we can separate alcohol from water by distilling it, as we do in making spirits. Because some of the other substances boil off with the alcohol, we can obtain special flavored spirits, such as brandies, rums, scotch, and bourbon.

If as much moisture goes back into a substance as leaves it, a state of equilibrium exists, and the item does not dry out. When we wrap foods in vapor-proof wraps, the wraps prevent moisture from escaping, and a state of equilibrium within the wraps is set up. Some foods are hydroscopic, which means that they draw in moisture. Brown sugar is hydroscopic, and so are many of the things that contain it. When the humidity is high, a beautiful sugar piece can begin to drip and melt because it pulls in so much moisture. When a warm gas strikes a cold object, it condenses or turns into a liquid. We see this happen when humid air strikes a cold glass of water. Freezer burn occurs when a surface dries out while frozen. Moisture evaporates from the frozen item, and—even though the item is in a moisture-proof wrap—it condenses and freezes so that no state of equilibrium arises; instead the surface continues to dry out, and tiny ice crystals continue to form. If there is a tight seal between the wrap and the item, however, no vapor forms and freezer burn does not occur.

Air can hold only so much moisture. When more moisture is present than the air can hold, the moisture condenses out. As air warms, it can hold more heat. But as warm air containing a lot of moisture cools, its ability to hold the moisture decreases, and rain results. Moist, warm air moving upward into the sky cools; then thunderclouds show, and it rains. The term *absolute humidity* refers to the maximum moisture air can hold at that humidity. In absolute humidity, things do not dry out. For this reason, we often try to have refrigerated spaces be high in humidity. *Relative humidity* is the quantity of moisture air actually has in it at a specific temperature, as compared to its absolute humidity at that temperature. The phrase "50 percent relative humidity" means that the air is holding 50 percent of all the moisture it could possibly hold. When we cook sugar solutions, we have to correct for the amount of moisture in the air: if the humidity is high, we cook the syrup to a slightly higher temperature because we get less evaporation.

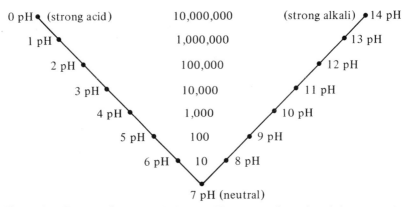

Figure 3-1. Diagram showing variations in pH: 7 is neutral; anything below 7 is acidic; and anything above 7 is alkaline. The figures in the center indicate the increase in acidity of alkalinity over neutral, which is the reference strength (1).

pH

The acidity or alkalinity of food can be indicated by a value called its *pH*. A food's pH can make major differences in cooking results. For example, many color pigments in vegetables are changed by slight differences in pH. Myoglobin, the color pigment in meat, changes to hematin, the color of cooked meat, more quickly and at a lower temperature if the meat is aged or relatively acidic. Legumes cook more quickly in an alkaline medium. A pH of 3.1 to 3.6 is needed to make a good jelly; under 3.1 produces a tough gel, and over 3.6 makes a too soft one.

A food's pH number indicates whether the food is neutral, acidic or alkaline. Neutral is 7, the strongest alkali is 14, and the strongest acid is 0. There is a tenfold increase in acidity from pH 7 to pH 6, a hundredfold increase between pH 7 and pH 5, and an increase of magnitude 10,000,000 between pH 7 and pH 0 (see fig. 3-1). The characteristic pH of various substances found in the kitchen is identified in table 3-2.

TABLE 3-2. pH values of various kitchen substances

Substance	pH	Substance	pH
Strong soap	11.0–13.0	Fresh milk	6.8
Mild hand soap	9.0	Some fruit cakes	6.4
Soda cracker	7.8	Good bread	5.0–5.4
Ripe olives	7.6	Bananas, beets	4.8
Deteriorated egg	7.5	Tomato juice	4.3
Egg white	7.2	Some vinegars	3.0
Distilled water	7.0	Lemon or lime juice	2.0
Meat	6.9–7.0		

METRIC CONVERSION

Today many quantity values and equipment measurements are given in metric values, while we often continue work in our old system of weights and measures. Thus, we frequently need to convert one value into another. Table 3-3 contains helpful information on doing this.

TABLE 3-3. Approximate unit conversions between English and Metric systems

	When you know:	You can find:	If you multiply by:
Length	inches	millimeters	25
	feet	centimeters	30
	yards	meters	0.9
	miles	kilometers	1.6
	millimeters	inches	0.04
	centimeters	inches	0.4
	meters	yards	1.1
	kilometers	miles	0.6
Area	square inches	square centimeters	6.5
	square feet	square meters	0.09
	square yards	square meters	0.8
	square miles	square kilometers	2.6
	acres	square hectometers (hectares)	0.4
	square centimeters	square inches	0.16
	square meters	square yards	1.2
	square kilometers	square miles	0.4
	square hectometers (hectares)	acres	2.5
Mass	ounces	grams	28
	pounds	kilograms	0.45
	short tons	megagrams (metric tons)	0.9
	grams	ounces	0.035
	kilograms	pounds	2.2
	megagrams (metric tons)	short tons	1.1
Liquid Volume	ounces	milliliters	30
	pints	liters	0.47
	quarts	liters	0.95
	gallons	liters	3.8
	milliliters	ounces	0.034
	liters	pints	2.1
	liters	quarts	1.06
	liters	gallons	0.26
Temperature	degrees Fahrenheit	degrees Celsius	$\frac{5}{9}$ (after subtracting 32)
	degrees Celsius	degrees Fahrenheit	$\frac{9}{5}$ (then add 32)

SOURCE: U.S. Department of Commerce

LIGHT EQUIPMENT

If an operation has the right equipment and uses it properly, labor is reduced, work is facilitated, and food is improved. Practice is the best teacher of how to use equipment. Thus, the information that follows should be considered more as an introduction to equipment use than as instructions on how to use it.

Written instructions for operating equipment should be posted in work centers. Operating manuals should also be available for consultation on how to use and maintain major appliances and pieces of machinery. It is essential that those who work in foodservices know what the equipment can do, how it is supposed to be used, and how it is maintained.

HAND TOOLS AND SMALL UTENSILS

Hand Tools

Hand-tool grasps should be big enough to permit holding without finger cramping but not so large that a good grasp cannot be maintained. Indentations give a more secure grasp, reduce fatigue, and facilitate use. Hardwood handles of rosewood or cherry are preferable to plastic handles. Balance is important. An offset spatula that tips every time it is used is undesirable. Metal should be firmly joined to the grasp. All hand tools should be sturdy, and strong, easy to clean, and easy to maintain.

Knife blades and some other cutting tools should be made of high-carbon steel or vanadium steel for extra hardness. Use stainless steel for fruit knives. Finger guards should be present, to prevent the hand from slipping onto the blade. Store knives in racks; magnetic racks with two magnets set 2 in. apart are preferred to slotted racks. Many workers have their own knives and hand tools, which they keep wrapped in a soft towel in a locker when they are off duty.

Various knives are used for different purposes (see fig. 3-2). A 10- to 12-in. French knife is used to slice, dice, or otherwise cut food. Usually, the knife point is set onto the cutting surface, and the handle is grasped firmly. As the food is pushed under the knife, it is rocked up and down on its tip, cutting through the food. The fingers holding the food should be kept curled in almost a clenched position, so that the knife's side rides against the second joints of these fingers. Do not extend the fingers. For greater control, the thumb of the hand using the knife can be on the left side and the forefinger on the right side of the blade. To cut long strips, lay the food flat, holding it firmly with the thumb and forefinger of the other hand. Then move the knife tip down along the length of the food in a sweeping motion, cutting the desired width. To cut a round, hard food, slice a thin strip off of one side. Rest the food on this flat spot, and place the blade at the cutting spot; then, using good pressure, press down. If this is not enough, take the palm of the other hand and press with this on the blade's top, forcing the knife through. Hold the knife firmly. An uneven cut results if the knife twists.

Figure 3-2. Examples of good grasps and riveting on small tools. Notice the finger guard on the boning knife.

Slicer knife blades are thinner and more flexible than the blade of a French knife. A roast-beef slicer is 12 to 14 in. long; a ham slicer, 12 in.; and a chef's slicer, 10 in. The chef's slicer is used to slice roasts such as legs of veal and lamb. To slice, insert a fork firmly or grasp the exposed hock bone firmly. Holding the slicer firmly, cut through with a drawing motion, putting even and good pressure onto the blade. Use as much of the blade as possible, making a long stroke. Hold the knife straight to get even slices. Cut through the meat or to the bone. If to the bone, do not detach slices until several are cut; then turn the knife at right angles and cut along the bone, starting at the hock end. Frequently, novices can slice faster and get more numerous and more even slices using a mechanical slicer.

A serrated or scalloped-edge slicer is used to cut bread, cake, and the like. Use a sawing motion with light pressure, cutting through. Hold the knife straight so that an even slice is obtained.

Boning knives have sturdy blades that are from 5 to 6 in. long. The boning knife is used for cutting around bones, and the tip is used more than the cutting edge is for this purpose. A finger guard should be on the handle. Grasp the knife with the thumb up and the little finger closest to the blade. Rotate the blade around bones by turning and twisting the wrist. For scalping (freeing the bone without the meat), reverse the cutting hand's position and use the cutting edge more than the point.

To pare fruits and other round items, start at the stem or flower end, and rotate the item with the other hand as the blade makes a thin, continuous peel. Pare all items before undertaking other manipulations, unless the quantity is so great that it cannot be stored or unless the items may tarnish if left to stand; then perform the remaining manipulations. Slotted or swivel parers can be used. The slotted parer is also a corer. Scalding and removing skins by rubbing them off can be done with peaches, tomatoes, apricots, and so on. Some items may be dipped into an antioxidant solution (such as ascorbic acid, citrus juice, or pineapple juice) to prevent tarnishing. A salt solution or water is not as effective for this purpose. Stainless steel blades reduce tarnishing.

Butcher or scimitar knives are used to slice or dice meats and for other general cutting. Cleavers are used to chop through bones, split chickens and do other heavy work. Light, sharp cleavers are used for some cutting. A bench knife or dough scraper is used in the bakeshop as a scraper and to cut dough and other items into desired sizes.

A steel edge is used to sharpen knives. To use one, hold the blade at a 20° angle and, working with the wrist, bring the blade against the tip of the steel; then sweep the blade down, running it from tip to base. Maintain an even, light pressure. Be careful not to sweep the blade onto the fingers. With the other side of the blade, at the same angle, sweep down similarly on the other side of the steel. Quickly reverse the action in this manner on either side of the steel and, with a twisting turning of the wrist, complete sharpening. Light pressure on the last strokes gives a finer edge.

Different cutting tools are used for miscellaneous work. Place the cutting edge of a ball cutter at about a 45° angle; then, with a twisting motion, turn the edge into the product and come out with a round ball. Failing to push outward at the start of the cut, downward during the middle, and inward at the end produces a misshapen ball. Egg slicers are quicker and slice eggs better than a knife does. A firm, even, downward stroke is needed. Biscuit, doughnut, cookie, and other cutters used in the bakeshop must be sharp to give desirable-shaped products. Dip cutters into flour and then cut down with an even, straight motion; twisting yields a misshapen product. Cut a large number of forms before stopping. Then, complete other manipulations. Roller cutters may be operated manually or mechanically; their use is specialized, and professional workers should provide instructions for running them.

Cutting boards should be made of laminated hard maple, hard rubber, or plastic—1 to 4 in. thick. Hard rubber and plastic boards are more sanitary and are not damaged by water, but they last a shorter time. Heat can cause plastic ones to warp. Use the cutting board on nonwooden working surface.

Serving Tools

Spatulas and servers should be made of high-carbon stainless steel or of chrome-vanadium steel. Plastic-covered blades can be used when they will not be subjected to heat. Grasps should be similar to those on knives. To scrape around mixing bowls or to spread frosting, use extra flexible spatulas. For sandwich spreading and for removing items from baking sheets, use flexible ones. For regular work, use firm ones. Larger offset spatulas are used for grill work and other cooking jobs. The offset keeps the hand away from hot surfaces. Its sides should be beveled so that the edge moves easily under products. It can be used for turning, for scraping, and for removing grease or other materials into grease troughs. Plastic or rubber spatulas are used in the bakeshop and in other settings where good flexibility is desired and strength is not important. A rubber or plastic spatula can be used for folding in foams, although normally a whip is used. Various servers, turners, spreaders, and cake and pie spatulas are used to meet specific needs.

Forks of high-carbon stainless steel or good forged steel are used for lifting and turning roasts and other items and for holding items during slicing. They should have good hardwood grasps and be sturdy and strong.

Ladles and dippers are used for portioning food or for moving it from one place to another. Various sizes are available for portioning. They should be sturdy, with handles firmly welded or riveted to strong seamless bowls. Care must be taken not to bang them against pot edges or against other equipment. Large scoops and dippers are used to move items; but if a worker knows how much they contain, amounts produced can be calculated by counting the number of units moved.

Ice cream scoops are used not only for dishing frozen desserts but for portioning puddings and other desserts, mashed potatoes, cottage cheese, and so on. A round type and a cone-shaped type have inside releases worked by the thumb. A rounded, hooked type that rolls frozen desserts into a ball instead of scooping increases the number of servings possible because it packs less. To work well, scoops should have sharp cutting edges and should be dipped into cold water and then drained before each use. Scoop, dipper, and ladle sizes are found in table 3-4.

In portioning thick foods, it is easier and quicker to use a smaller, rounded tool than to try to achieve a level full measure with an exact measure.

A perforated skimmer removes scum or other material from stocks, gravies, and other liquids. A regular skimmer is used to remove grease and other items, but a ladle placed into the liquid so that only the product to be removed can flow into it is preferable. A slotted spoon is frequently used to dish vegetables and other items that are cooked in liquid but are served drained. Regular spoons are used for basting, stirring, serving, and general work. Both serve about 3 oz when rounded. Do not bang them against pots or other utensils.

Extra strong grocer's scoops with handles integral to seamless bowls are used for dipping sugar, flour, and other dry items. Workers should learn the approximate the amounts these hold so that, in dipping items to be weighed, a quick, approximate amount can be scooped onto the scales.

TABLE 3-4. Cup, scoop, and ladle sizes

Cup size	Ounces	Scoop size	Measure	Ounces
$\frac{1}{4}$	2	No. 6	$\frac{2}{3}$ c	5
$\frac{1}{2}$	4	No. 8	$\frac{1}{2}$ c	4
$\frac{1}{3}$	2.7	No. 10	$\frac{3}{8}$ c	$3\frac{1}{4}$
$\frac{2}{3}$	5.3	No. 12	$\frac{1}{3}$ c	$2\frac{3}{4}$
$\frac{3}{4}$	6	No. 16	$\frac{1}{4}$ c	2
1	8	No. 20	$3\frac{1}{5}$ T	$1\frac{1}{2}$
		No. 24	$2\frac{2}{3}$ T	$1\frac{1}{3}$
		No. 30	$2\frac{1}{5}$ T	1
		No. 40	$1\frac{3}{5}$ T	0.8
		No. 60	1 T	0.5

Ladle size	Measure	Bowl diameter	Handle length
1 oz	2 T	$1\frac{3}{4}$ in.	10 in.
2 oz	$\frac{1}{4}$ c	$2\frac{3}{8}$ in.	$9\frac{3}{8}$ in.
4 oz	$\frac{1}{2}$ c	$3\frac{3}{8}$ in.	$12\frac{5}{8}$ in.
6 oz	$\frac{3}{4}$ c	$3\frac{1}{2}$ in.	$12\frac{3}{8}$ in.
8 oz	1 c	4 in.	$12\frac{5}{8}$ in.
12 oz	$1\frac{1}{2}$ c	$5\frac{1}{4}$ in.	$12\frac{1}{8}$ in.
16 oz	2 c (pt)	$4\frac{3}{8}$ in.	14 in.
24 oz	3 c	6 in.	$18\frac{1}{8}$ in.
32 oz	4 c (qt)	$8\frac{1}{8}$ in.	17 in.

Utility Items

A colander drains food from liquid; special colanders are used as for draining spaghetti. Allow food to drain, and then give one or two good shakes to free any liquid. Heavy-duty, rustproof strainers with mesh sizes of from 14 to 20 per sq in. are used for finer straining. Colanders are somewhat fragile and should be handled carefully. Wash immediately after use because dry food is hard to remove and creates extra wear on the mesh. Heavy-duty China caps are conical in shape; they may be used for draining or puréeing items. To force food through, use a roller around the edges, or insert a ladle into the center and pull and push it up and down to create a suction on the upstroke and pressure on the downstroke.

Small, fine wire whips about 8 to 10 in. long are helpful in working into corners and mixing foods such as hollandaise sauce and flour-and-water slurries. Larger whips with coarser, stronger, stiffer wires are used to work with large batches of sauces or with thicker items. For fast mixing, grasp the whip by the handle with the little finger toward the wires and the thumb up. Work with a quick forward and backward motion of the wrist. Reversing the hand allows the arm muscles to exert more powerful strokes for stirring larger or thicker batches.

Whips can be used to fold in foams or other ingredients and to whip eggs, cream, or other items, but this is most often done using mixers. Mix thick products with a mixer equipped with a paddle, not a whip. When quantities are small, use a hand rotary beater or an electrical beater. Both wire and rotary whips are harmed by rough handling. Do not bang them around; keep wires and blades straight and true. Cleaning may become a problem because of the inaccessible areas where food adheres. Washing soon after use helps in cleaning.

A stirring paddle or whip is used to mix food in steam-jacketed kettles and stock pots. Handles should have an outside diameter of at least $1\frac{1}{2}$ in. to allow a good grip. Put a scratch or mark on the handles to indicate the gallon volume at that level in a standard container; this will enable workers to tell how much of the food is being made. Aluminum paddles are lighter than stainless steel ones but are less durable. Electrolytic flow of particles between stainless steel and aluminum causes pitting in aluminum, so we avoid using these metals together; stainless steel also scratches aluminum.

Pots and Pans

Good heat conduction is needed in pots and pans. Aluminum, copper, and black cast iron are good conductors. Copper is best, but it must be tinned inside where food touches the surface. Copper destroys ascorbic acid and can form harmful substances in the presence of strong acids; it is also expensive. Nevertheless, with good care, copper is worth the price for its polished beauty and good heat conduction.

Pots and pans should be heavy-duty and seamless, with double-strength bottoms and tops or a strong bead at the top. Thick bottoms promote good heat spread and prevent sticking. Strong edges wear well and withstand the heavy rap of spoons and other utensils on them. Even, flat bottoms make broad, level contact with heating units. Rounded corners simplify cleaning. Loop handles should be firmly brazed or strongly riveted and welded to the pot. Sauce-pan handles should also be strongly attached and should be long enough to permit good handling at a safe distance from the hot surface. Some pots are equipped with a sanitary bib or with dairy-type faucets and strainers for use in draining stocks and other liquids. Special pots are used for making gravies, soups, and sauces. Sauce pots are shallower than stock pots, so working with them is easier. Braisers are special pots in which items are sautéed and then covered and braised. A covered pot comes to a boil faster than an uncovered one and needs less heat to cook. The working capacity of pots and pans is less than their stated volume. Food closer than 3 in. to the top is apt to spill during stirring, mixing, or boiling.

Deep sauce pans are used for making sauces, gravies, fillings, and other items in general kitchen work. Shallow ones are used when considerable work must done on the product or when substantial evaporative loss is desired. Deeper ones are used when the product is to be cooked for a long time.

Double boilers are used to cook foods that must not get too much heat, such as a stirred custard. The lower container holds water through which heat is transferred into the upper one holding the food. A rounded bottom in the top facilitates reaching all areas with a whip or spoon.

Frying or sauté pans are much like sauce pans except that they are shallower and have slanted sides to make work in them with a spatula or other hand tool easier. Fit the pan to the quantity of food to be fried. Otherwise, spots not covered burn and char. A straight-sided pan should be used for sautéing and braising and for uses where there is danger of foaming up.

When a large quantity of food is to be sautéed, use a large, thick heavy-duty griddle with two integral handles. After frying, remove the foods, put them into deeper pans, cover, and braise. Frying or sauté pans may be conditioned for use, through the same process recommended for griddles.

Heavy-duty roasting pans should be equipped with tight-fitting covers and should have two (or four, if large) strong handles. For reduced weight, they can be made of strong aluminum alloy, hardened to be dent resistant. Strap pans of black japanned steel or hotel steel are also satisfactory. Various sizes are needed, since pan size should be suited to the quantity of food to be roasted in it. Trivets or racks for allowing juices to drip through should be equipped with long handles to permit lifting the rack and meat from the pan.

Lighter-weight pans are used for storage, for transport, or as tote boxes. They should have strong beads at the top. Extra strength is gained by strapping. Stainless steel pans are suitable for storage or for serving food at steam tables, but not for cooking. Many of these miscellaneous pans can be made of plastic if heat is not applied.

Many 18 × 26-in. baking sheets are used. These usually are made of dent-resistant aluminum. Pebbly bottomed sheets make removing items such as cookies easier. Pie, cake, loaf, and other smaller pans are usually composed of aluminum, black japanned steel, or hotel steel which must be conditioned. To do this, wipe the new pans clean, place them in a 400°F oven, and allow them to remain until they are tinged with a bluish-black color. Remove, grease lightly with oil or a plastic fat, and return to the oven for 3 to 4 minutes. Then allow them to cool, and wipe clean. Aluminum pans do not need conditioning. All baking pans should be made of heavy enough material to withstand heavy wear. They should have strongly beaded edges. Handle them with care: do not bang them around or drop them to maintain their proper shape; avoid heat warping; use cake pans only for cake production. Glass pans are fragile and do not brown items well on the bottom.

Some muffin, popover, and other pans are conditioned as follows. Put them into a hot oven after liberal greasing. Remove them while hot, and rub them vigorously with a cloth dipped in salt. Repeat several times. Such pans are not washed but may be lightly greased before each use. After each use, clean the pan thoroughly with a clean, soft, absorbent cloth, and store it. Washing destroys the surface and makes the pan stick. Paper liners are used to prevent sticking.

Weighing and Portioning Equipment

Weighing is preferred to measuring in quantity work because of its greater accuracy, but occasionally measuring is done for reasons of speed or where accuracy is not critical. Pour—do not dip—thick fluids into a measure, and scrape well with a rubber or plastic spatula to empty. Use a glass measure for liquids, and see that the liquid reaches the measure mark at the edge, not the center.

Overfill a measure with dry ingredients, tap gently, and level off. Some items are sifted before measuring, but dry milk, presifted flour, leavening agents, and sugar are not sifted. Brown sugar is packed down lightly. Remove its lumps by rolling it or heating it gently in an oven. Stir before measuring packed items such as baking powder, graham flour, and dry milk. To measure by spoon or small measure, dip out a heaping measure and level it off. To get a fraction, use a fraction measure. Thus, to obtain $\frac{1}{2}$ teaspoon, use a $\frac{1}{2}$-teaspoon measure; do not attempt to fill a 1-teaspoon measure halfway. A pinch is $\frac{1}{16}$ teaspoon. To speed up work and improve accuracy, memorize equivalents between weights and measures. Use time-saving methods such as cutting a pound of butter in half to get a cup or 8 oz.

Measuring spoon sets contain a tablespoon (T), a teaspoon (t), a $\frac{1}{2}$ t, and a $\frac{1}{4}$ t. Cup measures are cup, one-fourth, one-third, one-half, two-thirds, and three-fourths. Large measures include pint, quart, half-gallon, and gallon. Tables 3-4 through 3-12 contain important weighing and measuring information.

Portion scales are used to obtain accuracy. Most are beam scales that measure in ounces or fractions of ounces (see fig. 3-3). An indicator shows when the amount is over, under, or correct.

A baker's scale is a balance-beam scale. Increments of ¼ oz, up to 16 oz, can be set on the beam. Additional weights are placed on the right side, with ounces or partial ounces put on the beam, and ingredients are placed on the left. A container on the left platform is used to hold ingredients, and a standard tare weight is used on the right to counterbalance it. Frequently an empty pan identical to the one being filled on the left is placed on the right to factor out its weight. Small quantities should be

TABLE 3-5. Conversion of water from measure to weight

Cups	Pints	Quarts	Fluid ounces*	Avoirdupois pounds	Avoirdupois ounces* weight
½	¼	⅛	4.15	0	4
1	½	¼	8.31	0	8¼
1½	¾	⅜	12.46	0	12½
2	1	½	16.62	1	½
2½	1¼	⅝	20.77	1	4¾
3	1½	¾	24.93	1	9
3½	1¾	⅞	29.08	1	13
4	2	1	33.24	2	1¼
4½	2¼	1⅛	37.39	2	5¼
5	2½	1¼	41.55	2	9½
5½	2¾	1⅜	45.70	2	13¾
6	3	1½	49.86	3	1¾
6½	3¼	1⅝	54.01	3	6
7	3½	1¾	58.17	3	10¼
7½	3¾	1⅞	62.32	3	14¼
8	4	2	66.48	4	2½
8½	4¼	2⅛	70.63	4	6½
9	4½	2¼	74.80	4	10¾
9½	4¾	2⅜	78.94	4	15
10	5	2½	83.10	5	3¼
10½	5¼	2⅝	87.25	5	7¼
11	5½	2¾	91.40	5	11½
11½	5¾	2⅞	95.56	5	15½
12	6	3	99.72	6	3¾
12½	6¼	3⅛	103.87	6	8
13	6½	3¼	108.03	6	12
13½	6¾	3⅜	112.18	7	¼
14	7	3½	116.34	7	4¼
14½	7¼	3⅝	120.49	7	8¼
15	7½	3¾	124.65	7	12½
15½	7¾	3⅞	128.80	8	1
16	8	4	133.00	8	5

* For whole milk equivalents, multiply by 1.032; for light syrups (20° Brix), multiply by 1.373.

TABLE 3-6. Weights, measures, and their abbreviations

Measure	Abbreviation	Equivalent
Teaspoon	t	3t = 1 T
Tablespoon	T	16 T = 1 c
Cup	c	2c = 1 pt
Pint	pt	2 pt = 1 qt
Quart	qt	4 qt = 1 gal
Gallon	gal	
Gram	gm	28.35 gm = 1 oz
Ounce	oz	16 oz = 1 lb
Pound	lb	

NOTE: 2 T of liquid or solid matter usually equals 1 oz; $5\frac{1}{3}$ T equals $\frac{1}{3}$ c; 4 T equals $\frac{1}{4}$ c; 1 pinch equals about $\frac{1}{16}$ t; and 1 dash is less than $\frac{1}{8}$ t.

TABLE 3-7. Dry and liquid measure equivalents

Dry			Liquid		
2 pt	1 qt	1.101 liters	4 gills	1 pt	473.25 cubic centimeters
8 qt	1 peck	8.808 liters	2 pt	1 qt	0.9465 liters
4 pecks	1 bu	35.24 liters	4 qt	1 gal	3.786 liters
			$31\frac{1}{2}$ gal	1 barrel	
			2 barrels	1 hogshead	

Figure 3-3. A mobile scale that has many uses in foodservice operations: it is excellent for use in receiving many items. (*Courtesy Hobart*)

TABLE 3-8. Liquid measure conversion table

	United States measure				Imperial measure (British)				Metric measure		Weight of indicated volume of water	
	Gallon	Quart	Pint	Gill	Gallon	Quart	Pint	Gill	Liter	Cubic centimeter	Pound (avoirdupois)	Kilogram
United States measure												
1 gallon	1	4	8	32	0.833	3.33	6.66	26.66	3.785	3,785.4	8.33	3.785
1 quart	0.25	1	2	8	0.208	0.833	1.666	6.67	0.946	946.4	2.08	0.946
1 pint	0.125	0.5	1	4	0.104	0.417	0.833	3.33	0.473	473.2	1.04	0.473
1 gill	0.031	0.125	0.25	1	0.026	0.104	0.208	0.833	0.118	118.3	0.26	0.118
Imperial measure (British)												
1 gallon	1.2	4.8	9.6	38.4	1	4	8	32	4.543	4,553.5	10	4.543
1 quart	0.3	1.2	2.4	9.6	0.25	1	2	8	1.136	1,135.9	2.5	1.136
1 pint	0.15	0.6	1.2	4.8	0.125	0.5	1	4	0.568	567.9	1.25	0.568
1 gill	0.038	0.15	0.3	1.2	0.031	0.125	0.25	1	0.142	142.0	0.312	0.142
Metric measure												
1 liter	0.264	1.057	2.11	8.45	0.220	0.880	1.761	7.044	1	1,000	2.20	1.
1 cubic centimeter	0.0003	0.001	0.002	0.008	0.0002	0.0009	0.002	0.077	0.001	1	0.002	0.001

TABLE 3-9. Conversion of grams, ounces, and pounds

Grams	Ounces	Pounds	Grams	Ounces	Pounds	Grams	Ounces	Pounds
28.35	1	0.06	198.45	7	0.44	340.20	12	0.75
56.70	2	0.13	226.80	8	0.50	368.55	13	0.81
85.05	3	0.19	255.15	9	0.56	396.90	14	0.88
113.40	4	0.25	283.50	10	0.63	425.25	15	0.94
141.75	5	0.31	311.85	11	0.69	453.60	16	1.00
170.10	6	0.38						

TABLE 3-10. Volume conversion: fluid ounces to milliliters

Fl Oz	Ml	Fl Oz	Ml
1	29.6	17	502.8
2	59.1	18	532.3
3	88.7	19	561.9
4	118.3	20	591.7
5	147.9	21	621.0
6	177.4	22	650.6
7	207.0	23	680.2
8	236.6	24	709.8
9	266.2	25	739.3
10	295.7	26	768.9
11	325.3	27	798.5
12	354.9	28	828.1
13	384.5	29	857.7
14	414.0	30	887.2
15	443.6	31	916.8
16 (1 pint)	473.2	32 (1 quart)	946.4

TABLE 3-11. Equivalents of household food measures

Quarts	Pints	Standard cups	Fluid ounces	Tablespoonfuls	Teaspoonfuls	Milliliters
1.0	2.0	4.0	32.0	64.0	192.0	946.4
0.5	1.0	2.0	16.0	32.0	96.0	473.2
0.25	0.5	1.0	8.0	16.0	48.0	236.6
0.125	0.25	0.5	4.0	8.0	24.0	118.3
—	0.125	0.25	2.0	4.0	12.0	59.2
—	—	1.125	1.0	2.0	6.0	29.6
—	—	—	0.5	1.0	3.0	14.8
—	—	—	—	0.33	1.0	4.9
—	—	—	—	—	0.2	1.0

TABLE 3-12. Guide for rounding off weights and measures

WEIGHTS

Item	If the total amount of an ingredient is:	Round it to:
	less than 2 oz	$\frac{1}{4}, \frac{1}{2}, \frac{3}{4}$ oz amounts
		oz. amounts
Various miscellaneous ingredients	2 oz to 10 oz	closest $\frac{1}{4}$ oz
	more than 10 oz but less than 2 lb 8 oz	closest $\frac{1}{2}$ oz
	2 lb 8 oz to 5 lb	closest full oz
	more than 5 lb	closest $\frac{1}{4}$ lb

MEASURES

Item	If the total amount of an ingredient is:	Round it to:
	less than 1 T	closest = $\frac{1}{8}$ t
Primarily spices, seasonings, flavorings, condiments, leavenings	{ more than 1 T but less than 3 T	closest $\frac{1}{4}$ t
	3 T to $\frac{1}{2}$ cup	closest $\frac{1}{2}$ t, or convert to weight
	{ more than $\frac{1}{2}$ cup but less than $\frac{3}{4}$ cup	closest full t, or convert to weight
	{ more than $\frac{3}{4}$ cup but less than 2 cups	closest full T, or convert to weight
	2 cups to 2 qt	nearest $\frac{1}{4}$ cup
	{ more than 2 qt but less than 4 qt	nearest $\frac{1}{2}$ cup
	1 to 2 gal	nearest full cup or $\frac{1}{4}$ qt
Primarily milk, water, eggs, juice, oil, syrup, molasses	{ more than 2 gal but less than 10 gal	nearest full qt
	{ more than 10 gal but less than 20 gal	closest $\frac{1}{2}$ gal
	over 20 gal	closest full gal

Source: *Standardizing Recipes for Institutional Use;* Circular 233, Agr. Ex. Station, Michigan State University.

scaled first, followed by heavier ones. For greatest accuracy, scale items singly. A scale will be inaccurate if it is not level. Jarring the scale leads to inaccuracy. Spring scales are used for speed in situations where accuracy is not important—such as where quantities of entrée items or other cooked foods are placed into pans for baking. A good supermarket scale is useful for some work, but a heavy-duty one with a large dial is often preferred. A heavy-duty-scale should be used for receiving. One that prints the weight and date is desirable; it should be equipped with a beam scale for taring container weights. Scales are good only if they are accurate. Therefore, they must be cleaned properly and handled carefully in order to prevent soil from interfering with their action. Lift scales from the bottom. Check their accuracy frequently, and do not leave objects on them when they are not in use.

HEAVY EQUIPMENT

HEATING EQUIPMENT

Heat is transmitted to food through air, metals, water, steam, or fat. Various types of equipment are used for this purpose.

Direct-heating Equipment

Range tops are the workhorses of many kitchens (see figs. 3-4 and 3-5). They can be used to fry, to deep-fry, to steam, to boil, or to braise. Most tops are heated by gas or electricity, but some may be heated by oil, coal, or even wood. Thermostat control for tops is standard. Most units come to a desirable cooking temperature quickly, making it possible to keep the units turned off until needed; leaving them on all the time would result in rapid deterioration or buckling, plus fuel waste. Tops should be covered as much as possible to make use of all the heat generated. By using more than one place, a cook can maintain different temperatures simultaneously, allowing shifting of items from faster to slower cooking or vice versa. A baker's stove is a small open-plate or solid top used to make sugar solutions, pie fillings, sauces, puddings, and the like. It is low, so

Figure 3-4. A heavy-duty electric range equipped with two hot plates and two high-speed cooking units. The 17 × 20 × 29-in. oven can hold six 18 × 26-in. bun pans and three 12 × 20 × 4-in. foodservice pans. (*Courtesy Lang Manufacturing Company*)

Figure 3-5. A 5-ft-long heavy-duty range unit with a hot plate, two high-speed units, and a large griddle. A convection oven and a cook-and-hold oven are underneath. (*Courtesy Lang Manufacturing Company*)

work is done more easily when tall pots are used. It is important to keep ranges clean. Check gas burners frequently to ensure that they are un-clogged and give a blue flame with a white tip. Adjust air flow to the burner until the flame achieves the proper color.

Griddles cook foods directly on the surface by sautéing or frying, a process of cooking in little fat. They should be heavy-duty and should be equipped with splash backs, grease troughs, and rounded corners for easy cleaning. Remove drip pans and grease catchers daily, and clean them well. Polish griddle surfaces with soapstone, a pumice brick, or a griddle cloth at the end of each day of use. Do not salt foods on a griddle, since this builds up gummy deposits that make cleaning more difficult. Have available a grease mop, an oil can, shakers of seasonings, forks, tongs, and spatulas, in addition to cleaning materials. Keep the griddle clean with a spatula, scraping charred materials and fat into grease troughs. Wipe the scraped griddle with a clean, soft cloth.

To condition griddles or sauté pans, cover the surface with high-quality oil or fat, sprinkle salt lightly on this, and heat the griddle until the fat almost smokes. Then, using soapstone, pumice, or a griddle cloth, polish the surface until it shines. Wipe clean with a dry cloth or soft paper towel. Repeat this procedure until a smooth, nonsticking surface is ob-tained. Water destroys this finish and makes complete refinishing ne-cessary.

A tilting skillet operates on gas or electricity; it sautés, deep-fries, braises, griddles, simmers, or boils items (see fig. 3-6). This gives it great flexibility in food production. It can be tilted to dump its contents. Gas models come equipped with tilting attachments. Tilting pans can be used

Figure 3-6. A tilting skillet. These versatile appliances save space and labor and can be used in various ways: for griddle-cooking breakfast eggs, bacon, sausage, hash browns, pancakes, and French toast; for pan-cooking stews, stir-fries, burgers, fish, grilled sandwiches, and soups; for braising chops and steaks; for preparing sauces; and for performing many other jobs. (*Courtesy Market Forge Company*)

in small foodservice operations if production is worked around the pan.

Some heavy-duty broilers come to full heat in 15 to 30 minutes (see fig. 3-7). Charcoal takes about 45 minutes to be ready, and some older gas and electric broilers take about the same time. In broilers the heat source is usually located over a grid, but some newer types have heating units situated underneath. A griddle may have a flanged top containing containing a broiler element. Huge broilers can use infrared lamps strung vertically in columns; items attached to hooks on a moving belt are broiled as they pass between them (see fig. 3-8). Some broilers are thermostatically controlled. Temperature control can also be achieved by raising or lowering the broiler grid. If the hand can be held for 2 seconds at broiling level, the temperature is from 350° to 400°F; if for 3 seconds, 300° to 350°F; and if for 4 seconds, 275° to 300°F. A salamander is a small overhead broiler designed to brown au gratin and other dishes, but it also is used to prepare some broiled items.

Figure 3-7. A heavy-duty broiler that can be operated with either gas or electricity. (*Courtesy Southbend Escan Corporation*)

Charcoal fires are started with hardwood or pieces of charcoal soaked in lighter fluid or wood alcohol. Fit the can with a good lid; keep the soaking can away from fire and covered tightly. Lighter fluid can also be poured or squirted over charcoal for starting. Some electric starters are available. Kerosene or other fuel oils give undesirable flavors. After the charcoal is well-lighted, spread it out. Add additional charcoal until a bed 2 to 3 in. thick is obtained, and let it burn until the charcoal is covered with a light white ash and glows. Make the bed slightly larger than the grid over the coals and a bit deeper at the edges than in the center because of the cooling that occurs at the edges. Some cooks adjust charcoal depth to control heat, but most vary grid levels for this purpose. A container of cold water and chipped ice or a syringe of cold water is kept nearby to control flames. Hardwood rather than softwood charcoal should be used, since softwood gives a resinous flavor. Some people

Figure 3-8. A combination broiler and griddle that cooks food on both sides simultaneously to reduce cooking time. The quartz heating unit turns on instantly when the hood is lowered and remains off when the hood is raised. Quartz heat is a swiftly generated infrared heat. (*Courtesy Lang Manufacturing Company*)

claim that the tars from softwood charcoal may be carcinogenic, as the tars and smoke from cigarettes may be.

Keep broilers clean, remove all grease, and empty the drain can daily. Broiler fires are extremely dangerous. A self-closing vent should be installed above the broiler to close in case of fire.

Deep fryers run on gas or electricity and are thermostatically controlled (see fig. 3-9). Keep these units scrupulously clean. Filter fat after every heavy use. After filtering, wipe the empty kettle free of fat and remove all gummy substances. Take removable kettles and equipment to a sink, and thoroughly scrub these with hot soapy water. Fill nonremovable kettles with a good detergent or deep-fryer cleaner and boil well. Drain, rinse with clean water, and repeat if necessary; then dry thoroughly. Check thermostat accuracy frequently.

Pressure fryers develop between 9 and 14 psi of steam while deep-frying foods at around 325°F. Some have water injectors, which add water to create steam; others utilize food moisture. Advantages claimed are increased flavor and tenderness of the food and reduced cooking time (half or less of conventional time).

(a)   (b)

Figure 3-9.   (a) A high-speed gas-fired deep-fryer. (*Courtesy Hobart*)   (b) A solid-state heat-controlled electric fryer that automatically raises the fry baskets when cooking time is complete. It can also be equipped with regular thermostats and mechanical timers. (*Courtesy Lang Manufacturing Company*)

One or several single ovens under range tops can satisfy the needs of a small operation, while a large revolving oven holding as many as eighty large baking sheets or a huge moving-belt oven over 100 feet long may be needed for large ones. Gas, electricity, infrared lamps, or microwaves may be the heat source.

In a revolving oven, shelves are suspended between turning wheels. Shelf stabilizers work to keep shelves in a continuously horizontal position. An indicator outside the oven shows shelf location so that an operator can stop at any shelf level. Good maintenance is required because jarring, uneven heat, or out-of-level shelves cause problems. To clean the oven inside, allow it to cool, and then lower a worker inside; some ovens have doors that permit access. Oiling of the wheels can also be done at these openings.

Ovens under range tops hold two 18 × 26-in. baking pans on two shelves. Because of heat variation, only one shelf is usually used. An item such as a tall turkey takes up all of the oven space on a single shelf.

Long ovens, in which items travel on a moving belt, are used for heavy production. It is possible to vary heat in different areas and to change belt speed to suit baking needs. Stack or deck ovens have baking shelves one on top of the other; shelves for baking are 8 in. high, and those for roasting are 12 in. high (see fig. 3-10). Each shelf may be individually heat-controlled. Often old-fashioned stack gas ovens give different shelf temperatures, with the hottest shelves being at the bottom (where the heat source is) and the coolest at the top.

Deep brick-lined or hearth ovens perform well in baking hard-crusted breads and other bakery goods; they can even be used for roasting. Because of their mass and size, a long warmup time is needed; some are left on at low heat overnight to cut down on reheating time. Wood- or charcoal-heated models are rare; most are electric and a few are gas-operated. Hard-crusted breads are baked directly on the hearth. A long peel or flat paddle is used for loading and unloading. Steam injection is desirable for making hard-crusted products. Workers should learn to open and close oven vents to suit different baking needs.

A convection oven is usually about the same size as a range oven, but some larger ones are also used (see figs. 3-11 and 3-12). The regular-size ovens take from 6 to 11 baking sheets. A fan at the back moves heat around, making it possible to have shelves quite close together and still obtain adequate heat between them. When fully loaded, some ovens bake unevenly, so workers must learn through experience how much of

Figure 3-10. A tiered baking or roasting oven widely used in foodservices. (*Courtesy Lang Manufacturing Company*)

Figure 3-11. A conventional range with a fry top and a convection oven. Such units can be purchased with different tops and different ovens, allowing considerable leeway in selecting cooking units. (*Courtesy Southbend Escan Corporation*)

different products can be loaded. Convection ovens are often used to warm large quantities of precooked foods, to toast sandwiches, or to bake pastries. The fan must be turned off for some baking. For instance, ripples form on cakes from strong air currents if fans are in operation while they are being baked.

Cathode-ray tubes in microwave ovens generate wave energy that penetrates food, disturbing the molecular structure and causing heat development (see fig. 3-13). These waves bound around inside the metal chamber (which they cannot penetrate), passing through foods, paper, plastics, and ceramics. Items cannot be cooked in metal containers because these would induce arcing that might destroy the cathode-ray tube. Microwave energy is very intense and cooks foods more quickly than conventional heat does. It can easily overcook. Thus, thick foods can be overcooked around the edges before the interior is cooked. This happen-

Figure 3-12. A free-standing conventional oven. Convection ovens contain a circulating fan that moves heat around, allowing greater oven capacity. (*Courtesy of Market Forge Company*)

Figure 3-13. A microwave oven operated by finger-touch solid-state controls. (*Courtesy Hobart*)

ing can be delayed by taping metal around the edge of the cooking unit so that microwaves cannot go through at this point. But be careful: *never allow such a metal wrap to touch any other metal in the oven.* Some items may have to be covered to reduce dehydration. Items leavened by chemical agents or foams may cook too rapidly to result in quality products. Meats have a higher rate of shrinkage when cooked in microwave ovens. In large meats, circular rings develop in the muscle portions.

Microwave ovens are efficient for warming frozen or other precooked foods. The depth and type of foods cooked together must be properly adjusted, however, because some foods can overcook faster than others. Cooking speed is indirectly related to the quantity of food. Small quantities cook the most rapidly, but cooking time increases as mass increases. It is possible to overload a microwave oven to the point where cooking time in it exceeds that in a conventional oven.

Before installing a microwave oven, management should make sure that it can be fully utilized. Employees unacquainted with its operational patterns may avoid using it. They must be taught how to use it and must be shown how helpful it is in doing many tasks.

Various ovens are used for warming foods (see fig. 3-14). Some refrigerate foods that are already dished for service; then at a set time they automatically begin to heat the food so that it will be ready for service at the correct time. Some have cycling heat inputs—on and then off, repeatedly—to warm foods more evenly without drying them out. Ovens using quartz tubes or quartz plates generate infrared waves that provide a steady, even heat. Some units have electrical contacts; serving dishes designed to work with these units contain elements that heat the food.

An experimental oven uses microwave, convection, infrared, and

Figure 3-14. A gas-fired unit for heating or broiling foods. It turns on when the weight of a plate touches it and turns off when the plate is removed. It can also be used for toasting foods or for warming plates or other items. (*Courtesy Lang Manufacturing Company*)

steam heat to warm foods. One of the simplest and most efficient methods is to place covered containers of bulk food into steam units and bring the food almost to serving temperature, after which the containers are removed and uncovered, and the food is brought to final temperature in a conventional oven. Covering foods in the steamer prevents condensation from thinning or watering them down. Special water-bath equipment, bains-marie, steam tables, or even deep fryers filled with water are used to reheat foods either in bulk or in individual packs.

A procedure that is extremely detrimental to food quality consists of holding food at high temperatures for long periods of time. Procedures should be worked out to keep foods as fresh as possible; failing that, the foods should be heated just before service. Some of the equipment mentioned previously as serving to warm food is suitable for this purpose.

Leaving ovens on at high heat burns out oven linings or warps and buckles shelving. Thermostats burn out, becoming inoperative or defective. Every oven has idiosyncrasies that must be learned to get best performance from it. Most ovens heat to a desirable temperature in 15 to 20 minutes, so they need not be left on continuously. For adequate performance, do not overload the oven, and do not allow pans to touch each other or the sides of the oven. Do not use heavily moistened cloths or water on interiors—especially of electrical ovens. Oven vents must be left open at the start of cooking so that moisture escapes. Unvented ovens may have the doors left open instead. Moisture can short out an electrical oven, or it can cause rusting or other deterioration. Operating, maintenance, and cleaning instructions for ovens vary: follow the manufacturer's instructions. Some new ovens are self-cleaning.

Food-handling Equipment

Food can be kept warm in standard equipment such as an oven or steamer, or it can be left on the range top after being set in a container of hot water to retard further cooking (see table 3-13).

A bain-marie keeps food hot in a shallow vat of water; it is heated by steam, gas, or electricity. Dry-heat or waterless bains-marie are sometimes used. A steam table is similar to a bain-marie but is designed to hold food for service rather than in reserve. It is covered with a top so that 12 × 20-in. serving pans (or their multiples) can be set into it. Meat

---

TABLE 3-13. Holding and serving temperatures

Type of food	Holding (°F)	At service (°F)
Soups, tea, coffee, thin gravies, sauces, etc.	180	160
Entrées, medium and well-done meat, thick sauces, etc.	160	140
Rare meats	140	135
Chilled foods such as salads, cocktails, and juices	35–40	45–50
Frozen foods	8–15	24

pans have tent-like covers for roasts and other foods. A bain-marie or steam table can be used to cook certain foods such as hollandaise sauce, scrambled eggs, poached eggs, eggs cooked in the shell, and sauces. Foods can overcook in bains-marie and steam tables unless temperatures are carefully controlled: rare roasts cook to medium or well-done; eggs turn dark and strong in flavor; vegetables lose flavor, texture, and color. To keep foods fresh for service, hold only a small amount ready for service and send in fresh batches from production periodically. This ensures highest quality to eggs, vegetables, and other items that lose quality quickly during holding. Steam tables may operate with water heated by steam, gas, or electricity. Units of dry heat, thermostatically controlled, are also used.

Special chambers may be built into walls or set in work areas to hold hot food. Some may be designed as pass-throughs so that the food can be taken out on the other side. For banquet service, where a lot of food often must be served at one time, a special heated room or unit may be designed into which carts loaded with food can be rolled (see fig. 3-15). These are usually located behind service areas, near the banquet or service areas.

Some food systems are built around the holding and transport equipment. Hot food carts resembling dry-heat steam tables hold bulk food,

Figure 3-15.   A walk-in refrigerated unit. Carts loaded with food can be rolled in and out of it as desired. (*Courtesy Victory*)

while other carts hold and transport dished foods. Some units are plugged into electrical outlets for preheating, and after transport are again plugged in to keep food warm. Refrigerated units are used in much the same way (see fig. 3-16). Trucks may also be designed to hold, transport, and dispense food. Hot food may be put into insulated containers of urethane, fiberglass, cork, or other materials, and then held for several hours. Large containers of bulk or portioned food may have to be handled by fork-lift trucks. Others may be easily handled by a single worker and may be constructed of disposable plastic foam. Some units hold already-dished food without benefit of heat or refrigeration. Hot and cold portions can also be set next to each other.

Special devices may be used to hold hot food. Placed over foods, infrared lamps diffuse a steady, dry heat that maintains the foods at the desired temperature. Such lamps are especially good for holding deep-fried foods because the dry heat stabilizes the level of crispness. A rare rib of beef can be held under infrared lamps for a long period without

Figure 3-16. A mobile cart into which foods can be loaded. Such carts can be constructed as heating, warming, or refrigerating units. (*Courtesy Victory*)

cooking further. Similar warmers on the market use Chromalux or other types of heating units. In these units, heated metal pellets are placed under foods to hold the temperature steady. The unit is then put onto a tray with cold foods, and the tray is transported to a service area.

Steam-cooking Equipment

Most steam cooking is done with pressure units, although some free-venting units are seen. Steam can be generated in the equipment, or it can be furnished by a central unit (see fig. 3-17). If outside pressure is too high, pressure reducers lower them. Some self-contained units automatically fill with water for steam. Manufacturer's directions should be followed. All units have protective devices that release excess steam or disconnect if the heating devices become too hot. Never tamper with safety pressure valves or other protective devices. Check the unit's operation frequently to see that all is in order. Some safety units are released manually as well as automatically. Most steamers cannot be filled with steam until their doors are properly sealed; these doors cannot be reopened until the steam pressure subsides. Many steamers automatically release air and water through a discharge valve before building steam pressure. Some steam-jacketed kettles have a bleeder valve for releasing condensed steam if it builds up in the kettle's jacket during operation.

Table 3-14 identifies the internal temperatures maintained at various pressures. High-pressure steamers rapidly process foods at pressures around 15 psi (see fig. 3-18). This facilitates fast batch cooking, where

(a)   (b)

Figure 3-17. (a) A heavy-duty self-contained steam-jacketed kettle. (*Courtesy Southbend Escan Corporation*) (b) A large heavy-duty steam-jacketed kettle that receives its steam from a central boiler. (*Courtesy Market Forge*)

TABLE 3-14. Steam pressures and
temperatures

Pressure (psi)	°F	Pressure (psi)	°F	Pressure (psi)	°F
0	212	8	235	25	267
2	218	10	240	30	274
4	224	15	250	40	287
6	230	20	259	50	298

small batches are rapidly produced in order to keep a fresh flow going to service. Two such units often can sustain a continuous flow of foods. Some have browning units in them. Large compartment steamers capable of holding 1 bushel (60 lb) per chamber cook at 5 to 8 psi. These may be equipped with timers and pullout shelves. Some vegetables are put into perforated pans to enable steam to reach them more easily; others must be put into water. If water is used, it is a signal that boiling in a

Figure 3-18. A high-speed high-pressure steamer. The pressure seals the door so that it cannot be opened when the steam is on. (*Courtesy Market Forge Company*)

steam-jacketed kettle or stock pot is a better procedure. Most frozen items cooked in steam are best if thawed before cooking to prevent the outsides from cooking before complete thawing has occurred. Food cooked in steam should be separated so that the steam gets around it. Food that packs—such as peas, spinach, or rice—may cook unevenly unless put into water. Since foods cook quickly, especially at high pressures, the use of timers to signal the end of cooking time is recommended. Food flavors build up in the water used for steam in self-contained units; therefore old, used water should be flushed out frequently, and new water added. Steam pressures should be released slowly. Too rapid a release causes liquids to leap from pans, peas to jump from their skins, and some other products to disintegrate.

Some steamers work on convection principles and do not involve any increase in pressure within the unit (see fig. 3-19).

Shallow steam kettles are easier to work into than deeper ones. Some deep units are so tall that workers must use special platforms or ladders to work into them. Both types of steam kettles are used for making stocks and soups, for braising meats, for preparing entrées, for cooking dry beans and other legumes, for boiling vegetables, and for performing other production work involved in range-top stock-pot cookery. Kettles may be sized from 2 to 4,000 gallons, and they operate usually at pressures of from 5 to 8 psi.

Figure 3-19. A convection (pressureless) steamer. (*Courtesy Southbend Escan Corporation*)

Most nontilt kettles have spigots and drains through which liquids can be drained. Large kettles may have electric stirrers so that paddles can be lowered into mixtures and mechanically agitated. These should have variable speeds and the agitator should tip out. Some may be cooled with cool tap water inside the jacket after the steam is turned off. For larger kettles, refrigerated water or glycol is used to obtain a more rapid cooling rate. Pumps for emptying kettles are also used.

Tilting steam kettles are used for cooking vegetables, pie fillings, puddings, salad dressings, gravies, entrée mixtures, and so on. Small units used for small quantities or batches are usually mounted on a table with a drain in front. Tilting is by lever. Larger units tilt by means of a wheel that moves the gears. Both tilting and stationary kettles may be self-contained or may operate with steam from a central boiler.

Most foods cooked in steam-jacketed kettles are cooked in liquids. Meat can be browned by placing it in the kettle without liquid and turning it frequently. Some foods are first washed, and the water allowed to run off. A closed lid saves heat and reduces evaporative moisture loss. Hard boiling water is no hotter than gentle boiling water. Besides its cost in wasted heat, hard boiling breaks up some foods and toughens others. It may also cause work areas to become uncomfortably hot.

Perforated containers are used to hold vegetables cooked in a steam kettle, thereby simplifying removal. Between two-thirds and three-quarters of the kettle's total capacity can be used; room must be left for boiling and for working in the kettle.

Clean kettles immediately after use or fill them with cold water to soak. Use warm water with a good detergent and a stiff brush on the interior. Disassemble the spigot, and clean it with a long-handled bottle brush; then run off the water, and rinse. Wipe dry, and leave the top open. Wipe down outside areas, and clean away soil with soapy water, brushes, cloths, and scrapers. Rinse the surfaces, and dry.

Beverage-making Equipment

Urns are sized from $2\frac{1}{2}$ gallons to over 100 gallons. Only three-quarters of the total capacity should be used. Two $2\frac{1}{2}$-gal urns give more flexibility than one 5-gal urn, since they allow a brew to be kept on hand in one urn while the other is being cleaned and readied for service. If service is slow, it is better to have smaller batches on hand. Some metals are attacked by coffee, giving a metallic flavor and an off-color to the brew. The most desirable metal for urns is stainless steel, followed by silver, nickel or chrome, copper, aluminum, and (last) tin plate. Glass, porcelain, and other ceramics are excellent, but they are fragile. Interiors should be stainless, for easy cleaning and good brew quality. Ceramic liners are acceptable; but if they craze, they retain coffee oils and sediment that harm the brew.

Urn brew is made by dripping water through grounds in a bag or basket. Most urns have automatic fillers that measure the water. Swivel arm sprayers are convenient. Filters with metal disks or perforated plates clean more easily than screen filters do, but they may allow more sediment into the brew. Metal baskets with paper filters are preferred. Cloth filters collect oils that may go rancid and give an off-flavor to the brew. Urns should be thoroughly cleaned after each use and should be disassembled and cleaned daily after a good soaking in an urn detergent.

Vacuum equipment consists of a top holding the coffee grounds and a bottom in which water is boiled; steam pressure forces the boiling water up into the upper bowl. Heat is then turned off; when the steam in the lower bowl condenses, the brew is sucked back into the lower bowl, leaving the grounds in the top on a filter.

Most coffee today is made in 8- to 12-cup-capacity drip units. They operate much as an urn does, with hot water coming from above, passing through the grounds, and filtering down into a bowl from which the coffee is served. Most are automatic, delivering the correct amount of water at a proper temperature, and are equipped with instant heaters that bring tap water to a proper temperature for brewing. Preportioned drip coffee packs are usually used. Some operations use a grinder that delivers the correct amount of fresh coffee. Ease of cleaning the equipment is an essential factor in selection.

Very little instant coffee is used. Equipment exists that delivers a brewed coffee from instant, but this type of machine is most often found as a self-dispensing unit.

Miscellaneous Cooking Equipment

Electric or gas toasters, with a belt that moves around a heating element, are used to make toast in quantity. For toasting at location, pop-up toasters are usually used. Items can be toasted with infrared lamps, salamanders, broilers, or griddles.

Waffle irons should be conditioned by heating a well-greased grid until it nearly smokes, holding this temperature 5 to 10 minutes, wiping the surface very clean with a soft cloth, and repeating the procedure.

Roll warmers heat breads and other foods at temperatures of around 180° to 200°F. Some of the drawers are vented, preventing products from becoming soggy as a result of moisture buildup. Pies, puddings, sauces, and other products that need to be warm for service can also be held in roll warmers.

MECHANICAL EQUIPMENT

Mechanical equipment can do much to facilitate work. Preparation time can be reduced, and quality of performance improved. Equipment also helps minimize work strain and fatigue.

Cutting Equipment

Food choppers (grinders) are used to chop or grind meat, nuts, vegetables, crumbs, and other foods (see fig. 3-20a). Particle size can be varied by using plates that have different-sized holes. The food is fed into a hopper and forced down with a mallet into a screw, which pushes the

(a)

(b)

(c)

(d)

Figure 3-20. Cutting equipment of various types: (a) countertop model chopper; (b) food cutter; (c) slicer adjustable for manual or mechanical operation; (d) vertical cutter/ mixer equipped with a see-through cover. (*Courtesy Hobart*)

food through the plate. A rotating blade helps divide the food. Some juice may develop, and this should be caught. Workers should never use their hands to push food down the hopper. Choppers should be soaked or cleaned immediately after use. Choppers may be acquired as separate pieces of equipment or as attachments to other power equipment.

Food cutters have two knives that spin on a rapidly rotating axle under a cover (see fig. 3-20b). The bowl turns so that all areas pass under the knives. Food can be fed into the knives with a mallet. Careless operation—especially pushing the food into the knives with the hands—can cause a serious accident. It is important that the knives be true and be well-sharpened if they are to cut rather than bruise the food. The bowl can be filled to between one-third and one-half of capacity. Food can be finely minced or coarsely chopped, depending on the length of time the cutter operates. Nuts, hard-frozen meat, whole grain cereals, and hard-crusted bread dull the knives. The chopper can be a separate piece of equipment, or it can be an attachment to other equipment.

Vegetable slicers, graters, and cubers that are obtained as attachments to food choppers or mixers find good use. The slicer forces food down into a rotating blade that can be varied to give different slice thicknesses (see fig. 3-20c). It is especially good for slicing cabbage, salad vegetables, potatoes, and the like. The grater operates much as the slicer does, and different-sized blades make different-sized gratings possible. A special feeding device and cutters are required for a cuber.

At least one type of cutter can cut slices from $\frac{1}{64}$ to $\frac{1}{4}$ in. thick, dice in various sizes, cut strips from julienne to french fry size, and perform other tasks. It has different openings and uses different cutters for each task. Food is fed into the machine with a mallet. The time required for assembly, disassembly, and cleaning is warranted only when a large quantity of food is to be processed through the cutter.

A vertical cutter and mixer has two knives on a vertical axle that spins in an enclosed bowl at high speed, operating much like a small blender (see fig. 3-20d). It processes a large amount of food in a short time. For example, it can process 20 lb of lettuce in $1\frac{1}{2}$ seconds. It can also be used to make fine emulsions such as mayonnaise. Some foods must be chopped with water to prevent bruising. The blade position can be varied to obtain different cutting results. If half or less of capacity is used, the blades should be on the bottom. Failing to keep blades sharp and true leads to poor results. Hard products such as nuts and dry bread dull knives.

The machine cannot be opened while it is in operation. Capacities are 15 to 80 quarts. On the 15-qt and 25-qt models, a hand-operated mixing baffle moves food into the rotating knives; on larger models, this baffle is mechanically operated. The baffle moves counterclockwise, opposite to the knife movement. A short jerk during turning helps to free food that is caught on the baffle. The manufacturer's instructions for operation and maintenance should be closely followed. Unless a program for use is carefully worked out, this machine may stand idle much of the time. With planning, it can be a big asset.

A meat slicer can be used to give uniform slices of different thicknesses to cheese, meat, vegetables, and some bakery goods (see fig. 3-21a). The slanted-blade types are easier to use because the slices made by vertical-blade units tend to fold as they are cut. To use, set the gauge and place the food on the carrier so that cutting proceeds across the grain and the most desirable shape and size are obtained. If necessary, pretrim and preshape the food to be sliced. Place an end weight at the back of the food to give steady pressure in forcing the food down into the rotating

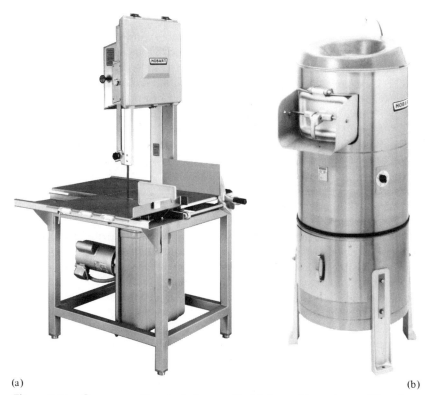

(a)   (b)

Figure 3-21. Common cutting tools in quantity kitchens: (a) meat saw; (b) peeler. Rather than peel, a peeler abraids items, taking off the outer skin.

blade. Hand pressure produces uneven slices and creates a safety hazard. Some machines have a carriage that operates automatically, going back and forth; others operate the blade only. Holding the hand in a plastic wrap under large or tender slices and lowering them carefully onto a container reduces food breakage. Some units catch and lower slices. Follow the manufacturer's instructions for maintaining and operating the unit. It is important that the blade be kept sharp and true. For this purpose, a special sharpening blade is used; it must be held against the blade at the proper angle as the motor turns the blade.

Peelers are used to remove the skins from hard vegetables such as potatoes, carrots, and turnips. A cylinder inside rotates, throwing the vegetables against an abrasive material on the top, bottom, and sides. Peelers vary in their capacity to hold vegetables, but those most commonly used process about 25 pounds per batch. Workers must be cautioned not to allow peelers to run too long since there can be a high waste of product. (Workers may be tempted to do so to avoid having to remove eyes and blemishes.) The abrasive material may have to be replaced from time to time.

Mixers

A mixer is used to mash potatoes and to mix foods (see fig. 3-22a). The pantry uses it to blend dressings and to mix or whip foods. The bakeshop uses it to mix batters and doughs, make frostings, whip foams, and do other jobs. In a large bakeshop, a horizontal mixer is used for large batches of bread dough, cookie dough, and other stiff doughs (see fig. 3-22b). Upright mixers are sized from 5 qt to 140 qt. Adapter rings and different-sized agitators make it possible to use mixing bowls of different sizes. Bakeshops usually have 20-qt and 80-qt mixers, with adapters. The cooks need mixers sized from 30 qt to 80 qt, with adapters, and the pantry needs a 20-qt mixer that adapts to 12 qt and 10 qt. Bowl dollies and trucks are used for large bowls and some have motors that raise or lower bowls.

Different agitators are used for different purposes on mixers (see fig. 3-23). Many mixers are designed to use other attachments, too, such as choppers, slicers, cutters, and dicers. Dough hooks are used for bread doughs; a special scalloped one is used for richer sweet doughs: it gives good mixing action but pulls the dough less. A pastry cutter has a wire or cutter on the front side to cut up the shortening. This should be removed and the dough hook or paddle used to finish making the dough after water is added. Flat beaters are used to make cookie doughs or cakes, to give good creaming and blending action. Wire whips are used to incorporate air into egg foams, whipping cream, and so on. Agitators are inter-

(a)   (b)

Figure 3-22.   (a) A small tabletop model mixer on a mobile stand. This design allows use by different operating units of the kitchen. (b) A floor model mixer that can handle large batches. (*Courtesy Hobart*)

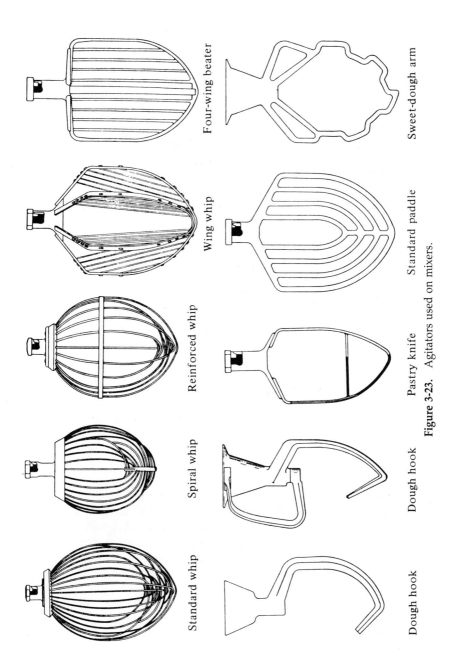

Figure 3-23. Agitators used on mixers.

Four-wing beater

Sweet-dough arm

Wing whip

Standard paddle

Reinforced whip

Pastry knife

Spiral whip

Dough hook

Standard whip

Dough hook

changed during production. Thus, a whip may be used to prepare an egg foam for an angel cake, and then a wing whip is used to blend in the flour, sugar, and other ingredients.

Agitators should reach to within about $\frac{1}{16}$ in. of all bowl parts. The machine should be stopped before scraping down is attempted. Using a flexible spatula that is sufficiently long to reach the bowl bottom, completely scrape down the sides with a twisting, turning motion of the wrist to remove all material and bring it into the center. This task is frequent in some mixing.

Refrigeration and Freezing Equipment

Reach-in and walk-in refrigerators are used to hold foods at sufficiently low temperatures that they retain their quality and stay safe (see fig. 3-24). Some foods cannot be stored together, so multiple units are required; eggs and dairy products easily absorb other food flavors and therefore must be kept separate. Walk-in refrigeration is used to store garbage and other waste in warm climates. Use increases if the floor is level so that mobile equipment can be moved in and out. Walk-ins are mostly used to store foods awaiting production, but they can also hold foods under production that cannot be conveniently stored in reach-in refrigerators. All foods in freezers and refrigerators should be covered with tight-fitting covers or moisture- and vapor-proof wraps because low temperatures dehydrate foods. Warm foods cool at room temperature nearly as fast as they do under refrigeration, so we often let items cool outside until they nearly reach room temperature before putting them under refrigeration. Stirring liquids or setting foods in the path of running water promotes faster cooling, as does placing foods in front of a fan or an open window in a good draft. If a knife or other instrument is placed under a container, cooling is faster. Thick foods such as puddings, gravies, and dressings should not be put into refrigerators in large masses but spread out into shallow lots so that they cool quickly. Storage is best at 0°F or lower. Fluctuating temperatures are not good for the texture, flavor, and color of frozen food. Shelving in refrigerated or frozen walk-ins should be removable, for easier cleaning.

Reach-in refrigerators are usually located in work centers. They are used for ongoing production—not storage—although foods used frequently in production but needing refrigeration are stored there. Some may have shelving that can be changed to suit storage needs. All foods should be covered and frequently checked to ensure that foods that should be used are. Do not pack foods too tightly, since they need air circulation around them. In refrigerators that depend upon natural convection, the bottom area is usually the coldest. If a fan operates inside, all areas should have about the same temperature. Open refrigerators and freezers as little as possible; plan ahead for withdrawals.

Mobile refrigerators are used for food storage and for distributing foods to wherever they must be transported. Chilled or hot foods can also be placed into insulated carts or units for transportation.

(a)

(b)

Figure 3-24. (a) A three-unit reach-in refrigerator. (*Courtesy Victory*) (b) A large walk-in refrigerator that can be installed into a space or left freestanding. (*Courtesy Hobart*)

Pass-through refrigerators hold foods so they can be quickly obtained without the problem of transport. They usually are sized to hold 18 × 26, 14 × 18, or 12 × 20-in. pans. Some are designed so that roll-in equipment can be moved into them.

Freezers in work areas arc rarely used except to hold frozen desserts or other frozen items. With the increasing use of frozen prepared foods, however, the use of on-location freezers is increasing.

Butchershop Equipment

The small amount of butchering done in small operations usually occurs at the cooks' unit, where a cutting board, hand meat saw, and knives are stored. In large units, a special area (usually equipped with a band saw) is used. Band saws do a good job cutting frozen meat. Novices should not be allowed to use them. A butchershop also uses meat grinders, meat cubers, tenderizers, and special chopping equipment. Poultry singers, tendon pullers, and other specialized equipment may be used.

Bakery Equipment

A combination dough divider and rounder is used to cut bread doughs into desired sizes and then roll them into rounded shapes for pan rolls; additional hand shaping can make these into hamburger buns, hotdog buns, Parker House rolls, and so on. Small operations usually rely on a manually operated divider; large operations commonly use mechanical dough dividers. In large operations, dough dividers and rollers are separate units. Fermented dough is moved through these two units and into an overhead proofer. Then it is panned, final proofed, and baked.

Dough rollers or sheeters are used for rolling out pie dough, break dough, and other products. Bench-type rollers are used on tables. Rollers require special settings for rolling out Danish doughs, puff pastes, and other specific items. Yeast products must be properly rested to be relaxed enough to go through a sheeter; other doughs, such as pie or cookie dough, must be stiff enough to go through the machine; refrigeration usually satisfies this need.

A proofing cabinet is used to proof yeast doughs after panning and before baking. It must maintain temperatures around 90°F and a relative humidity of 80 to 85 percent. Some are automatically controlled to hold temperatures and humidity within narrow limits. Others may require manual operation of heating units, and on some a pan of water may be placed over the heating unit on the bottom to give proper humidity. Proofers can be mobile or stationary; the latter may allow loaded carts to be moved in and out of them.

Dishwashers and Potwashers

Dishwashers and potwashers are important pieces of equipment from the standpoint of cleaning and sanitation (fig. 3-25). Both work by having 160°F (71°C) wash water containing a detergent being thrown with force

Figure 3-25. A flight-type dishwasher that can handle large loads. (*Courtesy Hobart*)

against dishes and utensils to remove soil. Often, moving arms throw this water, but some models have stationary units through which water is forced by strong pump action. These units then rinse, and most sanitize as well. Sanitizing can be done by increasing the temperature above 180°F (82°C) for at least 10 seconds or by increased temperature plus a sanitizing medium—usually one containing chlorine. Some wash detergents contain a sanitizing agent.

Dishwashers may be single-tank or multiple-tank. Multiple-tank units can have a prerinse tank, a wash tank, a rinse tank, and a sanitizing tank. Single-tank machines are basket type; that is, the dishes and utensils to be washed are put into a basket and the basket is then pushed into the machine. Multiple-tank units have either baskets or belts moved through by chain movement. If belts are used, the dishes and utensils are loaded directly onto the belt without using baskets, but small items that might drop through are first loaded into containers. Items are air-dried after coming out of the machine. Some machines have a chamber to facilitate this drying, especially for plastic ware that does not dry as well as china.

Potwashers are usually multiple-tank and belt-driven. Pump pressures are higher, creating more force for the removal of stubborn soil. Even then, some presoaking and scraping might be needed. The detergent used usually has a higher pH than that used for dishwashers so the alkaline substances can combine fats and make a soap that facilitates cleaning. Detergents should not develop too many suds since these stop the force of water directed at the items being cleaned. Methods of rinsing and sanitizing are similar to those used in dishmachines.

It is important to make sure that temperatures are correct in both dishwashers and potwashers. Both should be thoroughly cleaned after a day's use. In some areas where the water is hard and a white film forms on the inside of the equipment, a wash with some kind of phosphoric acid compound may be needed to remove the film. Workers should also check from time to time that food collecting on trays in the prerinse and wash sections is removed and the debris discarded. Better cleaning and sanitation result if temperatures are correct and the cleanliness standards are high.

Chapter Review

1. If the Celsius temperature is 20°, what is the Fahrenheit temperature?
2. If the Fahrenheit temperature is 32°, what is the Celsius temperature?
3. Define the following: conduction, convection, radiation, kinetic action, specific heat, heat of fusion, heat of vaporization, and absolute zero.
4. How can two liquids such as alcohol and water be separated? Describe the process.
5. How does evaporation work?
6. How is a French knife used for various manipulations?
7. How should a worker use a steam pressure unit?

CHAPTER 4

Work Improvement

Outline

Goals

1. To introduce the subjects of work study and work improvement.
2. To show how management can improve jobs in order to improve production and worker satisfaction.
3. To indicate how work improvement can be implemented in a kitchen.
4. To develop ideas on how equipment location and proper work flow can improve jobs.
5. To list different methods used in work improvement.
6. To explain how and why workers tire and lose productivity.
7. To show how storage can be made an effective part of the work flow.

INTRODUCTION

The way workers do their jobs has much to do with food cost and quality. Many industries use machines extensively to reduce labor, but foodservices have not been able to do so because too little is produced at one time, because production is geared to demand, or because machines cannot duplicate workers' skills. Consequently, the foodservice industry is highly labor-intensive: its products have a higher ratio of labor cost to dollar sales than do the products of other industries. Moreover, as a group, foodservices also use labor poorly: the average productivity is 50 percent, when it should be about 80 percent. Poor planning, poor work methods, and inefficiently planned work areas contribute to work inefficiency.

MANAGEMENT AND WORK METHODS IMPROVEMENT

Procedures aimed at work methods improvement try to teach workers how to work *smarter*, not *harder*. The ultimate aim is to reduce work so that time is reduced and energy is conserved. *Work methods improvement* is also called *methods engineering* or *work simplification*.

Methods engineering need not be a formal program. An alert supervisor can see how work is being done and can come up with improvements—especially if certain basic principles for improving jobs are known. Informal programs may be more successful than formal ones. It is better to think of work improvement as a philosophy than as a science. If workers are taught to think in terms of work simplification, many natural and spontaneous improvements can occur. Since workers often know their jobs better than anyone else does, they often have good ideas for improving them. Indoctrinate workers with the idea that there is always a better way; and emphasize that small savings, while insignificant in themselves, can cumulatively lead to a substantial reduction in work effort. Jobs that are easier to do and result in better-quality products quickly win employee approval.

MANAGEMENT'S ROLE

It is management's responsibility to see that workers achieve good productivity and have adequate equipment, tools, and environment to do the work. Work areas (centers) should be planned carefully, and tasks should be organized thoughtfully and effectively. Advance menu planning, purchasing, and work scheduling must be done. Workers need to be informed of production requirements and must have materials on hand when work starts. Coordination of work with other departments is management's job. If management fails in its job, workers will inevitably fail in theirs.

SELECTING WORKERS

Work improvement starts with worker selection. Job specifications should list the skills, education, ability to plan and organize, experience, age, personality, and so forth being sought in workers. Select workers who can perform jobs adequately or who have the potential to learn; then follow through with training, as needed. Good training programs increase productivity. From the day a worker is hired, he or she should increase in proficiency and value. If this is not the case, the worker should not have been hired. An operation's most valuable asset is its workers, yet many operations let this resource decline in quality while seeking to increase the worth of assets of less value. The developmental needs of every worker should be ascertained, and a program should be established to meet them. It is extremely important that workers feel sure about management's interest in developing the whole worker rather than in just developing skills and knowledge for the benefit of management.

Working toward employees goals in order to achieve management's goals is smart management.

TRAINING WORKERS

Training workers can be accomplished in different ways. A job description is an excellent training tool. It tells workers what the job is, and thereby serves to orient new workers so that satisfactory productivity is achieved more quickly. Many training programs rely on the "big brother" method, which uses an experienced worker as a teacher. If this method is used, make sure that the instruction being given is desirable, since older workers frequently pass on inefficient ways of working. On-the-job training under a planned program is effective. Workers, supervisors, and even management take part in instruction. Short courses combined with on-the-job training are also good. Even informal discussion of food standards, work methods, and other factors improve job proficiency. Operations should establish standards for work performance so that workers know what is expected of them. Visual aids, demonstrations, and talks are helpful. Job evaluation can do much to indicate what workers need to do in order to improve.

IMPROVING PRODUCTIVITY

New equipment, tools, foods, or ways of doing work should be constantly sought as means of improving worker productivity. A cook-chill method, for example, separates production from service and allows full concentration of production personnel on making larger batches for carry-over. Analysis of how work is done may suggest ways to reduce labor. Why receive bulky vegetables, move them into refrigeration, pull them out again and into vegetable preparation, and then move them back into storage, when they could go directly from receiving into preparation and then storage—or even, with good planning, bypass storage altogether and go directly to production? Bypassing storage often saves time and promotes quality by improving freshness.

The ingredient room is a big time-saver. Food needed for production is measured or weighed out in it, and then delivered to production sections. This eliminates worker travel to get materials and consolidates all orders into one, so everything is on hand for production.

Management should see that as large a volume of production as possible occurs when a job is done. If possible, larger batches should be made, since this can save time. Every job consists of three parts: getting ready; doing; and cleaning up and putting away. The getting ready and the cleaning up and putting away take about the same amount of time whether the job is large or small. Therefore, the more doing that occurs in comparison to the other two factors, the greater the productivity that is realized. Consolidating work or jobs may help increase the proportion of the doing. For example, if cinnamon rolls are made every day, why not do the entire week's needs at one time and freeze the excess? Then the amount needed for one day's service can be withdrawn in the morning, thawed in its wraps, proofed, and baked. Doing just this in one activity raised productivity 280 percent. Writing up ways to do jobs correctly is a good approach for establishing proper ways of doing work. Time management involves establishing a set time for doing specific tasks. A worker's schedule is set up with times blocked out for accomplishing jobs; at a set time, the worker is expected to be working on that job and to be on schedule. Once such a schedule is established, workers like it because it establishes a routine pattern that organizes and simplifies the work.

"A fair day's pay for a fair day's work" has long been an accepted motto in management–worker relations. Every worker must produce enough to justify the pay he or she receives. Today, if a worker makes $12,000 per year, the worker should produce at least $50,000 in sales per year.

PLANNING WORK

Work done according to plan is done more quickly and more easily than nonplanned work. A good worker quickly learns what to do upon coming on shift, and checks equipment, tools, and materials to see that the necessary things are on hand. Recipes are reviewed and equipment is readied. Items needing longer cooking are started first. Pre-preparation needed for production is done in advance. Production times are known and work is organized, so items are ready in time. Work is eliminated; for example, a butter cake is made before a chocolate cake, thus eliminating the need to wash the mixing bowl between uses.

A phrase used often in the kitchen is *"mise en place,"* which means literally "put in place" but is interpreted as meaning "keep things in order." *Lining up* means somewhat the same thing but also refers to getting things ready ahead of time. Lining up speeds production that must be performed at the last minute. Pantry work and fry-station work require good lining up. *Mise en place* includes cleaning up as one works; clutter slows work down, causes confusion, and lowers product quality. Workers should learn to conserve motion—for example, by placing dirty pots and pans on a mobile cart as they accumulate so that they can all be moved to the sink at one time, instead having to be carried one at a time.

WORK CENTERS AND WORK FLOW

Workers should be confined as much as possible to performing their jobs within a work center. Figure 4-1 shows the horizontal and vertical maximum and normal work areas in a work center. No required reach should extend outside the maximum area, and the most frequent ones should fall within the normal work area. Where two hands cross in the normal area, two-handed work is best done. Not only should horizontal space be used, but the vertical space between 88 in. and 30 in. from the floor should be used. Motions in a work center should follow the natural job flow, without crisscrossing or backtracking. Right-handed workers usually work best from left to right (see fig. 4-2).

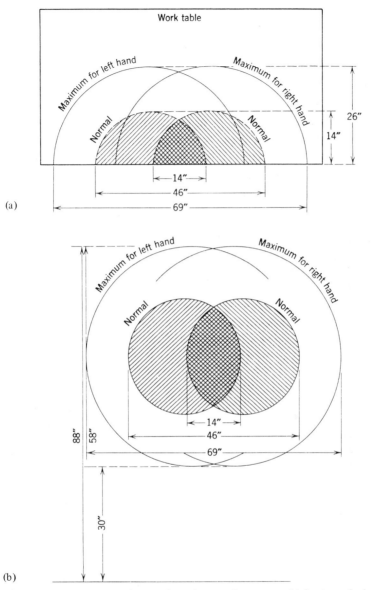

Work table

Maximum for left hand

Maximum for right hand

Normal

Normal

26"

14"

14"

46"

69"

(a)

Maximum for left hand

Maximum for right hand

Normal

Normal

14"

46"

69"

88"

58"

30"

(b)

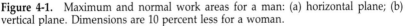

Figure 4-1. Maximum and normal work areas for a man: (a) horizontal plane; (b) vertical plane. Dimensions are 10 percent less for a woman.

When work in one center is done, it is moved to the next center in a progressive fashion. Instead of setting up different centers, planners may prefer to use the same one, after adding equipment, removing other equipment, or in other ways changing it. Using mobile equipment is a good way to do this, as shown in figure 4-3. Different work often requires

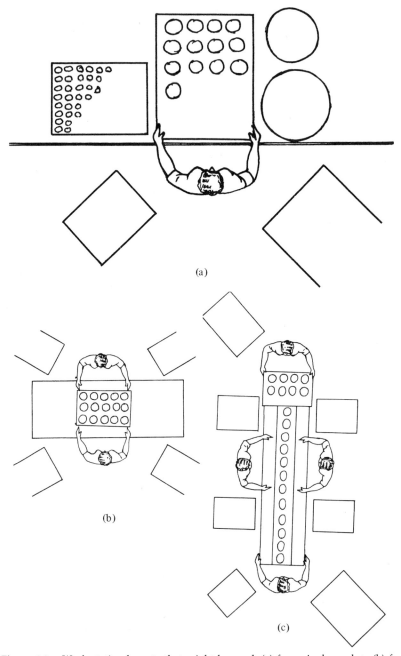

Figure 4-2. Work station layouts that might be used: (a) for a single worker; (b) for two workers; (c) for more than two workers. (*Taken from a student assignment by Andrew Castle, University of Montana, 1958*)

(a)   (b)

Figure 4-3.   (a) A work table in a bakeshop. The mobile pie dough roller at the end of the table dumps the rolled dough into a pie pan, so the worker stationed there can remove the excess crust and then pass the unbaked crust over to another worker to fill the shells and place the filled trays onto the mobile cart. The worker has the pie filling on a mobile cart to her left. (b) Placing this toaster on rollers allows it to be moved out of the way and replaced with more needed mobile equipment at other meal times.

different centers. Salad preparation usually calls for three: a preparation center, a make-up center, and an assembly center. If the vegetable center prepares salad items, the pre-preparation center is eliminated.

Much foodservice production does not involve the repetitive motions characteristic of factory production. This is because the work is so varied. Great flexibility must be incorporated into kitchen sections to that the centers can be changed as required. A takeout unit has much different needs than a drive-in.

If work can be done continuously or in assembly-line flow, better productivity is usually achieved. Such continuous flow may be straight-line, U-shaped, circular, or any other, as long as it is continuous. Many items must be made in order to use this flow efficiently, and motions must be identical and repetitive. It is used on soiled dish tables, salads, sandwiches, and for assembly of similar products; using a circling table or a moving belt helps promote continuous flow.

Most work in foodservices is done by shop or unit flow, where foods are processed to a certain point, then stored, and finally taken up later when final production begins. Small operations find this approach suitable to their needs. It requires less equipment than assembly-line flow, but production time is usually longer. A great many different motions are required of each worker, and storage requirements are higher. Jobs such as breading and then storing meat for future use and partially cooking and holding sausages at breakfast time are examples of this flow.

WORK MOTIONS

Productivity is promoted by combining, rearranging, or eliminating work motions. A sandwich-spreading spatula with a cutting edge combines

TABLE 4-1. Principles and examples of motion economy

Principle	Example
Move hands in unison, starting and stopping at the same time and leaving neither hand idle except at rest.	Worker reaches for a soup bowl with left hand while reaching for a ladle of soup with the other; hands are positioned in front when at rest.
Move arms simultaneously and in opposite and symmetrical directions for best balance in two-handed work.	The example above also shows this. Try holding an arm against the side while moving the other, and notice how much easier it is to move both arms.
Use the lowest movement classification to produce work with the least effort and time.	Using a finger to start a pot and pan machine is better than washing the pots in a sink.
Do work the easiest way.	Most work is most easily done with the right hand and the first two fingers.
Use natural rhythm and continuous, curved motions that are ballistic.	Use circular rather than back-and-forth motions. Ballistic or arched movements are more accurate, easier, and quicker to do than straight-line movements.
Use momentum or gravity, and reduce either (if possible) in doing work.	Use drop delivery to deliver water from a faucet at the cook's stove. Use an arching swing in lifting a loaded pan using the momentum in the swing to help lift the pan.
Use devices, tools, or equipment to free hands in doing work.	A recipe card holder keeps a recipe at eye level, so a worker need not lift it frequently to read.
Have tools, utensils, and materials within the normal and maximum work areas.	A cook stuffing a turkey should have the dressing, turkey, seasonings, and pans conveniently located in the work center.
Avoid hunt and search.	Train workers to return tools to the same place, so they know where they are.
Combine tools and equipment.	Use attachments to mixers for grinding, slicing, shredding, and so on.
Promote proper motion sequence by good location of tools and materials.	Locate a knife rack close to where knives are used. Have the most common spices in small bins over the baker's work table.
Provide good light.	Provide 50 to 100 foot-candles in areas where fine work is done.
Reduce equipment speed so as to promote motion rhythm.	A belt moving at 8 to 12 feet per minute does this on a dishmachine.
Arrange work heights so they are most comfortable for workers; have workers sit at work whenever possible.	A surface should be 2 to 4 inches below a worker's elbow when small hand tools are used. When a tool that extends the worker's arm is used (such as a whip or ladle) arrange the surface so that the worker can stand erect and place hands flat on the surface easily and firmly.
Provide good grasps on tools.	See the discussion on this in chapter 3.
Position all controls and levers so that they manipulate easily with the least change in posture.	A good mixer has levers and controls so that workers can stand and work and still reach them easily.
Minimize disturbing noises and vibrations.	A noisy fan can reduce work efficiency.
Provide heat and ventilation for comfort.	The best temperature for work is 65° to 75°F, with relative humidity not over 65 percent.
Allow appropriate rest periods.	This is discussed in the present chapter.
Provide good training.	This is discussed in the present chapter.
Establish good personnel relations.	Workers cannot produce well in an environment that is not conducive to trust and cordiality between workers and management.

spreading and cutting functions in one tool. Repeat motions without changing others, in order to speed work. For example, slice as much meat as possible, and then lift all slices into a tray, rather than cutting one slice and putting it on the tray before resuming slicing. Reducing motions to the lowest classification reduces time: fingers move faster than the hand, the hand moves faster than the arm, and the arm moves faster than the body. Following this guideline also improves accuracy. Using a finger to start a machine that whips a quart of cream is easier than whipping it by hand (and arm). Twenty-one principles of motion economy—motions that save effort—are outlined in table 4-1. Practicing these in the workplace can save much effort and time.

FATIGUE

As workers tire, their productivity drops (see fig. 4-4). All workers must have rest to perform satisfactorily. Workers are subject to both physical and mental fatigue.

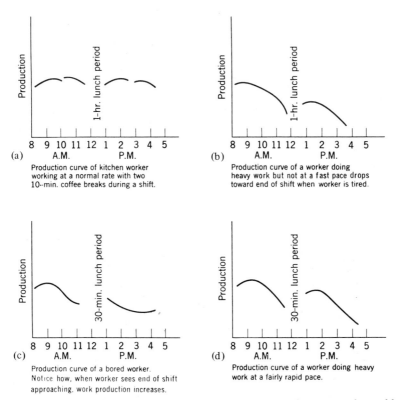

Figure 4-4. As workers tire, their productivity drops. (a) Production is enhanced by coffee breaks in the morning and afternoon. (b) Heavy work causes a significant drop in production. (c) Effects of mental (rather than physical) fatigue. (d) Heavy work at a rapid pace.

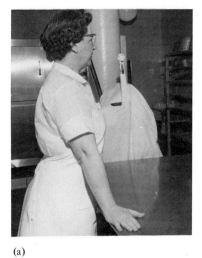

(a)

(b)

(c)

(d)

(e)

(f)

Physical fatigue occurs when muscular exertion uses up the body's readily available energy. Avoiding body strain and heavy work reduces fatigue. Normally, men should not lift more than 50 lb, and women should not lift more than 35 lb. Use mobile equipment to move heavy loads. Rest rebuilds energy. Sweets change rapidly into blood sugar, yielding energy fairly soon after they are consumed. Coffee stimulates the liver, causing it to release glycogen, which turns into glucose (our energy sugar). Proper work-area heights reduce fatigue significantly (see fig. 4-5). The body rests on an inverted T made by the spine and hips. When this T gets out of position, we use more energy and tire sooner.

Mental fatigue can be caused by dislike of a job, boredom, noise, poor light, or other environmental factors. Workers who are not physically tired can still feel so. This effect is thought to be the result of a slowing-down of nerve impulses, especially at nerve endings. Figure 4-4c shows a mental fatigue curve.

Three kinds of rest must be given workers to reduce fatigue. The first is rest between work motions. Our hearts must rest, and they do between beats. If a person's heart beats too fast, the person dies because the heart muscles get no rest. Motions made too rapidly tire muscles, which cannot renew the energy they need fast enough. Rhythmic, steady motions conserve energy by allowing muscles to renew energy between motions. The old adage, "Life by the yard is apt to be hard, but life by the inch is more of a cinch," has meaning in doing work. The example of the tortoise and the hare illustrates the benefits of a steady pace, although the tortoise's exact pace need not be overemphasized.

Workers should set paces that are suited to them. Some have excess energy and like to burn it by wasting motion. Let them: restricting the movements of such workers creates frustrations and mental fatigue. Others workers should conserve their energy so that they have some left at the end of the day. Normally, a worker is tired during about one-fifth of the shift, and most of this time comes at the end of it. Teach workers to use energy as they do paychecks—spending carefully so they are not penniless before the next one comes along. Plan for rest periods. If workers are not given adequate rest, they take it anyway by degrees, which is only half as good as authorized rest.

The second kind of rest workers need is a break from work. After several hours of work, a worker's energy is low and work slows. A longer rest than the one obtained between work motions is required. Short breaks of 3 to 10 minutes help reduce this physical fatigue, as well as

Figure 4-5. (a) When tools such as whips or spoons are used, the work table height shown here is correct. (b) When tools such as knives are used, the work surface should be 2 to 4 in. below the elbow. (c) A shallow kettle makes for easier work. (d) Lift heavy loads with the strong leg muscles, not the weaker back muscles. (e) The worker on the right, despite being seated, is using more effort than the worker standing on the left because of poor body posture. (f) In carrying objects, workers should walk out of step; if there is sufficient room at turns and corridors, the workers should have their heads on opposite sides of the object being carried, to increase the field of vision.

relieving mental fatigue. If a worker continues to work after fatigue sets in, it is unwise to give additional rest to compensate for it, since the rest required to eliminate such fatigue increases geometrically. Getting doubly tired requires more than twice the rest—perhaps four times more.

The third kind of rest is rest between work shifts, to rebuild interest and energy. Days off or vacations are needed. Working overtime or too long without rest causes productivity to drop. During the Battle of Britain in World War II, workers engaged in a 60-hour work week produced less than they did on a 48-hour one, in spite of high motivation to produce. Speed-up working, working the best workers longer than they should, and other factors that may seem desirable at first impression may actually lower production.

STORAGE

Use one-motion storage as much as possible. Send pots and pans to the work centers where they are used, rather than to central storage. Store items at points of first use, and arrange work so that the least possible distance exists between work and storage. Plan temporary storage to eliminate travel to central storage. Much storage is dead storage unconnected to any important sequence in production. Things in storage should be on the move. Use conveyors or mobile storage units to reduce handling. Plan production so that storage is located between two points in processing (see fig. 4-6).

JOB BREAKDOWN TECHNIQUES

Work improvement engineers use various techniques to study jobs and improve them. Many—such as time studies, flow process charts, travel

Figure 4-6. A principle of motion economy says, "Use drop delivery when possible."

charts, simo-charts, menomotion, and stroboscopic and cyclegraphic study—can be used by nonprofessionals.

The first step is to select the job. A job that is time-consuming, bottle-neck-inducing, difficult to do, or widely disliked has promise. Jobs that involve a lot of walking or a lot of repetitive motion may be attacked with profit, as may jobs that call for producing a lot of items. It is best to be sure of success on the first try. This builds confidence and wins over skeptics.

In breaking jobs down, identify their productive, rest, and waste components. Question each component for essentiality. Ask questions such as: what is done? what is the purpose? what happens? why is it done? is it necessary? could something else be used instead? could things be combined or rearranged to improve the job? when should it be done? where should it be done? how is it done? would doing it differently improve the job and make it quicker to do? These questions are most important in getting a true insight into the job. Constantly think about different ways a job can be done. Weigh all alternatives. It is sometimes surprising to discover how a job is actually done, who is doing it, and so on. Asking *what* and *why* might reveal that eggs are being hard-cooked, peeled, and chopped, when they could be cracked into lightly oiled pans, gently steamed until hard, and then chopped—eliminating shelling. Answers to *where*, *when*, and *who* (along with the always-recurring *why*) may lead to combining, eliminating, or rearranging tasks. If a product is batter-dipped instead of breaded, for instance, time is saved.

Job study methods are published in a number of books devoted to the subject; some of these books are identified in the references at the end of this text. Study in this area might be well worth the time and effort.

Chapter Review

1. What is work improvement, and how is it implemented in quantity food production?
2. What is management's responsibility in any work improvement program?
3. What are some of the ways in which jobs can be studied and improved?
4. If every job consists of a "get ready," a "do," and a "clean up and put away," how can we get more "do" accomplished for the same amount of work done in the other two categories? Give examples.
5. What is *mise en place*?
6. What are the dimensions of a work center?
7. What kinds of rest do workers need?
8. How should the issue of storage be addressed in the job improvement program?

Kitchen Production

CHAPTER 5

Pantry Production

Outline

V. **Beverages**
  A. Coffee
    1. Standards
    2. Brew Water
    3. Making Coffee
      a. Urn Coffee
      b. Automatic Drip Coffee
      c. Vacuum Coffee
      d. Miscellaneous Procedures
      e. Holding Coffee
    4. Variety Coffee
  B. Tea
    1. Standards
    2. Principles
    3. Making Tea
  C. Cocoa
    1. Standards

Goals

1. To cover the standards, principles, and techniques used in making foods prepared in the pantry.
2. To detail the making, ingredients, work methods, kinds, garnishes, and storage of sandwiches.
3. To discuss the standards, the parts, the kinds, and the methods of making salads and dressings.
4. To cover the standards and preparation of appetizers.
5. To cover the standards, principles, and techniques of making coffee, tea, and cocoa.
6. To cover some of the sanitary procedures used in pantry work.

THE PANTRY AND ITS WORK

The pantry makes salads, appetizers, sandwiches, and other cold items, and it may prepare breakfasts. In the continental kitchen, the pantry is usually separate from the *garde manger* section, which prepares cold meat and fish; however, the *garde manger* chef may be in charge of both. Some pantries make beverages, fountain items, and dish desserts. Beverages are discussed in this chapter, but fountain items and desserts are discussed in chapter 15.

Pantry work is characterized by the production of many small units; the work requires considerable hand labor and much dexterity, skill, and speed. The wide variety of foods made and the need to rely on last-minute assembly in order to preserve freshness and temperature make work simplification essential. While the technical knowledge required may not be as great as for cooking or baking, perhaps a better sense of artistry and proportion is needed. Workers should have the ability to organize their tasks and time well, keep work areas clean, and withstand pressure. Good space utilization is needed because the quantity of items produced is large (see fig. 5-1).

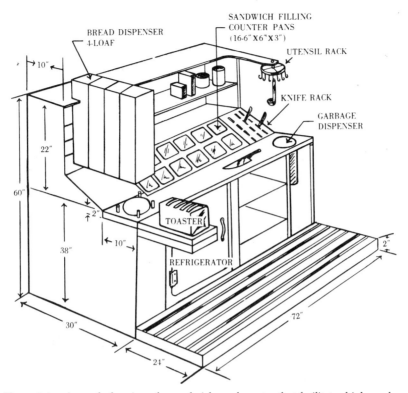

Figure 5-1. A rough drawing of a sandwich work center that facilitates high production with minimum utilization of space and worker effort. (*Courtesy Z. Eppel*)

Workers should know how to set up good work centers and how to maintain proper work flow between them. Necessary movements should require as little reaching as possible (see fig. 5-2). In making a number of similar items, workers should repeat one set of motions for a whole group of items; then another set for the same group; and so on until the work is done. For example, in making a large number of cocktails, workers should place all glasses on trays at one time, then fill them with the cocktail product, then cover them with sauce, and then garnish them with parsley and lemon slices. The cocktail product and sauce could be added in alternate motions using two hands, and the parsley and lemon slice could be added the same way to save time and energy. Groups of two or more workers facing each other across a table and sharing the work can limit motions and thereby save time. In addition, moving belts or moving circular tables may be used, moving at a steady speed of from 8 to 12 feet per minute. Highest production is achieved when the work pace is steady and even; excessive speed can destroy this rhythm. Some attention must be given to pantry resupply because of the bulky items that are transported to it.

Figure 5-2. The worker is reaching too far in making these baked cranberry and cheese sandwiches. Confine distances of reach to 14 in. if possible; never exceed 26 in. (*Courtesy American Baking Institute*)

High standards of sanitation must be practiced. Pantry foods often are not cooked, making them good culture for bacteria. All foods should be fresh and safe. A constant 40°F temperature should be maintained in refrigerators. Only food needed for the day's production should be made up at one time if it is perishable, and only food needed for a meal should be removed from the batch. Provide covers for food not in use. Do not allow materials to stand at room temperature for a total time of over 4 hours. Handle foods as little as possible. Keep all utensils, storage areas, and work spaces scrupulously clean. Scrutinize carry-over foods, which may spoil quickly and cause trouble. If production is to occur in front of patrons, have workers use tongs, forks, and other tools to handle foods. Plastic gloves are recommended.

Evaluate preparations that require large amounts of labor, such as fancy sandwiches, complex fillings, elaborate garnishes, and dishes requiring a great deal of arrangement. Attractiveness is essential, but it cannot justify excessive labor costs. Simplicity may create more eye appeal than elaborate design or garnish. A sprig of mint can do more for a fruit salad than an elaborately stuffed date. Fluting a cucumber or peeled banana with a fork before slicing them may create more interest than cutting them into fancy shapes. An unpeeled red apple slice not only adds color but saves time over peeling. Bite-size pieces in myriad forms and colors achieve a desirable artistic effect in a salad. Overworking foods gives them a fatigued appearance. Even though the cost of the ingredients is low, the time required to prepare such items as stuffed eggs, Waldorf salad, and sliced orange salad may make them costly.

Attractiveness can be gained by using good arrangements and by putting together food combinations in distinctive dishes. A balanced arrangement of sandwich pieces with a cup of hot soup or an arranged fruit salad on a chilled glass plate may be more appealing than elaborately decorated food. Cutting a sandwich into varied shapes may add more to them than an elaborate garnish. A cockle shell filled with seafood salad or a fruit salad served in half a cantaloupe may be very appealing. A large sherbet glass can be used for a chilled fruit salad. Different-shaped dishes can add interest and give form and variety to a buffet.

Pantry items are often low in food cost and high in labor cost. Because labor is sometimes quite high, these items are often priced differently than other foods, with a higher markup being taken on food cost.

SANDWICHES

Sandwiches are popular and satisfy many food needs. Most are used for a light meal or snack, but they may be used for desserts or even for breakfast, as is the case with a scrambled egg and bacon sandwich. A hot sandwich with vegetable salad constitutes a full meal.

A sandwich is bread filled with some food. A typical sandwich consists of a filling inside two bread slices, but this varies widely. Sandwiches fall into various classifications under the general headings *hot* and *cold*:

Hot	*Cold*
regular	regular
broiled	open-face
grilled	decker types (dagwood)
deep-fried	rolled or pinwheel
baked	finger, layered, or checkerboard

A regular hot meat sandwich consists of meat, bread, and gravy. It is either closed or open-face, and gravy can be omitted. Toasted bread can be used for either hot or cold sandwiches. Open-face sandwiches may be large, fancy small, or canapés.

Old favorites should be offered frequently, but good merchandising suggests offering new ideas with these. Unusual fillings, variety bread, service on attractive dishes, or unusual presentation may be used to increase sales. Wrapped sandwiches should show the cut side, identifying fillings.

STANDARDS

Bread, fillings, and garnishes for sandwiches should be absolutely fresh. Fillings should be pleasantly flavored, tender in texture, easy to eat, and rich enough to provide an appetite-satisfying sandwich. Excessive sweetness, tartness, harshness, and blandness should be avoided. Chopped fillings should be distinct and not messy. Soft fillings should contain some crisp material such as chopped celery, green pepper, lettuce, or thinly sliced cucumber. About one-third to one-half of the total sandwich weight should be filling. Fillings should not hang over the edge. Bread should be fresh and firm, with a close, smooth crumb of good flavor and moistness; a person should be able to pick up the sandwich without its bending or losing filling. Bread containing bread softeners soaks easily from moist fillings. Ragged or unevenly cut sandwiches that barely hold together are unattractive. Grilled or toasted sandwiches should have a crisp, outer crust. Try to achieve interesting color and design in sandwich presentation. Garnishes should be edible and suitable to the sandwich. Plates or containers should suit the size and type of sandwich.

SANDWICH INGREDIENTS

Bread

Fresh bread should be firm and should not have a pasty texture. It should be stored for immediate use at a temperature between 75° and 85°F in a dry place. Store soft-crusted bread in original wraps, but store hard-crusted bread without wraps in a place that has free air movement. A mobile rack or simple drawer is adequate for storage. Hard-crusted breads have a relatively short storage life. Bread easily absorbs odors: even cigarette odor on a worker's hands can flavor it. Have workers clean storage areas daily with a soft, dry brush or an industrial vacuum cleaner; scrub and dry these areas once a week. Keep old and new supplies separate, and use old bread for toasting, grilling, or making French toast. Plan supplies for only one day's needs. Refrigerating bread causes it to go stale faster than holding it at room temperature; freezing bread is the best way to preserve its freshness. Thaw frozen bread in its wraps. Frozen bread may be spread, filled, and then wrapped.

Spreads

Flavor, richness, or moistness may be the basis for selecting a spread. Among the spreads commonly used are margarine, butter, mayonnaise, salad dressing, cheese mixtures, peanut butter, and jelly. Soaking is increased when butter or margarine is either melted and used or softened with added milk or other moist products. A flavored butter or margarine spread may eliminate the need for fillings, but the spread should be soft and plastic, with no air incorporated as a result of softening.

Fillings

The filling gives a sandwich much of its character. Sliced meats or cheese are most common, and salad mixtures are also popular. Most salad fillings are made with one part chopped vegetable and one part chopped pickles to four parts meat or other product. Banana, bacon, peanut butter, and combinations with jellies, jams, or other sweet items are popular and give variety. Many vegetable combinations are used, including the always-popular lettuce and tomato sandwich. Fruit fillings such as date and nut are used for special purposes with variety breads. Many convenience fillings are available on the market.

Filling mixtures should spread easily and should be of good consistency for eating—neither too dry nor too moist. Messy fillings should be avoided. Mixed fillings with a fresh, distinct appearance increase acceptability. Limp or greasy bacon or wilted lettuce can ruin an otherwise good sandwich. Meat or cheese slices should fit the bread and be sliced evenly. Prepare fillings ahead of time and chill well. Carry-over foods may find good use in sandwich materials, but those of inferior quality should be discarded.

Garnishes

Suit the garnish to the texture, form, color, and flavor of the sandwich. The exact range of garnishes may be questioned. Perhaps we would include lettuce, parsley, romaine, radishes, potato chips, shoestring potatoes, nuts, cheese, catsup, chili sauce, and the like, but what about a cup of broth, a small coleslaw salad, or a spiced peach half? Are they garnishes or accompaniments? Since garnishes are usually considered decorations, they can be left out when speed is important.

QUANTITIES TO USE

The number of slices of bread per pound varies according to loaf size, width of slice, and bread density (see table 5-1). Thinly sliced bread is $\frac{1}{4}$ in. thick while $\frac{3}{8}$-in. slices are considered thick. A $\frac{1}{2}$- or $\frac{3}{8}$-in. slice is the usual thickness. Quick loaf bread is usually sliced $\frac{1}{2}$ in. thick.

If a No. 20 scoop ($1\frac{1}{2}$ oz) is used, a quart of filling makes twenty sandwiches. A quart of jelly or jam spreads about thirty sandwiches, at 2 T each, and a quart of peanut butter spreads about twice that at 1 T each. A pound of soft butter or margarine or a pint of mayonnaise or salad dressing spreads about 100 sandwiches at 1 t per slice. A 4-in^2 cheese slice is usually 1 oz, and about $1\frac{1}{2}$ to 2 oz of meat serves for a sandwich (although hot meat sandwiches may have over 2 oz of meat. Weiners run ten per

TABLE 5-1. Bread slices in standard loaves

Loaf	Size loaf (lb)	Slice thickness (in.)	No. slices (no ends)	Loaf	Size loaf (lb)	Slice thickness (in.)	No. slices (no ends)
Quick bread	$1\frac{3}{4}$	$\frac{3}{8}$	20	Rye, regular	1	$\frac{3}{8}$	23
Regular, white	$1\frac{1}{4}$	$\frac{5}{8}$	19	Rye, regular	2	$\frac{3}{8}$	33
Regular, white	$1\frac{1}{2}$	$\frac{5}{8}$	24	Sandwich, white*	2	$\frac{1}{2}$	28
Regular, whole-wheat	1	$\frac{5}{8}$	16	Sandwich, white*	2	$\frac{3}{8}$	36
Regular, whole-wheat	2	$\frac{1}{2}$	28	Sandwich, white*	3	$\frac{1}{2}$	44
Regular, whole-wheat	3	$\frac{1}{2}$	44	Sandwich, white*	3	$\frac{3}{8}$	56
Regular, whole-wheat	3	$\frac{3}{8}$	56				

* $4\frac{1}{2}$ inches square

TABLE 5-2. Yields of some common sandwich materials

Item	Portion*	Quantity for 100 sandwiches
Butter or margarine	2 to 3 t	2 to 3 lb
Jelly or jam	2 T	3 qt (1 No. 10 can)
Spread-type filling	2½ T	1 gal
Peanut butter	1½ T	2½ qt
Mayonnaise	2 to 3 t	1 to 1½ qt
Lettuce	1 leaf	5 medium heads or 5 to 7½ lb
American cheese	1 to 1¼ oz	6¼ to 8 lb
Meat	1½ to 2 oz	9½ to 12½ lb

* Two slices of bread per portion; rough-textured bread requires more spread than smooth-textured bread.

pound, and hamburger patties weigh from 1½ to 5 oz each. A deluxe open-face steak sandwich may use an 8- to 10-oz steak. Tables 5-2 and 5-3 identify yields of various spreads, fillings, and filling ingredients. Needs should be carefully calculated ahead of time, since stopping to prepare additional food in the midst of a busy period hampers efficiency.

WORK METHODS

Sandwich work centers differ depending on whether they are made in batches or to order, and on whether one or more workers make them. Normally, it takes as much time to line up for sandwich production as it

TABLE 5-3. Amounts obtained per pound of sandwich material used

Ingredient	Quantity per pound or other
Bacon, sliced	18 to 25 slices; 2½ c cooked and chopped
Butter or margarine	2 c
Cheese, cream or cottage	1 pt
Cheese, Swiss or cheddar	16 slices about 4 × 4 in., $\frac{3}{32}$ in. thick; 1 qt ground
Date and nut filling	1 pt (scant)
Eggs, hard-cooked	10 large eggs, chopped, equals 3 c
Fish, flaked	2½ c; each portion about 1½ oz or 2 T
Jelly, jam, or preserves	1¾ c
Lettuce	1 medium head yields 16 leaves about ¾ oz each, leaving about 3 to 4 oz of heart
Meat	chicken, sliced, 12 to 16 portions, 1½ to 1 oz each; ham, beef, or other, 8 to 12 portions, 2 to 1½ oz each; ground, cooked meat, 3 c
Olives, drained, chopped	3 c
Peanut butter	1⅞ c
Tomatoes, fresh	18 to 32 slices, 6 to 8 slices per tomato, $\frac{3}{16}$ inch thick; a large tomato (5 × 5), about 2 to 2½ per lb will give about the right size slice for a regular sandwich
Vegetables, chopped or diced (celery, onions, carrots, peppers, etc.)	2½ to 3 c

does to make the sandwiches; so the larger the amount to be made, the greater the production rate (see fig. 5-3). *Mise en place* is important because clutter causes confusion, poor-quality products, and time loss. Reduce search; have tools and materials in standard locations that follow the sequence of movements. Efficient use of vertical space reduces reach.

(a)

(b)

(c)

(d)

(e)

(f)

Figure 5-3. A one-worker method for making sandwiches in quantity. (a) Split bread wrappers in the center, and place each half loaf open-side-down on a tray. Remove wrappers as bread is used. (b) Pick up four slices of bread in each hand and starting from the center out, line slices to form four rows on the working surface. (c) An efficient spreading technique: spread filling with spatula in one motion; with tip of spatula, press filling lightly, moving from upper right to upper left corner; complete S motion to lower right and then lower left portions of the slice. (A left-handed person should reverse this procedure.) (d) Using both hands, cap. (e) An alternative method in which the worker tops completed sandwiches and adds another row of fresh bread simultaneously. This may be repeated until three tiers of sandwiches are laid out. (f) Each stack may then be cut at one time. (*Courtesy American Baking Institute*)

A foot lever can drop bread onto a work board or moving belt. An electric knife facilitates cutting of stacked sandwiches (see fig. 5-4). In one study, forty-four sandwiches per minute were made on a wooden board that was slightly longer than five slices of bread, making five sandwiches. When the sandwiches were stacked two high, they were cut in half; the board was then placed on a moving belt for transfer to a mechanical wrapper, and another board was moved in to replace it. The American Institute of Baking, 1213 Baker's Way, Manhattan, Kansas 66502 can be of assistance in working out methods for producing good-quality products at low labor cost.

FANCY SANDWICHES

Fancy sandwiches are often used for teas or receptions. They are served in assorted types and designs, attractively arranged on plates or trays covered with doilies (see fig. 5-5). They may accompany other foods and are themselves considered finger foods. Forms may be closed, open-face, pinwheel, rolled, or other (see fig. 5-6). Occasionally they may be hot. Variety breads such as date and nut, banana, or fruit bread may be used with interesting combinations incorporating cream cheese, fruit, vegetables, or meat salad. Day-old bread may be best for rolled or shaped sandwiches. Make fancy sandwiches as close to the time of service as possible. If they must be stored, cover them with a moisture- and vapor-proof wrap. A moist cloth may be used over a layer of wax paper for temporary storage. Oblong shapes should be about $1\frac{1}{2} \times 3\frac{1}{2}$ in., round ones not over 2 in. in diameter, and oval ones about $2\frac{1}{2}$ in. long and about $1\frac{3}{4}$ in. wide.

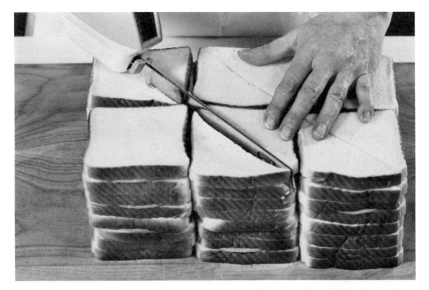

Figure 5-4. An electric knife speeds work and avoids tearing the sandwiches. (*Courtesy American Baking Institute*)

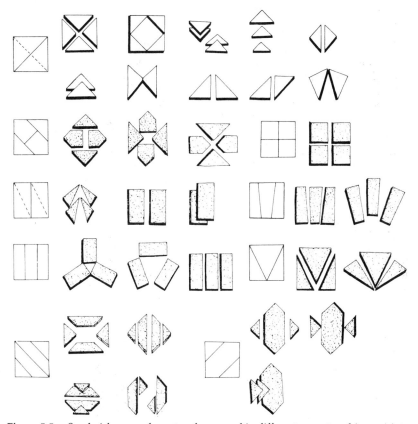

Figure 5-5. Sandwiches may be cut and arranged in different ways to achieve variety and interest. (*Courtesy American Baking Institute*)

HOT SANDWICHES

About 2 oz of sliced meat plus two slices of bread, $\frac{1}{4}$-in. to $\frac{1}{2}$-in. thick, makes a good hot sandwich. Spread may be omitted and the meat and bread covered instead with 2 to 3 oz of very hot gravy. If the meat is hot, a warmer product is served. Service often includes mashed potatoes and a salad or vegetable.

Grilled sandwiches are best made of one- or two-day-old bread, fairly dry and firm, buttered on the top and bottom outsides, and placed on a grill. A light weight placed on top gives more rapid and even browning. Fillings of sliced meats, cheese, ham, and some salad mixtures are most suitable.

A toasted sandwich uses toasted slices of bread but is otherwise made in the same way as a regular cold sandwich.

Deep-fried sandwiches are egg-coated and deep-fried (see fig. 5-7). They may be prepared ahead of service—cut into desired sizes so that, on order, they can be egg-dipped and fried. Do not thin the egg with milk

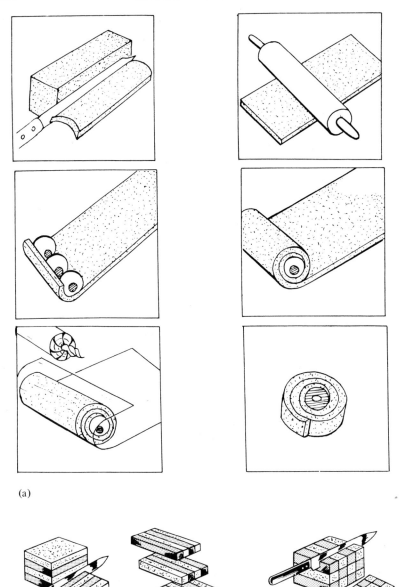

(a)

(b)

Figure 5-6. Techniques for making fancy sandwiches: (a) pinwheels; (b) fingers or checkerboards; (c) mosaics; (d) envelopes; (e) cornucopias; (f) roll-ups.

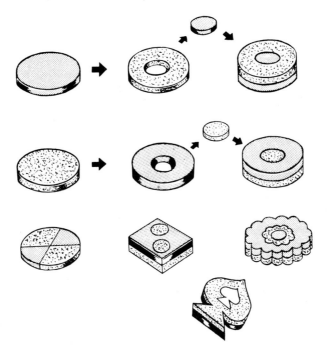

(c)

(d)

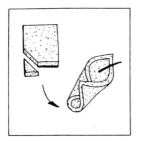

(e)

(f)

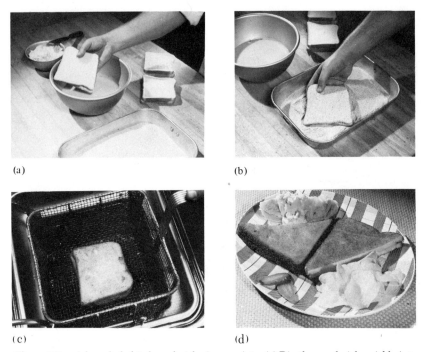

(a)   (b)

(c)   (d)

Figure 5-7. A breaded, fried sandwich gives variety. (a) Dip the sandwich quickly into an egg–milk mixture (six eggs to 1 pt milk gives best results, but more eggs to milk may be used). (b) Cover completely in crumbs, after draining off excess egg–milk mixture. Use bread crumbs or other crumbs that brown rapidly. (c) Place covered sandwich in frying basket, weight down lightly by covering with another basket or a metal screen, and fry for 1 minute at 375°F. (d) Slice and serve the sandwich.

or other liquid, unless the sandwich is to be coated in breadcrumbs. Fillings must adhere rather tightly to the bread to hold shape in frying. Sometimes these sandwiches are grilled or baked in a very hot oven on greased pans.

COLD SANDWICHES

Wrapping

Cold sandwiches may be served wrapped or unwrapped. Vended sandwiches or those held for some time need to be wrapped. Work out wrapping procedures so that a minimum of effort and time is used (see figs. 5-8, 5-9, and 5-10). Clearly label uncut wrapped sandwiches. Mark plastic or wax paper wraps with freezer marking pens. Display cut sides for identification. Only moisture- and vapor-proof wraps should be used for sandwiches to be held for a long time; heat sealing is recommended. Sandwich bags save labor. If sandwiches are to be heated or frozen in wraps, make certain that the wrap is suitable for the particular treatment.

Figure 5-8. Plastic or wax paper bags may be used for wrapping sandwiches; they are then flip-sealed. (*Courtesy American Baking Institute*)

TABLE 5-4. Sandwich filling ingredients and freezing

These freeze well	These freeze poorly
Cooked egg yolk	Cooked egg white
Peanut butter	Cream cheese or cottage cheese
Chopped or sliced cooked meats,	Process cheese
poultry, and fish	Chopped cooked bacon
Lemon juice, orange juice	Tomatoes, celery, lettuce, cucumbers, green peppers,
Butter, margarine	radishes, carrots, watercress, onion, cabbage,
Dried beef	apples
Bread, buns	Jelly, jam, preserves
Baked beans	Mayonnaise, salad dressing
Crushed or chopped pineapple	Sliced cheese
Roquefort or blue cheese	Cheese spreads
Milk	Nuts, whole or chopped
Sour cream	Chili sauce, tomato catsup
Applesauce	Whole frankfurters
Horseradish	Honey
	Swiss or cheddar cheese
	Liverwurst
	Olives, sliced or chopped
	Pickles, dill or sweet
	Pimiento
	Prepared mustard
	Sweet relish

NOTE: Freezing adds nothing to sandwich quality. Thaw sandwiches under refrigeration 24 hours prior to use; once thawed, they should be eaten; palatability is lost on standing. Keep refrigerated until used.

(a)

(b)

(c)

(d)

Figure 5-9. A method of wrapping uncut sandwiches. (a) Place an oblong piece of wrapping paper so that the short sides are parallel to the front of the counter top. Center the sandwich so that its top and bottom crusts are parallel to the long side of the paper. (b) Bring the ends of paper together in a pharmacist's fold. A neat, stay-in edge is formed that keeps air out. (c) Seal by tucking in the ends of the paper, folding the top side in first. (d) Fold in the bottom side to form a neat, secure package. (*Courtesy American Baking Institute*)

Storing

Store sandwiches with perishable fillings under refrigeration. Protect unwrapped sandwiches from drying out or absorbing odors. Put a protective medium over sandwiches when using a moist cloth cover. Place trays or wire baskets of sandwiches in large moisture- and vapor-proof wraps, allowing air space between containers in refrigerators. Such containers may be on mobile racks and may be wheeled into walk-in refrigerators.

Maximum storage time is 12 hr at 40°F. Freezing holds for longer periods, but not all fillings can be frozen (see table 5-4). Do not stack wrapped sandwiches more than three high, nor unwrapped sandwiches more than two high. Sandwiches with moist fillings soak easily when stacked.

SALADS

A salad usually consists of an underliner of crisp leafy greens, a body, dressing, and a garnish. All but the body can be omitted. Perhaps a salad is most familiar as a combination of cool crisp green ingredients. But

(a)

(b)

(c)

(d)

Figure 5-10. A method for wrapping cut sandwiches. (a) Wrapping paper should be precut to proper size. Place the paper on the working surface so that a corner points toward the worker. (b) Transfer the sandwich, cut-side-down, to the center, and turn in the paper on both sides. (c) Lay the sandwich over on its side, and fold the paper against the crust edges. (d) Tuck in the excess securely at the upper edge. All wrapping movements are away from the worker. (*Courtesy American Baking Institute*)

salads can be hot, and they can be dominated by nongreen ingredients. Salads may accompany meals, constitute a complete meal, or be a snack. A fruit salad is proper fare at a wedding breakfast, for instance.

STANDARDS

Salads must be light and refreshing and must balance the foods they accompany in flavor, texture, and color. Color and artistry are achieved through a set pattern, through uniformity and symmetry of design, or through an intentional avoidance of any set pattern (achieved by a light heaping of different greens, fruits, or vegetables). Avoid giving salads a fatigued or overworked appearance (see fig. 5-11). Ingredients should be distinct, neatly divided, and usually bite-size. Do not cut ingredients raggedly. Often greens are torn by hand and not cut. Bright, clear, fresh colors contribute to bloom and freshness; selection at proper maturity encourages these qualities. A salad should be framed as a picture, with about a $\frac{1}{2}$ inch of the brim acting as the frame (see fig. 5-12). Form and height should vary, and both soft and crisp foods should be used.

Figure 5-11. This baked bean and tomato salad is well merchandised because of its fresh and attractive appearance. (*Courtesy H. J. Heinz Company*)

Figure 5-12. A good standard for a molded salad. (*Courtesy General Foods*)

Cooked fruits and vegetables should not be overly soft. Flavors should be piquant and zestful, not harsh or bland. The salad should be complemented with a dressing that is more tart and flavorful than the body. A blend of flavors is desirable: a touch of chervil, mustard green, peppergrass, dill, mint, anise, or basil adds subtle interest. Nasturtium leaves, capers, and may other herbs offer flavorfulness and contrast.

SALAD INGREDIENTS

Underliner

Leafy greens are frequently used as underliners, but it is not unusual to use attractive bowls or dishes with no underliner. Iceberg lettuce, Bibb lettuce, leaf lettuce, cos (romaine) lettuce, escarole, curly endive, chicory, Whitloof endive, dandelion, watercress, and spinach all make good underliners. Chopped, pulled, or sliced greens are also used. The cost and labor of making lettuce cups are avoided by using leaf lettuce.

Body

The main salad part is the body, of which there are many kinds. Good-quality products should be used. Meats should be well-flavored and tender; fish is best cooked in court bouillon before flaking. Macaroni products should be made of semolina and should be cooked to have some texture left. The fresher, crisper, and more tender the green, the better the salad. Heavy ribbing, coarse stems, large leaves, and evidence of seeding in greens indicate age. Wilted greens may not recrisp.

Wash salad greens carefully, removing dirt, insects, imperfections, and coarse areas. Give iceberg lettuce and other greens that have hard cores a sharp rap and then finish with a firm twist, breaking the core from the head. Run a forceful water spray into the open heart to loosen tightly wrapped leaves. If no separation occurs, simply place the cored heads open end down to drain. Put washed greens into terry towel sacks, and whirl them around to throw off water; then store them. Moisture must be present in order for greens to crisp well. Some operations have units that centrifuge the moisture from items.

Many operations today purchase greens that are already prepared. These may be subjected to some type of permitted bleach that reduces discoloring. Such greens may be obtained in many different mixtures, cuts, and sizes.

Crisping occurs by osmosis. Plant cells contain salts that can draw moisture through cell walls. When many cells swell, they crowd each other, making a crisp product. Air encourages this swelling, so greens should not be too tightly packed. Chilling also helps. Soaking can be used to crisp, but this is not as effective. Too much water drowns rather than crisps. Wilting occurs when moisture is pulled from the cells, either by evaporation or by osmotic pull from salt, vinegar, salad dressing, or some other substance outside the cell. That is why these items are not added until service.

Greens are best stored in moistened cloth bags, baskets, or colanders covered with damp cloth. Light packing into polyethylene bags is good for short-term storage, and closed mobile bins work well. Fine cutting is done after crisping, using extremely sharp tools to avoid bruising. Pulling or tearing greens is also done. Cabbage, turnips, and other hard vegetables can be shredded, sliced, or grated without texture loss.

Mise en place is very important in salad preparation. Doing jobs at service peak that could be done beforehand is often the mark of an amateur or inefficient worker. Prepare molded or frozen salads 24 hours in advance. Carry all work as close to service as possible, with due regard to quality. Workers are assisted in producing good products by using pictures, patterns, or designs. Providing a listing of number of pieces and arrangement in written form is helpful.

Garnish

Salad garnishes should contribute form, color, and texture (see fig. 5-13). They should be suited to the salad and be edible. One of the ingredients used in the salad can be a garnish. Keep garnishes simple—for example, using a few caraway seeds over coleslaw, or using chopped cranberries on a Waldorf salad. Other attractive garnishes include flakes of green

Figure 5-13. Fluting a cucumber to give a simple yet attractive garnish. (*Courtesy General Foods*)

burnet (with its subtle flavor of cucumber), a pineapple slice edged with chopped mint, a crisp food such as cracker or toast croutons, and a brightly colored gelatin cut into a fancy shape.

Dressings

Dressings add flavor, moistness, and tartness to salads. The three main kinds are French, mayonnaise, and cooked, but each has many variations. Ingredient quality is important. Fresh corn, cottonseed, peanut, soy, or other oil is good for mayonnaise. Any of these or virgin olive oil is good for French dressing. Bacon fat, animal fats, butter, or margarine is used for cooked dressings. Mineral oil is not an edible oil and should not be used. Good, clear, double-strength vinegar and high-quality fruit juices are preferable to lower-grade products. Eggs should be of the highest quality. Use fresh, sterilized spices and seasonings, and use very clean tools and utensils to reduce chances of spoilage. Store dressings at 40° to 50°F in ceramic, glass, or stainless steel containers.

Oil is highly perishable, and open containers should be stored in a cool place; use the contents of such containers as fast as possible. Taste for rancidity before using. A thin film of oil oxidizes (gets rancid) quickly; thus, an oil held for some time should never be mixed with new oil, since the whole lot would then become rancid quickly. Clean oil containers must be used for oil. Winterized oil, treated so that it does not solidify when chilled, should be used for dressings that are refrigerated.

Emulsions. Most salad dressings are oil-in-water emulsions. Moisture forms a continuous network around tiny globules of oil; water is called the *continuous* phase, while oil is called the *dispersed* phase. Oil and water alone do not form a permanent emulsion. But by adding an emulsifier—such as whole egg, egg yolk, starch, agar, tragacanth, a hydrophilic colloid, gelatin, casein, gum arabic, pectin, Irish moss, or condensed milk—we can get a permanent emulsion. French dressings are often temporary or unstable emulsions. Mayonnaise is a permanent emulsion, but if too much oil is added to it, it breaks down and becomes unstable.

Mayonnaise should be semisolid and nonflowing, with a good, clear sheen and a yellowish cream color. The texture should be smooth, and the flavor sweet, with no trace of rancidity or off-flavor. There should be a distinct tartness. A power mixer makes a finer and more stable emulsion than does hand-whipping. Commercial manufacturers use powerful homogenizers that produce such a stable emulsion that freezing does not break it down. Undermixing an emulsion or beating air into it makes it unstable. Mayonnaise is unstable with less than 20 percent eggs or with more than 15 percent vinegar. Good commercial mayonnaise is 50 to 80 percent oil, 6 to 20 percent egg yolk, and 12 percent vinegar. Starch pastes can be added as extenders, but only a small quantity. Federal standards state that mayonnaise may not contain less than 50 percent edible oil and that the sum of the percentages of oil and egg may not be less than 78 percent. Emulsions are best made with ingredients at 60° to 70°F; freezing can destroy emulsions. Salt can draw out moisture, breaking the emulsion. For this reason, salt is added with the vinegar in a strictly controlled amount.

Re-form a broken emulsion by rapid mixing; if this fails, place a bit of liquid or emulsifier (such as eggs) in a bowl and then add the broken emulsion gradually, mixing well (see fig. 5-14). The bowl should be small enough to enable the agitators to pick up the emulsifier and mix it with the broken emulsion. Allowing an emulsion to have too great a surface area breaks it down. Thus, gravy containing considerable fat is more stable in a deep pan than in a shallow wide one.

Once a good emulsion is formed, oil can be added at an increasing rate; at the start, however, the addition of oil must be very slow. Some prefer to start mayonnaise with eggs, vinegar, and seasonings in the bowl, while others advise that no liquid be introduced until a good emulsion is formed, after which seasonings dissolved in the vinegar can be added. Some say that adding vinegar and oil to raw egg withdraws moisture from it, giving it better emulsifying properties.

French dressing is made with two parts oil and one part vinegar or lemon juice. Wide variety is achieved by adding honey, chives, Roquefort cheese, capers, or poppy seeds.

A cooked or boiled dressing is a mixture of liquids and seasonings thickened with starch and perhaps eggs. The liquids may include water, milk, vinegar, or lemon or other fruit juices; the seasonings may be salt, sugar, or spices; and the thickeners may be cornstarch, flour, arrowroot, or eggs. The final product is much like mayonnaise in texture, but it may be thicker and then thinned with other ingredients such as sour cream. Cooked dressings usually contain 5 to 35 percent oil or fat. They are excellent for potato salads, coleslaw, and many meat or fish salads.

Mayonnaise and oil dressings have many variations. Russian dressing, tartar sauce, thousand island, and many others are based on them. A sour cream dressing is a boiled dressing with sour cream, vinegar, and seasonings added.

Marinades.   A marinade is not a typical dressing but a sharply flavorful product like French dressing. Some marinades contain oil; others do

Figure 5-14.   A broken and a reformed mayonnaise. The broken emulsion is reformed by adding it slowly with good agitation to a liquid such as vinegar, water, or egg yolks.

not. Wine, vinegar, fruit juices, soy sauce, and other liquid ingredients are added, along with seasonings, to impart flavor. Firm-structured fresh fruits and vegetables such as cauliflower, carrots, cucumbers, and tomatoes, as well as certain cooked fruits or vegetables, are marinated. Tender, succulent greens cannot be marinated but can be quickly dipped into a marinade and served at once. Cooked or uncooked marinades are used to flavor meats, fish, or poultry. A sauerbraten (sour roast) is a German pot roast made from marinated meat.

TYPES OF SALADS

Molded Salads

Gelatin, agar, or other products can be used to set a liquid into a gelatinous solid. High-quality plain or dessert gelatins should have bright sparkle, clean color, good setting ability, and a true, pleasing flavor. Gelatin desserts consist of water, plain gelatin, sugar, flavoring, and coloring. Plain gelatin comes in sheet or granular form.

Normally, a 2 percent solution of gelatin gives a satisfactory gel. Proportions are 1 lb of gelatin to 7 gal of liquid, or $2\frac{1}{3}$ oz ($\frac{1}{2}$ c) per gal; for gelatin desserts, the proportions are $1\frac{1}{2}$ lb per gal or 3 oz ($\frac{1}{2}$ c) per pint of liquid. Sugar increases the gel's firmness. Gelatin foams and chopped ingredients weaken gelatins, so more gelatin per unit of liquid must be used. Milk gives a stronger set.

Gelatin sets at between 48° and 57°F. Cooling the mixture slowly to 100°F and then refrigerating it until it reaches 40°F takes from 1 to 2 hr but yields a firmer mass than does fast-setting. For rapid setting, add one-fourth to one-half of the total liquid hot to dissolve the gelatin, and then add crushed ice to make up the rest of the liquid; stir this until the ice is melted, and refrigerate. Plain gelatin must be soaked in cold liquid for about 5 minutes before being dissolved. Gelatin starts to go into solution at 100°F but goes rapidly into solution at 170°F. Uncooked pineapple, figs, papaya, and some other fruits contain enzymes that digest gelatin, so they must be cooked before being used with gelatin mixtures. If gelatin is allowed to set partially before other ingredients are added, they do not float on the top. Gelatin should be whipped when syrupy, while set in a bed of ice. Items may be folded into foams after whipping. If a gelatin mixture is to sit on a buffet or at room temperature for any length of time, it should contain more gelatin. Agar and some other items used to set liquids are not affected by the heat, so they may be used where warmth of the room is a problem.

Molded salads can be used to produce striking color contrasts; layered colors give good display. Interesting effects can be achieved by combining part solid and part foam or by mixing gelatin with other foods (see fig. 5-15). Using different molds or cutting pieces into different shapes provides design variation. Designs can be put on the bottom of molds and a thin layer of gelatin at the syrupy stage poured carefully over it. After this has set, additional gelatin can be added.

Figure 5-15. Folding fruit and gelatin into a mixture of mayonnaise and whipped cream to make a mousselike mixture. This may be frozen and then served as a frozen salad. Notice the garnish added to enhance the salad's appearance. (*Courtesy General Foods*)

Pasta Salads

Whether the popularity of pasta-base salads is ephemeral or permanent, a wide variety are now being merchandised. They combine a starch with meat, fish, poultry, eggs, cheese, vegetables, or fruit; consequently, they are rather substantial salads. The ratio of most is about one part (by volume) pasta to one part vegetable to one part protein product. The pasta should not be overcooked, so it retains good texture. Short-cut rigatoni, macaroni elbows, sea shells, and other different-shaped products enhance interest.

Tossed Salads

Greens for tossed salads should be cut or broken into small pieces and—as materials accumulate—drop-delivered into a large container. A baker's mixing bowl works well in this capacity, since it facilitates light, deft mixing. The bowl can be covered with a damp cloth to prevent the greens from drying out, and then it can be placed on a mobile stand and rolled into refrigeration.

Tossed salads are usually flavored with herbs, one of which is traditionally a member of the onion family. A *chapon* (piece of dry bread rubbed with garlic) is often added. A *ravigote* of chopped herbs can also be added. Add dressings and seasonings at the last moment to preserve their freshness (or let the guest add them). Chopped egg, sliced salami, and Parmesan cheese make attractive garnishes.

Service may be done at the table, in which case, setups should be arranged in the pantry so that all materials are available, possibly on a mobile cart. To hold dressing, the greens should be dry; excess moisture dilutes dressing. Add oil first, toss, and then add the acidic liquid; if coddled egg (as in a caesar salad) is to be added, add this first, followed by oil, acidic liquid, and seasonings.

Fruit Salads

Because they are fragile, most fruit salads are not tossed. Place broken greens on the bowl bottom, then add well-drained fruit, sized as desired; successively add more greens and more fruit, as needed. Drizzle salad dressing over the top, and serve at once; some people drizzle dressing on each layer, as it is made. The dressing, which is usually sweet, may be flavored with fruit juices. Arranged salads are easier to make if illustrations on fruit placement are provided. Prepare fruit salads on platters and plan for convenient dish-up if portions are to be self-served.

Frozen Salads

Usually fruit is the base of frozen salads, but vegetables are sometimes used. Nuts and some chopped crisp vegetables are added for texture in frozen fruit salads. Select for color and flavor, bearing in mind that not all fruits freeze well. A frozen salad base is usually composed of whipped cream, cream cheese, or cottage cheese into which fruit and mayonnaise are lightly folded. A contrasting tartness to accompany the sweetness lends interest.

Complete-meal Salads

Bodies of complete-meal salads are usually substantial. Meat, egg, fish, or cheese is combined with vegetables, legumes, potatoes, macaroni products, rice, and the like. The dressing can also be substantial, and it is usually mixed in with the ingredients.

Salad Bars

Even fastfood operations have adopted the salad bar, which is looked upon as a source of healthful foods. Salad bars allow individuals to make up their own salads, by offering a wide range of foods from which the patron selects the items and quantity desired. The typical salad bar serves the following items: greens (usually plain lettuce); corn, bean, or beet relish; sliced tomatoes, sliced cucumbers; pickled beets; potato salad; three-bean salad; carrot or green pepper strips; chopped celery; cottage cheese; chopped sweet, mild onions; molded canned fruit; croustades; salted sunflower seeds; chopped bacon; alfalfa sprouts; olives; pickle relish; and four dressings (mayonnaise, creamy French, oil and vinegar, and Roquefort). The cost of seafood, poultry, and meats in salad prohibits their being offered. It is therefore difficult to achieve a lot of originality, although this can be done by selecting different greens and by presenting the typical in a slightly novel form.

To make the salad bar different, search for items that patrons do not usually see but that are good and reasonably priced. Vary the greens from plain iceberg lettuce, introducing endive, romaine, escarole, and spinach, and offer sliced cooked celery root, raw turnip, carrot or lower broccoli strips,* pickled French beans, molded salads with different ingredients, a sweet-and-sour vegetable mixture flavored with soy and ginger, grated Jerusalem artichoke, cooked slices of anise root, chopped chives, and basil, dill, or other herbs. Change the pattern so that patrons do not always see the same thing. Change accompaniments; offer different-flavored croustades, spiced peanuts, salted toasted garlic slices, and low-cost dips. Unusual dressings such as a cucumber, basil and yogurt, or curried mayonnaise help add flair. It is not necessary to have everything different: several well-planned additions or alterations may be enough to escape from the routine and pique interest. Neatness of the bar is essential, and containers should not be allowed to get empty. Near the end of the service period, transfer the contents of a larger container into a smaller one, so patrons do not perceive the remainder as a nearly empty, scraping-the-bottom offering. It is highly desirable to store plates or bowls in a refrigerated leveler, as it is extremely distasteful to pick up a warm dish just out of the dishwasher and then dish chilled foods onto it. No matter how good the bar offerings are, everything can be lost through a failure here.

Hot Salads

Many hot salads must be served immediately. Quality rapidly diminishes in a wilted lettuce or dandelion salad. Therefore, make them in small batches. Hot salads such as celery root, German potato, slaw, and cauliflower hold fairly well and can be made in quantity either on the range

---

* Cut 2½ to 3 in. from the bottom of a broccoli stalk, and pare this deeply to get rid of the stringy part; then slice the inside tender part into strips.

top or in ovens. Limit quantities, however, so the salads do not become messy. At times, marinated items are used in hot salads.

To make a hot salad, put fat from fried bacon, salt pork, or ham into a pan, and add vinegar or other acidic liquid in a 2:1 ratio. Seasonings and a bit of sugar are optional. Add a bit of starch to give the dressing some cling. Heat the dressing, add the main salad ingredients, and toss them quickly, coating each particle with dressing. Skill is needed to preserve shape and texture. The salad must be served at once, with a crisp garnish such as croutons, diced radishes, celery, cucumber, or cabbage. Crisply fried bacon, bacon soyettes, ham, or other small pieces of meat often are added for flavor. Individual skillets, attractive in design and appearance, are used to make the salad; it is then presented to the guest in this.

QUANTITIES REQUIRED

The ratio of bulk to weight varies for different salads. From 4 to 5 gal of tossed salad—about 17 lb greens AP (as purchased) or 13 lb EP (edible portion)—yields 100 portions of $\frac{2}{3}$ cup each. If trim loss is high, more must be used. Heavier items, such as celery or tomatoes, may be 20 lb or more for 100 portions. A No. 12 scoop (3 oz level, 4 oz rounded) is frequently used for salads such as tuna salad, fruit salad, or potato salad, 8 to 10 portions being obtained per quart. About $\frac{1}{3}$ to $\frac{1}{2}$ cup of molded or frozen salad makes a portion; if cut from pans, a piece 1 in. deep and 2 in. square is $\frac{1}{2}$ cup; slightly over 3 gal gives 100 portions. When a complete-meal salad is served, these portions are increased twofold or more. Table 5-5 identifies portions and yields of various salad components.

TABLE 5-5. Yields of some common salad components

Item	Normal portion	Yield
Apples, raw, sliced	$\frac{1}{2}$ c, 2 oz	2 salads per apple, 113 size (3 to lb AP); 1$\frac{1}{2}$ lb AP equals 1 qt sliced
Apples, raw, diced	$\frac{1}{3}$ c, 2 oz	1 lb unpared yields 4$\frac{1}{2}$ c
Apricots, pitted	4 halves	22-lb lug yields about 100 salads
Artichoke, globe	1, medium size	Order 60s to 72s per container
Asparagus	3 to 4 stalks	12 to 15 medium stalks per lb
Avocados	$\frac{1}{2}$ medium, or 3 to 5 slices	16 slices per avocado, medium size (Calavo)
Bananas	$\frac{3}{4}$ banana, split or $\frac{1}{3}$ c slices	25 lb AP gives 100 salads
Cabbage, shredded	$\frac{1}{3}$ c	7 lb EP yields 50 salads
Carrot, grated	3 oz, $\frac{1}{2}$ c	1 lb AP equals 3$\frac{1}{3}$ c
Celery, diced	2 oz, $\frac{1}{2}$ c	3 c diced per lb AP
Cheese, sliced	1 oz, 1 slice	6$\frac{1}{4}$ lb for 100
Cherries, pitted	3 oz, $\frac{1}{2}$ c (12 fruits)	20 lb AP for 100 salads
Chicken, diced	2 oz, $\frac{1}{3}$ c	12$\frac{1}{2}$ lb EP for 100 salads; 30 lb AP ready-to-cook; 40 lb AP dressed

continued

TABLE 5-5. Yields of some common salad components (*continued*)

Item	Normal portion	Yield
Crab meat	2 oz, ⅓ c	
Cucumbers, sliced	5 slices	6-in. cucumber yields 30 slices
Dressing, blue cheese	1½ T	2¼ qt per 100 (use 5 oz blue cheese per qt dressing)
Dressing, French	1½ T	2¼ qt per 100
Dressing, mayonnaise	1½ T	2¼ qt per 100
Endive, curly, underliner	1/20 head	
Endive, curly, chopped	⅛ head	
Endive, French (Whitloof)	1½ to 2 oz	1 endive split makes a salad
Escarole	1/12 head	
Figs	2 to 3 medium, split	6 6-lb boxes, 48 per box, yields 100 salads
Grapes	½ c	14 lb AP for 100 salads
Grapefruit	5 sections	12 sections per grapefruit; 42 grapefruit for 100
Lettuce, Boston, underliner	⅛ head	
Lettuce, Boston, chopped	¼ head	
Lettuce, iceberg, underliner	1/15 head	Trimmed head usually weighs 1 lb
Lettuce, iceberg, wedge	⅙ head	
Lettuce, leaf, underliner	2 leaves	12 to 15 leaves per bunch
Lettuce, leaf, chopped	¼ bunch	
Lettuce, Romaine, underliner	1/10 head	
Lettuce, Romaine, chopped	⅛ head	
Lobster meat	2 oz, ⅓ c	
Meat, ground	1¾ oz, ⅓ c	
Meat, diced	2 oz, ⅓ c	
Meat, sliced	3 to 4 oz, 2 slices	
Melon, cantaloupe, ring	1 ring	8 rings per melon, 36 to 45 size
Melon, cantaloupe, balls	8 balls	30 to 35 balls per cantaloupe, 36 to 45 size
Onions, sliced	2 oz, 4 slices	1 lb AP diced yields about 2½ c; 1 lb AP yields 2½ to 3 c (buy Bermudas or sweet Spanish)
Onions, green, diced		
Oranges, sliced	1 half, 3 slices	6 to 8 slices or 8 to 9 sections per orange
Oranges, diced	3 oz, ½ c	8 to 9 doz medium size yields 100 salads
Pears	1 half	120 per box
Persimmons	1 whole	8 wedges per persimmon
Pineapple, sliced	2 half-slices	100 salads per case of 24-size pineapple (fresh)
Potatoes, new diced	3 oz, ½ c	2 lb AP yields 1 qt diced
Salmon, flaked		16 1-lb cans yields 100 salads
Shrimp, small or Pacific	2 oz, ⅓ c	
Shrimp, large, diced	2 oz, ⅓ c	Serve 4 25- to 33-per-lb shrimp per salad
Tangerine	5 sections	10 sections per tangerine
Tomatoes, sliced	3 slices ⅜ in.	about 6 slices per tomato; for 100 salads, purchase 17 lb AP
Tomatoes, diced	1¾ oz, ⅓ c	
Tuna, flaked	2 oz, ⅓ c	15 18-oz cans yields 100 salads
Turkey meat	2 oz, ⅓ c	12½ lb net, 25 lb AP dressed, 20 lb AP ready-to-cook
Watercress	¼ bunch	15 bunches per basket; 1 basket is about 3 lb

APPETIZERS

An appetizer is a small food that whets the appetite. It may be an hors d'oeuvre, a relish, a canapé, or a cocktail, served to patrons as a first course before or after seating or to guests as they mingle at a social gathering. When use for the latter purpose, wide variety is characteristic. Appetizers may be distributed, or guests may get them at buffets.

HORS D'OEUVRES

Originally, an hors d'oeuvre was a hot or cold food such as a timbale, a creamed dish, or bits of seafood in aspic served immediately after the soup at a formal meal. The Russians changed them into a food passed to guests before a meal or at receptions. They called them "flying dishes" because they were passed by hurrying servants. Today, a more common name for appetizers is *finger foods*. Any small piece of piquant, appetizing food served before a meal is an hors d'oeuvre.

A relish may be called an hors d'oeuvre, but it is a pickle, conserve, or sweetened vegetable or fruit served with a meal. Chilled relishes include celery sticks or hearts and raw cauliflower buds. Partially cooked vegetables may be marinated in spicy vinegar, or red or white cabbage may be sliced thinly and allowed to make a brine for four days in a refrigerator before being brought to boil in spiced sweet vinegar; these foods are then drained and chilled before being served.

Tidbits of cheese, smoked oysters, cantaloupe or watermelon pickles, pickled walnuts, mushrooms, and many other pickled items may be used for hors d'oeuvres. Smoked meats, fish, sausages, thinly sliced meat and cheese, cheese straws, and strips of green pepper and carrots may be offered for dipping in tangy dips. Hot hors d'oeuvres can include filled choux pastes, fritters, tiny patties, rissolés, oysters broiled in bacon, tiny croquettes, timbales, mousselines, rolled tiny pancakes filled with mixtures, deep-fried clams, fried frog legs, mussels, shrimps, snails borelaise, and hot casseroles such as golden duck, oyster or clam poulette, or deviled lobster. Picks or forks are often used to pick up foods that do not lend themselves to eating with the fingers.

Table 5-6 lists portions and yields of various hors d'oeuvre and canapé components.

CANAPÉS

Canapés are small pieces of bread, toast, wafer, or pastry, covered with a piquant food. They can be used as appetizers or, if slightly larger, as a first course to be eaten with a fork. For example, a crab-in-aspic canapé may be served on a 5-in. plate on a doily consisting of a thin slice of rounded toast, covered with a mold of aspic, capers, and crab and decorated with mayonnaise, green pepper, and pimiento strips. Canapés are usually decorated, but high decoration should be avoided. Blending some relatively ornate items with a larger number of simply decorated ones gives a pleasing effect. All should be neat and trim. Good flavor,

TABLE 5-6. Yields of some common appetizer components

Item	*Portion*	*Yield*
Carrot strips	2 to $3\frac{1}{8}$ in.; julienne, 3 in. long	90 strips per lb EP
Carrot curls	2 curls	8 per carrot, 6 to 8 carrots per lb EP
Celery curls	1 curl	$3\frac{1}{2}$ lb EP or $4\frac{1}{2}$ lb AP yields 100 curls
Cheese straws	1 or 2	32 per lb
Clams, cherrystone	4 clams in shell	300 per bushel
Crab meat	$1\frac{1}{4}$ to 2 oz	8 to 12 cocktails per lb EP
Crab legs	2 to 3 legs	about 18 to 22, dungeness, per lb
Crackers, saltine	1 or 2	130 to 140 per lb
Crackers, soda, 2 in.^{2}	1 or 2	100 per lb
Crackers, soda, large	1	50 per lb
Fruit cocktail	3 oz, $\frac{1}{3}$ c	2 $\frac{1}{3}$ gal for 100 cocktails
Melon cup, balls	9 balls	30 balls per cantaloupe, 36 per crate; 54 per honeydew melon, 8 per crate
Melon cup, diced	3 oz	12 oz per cantaloupe, 36 per crate; 30 oz per honeydew, 8 per crate
Melon slice		$\frac{1}{4}$ cantaloupe, 45s, $\frac{1}{6}$ Persian, $\frac{1}{8}$ casaba, and $\frac{1}{6}$ honeydew
Onions, green	3 whole	5 lb AP for 100
Orange cup	1 orange	8 to 9 sections per orange
Orange juice	4 oz	3 32-oz cans frozen concentrated; 11 qt juice from Florida oranges, and 9 qt from California per bu carton
Oysters, bluepoint, unshucked	4 oysters	300 cocktails per bushel; serve in shell
Oysters, Olympia, shucked	$1\frac{1}{4}$ oz	100 per gal
Oysters, small, shucked	2 oz, $\frac{1}{4}$ c	4 to 5 oysters, 60 per qt
Pineapple cup	3 oz, $\frac{1}{2}$ c	20 oz diced, 24 size pineapple per crate
Punch	3 oz	1 punch cup
Shrimp, small Pacific	$1\frac{1}{2}$ oz, $\frac{1}{3}$ c	9 lb EP for 100 cocktails
Shrimp, jumbo or large	4 to 5 shrimp	25 to 33 per lb green headless
Toast, Melba	1 or 2	30 per lb

form, color, texture, and freshness are needed. Overworked form, dried edges, or a wilted appearance makes them look ugly. Good tray or platter arrangement can do much to make canapés more attractive.

Canapés are usually made from day-old, unsliced pullman loaves, sliced longitudinally about $\frac{3}{16}$-in. thick, rolled lightly with a rolling pin to firm the bread, and spread first with basic butter and then with a filling or paste. Both butter and filling should be worked to the outer edges, as in making sandwiches, and then cut into the desired shapes. Decoration is usually added after cutting. Tangy pastes, mushrooms, truffles, anchovies, slices of stuffed olives, caviar, cheese, and other piquant foods are used for decoration. Some canapés are spread with tangy fillings and then toasted, broiled, or sautéed and served hot. Seasonings in a hot canapé are hotter than in cold ones, and less decoration is needed. Tiny choux pastes filled with tangy items, cheese straws, and other prepared items may reduce labor. Making canapés begins with setting up diagrams and listing tools and ingredients prior to preparation.

COCKTAILS

Cocktails are either alcoholic or nonalcoholic. The former are usually consumed before guests seat themselves. Hors d'oeuvres or canapés may be served along with cocktails, and the first course omitted. Alcohol in quantity blunts the appetite. Apéritifs or wines whose flavor qualities stimulate the appetite are recommended, such as vermouth, dry sherry, Madeira, Byrrh, or Dubonnet. A fruit punch with or without alcoholic spirits is sometimes offered. Cocktails should be served in their proper glass, but it is becoming increasingly common to use a roly-poly glass or a 4-oz glass for all drinks. Often cocktails are served "on the rocks" (over ice cubes), and a 4-oz glass is suitable for this.

Some common measures used in bar work are:

Dash	3 drops
Pony	1 fluid oz (2 T)
Jigger	1½ or (more often) 2 fluid oz (3 or 4 T)
Part	more or less than a jigger, depending on taste
Split	1 c (½ pt)

A silver, chrome, stainless steel, or glass shaker or large container is used for mixing cocktails. A glass rod or silver spoon is used to stir cocktails containing wine as an ingredient; others are shaken. Drain cocktails at once from their ice. Metals other than those mentioned may affect the flavor of cocktails. Service bars speed service. Make fruit or vegetable juices or a dry white wine available to those that want them.

Juice cocktails may be fruit- or vegetable-based. Colors should be natural, bright, and clear. Carbonized water or sweetened carbonated drinks may be added to fruit juices and served in frosted glasses. A coarse frappé, sherbet, or ice may be put into a glass of fruit juice at the last minute.

FIRST-COURSE OFFERINGS

Raw oysters or clams on the half shell, a slice of melon or mango with a wedge of lemon or lime, a juice, a fruit or vegetable cup, or a flaked fish or seafood cocktail can be a first course. Canapés or hors d'oeuvres are also proper, as are Italian antipastos or various hot foods in tangy sauce.

Fruit or vegetable cups should possess attractive colors and should look fresh. Colors should be bright and clear, and the cups should contain pieces of contrasting size and shape. Sameness of texture should be avoided. Fresh fruits in season, served in their own juice or in sweetened juice, and canned or cooked dried fruits combined with fresh fruit present interesting possibilities. Fruit cups should not be too sweet—the natural sweetness and acidity being sufficient to stimulate the appetite. Contrasts in flavors should be welcomed if they blend happily. Fruits that tarnish can be dipped into citrus or pineapple juice to keep colors bright, but usually the cocktail liquid itself is sufficiently acidic to accomplish this.

Flaked crab or other seafood served with a tangy sauce is popular. The delicate flavor of the basic ingredients should not be destroyed by the sauce; too much seasoning or too tart a sauce lessens eating pleasure. Chopped vegetables such as celery, cucumber, or other crisp foods that are combined to give texture should not extend the cocktail too much. Pieces should be bite-size and distinct in form. Color and flavor contrasts and interesting combinations create interest.

QUANTITIES REQUIRED

The quantity of finger food needed in a particular setting is difficult to determine. Variety and popularity are factors, as are the type of function, its length, and so on. Usually, allowing two to eight pieces per person is sufficient and, while the range is wide, individual factors of the function must be weighed to indicate this. Bowls of dips and crisp foods that are easy to replenish give flexibility. Some operations plan a run-out time, and toward the end of serving have only a few foods remaining.

About $1\frac{1}{4}$ to $1\frac{1}{2}$ oz base material plus $\frac{1}{2}$ to 1 oz (1 to 2 T) sauce makes a fish or seafood cocktail, if a standard cocktail glass of 3 oz is used. From 8 to 10 lb crab, lobster, or flaked fish is needed for 100 cocktails. The use of large cocktail glasses, with a heavy underline of lettuce or a lot of chopped celery in the cocktail to give the impression of a larger cocktail, is not recommended. Liquid or solid foods such as fruit cups need nearly a full 3-oz portion ($\frac{1}{3}$ c) or about 2 to $2\frac{1}{4}$ gal (16 to 18 lb) per 100 portions.

GARNISHES

Garniture is probably used more extensively in the pantry and *garde manger* sections than any other. The *garde manger* does much decoration on cold meats and buffet items. Wide variety may be obtained from a few basic sauces or soups by using only different garnitures.

The elaborate garnishes once popular in continental cooking are losing favor, and simplicity is now in fashion. Some garnishes may be traditional and more properly viewed as accompaniments than as garnishes, such as Yorkshire pudding with roast beef, sautéed mushroom caps on steak, and chopped parsley on new potatoes. Mushrooms, truffles, diced poultry breast, meat salpiçons, chicken livers, pâté de fois gras, julienne or macédoine of cooked vegetables, finely chopped or stuffed vegetables, parsley, chopped fine herbs, tiny deep-fried calves' brains or sweetbread pieces, purées of vegetables, small fritters or filled choux pastes, cooked cereals such as barley, glazes such as cranberry or brown sugar for ham, fish milt or roe, various forcemeats, tiny sausages or sausage slices, olives, pickles, cheese, fresh fruits, and many other items are used as garnishes. Table 5-7 lists the portions and yields of common garnishes.

Standards

All garnishes should be edible and should complement the flavor, color, and texture of the foods they garnish. They may be hot or cold. Excessive

TABLE 5-7. Garnish yields

Item	*Portion*	*Yield*
Apples, sliced	2 thin wedges	12 wedges per 113-size apple
Apples, ring	1 ring	5 rings per 113-size apple
Apricots	½ or 1	20 halves or 40 wedges per lb
Avocado	1 slice	30 slices per avocado, 24 per crate size
Banana, split, 1-in. slice	1 or 3 round slices	12 bananas or 2½ c slices per lb AP; 1 banana (3 to lb AP) yields 30 1-in. slices, split
Blackberries	3 berries	1 qt yields 100 berries
Blueberries	3 to 5	1 qt (1½ lb) yields 360 to 800 berries
Cantaloupe	3 balls or small wedges	30 balls or 45 wedges, 45 per crate size
Capers	1 t	10 to 15 capers per t
Cheese, shredded, moist	1 T (½ oz)	
Cheese, shredded, dry	1 T (¼ oz)	
Cheese, cream	2 T (1 oz)	for stuffing celery
Cheese, cottage	1 No. 20 scoop	1½ oz
Cherries, maraschino	½ or 1	640 per gal
Cherries, sweet, fresh	1 fruit	40 per lb
Chocolate tidbits	1 T	40 portions per lb
Coconut, long shred	1 T rounded	1 lb equals 6½ c or 60 portions
Currants	3 fruits	1 lb equals 150 currants
Dates	1 fruit	60 dates per lb
Decorettes	1 t	160 portions per lb
Endive, curly	1 leaf	45 per head
Figs	1 fruit	48 per box, 6 lb
Grapes	3 fruits	50 grapes per lb, medium size
Grapefruit	1 to 2 sections	12 sections per grapefruit
Kumquats	1 fruit	1 lb equals 24 fruits
Lemons, wedge	⅙ to ⅛ fruit	1 doz lemons yield 144 rind twists
Limes, wedge	¼ to ⅙ fruit	1 doz limes yield 62 twists or rind
Mint	2 to 3 leaves	300 leaves per bunch
Mushrooms, cap	1 cap	15 to 20 caps per lb AP
Nuts, chopped	1 T	1 lb chopped is 4 c
Nuts, salted for tea	1 T	1 lb nuts is about 4 c; use 3 lb for 100 people
Oranges, sections	3	8 to 9 sections per 82-size orange; 1 doz orange rinds yields 164 rind twists
Olives, green	1 or 2	1 qt (1¼ lb) equals 100 extra-large
Olives, stuffed, sliced	1 or 2	1 medium-size olive yields 6 slices
Olives, ripe	1 or 2	1 qt small-size yields 120 olives
Parsley, curly	1 sprig	80 sprigs per bunch
Peach	1 wedge	8 wedges per medium peach
Pear	1 wedge or slice	12 wedges per 5-oz pear
Pepper, ring	1	10 rings per medium-size pepper
Pickles, sweet, medium (3 in.)*	½ pickle	24 pickles per qt
Pineapple	1 wedge or 2 to 3 diced pieces	60 wedges or 150 diced pieces per 18-size pineapple
Plums, Santa Rosa	1 medium	70 per till (5 × 5 size)
Pomegranate	5 seeds	25 garnishes per fruit
Potato chips or shoe-string potatoes	¾ oz	1 c; 8 ounces is about 2½ qt
Prunes, dried	1	30 to 40 per lb AP
Radishes	1 or 2	15 to 20 per bunch; 1 bunch, 10 oz; 1½ c topped and tailed equals 8 oz or about 25 radishes
Raspberries	5	1 qt yields 300 berries

continued

TABLE 5-7. Garnish yields (*continued*)

Item	Portion	Yield
Rhubarb	1 or 2 curls	1 lb yields 100 curls
Sardines	1 (3 in. long)	1 lb yields 48 sardines
Strawberries	1	1 qt yields 60 medium-size berries
Tangerines	3 to 4 sections	10 sections per tangerine
Tomatoes	1 wedge	8 wedges per medium tomato
Walnuts, whole	$\frac{1}{2}$ nut	8 oz is 2 c or about 150 halves
Watercress	1 sprig	30 sprigs per bunch

* Pickles sized per gallon are frequently used: gherkins, 200; pickle rings or slices, 400; small sweets (3 in.), 80 to 100; large dills (4½ in.), 25.

pattern, color, or form should be avoided, but some contrast is desirable, as are natural colors and simple design. A high degree of garnish may be proper on a wedding cake, a chaudfroid piece, or something emphasizing an occasion. At times a red strawberry, a few sugar-glazed grapes, or a few pomegranate seeds suffice to garnish a fruit salad; likewise, a few capers, a sprig of chervil, or a cheese wedge does much to enhance a cold plate. A grilled ripe tomato slice, a lemon wedge, a broiler-browned spiced pear filled with currant jelly, or a sprinkling of spring vegetables increases interest by its goodness as much as by its color or design. Cream of corn soup is given extra appeal when garnished with a few croutons of popped corn. Labor should be considered in garniture. Freshness of appearance, tastefulness in color and form, and texture are essentials of good garnish. The appearance of overworked food, dried brown edges, and a wilted condition destroys appeal in spite of high design and color. Garnish size should be related to the size of the food it garnishes.

Elaborate garnishes may be desirable with chaudfroid. A chaudfroid is a cooked food that is chilled, covered with a gelatin glaze, and (usually) decorated with pieces of food. Two types of glaze are used: an aspic or clear gelatin seasoned with beef, chicken, or fish stock; or a chaudfroid glaze made by adding gelatin to a cream sauce or mayonnaise (the latter being especially desirable for fish). Designs made from pieces of pimiento, beets, ripe olives, truffles, cucumbers, green pepper, chives, leeks, lemon peel, carrots, or other fruits and vegetables are used. The glaze, when ready to set but still syrupy, is poured over the food until the food is covered. After the chaudfroid is chilled and the glaze is set, another layer is applied, until a complete covering is obtained. This may require five to eight layers. The design is set into the glaze on the last coating. A light wash of clear aspic is then used to cover the design set into the glaze.

Ice carvings, tallow or butter carvings, sugar work, and other food designs are used often as central garnishes—not for any particular food, but to garnish the entire function. They are cut from ice blocks, so the design must fit the shape and size of the block. Know ahead of time what is to be made, and have a good drawing prepared setting forth dimensions. A chisel, a chain saw, an ice shaver, or even an ice pick can be used. Start by cutting a rough outline, and then refine. Some carvers work with the block on a low table or even on the floor. The block's size usually dictates the work level. Rough cutting can be done with a chain saw. If cutting is done at room temperature, the carving may have to be returned to freezer space periodically and then withdrawn for more work. Working in a refrigerated area allows completion without enforced pauses. Keep the carving in a rather solid piece. Do not attempt to carve thin extensions or fine units since they may be lost when the unit is on display.

Ice carvings are displayed at temperatures at which they melt. Bring them out only at the last minute. Mount them on a pan that catches the water and then drains into a unit under a draped table. Sometimes the pan beneath the carving can be covered in such a way as to hide the water caught in it; if so, draining is not necessary. Sometimes colored lights are set underneath the carving to give special effects. Carvings may be made from blocks of different-colored ice or may incorporate special designs.

BEVERAGES

Beverages provide an important accompaniment to a meal or snack, and patrons often judge facilities on the basis of their beverages' quality. They are delicate substances and require exacting care in their making.

COFFEE

Standards

Evaluate brewed coffee for flavor (taste and aroma), clarity, color, and body when it is not over 30 minutes old. Add no sugar; add cream only at the last, to test body. To identify flavors, swish the coffee brew around the mouth so that the aroma rises into the nostrils. The taste and aroma should be balanced and sufficiently strong to give a pleasing flavor. Turkish, espresso, or after-dinner coffee should be strong and heavy. Many people mistakenly judge coffee strength by color.

Coffee taste should be pleasing and properly balanced between bitterness (astringency), acidity, and sweetness, with no off-flavors. The aroma should be fragrant, mellow, heavy, and rich with coffee bouquet—not acrid, burned, rancid, or oily. No excessive bouquet or fruitiness associated with aldehydes should be present, nor any trace of oiliness.

Clarity is inversely related to the amount of insoluble solids in a brew. Grinding and handling influence brew clarity. Coffee should be bright and clear enough to show a silver spoon lowered into the cup bottom. There should be no evidence of grounds, flocculent material, cloudiness, dullness, or muddiness. Brew color should be a rich, deep brown; lightness or paleness on the one hand or a heavy almost blackish dark brown on the other indicates lower quality.

Body refers to brew density and is directly related to the quantity of solubles in the brew, as measured by a hydrometer. Body is detected in the mouth as something heavier than water. Espresso or demitasse have a heavy body, giving the feeling of thickness or syrupiness. Body should not come from fine or pulverized grounds suspended in the brew. If 18 percent cream is added, it should not immediately blend with coffee, as it would with hot water, but should feather or layer out. Stirring should be necessary to blend it. Heavier creams feather more than lighter ones do.

Use a high-grade blend of coffee with the proper grind and roast. Heavy roasts are needed for demitasse, espresso, Turkish, and some foreign coffees. Make certain that equipment is very clean, since coffee oils can easily give a rancid flavor if left on equipment. Test products carefully before deciding on what to serve.

Coffee flavors are highly volatile, and they readily deteriorate if oxidized. Flavor loss increases with time and temperature, so store ground coffee in a cool dry place. Refrigeration retards this loss; holding at $-4°F$ almost stops it. After five to eight days at room temperature, a ground coffee grades at fair to poor quality. In three days at room temperature, it loses 20 percent of its aroma; and at the end of twenty days, 50 percent is gone. Whole-bean coffee deteriorates more slowly. Coffee easily absorbs odors. Plan deliveries so fresh coffee is always used, and use the oldest first. Some operations grind their coffee on the premises, one day's supply at a time. Vacuum-packed coffee is freshly ground and then compressed and sealed to reduce flavor loss. Ground coffee releases carbon dioxide, and this may swell cans. Much coffee is vacuum-packed in moisture- and vapor-proof bags. Purchasing coffee in the right quantity to make even batches in the equipment on hand is recommended. Table 5-8 identifies the proportions needed to produce various large quantities of brewed beverages.

Brew Water

Moderately hard or mildly soft water produces a good brew; extremely soft or hard (alkaline) water does not. Chlorine, sulfur, ammonia, and

TABLE 5-8. Proportions for making coffee in quantity

Number of people	Number of portions (5½ oz each)	Coffee required (lb)	Water required (gal)
25	40	1	2
50	80	2	4
75	120	3	6
100	160	4	8
125	200	5	10
150	240	6	12

other compounds must be present in greater than normal concentrations in order to hurt coffee. Unrinsed detergents can harm. Water containing more than 4 ppm (parts per million) of iron gives a greenish brew when cream is used. If water comes from rusted pipes or from some other iron-yielding source, the water may have to be treated to remove the iron.

Water softened by sodium may turn dissolved carbonates into sodium bicarbonate. Sodium bicarbonate combines with coffee grounds to make a gel, slowing the flow of water through grounds and producing a bitter, harsh brew. Polyphosphate softeners correct this problem.

Making Coffee

Use fresh coffee of the proper grind. Measure coffee and water accurately. Have equipment scrupulously clean. Coffee is made when hot water extracts soluble flavors from the ground beans. Particle size governs how long water should stay in contact with the grounds. Contact should be shorter with fine grinds. The aromatic and milder flavors are extracted first, and the bitter and more pungent ones last. Too long a contact time results in overextraction, and too short a time produces a weak coffee. Fine, automatic drip needs 2 to 4 minutes; drip or urn coffee, 4 to 6, and regular or percolator coffee, 6 to 8 minutes. Agitating the grounds reduces the amount of contact time needed. From 18 to 22 percent ($2\frac{3}{4}$ to $3\frac{1}{2}$ oz) of solids per lb should be extracted. A ratio of 1 lb coffee to $1\frac{3}{4}$–$2\frac{1}{2}$ gal water does this. Best extraction occurs at between 195° and 203°F; do not use water that has been sitting too long after being heated, since it lacks vitality. If the right amount, kind, and temperature of water comes into contact with the right grind and amount of good coffee in good, clean equipment, a brew containing between 1.15 and 1.35 percent total coffee solids should result. A starting volume of 2 gal water gives $1\frac{3}{4}$ gal brewed coffee. If 3 gal water is used per pound, a 24 percent extraction would have to occur to give a 1.15 to 1.35 percent solid content, but this would involve excessive extraction. Figure 5-16 shows how varying the water/coffee ratio and the extraction quantity affects coffee quality. If coffee has to be stretched, make the smaller amount of coffee correctly, and add hot water directly to this. While the resulting brew will not be of proper strength, body, or color, it will at least be in somewhat proper balance and not overextracted, as would be the case if the entire quantity of water were to come into contact with the grounds.

Urn Coffee. For urn coffee, spread grounds evenly 1 to 2 in. deep in a clean bag or basket; then spray or pour water over the grounds, wetting all. If the water is boiling, its temperature will be correct when it strikes the coffee, unless the elevation is so high that the water boils at less than 200°F. See that proper contact time occurs, and then remove the grounds. Draw about 1 gal of brew and dump it back at the top, thereby mixing up layers of different density. Do not pour brewed coffee over grounds. Keep the cover on to prevent heat loss during brewing.

Automatic Drip Coffee. Automatic brewers give the proper amount of water at the proper temperature and the correct contact time, if they

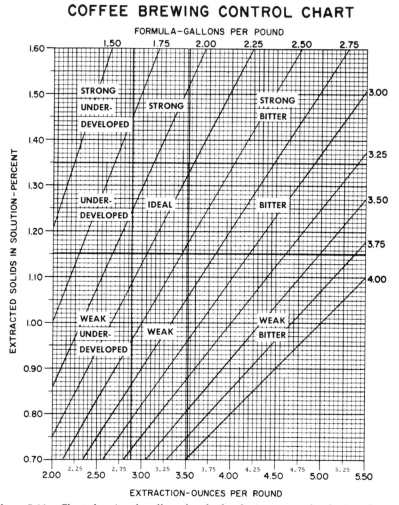

Figure 5-16. Chart showing the effect of underdeveloping or overdeveloping a brew. (*Courtesy Coffee Brewing Institute, Inc.*)

are working properly. Merely add the right amount of coffee to the container, set it in place, and push a button. Remove the grounds and clean the filtering unit as soon as the brew is made.

Vacuum Coffee. Vacuum coffee makers are used much less today than in the past. To use one, fill the lower bowl with fresh water at the proper level, place the bowl on heat, and adjust the filter on the upper bowl, adding the right amount of coffee. When the water is boiling briskly, set the upper bowl firmly into the lower bowl, twisting slightly to make a tight seal. Turn the heat down, and as the water rises, stir the brew for about 30 seconds; at the end of 2 to 4 minutes, allow the brew to filter back into the lower bowl.

Miscellaneous Procedures. Coffee can be made in a drip pot, a percolator, an old-fashioned pot, or a steam-jacketed kettle or pan on the range. Never boil coffee: this causes overextraction. Use 2 T of ground coffee per 6-oz cup.

Drip pots make good coffee. Usually paper filters are used. Follow procedures for making urn coffee. Correct contact time is 4 to 6 minutes. Stir to mix strata of different density.

Percolators work by causing steam to force hot water up through a central core and over coffee grounds. The coffee is good as long as the water is not allowed to get too hot and the percolating time is controlled.

To make kettle coffee (either steam-jacketed or a pan on the range), put the proper amount of coffee into a cloth bag—about half-filling it, so the coffee can expand. Submerge this in the proper amount of simmering water, pushing the sack down frequently to enable the water to move through it easily. Allow a contact time of 8 to 10 minutes.

Boiled coffee is made in old-fashioned coffee pots. Add the right amount of fresh cold water to a clean pot and place it on the heat source. When the water starts to boil, reduce the heat so that the water barely boils. Add the correct amount of coffee, and stir. Steep for 6 to 8 minutes. If the grounds do not settle, add a bit of cold water, or strain the brew to remove grounds.

Instant coffee may be used for some occasions. The proper amount of instant coffee should be measured and added to freshly boiled water. Stir and let stand two minutes. Then serve at once. Freeze-dried coffee is of better quality than plain instant coffee.

Iced coffee is made by brewing extra-strength coffee (using two-thirds the usual amount of water) and then pouring this over ice cubes. Alternatively, regular-strength coffee may be brewed and frozen (as quickly as possible, to prevent coffee solids from separating out) into cubes in a nonmetallic container, to be used to chill regular coffee. A third possibility is to mix extra-strength instant coffee with a small amount of cold water and ice cubes to bring it to proper strength. Stir well.

Holding Coffee. Coffee holds best at between 185° and 200°F—preferably for under 1 hr, but never for over $1\frac{1}{2}$ hr. Excessive grounds or flocculent material reduces effective holding time. A fluctuating temperature can cause solids to precipitate, making the coffee turbid. Do not cool and then reheat coffee. Patrons should receive coffee at 160°F or higher.

Variety Coffee

Demitasse coffee is made using $1\frac{1}{2}$ to $1\frac{2}{3}$ gal water to 1 lb coffee, using standard equipment. Use a dark roast. Serve in demitasse cups. Sugar, lemon peel and liquors may be offered with it. A mixed spice of equal parts of cardamom seed, whole cloves, and broken cinnamon stick goes well with it, as does cardamom alone. This mixture is also served with Italian coffee. Sugar is proper with demitasse coffee, but cream is usually not.

Espresso coffee (*caffè esprèsso*) or Italian coffee is made with a drip pot, a macchinetta, or an espresso maker (see fig. 5-17a and b). The macchinetta is a drip pot with two units, one of which has a spout. The nonspouted cylinder includes a container for the coffee at the top, with top and bottom sieves. Water is measured into the nonspouted cylinder, and the sieved container containing coffee is fitted into this. The spouted cylinder is then fitted over both, spout down. When the water is at full boil, stop the heat and turn the macchinetta upside down, allowing the water to drop through the grounds and into the spouted unit. Espresso makers use steam pressure to force water up and through grounds, much as is done in making vacuum coffee. Service should be in special 4-oz cups or glasses, with a twist of lemon. Sugar, brandy, or other liquors may be offered, but no cream.

Cappuccino coffee (*caffè cappuccino*) is Italian coffee blended with an equal quantity of hot milk; both are poured simultaneously from two separate pots into a tall cup; a bit of cinnamon, nutmeg, or grated orange is then sprinkled over the top, or whipped cream is added.

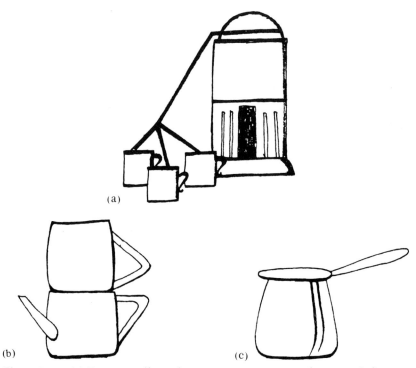

(a)

(b)   (c)

Figure 5-17. (a) Espresso coffee-makers use steam pressure to brew true Italian espresso coffee. Small, electric espresso machines are available for home use. (b) The two-tiered macchinetta is the Italian version of our drip coffee-maker. It makes excellent demitasse and Italian coffee. (c) The *ibrik* is commonly used in Egypt, Syria, and Turkey. Only coffee made in the style of the Middle East and Near East requires boiling.

About twice as much ground coffee to water is used for Turkish coffee as for regular coffee. The roast is dark, and the grind almost pulverized. The brew is made in a pot (*ibrik*) with high sides (see fig. 5-17c). Sugar is added at the start, and the mixture is brought to a boil and allowed to froth up three times. The froth is called *face*. After the coffee is removed from the heat, a few drops of cold water are added to settle the grounds; then the face is spooned into tiny, egg-shaped cups, and the brew is poured in over it. The key to good Turkish coffee is to avoid "losing face." The flavor is strong.

Viennese coffee is about the same strength as demitasse coffee. It may be thinned with hot milk or served plain, but it is always topped with whipped cream (*mit schlag*). It may be sweetened.

French coffee (café au lait) consists of equal quantities of regular-strength (or slightly stronger) coffee and hot milk; these are poured from two different pots into a cup at the same time. It is usually served at breakfast but may also be served at other times.

TEA

The quality of brewed tea is governed partly by leaf size—tiny leaves or buds being best. Tea grown or picked late in the season is lower in quality than that picked early or in midseason. The place where it is grown, the soil, the weather, the elevation, and the method of processing also affect quality. Green tea is made without allowing the tea leaves to ferment (oxidize); oolong tea (semigreen) is partially fermented; and black tea is fully fermented. Green tea contains the most tannin, and black the least. A good tea may be a blend of as many as thirty different varieties of tea.

Standards

Judge tea by its flavor, strength, clarity, and color. Unlike with coffee, body is not considered in evaluating tea. Tannin gives tea a slightly bitter flavor. Some sweetness and acidity may be present. Aroma should be fruity and fragrant; an excess, however, lowers quality. As with coffee, swish tea around the mouth to blend taste and aroma at the same time. Tea lacking flavor is called *thin* or *weathery*. A good tea is called *brisk*, indicating a zestful, stimulating quality. There should be no oiliness, and clarity is essential. No tea leaves or silt should be present. Typical colors are for each main type are as follows: green, a pale greenish yellow; oolong, a light yellow-green with a hint of tan; black, amber to reddish copper. Oolong and green teas show some green from chlorophyll.

Principles

Tea's soluble substances are the alkaloid theine (caffeine), tannins, other astringent compounds, acids, sugars, carbohydrates, some essential oils, and coloring matter. As water temperature increases, tannins become more soluble. The best contact time for water and tea is 3 minutes at 200°F. The cooling effect of equipment should be considered in judging water temperatures. Overcontact results in excessive tannin extraction, plus the drawing out of other undesirable compounds. The essential oils are highly volatile, especially in brewing, and may rapidly dissipate in boiling. Thus, tea should be made and served at once. Tea infuses more rapidly in soft or mildly hard water than in hard, alkaline water. Clouding from precipitated tannins occurs easily with hard water, producing a dark, dull tea that sometimes has a thin film on top. Flavor can be affected by hard-water salts. A bit of additional acidity—in the form of lemon juice, for example—changes the pH, dissolving tannates, lightening color, and giving a brisker flavor. At times, acid has no effect, however, as in an acid punch, where clouding occurs from iron tannates. Rapid cooling induces clouding if the tea is high in tannins. Tea stored in a refrigerator may cloud. Hold strong infusions for use in iced tea at room temperature; discard leftover brewed tea at the end of the day. Metals such as aluminum, brass, and iron give a metallic taste; glass, earthenware, vitrified china, enameled ware, or stainless steel are good materials for tea-making equipment.

Making Tea

A teaspoonful of tea gives one strong cup of tea or two cups of milder tea. A tea bag holds this amount; there are 48 teaspoons in an ounce. Between 5 and 8 oz tea serves 100 people, producing 4 to 7 gal (100 to 150 cups). A tea bag holding 1 oz tea makes 1 gal strong tea. Tea in quantity is made by tying leaf tea loosely in a cloth bag and steeping it in hot water for 3 minutes. A volume of 1 cup dry tea (16 T or 1 oz) makes about 50 cups (a little more than 2 gal) regular to mild tea. Decant and serve the brewed tea immediately.

Rinse the tea containers in very hot water, add tea, and pour boiling water over it. This is called wet service. It is incorrect to pour water into the container and then add the tea or to serve a tea bag on the side of a cup or pot of hot water. Tea is frequently served with lemon; often cream or milk is desired—milk allowing the tea's subtle flavor to be smoothed out but not lost. A clove may also be served.

Iced tea should be made with a slightly greater proportion of tea to water since dilution by ice occurs. Make the brew as for regular tea, using care in steeping; too much extraction produces a tea that clouds easily. Green tea clouds easily but is rarely served as iced tea. Certain black teas from India also cloud easily. Hold infusions in glass or crockery containers equipped with a spigot. Fill a tall glass with ice, and run the brew over this. Quite strong fresh hot tea may be poured over ice in a glass, the ice melting to give a proper concentration. Instant tea is often used in making iced tea. Mint or lemon may be served with it. The Tea Council recommends the 1–2–3 method for making iced tea. For 1 gal of tea pour

1 qt boiling water over
2 oz tea; steep 6 minutes, stir, remove tea, and pour
3 qt cold tap water

For larger quantities, multiply the 1–2–3 quantities by the number of gallons desired.

Teas may be blended with fruit juices and other liquids for special occasions. Russian tea is sweetened tea blended with orange, lemon, and pineapple juice, and seasoned with cinnamon. Spiced tea is steeped with orange and lemon rind, whole cloves, cinnamon sticks, and sugar.

COCOA

Where the service of cocoa is infrequent, it is best to use individually packaged mixes. Where service is regular or large, make the drink from dry cocoa, sugar, and either liquid or dry milk.

Standards

The color of cocoa or hot chocolate should be a pleasing rich brown color. A pale, weak color or a gray, muddy one indicates low quality. No scum should be present on the surface. Foam from added whipped cream or marshmallows is acceptable. The flavor should be delicately sweet, with the rich, aromatic flavor of cocoa evident. There should be a richness of flavor, especially in hot chocolate, which also has a richer color. Flatness, lack of flavor, or a scorched or raw flavor is undesirable. Poor blending, a large quantity of sediment, definite wateriness, or a syrupy consistency signals poor quality. Cocoa has more body than hot milk. Starch in cocoa and hot chocolate causes thickening, but this should be evident as body only in a minor way. Adding starch to increase body is not recommended.

Chapter Review

1. What are the major parts of sandwiches?
2. What items would you offer in a salad bar, and how would you set it up?
3. If you wanted to serve 100 4-oz portions of fruit cocktail, how many gallons of fruit cocktail would you need?
4. What are the ingredients in a French dressing, and how is it made? What are the ingredients in a mayonnaise, and how is it made?
5. List kinds of salads, each of which is distinctly different from the others.
6. What are some of the basic principles for making good coffee, tea, and cocoa?
7. Match the following terms to their definitions:

Mise en place	Marinade
Garde manger	Hors d'oeuvre
Emulsion	Canapé
	Chaudfroid

_____ A piquant food served as an appetizer.
_____ Means "to put in place," but expresses the idea that the workplace should be kept in good shape while working.
_____ Oil held in suspension in a water cover.

—————————— A small finger food served as an appetizer.
—————————— The *chef de partie* in charge of the cold meat section and sometimes of the pantry.
—————————— A piquant liquid in which foods are dipped or soaked to take on added flavor.
—————————— A food that is cooked and then served cold as a highly decorated piece.

CHAPTER 6

Stocks, Soups, Sauces, and Gravies

Outline

Goals

1. To discuss the standards, principles, and techniques needed to produce good stocks, soups, sauces, and gravies.
2. To show how stocks perform as a base for many foods.
3. To define many of the terms used in describing the making of stocks, soups, sauces, and gravies.
4. To cover sanitary procedures to use in preparing stocks and stock products.
5. To differentiate among the various kinds of stocks, soups, sauces, and gravies.
6. To show how sauces develop progressively from mother (basic) sauces into secondary (small) and other sauces.
7. To describe the preparation of butters, liaisons, and thickening agents.

INTRODUCTION

Soups, sauces, and gravies are related in that they are made from stocks. Their differences frequently are matters of consistency, a few ingredients, or seasoning.

STOCKS

Ingredient quality is directly related to stock quality. Stocks are not made; they are built, by careful blending of ingredients, until a rich, flavorful liquid is obtained. A stock is a thin liquid flavored by substances of meat, poultry, fish, vegetables, and seasonings and used as a base for soups, sauces, and other items. The terms *stock, broth,* and *bouillon* refer to different things. A broth is a simple stock served as a soup, with perhaps a few added ingredients. A bouillon is a clarified broth of definite beef flavor. Stocks are widely used for many foods other than soups, sauces, and gravies.

Reducing a rich stock by one-fourth makes it a *glaze;* reducing it to half its volume makes it a *demiglaze.* These are used to enrich soups, sauces, and gravies. Prepared food bases often replace glazes, stocks, sauces, and many gravies. A demiglaze from meat is called a *glacé de viande;* from fish, a *glacé de poisson;* and from chicken, a *glacé de poulet.* Fish and game are frequently simmered in or steamed over a concentrated stock called a *fumet* or *essence.** A rich fish stock used similarly is called a *court bouillon.* Often when meat drippings are removed from the bottom of a pan by adding a liquid and scrapping over heat, the process is called *deglazing.*

INGREDIENTS

Not all components of meat flavor have been identified. Meat proteins, nonprotein nitrogenous fractions, and fat give meat its primary flavor. Fat contains aromatic substances that carry much flavor and contribute richness. Flesh from different animals—and even different cuts from the same animal—differ in flavor. We often blend different animals' meats or bones to get a certain flavor blend in the stock. Pork is acidic, turkey and lamb are distinctively astringent and pungent, and chicken has a mild, sweet flavor.

Stock should possess body, and this comes largely from gelatin from meat and bones. Stock gels if it contains about 2 oz gelatin per gallon; gelatin can be added to stocks to produce this effect. Stock flavor is often modified by vegetables and seasonings. Its color is governed by its ingredients and sometimes by browning of meat, bones, and vegetables. Meat flavors are more soluble in salted water than in unsalted water.

Bones for stock are usually well-trimmed, cut into 3- or 4-in. lengths, and split. Knuckle, shank, and neck bones are preferred, in that order. Young animals' bones have rich red centers and good marrow for good

---

* The terms *fumet* and *essence* are also used to indicate the use of concentrated flavors, as in *essence of mushrooms* or *fumet de concombre.*

flavor. Bones, trimmings, and skin from cured, smoked pork may be used for specific flavor. Uncured pork bones are used to give richness to some stock.

Bones are often washed in a stock pot with cold water that runs over them and then flows out through a spigot at the bottom. Meat is usually not washed. Tougher cuts from older animals give a richer flavor and darker color. Lean meat is preferred; it may be diced into 1-in. cubes, but if it is to be used for other dishes, leaving it in larger chunks may make it easier to remove when done.

Use 5 qt water, 4 lb meat and bones, and 1 lb mixed vegetables (*mirepoix*) for 1 gal of stock (see fig. 6-1). Extra-rich stocks usually have twice as much meat and bones. Many good stocks are by-products from steaming or boiling meat or poultry. Often stocks are enriched with bases. Seasonings are light, since stocks are often reduced. Bouquet garni or sachet bags (mixed spices in a cloth bag) should be removed when the seasoning is correct. Leeks may be preferred to onions because of their milder flavor. Vegetables and seasonings are often added midway through the cooking to prevent them from giving harsh or bitter flavors to the stock. The small round nubs of whole cloves may be removed after use to give a less bitter flavor to the stock.

Steam-jacketed kettles or stock pots equipped with spigots for stock withdrawal are normally used for stock building. Simmer beef bones and meat for 6 to 10 hr. Meat and bones from young animals or poultry are cooked a shorter time; fish is usually simmered for no longer than $1\frac{1}{2}$ hr. Flavor in meat develops in the course of 3 to 4 hr of boiling, and then declines. The smooth, mellow flavor of a stock does not develop until gelatin and other compounds are extracted. Simmer stocks at 185°F; avoid prolonged boiling, which causes clouding. Starting the ingredients in cold water extracts slightly more flavor but probably no more nutrients. (In any case, the nutrient value of stock is small, but meat flavors in the stock whet the appetite and start the flow of gastric juices.) Many meat substances that are soluble in cold water coagulate, and this mate-

(a)   (b)

Figure 6-1. (a) A mixture of chopped vegetables for flavoring stocks. (b) Meat, bones, mirepoix, and seasonings being simmered for a stock.

rial is usually skimmed away. Starting the ingredients with hot water gives a clearer stock. To achieve a mild flavor, some cooks recommend bringing bones and meat (especially chicken) quickly to boil from a cold-water start, running this off, and then starting again—with cold water, a bit of salt, vegetables, and seasonings—and simmering. Salt helps make some substances more soluble. Stock is strained through several thick-nesses of cheesecloth. Cooling is rapid, during which the pot should be covered. Meat on bones may be trimmed and used for prepared dishes.

Many cooks keep a stock pot simmering continuously; this is often called *pot-au-feu*. In pot-au-feu, fresh bones are added to lightly salted water; then, as clean, edible foods—vegetable trimmings, vegetables from the steam table at the end of service, liquor from cooked or canned vegetables, bones from roasts and poultry—accumulate, they are added. Stock is withdrawn as needed, and the lost liquid is replaced with fresh water. Once started, such a stock pot can be kept going for four or five days. After this, the stock becomes too weak to use and may begin to cloud. The materials are then discarded, and a new stock pot with fresh bones is started.

STOCK CARE

Stock makes an excellent bacterial culture and spoils quickly. Keep stock pots simmering very slowly overnight. Otherwise, cool by placing in a running-water bath or in a cool, well-ventilated area (see fig. 6-2). Put

Figure 6-2. To cool a stock, place it into a sink and cover it. Allow cold water to fill the sink slowly, exiting through the overflow. Insert a trivet under the pot so that cold water can flow under the bottom.

something underneath the bottom to allow water or air circulation there. Keep the pot covered. Stirring, to speed cooling and vary the exposed surface area, also helps. After cooling, place the stock pot under refrigeration. Fat congealed on the top serves as a protective seal. Stocks that remain for over 4 hr at 50° to 140°F should be reboiled and then cooled and chilled. Maximum storage time is seven to ten days at 40°F. Quality declines if a stock is reheated, recooled, and again refrigerated.

CLARIFICATION

Stock can be clarified either by cooling and decanting or by clarifying with egg white (see fig. 6-3). To decant, chill the stock for 24 hr; if the stock will gel, chill it until syrupy and then decant, leaving flocculent material on the bottom. A better method is to blend two raw egg whites in a cup of cold water, mix this with 1½ lb lean, ground beef, and add this to 5 qt cool, rich stock. Seasonings and chopped vegetables may be added at this time. Bring to a slow, rolling simmer. After the egg whites and meat begin to cook, the stock must not be disturbed. The coagulated mixture, called the *raft* or *crust*, rises to the top with the vegetables,

(a)

(c)

(b)

Figure 6-3. (a) Strain stock through several thicknesses of cheesecloth. Be careful in taking the last bit not to allow flocculent materials to come off with the stock. (b) One method of clarifying is to decant after chilling. Here, a stock about to gel is decanted away from flocculent materials on the bottom. (c) Ingredients used for clarifying a stock. The well-browned onions are added to increase color and flavor. (d) To use the raft as a filter, break away a small piece of it; then allow the stock to bubble up through the resulting hole and over the raft in a slow roll.

seasonings, and most flocculent material. A small piece of the raft is broken carefully at the edge, so that the stock bubbles up at this point, filtering through the raft. After several hours the clarified stock is carefully drawn through a spigot and strained through several thicknesses of cheesecloth. Clouding materials on the bottom of the stock pot or from the raft must not be allowed to run off with the stock. The remaining liquid and the raft are added to a new stock. The yield should be 1 gal clarified stock.

TYPES OF STOCK

Brown stock is made from well-browned meat, bones, and vegetables (see fig. 6-4). White stock is made from the same materials, unbrowned. Fish stocks are usually white. Beef or veal is used to make a brown stock, with a mirepoix of vegetables and a sachet of seasonings. A bit of fat aids in browning meat and vegetables. To add flavor and color, thick onion slices are browned evenly on a hot griddle or range top and thrown into the stock. Salt delays meat from browning, so it is added afterward. Tomatoes, tomato purée, and tomato trimmings may be added. The finest white stocks are made from veal or chicken. To give a delicate and light stock, a light-colored mirepoix is used. To ensure a lighter color, some chefs avoid using carrots in such a stock. A fish stock is made from white, lean deep-sea fish such as cod, whiting, or flounder; bones, heads, skins, and trimmings may be used. Fat fish such as salmon or

Figure 6-4. Browning bones, meat, and vegetables to make a brown stock.

mackerel give a dark, heavily flavored stock. Seasonings are slightly more pungent in fish stock.

SOUPS

STANDARD

Often light soups are used as a first course, and heavier soups as a complete or nearly complete meal. Soup is a liquid food. Unlike a sauce, it does not complement another food. Standards vary according to the type of soup. Hot soups should be served at a temperature above 170°F, and cold soups should be served at between 40° and 50°F. Portions vary. For a first course, the serving size is 6 oz ($\frac{3}{4}$ c); a more substantial portion is 1 cup (8 oz). Where the soup constitutes a substantial part of the meal, a 10-oz (1$\frac{1}{4}$-c) portion is served.

A soup's thickness depends on its type and ingredients. Clear soups should resemble a thin broth but have more body and not be thin or watery. A cream soup, bisque, or light purée should delicately coat a spoon. Heavy, thick, country-style (*paysanne*) soups can build a mound of ingredients when placed in a bowl. Some soups may be almost as thick as a stew or ragoût. Whether bouillabaisse or gumbo is a stew or a soup has long been argued. The form of ingredients should be distinct and clear—not mushy or broken—except in a purée, where no evidence of form is desirable. Thickened soups should be free of lumps.

Flavors should be distinct, mild, pleasant, and characteristic for the soup. Seasonings should be delicate, not predominant; colors may vary according to the ingredients but should be natural and pleasing. Contrasting colors are desirable. In chicken gumbo, for example, the red of tomato, the green of okra, and the white of rice give a pleasing variety of color.

A clear soup, such as consommé or bouillon, may show a sheen of minute globules of fat, but only a trace. Heavier soups that have more fat bound in them should have only slightly larger fat globules on the surface. Fat should never appear in pools or large, round globules. Clear soups should have bright, sparkling clarity. A purée or cream soup should have a smooth texture. All particles should be bite-size except in special soups. Purées should remain in suspension. Cold soups should be seasoned more highly than hot ones, since chilling reduces flavor. Cream soups should not be flat or dead white but should have a rich cream color unless modified by other ingredients, as in cream of tomato soup. There should be no curdling.

TYPES OF SOUPS

It is difficult to classify soups. Perhaps consistency is the best indicator, for it determines use; thus, we may identify three classifications: thin, medium (or lightly thickened), and heavy (or thick). Table 6-1 shows a different simple soup classification. A soup made *without* meat stock is called *neutral* in this system.

TABLE 6-1. Soups and their derivation

MEAT BASE

Brown Stock
Bouillon (beef base)
  French onion (onions)
  Tomato bouillon with rice (tomato ragout
    and cooked rice)
  Windsor bouillon (spaetzels of egg, flour,
    and cream)
Jellied bouillon
  Avocado jellied bouillon (purée of avocado,
    sour cream garnish)
  Beet bouillon, polonaise (minced beets, beet
    juice, sherry, lemon juice, sour cream
    garnish)
Consommé
  Argenteuil consommé (asparagus tip
    garnish)
  Vaudoise consommé (leeks, white turnips,
    parsnips julienne)
  Vert-pré consommé (tapioca, green peas,
    string beans, asparagus tips, spinach
    purée)
Broth
  Beef broth (rice or macaroni products are
    usually added)
  Scotch broth (lamb or mutton stock, pearl
    barley, diced vegetables)
  Vermicelli broth (vermicelli)

White Stock
Consommé
  Printanière (spring vegetables)
  Florentine (chopped spinach, almonds)
  Princess (princess royal garnish)
Broths
  Chicken noodle soup (noodles)
  Mulligatawny soup (apples, curry, egg-
    plant, cream)
  Chicken Creole (onion, okra, rice, toma-
    toes, celery)
Veloutés (creams)
  Crème de cressionère (watercress, liaison)
  Cream of chicken (diced chicken, rice pulp
    thickening, liaison)
  Crème d'amandine (almond paste, al-
    monds, liaison)
  Cream of mushroom (mushroom essence,
    liaison)
Veloutés fish (bisques)
  Clam bisque (chopped clams, clam juice,
    cream finish)
  Lobster bisque (lobster essence, brandy,
    cream finish)
  Shrimp bisque (shrimp essence, cream,
    sherry, diced shrimp meat)

NEUTRAL*

Tomato
  Cream of tomato soup (blend tomato
    velouté with hot milk or cream)
  Moute rouge soup (carrots, potatoes,
    marjoram, tarragon)
  Mongole soup (equal parts purée of split pea
    and tomato ragoût
  Madrilene soup (consommé in equal parts to
    tomato and beet juice)

Milk
Cream soups
  Cream of asparagus (white sauce, aspara-
    gus, liaison)
  Cream of broccoli soup (white sauce,
    broccoli, liaison)
  Cream of spinach soup (white sauce,
    spinach, liaison)
Bisques
  Oyster bisque (crushed and mashed
    poached oysters in cream sauce, hot
    milk)
  Scallop bisque (pulp of cooked scallops in
    cream sauce, hot milk)

continued

TABLE 6-1. Soups and their derivation (*continued*)

MEAT BASE	NEUTRAL
White Stock	
Chowders	
Manhattan clam chowder (potatoes, salt pork, clams, tomatoes, onions, celery, green peppers)	
Washington chowder (salt pork, onions, potatoes, corn, celery, green peppers, tomatoes, milk)	
Okra chowder (tomatoes, okra, onion, parsley, peppers, celery, potatoes)	
Purées (may include cured meat stock)	
Split pea (split peas)	
Navy bean (navy beans)	
Potato and leek (leeks, potatoes)	
Purée of artichoke (artichoke heart purée, starch thickened)	

1. A cream or white sauce, a velouté sauce thinned with rick milk or cream, or a béchamel may be used interchangeably in making the numerous cream soups.
2. The stock used may vary. Chicken, beef, or fish stock may be used for the various types of soups, sometimes interchangeably, and so exact definition is difficult.
* *Neutral* means that meat stock is not used.

Thin Soups

Most thin soups are clear, being composed largely of rich stock. *Bouillon* is made from clarified brown stock, often beef-flavored. The word *consommé* comes from the same root as the word *consummate*, which means to bring to completion or perfection. It is highly clarified, and its delicate flavor is built on a stock made from two or more kinds of bones, one of which is usually veal or chicken. Broths are rich stocks frequently containing a few vegetables, rice, and the like. Some milk soups such as oyster stew, cream soups, bisques, and vichysoisse are thin. Light oxtail soup, light purées, and turtle soup are other examples of thin soups.

Curdling is a problem often encountered in making cream soups. For best stability, begin by making a moderately heavy velouté (a base sauce made from white stock), and add to this the vegetable purée that gives the soup its distinguishing flavor (1 or 2 pints per gallon of velouté); then add the velouté to hot rich milk or thin cream—*not the other way around*—stirring well to blend them (see fig. 6-5). The milk or cream can be lightly thickened for soups that curdle easily. Only make the amount required for a 20- to 30-minute serving period, and never mix an old batch with a new batch. Excess salt or heat encourages curdling. Some cream soups are finished with a liaison (a mixture of one part egg yolk well blended into three parts cream). The soup is then cooked only enough to thicken the eggs; it is never boiled.

A fairly stable cream soup is made by starting with béchamel sauce, blending in the flavoring purée (1 pint per gallon of soup), and then

(a)   (b)

Figure 6-5. (a) The first step in preparing a cream soup is to make a velouté base. Here a stock is being added to a mixture of roux and vegetables for the velouté. (b) Making a cream soup. After a thickened velouté containing the main flavoring agent and seasonings is made, the thickened mixture is added to slightly thickened rich hot milk; the velouté mixture is blended in with good, rapid agitation.

thinning to the desired consistency by pouring the béchamel mixture into hot milk or cream.

Another method is to prepare a white sauce, blend in the purée, and thin with milk or cream if the sauce is too thick. This last method is the least stable of the three. A good cream soup should have the consistency of moderately heavy cream. A bisque is a cream soup that contains shellfish as the main flavoring ingredient.

Medium (Lightly Thickened) Soups

Soup thickness can be caused by rice, macaroni, dumplings, vegetables, puréed potatoes, flour, starch, eggs, or panadas. Most medium-thick soups are less clear, thin, and delicate than thin soups. They can serve as the first course of a light meal or as part of a luncheon. Purées gain their thickness in two ways: from the pulp of succulent vegetables such as carrots, asparagus, turnips, celery, or green peas; and from some starch. For a medium consistency, about 2 lb legumes or 1 qt puréed product is needed per gallon of soup (see fig. 6-6). Doubling the quantity of solid ingredients gives a heavy soup. In some purées, starch can be used to hold items in suspension.

Heavy Soups

Thick or heavy soups such as potages, heavy purées, gumbos, chowders, or French onion usually gain their thickness from their ingredients rather than from added starch. The base may be stock or milk. Most chowders

Figure 6-6. Forcing split peas through a china cap with an up-and-down motion of the ladle to make a purée.

contain chopped onions, diced potatoes, and sautéed bacon or salt pork. Items such as clams, corn, mussels, lima beans, or mushrooms give each chowder its name. Fish stock and tomatoes form the base for Coney Island (Manhattan or Philadelphia) chowder. Chowder with a milk base is called Boston or New England chowder.

Cold Soups

There are numerous cold soups, including vichyssoise, borscht, and jellied consommé. Scandinavians serve a cold, slightly sweetened soup that contains dried fruits. Such soups give a meal variety and interest.

SOUP GARNISHES

A change in garnish can effectively change the soup. If garnishes are used, they are usually cooked separately and added at service. Starchy products must be blanched thoroughly after cooking so that they do not cloud the soup.

SAUCES AND GRAVIES

A sauce or gravy is usually a richly flavored stock or liquid that gives moistness, richness, flavor, or some other complementary character to another food. They may or may not be thickened. Some give color and form to foods and should contrast in flavor with the food they accompany. Others may be garnishes. A sauce should never mask or disguise the flavor of a food; instead it should heighten it. A portion is usually 2 oz, although this may be varied according to need.

STANDARD

Sauces or gravies should have a soft sheen imparted by tiny pinpoint globules of emulsified fat; some may have the sheen of varnish. The texture should be smooth and velvety with no lumps. No flavor should predominate in sauces, but gravies should possess the flavor of the meat from which they come. No evidence of starch should be apparent in taste or texture. Brown sauces should have a rich mahogany color, modified by added ingredients. A white velouté should be a clear, creamy white color. A béchamel, white, or cream sauce may be slightly opaque; a dead, pasty, white color and a lack of sheen indicate poor quality.

The sauce's consistency may vary, but pasty, excessively thick sauces are undesirable. Thin sauces are served over or with foods needing flavor. Some sauces should be fairly thick to give cling; for example, hollandaise must hold to broccoli. Pan gravy, au jus, or meat essences are almost as thin as broth. They are just the juice of meat obtained from drippings or deglazing. Clarity may vary according to the ingredients, but no sauce should be murky or cloudy. Many sauces should have brilliance.

Neutral sauces contain no meat flavor. They vary widely in characteristics. Some, like mayonnaise, have a high oil content and possess a high sheen. The color of these should be delicate yellow. The consistency and texture of fruit sauces, such as applesauce and cranberry sauce, should be sufficiently firm to stay in a mound when served and leave little or no liquid seepage on standing.

INGREDIENTS

High-quality stocks should be used. Some stocks are reduced before being used, and wines may be added and reduced. Frequently shallots rather than onions are used because of their milder flavor.

Finishing is the final addition of cream, butter, a liaison, or wine, followed by heating (*never* to boiling). To prevent scum formation, cover a warm sauce or brush the surface lightly with melted butter; oiled paper can also be laid on the surface. Brushing the surface with liquid works well for warm sauces held for only a short time.

The most commonly used thickening agents for sauces are flour and cornstarch, but other starches are also used. A mixture called a *roux*— half fat and half flour by weight—is most often used. The fat is melted, flour is added, and the mixture is cooked for about 10 minutes, until it is quite frothy and leaves the pan bottom easily. A roux should have a light hazelnut odor and a slightly gritty texture. Chicken fat is highly prized in roux for béchamel, velouté, or white sauce. Brown, pale (blond), or white (light) roux are made from well-browned, lightly browned, or unbrowned flour, respectively. A dry roux is made by heating flour in an oven without fat until it becomes slightly gritty. Dry roux is used when a regular roux would give an overly rich product and perhaps a broken emulsion.

Some starches or flour are blended with liquid to make a slurry for thickening called *whitewash*. It gives a less smooth flavor and is more apt to lump. A *beurre manié* is equal parts butter and flour kneaded together and used to give final consistency to a product. Figure 6-7 shows the various manifestations that roux and its components may take.

Roux can be stirred into a moderately hot liquid or the liquid can be stirred into the roux (see fig. 6-8). Some chefs use a cold roux with a hot liquid, and a hot roux with a cool liquid. Good agitation should be employed when the two are blended. The mixture should cook for at least 10

(a)

(b)

(c)

(d)

Figure 6-7. (a) Fat and flour for a roux. (b) Unbrowned flour, lightly browned flour, and heavily browned flour in quantities required to give equal thickening to 1 gal. of stock. (c) A dry roux. (d) A *beurre manié* is a kneaded mixture composed of equal parts flour and butter; it is used to give final, correct thickness to a sauce or soup.

(a)

(b)

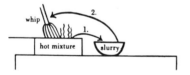

Step 1.   After making a smooth thin paste of
           the starch thickener and liquid, add
           some of the hot mixture to the
           slurry and blend well.

Step 2.   Then add all the warmed slurry to
           the hot mixture, giving good agita-
           tion as it is poured in slowly.

(c)

Figure 6-8. (a) Roux may be added to a stock in the manner shown. (b) Alternatively stock may be added to a roux in thickening a sauce or soup. (c) To use a flour or starch slurry, add some of the hot mixture to the slurry and blend well; then with good agitation add this mixture to the hot mixture. This method is also used in adding a liaison to a soup.

minutes to complete gelatinizing the starch. Flour, cornstarch, and most other starches thicken at around 144° to 162°F, and they complete their thickening at around 203°F. Failing to cook such starches completely gives graininess and a raw starch flour. Waxy maize starch starts to thicken at 155° to 167°F, and no second thickening occurs. If this starch is heated to a temperature above 195°F, a slight rethinning occurs. If a sauce is to be frozen, a waxy maize or modified starch should be used, because these remain smooth when melted and do not break down into a curdled mass. Instant starches are little used in sauce cookery.

Acids break down starch. For this reason, acidic ingredients may not be added until cooking is completed. Meat stock and drippings are slightly acidic, and sauces containing these (or wines) require more starch. More starch per gallon is required to thicken large batches than small ones, because large batches may not reach as high a temperature during cooking as small batches do.

The process of starch gelatinization or swelling is not completely understood. There are about 770 billion starch granules in 1 lb of cornstarch. They are insoluble in cold water but in hot water they dissolve and swell. When enough are in solution, the swelled units crowd one another and cause thickening. Lumping occurs when the starch particles are not separated before swelling occurs. Separation by fat in a roux or by liquid in a slurry divides the starch. The starch can be also blended with sugar and poured without moistening directly into hot liquids. In any addition, good agitation is needed.

Starches differ in their thickening power, viscosity, and clarity. Flours differ in their clarity and thickening power because of differences in gluten and starch content. Pastry and cake flours have more starch and less gluten than bread flour, and so they thicken better; bread flour gives a more opaque and stringy sauce because of its higher gluten content. Cornstarch gives a fairly clear paste because it is largely pure starch. Waxy maize and modified starches give a clear paste that remains as thick when it is cold as when it is hot, and they do not break down after freezing. Tapioca, sago, rice, potatoes, rice flour, potato flour, bread crumbs, egg yolks, and other ingredients are also used for thickening. Table 6-2 identifies the relative thickening power of various thickeners.

TABLE 6-2. Approximate equivalent thickening power of thickeners

Ingredient	Ounces	Cups	Ingredient	Ounces	Cups
Pastry flour	4	1	Tapioca	$3\frac{1}{2}$	$\frac{2}{3}$
Bread flour	5	$1\frac{1}{4}$	Bread crumbs, dry	$3\frac{1}{2}$	$\frac{3}{4}$
Cornstarch	$2\frac{3}{4}$	$\frac{3}{4}$	Whole eggs	22	$2\frac{3}{4}$*
Waxy maize starch	2	$\frac{3}{8}$	Egg yolks	20	$2\frac{1}{2}$**

* approximately 14 large eggs.
** approximately 28 large yolks.

TABLE 6-3. Sauces and their derivation

MEAT

Brown Stock
Brown sauce (espagnole)
  Bordelaise sauce (red wine, shallots, beef
    marrow)
  Château sauce (white wine, shallots, butter)
  Chasseur sauce (tomato ragoût, fine herbs,
    mushrooms, white wine)
  Madeira sauce (Madeira wine)
  Mushroom sauce (mushrooms, red wine)
  Poivrade sauce (tarragon vinegar, red wine,
    tabasco, tomato ragoût)
    Grand veneur sauce (game essence,
      truffles)
    Sauce Diane (whipped cream, truffles,
      hard-cooked egg)
    Moscovite sauce (juniper berries, malaga
      grapes, almonds, raisins)
  Provençale sauce (tomato ragoût, garlic)
  Robert sauce (mustard, red wine, shallots,
    tomato ragoût)
  Salmi (currant jelly, mushrooms, port wine)
  Fruit sauces[2] (sweetened brown sauce)
    Bigarade sauce (orange juice and peel,
      lemon juice, brandy)
    Cumberland sauce (orange and lemon
      peel and juice, ginger, cayenne, port
      wine, mustard)
    Brancy peach sauce (peach preserves,
      brandy)
    Pineapple sauce (pineapple)
    Raisin sauce (vinegar, raisins)

White Stock
Velouté sauce
  Allemande sauce (egg yolks)
    Poulette sauce (cream)
    Soubise sauce (onion purée)
  Supreme sauce (cream)
    Princes sauce (mushroom essence, glacé
      de poulet)
  Reine sauce (almond butter, truffles)
  Vin blanc sauce (fish velouté)
    Cardinal sauce (cream, chopped shrimp
      or lobster meat)
    Flamande sauce (mussel essence, parsley,
      mustard, lemon juice)
    Normandy sauce or Nantua (egg yolks,
      cream)
    Nantaise sauce (chopped crayfish,
      chopped lobster, or chopped shrimp)
  Béchamel sauce (chicken or veal stock)[3]
    A la king sauce (green peppers, mush-
      rooms, pimientos)
    Bretonne sauce (fish stock, leeks, onions,
      mushrooms, celery)

NEUTRAL

Tomato
Tomato ragoût sauce[1]
  Creole sauce (onions, garlic, tomatoes,
    green peppers)
  Spanish sauce (onions, celery, okra, mush-
    rooms, garlic, tomatoes, green pep-
    pers, stuffed green olives)

Milk (white sauce)
Cheese sauce (cheddar cheese)
Cream sauce (cream finish)
Curry sauce (curry, apples, onions)
Egg sauce (hard-cooked eggs)
Mornay sauce (Parmesan cheese)
Mustard sauce (prepared mustard)
Newburg sauce (sherry wine)

Egg Yolk, Vinegar, and Oil Emulsions
Hollandaise sauce
  Béarnaise sauce (tarragon vinegar)
  Figaro sauce (tomato purée, celery)
  Glacé royale sauce (mousseline sauce,
    mornay sauce, or cream sauce)
  Grimod sauce (saffron)
  Maltaise sauce (orange juice and grated
    peel)
  Mousseline sauce (whipped cream)
Mayonnaise
  Chaudfroid sauce or mayonnaise collée
    (gelatin)
  Imperial sauce (onion, mushrooms, mus-
    tard, pickles, pimiento, cream sauce)
  Ravigote sauce (shallots, chives, capers,
    chopped eggs)
  Rémoulade sauce (dill pickles, anchovy,
    capers, mustard)
  Russian sauce (chili sauce, chopped pimien-
    tos, chives)
    Chiffonnade sauce (chopped eggs, beets)
  Tartar sauce (dill pickles, onions, parsley)

Butters
Compounded butters
  Anchovy butter (anchovy paste)
  Caper butter (capers)
  Garlic butter (garlic juice or crushed garlic)
  Lobster (lobster pulp)
Melted butters
  Clarified butter (pour melted butter from its
    curd)
  Noisette butter (brown to hazelnut color)
  Maître d'hôtel butter (lemon juice, cayenne,
    parsley)
  Caper butter (capers)
  Irish butter (tomato catsup, nutmeg)

continued

TABLE 6-3. Sauces and their derivation (*continued*)

MEAT

White Stock
Caper sauce (capers))
Dill sauce (fresh dill)
Newburg sauce (sherry wine)

Tomato
Tomato ragoût sauce[1]
Barbecue sauce (onions, garlic, sugar, mustard, vinegar, lemon or lime juice, worcestershire, barbecue spice)
Italian or spaghetti sauce (garlic, onions, celery, green peppers, basil, oregano, bay leaf, olive oil)
Milanaise sauce (mushrooms, ham, tongue)

NEUTRAL

Butters
Mustard butter (dry mustard)
Polonaise sauce (fine bread crumbs)
Meunière butter (brown maitre d'hotel butter)
Amandine butter (sliced almonds, onion juice)
Lemon butter (lemon juice)
Noir butter (brown until very dark)

Bread Sauce
Gooseberry bread sauce (gooseberry preserves)
Horseradish bread sauce (horseradish, cream)
Mustard bread sauce (dry mustard)
Onion bread sauce (minced onions or onion purée)

Sour Cream Sauces
Horseradish sauce (horseradish)
Smitane (onions, white wine, lemon juice)

French Dressing Sauces
Avocado sauce (avocado, hard-cooked egg yolk, tarragon)
Cambridge sauce (hard-cooked egg yolk, anchovy, capers, fine herbs, mustard)
Chiffonnade sauce (fine herbs, hard-cooked egg, beets)
Vinaigrette sauce (capers, pickles, pimiento, mustard, hard-cooked eggs, chervil, tarragon, parsley)

Wine Stock Sauces
Spadoise sauce (dry red and port wine, bread crumbs, currants, nutmeg)
Raisin sauce (burgundy wine, raisins, currants, mustard, sugar, cloves, nutmeg, cinnamon)
Port wine sauce (port wine, orange and lemon juice, orange rind, thyme, velouté sauce)

1. Tomato ragoût sauce may be made from tomato purée which is combined with a meat stock as well as from a stock brought up from the start with tomatoes in it; sauces made with a neutral or meat tomato ragoût are used interchangeably.
2. Melt several teaspoons of sugar over low heat until it is caramelized; add brown stock and a bit of vinegar, and then proceed with the derived sauce.
3. Variations found in béchamel sauce are applicable also to secondary sauces made from cream sauces; likewise, some sauces made from béchamel or from cream sauce may also be derived from allemande or supreme sauces. A *béchamel maigre* is made from fish stock and can be used for some sauces that otherwise would be made from a fish velouté sauce base.
SOURCE: Adapted from a classification made by Murray Schuman.

TYPES OF SAUCES AND GRAVIES

Many sauces are made from one of several basic sauces called *foundation* or *mother* sauces. The sauces made from them are called *secondary* or *small* sauces. Table 6-3 classifies sauces and gives some derivations of small or secondary sauces from mother or basic sauces. The amount of roux to add to a sauce depends on the type of sauce being made. Table 6-4 gives approximate roux proportions to use in making various sauces.

The basic meat sauces with meat stock as a base are brown (espagnole), velouté and béchamel. Another basic sauce, tomato, may or may not have meat stock; it usually does. Brown stock thickened with a brown roux, seasoned with mirepoix, bouquet garni, tomatoes, and perhaps red wine is a brown sauce or *sauce espagnole*. It is used for red meats and game. Velouté is made from white roux, white stock, and seasonings, while a fish velouté (also called a *sauce vín blanc* or *white wine sauce*) is made from fish stock and dry white wine. A fricassée gravy is a velouté. Escoffier made béchamel sauce by using a rich veal stock, thickening it with a roux of butter and flour, and then thinning it with thin cream. It is usually made today by thickening rich chicken or veal stock with white roux, and thinning this with rich milk or cream. A white sauce is made by heating milk with mirepoix, bouquet garni, salt, and seasonings, straining the liquid, and thickening with a white roux; if cream is then added, it becomes a cream sauce. Often what is a velouté, béchamel, white, or cream sauce is confused, and chefs may argue which is which. The definitions given here should be helpful in giving what, traditionally in cooking, is the proper terminology.

Thickened tomato purée or tomato purée or brown stock flavored with

---

TABLE 6-4. Proportions of roux for soups and sauces per gallon of liquid

	Fat		Flour		
Product	*(oz)*	*(cups)*	*(oz)*	*(cups)*	*Use and consistency*
Soups:					
Thin	6	¾	4	1	Light cream soups or other thin soups
Medium	8	1	6	1½	Succulent purées, light chowders, medium creams
Thick	12	1½	10	2½	Heavy, thick soups
Sauces:					
Very thin	6	¾	4	1	Escalloped potatoes; thin, creamy sauces
Thin	8	1	8	2	Thick enough to coat a spoon
Medium	12	1½	12	3	Creamed dishes, newburg or mornay sauce, escalloped dishes, and gravies
Heavy	16	2	16	4	Soufflé bases, heavy sauces thinned by the addition of other liquids
Very heavy	20	2½	20	5	Croquettes, cutlets, and so forth

If pale roux, double flour. If brown roux, increase three times; fat may be increased in proportion. If cornstarch, potato starch, or arrowroot is substituted for plain flour, reduce amount to about three-fourths of flour amount given here.

vegetables and seasonings may be called *tomato sauce* or *tomato ragoût*. Tomato predominates in color and flavor; the seasonings are pungent.

Gravies are meat drippings that have been thinned with stock or other liquid and then thickened. Pan gravy or *au jus* is not thickened. Red-eye gravy, used in Southern cooking, is made from ham drippings. Some pan gravies contain milk.

Brown meat drippings after sautéing are called *fond brun*. They are extracted by a process called "swishing and swirling," in which liquid is added and the drippings are brought into solution through vigorous use of a fork or spoon to scrape them up from the bottom (see fig. 6-9). The sauce is frequently poured over the items being sautéed in the pan.

Bread is used to thicken sauces, and many sauces are made this way. American bread sauce is made by sautéing minced shallots or onions in butter, then adding hot milk, soft bread crumbs, and seasonings, then stirring the mixture over low heat, and finishing with cream. The English make virtually the same sauce, seasoning it with onion juice instead of shallots and onions. The French use no milk or cream, but instead a rich velouté and wine.

BASIC BUTTER SAUCES

Basic butter or butter sauce is made from butter or margarine, a bit of strained lemon juice, and few grains of cayenne. Compounded butter is basic butter plus a minced or pulped item such as anchovy paste, garlic, or mushrooms; it is used as a spread for canapés. Maitre d'hotel butter is melted unbrowned butter. Meunière butter is lightly browned basic butter, often called *hazelnut* or *noisette* butter; adding slivered almonds to it makes *sauce amandine*. *Beurre noir* (black butter) is darkly browned basic butter. Maitre d'hotel and meunière butters are served over steaks, chops, or fish. Black butter is good served over scrambled eggs or calves' brains.

CONVENIENCE PREPARATIONS

The preparation of many soups and sauces is shortened by the use of prepared items that do not require the use of traditional methods. Many dried prepared stocks or canned items can be used either to supplement stocks or to replace them completely. The use of portion meats, fish, and poultry products has eliminated many of the products used for stock making; some operations, needing stocks, have adopted these products with no great loss in the palatability of items made from them. It is also possible to purchase dried or canned soups that meet with customer approval, eliminating the tedious process of making stocks and the derived soups. Similarly, many sauces are available from bases or canned products that duplicate well the original product, which requires so much more labor. Many fine chefs today use these preparations, and at least one company sells its product only to chefs in operating facilities.

(a)

(b)

(c)

Figure 6-9. (a) A process called *deglazing* or *swishing and swirling* is used to extract encrusted materials and drippings from the sauté pan. A stock, wine, or other liquid is added, and the encrusted materials on the bottom are scraped up and brought into solution with the drippings and the liquid. (b) Some of the fat and drippings may be left in the pan to start a roux. (c) Stock is then added, and the mixture is cooked for about 10 minutes to give a thickened gravy.

The products derived are of high quality, as can be seen by comparing the duplicates with originals.

Chapter Review

1. What is compounded butter? maitre d'hotel butter? meunière butter? hazelnut (noisette) butter? beurre noir (black butter)?
2. How does a gravy differ from a sauce?
3. What is a mother sauce, and how can it be developed into a secondary (small) and other sauces? Give an example.
4. Define the following items, and describe how are they made and used:
   roux   beurre manie   slurry or whitewash   dry roux   finish
5. Match the following terms to the correct description:

Stock	*Paysanne*	Essence	Purée
Broth	*au jus*	Court bouillon	Pot-au-feu
Bouillon	Liaison	*Glacé de viande*	Bisque
Raft	*Glacé de poisson*	Consommé	Mirepoix
Glaze	*Glacé de poulet*	Sachet	Bouquet garni
Demiglaze	Fumet	*Fond brun*	

_____ The browned drippings collected after sautéing meat, fish, or poultry.

_____ Rich stock reduced by one-fourth.

_____ A simple, plain stock.

_____ A thin liquid made from vegetables, flesh, and seasonings; used as a base for soups, sauces, and other dishes.

_____ Stock reduced by one-half.

_____ A clarified broth with a definite beef flavor.

_____ A cream soup in which seafood is the main flavoring ingredient.

_____ Demiglaze from meat.

_____ A mixture of egg yolks and heavy cream that is used as a finish.

_____ Fish or game are steamed over this kind of stock. (Two of the terms listed fit this description; give them both.)

_____ Rich fish stock over which fish is steamed.

_____ Glaze made from rich poultry stock.

_____ Chopped vegetables that are used to season a stock, sauce, or other dish.

_____ A small sack of mixed spices. (Two of the terms listed fit this description; give them both.)

_____ A pot kept going continuously to make stock.

_____ A crust or floating mass of meat and vegetables floating on top of a clarified liquid.

_____ A soup whose name is derived from a word that means perfection.

_____ A thick, country-style soup.

_____ Soup made from something such as beans that gives it a slight thickness.

_____ The plain, unthickened juice of meat.

_____ A glaze made from fish.

CHAPTER 7

Eggs and Dairy Products

Outline

Goals

1. To detail standards, principles, and techniques for the preparation and cooking of eggs.
2. To indicate how egg quality and cooking affect final product quality.
3. To cover various methods of egg cookery.
4. To enumerate equivalents and detail preparation treatment of processed eggs to bring them to a form equal to fresh eggs.
5. To show how proper techniques can avoid problems in dairy product handling and cooking.
6. To indicate how dairy foams are produced, how different milk products can be substituted for each other, and how cheese must be handled in cooking.

Eggs and milk products are often studied together because many of the principles for cooking them are related.

EGGS

Egg cookery makes use of some of most difficult and exacting techniques of any food. Many reactions can occur in eggs that lead to an undesirable product.

Eggs are used as entrées, as appetizers, and in salads, for thickening or binding agents in custards, pie fillings, puddings, and meat loaves, and for covering French toast and breaded or batter-fried items. They incorporate air into cakes and soufflés, and they are excellent emulsifiers (especially yolks). Their ability to coagulate and improve cell strength gives them utility in baking. They can be used to clarify stocks. Eggs give richness, color, and flavor to food; they are complete proteins, are easily digested, and contribute significant amounts of vitamin A, thiamine, riboflavin, niacin, vitamin D, fat, minerals, and calories.

EGG QUALITY

Fresh eggs of high quality are important in breakfast preparations. The quality of frozen, freeze-dried, or dried eggs depends on the quality of the fresh eggs from which they came and on the subsequent care given them in processing and storage. For many purposes, such eggs produce foods of the same quality as would be obtained using fresh eggs (see fig. 7-1).

A good egg has a well-centered yolk with a firm membrane. The white should be firm, thick, and viscous, and the air sac should be small. When broken, an egg should have a white that forms a rounded mass close to

Figure 7-1. Dried eggs like the ones shown in the scoop were used to make the angel cake shown on the right. Prepared cake mixes also make excellent finished products.

the yolk, with only a small quantity of thin, watery white and a high-standing yolk. A fresh egg is slightly acidic; as it ages and loses quality, it becomes more alkaline. The white becomes thin, and the yolk loses its central position and breaks easily on shelling. Eggs lose quality rapidly at room temperature. Older eggs have a strong flavor or may develop such flavor easily in cooking. Some off-flavors bake out in old eggs used in baking, unless they are caused by bacteria, yeasts, or molds.

EGG STANDARDS

Standards for eggs vary with each cooking style (see fig. 7-2). A soft-cooked egg has a partially coagulated white with one-half to three-fourths of the white firm, depending upon doneness. The yolk should be warm throughout, but still liquid. A medium-cooked egg has a white cooked only to the yolk, which remains liquid. A hard-cooked egg has a firm, glossy white and a solid, mealy, bright yellow or orange-yellow

(a)

(b)

(c)

(d)

Figure 7-2. (a) High-quality country-style eggs show a good sheen, high yolks, and soft-cooked edges. (b) A high-quality poached egg on the left and a poor one on the right. (c) Well-scrambled eggs; notice the soft texture and good sheen, indicators of good quality. (d) Hard-cooked, medium-cooked, and soft-cooked eggs, all of good standard.

yolk. The yolk should be uniformly coagulated and not dark on the outside. Eggs cooked in the shell should have a pleasing egg flavor and should appear bright and fresh. Colors should be natural and clear. There should be no toughness, rubberiness, crumbliness, stickiness, or other undesirable texture. Boiled eggs are firmer than those cooked at lower temperatures, and boiling may be done purposely to produce eggs that are firm enough to slice or stuff. Eggs processed by being dipped in oil may leave a film of oil on the surface of cooking water that in no way indicates an egg of poor quality.

A fried egg has a bright, glossy appearance and is compact, like a poached egg but not quite as bunched (see fig. 7-3). A sunny-side-up egg should have a bright yellow or orange-yellow, well-rounded yolk. If cooked country-style (with the pan covered tightly), the yolk is covered with a thin film of coagulated white and (depending on the degree of cooking) is firmer than when cooked sunny-side-up. The egg should be shiny, not dull, wrinkled, porous, or watery, and should be soft underneath with no hard edges. The coagulated areas should be firm, yet tender—not tough or rubbery.

Poached eggs should have a bright appearance with some shiny white adhering closely to bright yolks. They should not be spread out or porous. Raggedness, wrinkling, dullness, or other undesirable qualities indicate poor-quality eggs or poor cooking. A shirred egg's standard closely resembles the standard for a country-style fried egg: it should be bright, tender, not overcooked or dry on the surface or edge, and free of any dark ring around the yolk.

Scrambled eggs should be bright and clear, with a soft sheen, a uniform, pale color, and no evidence of browning. A hard bottom or foaminess on top should be avoided. A strong flavor, a dark, green color, or rubberiness is a sign of overcooking or poor quality eggs.

A plain (French) omelet in many ways resembles scrambled eggs, except that the outside of an omelet is browned a delicate light tan. It also may be firmer and have a more continuous mass. No moist, large segments should be seen. Moistness, tenderness, and delicacy of flavor should be evident. The folded or rolled shape should be even, uniform,

Figure 7-3. A fried egg should have no brown or crisp part on the bottom.

well-rounded, and lacking any sign of raggedness or separation. A foamy omelet may be served unfolded, but it is usually folded in half or rolled. It should be well-puffed, large, and well-rounded, not fallen or collapsed, with a uniform, delicate tan top and a delicate brown bottom. Uneven or pale color, excessive browning, and raw egg in the center are all undesirable. The texture and consistency should be uniform, well-blended, tender, firm, and moist. No unmixed egg white should be apparent, and neither foaminess on top nor toughness on the bottom should be present. The flavor should be delicate, not pasty, flat, raw, or burned. A foamy omelet depends for its quality upon the light, airy leavening of beaten whites and yolks; its texture should be the primary consideration in evaluating it.

A soufflé should have many of the textural qualities of a foamy omelet (see fig. 7-4). The top should be slightly rounded, well-puffed, and only slightly cracked, with a smooth, shiny, unsunken surface and an even, delicate brown color.

Baked custard should be clear, creamy, shiny, and delicately flavored. An eggy, flat, or tasteless flavor is undesirable. Texture should be smooth—not stiff, tough, rubbery, curdled, or uneven; no wateriness or porosity should be evident. Tops should be shiny, clear, and touched with a light tan. Stirred custards should be creamy and smooth with a delicate, light flavor.

PRINCIPLES

Coagulation

Eggs coagulate (become firm) and change color at certain temperatures. Although this change is not instantaneous, it occurs at around 156°F for whole eggs, at between 144° and 158°F for yolks, and at 140° to 149°F for

(a)   (b)

Figure 7-4. (a) This cheese soufflé shows a high standard and good stability. (b) A foamy omelet is prepared in much the same way as a soufflé, but it is cooked differently.

whites. Mixing eggs with liquids, sugar, or other substances raises the coagulation temperature; thus, custards coagulate at around 175° to 185°F. Slowly raising the temperature gives a low coagulation temperature. Coagulation can also be caused by beating or by chemical actions, such as reactions with strong acids or alcohol. Low or moderate temperatures are best for egg cooking. High temperatures toughen eggs and cause them to develop unpleasant flavors. Mild acids make eggs more tender, retard the development off-flavors, increase their thickening power, and lower their coagulation temperature.

Egg proteins hold moisture loosely in a raw egg; coagulation binds it in firmly. If the protein is diluted with moisture (as in meat), moisture breaks away, producing an open, curdled texture called *syneresis* in eggs, and producing drip in meat. The protein bunches together separate from the moisture. Additional heat toughens and hardens this curd. Milk is also subject to syneresis or curdling. Syneresis is seen in overcooked custards, in grainy rarebits, and in sour milk.

Coagulation is an endothermic reaction; that is, heat is absorbed in the process. A thickening custard does not rise in temperature until coagulation is complete. The second rise in temperature indicates that the custard should be removed from the heat or curdling will occur. Custards usually curdle at around 190°F. Stirring a custard gives a smooth, slightly thickened liquid, and baking it undisturbed gives a smooth, solid mass.

Eggs, especially whites, contain sulfur that can give off-flavors or off-colors to eggs, especially in an alkaline medium. If this sulfur joins with iron in the yolk, it forms iron sulfide, which has a strong flavor and a dark greenish color. Overcooking can produce this compound. Sulfides form at around 155°F, but formation does not become rapid until 185°F or above. It is slowed by cooking at lower temperatures, by using fresh eggs, by using some acid in cooking, or by shortening cooking time. Fast cooling of cooked eggs helps reduce sulfide formation.

Foams

Age, temperature, egg quality, and pH are factors that affect foam formation and stability. Fresh eggs may lack good foaming ability. Aging tenderizes egg proteins, making them more extensible; as a result, old, dried, or frozen eggs may foam more satisfactorily than fresh eggs. Yolks and whites separate best when the egg is at a temperature above 60°F.

Eggs form a good foam at 50°F, but the foam is unstable. The best volume and stability is obtained at temperatures greater than 115°F. In quantity work, eggs are whipped at between 75° and 110°F. Thawed, reliquefied dried eggs should be whipped at around 110°F. Like fresh eggs, they can be overbeaten.

Eggs foam best if their pH is 6.5 or lower. About $\frac{2}{3}$ T ($\frac{1}{4}$ oz) cream of tartar for each 1 lb (2 c) eggs is normally used to lower the natural pH, although lemon juice or other acids are also effective. Acid tenderizes protein and makes it more extensible; it also lightens the pigments in the yolk. Salt seems to encourage foaming. Sugar gives foam stability; it also helps draw air into the foam. Acid and salt are usually added at the start of beating, and sugar is added later, when the eggs become foamy or nearly whipped. Early sugar addition aids in buffering the eggs—especially the whites—against overbeating. Egg whites do not foam if fat is present. Even the presence of a small amount of yolk may suffice to make whites unwhippable. Therefore, utensils for beating whites should be scrupulously clean and fat-free. Egg color lightens as foam increases. The most common fault in beating yolks is to underbeat them.

Dried egg whites, which are used for meringues and angel cakes, can be beaten to a stiffer, drier foam without overbeating than can regular egg whites; this is because they contain stabilizers that give them a durable and elastic foam. Phosphoric acid salts, bile salts, or triethyl citrate increases stability and volume. Dried eggs, especially whites have a longer shelf life if the small amount of glucose they contain naturally is removed in processing. If dried egg products are acidified and packed in gas, their shelf life is extended. Storage under refrigeration also increases shelf life and stability.

Recipes should state the stage to which eggs must be beaten and should indicate in some cases whether the upper or lower range of the stage is appropriate. The four stages to which foam can be beaten are identified in table 7-1.

TECHNIQUES OF COOKING

Breakfast eggs should be cooked to order whenever possible. The rapid degeneration of cooked eggs from optimum quality makes it difficult to prepare and hold them in large quantities. Fried, shirred or scrambled eggs can be cooked in quantity until almost done and then finished in an oven.

TABLE 7-1. Appearance and uses of foam at different stages of beating

Stage	Appearance	Use
First	Liquid, but well blended; foam is in large bubbles.	Clarifying soups, making French toast, coating foods, and blending into mixtures as a liquid.
Second	Medium-size air cells throughout mass; foam is shiny, moist, and fluid; tips fold over into rounded peaks, and liquid separates out upon standing.	Sponge or angle cakes, soufflés, foamy omelets.
Third	Stiff foam; small air cells; no longer fluid, especially whites; still moist, smooth, and glossy; points stand when peaked.	Cooked frostings, divinity, soft or hard meringues, tortes, sponge cakes.
Fourth	Dry, dull, brittle foam; flakes off and can be cut into rigid parts; curds may appear, indicating coagulation. It is difficult to beat whole eggs or yolks to this stage.	Has no use in food work; eggs are so overextended that they will not extend further in baking, causing failure in the product.

TABLE 7-2. Cooking times for shell eggs at different heats

Style	212°F*	190°–195°F	7 psi Steam
Soft-cooked	3 min	6 min	1 min 25 sec
Medium-cooked	4 min	8 min	
Hard-cooked	12–15 min	20–25 min	3 min 10 sec

* These times are not long enough for eggs cooked at elevations above 3,000 ft.

Cooking in Water

Have eggs that are to be boiled at room temperature or warm them slightly in lukewarm water before adding them to hot water; cold eggs may crack. Cooking times for shell eggs are given in table 7-2.

Egg boilers operated by service personnel usually hold four eggs. To hard-cook shell eggs in quantity, place them in a perforated insert; set this in tepid water in a steam-jacketed kettle or pot, and bring the water quickly to boil. The water should cover the eggs about 1 in. deep. For breakfast eggs, bring the water to a temperature of between 190° and 195°F, add the eggs, and bring the water to a slow boil. When they are done, plunge them immediately into hot water to stop the cooking, and send them to service. Hard-cooked eggs should be water-cooled for 5 to 10 minutes and peeled immediately; to peel, crack the shell well and roll to ensure good shell breakup. Start at the large end and peel downward, using running water, if necessary, to loosen the shell (see fig. 7-5a). If hard-cooked eggs are to be chopped, crack them into lightly greased pans and steam or bake them; then chop. If eggs are steamed, cooking times must be carefully watched. A frozen, hard-cooked tubular egg is available on the market that only requires thawing and slicing to give well-

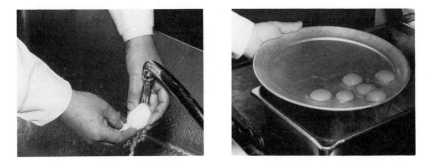

(a)   (b)

Figure 7-5. (a) To peel a hard-cooked egg, crack it well and start peeling at the broad end, using water to assist in loosening the shell. (b) To poach eggs, let them slide gently into the hot water, striking the side of the pan; this cushions their entry and allows them to bunch up.

formed center slices. It is of high quality and has many advantages over the old way of getting slices.

Eggs for coddling should be readied at room temperature; then add boiling water, using a pint of water for each egg. Cover tightly, and allow to stand without heat until done.

Have the water for poached eggs 2 to $2\frac{1}{2}$ in. deep, using 1 T salt and 2 T vinegar per gallon of water. The salt and vinegar cause the egg proteins to bunch together, retarding spread. Bring the water to a gentle boil. Eight to sixteen eggs can be poached per gallon of water. The water can be used for three to four batches of eggs before being discarded. Crack eggs onto platters, and slide them in toward the pan side—not in the center (see fig. 7-5b). This helps keep the yolks centered in the white and prevents spread. Cook for 3 to 5 minutes, depending on the desired level of doneness. Remove poached eggs with a perforated ladle or slotted spoon, for good drainage. Eggs may be partially poached and sent to the steam table for final cooking. Eggs poached at too low a temperature may be too delicate to handle in fast service. Another option is to steam-poach eggs in greased cups set in steam-table wells.

Dry-heat Cooking

Eggs are frequently fried to order, even when many are needed. Single-egg pans should be about 4 in. in diameter at the bottom, and double-egg pans 6 to 8 in. in diameter. Condition pans well and use only for egg frying.

Add fat or butter about $\frac{1}{8}$ in. deep in the pan. For sunny-side-up eggs, have the fat hot, and slide the eggs into it, immediately reducing the heat to avoiding a hard surface under the egg or at the edges. The hot fat retards spreading. Covering the pan tightly gives country-style; adding a few drops of water before covering encourages a bit more steam to coat the egg. Basting with hot fat also coats an egg. Turning the egg over and cooking it lightly gives an over-easy egg. Figure 7-6 shows good products of all three styles.

Grilled eggs are not as attractive as pan-fried eggs, but production is faster. Use plenty of butter or fat on a clean, conditioned grill heated at 300° to 325°F. Place eggs on the grill in the same sequence in which they will be removed. Eggs may be prebroken into a device containing many cups so that they can be placed on the grill at one time. If eggs are to stand for service in a steam table, cook them until they just set, and send them to the steam table for finishing; the heat there finalizes setting.

To fry in mass quantity, break the eggs onto platters, and slide them into hot fat at a temperature between 265° and 280°F. Drain well, and send to service. Some cooks grease 18 × 26-in. hamburger bun pans, place the eggs in the indented spaces, and put them in the oven.

Place eggs destined for shirring (baking) in well-buttered cassolettes or shallow baking dishes, and season. For large quantities, break the eggs into well-buttered 12 × 20-in. pans, place the pans over low heat until the eggs begin to set, and then finish them under a broiler or in an oven. Do

Figure 7-6. Eggs country-style (left), over-easy (center), and sunny-side-up (right).

not overcook; some heat remains after removal for final cooking. Cream, milk, cheese, bacon, chicken livers, or other foods may be added to the eggs before cooking, or sauces may be added during the last stage or at the end of cooking.

Scrambled eggs are easily prepared in quantity. Usually 4 oz of cream, milk, or some other liquid is added to each 1 lb of whole eggs. Cooking may be done in a large greased pan in the oven, under a broiler, in a steam-jacketed kettle, in a bain-marie, in a steam table, in individual skillets, or in a steamer or double boiler. Have the heat set high at the start; then lower it as the eggs coagulate. Lift the eggs carefully from the bottom, allowing the uncooked portions to flow down and cook. Allow the eggs to cook in about $\frac{1}{4}$-in. segments; excessive stirring yields pieces that are too fine. Remove them while still soft, and send to service so that they are just about the right consistency when served. Too much heat or prolonged cooking toughens the eggs and promotes off-flavors and off-colors. Whole eggs are sometimes combined with a medium white sauce and cooked until just set. They hold well at 200°F for 30 minutes—considerably longer than eggs prepared without the sauce.

Foamy omelets are little used in quantity cookery because of their delicate nature and the skill required to make them. Plain or foamy omelets are usually cooked to order. Plain omelets can also be baked in large pans, steamed in pans, or cooked in a bain-marie or steam table. A frozen prepared omelet is available that needs only slight warming to be ready for service. Airlines use this product. If it is to be baked in an oven, bake it at 325°F for 25 to 30 minutes.

One egg makes a small omelet; two, a medium one; and three, a large one. Adding liquid is not recommended. Beat the eggs well but not to frothiness. Use a well-conditioned pan covered with about ⅛ in. of clarified butter or oil. Bring the pan to a fairly high temperature so that the eggs bubble as they are poured in (see fig. 7-7a). Tilt the pan in all directions, spreading the eggs to the outer edges. Lower the heat, and cook at a moderate temperature. Lift cooked portions up carefully to allow uncooked eggs to flow underneath, but do not break up the egg mixture or allow it to bunch or form a mass in the pan center (see fig. 7-7b). While the surface is moist, increase the heat in order to brown the bottom. To fold or roll the omelet tip the pan to about a 60° angle and shape the omelet with a spatula. Before folding, fill it with creamed items, chicken livers, chopped bacon or ham, cheese, or a sweet mixture. Fold over, pressing the still-moist edges together lightly to seal them; then turn the omelet and cook it a short time. Turn it onto a plate, shape it with a clean cloth, and serve (see fig. 7-7c). Omelets with sweetened centers are frequently "burned"—a process in which the omelet is sprinkled liberally with powdered sugar, and a hot metal instrument is then used to burn a design on the omelet top (see fig. 7-7d). Foamy omelets are made by whipping yolks and whites separately and then folding

(a)

(b)

(c)

(d)

Figure 7-7.   (a) To make a French omelet, heat the fat to a fairly hot temperature, and pour the stirred whole eggs into the pan. (b) Lift until the entire mass is well-coagulated; then fill and fold. (c) Shape, if desired. (d) If the filling is sweet, dust with powdered sugar and burn with a poker.

them together. Bake foamy omelets in an oven, or cook them covered over heat. Like regular omelets, they can be filled, folded, and scored.

For a soufflé, blend stage-one yolks into a thick starch base, and carefully fold stage-two (upper level) whites into this mixture. Chopped meat, cheese, or other foods can be added. Sweetened soufflés are used for desserts. Tapioca-thickened soufflés perform well in quantity service. Bake soufflés at around 300°F to obtain a dry and stable product. Baking a shorter time at 375°F in a pan of water also gives a good product. To guard against sudden collapse after baking, leave the soufflé at the oven entrance with the door open so that it stabilizes. As it cools, its volume decreases, although a well-made one shrinks only slightly.

There are many fondues. One is made of cheese, white wine, starch, and kirsch; another by deep-frying small pieces of meat and serving these with tangy sauces; still another is a custardlike dish, with bread or bread crumbs added for lightness. Chopped chicken, cheese, or other items may be added. The custardlike fondue is somewhat similar to a soufflé. A timbale is a baked dish that uses a strong custard to bind in chopped items such as vegetables or meats.

PROCESSED EGGS

All processed eggs must be pasteurized. Many prepared egg products are now on the market. Dried egg mixtures are available that, when water is added, make custards, scrambled eggs, omelets, and other egg dishes. Frozen egg products (in addition to the omelets and hard-cooked tubular eggs previously mentioned) are also on the market. Operations should test these products to see if they achieve the desired quality in finished foods while saving money.

Frozen or dried eggs are used extensively in cooking or baking. Even though they are pasteurized, it is best not to use them as raw eggs in such products as mayonnaise and eggnog. Frozen whole eggs, frozen yolks, frozen whites, a sugared yolk containing approximately 10 percent sugar, and whole eggs containing added yolks (proprietary eggs) are available. A high-quality frozen whole egg is available for omelets, scrambled eggs, French toast, and other breakfast items. For the most part, dried and frozen eggs come from low-quality eggs and consequently should not be used for breakfast eggs. Store frozen eggs at 0°F or lower. Thaw eggs under refrigeration; a 30-lb can takes two or more days to thaw at 40°F. Mix well after thawing, to redistribute egg solids.

A case (30 doz) of large eggs weighs approximately 45 lb net and yields about 40 lb shelled egg—20 to 22 lb whites, and 16 to 18 lb yolks. A 30-lb can of frozen eggs contains about 300 large whole eggs or 670 yolks or 540 whites. If whites and yolks are to be blended to make whole eggs, a 55:45 ratio of white to yolk should be used. This is not the proportion of the two in the shell, but it corrects for the fact that, in separating, some white is always left in the shell or with the yolk. Frequently, to obtain 1 lb (1 pt) whole egg, $1\frac{1}{8}$ c whites and $\frac{7}{8}$ c yolks are mixed. Eggs by count in recipes are calculated as large eggs (24 oz per dozen in the shell); if

TABLE 7-3. Frozen and fresh egg equivalents

Type egg (frozen)	Weight (lb)	Volume (pt)	Fresh EP equivalent (large eggs)* (24 oz per dozen)
Whole eggs	1	1	9 to 11 whole eggs
Whites	1	1	17 to 19 whites
Yolks	1	1	20 to 24 yolks

* If medium eggs, increase count by about 10%; for 1 lb (1 pt)
of whole eggs, use 9 oz whites to 7 oz yolks.

medium or extra large eggs are used, the amount called for should be
decreased or increased, respectively, by 10 percent. Table 7-3 lists frozen
and fresh egg equivalents.

The ratio of water to dry whole eggs is about $2:1$ by weight; whites,
$3:1$; and yolks, $1:1\frac{1}{4}$. As much as possible, we try to mix dry eggs with
the other dry ingredients first, adding the extra water with the rest of the
liquid. Tables 7-4 and 7-5 give quantity, volume, and weight equivalents
between dried and fresh eggs. Notice that the equivalents for yolks in
these tables are not the same; bakers prefer to use more yolks. The
manufacturer's directions should always be consulted for proper ratios.
Dried eggs are available as whole eggs, whites, yolks, special fortified
blends (70 percent whole, 30 percent yolks), and baker's special blends
(20 to 30 percent sucrose, to improve foaming ability). Dried eggs should
be vacuum-packed in nitrogen gas. If acidified, they are more stable in
use. Store dried eggs in quite cool areas. After opening, store them at 32°
to 40°F in a tightly sealed container, to reduce lumping. If they are to be
measured, stir them lightly with a fork before measuring; it is preferable,
however, to weigh them. To reconstitute, spread evenly over lukewarm
water, stirring constantly with a wire whip, or use a mixer. Let stand for 5
to 10 minutes; stir again, and use.

TABLE 7-4. Miscellaneous equivalents of dried and fresh eggs

Dried product	Ratio of egg to water	Fresh equivalent EP (large eggs)
No. 10 can (3 lb) dried whole eggs		100 whole eggs
1 lb dried whole and $2\frac{1}{2}$ pt water	$1:2\frac{1}{2}$	$3\frac{1}{2}$ lb whole eggs
1 lb dried yolks and $1\frac{1}{2}$ pt water	$1:1\frac{1}{2}$	$2\frac{1}{2}$ lb yolks
6 oz dried whole and $1\frac{7}{8}$ c water	$3:7$	1 doz whole eggs
1 lb dried whole and $2\frac{1}{2}$ pt water	$1:2\frac{1}{2}$	3 doz whole eggs ($3\frac{1}{2}$ lb)
1 lb dried whites and 5 pt water	$1:5$	100 whites (6 lb)
1 lb dried yolks and $1\frac{3}{4}$ c water	$8:7$	47 yolks

TABLE 7-5. Dried eggs required to make 1 lb
fresh EP equivalent

Type egg and quantity to give 1 lb	Quantity for 1 lb equivalent			
	Dried egg		Water	
	Ounces	Measure	Ounces	Measure
Whole egg, 9	$4\frac{1}{2}$	1 c 2 T	$11\frac{1}{4}$	1 c 7 T
White, 17 to 19	$2\frac{1}{4}$	$\frac{1}{2}$ c	$13\frac{3}{4}$	$1\frac{3}{4}$ c
Yolk,* 20 to 24	$7\frac{1}{4}$	1 c	$8\frac{3}{4}$	1 c 1 T
Yolk,† 25 to 27	$7\frac{1}{2}$	1 c	$8\frac{1}{2}$	1 c 1 T
Yolk,‡ 16 to 20	$6\frac{1}{2}$	1 c	8	1 c

* 43% solids
† 45% solids
‡ Add 1.6 oz of sugar to give yolks with 10% sugar, as used in the
bakeshop for frozen sugared yolks.

DAIRY PRODUCTS

Milk is a fluid commonly used in cooking as a medium for suspending or
dissolving foods. It contributes flavor, color, and richness, plus valuable
minerals and vitamins. Cream offers moistness, richness, and smoothness of flavor. Butter and cheese contribute flavor and nutrients. Dry
milk is low in cost, easy to handle, and low in perishability; its products
are equal in quality to those made from regular milk.

STANDARDS

Identify the standard of the particular food with which dairy products are
combined, rather than the standard of the dairy products themselves.
Foods containing a high proportion of dairy products are significantly
modified by them; these foods should be smooth and noncurdled in
texture and should be tinted considerably by the color of the milk,
cheese, or butter. The flavor should be mild, sweet, and pleasant, as well
as rich. Cooking, together with the addition of other ingredients, modi-
fies dairy flavors, and this should be considered in evaluating products.
Margarines are considered dairy products.

TYPES AND PROCESSING

Table 7-6 lists the approximate composition of different milks and
creams. Coffee cream has 18 percent milkfat, light whipping cream has 30
to 34 percent, and heavy whipping cream has 34 percent or more. Half-
and-half (not a cream) has about 12 percent milkfat. Sour cream must
have at least 18 percent milkfat and about 0.2 percent lactic acid.

Buttermilk was originally a by-product of butter, but today it is made
by souring pasteurized nonfat milk with lactic acid–producing bacteria.
Pasteurization destroys pathogens. In cooking, when unsoured products
must be used for soured ones, add $\frac{1}{4}$ c vinegar per quart of product.

**TABLE 7-6. Approximate composition of milks
used in cooking**

Type milk	Fat	Nonfat solids	Water	Sucrose
Fresh whole milk	3.5	8.5	88	0
Fresh nonfat milk	trace	9	91	0
Evaporated whole milk	8	18	74	0
Evaporated nonfat milk	trace	20–30	80–70	0
Sweetened condensed whole milk	8	20	30	42
Dry whole milk	27	70	3	0
Nonfat dry milk	trace	96	4	0

Yogurt is a fine, smooth, semisolid clabbered milk containing 20 percent milk solids. Butter is churned from cream and has 80 percent milkfat. Clarified butter is melted butter without the liquid that forms under it. Margarine is vegetable or animal fat flavored with dairy products; like butter, it is 80 percent fat. Margarine containing lecithin foams and browns. Cheese is a food high in milkfat and milk proteins. Most cheese comes from the curd of milk but some may be partially whey (see fig. 7-8).

Milkfat is held in suspension by protein adsorbed on the fat surface. Its binding power declines as milk cools; thus cream comes slowly to the

Figure 7-8. The upper curd is set with rennet and can be used to make a firm cheese. The lower curd is set with natural souring from bacterial action and can be used to make cottage cheese.

top, being lighter than the milk. Milk fat is separated from milk by centrifuging. Dividing individual fat globules finely by homogenization increases the surface area of the fat and leaves each small globule with less upward pull, so the fat globules are held in suspension. Homogenized cream whips less well than natural cream because the globules are too finely divided to bunch together—a factor needed in order for the cream being whipped to form a fine network around air bubbles.

Pasteurization—the destruction of harmful bacteria through heating—can occur in milk if the milk is held for 30 minutes at 143°F or for 15 seconds at 160°F or for even less time at still higher temperatures. The higher temperatures (ultrapasteurization) may give a cooked flavor to the product, however, and may even change the reaction of the product. Some chefs complain, for example, that milkfat-rich creams that have been subjected to these high temperatures do not react in cooking the same way that creams do after being pasteurized at lower temperatures. Milk that is to be used to make bread is heated to destroy thermophilic bacteria and enzymes that remain after pasteurization. Pasteurization gives a more tender clabber in milk and produces custards with a softer, finer curd.

PRINCIPLES

Fresh milk has a pH of from 6.5 to 6.6. Casein, the major milk protein, is held in stable colloidal suspension at this pH, but at 4.6 it becomes unstable, curdling or precipitating out. This is why acids such as lemon juice (with a pH of 2) curdle milk so easily. Evaporated milk is most stable, fresh milk is next, and dry milk is least stable. Curdling is a process in which casein separates into curds, leaving whey behind. Clabber is a smooth, soft, shiny solid mass that resembles custard. When a clabber is broken—for example, as a result of agitation or heat—curdling occurs. Compounds such as salts, tannins, and strong food acids curdle milk that is in clabber form, while mild acids or rennet clabber milk. The acidity of milk can be increased in a number of ways. The natural loss of carbon dioxide in the course of standing increases acidity; alternatively, acid may be introduced in cooking, or bacteria may sour milk. Tannins act as denaturing agents, drawing moisture from proteins and causing curdling. Cooking salt, curing salts, and other salts such as calcium chloride in food encourage curdling, as does heat.

Some milk proteins are heat-coagulated—for example, the scum that appears on heated milk or the deposits that form at the bottom of utensils in which milk is heated. Scum can be avoided by covering pots tightly during cooking, by whipping to create a foam on top, or by allowing fat to cover the surface.

TECHNIQUES

Curdling

Milk curdling can be reduced by various means. Low salting helps. Adding the acid- or tannin-containing food slowly into the milk, accompanied by good agitation, or thickening both the milk and the acid- or tannin-containing food reduces the potential for curdling. The gelatinized starch in the thickened milk binds casein so that it separates with more difficulty. Some authorities recommend adding milk in several portions during the cooking of such items as a cured ham baked in milk. Having both the milk and the curdling agent at the same temperature when they meet may help. Adding bicarbonate of soda or other alkalies reduces acidity, but the practice is not recommended because alkalies destroy vitamins. Shortening cooking time or reducing the temperature helps in some cases. Escalloped potatoes often curdle. Sometimes a slightly thickened white sauce poured over the potatoes stops it; alternatively, dry milk, flour, and seasonings can be blended together with the raw potatoes, and then water added to give greater stability (see fig. 7-9). The methods for making cream soups in the previous chapter should be reviewed. If proper techniques are used and service is fairly soon after preparation, tart foods can be combined with milk. For example, horseradish can be whipped into a rich béchamel sauce with minimal curdling to make a horseradish sauce for roast beef. Acids in molasses or brown sugar sometimes curdle puddings or pie fillings, but if the sweetener is blended with the thickening agent or is added after thickening occurs, curdling is reduced.

Table 7-7 gives the proportions used in making sauces from nonfat dry milk. These proportions differ slightly from those given in chapter 6. About 13 oz nonfat dry milk per gallon gives the equivalent of fresh nonfat milk, although normally 1 lb is used. Adding 5 oz butter, margarine, or fat to this mixture makes the equivalent of 1 gal of whole fresh milk. Increasing the proportion of milk solids in some bakery products and frozen desserts improves their quality. Recipes may have to be adjusted when this is done. Normally, 1 lb dry milk is 4 cups, but 5¾ cups instant dry milk is 1 lb (see table 7-8). Instant dry milk goes into solution

Figure 7-9.   On the left, a slightly thickened white sauce is being poured over parboiled potatoes for escalloping. On the right, dry milk, flour, and seasonings are blended together with raw potatoes, and then water is added before baking. In either method, the chances of curdling are reduced.

**TABLE 7-7. White sauce proportions using
nonfat dry milk (per 1 gal sauce)**

Type sauce	Water	Nonfat dry milk	Butter, margarine, or fat	Flour*
Thin	3½ qt	1 lb 6 oz	6½ oz	4 to 8 oz
Medium	3½ qt	1 lb 6 oz	8¼ oz	8 to 12 oz
Thick	3½ qt	1 lb 5 oz	10 oz	1 lb
Very thick	3½ qt	1 lb 5 oz	12½ oz	1¼ lb

* Quantity of flour used depends on type of flour and thickness
desired.

more easily than regular dry milk does. Usually dry milk is added to the
other sifted dry ingredients, and the required liquid is added with the
other liquid in the recipe. The milk is more stable if it is made the day
before it is used; even making it 20 minutes ahead helps. Make dry milk
with less water than needed, and thin it with water just before use. Blend
dry milk into water by sifting it over the top; then use good agitation to
bring it into solution. Weigh rather than measure. Because of dry milk's
poorer stability, heat it for as short a time as possible. Thicken its solutions more than is normally necessary, and thin to proper consistency
just before service, adding salt at the last minute. Custards made with
dry milk are unstable. Even dishing them up while they are hot causes
syneresis. A strong custard with 2 to 2½ lb eggs per gallon of milk must be
made when dry milk is used; as a result, it is less expensive to use fresh
or evaporated milk and fewer eggs than to use dry milk and extra eggs.

Scorching

Milk scorches easily. It is best heated over water, in a steam-jacketed
kettle or steamer. Prolonged heating below scorching temperatures can

TABLE 7-8. Equivalents for 1 gal liquid milk

For 1 gal whole liquid milk use:	For 1 gal nonfat liquid milk use:
18 oz dry whole milk + 7½ lb or 3¾ qt water	13 oz dry nonfat milk + 7¾ or 3 qt 2½ c water
or	or
13 oz nonfat dry milk + 5 oz melted fat + 7½ lb or 3¾ qt water	4½ lb nonfat evaporated milk + 4¼ lb or 2 qt ½ c water
or	or
4¼ lb evaporated whole milk + 4½ lb or 2¼ qt water	3 lb condensed nonfat milk + 7 lb or 3½ qt water†
or	
4 lb condensed whole milk + 6¼ lb or 3¼ qt water*	

* Will also contain 1 lb 10 oz sugar.
† Will also contain 1 lb 5 oz sugar.

darken milk and give it a somewhat carmelized flavor, or it cause milk to become flat and less flavorful—probably because of loss of gas or air.

Foams

Air can be beaten into milk or cream to make a stable foam. Special methods or ingredients are used to whip cream that contains less than 30 percent milkfat. Recipes usually state quantities of whipped cream in unwhipped measure; volume increases two to three times upon whipping. Use it soon after whipping; drainage is evident about an hour afterward. To whip whipping cream (30 to 40 percent milkfat), use pasteurized, unhomogenized cream that has aged at least two days to give improved stability and volume. (Pasteurization slightly decreases volume and stability.) To improve stability, add $1\frac{1}{2}$ oz nonfat dry milk per quart of cream (preferably before use), or use $1\frac{1}{2}$ t of a 10 percent suspension of lime per quart. Using powdered sugar instead of granulated sugar seems to improve stability. Have utensils cold, and keep the cream chilled below 40°F. The bowl should be deep enough to allow good agitation. Do not overbeat; this produces butter. After whipping, add sugar and flavor-

Figure 7-10. To whip evaporated milk, add a bit of dehydrated gelatin to the scalded milk, and then chill. Whip in a bowl sitting in ice. Many operations omit the gelatin, but a slightly more stable product is obtained if it is used.

ings, and store in a cold place. Cream with as little as 18 percent milkfat can be whipped, but it is not as stable and does not give the same volume.

To whip evaporated milk, scald the milk or place the cans into boiling water for from 5 to 10 minutes. Soaking half a teaspoon of gelatin in 2 T tap water and adding this to 1 pt of hot evaporated milk improves stability (see fig. 7-10). Chill to 40°F, and whip using chilled equipment and a deep enough bowl. When the milk is almost to the desired foam, add 3 T of lemon juice per pint of milk. Add the sugar and flavoring, and finish whipping. Hold chilled at a temperature below 50°F.

Whole or dry milk may be whipped. The volume increases about fourfold, but the foam is not stable. Poor-quality milks do not develop good foams. Use ¾ qt regular dry milk or 1 qt instant to 1 qt ice water, and beat to a soft peak. Add 1 c lemon juice, and beat until stiff. Add 2 c sugar and flavoring, and complete the beating. Hold the whipped milk chilled at a temperature below 50°F.

Imitation products are available that can be whipped to make products similar to dairy foams (see fig. 7-11). They are widely used and—besides giving fairly good products—are lower in cost than whipping cream. Aerosol-type containers are frequently used for dispensing these and regular dairy foams.

Figure 7-11. Many processed dairy products are used today in quantity food preparation. Here a packaged dairy whip is shown used on three products. (*Courtesy General Foods*)

CREAM

Patrons add coffee cream to coffee until the beverage attains the desired color. The more fat in the cream, the more whiteness is reflected in the coffee. About 1 T or ½ oz 18 percent cream is sufficient for a portion. Portioning loss from pouring cream into individual containers is around 6 percent; this loss is avoided if cream is purchased and served in individually packaged portions (also a more sanitary serving procedure). Homogenized cream gives a smoother flavor to coffee than does nonhomogenized cream. Patrons today tend to drink their coffee without cream or use half-and-half. A number of nondairy products are marketed. Cream or sour cream is used as a finishing agent for sauces and other products being blended into the product just before service; the food is never boiled after the addition. The effect of this finishing is to smooth out flavors and increase richness.

CHEESE

Like eggs and milk, cheese should be cooked at low heat. Ripened or processed cheese blends into sauces and other foods better than do other cheeses; the best temperature for blending is 125°F. A hard, dry cheese blends better if it is grated and moistened with warm milk a short time before being added to the product. In adding cheese to a thickened starch mixture that also uses eggs, add the eggs or egg yolks first, and then add the cheese; the eggs aid in blending in the cheese.

CHAPTER REVIEW

1. List the factors to look for in checking eggs for freshness.
2. What are the various stages of egg foams, and what do they look like?
3. Why does an egg coagulate? Why does the yolk of an overboiled egg have a dark greenish ring around it? Why do eggs become hard, rubbery, dark, and strong-tasting when cooked too much?
4. What is syneresis?
5. How do you shir an egg? coddle an egg? fry an egg country-style?
6. How can a cook help prevent milk from curdling in making escalloped potatoes?
7. How much dry milk is needed to make 1 gal of regular milk? 1 gal of evaporated milk?
8. What is homogenization? pasteurization?
9. How can evaporated milk be whipped to a stable foam? How can dry milk be whipped to a stable foam?

CHAPTER 8

Vegetable Cookery

Outline

Goals

1. To discuss the standards, principles, and techniques required to produce good vegetables.
2. To indicate how proper flavor, color, and texture are obtained in vegetable cookery.
3. To classify different kinds of vegetables according to how they should be cooked.
4. To illustrate different cooking methods used to prepare good finished vegetables from different kinds of raw vegetables.
5. To list ways to preserve nutrients in vegetables.
6. To discuss how cereal products and stuffings (dressings) should be prepared.

INTRODUCTION

Good vegetables are sure to be served if the product purchased is good and if good preparation procedures are used. Quality depends to a great extent on characteristics easily destroyed by improper preparation or cooking. Cooking vegetables well takes skill and knowledge. The wide variety of vegetables is matched by the number of different ways they must be handled. Processing differences also change cooking requirements. Vegetable cooking includes some items that are not truely vegetables but are served in place of them, such as dressings, rice, macaroni, and cooked cereals.

Vegetables are an important part of the diet, and they must receive proper care, handling, and preparation if they are to preserve their healthful qualities. Vegetables contribute significant quantities of vitamins and minerals to the diet and are one of the main sources of fiber. Patrons want them not only for these reasons but because they are highly palatable and appetizing and because they contribute to the appearance of food on the plate.

STANDARDS

Cooked vegetables are judged on the basis of their texture, flavor, and appearance (including form and color). Their temperature at the time of service affects quality, too. A vegetable is usually not the dominant meal item, so it must be judged in relation to the other foods served with it. Vegetable flavors should be neither bland nor strong, but natural, sweet, pleasant, and free of any trace of rawness. Seasonings and sauces that mask natural flavors should be eschewed in favor of those that give mild contrasts and blend happily as a light, delicate complement to the vegetable. Texture requirements vary according to the vegetable. Some firmness is good in high-moisture vegetables such as carrots, string beans, and cabbage; cook them to a slight underdoneness. An overly soft, sloughy, or hard texture is undesirable. Starchy root vegetables, legumes, and cereals should be soft; fried vegetables may be crisp outside and soft inside. Potatoes can be mealy, but in other vegetables this texture is objectionable. Excessive wateriness, dryness, softness, crispness, hardness, woodiness, stringiness, and other poor textural qualities should be absent.

Form should be distinct, not messy or broken. Uniformity is often desirable. Vegetable firmness should show as a soft sheen. When dished, vegetables should be rounded, rather than flat or runny. Colors should be bright, lively, attractive, clear, and natural—not dull, pale, muddy, intensified, or false. Poor quality is often indicated by color loss.

PRINCIPLES

Cellulose and pectins (fiber) constitute most of the skeletal structure of vegetables (see fig. 8-1). Cooking softens them. The amount of cellulose varies according to the vegetable's type, age, and growing conditions. Spinach has less fiber than carrots; old vegetables have more fiber than young ones; and vegetables grown under good conditions are tenderer than those grown under adverse conditions. One part can be tougher

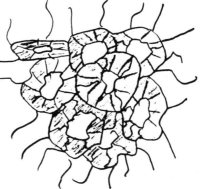

Branching filament of cellulose
chain

Large thin-walled parenchyma
cells of a pear

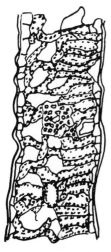

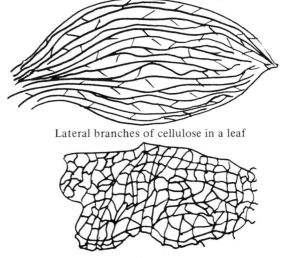

Lateral branches of cellulose in a leaf

Cross section of
spinach leaf

Cellulose network in a carrot

than another on the same vegetable, as in the case of stems and tips of broccoli or asparagus. We often cook the stems first, and then tip the vegetable over into the boiling water to cook the stems and tips completely; or we split or pare the stems to help speed cooking. Cutting vegetables on the bias (slant) or lengthwise cuts through more fiber, giving a tenderer product.

Sugar and calcium chloride strengthen cellulose; the latter gives firmness to pickles and canned vegetables. Alkalies, on the other hand, soften cellulose. Where water is hard (alkaline), boiled vegetables can easily become too soft. Adding a bit of acidity (in the form of cream of tartar or lemon juice) reduces the cooking water's alkalinity. Acids may bring about undesirable reactions in cooking, and they strengthen cellulose. Adding catsup and molasses to baked beans before the beans are softened extends the required cooking time because of the acid content of these foods (see fig. 8-2).

Cooking changes vegetable flavors; some people like a vegetable cooked but not raw, while other people may feel exactly the opposite way. Many today prefer their vegetables slightly undercooked. Vegetables contain salty, sweet, bitter, and acidic compounds, but their characteristic flavor comes mainly from aromatic esters or essential oils that are volatile (escape easily upon cooking). To avoid losing them, shorten cooking time. Fat or oil absorbs these esters, so sometimes 1 T oil per gallon of water is used to hold flavors in the cooking water. Some flavor loss may be desirable in strong-flavored vegetables; they may be cooked uncovered to allow flavors to escape. Most vegetable acids are also volatile. Acid destroys the green color in green vegetables and promotes the development of strong flavors in others during cooking. The mustardy, pungent flavor characteristic of the cabbage and turnip families comes largely from a glucoside called sinigrin. Heat favors its separation, and acids speed this process. The sharp flavor of the onion family comes from allyl sulfide. Cooking breaks it down and renders its flavor less pungent.

Vegetable freshness is an important quality factor. Sugars change rapidly to starch at temperatures above 50°F in corn, green peas, and the like. Freshness is also associated with the presence of glutamic acid. Corn loses 30 percent of its glutamic acid 24 hours after harvest, and fresh peas lose 25 percent. Refrigeration reduces its loss and the change of sugar to starch. Dehydration, oxidation, and poor handling may also contribute to a loss of freshness, nutrients, and quality.

Care is needed in preparing and cooking vegetables. Poor preparation techniques can lead to messy, poorly shaped vegetables that look unattractive and cook poorly. Hard boiling, excessive manipulation or stirring, and overcooking can produce a very unpleasant product. Cooking by means other than boiling often reduces movement and helps vegetables retain their form.

Vegetable color pigments are *anthocyanins* or *lycopenes* in red vegetables, *carotenes* in yellow or orange ones, *chlorophyll* in green ones, and *flavones* in white ones. Acids turn anthocyanins bright red, while alkalies turn them a dirty blue or purple. When red cabbage turns green, it is because the red pigments have turned blue and the white pigments have turned yellow. Iron combines easily with anthocyanins. Red cabbage or beets when cut with a steel knife or cooked in an iron pan may darken or turn a muddy brown. Iron salts in canned pineapple juice may combine with raspberry juice in a red punch to make a brownish red or muddy-looking punch. Anthocyanins also join with tannins to form a cloudy precipitate. Acid retards the reaction of iron with anthocyanins. Because

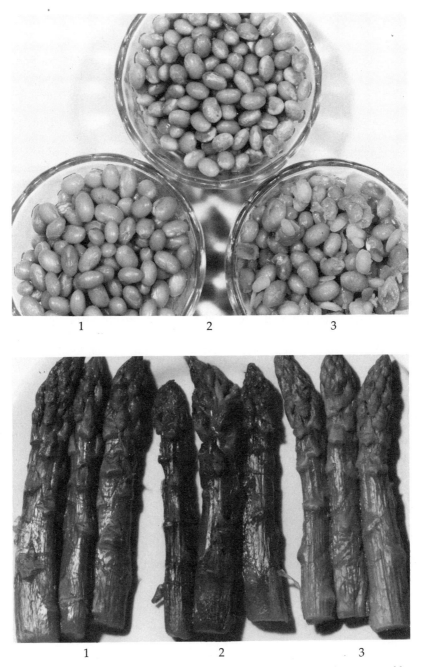

Figure 8-2. The effects of neutral, alkaline, and acidic cooking media on vegetables: (1) neutral; (2) alkaline; (3) acidic.

anthocyanins are water-soluble, they can be leached into water, leaving a pale vegetable behind.

Carotenes and lycopenes are closely related. Both are stable when exposed to heat, acids, and alkalies. Lycopenes are red pigments found in tomatoes; carotenes are yellow pigments found in carrots, squash, peaches, and cantaloupe. Oxidation destroys them, but they are not water-soluble. Carotenes make vitamin A in the body.

Chlorophyll (green pigment) is easily destroyed by heat or acid, but an alkaline medium preserves it. Chlorophyll is not water-soluble.

The white pigments, flavones, are white in an acid medium and yellow in an alkaline one. Onions can turn deep yellow if cooked in hard water. Other white vegetables may darken. Adding a bit of acid such as cream of tartar or vinegar quickly corrects the color change. Flavones are water-soluble and are unaffected by heat.

Many nutrients are concentrated under the vegetable's skin, and deep paring causes a large loss of nutrients. To reduce leaching loss, pared items should be soaked and cooked for as short a time as possible. Using an antioxidant dip so that vegetables do not have to be soaked reduces leaching loss, as does cooking by steaming, baking, or another method that uses little or no water. Vitamins such as ascorbic acid and thiamine are destroyed by heat. Soda and hard-water salts are not harmful to these nutrients, but as the concentration of the former increases, destruction of the latter becomes more rapid. Salt reduces the loss of ascorbic acid somewhat. Copper is harmful to ascorbic acid. Light destroy riboflavin, and oxidation destroys ascorbic acid.

The best method for preserving nutrients cannot always be used. For example, pressure-steaming reduces leaching but the higher temperature at which it operates harms heat-labile nutrients. Using lots of water yields a milder-flavored rutabaga but increases leaching loss. The best method is the one that gives the most flavorful and attractive product; usually, this is the most nutritious product, too. Little is gained when vegetables are cooked to retain all of their nutrients, only to end up rejected and uneaten.

Fresh, tender vegetables that receive proper care and are quickly used have a maximum chance of being made into good cooked vegetables. Corn-on-the-cob consumed a few hours after picking is far superior to corn that is 24 hours old. Fresh, tender spinach loses much of its excellence if stored. Cauliflower, artichokes, and broccoli are blossoms that must have tight buds to be of good quality. An old and fibrous beet, carrot, or other root vegetable is tough and unflavorful. Potatoes high in starch and low in sugar are good for baking, mashing, or french-frying, while these same qualities make them less desirable for salads, hash browns, or steamed potatoes. High-starch potatoes (ones containing at least 17 percent starch) have a specific gravity of 1.08 or more, whereas low-starch potatoes (ones containing at most 13 percent starch) have a specific gravity of 1.07 or less and are moist or waxy. Mature potatoes are higher in starch than new ones. Potatoes that are high in sugar or have been frozen streak or darken when fried. Store potatoes at temperatures above 50°F; if stored at lower temperatures, they develop sugar and lose starch. Sprouting potatoes are high in sugar.

Some fruits and vegetables tarnish easily because the tannins they contain oxidize. Soaking in water or dipping in an antioxidant stops discoloration. Dipping fruits or vegetables into citrus, pineapple, or other fruit juices retards tarnishing. Adding salt to water may help somewhat, but not much. Stainless steel or plastic tools can be used to cut items that tarnish easily, since these do not leave iron salts to combine with tannins and produce dark substances. Never use sodium sulfite as an antioxidant dip: asthmatics and others who are allergic to it can be seriously harmed by their reaction to it and may even die as a result.

Many vegetables contain starch. Corn, green peas, and some others contain a moderate amount, while potatoes, macaroni pastas, rice, dry beans, and others have much more. Cooking swells and gelatinizes the starch, giving a soft, tender product. Because starch imbibes water, high-starch products are cooked in a lot of water.

TECHNIQUES

PRE-PREPARATION

Table 8-1 lists recommended procedures for preparing fresh vegetables for cooking. Proper pre-preparation starts with receiving. Handle vegetables with care to prevent damage, move them to storage quickly, and use them soon.

Vegetables continue to live after harvest, but their quality diminishes rapidly as a result of the action of yeasts, bacteria, and other organisms, from chemical changes, from surface dehydration, from odor absorption, or from aging. Refrigeration retards many undesirable changes. Clean vegetables keep better, and many vegetables should be cleaned upon receipt. Soak to loosen soil; a bit of salt in the water helps accomplish this and also drives mites from the vegetables. Store clean, drained vegetables in covered units.

Good pre-preparation techniques can reduce vegetable waste. Crisping or freshening in cold water reduces wilting and produces a firm product that handles better. Limp root vegetables pare poorly. Presoaking in cold water firms them, reducing waste. Bruised parts of leaves should be trimmed and discarded. Use edible, clean vegetable trimmings for stocks. Woody stalks, tough stems, and other otherwise unusable parts can be cooked and pulped for use in cream soups, purées, and other dishes. Using proper tools and observing proper peeling times reduces loss. Selecting for even size gives more uniformly cooked products and should also be done for machine paring.

Most dried, dehydrated, or freeze-dried vegetables require some soaking before cooking. Use lukewarm or cool water containing 3 T salt per gallon. Do not use hot water unless the manufacturer recommends it.

TABLE 8-1. Procedures for preparing vegetables for cooking

Vegetable	Preparation procedures
Asparagus	Cut off tough or woody portion, $\frac{1}{2}$ in. above white portion. Scrub well; remove lower scales, as dirt or grit may be under them. Scrape lower portions. Clean and rinse thoroughly. Tips may be cut from ends. Toughest ends may be set aside for puréeing for soup.
Beans, snap	Use only young, tender beans that snap readily when bent to a 45° angle. Cut into 1-in. sections or French-cut lengthwise into strips. Rinse thoroughly. Beans cook more readily if cut lengthwise or at an angle instead of crosswise.
Beans, lima	Purchase fresh shelled beans or frozen beans.
Beets	Leave uncut 1 in. of steam and all of root. Trim and wash, scrubbing if necessary to remove soil. Beets may be machine-peeled, but a heavy loss of red pigment occurs when this is done.
Broccoli	Wash well, and cut off tough ends of stalks. Remove tough outer leaves. Clean and rinse thoroughly. Split ends of thick stalks, or cut ends from tops. Cut into $2 \times \frac{1}{2}$-in.-wide strips.
Brussels sprouts	Trim yellowed or coarse outer leaves. Soak in salted water $\frac{1}{2}$ hour, clean, and rinse.
Cabbage	Strip off wilted outer leaves, remove core, rinse thoroughly, and cut into sections or shred. For sectioning, coring is often omitted.
Carrots	Remove tops, if present. Pare in peeler. Less flavor loss occurs in cooking if carrots are sliced lengthwise, since this avoids cutting across the fibrovascular structure (juice-retaining fibers).
Corn-on-the-cob	Strip husks, and remove silk. Trim any inedible portions. Keep cold.
Onions	Trim. Peel outer skins with paring knife. Rinse. Chop, slice, or prepare as required.
Parsnips	Peel. Trim and rinse. Slice lengthwise to avoid cutting fibrovascular bundles.
Peas, green	Shell. Rinse in colander in cold water.
Potatoes, Irish	Scrub well, if for baking; pare others.
Potatoes, sweet	Best cooked in skins and then pared, but may be machined-pared if uniform in size and not long and thin. Machine-paring loss may be high with some shapes. Wash before cooking in skins.
Rutabagas or Turnips	Pare in peeler. Trim and rinse thoroughly. Slice into slices $\frac{1}{2}$ in. thick or dice into $\frac{1}{2}$-in. cubes.
Spinach	Remove tough stems, wilted leaves, and roots. Wash in large quantity of water, lifting spinach up and down to loosen dirt. Lift spinach from water and drain well. Continue washing until no evidence of soil or grit shows. The water clinging to the leaves of fresh spinach may be sufficient to cook it in a steam-jacketed kettle.
Squash, summer	Trim ends. Rinse. Cut into slices approximately $\frac{1}{4}$ in. thick or into bite-size pieces.
Squash, winter	Cut into pieces of convenient size. Remove seeds and fiber.

NOTE: Vegetables that must be held for long periods before cooking should, after pre-preparation, be placed into containers or polyethylene bags and held under refrigeration.

Soaking is usually done for 20 to 30 minutes but the yield is higher if soaking occurs overnight. Weigh rather than measure. High-moisture dried vegetables require 2 gal water for 1 lb vegetables, and starchy ones such as potatoes, rutabagas or turnips require 1 gal water for 1 lb. Do not discard the soaking water; use it for cooking the vegetable. Follow the purveyor's directions. Dry beans, split peas, and other legumes cook quicker if presoaked. Sort, wash, drain, and cover with water; then soak for 2 to 6 hours. Washing, soaking, and cooking in a steam-jacketed kettle saves labor, since all work takes place in one unit.

Blanching vegetables to remove their skins facilitates the work. Heat the water to boiling, and drop items into the water, turning them so that all areas are blanched. Do not leave them in too long. Drop into cold water and remove skins. As rapidly as possible, treat items that tarnish easily.

The labor cost of separating potatoes into small, medium, and large sizes is repaid in food savings and quality. Large potatoes can be used for baking or for french-fry strips. Paring waste increases when different-sized, crooked, or knobby items are used. After paring, all peel and blemishes must be removed. Mold spots show as dark spots on deep-fried potatoes. Pare only long enough to remove peels; any remaining portions needing to be trimmed can be processed after paring. It is common today to serve french-fried, fried, and other styles of potatoes in their skins.

Potato strips for deep-frying are 3 to 4 in. long and $\frac{3}{8}$ to $\frac{1}{2}$ in. thick. Shoestrings are $\frac{1}{4}$ to $\frac{1}{8}$ in. thick, and juliennes are closer to $\frac{1}{4}$ in. thick. The length of both should be 2 to $2\frac{1}{2}$ in. Whether or not soaking reduces the tendency of potatoes to stick together during frying, it may be required to give potato chips an even color. Soft, flabby strips do not fry well, so they may be presoaked under refrigeration to crisp them up. Wafered or waffle potatoes are made with a device that cuts across the width of the whole potato, giving a round slice with tiny waffled holes. Parisienne ball potatoes are cut from raw, pared potatoes with a round melon-ball cutter. Soufflé potatoes are made by cutting crisp, high-quality, mature potatoes into slices about $2\frac{1}{2}$ in. long, $1\frac{1}{4}$ in. wide and $\frac{1}{8}$ to $\frac{3}{16}$ in. thick. All pieces should be even and of the same size; crisp them in ice water for 30 minutes. Browned or rissolé potatoes are usually selected on the basis of one potato to a portion, about 5 oz pared. Brown them well in fat, and bake. French-fry strips are often dipped into an antioxidant, put into polyethylene wraps, and stored at a temperature of from 32° to 40°F. Prepare only the amount of strips needed in a 24-hour period. Many operations today purchase their potatoes and other vegetables already prepared and ready for cooking.

COOKING CONSIDERATIONS

Planning

The fragile quality of vegetables makes continuous batch-cooking desirable. With proper planning, labor need not be increased by batch-cooking. Regular steamers, steam-jacketed kettles, or pots on the range top can be used, but work is facilitated if high-pressure steamers or tilt steam-jacketed kettles, (in 1-qt to 4-qt sizes) are used. These can be situated directly behind service areas to shorten transport. Perforated, stainless steel inserts that can be set into the kettle facilitate introduction and removal of foods to be cooked. On steamers, a timer set to operate auto-matically exhausts steam and guards against overcooking. Vegetables may remain in the open chamber for a few minutes without loss in quality.

Production schedules should list the meal, the vegetable, the batch quantity, the total amount needed, the time required, and the service area to which the vegetable is to be sent (if several exist). Time is needed for loading, cooking, removing, and sending to service. Most vegetables should be served no later than 20 to 30 minutes after cooking. Serve all of a batch before going to a new one, do not mix batches. Experience can guide the proper timing of batch starts, and the cook in charge should be responsible for this. Some operations use the rule that a new batch is started when half the preceding batch is served. Cook only to tender-ness, with some resistance at the center. Such vegetables are more nutri-tious, have a brighter color, and are more flavorful. Test the doneness of large vegetables by piercing then with the tip of a sharp knife or long-tined fork. Smaller vegetables may be pressed between the thumb and forefinger or pressed against the container side with a spoon.

Canned Vegetables

Careless preparation of canned vegetables is undoubtedly responsible for much of the criticism directed at institutionally prepared vegetables. Just warming them does not increase their acceptability. String beans deli-cately seasoned with crisp bacon bits, peas lightly flavored with mint leaves, succulent kernel corn bright in contrast to bits of pimiento and green pepper, sauerkraut simmered with juniper berries, and crisp crack-lings sprinkled over succotash present examples of how to increase the interest and acceptability of standard canned fare. Use a light hand with seasonings. Canned vegetables are already cooked and require only sea-soning and heating in about half of their own liquor for service. Heat as close to service as possible. Botulinum toxin is destroyed in canned vege-tables if they are heated above 190°F for 10 minutes or more, but beets, spinach, and other nonacidic foods are frequently heated for 20 to 30 minutes.

The drained weight of many canned vegetables is about 65 percent of the net weight. A No. 10 can gives 20 to 25 3-oz portions of drained vegetables or 35 3-oz portions of vegetables that are not drained, such as cream-style corn.

Frozen Vegetables

To cook frozen vegetables, simply break them into chunks and drop them (still frozen) into boiling salted water (see fig. 8-3). Use 1 to 2 T salt per gallon of water. Corn-on-the-cob and some leafy greens cook better if thawed, especially if they are to be steamed. Cooking time for frozen vegetables is shorter than for fresh vegetables because the blanching they receive prior to being frozen partially cooks them. Dehydro-frozen vege-tables have had about 50 percent of their moisture removed, and this

Figure 8-3. Break mild-flavored, high-moisture frozen vegetables into chunks and drop into boiling, salted water. Bring the contents to a boil and cook rapidly until tender. Cook in quantities of about 5 lb per batch.

must be replaced in cooking; thus, more water than normal is required in cooking them. Follow the manufacturer's instructions for cooking its frozen products.

Dried Vegetables

After soaking, succulent dried vegetables are cooked similarly to fresh ones. Simmer to encourage plumping. Cooking time is often slightly less for dried vegetables than for fresh ones. Bring dry legumes to a boil, and then drop the heat to allow simmering. Cook covered to preserve heat. Use from 2 to 3 T salt per gallon of water.

COOKING METHODS

Vegetables can be cooked by boiling, steaming, baking, oven-roasting, deep-frying, sautéing, or broiling. The proper method to use depends on the final product desired, plus whether the product is mild- or strong-flavored, high or low in moisture, and high or low in starch. Table 8-2 identifies the cooking times for various vegetables by several cooking methods. For the most part, the discussion in this section is directed at the cooking of fresh vegetables; however, these methods also apply to other types.

Vegetable Classification for Cooking

Vegetables are usually separated into the following four classes for cooking:

1. High moisture, mild flavor: celery, spinach, summer squash
2. High moisture, strong flavor: cabbage, turnip, onion
3. Moist and starchy: Irish potatoes, sweet potatoes, parsnips
4. Dry and starchy: dry legumes, macaroni products, rice, cereals

Boiling

Boil mild-flavored, high-moisture vegetables by dropping them into boiling water, covering the pot, and bringing it back to a boil as fast as possible, removing the cover immediately after boiling starts again. Use $\frac{3}{4}$ gal water, 3 T salt, and 2 T salad oil for every 5 lb EP vegetables (twenty-five 3-oz portions). Add about $\frac{1}{4}$ to $\frac{1}{2}$ c sugar, if desired. After the cover is off for 3 to 5 minutes, put it back, if desired, and cook slowly. Send immediately to service. It is common to use only enough water to achieve boiling; some items such as carrots can be cooked covered in a very heavy pot without any water. This method reduces the extent of nutrient losses due to leaching. It has been shown, however, that using a large quantity of boiling salted water, adding the vegetables, and covering them until boiling starts shortens cooking time; therefore, nutrient losses are about the same as when vegetables are cooked in only a small amount of water.

In quantity preparation, vegetables may have to be cooked in advance. If this must be done, boil the vegetables to just on the verge of doneness; then drain off the cooking water, saving some of it for use in reheating the vegetables. Plunge the vegetables immediately into cold water to stop them from cooking. Then drain the vegetables well, place them in a covered container, and store the container under refrigeration. If the vegetables are leafy greens, press out the excess water after blanching, place them in about 1-lb mounds in a pan, cover the pan, and store it under refrigeration. To serve any vegetable handled in this way, reheat some of the cooking water, add the vegetable, season, heat as quickly as possible, and serve. Heat only the quantity that can be used in a short period. This method retains nutrients and quality better than does holding a large batch for service.

Strong-flavored, high-moisture vegetables are best boiled to reduce flavor. The best procedure is to cook them. If they must be cooked ahead, boil and then blanch them, as described previously. Avoid holding vegetables of the cabbage and turnip families at high heat. Use 1¼ gal water and 3 T salt per 5 lb EP of vegetables; this yields twenty-five 3-oz portions. Add the vegetables to rapidly boiling water, and cover until boiling starts again. Removing the cover during cooking allows volatile acids to escape. If retained, these acids help develop strong flavors. Old vegetables and vegetables stored for a long time are stronger in flavor than young and briefly stored vegetables. Cutting into small pieces increases surface area, permitting strong flavors to be more easily lost into the cooking water, and also shortens cooking time. Members of the onion family should be cooked longer to dissipate pungent flavors from allyl sulfide. Fine division is also recommended to help break down pungent flavors. Onions are often sautéed or precooked in some other way to give a milder flavor in sauces, dressings, and the like. We may also add these vegetables early to stews, soups, and other foods, so they cook longer and lose some of their pungent flavors.

Moist, starchy vegetables such as potatoes are best steamed. To boil, drop them into boiling salted water (about 3 T salt to 1 gal water). Cover and gently boil. Drain well, and serve as soon as possible. Do not hold under water; this would create a soggy product.

Dry, starchy vegetables such as dry beans and other legumes are presoaked in 1½ gal salted water (3 T salt to 1 gal water) for every 5 lb legumes; 11 lb serves about 100 6-oz portions. After soaking, bring the legumes to a boil, cover, and cook gently until tender when pressed with a spoon on the kettle side or between the fingers. Breaking of the skin indicates doneness or perhaps overdoneness. Add no acid until legumes are fully cooked. Cooking time varies; lima beans and split peas may cook in less than 1 hour; others may take 3 hours.

Drop macaroni products, rice, and other cereals into boiling salted water, stirring while adding. Use 2 T salt and 1 gal water to 1 lb product. Cover until boiling begins; then stir, re-cover, and cook until tender. (A small amount of salad oil mixed into rice before moistening helps to prevent it from sticking together. For added flavor, lightly sauté rice in oil before boiling.) Test doneness by pressing with a fork or spoon against the kettle side or between the fingers. If it breaks cleanly and easily, it is done. Do not overcook. Blanch immediately. Macaroni products should be cooked until they are tender but still have some chew or resistance left—a condition known as *al dènte* ("to the tooth"). Rice should be tender but not too soft.

Another method for cooking dry starchy items is to use 3 qt of water and 2 T salt with 1 lb product. Bring the water to boiling, and stir it slowly while adding the product. Then cover, and remove from direct heat (if a steam-jacketed kettle is used, turn off the heat). Let stand 10 minutes or until the product is tender. Drain and blanch. Heavy, thick-walled macaroni products cannot be cooked this way, but thin-walled ones can.

TABLE 8-2. Cooking times and quantities required in vegetable preparation

Vegetable	Cooking times (minutes)					Approx. prep. time for 100 portions (minutes)	Quantity per 100 3-oz portions	
	Boiling	Steaming			Baking			
		Free vent	15 lb psi	5 lb psi			AP (lb)	EP (lb)
Artichoke, French, whole, fresh	30–45		10–12	20–25		30	56	$8\frac{1}{3}$ doz
Artichoke, Jerusalem, whole	25–35	35			30–60	40	25	18
Asparagus, whole or butts, fresh	9–15	10–16	$1–1\frac{1}{2}$	8–10		85	38	25
Asparagus, tips, fresh*	7–9	8–12	$\frac{1}{2}–1\frac{1}{2}$	6–8			20	20
Beans, lima, green, fresh	15–25	20–30	1–2	10–15		120	48	20
Beans, lima, green, frozen	6–12	8–15	$1–1\frac{1}{2}$	8–12			20	20
Beans, lima, dry	60–150	60–150	15–25	20–30			6	6
Beans, snap, cut, fresh	15–25	20–30	$2–3\frac{1}{2}$	20–30		60	24	20
Beans, snap, Frenched, fresh	10–20	15–25	$1–2\frac{1}{2}$	18–25		75	24	20
Beans, snap, frozen, cut	8–10		$2–3\frac{1}{2}$	15–20			20	20
Beans, snap, frozen, Frenched	5–10		1–2	12–18			20	20
Beans, dry, navy or kidney	60–150	60–150	20–35	25–35			$5\frac{1}{2}–6$	$5\frac{1}{2}–6$
Beets, new, whole, medium, fresh	30–45	40–60	5–10	40–50	40–60	15	25 (topped)	20
Beets, old, whole, medium, fresh	45–90	50–90	10–18	60–75	50–75	15	26 (topped)	20
Broccoli, cut or split, fresh	7–12	12–18	1–3	7–10			35	22
Broccoli, cut or split, frozen	5–8	10–15	1–2	4–6			20	20
Brussels sprouts, whole, fresh	10–15	10–20	$1\frac{1}{2}–3$	10–12		30	24	20
Brussels sprouts, whole, frozen	4–9	8–15	1–3	8–10			20	20
Cabbage, shredded, fresh	6–10	6–10	$\frac{1}{2}–1\frac{1}{2}$	5–10			25	20
Cabbage, quartered, fresh	8–15	15	$1\frac{1}{2}–3$	8–12			25	20
Carrots, whole, fresh	15–25	20–30	2–5	15–20	35–45	30	26 (topped)	20
Carrots, sliced, fresh	10–20	15–25	$1\frac{1}{2}–4$	12–15	30–40		26 (topped)	20
Carrots, sliced, frozen	10–20	15–25	$1\frac{1}{2}–4$	10–12			20	20
Cauliflower, whole, fresh	10–25	15–25	10	15			50–60	26
Cauliflower, broken up	8–12	8–12	2–3	8–10			50–60	26
Cauliflower, frozen	4–8	6–10	$1\frac{1}{2}–2\frac{1}{2}$	6–8			20	20
Celery, cut up, fresh	6–15	8–20	2–3	10–12			27	20
Corn-on-the-cob*, fresh	5–15	10–15	3–4	8–10	30 (in husks)	30	50–75	$8\frac{1}{3}$ doz
Corn-on-the-cob, frozen	5–8	8–12	2–3	6–8			$8\frac{1}{3}$ doz	$8\frac{1}{3}$ doz
Corn, kernel, frozen	2–3		$\frac{1}{2}–1$	2–3			20	20
Eggplant, sliced	10–18	10–20					26	20

Greens

(Greens in quantity are difficult to steam because of packing.)

Beet, fresh	3–10					33	20
Beet, frozen	3–10					20	20
Chard, fresh	8–15					27	20
Dandelion, fresh	10–20					35	20
Kale, fresh	10–20					27	20
Mustard, fresh	20–30					32	20
Mustard, frozen	8–15					20	20
Turnip, fresh	10–30					27	21
Kohlrabi, sliced	15–20	25	4–5	15–25		35	20
Mixed vegetables, frozen	10–20	15–25	1–2	8–15		20	18
Okra, sliced, fresh	10–20	20	2–4	10–18		23	22
Onions, small, whole or cut	15–25	25–35	3–5	15–20	50–60	25	22
Onions, large, whole	30–35	35–40	5–8	25–30	30–45	25	21
Parsnips, whole, fresh	20–40	30–45	8–10	15–20		24	20
Parsnips, quartered, fresh	15–30	25–40	4–8	12–18	100	24	20
Peas, green, fresh	6–8	10	1	4–5		53	20
Peas, green, frozen	4–7	8	1	3–4		20	20
Peas, dry, split	90–120					5	6¼ gal (soup)
Potatoes, Irish, whole, fresh	25–40	30–45	9–15	20–25	45–60	39	28
Potatoes, Irish, quartered, fresh	20–25	30–40	4–12	18–22		39	28
Potatoes, Irish, diced, fresh	10–15		5	10		39	28
Potatoes, sweet, whole, fresh	25–35	30–35	5–8	20–25	30–45	35	26
Potatoes, sweet, quartered, fresh	15–25	25–30	6			35	26
Rutabagas, diced ½ in, fresh	20–30	35–40	5–8	15–25		32	28
Rutabagas, sliced ½ in, fresh	15–25	25–35	4–7	15–20	20	32	28
Spinach, fresh	3–10	5–12				31	26
Spinach, frozen	1–4	2–6				20	20
Squash, hubbard, pieces	20–30	25–40	6–12	15–20	40–60	46	32
Squash, summer, sliced	10–15	15–20	1½–3	8–12	30	24	20
Tomatoes, fresh	7–15		½–3	5	15–20	23	22
Turnips, whole, fresh	20–30	20–25	8–10	10–15		25 (topped)	22
Turnips, sliced or diced, fresh	15–20	20–25	1½–2	10		25 (topped)	22

Boiling time is calculated from the time water comes to boil after the vegetable has been added; corn-on-the-cob is sometimes placed into cold water, brought to a boil, and then sent to service.

Steaming free vent times must be increased at higher altitudes. Steam time will depend on type of pan; fill solid pans less full; solid pans increase steaming time over perforated pans. Thaw frozen corn-on-the-cob before cooking it.

* Reduce times slightly for frozen tips.

Rice is cooked successfully by boiling, steaming, or baking. All methods require, by measure, two parts water to one part rice. Add the water and salt to the rice. To boil, cover the pot tightly, and bring it to a boil. Then stir, and replace the cover tightly. Cook very slowly for about 30 minutes. During the last 10 minutes, uncover the pot so that the rice steams dry, leaving the grains light and separate. If the rice absorbs all the water but is still dry and hard, add more water. Too much water yields soft, mushy rice. A steam-jacketed kettle or heavy pot can be used for this method. For steaming, place the rice in a covered container, set this into the steamer, and steam until done (about 25 minutes). To bake, place the rice in a pan, cover, and put into the oven. When cooking starts, stir once, re-cover, and bake until the rice is done. Some people cook rice in plenty of water (1 gal water to 1 lb rice), blanch it in cold water, and then reheat it.

Add breakfast cereals to boiling salted water. Stir well during the addition, continuing until some thickening is apparent. Then reduce to a simmer, and cook covered until the cereal reaches proper thickness and no taste of raw starch remains. The more a cereal is stirred during thickening, the more slick and pasty it becomes. Therefore, avoid stirring once thickening starts. Fine cereal that might lump can be mixed with a part of the cooking water and then added to the remainder as a slurry. Coarser cereals may be added slowly. For 100 5-oz portions, use 4 gal water, $\frac{1}{4}$ and $\frac{1}{3}$ c salt, and 4 lb fine-grained cereal (cornmeal, grits, or farina) or 5 lb coarse-grained cereal (oatmeal or cracked wheat). For best quality, cook as soon before service as possible; holding harms quality.

Steaming

Many vegetables steam well under proper cooking conditions (see fig. 8-4). Others, however, do not. Normally, if the cooking directions indicate that the vegetable should be placed in water in a pan for steaming, the vegetable does not respond well to steaming and instead should be boiled. Small, high-pressure units are often used for batch-cooking, but compartment steamers are commonly used for large quantities. Most vegetables are cooked in perforated pans to allow steam to circulate freely around them. Vegetables that leave some space between pieces steam much better than those that do not. Fresh peas or spinach, for instance, cook thoroughly on the outside but not on the interior of the pack, because steam cannot infiltrate the pack. Moist, starchy vegetables steam well. Use care in cooking with steam because the higher temperature involved can quickly lead to overcooking. Table 8-3 summarizes steaming procedures.

Baking

Baking consists of roasting in an oven with dry heat. Moist, starchy vegetables such as Irish potatoes, sweet potatoes, winter squash, and parsnips bake well. A few high-moisture vegetables such as tomatoes may also be baked. In the baking process, vegetables often are parboiled

Figure 8-4. Mild-flavored, high-moisture vegetables may be steamed if they are not packed too deeply into pans.

TABLE 8-3. Recommended practices for steaming vegetables

Vegetable	Recommended procedure at 6 psi
Asparagus	Lay flat in counter pans, 2 in. deep; add small quantity of warm salted water. Steam until stalks are tender. If desired, cut off tips, sizing end pieces to equal length of tips. Steam ends 1 minute, add tips, and steam until tips and ends are soft and done.
Beans, dry	Soak 2 to 6 hours. Cover with salted water in a solid basket, and steam until skins just crack.
Beans, lima, fresh	Place in a solid basket to a depth of not more than 3 in. Add small quantity of salted water. Steam until tender.
Beans, snap	Place in a flat, perforated basket up to $2\frac{1}{2}$ in. deep. Steam until tender. For large quantities, half-fill a tall, narrow, solid basket together with a small quantity of salted water. Avoid overcrowding. Steam until tender.
Beets	Top only. Steam in a perforated basket. Cool, and remove skins after steaming.
Broccoli	Lay flat in counter pans with enough warm salted water to cover stalks. Steam only until tender. Split heavy or thick stalks. Avoid overcooking to retain color.
Brussels sprouts	Place in a counter pan about 1 in. or one layer deep. To shorten cooking time, stem ends may be split slightly.
Cabbage	Place in a half-filled flat, solid basket, together with a small quantity of warm salted water.
Carrots	Steam in a perforated basket, half full.

continued

TABLE 8-3. Recommended practices for steaming vegetables (*continued*)

Vegetable	Recommended procedure at 6 psi
Cauliflower	Steam in a flat, perforated basket, one-quarter full. Should be tender when cooked, with stems having waxy appearance, but should possess firm texture, maintaining original form characteristics.
Cereals	For each 4 lb of the flaked or coarse type, use 4 gal water and $\frac{1}{4}$ cup salt. Bring water to boil, and add cereal. Stir to blend thoroughly. Use 5 lb of fine granular cereal to 4 gal water and $\frac{1}{3}$ cup salt. Steam until done.
Corn-on-the-cob	Thaw frozen corn-on-the-cob before steaming. Use about 25 ears per perforated basket. Steam. Doneness is indicated when kernels are pierced with a fork and no milk comes out.
Corn, kernel	Place in a counter pan with a small quantity of warm salted water.
Dumplings	Drop on greased baking pans, separated sufficiently to allow for expansion. Steam for 15 minutes.
Macaroni products	Bring salted water to boil in a solid basket. Add macaroni product, 1 lb to 1 gal water, stirring to separate for 2 minutes. Steam for 12 to 15 minutes.
Onion	Steam mild onions in a perforated basket, one-third full. Strong, old onions should be steamed in a solid basket with a small quantity of warm salted water.
Parsnips	Place in perforated basket, one-quarter full; steam only until tender.
Peas, green	Place in counter pans without water to a depth of not over 2 in. If necessary, midway through cooking, pressure may be released and peas stirred.
Potatoes, Irish	Steam in a perforated basket, three-quarters full. May be partially steamed in skins and baked. Steaming french fries to a partially done stage is also satisfactory.
Potatoes, sweet	Steam in a perforated basket, three-quarters full, with skins on. Cool and peel. May also be partially steamed and then baked.
Rice	Wash rice well. Use approximately 2 qt salted water per 1 qt washed rice. Bring this water to boil in a solid basket. Add rice, stirring to separate, for 2 minutes. Cook until tender. Rinse with hot water, and steam without water until grains are tender and separated.
Rutabaga	Steam in a perforated basket, half full. Old rutabagas should be steamed in a solid basket, covered with warm salted water.
Spinach	Steam in small quantity until almost cooked in a solid basket containing some warm salted water. Remove and stir. Complete cooking. Heat retained in spinach just before doneness may be used to complete cooking without further external heat.
Squash, summer	Steam in a perforated basket until soft. Do not place more than 2 in. deep.
Squash, winter	Place in a perforated basket, half full, and steam.
Turnips	Place in perforated basket, half full, packed loosely. Place old turnips in a solid basket with some salted water, and steam.

NOTE: Where salted water is required, use $2\frac{1}{2}$ to 2 T salt per gallon of water.

or steamed and then finished in an oven. This reduces baking time and is an excellent method for cooking winter squash, sweet potatoes, and parsnips; Irish potatoes, however, usually are best when baked without such precooking. Combination dishes containing vegetables such as turnip soufflé, spinach timbale, or corn pudding are commonly baked. Baked beans, au gratin potatoes, zucchini in tomato sauce, and glazed onions or carrots are braised in an oven or are covered with some moisture before baking. At times, vegetables are baked with meat, such as a roast; if so, they are added near the end of the roasting period.

Deep-frying

Deep-frying imparts a nutty flavor and a crisp outer texture to vegetables. Potatoes and some other vegetables deep-fry well. Some may be breaded or dipped into a batter. Partial cooking by boiling or steaming, followed by finishing in deep fat is also done. Different types of vegetable fritters are popular. Table 8-4 summarizes deep-frying procedures.

Dry potato strips before deep-frying. If orders are sporadic and demand is light, use the one-operation method for cooking $\frac{1}{2}$-in.-thick potato strips at 375°F in about 7 minutes. If volume is high and a large amount is produced, the two-operation method is used. Blanch the potatoes at 375°F until they are tender but not colored. Then later, for service, fry for about 2 minutes at 350° to 380°F. The potatoes, after being blanched, can be held refrigerated for up to two days, and even longer if frozen. Potatoes that begin at room temperature or have been slightly warmed in an oven cook more quickly. Another approach is to preblanch in a steamer until partially done, and then fry. Commercially blanched frozen strips are commonly used in foodservices. Potatoes smaller than $\frac{1}{2}$ in. thick are fried at 360° to 380°F for 4 to 6 minutes to give a crisp product with a soft center. If complete crispness is desired, as in shoestrings, fry for 6 to 9 minutes in 335°F to 340°F fat until golden brown. If still not crisp, drain the strips, raise the temperature to 375°F, and crisp for a few seconds. These potatoes keep for a week if unsalted and held in a cool place in an airtight container.

Soak potatoes to be used as soufflé potatoes for at least 30 minutes in ice water; dry well, and cook for 4 to 5 minutes in 275°F fat, keeping the potatoes separate. Drain well and chill for at least 5 minutes. Raise the temperature of the fat to 400° to 425°F (this requires good fat), place a few potatoes into the basket, and lower them into the fat. The potatoes puff, become crisp, and acquire a golden-brown color. Remove, drain, and serve at once. Sweet potatoes and some other starchy vegetables are also sometimes souffléed.

Sautéing

Grilling, pan-frying, or sautéing of cooked or raw vegetables is common, especially for short orders. Hash browns, potatoes lyonnaise, and many other potato dishes are sautéed. Mushrooms, string beans with bacon, breaded tomato slices, onions, parsnips, squash, shredded cabbage, and other items may be sautéed. Pan-braising may be done in a pan, steam-jacketed kettle, or oven. Shredded, diced, or thinly sliced vegetables high in moisture are placed into a skillet with 1 T of oil, butter, or margarine, 1 t of salt, and 2 T of water per quart of vegetables. The container is covered tightly and allowed to steam or braise, with occasional stirring. Small quantities should be prepared.

TABLE 8-4. Recommended practices for deep-frying vegetables

Vegetable	Quantity per 100 portions (lb EP)	Temperature of fat (°F)	Frying time (min)	Procedure
Asparagus	24	360	1–3	Boil until almost done; cool; dip into batter, and fry until golden brown.
Carrots or Parsnips	24	360	3–5	Boil or steam until almost done; cut lengthwise into quarters; batter or bread, and fry.
Cauliflower	20	360	1–3	Partially steam or boil. Bread or batter, and fry.
Corn-on-the-cob	100 ears	350	3–5	Husk ears and remove silk; fry in fat, turning frequently. If frozen corn is used, be sure it is thawed before use; frozen corn is not as satisfactory as fresh.
Cucumbers	35	360	3–5	Wash only. Cut into quarters and cut these quarters lengthwise into halves. Batter or bread, and fry.
Dill pickles	50 pickles	350	3–5	Split pickles in half lengthwise. Batter or bread, and fry.
Eggplant	16	370	5–8	Do not pare. Cut into slices $\frac{1}{2}$ in. thick or cut into $\frac{1}{2}$-in. strips. Soak in salted water, $\frac{1}{4}$ cup salt per gallon for 1 hour. Batter or bread, and fry.
Onions	16	375	2–3	Cut peeled onions into rings $\frac{1}{2}$ in. thick. Separate into individual rings. Dip into evaporated milk and then into flour, repeating until well-coated, or dip into batter. Fry.
Potatoes, Irish (rissolé)	24	360	5–8	Steam or boil until almost done, if desired. Brown in fat. Finish baking in oven. If not partially cooked before browning, extend baking time.
Potatoes, Irish (french-fried)	24	375	7	See text.
Potatoes, sweet	24	360	5–8	Parboil or steam $\frac{1}{4}$-in. sticks or slices; then deep-fry.
Squash, winter	24	360	5–8	Parboil or steam pieces $\frac{1}{2}$ in. thick; then deep-fry.
Tomatoes	20	360	2–4	Slice $\frac{1}{2}$ in. thick, dip into batter or bread, and fry.
Zucchini	16	360	3–5	Dip into batter or bread, and fry.

Stir-frying is becoming common. This is a method of adding succulent vegetables to very hot fat in a pan, and frying them furiously for only 1 or 2 minutes. The vegetables are only partially done; after first frying them in fat, the cook may add some moisture and thickening, afterward cooking the vegetables only until thickening occurs. The moisture may be chicken stock, water, or other stock—perhaps rice wine or dry sherry and soy sauce.

Oven-roasting

Oven-roasting (also called *ovenizing*) produces results similar to sautéing, but different equipment is used. Vegetables are placed onto well-greased pans and put into a hot oven, where they fry. They are stirred frequently. Some vegetables can be parboiled or steamed and then finished with a brief baking in a well-greased roasting pan. Rissolé potatoes are frequently parboiled or steamed, browned in deep fat, and then browned well in an oven.

Broiling

Raw tomato slices broil well if cut about 1 in. thick, brushed with oil, and broiled at a distance of about 4 in. from the heat. They should be turned only once. Unpeeled eggplant may be sliced about $\frac{1}{2}$ to 1 in. thick, soaked in salt water for an hour, parboiled, and then spread with mayonnaise and broiled. Other items may be partially parboiled or steamed and then broiled—including mushrooms, zucchini, onion slices, carrots, and parsnips. Some almost-cooked vegetables are glazed under a broiler, while some broiled vegetables are braised in an oven and given only a last-minute finish under the broiler.

STUFFINGS OR DRESSINGS

Bread dressings are often served in place of a moist starchy vegetable or cereal. Such a dressing (*panada*) should blend with the main dish or meat, complementing its flavor. Strong meats should have mild dressings; and rich meats, lean dressings. Dry dressings may be desirable when a moist, rich sauce or gravy is served with the meal. A moist dressing is best if the meat is dry. With a 2- to 3-oz meat portion, 4 oz dressing is adequate and about 2 oz is enough to stuff a pork chop or serve with a heavier meat portion. Use 3, 4, or 5 lb stuffing, respectively, for a 10-, 15-, or over-15-lb bird (ready-to-cook weight), or 10 oz ($1\frac{1}{4}$ c) dressing for each 1 lb of ready-to-cook bird.

Bread dressing is the most popular, but rice and other cereals can be used (see fig. 8-5). Cornbread dressing is popular with some poultry. Almonds, chestnuts, apples, cranberries, crabmeat, shrimp, oysters, giblets, or sausage may be added. For each 12 lb of dressing, use the following: 3 c chopped or sliced almonds or chestnuts; 1 qt chopped apples; 1 qt ground cranberries with $\frac{1}{4}$ c sugar (omitting onion and poultry seasonings); 1 lb crab, shrimp, or oysters, with 2 eggs; 1 qt cooked chopped giblets; or 2 lb sausage. Table 8-5 presents a bread stuffing guide for poultry of different weights.

Refrigerate dressings immediately after preparing them, unless they are to be baked at once. At no time—either before or after baking—allow dressings to stand at temperatures between 40° and 125°F for several hours. Place only chilled dressings into chilled birds, and bake at once.

(a)

(b)

(c)

(d)

(e)

Figure 8-5. (a) For a moistened dressing, wet the bread and then press out the excess moisture with the palms of the hands. (b) A dry dressing is made with firm, fresh bread. (c) To either type of bread, add sautéed vegetables, salt, and seasonings. Mix well. (d) Spread into a baking pan. Plastic gloves prevents hands from contaminating the dressing with bacteria. (e) Never let dressings stand at room temperature. Always cover and refrigerate.

Remove dressings from cooked birds before refrigerating. It is best to bake the birds separately and to dish the dressing with the meat or poultry at service. Bake in pans with the dressing about 2 in. deep. Hot dressings should be spread out in shallow pans to cool before being stored under refrigeration. After cooling the dressing, cover it. Reheat

TABLE 8-5. Bread stuffing guide

	Poultry weight (ready-to-cook)				
Stuffing ingredients	*4 lbs*	*6 lbs*	*10 lbs*	*12 lbs*	*20 lbs*
Shortening	$\frac{1}{4}$ cup	$\frac{1}{3}$ cup	$\frac{1}{2}$ cup	$\frac{2}{3}$ cup	1 cup
Chopped onion	$\frac{1}{2}$ cup	$\frac{2}{3}$ cup	1 cup	$1\frac{1}{3}$ cups	2 cups
Chopped celery	$\frac{1}{2}$ cup	$\frac{2}{3}$ cup	1 cup	$1\frac{1}{3}$ cups	2 cups
Fresh enriched bread: $\frac{1}{2}$-in. cubes or number of $\frac{5}{8}$-in. slices	6 cups or 6	9 cups or 9	15 cups or 15	$1\frac{1}{8}$ gal or 18	$1\frac{7}{8}$ gal or 30
Salt	$\frac{2}{3}$ t	1 t	$1\frac{1}{2}$ t	2 t	1 T
Pepper	dash	$\frac{1}{8}$ t	$\frac{1}{4}$ t	$\frac{1}{4}$ t	$\frac{1}{2}$ t
Poultry seasoning	$1\frac{1}{3}$ t	2 t	1 T	$1\frac{1}{3}$ T	2 T
Water	$\frac{1}{3}$ cup	$\frac{2}{3}$ cup	1 cup	$1\frac{1}{3}$ cups	2 cups
Average number cups of stuffing	4	6	10	12	20

SOURCE: Courtesy of the American Institute of Baking.

under steam pressure or in an oven until the temperature is well above 180°F.

Dumplings, hot biscuits, and pastry may also be used as meat accompaniments in place of a moist, starchy vegetable.

Chapter Review

1. What substance gives vegetables their green color? their red color? their yellow or orange color? their white color? What are the correct cooking techniques to hold each of these colors?
2. What harmful effects does the alkaline reaction that occurs when soda is added to cooking water have on vegetable texture and nutrient values?
3. How should various vegetables be stored?
4. How should canned vegetables be cooked? frozen ones? dried ones?
5. Can you list the proper ways to cook each of the following:
   a. high-moisture, mild-flavored vegetables
   b. high-moisture, strong-flavored vegetables
   c. moist, starchy vegetables
   d. dry, starchy vegetables such as dry legumes, rice, and cereals
6. What are the sanitary procedures to follow in preparing and holding dressings (stuffings)?

CHAPTER 9

Deep-frying and Sautéing

Outline

Goals

1. To discuss the standards, principles, and techniques needed to obtain good deep-fried and sautéed products.
2. To describe how fats and oils perform in deep-frying and sautéing, and to indicate how to avoid problems in using them.
3. To explain how to deep-fry items properly.
4. To explain how to sauté items properly.
5. To detail the different methods of preparing foods for deep-frying and sautéing.

INTRODUCTION

The simple procedure of cooking foods in fat belies the amount of technical knowledge needed to do a good job. Fat is a delicate product that breaks down under high temperatures or hard use. Knowing something about fats, about how they break down, and about what procedures, equipment, and fat to use can do much to ensure good results. Poor frying occurs when one or more of these three things is handled incorrectly.

PRINCIPLES

Fat and oil are the same chemically, except that a fat is solid and an oil is liquid; whether they appear as one or the other depends on temperature. Fats and oils are both known as *triglycerides*, which means that in each molecule a glycerine is attached to three fatty acids. The fatty acids are

258

long chains of carbon atoms, to which hydrogen and oxygen atoms are attached. All of the carbons have four bonds by which they join to other atoms. If the carbons are attached as in figure 9-1a, they form a *saturated* molecule, but if they are attached to each other with double bonds, as in figure 9-1b, they form an *unsaturated* molecule. A fat that has only one unsaturated carbon connection is called *monounsaturated*, while a fat that has two or more unsaturated connections is called *polyunsaturated*.

As was discussed in chapter 2, unsaturated fats—especially polyunsaturated ones—are considered more desirable in the diet than saturated fats. Solid, hard fats tend to be more saturated than oils. Fats from red meat tend to be more saturated than fats from poultry and fish. Aside from the issue of nutritive value, we are interested in the properties of saturated and unsaturated fats because saturated fats tend to be more stable than unsaturated ones under the rigorous treatment of deep-frying and sautéing.

FAT BREAKDOWN

Fats do not boil away, as water does. Instead, at certain temperatures or under certain conditions, they break down and develop undesirable flavors and cooking characteristics. Normally, a good frying fat can be heated to nearly 450°F without breaking down (it bursts into flame at around 600°F), but we do things to fat that cause it to break down at lower temperatures. Breakdown is indicated by a white smoke called *acrolein*—a sharp, acrid vapor irritating to the eyes, nose, and throat.

Because unsaturated fats break down at lower temperatures, saturated fats are preferred for frying. Unsaturated fats can be made into saturated fats by hydrogenation. Fats that contain a lot of free fatty acids (acids not attached to the glycerol) have a low smoking temperature. Butter, olive oil, fish, and some animal and poultry fats are high in free fatty acids; vegetable oils contain less of them and are often preferred for deep-frying. Frying fats are treated to remove free fatty acids. When fats break down, they release fatty acids, which speed the breakdown. Fatty acids are also introduced when foods high in free fatty acids, such as fish, pork, or poultry, are fried in the fat. Some low-cost frozen potato strips are blanched in poor-grade fat, and these can contaminate good fat when they are fried in it. Enzymes called *lipases* can help break down fats, too.

Metals encourage fat breakdown. Copper and brass are twenty times worse than iron in this regard, while nickel, chrome, and stainless steel are not harmful. Watch for exposed iron on frying baskets or other equip-

Figure 9-1. Types of carbon bonding. (a) Single bonds are characteristic of saturated fats. (b) Double bonds are characteristic of unsaturated fats.

ment. Keep iron tools out of fat. Do not use steel wool or other abrasives on thermostats, exposing the copper. Curing salts and cooking salt also help break down fat; therefore, do not salt over the fryer or griddle. Water encourages break down, so foods should be as dry as possible when put into fat. Sediment in the fat and unclean equipment are harmful, too. When fat spreads out into a thin film, it breaks down more easily: a fat at a particular temperature smokes much more readily on a griddle than in a larger mass in a fry kettle.

When oxygen joins a fat, rancidity develops; unsaturated bonds tend to pick up oxygen. A film of oil oxidizes quicker than a larger mass does. Failing to wash a coffee maker that still has a film of coffee oil on it encourages a rancid flavor in the brew. Fat mixtures get rancid faster than do individual fats. High storage temperatures and exposure to air or light also favor rancidity development. Store fats in a cool, dry, dark place. Use them as soon as possible after opening, and store them covered in a cool place.

Some fats develop off-flavor when they lose oxygen, a process called *reversion*; this is first detected as a beany flavor, then as a metallic one, and finally as a fishy flavor. Soybean oil reverts easily, and sometimes potato chips fried in it have a fishy flavor as a result. Salting also favors reversion. When fats or free fatty acids join together, they form *polymers*—resins, gums, and waxes that appear as gummy substances on griddles, deep-fryers, and broilers. Polymers give off-flavors to fats. Manufacturers of frying fats introduce stabilizers to retard their breakdown. One high-grade frying fat on the market contains silicon for this purpose.

Fat that is highly broken down develops a soft, yellowish foam when heated and should be discarded. A good fat should have white bubbles that break sharply; if handled correctly, it should never need to be discarded, because from 15 to 20 percent of the fat is used each day, and enough fresh fat is added to keep the fat that remains in good condition. Replacing fat in this way is called *turnover*. A 15-lb fryer should use 2¼ to 3 lb new fat per day to have proper turnover. A dozen doughnuts absorb 3 oz fat in frying; 10 lb potatoes absorb 1 to 2 lb (if preblanched, 1 lb); and 10 lb batter-covered or breaded food, 18 oz fat. If a 15-lb fryer each day fries 25 lb potatoes, 20 lb batter-covered or breaded items, or 12 dozen doughnuts, the turnover requirement should be met. Strain fats frequently, since sediments speed breakdown. Keep all equipment clean.

DEEP-FRYING

The right fat, frying equipment, and cooking techniques yield good deep-fried products. The fat should be flavorless, have a smoking temperature of not less than 425°F, and contain antioxidants and stabilizers to protect it. Packing solid fat around the elements and setting the temperature at 200°F until melted fat surrounds the elements prevents the fat from charring as it melts. Do not underfill or overfill the fryer with fat. Refill as the level of fat in the fryer falls. If large or many small batches are fried, or if production volume varies, install several fryers rather than a single large one; then during periods of low demand, operate only one. Since the crumbs and flour on breaded food harm fat, a kettle is often reserved just for them. Materials should be skimmed off as they collect on fat.

Check the thermostat's accuracy by using a thermometer to see if the fat temperature matches the temperature shown on the dial. A 1-in. cube of soft bread becomes a delicate brown in $1\frac{1}{4}$ minutes in 350° to 360°F fat, in 1 minute in 360° to 370°F fat, in 40 seconds in 375° to 385°F fat, and in 20 seconds in 385° to 400°F fat. Table 9-1 identifies correct frying temperatures and cooking times for various foods. Escoffier said, "Fat is moderately hot when, after a sprig of parsley or a crust of bread is thrown into it, it begins to bubble immediately. It is hot if it crackles when a slightly moist object is dropped into it, and very hot when it gives off a thin white smoke perceptible to the smell."

To deep-fry successfully, the temperature of the fat must be right. Cold fat colors food poorly and gives a greasy, soggy product; too hot fat burns the food without properly cooking it inside. Food pieces of the same kind and size should be used to obtain uniform cooking and browning. Add only the correct amount of food to the fat. Food totaling about $1\frac{1}{2}$ to 2 times the fat's weight can be fried in a deep-fryer every hour. The food : fat ratio in a good fryer can be 1 : 5 to 1 : 8, and for potatoes 1 : 6. In an old-fashioned fryer, it is 1 : 10. Overloading lowers temperatures significantly, leading to excessive fat absorption and a poorly cooked product (see fig. 9-2). This also increases fat consumption. Many frying fats are made to have sharp melting points so that when they solidify they lose their greasiness. Other factors increasing fat absorption include cold food, cold fat, rich batter or dough, large surface area, excessive leavening in a batter or dough, poor shape, rough surfaces, poor-quality fat or poor fat handling. Table 9-2 describes various bad frying conditions, their causes, and their proper treatment.

Lower baskets carefully to avoid a spillover upon bubbling up. Shake baskets occasionally to prevent foods from sticking together. Fat should cover the food (see fig. 9-3). Fry until golden brown; then lift the basket, and drain. Spill the basket's contents into a pan or onto an absorbent paper. Serve hot. If storage is necessary, keep in a dry, warm place or under an infrared lamp. Salt immediately upon service, not before, because salt destroys crispness.

Fat is very combustible, and a grease fire is very dangerous. Never overheat fats or allow them to come into contact with open flames or substances at temperatures above 500°F. Never leave grease unattended over heat. Keep handles of utensils that contain hot fat pointed inward when not in use. Lower wet foods carefully into heated fat. Fat can give terrible burns, and care should be used in handling it. Strain used fat when it is below 150°F, using several thicknesses of cheesecloth, a special

TABLE 9-1. Deep-frying temperatures and times

Type of food	Frying temperature (°F)	Frying time (minutes)
POTATOES		
One operation, ½ in. cut	350	7
One operation, ⅜ in. cut	350	6
One operation, ¼ in. cut	350	5
One operation, ⅛ in. cut	360	4
One operation, ⅛ in. cut, completely crisp	330	6–9
Two operations, ½ in. cut to ⅜ in. cut		
Blanch	350	4
Brown	350	3
Two operations, ⅛ in. cut		
Blanch	350	2½
Brown	350	2½
Two operations, ⅛ in. cut		
Blanch	360	2½
Brown	360	2½
Frozen, blanched, ⅜ in. cut	350	2
SEAFOODS		
Frozen breaded shrimp	350	4
Fresh breaded shrimp	350	3
Frozen fish fillets	350	4
Fresh fish fillets	350	3
Breaded clams	350	1
Breaded oysters	350	3–5
Fresh breaded scallops	350	4
Frozen fish sticks	350	4
Abalone, breaded	375	2–3
Sliced fish, breaded	350	6–8
CHICKEN (1½ to 2 lb, sectioned)		
Raw	325	12–15
Steamed 20 min, then breaded	350	3–4
MISCELLANEOUS		
Breaded veal cutlets	350	3–4
Breaded onion rings	350	3
Croquettes, meat	350	3–4
Precooked cauliflower, breaded	350	3
Eggplant, breaded, raw	350	3
Tamale sticks, breaded	350	3
French-toasted sandwiches	350	1–2
Yeast-raised doughnuts	350	1–3
Hand-cut cake doughnuts	350	1–3
Glazed cinnamon apple rings	300	3–5
Corn-on-the-cob	300	3
Fritters	350	3
Turnovers, meat	350	5–7

SOURCE: Adapted from Procter and Gamble, *Deep Frying Pointers.*
NOTE: The potato ratio should be 1:6 in the new type of fast-recovery kettles and 1:8 in the old type of kettles. If smaller loads of potatoes are used, use slightly lower temperatures.

(a)

(b)

(c)

(d)

Figure 9-2. (a) A properly filled deep-fryer basket. (b) An overfilled basket. (c) Quantifiable results of the overload. Notice that cooking time was longer and cooking temperature was lower on the overfilled baskets. Product quality was poorer, too, and a smaller quantity was produced per hour. (d) Potatoes in a properly filled basket being fried in a good fat. Notice the sharp white bubbles. (*Courtesy Procter & Gamble*)

(a)

(b)

Figure 9-3. (a) Fried pies are a most popular dessert, but good deep-frying techniques must be used to get a good product. (b) Deep-frying chicken. Notice again the sharp, white bubbles of fat.

TABLE 9-2. Problems, causes, and correction in deep-frying

Problem	Causes	Corrections
Objectional smoke	1. Temperature too high 2. Failure to strain fat frequently 3. Old fat	Use lower temperature; strain fat and store in cool place after use. Set up filtering schedule; check fat turnover.
Fat bubbles over	1. Too much fat in kettle 2. Too much food in kettle 3. Excessive moisture in food	Check fill of deep kettle; add smaller quantities to be fried in basket; drain batter-dipped or egg-and-crumbed foods; dry potatoes thoroughly.
Foods not crisp	1. Frying temperature too low	Use higher temperature for frying; use frying thermometer, or check temperature with bread cube.
Strong flavor and color	1. Old or deteriorated fat 2. Wrong fat for frying	Keep used fat in cool place; select proper type of frying fat; strain after use; if too many strongly flavored foods must be fried in fat, discard after use.
Excessive foaming	1. Failure to strain fat 2. Deteriorated fat 3. Extremely cold foods added to hot fat 4. Too much egg and crumb or batter 5. Frying temperature too low	Strain fat before storing in cool place; do not take foods direct from refrigerator to kettle; drain batter-dipped or egg-and-crumbed foods; use correct temperature for frying; use thermometer or check temperature with bread cube; discard deteriorated fat.

SOURCE: Adapted from Procter and Gamble, *Proper Frying*.

filter bag, or a filtering machine. If sediment does not settle, cool the fat to below 200°F and sprinkle it lightly with water to help the fine particles fall to the bottom. Pour or siphon the fat off from this water sludge. Allow solid fat to solidify, pour off the sludge, and undesirable portions from the chunk.

Few operations still use the old-fashioned frying kettle; if it is to be used, select one with straight or almost straight sides to minimize boiling over. Select a size large enough to permit fat to bubble up after adding food. Fill the kettle with fat to about half full, and fit the basket to the kettle. Use heavy-gauge kettles that have good flat bottoms and are composed of good heat-conducting material. The ratio of fat to surface area should be large. If the kettle is to be used over gas, do not allow flames to rise around its sides and set fire to the fat. Cool the kettle before removing it from the stove.

SAUTÉING

Cooking food in a thin layer of fat is called *sautéing* or *pan-frying*; a fry pan, sauté pan, or griddle is used for this purpose. To pan-fry, select a

**TABLE 9-3. Recommended quantities of fat
for sautéing**

Pan size (diameter in in.)	Uncovered foods	Breaded or butter-covered foods
8	3 T	$\frac{1}{3}$ c
9	$\frac{1}{4}$ c	$\frac{1}{3}$ c
10	$\frac{1}{3}$ c	$\frac{1}{2}$ c
12	$\frac{1}{2}$ c	$\frac{2}{3}$ c

low-edged heavy skillet or frying pan of good heat-conducting metal. Use a straight-edged pan (with or without a handle) when foaming is a problem. When foods must be fried, covered, and cooked or turned during cooking, use a slant-sided pan to facilitate working in the pan. Fit the pan to the quantity of food to be fried. Some pans may be 12 to 14 in. in diameter or larger. Table 9-3 lists quantities of fat to use in pans of different size. Sauté small or thin items quickly to prevent them from drying out. Put foods into hot fat, gently sliding them in to avoid splashing. Cook until half-done, and turn. Add fat as required. Table 9-4 identifies recommended temperatures and sautéing times for various foods.

Thick foods may be sautéed or grilled, and then finished in an oven or covered in a pan and cooked over low heat to complete cooking. Some added moisture may be needed. When a great deal of food is to be sautéed, fry in this manner and recrisp just before service by uncovering the food and drying it out in a hot oven. If a breaded or batter-covered food is to be grilled, allow 3 to 4 oz oil per square foot of griddle. If the foods are not covered, use 2 to 3 oz per square foot. Spread the oil lightly over the surface. Drizzle oil with an oil mop around the edges of the food during frying. The oil conducts heat from the grill to the food. Bacon,

**TABLE 9-4. Temperatures recommended for sautéing
and grilling**

Item	Temperature (°F)	Approximate cooking time (min)
Hamburger, thin	340–350	5–8
Griddlecakes	350–360	3–4
Eggs, fried	300–325	3–4
Bacon, ham, sausages	325	4–5 (if thin)
Steak, $\frac{1}{2}$ in. thick	350	10–15 (well done)
Steak, 1 in. thick	340	10–15 (medium)
Steak, over 1 in. thick	330	10–15 (rare)
Pork or veal cutlets	325	6–8
Small fish or fillets	350	10–15
Small steaks or chops	340–350	10–15
Potatoes, hash brown or American fries	350–360	8–10
Toasted sandwiches	350	4–5
French toast	325–330	3–4

TABLE 9-5. Problem, causes, and corrections in pan and griddle sautéing

Problem	Cause	Correction
Food sticks	1. Not enough fat 2. Food too cold 3. Surface needs conditioning 4. Surface too hot or cold	Use more fat or oil. Thaw or warm food slightly. Condition with fat. Adjust temperature.
Food burns	1. Surface too hot	Adjust heat.
Food does not brown	1. Surface too cold	Adjust heat.
Spattering	1. Moist foods added to too-hot fat	Drain moist foods thoroughly; reduce cooking temperature.
Foods not crisp	1. Food too cold 2. Insufficient fat 3. Too low cooking temperature	Warm food. Add more fat. Adjust heat.

SOURCE: Adapted from Procter and Gamble, *Proper Frying.*

unbreaded pork chops, and other fatty foods require less oil than leaner products. Table 9-5 identifies various problems that may arise in sautéing, together with their causes and means of correction.

PREPARATION FOR FRYING

Breading, batter-dipping, or wrapping food in dough may be preliminary treatments before frying it (see figures 9-4 and 9-5). Providing excessive cover to extend products is not recommended. Heavy covering can become tough and dark and can separate from the product. Ratios of cover to product should be as follows: small pieces (shrimp, chicken nuggets), 1:2; larger pieces (veal cutlets, croquettes), 1:3 or 1:4. On the average, 100 lb batter or crumbs should cover 200 to 400 lb food. Lightly

(a)   (b)

Figure 9-4. (a) Flouring liver prior to sautéing it. (b) The proper flow for breading: the partially thawed veal cutlets are covered with flour, then dipped into the egg-and-milk mixture, and then dipped into crumbs.

Figure 9-5. The liver shown floured in figure 9-4, after being sautéed in a thin layer of fat on a griddle.

breaded items such as chicken should not increase in weight by more than 10 to 15 percent (see fig. 9-6). Dough-wrapped items should have a ratio of between 1:1 and $1\frac{1}{2}:1$. High-moisture foods require a heavier and tighter cover than drier ones; firm foods need less cover. Plan good work centers and production centers for covering food.

Breading usually requires three steps: flouring, moistening, and crumbing. Paprika may be added to the flour for color, and seasonings may be added for flavor. Flour absorbs the moistening agent, setting up a good base for crumb adherence. Moisteners (in order, from strongest to weakest cover formed) include eggs, egg and liquid, evaporated milk, regular milk, and other liquids. Milk gives less crispness than eggs or water. Crumbs may be from crackers, bread, other cereals, or prepared mixes; particle size should be even. Sift if necessary to give uniformity. The finer the crumbs are, the firmer is the coating. Place products on a rack to dry at least 15 minutes before frying. If they are to be placed into pans, sprinkle a few crumbs on the bottom of the pans to avoid bottom soaking. Prepared breadings contain monosodium glutamate and other seasonings, plus substances to improve adherence. Operations making their own breading mixtures can add these. Consult a good food technologist on what to use.

Modify breadings to suit the food. Veal cutlets, oysters, tomatoes, eggplant, croquettes, partially cooked cauliflower, and other firm products may be breaded in a standard way, but some vegetables and other foods that are high in moisture may work better if dipped into flour at the third step and not into crumbs. This gives less grease absorption in a product that nonetheless resembles a batter-dipped one. Some meat and

Figure 9-6. Chicken dipped into batter and then sautéed in a liberal quantity of fat to give a product much like deep-fried chicken.

fish items may be floured only; the method of frying them is usually sautéing rather than deep-frying (see fig. 9-7). If frozen breaded items are to be deep-fried, allow them to stand at room temperature to thaw partially and then deep-fry them just as for other breaded items.

Batter-dipped items should be dipped into a batter that is thick enough to adhere and give an adequate coating. Dipping the food into the batter and then holding it over the batter allows the excess to drop off. The dipped food should then be dropped easily into the hot fat, without splashing. Dough-wrapped products should be tightly sealed in dough so that the fat does not get into the product but cooks from the outside. In

Figure 9-7. Sautéing cube steaks prior to braising them covered in an oven.

a breaded, batter-dipped or dough-wrapped product, it is desirable to obtain rapid cooking on the outside so that fat does not penetrate. This is also true of egg-dipped items such as Monte Cristo sandwiches. The coating should cover all areas that protect the interior. The dough for dough-wrapped items should be less rich than pie dough and should more nearly resemble biscuit dough. Fat adds richness to such dough in frying.

Dough-wrapped and breaded products can be placed into baskets and lowered into fat, but batter-dipped ones (as well as pastes or batters such as crullers and fritters) that are soft enough to stick to the basket should be dropped carefully into hot fat after the basket is lowered. The basket can then be raised to remove the products once they are cooked. Sometimes items must be turned in the hot fat. Placing a screen or another basket over these items so as to submerge them makes turning unnecessary. Items should not be crowded in a basket, since—even though they may not stick together—crowding gives uneven and poor cooking results.

Chapter Review

1. What is a saturated fat? a monounsaturated fat? a polyunsaturated fat?
2. What is acrolein, and what does it signify?
3. When a small, yellow foam rises when items are added to a fat, what has happened to the fat? What should be done with it?
4. What requirements must equipment, fat or oil, and food items meet in order to produce good deep-fried items?
5. What are the dangers in deep-frying?
6. What is deep-frying? sautéing?
7. What are the proper ways to bread a food? to batter a food? to dough-wrap a food?

CHAPTER 10

Meats, Poultry, and Fish

Outline

Goals

1. To identify the standards and principles needed to cook meat, poultry, and fish properly.
2. To elaborate on the nature of meat, poultry, and fish, explaining how various treatments affect their cooking and how different modes of cooking promote flavor, tenderness, and doneness in them.
3. To describe the various techniques used to cook meat, poultry, and fish.

INTRODUCTION

Meat is usually the main meal item. Its selection often dictates the choice of other foods in the meal, and it is usually the meal's most costly item.

Acceptable cooked meat is served if good meat is purchased and proper procedures for preparation are followed. Escoffier thought a good meat cook could be trained with "application, observation, care, and a little aptitude," disputing Brillat-Savarin's assertion that "good roast cooks are born, not made."

PRINCIPLES

The flesh of warm-blooded animals, poultry, and fish is much alike, and the basic principles dealing with their cooking are quite similar.

COMPOSITION

Meat is about 25 percent solids and 75 percent moisture. Of the solids, 20 percent consist of fat, fatlike compounds, ash, and other substances; the remaining 80 percent are proteins. Meat contains a small quantity of glucose, which is quite important to color and flavor development in browning. The protein, moisture, ash, vitamins, and other compounds are mostly found in the flesh and not in the fat.

Most meat proteins are soluble in cold water, but heat coagulates them and makes them insoluble. Fat is found in three forms: emulsified in fibers; as marbling; and as finish. Finish is the covering of fat over the outside and inside of the carcass. Young and old animals have less fat than middle-aged ones. Body fat contains from 15 to 50 percent moisture, which keeps meat from drying out in cooking. For this reason, roasts are cooked fat-side-up. Similarly, some poultry is cooked with its fat back up so that the fat and its moisture baste the breast. Meat is larded or pieces of fatty tissue are laid over it (barded) to give moisture in cooking. Marbling contributes to tenderness by separating meat tissues. Fatty tissue is more tender when hot.

STRUCTURE

Lean meat is composed of tubelike rods or fibers tapered on both ends (see fig. 10-1a). An individual fiber may measure from $\frac{1}{200}$ to $\frac{1}{1100}$ in. in diameter and may be up to 2 in. long. These fibers appear as strings or shreds of meat when well-done chicken breast or boiled short ribs are pulled apart. Fibers are cells that have many nuclei and are filled with a liquid containing proteins, emulsified fat, fatlike substances, minerals, and vitamins (see fig. 10-1a and b). Connective tissue binds these fibers together in bundles like straws in a broom and spreads in a network around the fibers, holding them in place. Tendrils of connective tissue even enter into the fibers (see fig. 10-1d). Additional connective tissue binds bundles together to make a muscle. At the end of each muscle, long ends of connective tissue join to form a tendonous mass attached to bone.

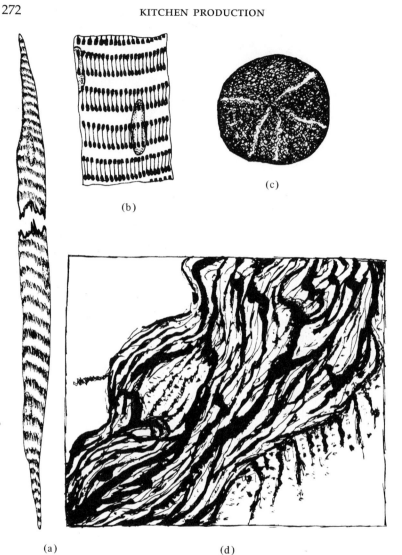

Figure 10-1.   Meat fibers: (a) long, tapered, tubelike muscle fiber; (b) close-up of a section; (c) cross section of a fiber; (d) dark areas show connective tissue in meat tissue.

Fiber size influences the texture of meat. Fine fibers indicate a fine, smooth texture and tender meat. Buyers look for a velvety, smooth, soft surface indicating fine grain. These characteristics remain visible after cooking (see fig. 10-2). The surface should have a soft, moist sheen and should show marbling. Young animals, males castrated when young, and females have finer-grained flesh than mature males or stags. The outer sheath or membrane strength of the fibers also affects tenderness. Exercised muscles develop stronger sheaths and more connective tissue than do those receiving less exercise. Feed, care, and breed also affect

Figure 10-2. Excellent quality is evident in this roast beef. The moist, shiny surface, glittering fat, and fine texture indicate superior eating quality. (*Courtesy Armour and Company*)

tenderness, although tenderness may vary considerably among animals of the same breed.

The type and quantities of connective tissue in meat also affect tenderness. White connective tissue consists largely of collagen, while yellow connective tissue is primarily elastin. Collagen can be converted into gelatin and water by moist heat. Acids speed the change. Marinating meat in an acid solution tenderizes the meat and adds moisture. Elastin is not changed by cooking. To be made tender, it must be broken up by mechanical treatment such as grinding, pounding, or cubing.

As an animal gets older its flesh toughens. Some increase in connective tissue may be the cause, but it is more probable that the type of connective tissue changes with age. Usually muscles that are exercised a lot contain greater quantities of connective tissue (especially elastin) than do those exercised less. Meat is tenderized by enzymes—usually papain, which digests connective tissue. Injection of a tenderizer just before slaughter provides wide distribution of the enzyme throughout the capillary system, giving more satisfactory results than are obtained by coating or spraying the meat with tenderizer after slaughter.

RIPENING

Rigor mortis is a muscle stiffening that appears after death. Cooking meat while rigor is present gives tough meat; such meat is called *green*. Rigor disappears after three or four days, and the meat becomes more tender. Since most meat takes about seven days to go through marketing channels, few operations are troubled with green meat. Pork develops little rigor, while chickens develop and lose it quickly.

Ripening or aging can be accomplished by holding meat at 35° to 40°F under controlled humidity; this is often called *dry aging*. Beef, lamb, and mutton are aged, but pork and veal seldom are. Aging increases flavor, tenderness, and moistness. After twenty-one days, meat ages little. A good fat cover prevents bacteria from invading meat during aging, but mold will grow on it. Because of weight loss, the cost of refrigerated storage, the tie-up of money, and the need to trim fat later, aging increases cost. Game is aged—sometimes almost to putrefaction, as in game birds. Cryovac aging—a process in which meat is placed into moisture- and vapor-proof wraps, air is exhausted, and the pack is held under refrigeration—is used a great deal more than dry aging. No fat cover is needed because molds and bacteria cannot invade the packaging. The resulting meat is often moist from exuding juices. It loses more weight in cooking than dry-aged meat, so final yields are about the same. Cryovac meat when first opened may have a musty aroma, but this soon dissipates.

COOKING

Meat proteins coagulate at temperatures of from 160° to 175°F, changing color and flavor and becoming firmer. Just before coagulation begins, denaturation (loss of moisture) occurs, at around 140°F. Shrinkage loss varies according to cut, type of meat, amount of fat, and other factors, but the most important factor is temperature. Minimum cooking shrinkage for a beef rib is as follows: rare, 10 percent, medium, 15 percent, and well done, 25 percent. That searing heat "seals the pores" and thereby reduces shrink has not been proved. Rather, searing at a high temperature and then cooking at a low temperature increases shrinkage over cooking at a constant low temperature, although it may be done anyway to give a browned surface and a caramelized flavor. A constant low temperature saves labor and fuel and reduces spattering. Salt delays browning; since its penetration is small in any case—from $\frac{1}{4}$ to $\frac{1}{2}$ in.—it is frequently omitted until serving. Excess cooking dries meat out and toughens it.

COLOR

The pigment myoglobin gives meat its red color. Milk-fed animals have light-colored flesh because it contains little myoglobin; fish flesh is light because it lacks myoglobin altogether. Acids darken myoglobin, and ripened meat is darker because of its increased acidity. Oxygen joins myoglobin to form oxymyoglobin, a bright red pigment. Heat turns myoglobin into hematin, a gray or grayish brown substance. Myoglobin and nitrogen combine to form nitrosomyoglobin, a red pigment that does not change color in cooking; we see this in cured meats because they contain nitrogen salts. Onions dehydrated in nitrogen gas can give a red, uncooked appearance to cooked meat loaf. Ground meat patties that are presalted and frozen can turn red after cooking, although the reason why is not known. When meat spoils, myoglobin is changed into a brownish, odorous substance called *metamyoglobin*. An iridescent green that is sometimes seen on cured meat and some commercially cooked uncured meats, results from a chemical reaction; it has nothing to do with the edibility or wholesomeness of the meat.

FLAVOR

Nitrogenous substances, nonnitrogenous extractives, and waste products were once thought to account for the primary flavor in meat, but now we know that much flavor also comes from fat. Cooking develops flavor as well, with amino acids breaking down into flavorful products and free fatty acids and carbonyl fractions giving the rich aroma of cooked meat. Flavor develops in cooking for up to 3 hours and then declines.

An animal's diet affects its meat's flavor. A milk-mash diet for chickens produces mild-flavored flesh. Cattle fattened on distiller's mash have sharply acidic meat with a fermented flavor. Good care and feed and a good environment foster mild flavors; animals exposed to rigorous weather and given poor diet and shelter have strong-flavored meat. The marine diet and iodine content of sea fish give their flesh its characteristic "fishy" taste. Breed, sex, and age may also affect flavor. The meat of males, unless they were castrated when young, is stronger than that of females; the flesh of young animals is milder than that of older ones. The sulfurous flavor of cooked meat varies according to animal's breed, its diet, the degree of cooking, and other factors. Muscles of the same animal may differ, as between the breast and the leg of a chicken. Poultry is especially acidic and astringent; turkey has an almost pungent flavor. Pork is sweeter but more acidic and sulfurous than beef. Lamb and mutton seem to taste more alkaline than beef or pork; their strong flavor is associated with caproic, caprylic, and pelargonic acid compounds. MSG (monosodium glutamate) heightens meat flavor.

DONENESS

Meat is cooked to make it more palatable and perhaps more digestible. When tenderness must be developed, moist heat is used; dry heat seldom tenderizes, and overcooking with dry heat often toughens. High heat toughens more than low heat does. Extended cooking also toughens, and some shellfish toughen with long cooking even in water. Simmered fowl is more tender than fowl steamed at 250°F steam pressure when both are cooked to the same doneness. Often the meat's outside and inside appearance indicates doneness. The surest way of gauging doneness is by thermometer, although it is difficult to use thermometers in small pieces of meat such as steaks and chops. Six stages of doneness can be distinguished:

Very rare: The meat has only a thin portion of cooked meat around the edge; red, almost bloody juices exude. Under finger pressure, the meat is soft and jellylike inside.

Rare: The raw, red portion is smaller and the meat around it is pink; a good brown outer surface is present. There is a full, plump appearance and still some give to pressure. The juices are red but not bloody.

Medium rare: The interior is a rich pink. The meat is still plump; the juices are pink. Firmness to the touch is more apparent; the amount of gray outer surface has increased.

Medium: The interior color is a modified rose. Pink juices are apparent but less widespread. The exterior is well-browned. The surface does not appear as plump or full. When the meat is pressed, there is definite resistance.

Medium well: The pink color has disappeared. Juiciness is still evident, but the juices are clear or gray, not pink. There is no plumpness; the meat is firm to touch.

Well: The meat is completely gray inside. Little or no juice appears. The meat is hard and flinty to the touch and has a shrunken appearance. The surface is brown and dry.

Temperatures indicating doneness are identified for various meats in table 10-1.

Aged beef at 140°F may appear to have been cooked medium rather than rare because the meat's greater acidity causes myoglobin to change to hematin at a lower temperature. Large meat pieces increase in internal temperature after cooking has ceased, so cook rib roasts 15° to 25°F lower than desired and remove from the heat; the heat on the outside will continue to flow in raising the internal temperature to the desired level. Meat at room temperature cooks more rapidly than chilled or frozen meat; frozen meat takes two to three times longer to cook than chilled meat. As cooking temperature increases, the cooking time required falls; however, high temperatures increase shrinkage and reduce appearance,

TABLE 10-1. Internal temperatures indicating doneness

Meat	Rare	Medium	Well Done
Beef	140°F	160°F	170°F
Lamb		165°F	175°F
Pork, fresh			165°–175°F
Pork, cured			155°F
Poultry		165°F	180°F
Veal			170°F

NOTE: Pork should always be cooked to well done.

juiciness, tenderness, and flavor. Usually, large pieces take longer to cook than small ones, but a flat roast with a large surface area cooks in less time than a compact roast of the same mass. Boned meats take longer to cook than unboned ones. Fat can act as an insulator, so meat with a fat cover may take longer to cook. Using aluminum foil increases shrinkage and cooking time and hastens flavor loss. To cook meat by the pound, calculate cooking time by the piece, not by the entire pan weight. For example, a roast pan containing six 7-lb roasts should be timed for 7 lb and not for 42.

STANDARDS

The wide variety of meats and the many ways in which they can be cooked make it difficult to establish one standard for cooked meat. Standards for poultry, fish, and shellfish differ somewhat from those given here, but not appreciably.

All meat should be of good flavor and pleasing appearance, and drippings should be rich and of good color. The texture should be moist—not dry or crumbly—with firmness consistent with doneness. It should be tender—not pulpy, stringy, excessively soft, greasy, or oily. The color should be natural to the meat, given the style of cooking and the degree of doneness, with no burned portions and no burned taste. Roasts should be well-browned. Veal roasts should have a reddish brown surface, and roast pork a uniformly rich brown surface. Roasted poultry skin and the outer surface of lamb and pork roasts should be crisp, not dry or tough. Sliced meat should be firm, juicy, and tender and should hold its shape. Broiled exteriors should be evenly browned, juicy, and glossy in appearance. Bacon should be crisp but not brittle. Browned meats should have a rich brown color with well-developed flavor and aroma. Braised meat should be tender and juicy—not stringy—and should hold its shape and not fall apart. A rich gloss should be visible on the meat surface. Pieces should be uniform, even, symmetrical, and attractive. Unbrowned meat lacks the color and characteristic flavor that are developed by browning, but otherwise it has similar qualities.

COOKING TECHNIQUES

MEATS

The tenderness of a meat largely dictates its cooking. Tender cuts are usually cooked in dry heat, while tough cuts are usually cooked in moist heat. Some tough cuts may be mechanically tenderized or treated with tenderizers and then cooked with dry heat. Dry-heat methods include the following:

Broiling, pan-broiling, or griddle-broiling
Roasting or baking
Barbecueing

Sautéing, pan-frying, or grilling
Deep-frying
Oven roasting

Moist heat methods include the following:

Braising (pot-roasting, fricasséeing, casseroling, Swissing, or stewing)
Simmering (poaching or stewing—seldom boiling)
Steaming
Blanching

Work areas for cooking meats must be well-planned. Broiling, sautéing, and deep-frying require fast work. Adapt equipment to needs and workflow, giving proper work space and landings. Locate small tools, salt and pepper, oil, oil mop, and cloths within easy reach. Provide refrigerated storage in the work area.

Broiling

Cooking by radiant heat is called *broiling*. *Grilling* once meant broiling, but now it means sautéing or frying. Broiling temperatures are slightly higher than roasting temperatures. The cut, type of meat, and piece size governs the temperature. Meat with low fat content and meat cut in small pieces are cooked at higher temperatures to shorten cooking time and to reduce their chances of drying out. Thin pork chops or steaks, bacon, and other small units are cooked within 2 to 3 in. of the heat (see fig. 10-3). Thick turkey breasts, chateaubriands, and similar pieces are cooked 8 in. or more from the heat source. Larger pieces may be scored to promote heat penetration; putting metal skewers into meat speeds cooking, too.

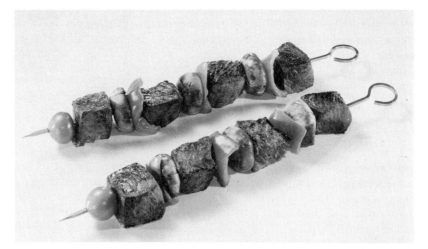

Figure 10-3. Small items like these shish kebabs should be broiled at a higher temperature than larger items. This is accomplished by placing them closer to the heat. (*Courtesy Armour and Company*)

High temperatures lead to a hard, dry crust that slows heat penetration, giving a charred outside and an undercooked inside. Very thick pieces may be broiled for 5 to 8 minutes on each side and then completed in a 350°F oven.

Broiled meat, poultry, or fish may be planked. In this method, the item is broiled almost to doneness and then placed in the center of a heated oak plank that is about 2 in. thick. A border of duchess potatoes is piped around the edge, the open spaces are filled with various hot cooked vegetables, and the whole is garnished with broiled mushrooms or other items. The plank is put into a hot oven or under a broiler to warm and brown, and then the item is sent to service, liberally drizzled with melted butter (see fig. 10-4).

Dip meat into vegetable oil, hold over the oil pan for a moment and then place gently onto the grid, giving good contact (see fig. 10-5a). Cook to half doneness (100°F for rare to medium, and 135°F for medium to well done), turn, and season with salt; earlier salting retards browning. For large pieces, four turns may be needed; seasoning is done on the third and fourth turns. Items turned once should show parallel grid marks (///) (see fig. 10-5b). Those turned twice should show crisscrossed grid marks (×××), achieved by making a 90° turn of the meat on successive turns. Press meat gently onto the grid each time it is turned. Score (cut) meat at the edges to prevent it from curling. Flesh that is low in fat content is too dry to broil well. To broil such meat, first flour it, and then dip in oil. Put the item on a double grid to hold it firmly in place; then slow-broil, basting the meat with oil to help it retain moistness.

Figure 10-4. A tenderloin butt broiled and then planked. After being placed under the broiler, it is sent to service.

(a)   (b)

Figure 10-5. (a) Items to be broiled are dipped into oil before being placed on the grid. (b) Grid markings on these steaks indicate that they have been turned only once. (*Courtesy Armour and Company*)

Small meat pieces, extremely tender flesh such as fish, and breaded foods that might stick to a grid or break in turning may also be cooked in a well-oiled double grid. This utensil is designed to fold like an old-fashioned toaster, holding foods securely (see fig. 10-6).

Do not allow drippings to catch fire. Sooty smoke and off-flavors can ruin meat. Grease fires are dangerous. Have at hand a bottle of cold water with a perforated top, or a syringe of cold water or small container of water with chipped ice to stop flaming. Rotating horizontal spits should revolve so as to keep drip as much as possible on the meat. Some people claim that burned fats on red meat or heavily browned products contain carcinogenic substances.

Whenever many items are broiled at one time (such as for a banquet), have the broiler set at the correct temperature, but move the grid closer to the flame. Broil the foods only to the proper color; then remove, placing the items into pans. Before service, finish them in a 350° to 400°F oven. Prepare lobsters similarly, broiling them to a desired color, setting them

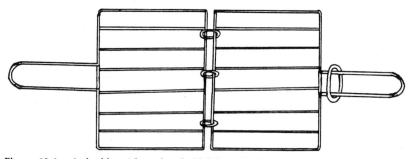

Figure 10-6. A double grid used to hold fish and other items under a broiler. This device enables cooks to turn fragile items without breaking them.

into pans, and placing a weight on their tails to prevent these from turning up and charring in the oven.

Table 10-2 identifies the proper cooking times for rare, medium, and well-done meats of various kinds, for regular broilers and for griddle- and pan-broiling.

Pan-broiling or Griddle-broiling

Pan-broil meats in fairly heavy skillets; if heavy production is called for, griddle-broil them. Select pans suited to the quantity to be made, so drippings do not burn. Rub the bottom interior of the pan lightly with fat and preheat. Cook the meat on one side and then on the other, turning as often as necessary. Pour off the fat as it gathers. Do not cover or add water. Only pan-broil meats that are high in fat. To griddle-broil, place the item onto a lightly greased 325°F griddle, and cook with no fat. Pan-broiled and griddle-broiled foods resemble sautéed foods more than they do broiled ones.

TABLE 10-2. Timetable for broiling various meats

Cut	Thickness	Rare	Medium	Well done
CHARCOAL, GAS, OR ELECTRIC BROILER				
Rib, club, T-bone, porterhouse, tenderloin or	1 in.	15	20	30
individual servings of sirloin beef steak	1½ in.	25	35	
	2 in.	35	50	
Sirloin beef steak (whole steak)	1 in.	20–30	30–40	
	1½ in.	30–40	40–50	
	2 in.	40–55	50–65	
Ground beef patties	1 in. (4 oz)	15	20	
Shoulder, rib, loin, and sirloin lamb chops or steaks	1 in.		12–15	16–18
	1½ in.		17–20	
	2 in.		20–25	25–30
Ground lamb patties	1 in. (4 oz)		16–18	
Smoked ham slice	½ in.			10–12
Bacon				4–5
GRIDDLE- OR PAN-BROILING				
Individual servings of beef steaks	¾ in.	4	8	12
	1 in.	6	10	15
	1½ in.	10–12	15–18	20
Ground beef patties	¾ in.	4–5	8–10	12
	1 in. (4 oz)	6–8	10–12	15
Lamb chops	1 in.		10	15
	1½ in.		15	20–25
Ground lamb patties	¾ in.		10	12–15
	1 in. (4 oz)		10–15	15–20
Smoked ham slice	½ in.			6–10
Bacon				2–3

NOTE: For automatic speed broilers, which cook both sides of the meat at once, decrease the time to one-half or even one-third of the figure given for regular broilers.
SOURCE: National Livestock and Meat Board.

(a)   (b)

Figure 10-7. (a) The wrong way to roast a piece of meat, since the fatty side does not get a chance to drip over the meat and keep it moist. (b) The right way.

Roasting

Meat intended for roasting should cover the pan and not leave space for drippings to burn. Sometimes a trivet or perforated underliner is put on the bottom to keep meat from resting in its own juices and fat. The trivet is omitted for meats such as leg of veal that need to be turned in their own juices as they roast. Some cooks add roughly chopped vegetables at the start. Salt is not added until browning is complete. Never pierce lean flesh in turning a roast or broiled item; merely roll it over or insert the fork in fatty tissue. Use no liquid. Do not cover, except in the case of fish and a few other items that required covering. Place the meat fat-side-up (see fig. 10-7); place poultry breast-down. Meat lacking in fatty tissue may have to be basted, larded, or barded (see fig. 10-8a). To minimize drying out, roast small pieces at higher temperatures. In roasting batches, select the smallest piece in the lot, and insert a thermometer in

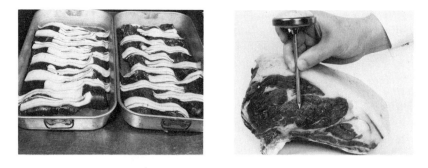

(a)   (b)

Figure 10-8. (a) Barding lean tenderloins with bacon to keep them moist. Larding is similar to barding except that the strips of fat are pulled through the meat. (b) Set the meat thermometer in the center of the muscle to record the roasting temperature.

the center of it (see fig. 10-8b). When the proper internal temperature is reached, remove the thermometer and the meat. Repeat the process with the next smallest piece, until all pieces are done. Roast meat in a 300°F oven, or preheat the oven to 475°F, sear the meat until well-browned, and then drop the temperature to 300°F to complete roasting. Gentle roasting gives tenderer, more flavorful meat. Table 10-3 lists roasting times and temperatures for various cuts of meat.

En papillote means wrapped in paper and roasted; this is most frequently done with fish or chicken. Often cured meats require soaking and/or parboiling before roasting. Do not sear cured ham.

If thermometers are not available, test doneness with the thumb or forefinger by pressing down on the meat to feel its firmness or resistence. If the meat feels flabby, it is undercooked; if it feels soft, it is rare. The meat feels firmer at medium and hard at well done. Experience is required for this method of testing, and even experts are sometimes fooled. Allow roasts to stand for 30 minutes before carving. Hold rare or medium roasts at gentle heat to avoid further cooking. Carve meats against the grain, and serve at once. Machine-slicing gives, on the average, more portions per pound than hand-slicing.

Delayed-service cookery is a method of roasting meat and poultry so that it can be prepared ahead of time and held. The items are roasted in a regular 325°F oven until they reach an internal temperature of about 125°F (poultry, 140°F); then they are removed and put into a holding oven that does not vary more than ±5°F from 140°F. (New ovens bring the products up to the desired temperature and hold them with little fluctuation, avoiding this two-step method.) Items can be held this way for 48 hours or more without diminution in quality. Shrinkage is low, and flavor, tenderness, juiciness, and evenness of cooking are increased. If desired, the meat can first be browned at a searing temperature. Ground meats should not be cooked in this manner, since the temperature may not be high enough to kill all bacteria. Wrapping the product in aluminum foil (bright side out) after roasting it holds it better.

Barbecueing

Broiled or roasted meats basted with a tangy sauce, meats cooked on a spit or rotisserie over an open fire, and meats cooked in a covered pit are called *barbecued*. All are served with a tangy barbecue sauce.

Frying

Cooking meat in a thin layer of fat is called *sautéing* or *frying* (grilling). Cooking meat immersed in deep fat is called *deep-frying*. These procedures are discussed in chapter 9.

Ovenizing

The term *ovenizing* was coined to describe the process of baking meats by placing them onto well-greased baking sheets or pans and then putting them into an oven to fry or sauté. Drizzle breaded items with additional

TABLE 10-3. Time and temperatures for roasting meats

Cut	Approx. weight of single roast (lb)	No. of roasts in oven	Approx. total weight of roasts in oven (lb)	Oven temperature (°F)	Interior temperature of roast when removed from oven (°F)	Minutes per lb (based on one roast)	Minutes per lb (based on total weight of roasts in oven)	Approx. total time roasting (hr)
BEEF								
Standing rib (7-rib)	20–25	1		250°	125° (rare) 140° (medium) 150° (well)	13 15 17		4½ 5 6
Standing rib (7-rib)	23	1		300°	125° (rare) 140° (medium) 150° (well)	11 12 13		4 4½ 5
Rolled rib (7-rib)	16–18	1		250°	150° (well)	26		7–8
Rolled rib (7-rib)	17	1		300°	150° (well)	24		6
Standing rib (7-rib)		2	56	300°	140° (medium) 160° (well)		6 7–8	6 7
Chuck rib	5–8	1		300°	150°–170°	25–30		2½–4
Rump	5–7	1		300°	150°–170°	25–30		2½–3½
Round (rump and shank off)	50	1		250°	140° (medium) 154° (well)	12 14		10 11–12
LAMB								
Leg	6–7	2	16	300°	180°		15	4
Cushion shoulder (with stuffing)	4½–5½	1		300°	180°	30–35		2–3
Rolled shoulder	3–4	1		300°	180°	40–45		2½–3

Rolled shoulder		5	29	300°	180°		10	5
Square cut shoulder		8	40	300°	180°		7	4–5
FRESH PORK								
Loin (bone in)	12–15	1		300°	185°	16		3–4
Loin (bone in)	11–15	1		350°	185°	15–18		3–3½
Rolled loin (two halves tied together)		3	21	300°	185°		14	5
Rolled loin (two halves tied together)		3	23	350°	185°		11	4
Half loin (bone in)		6	33	300°	185°		11	6
Half loin (bone in)		6	33	350°	185°		8	4½
Center cut loin	3–4	1		350°	185°	35–40		2–2½
End cut loin	3–4	1		350°	185°	45–50		2½–3
Shoulder	12–14	1		350°	185°	30–35		6½
Cushion shoulder (with stuffing)	4–6	1		350°	185°	35–40		3–3½
Cushion shoulder (with stuffing)		3	30	350°	185°		9	4½–5
Rolled shoulder	4–6	1		350°	185°	35–40		3–3½
Boston Butt	4–6	1		350°	185°	45–50		3½–4½
Ham (leg)	15	1		300°	185°	30		8
Ham (leg)	10–12	1		350°	185°	30–35		6
Ham (leg)		3	34	300°	185°		10–12	6–7
Ham (leg)		3	38	350°	185°		10	6–6½
Ham (leg) boned, split, and tied in two rolls	10–12	1		350°	185°	30–35		5–7
Ham (leg) boned, split, and tied in two rolls	10	1		350°	185°	20–25		4–5

continued

TABLE 10-3. Time and temperatures for roasting meats (*continued*)

Cut	Approx. weight of single roast (lb)	No. of roasts in oven	Approx. total weight of roasts in oven (lb)	Oven temperature (°F)	Interior temperature of roast when removed from oven (°F)	Minutes per lb (based on one roast)	Minutes per lb (based on total weight of roasts in oven)	Approx. total time roasting (hr)
SMOKED PORK								
Whole ham	10–14	1		300°	160°	15–18		3–3½
Half ham	6–10	1		300°	160°	20		2–3½
Ham, sweet pickled	16	1		350°	170°	15		4
Shoulder butt	2–4	1		300°	170°	30–35		1–2
Picnic	3–10	1		300°	170°	30–35		2–5
Canadian-style bacon (casing on)	7	1		350°	160°	10–12		1–1½
Canadian-style bacon (casing on)		3	19	300°	160°		5	1½–2

VEAL

Leg	7–8	1		300°	170°	25		3–3½
Leg	16	1		300°	170°	22		6
Leg	23	1		300°	170°	18–20		7–7½
Loin	4½–5	1		300°	170°	30–35		2½–3
Rack (4 to 6 ribs)	2½–3	1		300°	170°	30–35		1½
Shoulder	7	1		300°	170°	25		3
Shoulder	12–13	1		300°	170°	25		5–5½
Cushion shoulder (with stuffing)	9–10	1		300°	170°	30–35		5–5½
Cushion shoulder (with stuffing)		3	24	300°	170°		10–12	4–5
Rolled shoulder	5	1		300°	170°	40–45		3½–4
Rolled shoulder		3	20	300°	170°		14	5
Rolled shoulder	9–10	1		300°	170°	35–40		6–7
Round (rump and shank off)	20	1		300°	170°	20		6½

SOURCE: National Livestock and Meat Board.

fat as they cook. In total, the amount of fat needed for ovenizing is less than the amount needed for sautéing. Temperatures from 325° to 425°F are used. Smaller foods should be cooked at higher temperatures than larger ones. This style of cooking is used when large quantities must be produced.

Braising

Meat cooked in its own juices or in added moisture is called *braised*. Stewing, pot-roasting, fricasséeing, and Swissing are all forms of braising. Stewing and simmering require more liquid than does braising. Braisers or casseroles with straight sides 6 to 8 in. high are used for small quantities; large quantities are cooked in roasting pans, large pots, or steam-jacketed kettles. Marinating may occur before braising, as is done in the case of the seven-day marinade for sauerbraten. Lean meat may be blended with some fat to give moistness, or it may be larded. If meat is unbrowned, the item is called *blond* or *white*, as in a blond stew or a white fricassée. Braised meats are usually served with vegetables. If served without vegetables in an earthenware casserole, they are *en casserole*; if served with vegetables, they are *en cocotte*. *Jugged* means braised in a pot, as in jugged hare. The verb *poêler* means to brown well and then braise in juices while basting with butter. Poêlering temperatures are high; the process consists partly of roasting, partly of sautéing, and partly of braising. It is good for young, tender meats.

The piece size of braised meat can vary from pot roasts to hamburger. Poultry is portioned and braised. Often meat is floured before braising, especially if browning occurs. Browned meat is called *brun*, and unbrowned meat is called *blond*.

Browning is done over direct heat, in an oven, or in a steam-jacketed kettle. Add fat to cover the bottom of the container ($\frac{1}{8}$ in. deep), bring to about 350°F and add the meat, filling the containers well so that it builds moisture. For brun, turn the meat until it is richly browned; for blond, do not brown, but instead add water at once. Add moisture such as water, stock, milk, or tomato juice, or cover tightly and allow the meat to build its own moisture. Diced or minced vegetables may be added for flavoring. Simmer the meat until tender, replacing moisture if needed. When the meat is tender, remove the cover and reduce the liquid until it reaches the desired consistency. If necessary, remove the meat, thicken the gravy, and return the meat. Braising times for various cuts of meat are given in table 10-4.

Meats and poultry in quantity are best braised in a shallow steam-jacketed kettle. Heat the kettle, with cover down and steam on full, then add some melted fat and drop in even-sized meat pieces. Pot roasts should be evenly sized, between 5 and 10 lb. Turn the meat every 15 to 25 minutes until all sides are browned. After browning, add a small quantity of liquid, cover, reduce heat, and simmer. When the meat is done, remove it, make a gravy with the liquid, and return the meat. Again, for a blond product, omit the browning.

TABLE 10-4. Timetable for braising

Cut	Average weight or thickness	Approximate cooking time
Pot roast	3–5 lb	3–4 hr
Pot roast	5–15 lb	3–5 hr
Swiss steak	1–2½ in.	2–3 hr
Round steak or flank steak	½ in. (pounded)	¾–1 hr
Stuffed steak	½–¾ in	1½ hr
Short ribs	Pieces 2 × 2 × 2 in.	1½–2 hr
Fricassée	1–2 in. pieces	2–3 hr
Beef birds	½ × 2 × 4 in.	1½–2 hr
Stuffed lamb breast	2–3 lb	1½–2 hr
Rolled lamb breast	1½–2 lb	1½–2 hr
Lamb shanks	½ lb each	1–1½ hr
Lamb neck slices	½–¾ in.	1–1½ hr
Lamb riblets	¾ × 2½ × 3 in.	2–2½ hr
Pork chops or steaks	¾–1 in.	¾–1 hr
Spareribs	2–3 lb	1½ hr
Stuffed veal breast	3–4 lb	1½–2 hr
Rolled veal breast	2–3 lb	2–3 hr
Veal cutlets	½ × 3 × 5½ in.	¾–1 hr
Veal steaks or chops	½–¾ in.	¾–1 hr
Veal birds	½ × 2 × 4 in.	¾–1 hr

Source: National Livestock and Meat Board.

Simmering

Cooking meats in a quantity of water or other liquid may be called simmering, poaching, boiling, or stewing. Few flesh foods are boiled, since this tends to toughen them. To simmer, bring the water to a boil, add the product, and hold the temperature at between 185° and 205°F. For added flavor, use stocks or rich broths. Poultry should be simmered at around 190°F. Meats may be marinated, prebrowned in fat, and then simmered. Avoid heavy seasoning; the stock may later be reduced. Test doneness by inserting a fork about ½ in. deep and twisting. Small pieces break under pressure. Do not overcook, as this would produce dry, shreddy meat. Skim the liquid as necessary.

Vegetables are often boiled separately in stock and served with the meat. If they are to be cooked with the meat, add them about 30 minutes before serving. Cabbage and some other vegetables that cook relatively quickly are added later; members of the onion family are added earlier. Meat may be sliced and kept warm in stock. Meat, fish, or poultry to be used later should be cooled in its own stock or in cold water, removed, and refrigerated.

Steaming

Meats, fish, or poultry may be steamed over rich stock, a process called *free-venting*. Cooking under steam pressure reduces cooking time. It is easy to overcook meats when using steam pressure. Many meats may be given preliminary treatment such as prebrowning, then finished in a steam chamber. Fish is steamed over a flavored stock called *court bouillon*.

Blanching

Dropping meat momentarily into boiling water or simmering to partially cook it is called *blanching*. This procedure is more properly a form of preparation than a style of cooking. Some cooks presoak meats in cold, salted water before blanching, in order to remove undesirable parts or to firm the meats. After blanching, the item is dipped into cold water. Sweetbreads or brains are blanched in slightly acidulated water to whiten them. Cooking then proceeds by some other method.

Frozen Meat Cookery

The ability to freeze meat rapidly, avoiding heavy rupture of its cellular structure, and improved methods of packaging, storage, and transportation have improved frozen meats to such an extent that many operations now use them. Frozen meats are cooked according to the same methods used for nonfrozen meats. Better flavor and higher nutrient values result if meat is cooked from a frozen or partially frozen state than from a thawed state. The drip from frozen meat is high in nutrient and flavor values, and beginning the cooking while the meat is still frozen reduces drip loss. Constraints on time and equipment may disallow cooking meat from the hard-frozen state, but partial thawing reduces oven time without causing undue nutrient and flavor loss. If meat is thawed, the procedures and times for cooking it are the same as for regular meats. Meat needing shaping, grinding or breading is thawed and then prepared. Hard-frozen meats take about three times longer to roast than refrigerated meats. Prepare frozen meats for roasting as if they were unfrozen: place them fat-side-up, and roast in a 325°F oven. Cook until thawed; then insert a thermometer, and roast at 300°F.

Thin frozen steaks need only slightly longer cooking time than regular ones; thicker ones, however, required two to three times as much. To broil, place thin or medium frozen steaks 4 in. from the heat, and place larger steaks 8 to 12 in. from the heat. Reduce heat and thaw; then cook as for regular items. To pan-broil, cook frozen meats covered until thawed; then remove the cover and cook similarly to normal steaks. Dropping thick items into 325°F fat speeds thawing without giving an overcooked outside. Sautéing may be preferred to pan-broiling because thawing is more rapid. Sauté or grill at lower temperatures than normal. Covering the meat until it has thawed speeds thawing. To sauté or grill frozen breaded items, partially thaw them first. Braising small pieces takes only slightly longer for frozen than for unfrozen items, but larger pieces take much longer. Brown these while still frozen. If frozen pieces can be separated, they may be dredged with flour before browning. The procedure is then the same as for regular meat. Simmering frozen meat in water differs little from handling unfrozen meat in the same way.

To thaw meat, leave it wrapped under refrigeration; thawing takes $1\frac{1}{2}$ hours per pound. Thawing at room temperature takes about 1 hour per pound. Placing the frozen item in front of an electric fan reduces time. Meat frozen in waterproof wraps can be thawed in cold water or under running cold water, but unwrapped meat cannot. Water-thawing takes about 1 hour per pound.

For items that have been refrigerated but not frozen, table 10-5 identifies the day-limit for storage before use without diminution in quality.

Breakfast Meats

Breakfast calls for fast service, so some precooking of meats for this meal is advisable. Corned beef hash, steamed salt mackerel, finnan haddie, sausages, ham, and bacon all need some precooking. Hash is shaped ahead of time and browned, so it only needs heating. Mackerel and finnan haddie are partially poached and left in warm water for quick cooking. Thin ham grills rapidly enough to be done to order, but thick slices may be grilled and placed in a steam table in a small amount of stock or water. Bacon may be partially baked in 18 × 26-in. baking sheets or on wire racks; the grease is then poured off, and the bacon is stacked in a shallow pan, after which it can be recrisped in only a few minutes. Some cooks place a weight on the bacon to prevent it from curling. Sausages or sausage patties may be parboiled or steamed. Parboiling usually occurs from a cold-water start. Sausages are then removed and held; as orders for them arrive, they are browned on a griddle. Some cooks fry sausages and hold a small quantity of them in the steam table. If necessary, they can be given a quick sauté before serving. Brown 'n' serve sausages require 3 to 4 minutes of browning under a broiler or on top a griddle. About 2 minutes in deep fat cooks sausages, but the contamination of the fat from the sausage's free fatty acids is so great that this method is not recommended.

POULTRY

Methods for cooking poultry are much the same as those for cooking meat. Raw or cooked poultry and its stock are very perishable. Freshness is essential to quality. Fresh poultry should be received chilled. Hold it at a temperature below 34°F, and use it within a few days. Cool stock and cooked birds to 100°F, cover to prevent drying out, and refrigerate; use within 24 hours. Hold frozen poultry at 0°F or lower. At 10°F, poultry

TABLE 10-5. Refrigerator storage time chart
(at 36° to 40°F)

Meat (loosely covered)	Limit of days for maximum quality
BEEF	
Standing rib roast......................	5–8
Steaks	3–5
Pot roasts	5–6
Stew meat	2
Ground beef	2
Liver (sliced)	2
Heart................................	2
PORK	
Roasts	5–6
Chops...............................	3
Spareribs	3
Pork sausage........................	2–3
CURED AND SMOKED MEATS	
Hams, picnics	
whole or half.......................	7
slices	3
Bacon	5–7
Dried beef	10–12
Corned beef.........................	5–7
Tongue	6–7
LAMB	
Roasts	5
Chops...............................	3
Heart................................	2
Liver (sliced)	2
VEAL	
Roasts	5–6
Chops...............................	4
Liver (sliced)	2
Sweetbreads (cooked)	2
COOKED MEATS	
Home-cooked meats	4
Hams, picnics........................	7
Franks..............................	4–5
Meat loaves (sliced)	3–4
Luncheon meats (sliced)...............	3
Bologna loaves (unsliced)..............	4–6
Dry and semidry sausage (uncut)	14–21
Liver sausage (sliced)	2–3
Liver sausage (uncut)	4–6
POULTRY	
Chickens (drawn, whole)..............	2
Chickens (cut-up)	2
Turkeys (drawn)......................	2
Ducklings (drawn, whole)	2
Cooked poultry.......................	3–4

SOURCE: Swift & Co.

holds its quality for eight months, while at 20°F, it holds it for only two to four months. To thaw, place in a 40°F area. Most chickens thaw in one to two days, but larger birds take two to four days. Poultry can remain in moisture- and vapor-proof wraps and defrost in cold water or under cold running water; thawing time then takes 1 to 2 hours for chickens and 2 to 6 hours for turkeys. Placing frozen poultry before a fan reduces thawing time. To speed thawing, as soon as the legs are pliable, remove the giblets and neck and spread the legs and wings. Cut-up poultry can be separated as soon as it is crinkly. Wash thawed poultry in cold water, drain, and prepare for cooking. Never refreeze.

As with meats, poultry cooked at low temperatures (250°F) shrinks less and yields a moister, better-looking product. Cook old birds in moist heat and young ones in dry heat. Most poultry (except perhaps duck) is cooked well done. Small birds such as squab or quail are best when baked at temperatures around 400°F to reduce drying out. Cook rabbit according to the same criteria as poultry.

The larger the bird, the greater the yield of meat. About 9 percent of a turkey that weighs over 18 lb consists of skeletal structure, regardless of the bird's exact size. The abdominal cavities of 20- to 30-lb birds are about equal in size. A $3\frac{1}{2}$-lb duckling cuts nicely into four portions, each of which is cut into quarters and served with bones and skin still attached. A $2\frac{1}{2}$-lb chicken, with no neck or giblets, gives four cooked portions 6 to 7 oz each. Use about $\frac{3}{4}$ lb of uncooked turkey (dressed weight) per portion. Increase the size of this portion for geese. A 5-oz serving of boned chicken breast makes a fair portion, as does a 7-oz serving of unboned chicken breast. Size poultry as carefully as steaks or other meats.

Roasting

Truss legs and wings of small birds—but not of large birds—for roasting. Brush with fat, and season inside and out. Add paprika to aid in browning. Have pans full, but do not crowd birds together. Put large lean birds breast-down on trivets (see fig. 10-9). Small ones may be placed breast-up if basted frequently or covered with bacon, salt pork, other fatty tissues, or an oil-soaked cloth. Fat birds, such as geese and ducks, may be roasted breast-up without basting. Pour off fat as it accumulates. Ducks and geese are sometimes presteamed and then finished by roasting; this reduces their fattiness.

Place chickens in a preheated 325°F oven; place larger birds in a 250°F oven. When almost done, turn large birds breast-up and complete roasting, basting if necessary. Breaking the legs from the side at this stage improves heat penetration. Large birds may be split lengthwise and roasted, or breasts, legs, and wings may be roasted separately and the bony parts used for stock. Simmer giblets $1\frac{1}{2}$ to $2\frac{1}{2}$ hours. If turkey is to be roasted in heavy-duty ovens overnight, use a 225°F or slightly lower-temperature oven.

Doneness is indicated by a 180°F temperature in the thigh or breast center (see fig. 10-10a). When the meat on the thigh or breast feels soft, or

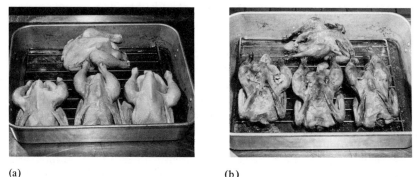

(a)   (b)

Figure 10-9. The wrong way to roast chickens, turkeys, and other lean birds: placing them breast-up prevents the fat on the back from running down and keeping the product moist.

when a fork inserted into the shoulder muscle twists out easily, the bird is done (see fig. 10-10b). Some cooks roast large, tender birds to a state of slight underdoneness, and then cool and slice. The slices are placed over mounds of dressing—dark meat first, covered with broad slices of white meat. The mounds are then covered with a moist cloth and refrigerated. For service, the cloths are removed, and the mounds are warmed in an oven or steamer and served, one mound per plate, covered with *very hot* gravy. Yield is always greater if poultry is chilled and then carved.

Poach-roasting of poultry is a common procedure that usually results in a product that is plumper, tenderer, juicier, and more flavorful. Prepare the poultry as shown in figure 10-11. Place poultry parts into pans skin-side-up, and fill the pans with water or stock until it covers about two-thirds of the poultry. Bones are usually left in. Season lightly and

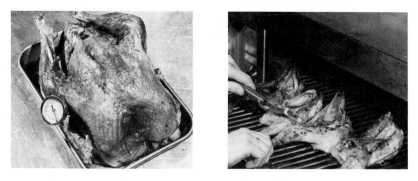

(a)   (b)

Figure 10-10. (a) Put the thermometer into the deepest part of the thigh to measure the internal temperature; the reading should be around 180°F for immediate serving or 160°F if service will occur after slicing and holding. (b) A test for doneness of broiled chicken. Notice that the worker does not pierce the meat in checking for movement of the joint, which indicates doneness.

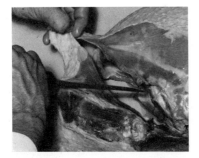

(a)

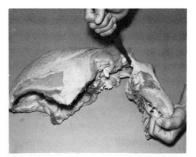

(b)

(c)   (d)

Figure 10-11. (a) To prepare a turkey for poach-roasting, first remove the legs and wings. (b) Then remove the back. (c) Separate the breast from the breastbone. (d) Use the back, wings, and other body parts for broth and picked meat, leaving the bony parts of the wings, legs, thighs, and breast for poaching.

roast in a 325°F oven until tender. Let the poultry cool in its stock. The tops of the poultry are a delicate brown and the meat is moist (see fig. 10-12).

Poaching

Poaching reduces cooking time and increases yield, flavor, and tenderness over roasting—especially with larger birds. More attractive and uniform portions are obtained, and less cooking space is required. Poach the poultry boned, and slice on a machine. Section and bone large birds, using bones and bony parts for stock. Pick cooked meat from these, using it in salads, made-up dishes, and the like. Place the parts skin-side-up in a stock pot, roasting pan, or steam-jacketed kettle, and cover with hot, salted water or stock, using 1 T of salt and 1 t of white pepper for every 6 lb of bird. Simmer at low heat for 2 to $2\frac{1}{2}$ hours or until fork tender. Cool covered in the stock, or plunge into cold water. Place in an area refrigerated to 40°F or lower, and chill; then slice. Use meat and stock within three days.

Figure 10-12. Poach-roasted turkey.

Simmering

Whole or sectioned birds are simmered in stock kettles or steam-jacketed kettles. They are covered with 1 gal of stock or water seasoned with 1 T of salt for every 5 lb of bird. Vegetables may be added. Bring the kettle to a simmer, cover, skim, and cook the poultry until tender, adding water as required. Cool as for poaching.

Steaming

Older birds may be cooked under steam pressure, giving a light-colored meat that can be used as picked cooked meat. Steaming takes half as long as simmering. Place the poultry into a pan, add a small quantity of water, and steam. Watch times, since cooking is rapid and overcooking occurs easily. Steam-pressure cooking may toughen the flesh more than simmering would.

Braising

Poultry may be braised like meat. Fricasséed or stewed poultry is braised poultry. This cooking method is used frequently for tougher birds, but tender ones may also be prepared by this method.

FISH AND SHELLFISH

Good fish, properly prepared, can vie in quality with the finest meat or poultry. Fish flesh contains little connective tissue and little pigment that changes color in cooking. Almost any method cooks it to the desired degree of tenderness. Fish is usually best when cooked to just done.

When properly done, the flesh should flake easily and be moist. Over-cooked fish breaks up too easily, and the meat is dry, pulpy, and tough.

Both raw and cooked fish are highly perishable; caution should therefore be observed in their handling. When not needed for preparation, hold fish at a temperature under 35°F. Make certain that fresh fish is used quickly, and take care that cooked items are covered, lightly packed in shallow layers, and used quickly. Discard suspicious items.

As with poultry and meats, it is important that fish be sized for proper portions. About 4 or 5 oz makes a portion, if there is not too much bone and skin. Many fish have a high proportion of preparation waste—some whole fish losing half of their weight with the removal of scales, head, fins, and entrails. Whole fish is scaled and drawn for baking or steaming, leaving the head on only if the fish is for display. It should be washed thoroughly. An 8- to 12-lb fish that has been baked, steamed, or poached portions well. A long and tapering 12-lb fish cuts into desirable steaks. Filleting aids portioning (see fig. 10-13).

If of good quality and correctly cooked, fish should not have a strong fishy flavor. While the flavor of cod, mackerel, herring, and others may

(a)

(b)

(c)

(d)

Figure 10-13. Preparing fish fillets. (a) Whole or round fish are scaled, except for trout and certain others that may be skinned, such as bullfish. (b) The head may be cut or broken off, or it may be left on to facilitate holding during boning. The fish is cut open on the underside, and the entrails are removed. The fish is then washed well. (c) The fish is laid flat on a cutting board and grasped by the tail. A cut is made about ½ in. from the tail, slanting downward to the bone, and then the flattened knife is set forward to obtain a strip. (d) The skin is peeled off with the knife. (*Courtesy U.S. Department of Interior*)

be abundant, it should never be objectionable. Fish that have abundant flavor are cooked in ways that lessen or modify the flavor.

The fat content of fish is from 1 to 20 percent. Marbling and finish are lacking, the oil being spread throughout. Fat fish such as salmon, mackerel, shad, and trout can be baked, broiled, or poached with good results. Lean fish such as flounder, halibut, and cod are best poached, deep-fried, sautéed, or simmered. Sauces are often used to give such fish richness and moistness. Lean fish are frequently breaded or batter-dipped for deep-frying, and they may be baked if basted or barded. Baking quickly at high temperatures helps keep lean fish moist. Most fish, fat or lean, are served accompanied by tart sauces such as hollandaise, lemon butter, or Bercy sauce.

Fish—especially lean fish—are baked covered. They should be cooked only until done and served soon. Use moderate roasting temperatures. Portion by lifting skin and serving in as complete a piece as possible. Fat fish broils well but lean fish gives a dry, pulpy product that lacks color and flavor and is apt to curl under the broiler. If dipped in flour, put into a double-grid, and basted frequently with butter, lean fish can be broiled. Follow the broiling procedures given for meat.

Fish is sautéed in slightly more fat than meats and poultry are—especially lean fish, which is often floured lightly, breaded, or batter-dipped. Because such coverings char quickly, care must taken to ensure that cooking occurs inside while a desirable outer appearance is maintained. Serve sautéed fish as soon as possible, since part of its quality depends on its having a crisp outer layer and a fresh, moist interior. Fish can be marinated for 5 minutes in a tart sauce and then cooked. Some cooks feel that sautéed fish is better if salted 5 to 10 minutes before cooking. Sautéed fish served with some of the frying fat over the fish is called pan-fried or à la meunière.

To steam, simmer, or poach, barely cover the fish with liquid and cook gently. Cook large fish in a cloth so that it can be lifted easily, or use a lightly greased trivet with handles for this purpose. If fish is to be served cold or decorated, allow it to cool in its own stock. Do not overcook such products. A whole fish should fit freely in the pan. Use good fish stock, salted water, court bouillon, wine, or other liquid. Mild-flavored fish may be cooked in a liquid consisting of one-quarter milk and three-quarters water. Large pieces are best started in cold liquid, since hot liquid encourages breaking up. To cook, quickly score the sides so that heat penetration is faster. Strong-flavored fish are best started in cold liquid. Put small pieces into boiling liquid, and immediately reduce the heat to a simmer. Cook for 8 to 10 minutes. Some white-fleshed fish may be baked in milk. Fish cooked in nonmilk liquids are often served with a bit of rich court bouillon poured over them. *Truite au bleu* is very fresh trout that has been killed, dressed, and immediately poached; they turn a bluish color and may be served hot or chilled. Steamed, simmered, or poached fish are good served cold—especially fat fish such as salmon.

Only firm-fleshed fish are braised, using a straight-sided braising pan. Live, firm, fleshed fish may be killed, scored (slash-cut), dressed, and then soaked in cold water. This toughens the flesh so that braising is possible. Fat fish should be used, as lean fish yields a dry item. Fish can be skinned for braising; leave it in large pieces. Good braising liquids include court bouillon and wine; if the fish is browned and a brown roux is used, red wine is common; otherwise, white wine is used, especially with white-fleshed fish. Because of a short cooking time, the cover may be left off or loosely fitted so that evaporation can reduce the sauce. A *matelote* is fish braised with vegetables and lightly thickened. *Bouillabaisse* and *chioppino* are fish stews; the fish may be served with its stock, or stock and fish may be served in separate bowls. The former style is French from around Marseilles, and the latter is Italian.

Shellfish, if cooked at too high a temperature or for too long, becomes tough and rubbery. Simmering at 190°F is preferred to boiling. Water at 140°F immediately kills shellfish. Simmer shellfish at 190°F in salted water (lobsters at 205°F—see fig. 10-14) to get a tender and flavorful item. After cooking, crab meat may be removed from the shell as outlined in figure 10-15. Where a large quantity of clams or oysters are to be shucked, mechanical shuckers are used.

Green (uncooked) shrimp may be purchased fresh or frozen, with heads on or headless. Cooked shrimp maybe purchased in the shell, shelled, or shelled and deveined. Prepare shrimp by removing the shell and cutting along the back to remove the vein; then wash. Shrimp may be butterflied by splitting it to the tail, which is left on. To cook shrimp, use $\frac{1}{2}$ cup salt to 1 gal water and 5 lb raw, headless shrimp. Do not overcook. Yield after cooking, peeling, and deveining is 50 percent. PDQ shrimp is peeled, deveined, and quick-cooked shrimp. It may be purchased fresh or frozen.

Wash clams or oysters in the shell thoroughly before steaming or using. To shuck oysters, follow the procedure outlined in figure 10-16. To rid clams of sand, add $\frac{1}{3}$ cup salt per gallon of water. Soak the clams for 15 to 20 minutes, and wash. Repeat until the clams are sand-free. Salted water must be used, since clams will not disgorge sand in freshwater. Some cooks put clams into salted water, add cornmeal, and leave them overnight under refrigeration. The clams eat the cornmeal and disgorge the sand.

To steam, use six to eight clams ($\frac{3}{4}$ lb) per portion. Place into a container with a perforated bottom containing 1 cup of water for every 1 lb clams. Steam for 5 to 10 minutes or until the clams are partially opened. Serve them on a plate with an accompaniment of clam nectar in a cup and a side dish of melted butter. Clams or oysters may also be roasted: place them in a baking pan, and roast them for 15 minutes at 450°F or until they are open. Alternatively, oysters and clams may be baked or barbecued in the half shell.

Lobster tails should be poached for 5 minutes and then split for broil-

(a)

(b)

Figure 10-14.   (a) To cook a live lobster, plunge it head first into water heated to about 150°F. Bring the water to a simmering temperature of about 205°F, and cook the lobster for about 20 to 25 minutes. (b) To split a lobster, lay it on its back, and cut through to the shell. Remove the stomach, the back of the head, and the intestinal vein that runs from the stomach to the end of the tail; do not discard the green liver and the coral roe, since many people like them. Claws may be cracked before the lobster is sent from the kitchen.

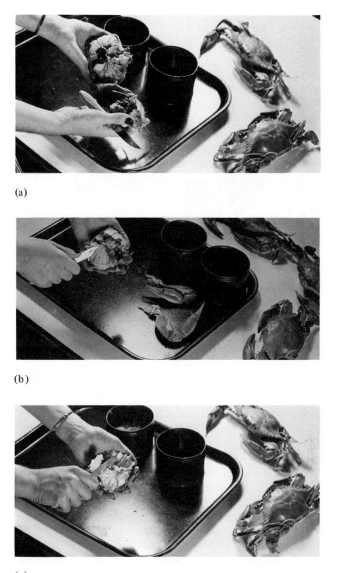

(a)

(b)

(c)

Figure 10-15. Obtaining crab meat from cooked crabs. (a) Break off the large claws, pull off the top shell, and break off the legs. (b) Remove the gills and other internal material by scraping and washing. (c) Slice open the top right side of the inner skeleton, starting at the top, and remove the meat. Repeat the slice on the left side, and remove meat. Crack the claws, and remove meat. (*Courtesy U.S. Department of Interior*)

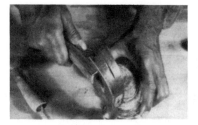

(a)

(b)

(c)

(d)

Figure 10-16. Shucking an oyster or clam. (a) Break the shell with a sharp rap of a hammer. This is called *billing*. Bill at the thinnest area of the shell. (b) Hold the oyster or clam with the hinge part of the shell at the palm, or hold it flat on a cutting board, and insert the tip of a knife where the shell is broken. (c) After inserting of the knife, twist it slightly to open the shell and then run the knife in and up close to the top, cutting through the adductor muscle that joins the clam or oyster to the shell. (d) Cut the adductor muscle attached to the lower shell. The clam or oyster is now ready to be served on the half shell or removed from the shell for other preparation. (*Courtesy U.S. Department of Interior*)

ing; this leads to a moister and tenderer product than results from broiling alone. The time for broiling when this method is used is about 5 to 6 minutes. To reduce curling of the tails, thaw and split them, or remove the thin undershells and bend the tails back firmly to break the connective tissue that causes curling.

Chapter Review

1. How do the composition and structure of flesh influence the way it is handled, treated, and cooked? In answering this, consider how connective tissue, ripening, fibers, and other factors enter into determining the proper way to proceed.
2. What makes up the flavor of cooked meat?
3. What are the different stages of doneness of meat, poultry, and fish?
4. What are some of the proper techniques to use in broiling meat, roasting it, pan- or griddle-broiling it, barbecueing it, and braising it?
5. What different techniques should be used in cooking frozen meat (versus meat that is not frozen)?

6. How should young birds be roasted? How should old birds be cooked?
7. What are the characteristics of fish flesh that influence the way it should be cooked?
8. Match the following terms with their correct definition:

matelote	nitrosomyoglobin	brun
rigor mortis	broil	jugged
hematin	*en papillote*	blanch
au bleu	trivet	*à la meunière*
collagen		

_____ fish braised with vegetables and served as a slightly thickened stew

_____ to cook by radiant heat

_____ white connective tissue

_____ a stiffening of the muscles after death

_____ roasted in paper

_____ myoglobin changes to this in cooking

_____ to sauté fish and then serve it with a bit of the frying fat over it

_____ a perforated pan on which meat rests while roasting

_____ braised in a pot

_____ trout that is boiled soon after it is killed

_____ browned meat

_____ to dip into boiling water

_____ a pigment that keeps meat such as ham or corned beef always red

Bakeshop
Production

CHAPTER 11

Bakery Ingredients

Outline

Goals

1. To cover the major ingredients used in bakery goods, and to list the properties each exhibits in products.
2. To discuss the action of leavening agents.
3. To explain what different flours do in bakery products and why specific ones are used to achieve certain results.
4. To identify the proper principles and techniques for obtaining successful products from sugar.
5. To describe how different leavening agents work.

INTRODUCTION

Perhaps no other food production work requires as much technical knowledge and skill as baking. While very similar ingredients are used, slight variations in proportions, preparation, or baking produce extremely different products. Success or failure thus becomes a matter of handling fine details. Knowing the properties of ingredients in baking is essential to producing successful items.

FLOUR

Flour has been described as finely ground cereal, but some flours (such as potato and almond flours) are not made from cereals. Moreover, some ground cereals (such as cornmeal and oatmeal) are meals, not flours. For baking purposes, flour can perhaps best be defined as a ground starch-like product that gives structure and body to bakery products.

WHEAT FLOUR

Different kinds of wheat flour are needed to satisfy the many different baking needs of a bakeshop. The average wheat flour contains 63 to 73 percent starch, 7 to 15 percent protein, 1 to 2 percent fat, 0.4 percent ash (minerals), 1 to 2 percent sugar, and 11 to 13 percent moisture. Variations in these relative quantities make a great deal of difference in flour's baking properties.

Soft flour made from soft or winter wheat is used for pastry, for many quick breads, for cakes, and for cookies. It has a clear white color and a soft velvety consistency. Its ratio of starch to protein is high. Spring or hard wheat is best for yeast breads and pastry goods that require strong structures. It contains a higher percentage of protein and a lower percentage of starch than does soft flour. The color is slightly creamy, and the texture is rough when the flour is rubbed between the fingers. Soft flour squeezed in the hand stays together, but hard flour crumbles.

Both the quality and the quantity of protein influence flour's structure-building properties. Yeast breads, puff paste, and éclairs are examples of items that need strong protein, while cakes, cookies, and muffins need weaker protein. Hard flour is called *strong* because it produces strong structures; soft flour is called *weak* because it produces tenderer, more delicate structures. When the word *strong* is applied to soft flour, it means that the flour has the ability in a batter to carry high percentages of sugar and fats.

The best wheat flours are called *patents,* and the poorest are called *clears*; *middlings* fall between the two in quality. Patents come from the first flour in milling, middlings next, and clears last. A straight flour contains all of the wheat kernel except the bran. Rye flour, straight flour, flour high in clears, or flour containing bran may have to be mixed with good patents to improve their structure-building properties.

Gluten is a group of six proteins present in flour; it is able to absorb about 200 percent of its weight in moisture. When completely moistened, it forms a tenuous, elastic, viscous, pliable mass extending as a thin, structural network in batter or dough. Salt and milk strengthen gluten, and sugar tenderizes it. Alkalies weaken it, while acids make it more pliable and extensible. Fat, sugar, and starch interfere with gluten formation; fat surrounds gluten particles, preventing them from joining, and thus gives a more tender product. Too much liquid causes gluten to become overextended and unable to form a strong network. To perform properly, gluten must form a strong enough mass to retain leavening gases and hold other ingredients in suspension (see fig. 11-1). For this reason, even delicate cake flours need some gluten.

Moisture is needed to make gluten sticky. Working then brings gluten particles together to form a network. This is why mixing (kneading) is performed for some items and avoided for others. When gluten is cold or not completely hydrated, it sticks together less easily; but when warm and given moisture, it develops readily—especially when worked. Keep-

(a)

(b)

Figure 11-1. (a) Three gluten balls showing approximate gluten content of (left to right) cake, pastry, and bread flours. (*Courtesy Wheat Flour Institute*) (b) Gluten development is shown in these baking powder biscuits. Notice the tiny strands and the layering of the dough from gluten development and gas pressures during baking. (*Courtesy General Foods*)

ing muffin batter cold retards gluten formation; limiting water in a pie dough reduces the opportunity for gluten networks to form.

Gluten development can be demonstrated by mixing hard wheat flour into a stiff dough and kneading it for 10 minutes. Rest or condition it for 20 to 30 minutes, and then carefully wash the starch from the dough. A yellowish, viscous and elastic mass remains; it is crude gluten. If this mass is formed into a ball and baked in a 380°F oven, steam develops inside, swelling it into a large honeycombed ball.

Green flour is flour aged less than six weeks. It is usually bulky or rigid and inflexible in baking. Products made with green flour are tough; bread forms odd humps on top or may break or tear because its gluten lacks elasticity. Overaged flour lacks extensibility and gives poor volume. Rye flours should not be aged because they do not have a gluten that requires it.

Moisture absorption is an indicator of flour quality. A flour capable of binding in a lot of water gives a moist product that performs well in mixing and baking and has good keeping qualities. A good hard or soft flour absorbs from 60 to 65 percent of its own weight in moisture and still makes a firm, pliable dough. Soft flours absorb less moisture than hard ones do. Failure to absorb moisture indicates weak gluten and signals the inability to form a stable batter. Sugar and acid increase moisture absorption. A yeast bread is sticky during mixing, but fermenting increases its acidity, and this (plus additional hydration time) produces a soft, pliable dough. Salt reduces moisture absorption and raises gluten's coagulation temperature.

Heat coagulates gluten and gelatinizes (swells) starch, producing a firm product. Coagulation occurs at around 165°F; starch starts to swell at 144°F and stops doing so at around 203°F. Additional ingredients, such as eggs, may coagulate and help make a firm product. A moisture loss of 8 to 16 percent also helps in firming. A highly complex balance must be established among the various actions of leavening agents, moisture, structure-forming ingredients, and heat.

Many things affect flour's performance. If ash content is above 0.5 percent, flour performs poorly, especially in yeast goods. Size and uniformity of grind is also important. Too-large granules do not absorb the right quantity of liquid to help in carrying sugar, shortening, and other ingredients. Bread from flour that is too coarsely ground is heavy and shapes with difficulty. A very fine grind gives a pasty, tight-grained, overly fermented product with excessive starch swell in baking. Unevenness of grind mixes together large particles, with slow moisture absorption and low stabilizing ability, and small granules that absorb too much moisture and have excessive stabilizing ability. Good milling produces properly ground flours. Proper size yields products with uniform cell structure, good oven spring, maximum volume, and good texture.

Store flour in a well-ventilated, dry place at about 70°F. Foodservice operations usually purchase flour by the barrel (196-lb or two 98-lb bags or four 49-lb bags). Cakes flours can be obtained in 100-lb bags. Do not stack flour over eight bags high. Some flours come in 50-lb boxes.

Bread (Hard Wheat) Flour

Strong hard wheat is used to make bread flour. Its gluten is capable of development and retains strength in kneading, fermenting, and baking. Its gluten content should be higher than that of regular flour—about 12.5 to 12.8 percent. If white flour is used, it must be enriched with iron, thiamine, niacin, calcium, and vitamin D. The flour should have good moisture absorption and should form a pliable, elastic, soft dough that is sufficiently viscous and tenacious after mixing to give good rising spring and good gas-holding properties. Too much viscosity leads to a bucky, unyielding dough that breaks or humps during baking. Good flour does not become slack as a result of fermentation. Overly elastic dough is hard to handle. A 15.5 percent protein flour is desirable for blending with flours lacking in good-quality gluten.

Pastry (Soft Wheat) Flour

The best pastry and cake flours come from the first patents. Cake flour contains about 7 to 8.5 percent protein; if less, the product lacks volume and is not of the best quality. The flour should produce a stable batter and should carry large quantities of liquid, fat, sugar, and eggs. Cake flours that are low in moisture absorption cannot carry the liquid and fat needed to give a good product. Pastry flour has more and stronger gluten than cake flour does—between 8 and 10 percent. If more gluten than this is present, it lacks some spring strength. Pastry flour is used for quick breads, pie dough, and other products requiring limited structure strength. It is also used for general cooking, since it is inexpensive.

If necessary, strong flour can be used to make cakes or pastries; in such a case, $2\frac{1}{2}$ oz cornstarch and 14 oz bread flour replace 1 lb of cake or pastry flour. The amount of shortening is also increased to weaken the bread flour's strong gluten. All-purpose flour is suitable for making cakes, cookies, breads, and so on, but it is little used in foodservice work.

SHORTENINGS

At one time, the shortenings used for baking were limited to plain butter (for cakes, cookies, and other pastries), washed butter (for puff pastes and rolled-in doughs), lard (for pastries, pies, and breads), and oleomargarine or suet (for crackers and bread). Chicken fat was prized for making cream sauces, and goose grease was blended with other fats to make mealy, tender pie crusts. Today, however, shortenings are available to do any specialized job.

Hydrogenation was a big step in the development of shortening because it made vegetable oils solid. We use it to achieve different results in fats. As much of 12 percent of lard can be hydrogenated in order to improve lard's plasticity, increase its waxiness, or raise its melting point. Margarines are given special hydrogenation treatment that makes them better than washed butter for puff pastes and rolled-in doughs. Chemists can bleach, deodorize, decolor, or deflavor oils and fats. They can add flavors such as milk solids and diacetyl to make a shortening taste more like butter. Margarine can be made to brown if lecithin is added to it, and fats can be protected against rancidity through the addition of antioxidants (see figs. 11-2).

Fats give slip to a batter or dough—a characteristic that is important in getting correct leavening and baking movement. A product lacking slip may not develop correctly and may have poor shape and crumb. Shortenings tenderize (shorten) by surrounding gluten and other ingredients,

Figure 11-2. A special deep-frying fat containing an ingredient called Metsil that stabilizes the fat against frying rigors. (*Courtesy Procter & Gamble*)

lubricating them so that they do not stick together. Free fatty acids increase shortness; chemists vary the number of these to produce more or less shortening power.

Shortenings must vary in plasticity for different purposes. For a flaky pie crust or rolled-in dough, a waxy, tough, extensible, plastic, firm fat is needed to ensure that, when the dough is rolled out, fat layers will remain in the dough. For icings, a flavorless, plastic fat that creams (aerates) well, has no greasiness, and carries a high amount of sugar is necessary. A shortening with good aeration ability, waxiness, and plasticity is needed to increase cake batter lightness and cake volume. Some shortenings are precreamed to ensure that this occurs. Baking shortening is conditioned so that it possesses the right characteristics at room or mixing temperature.

Plasticity and shortness are related. A fat that lacks plasticity may not spread well and thus may not shorten. Tallow (suet) is too firm and brittle to spread well. Some other fats, such as chicken fat, are too soft and shorten too much. Products such as cookies must be so short that they almost crumble, while cakes and quick breads must be sufficiently tender to have a delicate texture but still retain enough structure to be handled.

Emulsifiers such as monoglycerides and diglycerides help spread a plastic shortening in fine globules in batters or doughs, producing more stable batters and finer-grained products. An old rule for cake recipes was that the weight of the sugar should not exceed the flour weight; but with today's improved shortenings and flour, the sugar weight should exceed the flour weight, giving us sweeter and tenderer cakes. Emulsifiers increase shortening power without reducing plasticity. They also increase volume, give a smoother, finer texture to the crumb, and yield thinner cell walls, allowing the use of simplified mixing methods. Batters made with emulsified shortenings handle better, are smoother and more stable, and resist curdling better. Emulsified shortenings, by spreading more completely, retard moisture loss and thus enhance product moistness and freshness. Emulsified shortenings do have lower smoking temperatures, however, so they should not be used for deep-fat frying or for general cooking use. They are also expensive in comparison to other shortenings.

SUGARS

Sugar is used in baking to provide sweetness, tenderness, color, food value, good crumb texture, and attractive crust color to baked goods, and to serve as food for yeast. There are a number of different kinds of sugar. Sanding sugars are used to coat items such as doughnuts, crullers, cake tops, and coffee cakes. The coarsest of these, *confectioner's coarse AA*, comes in about $\frac{1}{10}$-in. cubes. *Sanding coarse* sugar is about half this size. *Fine granulated—also called bottler's sugar* because it is used for carbonated beverages—is sometimes used as a sanding sugar, too. *Regular granulated* is used for table sugar, as is *extra-fine standard*. *Fruit* sugar is slightly finer and is used for breakfast cereal and fruit. *Baker's special, extra fine,* is used for cakes and cookies; it goes into solution rapidly and promotes uniform cell structure and good volume. If such a sugar is not available, a baker may approximate it by rolling regular sugar under a rolling pin. *Standard powdered (6X)* sugar is used for toppings for sweet doughs and the like. *Extra-fine powdered (10X)* gives a creamy icing and is also used for dusting. *Icing* sugar is the finest powdered sugar, giving a creamy and fine-textured icing. Icings made with this sugar quickly develop a thin soft crust with a high gloss; they also have good spreadability.

Dehydrated fondant is a dried fondant, not a powdered sugar; it is used for icings and is sold under such trade names as Drivert and Dri-Fond. Bakeshops also use syrups such as honey, sorghum syrup, and corn syrup. Since these syrups contain about 25 percent moisture, moisture reduction is necessary if they are to replace sugar in a recipe. Glucose and other sugars are used to replace sucrose. Brown sugars contain 1 to 5 percent invert sugar—sugar whose natural direction of crystallization in solution has been reversed, inhibiting crystallization. Darker varieties of brown sugar are stronger in flavor than lighter ones. Molasses is also used; its flavor may be mild to strong. Granulated sugar is almost 100 percent sucrose and is made from sugar cane or sugar beets. Molasses and brown sugar contain a lot of sucrose but also acid, minerals, and other sugars, so they react differently from regular granulated sugar. Maltose, which comes from sprouted barley, is used often as a yeast food or (in other foods) as a sweetener and flavorer. Lactose—milk sugar— has low solubility and is not widely used in food preparation; yeast cannot digest it. Many plant or fruit sugars contain glucose (dextrose) or fructose (levulose). The sugar in honey is about half glucose and half fructose in simple sugar form. Sucrose is a crystallized chemical union of equal parts fructose and glucose; maltose breaks down entirely into glucose; and lactose breaks down into equal parts glucose and galactose. Starches and dextrins break down into complex sugars and then into simple sugars. For instance, starch changes into dextrin, then into maltose, and then into glucose (see fig. 11-3).

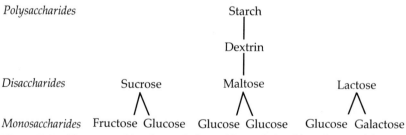

Figure 11-3.   The compositional complexity and interrelationships of some of the saccharides. Starch and dextrin are complex substances that can break down into maltose, a disaccharide sugar. Like maltose, sucrose and lactose are complex sugars. All break down into monosaccharides or simple sugars.

Changing starch to complex sugars or changing complex sugars to simple ones may be desirable or undesirable. It is desirable when enzymes are used to make corn syrup from corn, or when an acid is used to invert (break down) sucrose to glucose and fructose in cooking fondant; but it is undesirable when acid breaks down a starch paste, as in lemon pie filling. If 2 oz cream of tartar is added to 5 lb sugar and 1 qt water and this mixture is heated to 240°F, about 40 percent of the sucrose becomes inverted. Thenceforth the mixture will not crystallize, because the inverted sugar interferes with crystallization; if $\frac{1}{4}$ to $\frac{1}{2}$ oz cream of tartar is used instead of 2 oz, however, a 16 to 23 percent inversion occurs, and a soft, plastic, moldable crystalline mass is obtained. If too little acid is used, giving a 7 to 12 percent inversion, a hard fondant results (see fig. 11-4). Heating the mixture to a higher temperature gives other results. If 5 lb sugar, 1 qt water, and $\frac{1}{4}$ oz cream of tartar are cooked to 280°F, a good stiff fondant is obtained—one that is too stiff to use for frostings. Alternatively, we can omit acid and just add invert sugars. Thus, if $\frac{1}{2}$ to $\frac{3}{4}$ lb corn syrup (mostly invert sugar) is added to 5 lb sugar and 1 qt water, a mixture of 15 to 18 percent invert sugar is obtained, giving a good fondant; 1 lb corn syrup yields a mixture containing 20 percent invert sugar. Acids in molasses, vinegar, brown sugar, honey, and other foods can react in undesirable ways with carbohydrates during cooking or baking.

Some sugars, (especially fructose) are hydroscopic; that is, they attract moisture. Such sugars may be used to produce soft cookies but not crisp ones. A fruit cake containing invert sugar slowly draws moisture into it. Pulled sugar work or hard candies may attract moisture on humid days

Figure 11-4. The chocolate on the left was filled with a fondant center containing an enzyme that inverted the sugars, turning them into a syrup. The chocolate on the right was filled at the same time with a fondant center having no enzyme added; as a result, it remains firm.

and may therefore have to be stored in airtight chambers. Sugar products are sometimes stored in chambers containing calcium chloride, to remove moisture from the air. When calcium chloride becomes too wet to be effective, it can be regenerated by being heated in an oven. A sugar solution containing a hydroscopic sugar is often cooked to a slightly higher temperature to correct for the moisture it may later attract. Acids contained in sugar-coated candied fruit may invert the fruit's sugar coating, making it sticky.

Soda and other weak alkalies decompose sugars. Sucrose is more resistant to alkalies than are maltose, lactose, glucose, or fructose. Breakdown from exposure to alkalies is shown in most sugars by the development of a deep cream or light yellow color, although glucose turns a dirty gray. Cooking a sugar solution for a long time in an alkali produces caramelization and an off-flavor. Adding a bit of acid, such as cream of tartar, to water before dissolving sugar in it reduces the chance of its having an alkaline character.

In order, the sweetest to least sweet sugars are fructose, sucrose, glucose, maltose, and lactose—the same order as their solubility. The sweetness of a solution composed of 50 percent fructose and 50 percent glucose is just under that of sucrose. Acids present in molasses, honey, and sorghum syrup lessen their sweetness.

Lactose crystallizes easily, as is evidenced by the lactose crystals sometimes seen in evaporated milk. Mixing dry milk a day ahead of time helps the lactose go into solution, giving a more stable and flavorful product. Glucose also crystallizes easily, as we can see in crystallized jams, jellies, and honey. The uncrystallized portion of crystallized honey is fructose, which only crystallizes with difficulty.

Sugars become more soluble as the temperature of the liquid increases. While fine sugar dissolves more rapidly than coarse sugar, the total volume of each kind that can be dissolved in a given amount of water is identical. Salt, acid, or invert sugar increases the solubility of crystallized sugar.

If a solution holds all the sugar it can, it is called *saturated*; if it holds more than it should be able to under normal conditions, it is called *supersaturated*. Disturbing a supersaturated solution (for example, by shaking it) causes the excess quantity to crystallize. Sucrose's solubility in water is two parts to one part; a simple syrup made with a higher ratio of sugar to water than this is very apt to crystallize. When a sugar solution is boiled, water is lost. This changes the sugar : water ratio to one of higher sugar. As the temperature of a sugar solution rises, less and less sugar is needed to produce a saturated solution. As temperature drops, the reverse is true. If a sugar solution boiled at 240°F is saturated, when it is cooled to 104°F it will be supersaturated. Crystallization is faster and larger and fewer individual crystals result when a supersaturated solution is stirred while still warm. The more sugar there is in a solution, the higher the solution's boiling point becomes. A 10 percent sucrose solution boils at 213°F; a 50 percent solution, at 216°F; and an 80 percent

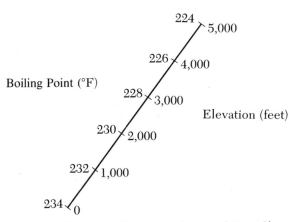

Figure 11-5. Elevation affects the boiling point of sugar solutions. If a sugar solution (4 sugar to 1 water) boils at 234°F at sea level, then at the various elevations shown on the right side of the line, the solution boils at the corresponding temperature indicated on the left side.

solution at 234°F. When heated until no more moisture can be lost, sugar begins to burn. Granulated sugar melts at 320° to 356°F and begins to burn at 410°F. A sugar solution's boiling point drops as altitude increases, at a rate of about 1 Fahrenheit degree for every increase of 500 ft. A correction for altitude is applied at elevations above 1,000 ft (see fig. 11-5).

When relative humidity (RH) is above 50 percent, syrups are cooked 1 Fahrenheit degree higher for every 25 percent or fraction of 25 percent in relative humidity that exceeds 50 percent. Bakers cook sugar solutions 2 Fahrenheit degrees higher in the summer than in the winter, because the air's humidity in summer is usually higher than it is in winter. Extra mixing after crystallization begins overcomes some humidity excess. Temperatures used in this text are for sea level with RH below 50 percent.

A syrup's viscosity (thickness) increases as its temperature drops. Caramels, peanut brittle, and cooked frostings may be liquid at higher temperatures, plastic at lower ones, and hard at still lower ones (see fig. 11-6). Cold fondants are warmed to 100°F to make them more workable; heating them above 100°F, however, makes them dull and grainy. Caramels and taffy should be warmed before cutting. Sugar work is done before a batch warmer to keep the mixture workable. Moisture, invert sugars, butter, and other ingredients increase creaminess and plasticity. Butter or fat in quantities up to 7 percent of the sugar does not interfere with crystallization; thus, 5.5 oz butter to 5 lb (80 oz) sugar causes no problem. To handle larger percentages of butter or fat, bakers raise cooking temperatures $\frac{1}{2}$ Fahrenheit degree for every 3 percent increase over 7 percent of fat, to counteract the extra softness caused by the fat. Adding about 0.5 percent of the sugar's weight in glycerine to the sugar mixture gives good softness in cases where butter or other fats are not used.

Figure 11-6. The viscosity or thickness of sugar solutions changes with their temperature. The melted caramel mixture on the right has the same composition as the firm caramels on the left. The temperature difference between the two accounts for the change.

Starch or dextrin makes crystalline mixtures firmer; when either is added to a mixture, allowances must be made for it. For every 3 percent of cocoa or chocolate over 10 percent (by weight) of the sugar, final temperature may be lowered by $\frac{1}{2}$ Fahrenheit degree. Thus, if $6\frac{1}{2}$ oz cocoa to 40 oz sugar is used, the temperature is dropped 1 Fahrenheit degree because 6.5/40 = 16 percent (two 3 percents over 10 percent). Chocolate may require a slightly lower correction factor because of its higher fat content.

Crystal size and quantity influence a crystalline mass's creaminess. Tiny crystals are appropriate in a fondant, but coarser ones may be desirable on items such as sugar-coated fruits. Amorphous mixtures—formless crystallized sugar—are desirable in caramels and brittles.

Stirring a supersaturated solution encourages crystal development. Smaller and more numerous crystals are formed if the solution is cool and if stirring is continuous and vigorous. If few crystals are formed, they are large; while if there are many, they are small. Agitation from stirring or kneading encourages development of small crystals. The first crystal that is formed influences the size of all others. To promote tiny crystal size, some fine fondant from a previous batch may be added to a new batch just before it crystallizes. This process is called *seeding*. The sides of pans are moistened during cooking to wash down any undissolved sugar crystals, or the pan may be covered during boiling so that steam dissolves them; failing to do this may leave a crystal that seeds the whole mass later. Dust or other particles can also seed solutions, so cover cooked solutions that must stand. Butter, acid, or other ingredients are added to discourage crystal growth during storage. To avoid agitation, a solution upon doneness is immediately poured onto a cold, flat, smooth surface such as a greased marble slab, baking sheet, stainless steel table, or platter. All the syrup should be allowed to run freely from the pan, but the pan should not be scraped, as this would cause large crystallization. Rough spots on the surface onto which the syrup is poured can start crystal growth, as can putting a thermometer into the mass after boiling has ceased. Laying the thermometer down on the slab and then pouring hot fondant over it avoids this problem.

When a liquid changes into a solid, heat is released; this is called an *exothermic reaction*. When a syrup crystallizes, the exothermic heat causes the mixture to thin slightly, and a loss of sheen is noticeable. Many cooks use these appearances as a signal to begin spreading, dropping, or performing other required manipulations before the mixture becomes too firm to handle.

The doneness of a sugar solution is best determined by using a thermometer; a Brix or Baumé scale reading can also be used. A Brix of 14° to 16° is a light syrup; 16° to 19°, medium; 19° to 21°, heavy; and 21° or over, extra heavy. Objective tests include the following:

Water test: Drop syrup into 50°F water; firmness indicates doneness; time in the water affects firmness obtained.

Finger test: Dip the finger first into cold water, then quickly into hot syrup; doneness is indicated by the thread or ball formed.

Spin test: Judge doneness by the length of the thread formed or the manner in which the syrup flows from a spoon or through a perforated ladle.

Bite test: Place a bit of syrup into the mouth. The bite or crack of the syrup indicates doneness; a syrup that breaks between the teeth without adhering to them is at the crack stage, about 310°F.

Appearance test: Color and appearance are good indicators; the size, type, and viscosity of the bubbles formed in cooking caramels, fudge, penuche, fondant, and other mixtures may be used to tell doneness. When a syrup begins to turn slightly brown, it is at the caramel stage. Because thermometers are difficult to use in burning sugar, sight is a more reliable method for evaluating the doneness of sugars cooked above the caramel stage.

Sound test: When a syrup cracks loudly twice as it is dropped into cold water, the moderately hard crack stage of 310° to 315°F has been reached. When a sugar thread cracks very hard three times as it is wrapped around the finger, the temperature is between 316° and 320°F; sugar may discolor slightly at this high a temperature.

Thermometers are the only reliable guide for nonexperts, and even the experts use them. Table 11-1 lists the characteristics and uses for sugar solutions cooked to various temperatures.

TABLE 11-1. Production data for use in sugar cookery

Temperature of syrup (°F)	Physical characteristics at this temperature	Cooking term used to indicate this doneness	Use of the product
215–217 (30° Baumé)	Faint thread forms between thumb and finger when they are separated.	Small thread (*lisse* or *petit filet*)	Light syrups (1 sugar to 3 water)
217–220 (31° Baumé)	Longer thread forms between thumb and finger when they are separated.	Large thread (*grande lisse*)	Heavy syrup (1 sugar to 1 water)
221–222 (32° Baumé)	Thread breaks between thumb and finger.	Little pearl (*petite perle*)	Extra-heavy syrups; can crystalize (2 sugar to 1 water)
222–223 (33° Baumé)	Holds as thread from thumb to finger.	Large pearl (*grande perle*)	Working almond paste, flowing fondants
223–225	Strong thread from thumb to finger.	Thread	Large crystals for crystallizing fruits
230–232	Use spin test; dip perforated ladle into hot syrup; tap lightly on side of container; blow through holes and make bubbles fly out.	The blow (*au soufflé* or *glue*)	Soft, pliable fondant mass; used to glaze fruits and nuts; dip singly and dry; adding a bit of lemon juice retards sugaring
236–239	Soft ball in 50°F water; in finger test, small ball can be rolled between fingers.	Small ball (*petite boule*)	Fondant for flowing icing on petit fours; thin fudge, penuche.
239–243	Medium ball in 50°F water; in finger test, ball has more firmness than soft ball.	Medium ball	Firm fondant for dipping bonbons, fruits, and mints; knead when too firm to stir
245–252	Firm ball in 50°F water; in finger test, ball is firm.	Large or firm ball (*grande boule*)	Soft caramels at lower temperatures; higher temperatures for taffies
250–258	Ball quite firm but still pliable in 50°F water.		Frostings at lower temperatures; divinity syrup, etc. at higher
258–266	Hard ball in 50°F water; in finger test, syrup detaches as hard material when finger is placed into cold water.	Small crack (*petite casse*)	Fondants where fruit juice is added last and temperature brought down to 242°F; nougats, hard taffies, popcorn ball mixtures
270–290	Syrup spins thread; above 285°F thread snaps between the teeth.	Crack (*casse*)	Butterscotch and hard candies; taffies
290–295	Cracks between teeth; crack is quite sharp.	Hard crack, lower range	Hard nougats; ribbon, English, and rock candy.
295–310	Very sharp crack between the teeth.	Hard crack, middle range	Coating fruits and nuts; some sugar work
310–316	Very brittle and hard between the teeth.	Hard crack, upper range	Pulled sugar work.
316–318	Hard to bite; may shatter.	Hard crack, top range	Flowers in pulled sugar work
318–320	Hard to bite; may shatter.	Hard crack, upper limit	Baskets and woven items in sugar work
338	Light caramelization noticed.	Caramel sugar	Caramel-flavored sugar
400	Almost black.	Burned sugar	Coloring material

LEAVENING AGENTS

Leavening is the aeration of a product during fermentation, mixing or baking to develop shape, volume, and texture. Leavening agents may yield other benefits, too, such as increasing spread or reducing the viscosity of a batter or dough, darkening pigments, and tenderizing or toughening proteins. Air, steam, chemicals, and yeast are used as leavening agents. Leavening is seldom caused by one of these acting alone; more often it is the result of a combination of two or more of them working together. Their relative contributions can vary. A cake made by the conventional creaming method is leavened equally by steam, air, and baking powder. Popovers are leavened mostly by steam.

The type and quantity of leavening required vary with the product, the amount and method of creaming, mixing, or beating, the type and quality of ingredients, the sequence of ingredient addition, the altitude, and the operator's technique. For an agent to leaven properly, leavening gases must be retained in the mixture until the structure is set by heat. Structural firmness after cooking should be sufficient to hold shape and retain desirable eating qualities. Excessive shrinkage after oven removal is frequently caused by a lack of structural strength to support the volume. Overdevelopment of gluten in mixing can restrict the movement of leavening gas, producing misshapen items of poor texture and volume. In some products, a batter or dough is so strong that gases cannot spread but instead gather and force their way upward in vertical vents called *tunnels*.

While only a small quantity of leavening is used in proportion to other ingredients, its influence on the quality of baked goods is so great that exact measurement is necessary. Insufficient leavening yields poor volume and color, a heavy close grain, and a crumbly, hard, dry texture attended by poor flavor; excessive leavening may lead to overexpansion of cellular walls, rupturing them and causing the product to fall. Leavening quantities must be tied to the loss of gas that occurs during mixing, benching, and baking. Fluid or soft batters leak more gas than do stiffer ones, and as a result they need more leavening.

The cell or grain size produced as a result of leavening may be important. A large cell is desirable in a cream puff or popover, while fine cells are sought in most cakes. Structural strength must be related to cell wall size. A cream puff must have a strong outside structure to support the large cells that are developed. A tender structure supports the fine texture in a cake. Too fine a cell leads to a compact, heavy item.

Leavening speed must be controlled. Usually, the more rapidly the item develops in baking, the more quickly the structural walls must be set. Most leavening action from chemicals should be obtained during baking and only a small amount during mixing or benching. Baking temperatures and times should permit free batter movement until maximum volume is obtained, at which point the structure should set and no further leavening should occur. An overly dark crust and a cracked high center indicate that the outside of a cake set before leavening was completed in the interior. If the crust on a pie shell sets before steam develops between the dough layers, the result is a loss of lightness and flakiness. In popovers, éclairs, and the like, the outside portion should set only at the time that steam develops in the interior. If more of the item is set, it will not rise.

AIR

Creaming fat, eggs, and sugar incorporates air into them, which serves to leaven baked items. Pound cakes and cookies are leavened almost completely by creaming. Air in egg foam leavens products such as angel cakes, sponge cakes, and meringues. Air is incorporated in the course of sifting flour, beating batter, or manipulating dough. Once it is incorporated, care must be taken to ensure that it is retained. Air expands by about one-third in baking. The quantity of leavening contributed by air depends on the quantity incorporated, the subsequent treatment of the product, and the kind and amount of leavening contributed by other ingredients.

STEAM

When water changes to steam, it increases in volume 1,600 times, making it an effective leavening agent. Popovers, cream puffs, crackers, and pie crust depend almost solely upon steam for leavening. Usually, 1 qt liquid is considered sufficient to produce the steam required to leaven 1 lb flour in a product.

CHEMICAL LEAVENING AGENTS

Soda, baking powder, and baking ammonia are chemical leavening agents. Baking ammonia is little used. To leaven 1 lb flour, one of the following is needed: 2 oz single-acting powder, 1 oz double-acting powder, or $\frac{1}{4}$ oz soda. Chemical leaveners should be finely divided and mixed thoroughly into the product, so leavening is even. Coarsely ground agents give grainy, open products. The finer the grind, the smaller the quantity required. Many old-fashioned recipes call for soda to be added to a liquid and then added to the mixture. This is because soda long ago was not so fine as it is today, and the prescribed mixing technique gave a more thorough incorporation of the leavener. Today, since soda is quite finely ground, this practice is unnecessary.

Soda

Sodium bicarbonate (soda) produces carbon dioxide gas for leavening foods. Moisture is also needed, and heat speeds the reaction. If an acid such as sour milk or molasses is present, the reaction can be complete and rapid in the cold stage; without an acid, soda reacts slowly when in a cold solution (see fig. 11-7). In the absence of acid or when there is an excess of soda over acid, an alkaline reaction occurs that may or may not be desirable. Cocoa and chocolate are reddened, and molasses, spices,

Figure 11-7. Acidified water has been poured into baking soda in the glass on the left, and an equal amount of neutral water has been poured into soda in the glass on the right. Pouring boiling (acidified and neutral) water and cold (acidified and neutral) water into identical samples of baking soda produces similar reactions.

fruits, nuts, vegetables, and some other foods are darkened when an alkaline reaction occurs. Leaving chocolate cakes to stand an extra-long time before baking encourages a higher development of red color. The flavone pigments in flour and other items turn yellow in an alkaline medium, and anthocyanin pigments turn blue or purple.

Acids in many products are used to react with and to neutralize soda; baking powder may be used to give extra leavening. An alkaline reaction softens gluten and toughens eggs. Gingerbread may sink in the middle if the soda in the batter softens the gluten too much. This can be counteracted somewhat by increasing mixing action. If it reacts alone, soda leaves sodium carbonate, a soapy, bitter-flavored residue. Some acid reactors, when combined with soda, leave a tasteless residue; sour milk combined with soda, for example, leaves a tasteless substance called *sodium lactate*.

Frequently, the quantity of soda required in recipes is guided more by the acid reactor quantity present than by the flour quantity to be leavened. Cream of tartar, an acid, is often used to react with soda; slightly acidic foods such as honey, fruits, cocoa, chocolate, and spices—as well as more acidic foods—are used as acid reactors, at least in part. Table 11-2 gives the approximate amount of various acidic foods needed to produce a balanced reaction with soda. This can vary from one recipe to another.

TABLE 11-2. Approximate balanced reactions between liquids and soda in food preparation

Liquid	Weight	Measure	Soda required for complete reaction Weight	Soda required for complete reaction Measure
Sour milk or buttermilk	8.3 lb	1 gal	$\frac{1}{4}$ oz	$2\frac{2}{3}$ T
Molasses	11.5 lb	1 gal	$1\frac{3}{4}$ oz	3–4 T
Sorghum	11.3 lb	1 gal	1 oz	$2\frac{1}{4}$ T
Honey	11.3 lb	1 gal	$\frac{1}{2}$–1 oz	1–$2\frac{1}{4}$ T
Vinegar, 40–50 grain	3 oz	$\frac{1}{3}$ c	$1\frac{1}{4}$ oz	$2\frac{2}{3}$ T
Orange juice	4 oz	$\frac{1}{2}$ c	$1\frac{1}{4}$ oz	$2\frac{2}{3}$ T
Cream of tartar	5 oz	1 c	2 oz	$4\frac{1}{2}$ T

Baking Powder

Baking powder is the most commonly use leavener. It consists of soda (bicarbonate of soda) and an acid reactor, giving a product that, by government standards, "yields not less than 12 percent available carbon dioxide"—although baking powders used in baking yield 17 percent. Acid reactors may include tartaric acid or one of its salts, compounds of aluminum, acid salts of phosphoric acid, or a combination of these. Starch is a dilutent acting as a drying agent to reduce caking of the leavener. Calcium lactate may be added to help control the reaction rate.

Certain baking powders evolve carbon dioxide gas immediately when moistened. Because they produce a complete reaction in the cold stage, they are called *single-acting*. *Double-acting* baking powder gives one-fifth to one-third of its gas in the cold stage; heat is required to produce the rest. A double-acting powder may contain one reactor that reacts cold and another that reacts hot. Figure 11-8 plots the reaction rates of different baking powders, cold and hot.

Baking powders made of tartaric acid, monocalcium phosphate, or monosodium phosphate are single-acting. Tartaric acid (cream of tartar) and soda, when placed into water, react completely within 2 minutes. Monosodium phosphate and soda react almost as rapidly, but monocalcium phosphate and soda take a bit longer. A baking powder containing sodium acid pyrophosphate releases gas slowly in the cold stage but more rapidly when heat is applied. Sodium aluminum sulfate reacts even more slowly than sodium acid pyrophosphate does. While it and SAS reactors are called *semi-double-acting*, they are actually single-acting, with the action slow when cold and fast when hot. A true double-acting powder used in quantity food production contains calcium acid phosphate for reacting cold and sodium pyrophosphate or sodium aluminum phosphate for reacting hot. Sodium acid phosphate and monocalcium phosphate are used a great deal in quantity food work. The sodium in all of these products may be significant to patrons who are on low-sodium diets.

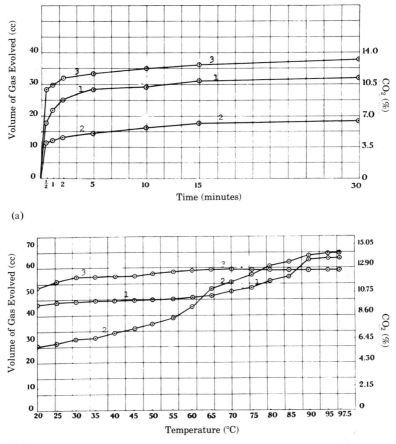

(a)

(b)

Figure 11-8. Reaction rates measured in batters containing baking powder (a) in the cold stage, and (b) in the hot stage. Baking powders are (1) pyrophosphate (double-acting), (2) calcium-acid-phosphate (SAS or semi-double-acting), and (3) tartrate (single-acting).

A high level of gas loss before baking sometimes occurs with single-acting baking powders; for this reason, mixing procedures may call for its addition at the end of mixing. From 1 to 2 oz single-acting powder is usually used with 1 lb flour, compared with $\frac{1}{2}$ oz for double-acting powder. Producing a small amount of gas is important in mixing, panning, and on the bench, but most of the gas is needed in baking. An excess of some baking powders can leave an undesirable flavor, so only the amount needed should be used. Tartaric acid baking powders leave no aftertaste, but their single-action makes them undesirable in quantity production; double-acting powders are best-suited to this work. Good tolerance in mixing and benching is needed, too, because preparation times and conditions may require a stable powder.

Baking Ammonia

Ammonium carbonate (baking ammonia) in the presence of moisture and heat changes into carbon dioxide, ammonia gas, and water. With a complete reaction, it leaves no aftertaste; however, aftertaste can result if baking ammonia is used in thick products, so experienced bakers use it only in thin products such as cookies and choux pastes. It gives rapid expansion that is desirable for spread in cookies and for a rapid rise in choux pastes. Recipes for machine-deposit cookies usually call for baking ammonia or at least a part. If baking ammonia is to replace baking powder in part, replace 40 percent of the omitted weight of baking powder with baking ammonia; if it is to replace soda in part, replace 80 percent of the omitted weight of soda with baking ammonia. Thus, if a recipe calls for $2\frac{1}{2}$ oz baking powder or $1\frac{1}{2}$ oz soda, the substitution would be, respectively, $1\frac{1}{4}$ oz baking powder and $\frac{1}{2}$ oz baking ammonia or $\frac{3}{4}$ oz soda and $\frac{6}{10}$ oz baking ammonia.

Yeast

Yeast is a single-celled fungus that feeds on carbohydrates. Wild yeast in the air can be allowed to culture a potato or some other moist product containing sugar or starch. It can then be used for leavening, or old bread dough can be added to a new one to supply a yeast culture—but this technique is used for specialized products such as sour-dough breads. Compressed and active dry yeasts are the types most commonly used, but instant yeasts that require shorter fermentation and proofing times are finding more and more acceptance. Follow manufacturer's directions for the correct quantity to use of instant, active, or compressed yeasts. Table 11-3 lists the relative weights of compressed and dry active yeasts to add to various quantities of water.

TABLE 11-3. Amounts of compressed and dry yeasts to combine with water

Compressed yeast	Active dry yeast	Water	
		Weight*	Approximate measure
1 oz	$\frac{1}{2}$ oz	2 oz	$\frac{1}{4}$ c
2 oz	$\frac{3}{4}$ oz	3 oz	$\frac{1}{2}$ c
4 oz	$1\frac{1}{2}$ oz	6 oz	1 c
8 oz	$3\frac{1}{4}$ oz	13 oz	1 pt
12 oz	$4\frac{3}{4}$ oz	1 lb 3 oz	$1\frac{1}{4}$ pt
1 lb	$6\frac{1}{2}$ oz	1 lb 10 oz	$1\frac{3}{4}$ pt
2 lb	$12\frac{3}{4}$ oz	3 lb 3 oz	1 qt $1\frac{1}{4}$ pt
3 lb	1 lb $3\frac{1}{4}$ oz	4 lb 14 oz	2 qt 1 pt
4 lb	1 lb $9\frac{1}{2}$ oz	6 lb 6 oz	3 qt 1 c
5 lb	2 lb	8 lb	4 qt

NOTE: Water temperatures should be 90° to 100°F for compressed yeast and 5 to 10 degrees higher for dry active yeast.
* Corrected to nearest $\frac{1}{4}$ oz.

Yeast grows best at between 78° and 90°F. Growth is slowed at temperatures above 98°F for regular yeast but not for dry active or instant; for these, 110°F seems to be the limit. Moisture must be present to foster good growth. Salt and other chlorides retard yeast activity; sulfates and phosphates promote it. Phosphates are essential for yeast nutrition. Use less yeast in warm weather than in cold. Keep compressed yeast in storage at 45°F. Freezing affects some of yeast's activity; even so, if it is not frozen for more than thirty days, and if it is thawed at 40°F and slightly more is used, good results are obtained. Active dry yeast, the most widely used yeast, is shaped into small pellets, dried, and packed into sealed cans. Freezing does not harm it. Crumble compressed yeast or sprinkle dry active yeast into water. Allow it to stand for 3 to 4 minutes, and then stir. The water used for this purpose constitutes part of the total amount needed. Instead of soaking in water, instant yeast is mixed with the dry ingredients.

Yeast's food is glucose, which it converts into heat, alcohol, water, and carbon dioxide. Flour's starch, dextrin, and other carbohydrates are changed by enzymes in the yeast into maltose, which in turn is converted into glucose. Malt syrup (maltose) helps yeast action. Yeast carries an enzyme called *invertase* that changes sucrose into glucose and fructose. Too fast a growth of yeast produces acid, as well as other products.

EGGS

Leavening is only one of the roles played by eggs in baking. They are also used to give tenderness, structure, nutritional value, flavor, color, and moisture; and they aid in binding ingredients together, in emulsifying fats and (when they coagulate) in developing a firmer structure. Eggs are often counted as moisture; egg whites contribute about two-thirds of their weight as liquid, and yolks about one-half. Eggs are discussed in detail in chapter 7.

FLAVORINGS AND SPICES

COCOA AND CHOCOLATE

Cocoa and chocolate contribute flavor, richness, and color to bakery goods. Unsweetened chocolate is 8 to 16 percent starch (about 30 percent carbohydrate in all) 14 percent protein, and about 52 percent cocoa fat. Cocoa is ground chocolate from which more than half the cocoa fat has been removed. The starch in cocoa and chocolate is sometimes treated as part of the flour in recipes. If a cocoa is low in cocoa fat, a suitable amount of butter, shortening, or oil can be added to make up for the lack. Dutch chocolate or cocoa is treated with alkali, which makes it darker, increases its solubility, and gives it a smoother flavor. This treatment also swells some of the cellulose and partly gelatinizes the starch.

SPICES

Many different spices are used in the bakeshop. They should be of the highest quality, since a small amount at little expense can make a big flavor difference. Limited supplies should be kept on hand to ensure freshness and flavor. Store spices in tight containers away from heat and moisture. Weigh spices for adding; do not measure them unless the amount to be used is so small that weighing is not possible. Some of the more important spices used in the bakeshop are briefly described here.

Allspice is the pea-sized fruit of a tropical evergreen that grows in Guatemala, Mexico, and Jamaica. Jamaican allspice is the best. The flavor is a blend of cinnamon, nutmeg, and cloves, with cloves predominating. Approximately 5 T equals 1 oz.

Aniseed is the seed of a plant belonging to the parsley family. It is grown in Spain, Mexico, Turkey, and elsewhere and has a flavor reminiscent of licorice. Star anise from China has a slight clove and licorice flavor.

Caraway is the seed of another plant of the parsley family. The best comes from Poland. A black or chocolate caraway used to top some European and Russian breads differs from regular caraway. Approximately 3 T equals 1 oz.

Cardamom is the dried fruit of a ginger plant of India, Guatemala, and Ceylon. Use decorticated cardamom (chaff and pods removed). Indian and Guatemalan cardamoms are best. About 5 T equals 1 oz.

Cinnamon is the bark of the cassia evergreen from Ceylon, Vietnam, and Indonesia. The best comes from Ceylon and Vietnam and is a light grayish brown powder. Lower-quality cinnamon is reddish brown and is hard to mix into batters; mix it with water to form a paste to simplify addition. Approximately 6 T equals 1 oz.

Cloves are the unopened buds of an evergreen from the islands of Molucca (Indonesia), Zanzibar (Tanzania), and Madagascar. All of these sources are good. About 5 T equals 1 oz.

Ginger is the root of a reedlike plant grown in Jamaica, India, and Africa. Jamaica's is lighter in color than the other and lighter and smoother in flavor. Indian Cochin ginger is good in baking. African ginger has a harsh flavor, and is usually used only for ginger snaps. Approximately 5 T dried ground ginger equals 1 oz.

Nutmeg is the inner part of a pecan-sized seed from the West Indies and Indonesia. About 4 T ground nutmeg equals 1 oz. The outer network around this seed is called *mace*; it is slightly more pungent in flavor. About 5 T mace equals 1 oz.

Paprika comes from both Spain and Hungary. Bright red Spanish paprika is preferred to the darker Hungarian variety.

Poppy seed is grown in many areas; the blue seed is preferred to the black because of its color and flavor. Approximately 4 T equal 1 oz.

Saffron is the stigma of a small crocus of the Mediterranean and Asia Minor. It is expensive, but a small amount gives much flavor. It is used to season breads and other items.

FLAVORINGS

Flavorings and seasonings should be of the highest quality, since the flavor contribution is considerable even though only a small quantity is used. Some flavors bake out; purchase these locked to glucose to prevent this. Freshness is essential to their strength and quality.

Flavorings are extracts made from natural esters (essential oils) or are imitation substances dissolved in a solvent, usually alcohol. Some are emulsions held in solution by gums or other emulsifiers. Often natural oils give the finest and truest flavor, but in some cases the imitation flavors are better.

Chapter Review

1. What is gluten, and what role does it play in bakery goods?
2. What is the role of shortenings in bakery products?
3. What is a hydroscopic sugar, and what action does it perform in cookies? cakes? crystalline candies?
4. Why does the cooking temperature have to be varied when relative humidity is over 50 percent?
5. What are the techniques required to produce a smooth, fine fondant?
6. How does water work as a leavener? What is the chemical action that occurs when baking powder leavens? How does yeast produce carbon dioxide?
7. What is the role of eggs in bakery products?
8. How can a chocolate cake be made to have a reddish color?
9. What are cloves? ginger? cardamom? saffron?

CHAPTER 12

Yeast Breads and Quick Breads

Outline

Goals

1. To indicate the standards, principles, and techniques needed to make good yeast breads.
2. To enumerate the different kinds of yeast breads and their products.
3. To discuss the ingredients used in yeast breads, and to list their properties.
4. To explain the different methods used to produce yeast breads.
5. To identify the steps involved in yeast bread making.
6. To present the standards, principles, and techniques needed to make good quick breads.
7. To describe the techniques needed to make good quick breads.

INTRODUCTION

Most operations purchase their loaf breads ready-made but make their own rolls and quick breads to ensure top quality. Prepared mixes make it easy to produce a wide variety of breads; their quality has been found to be good, and the cost is equitable.

YEAST BREADS

STANDARDS

Quality factors to consider in evaluating yeast bread include volume, crust color, symmetry of form, evenness of bake, crust character, break or shred, grain, crumb, color, texture, and flavor (see fig. 12-1a). Since breads differ in character, these factors vary according to each particular type.

The ratio of size to weight is used for judging volume; regular bread occupies 125 to 155 in.^{3} per lb. Too brown a crust, spotting, or unevenness of color lowers the crust-color grade. An even, rich golden brown or bloom is sought. Evenness of shape, good proportion, and absence of deformities are desirable. Even baking gives uniformly browned sides, ends, and bottoms with no excessive browning. Crusts should be tender, moderately thick, and uniform, although hard-crusted breads should have thick and crisp crusts. Break or shred is judged by the condition of the areas between the top and side, where a last-minute rise inside the loaf creates a break that is open and evenly shredded. A ragged, gaping break is undesirable. Small rolls do not have this break.

Grain character (internal appearance) is judged on the basis of cell size, shape, distribution, and porosity. Cells should be even-sized and evenly spaced. Held at a 45° angle to the floor in good light, a cut piece of bread should have a creamy white color and a soft sheen. A gray, uneven color is undesirable. Texture is determined by rubbing the finger tips against the cut surface. Judges may roll a bit into a ball to test its texture. Velvetiness, softness, moistness, and elasticity are sought, not harshness or

(a)   (b)

Figure 12-1.   (a) High quality in a loaf of bread is evidenced by straight sides and good color and shape. (b) Good bread should spring back to almost its original shape when squeezed.

graininess. Overly soft, doughy, crumbly, or lumpy bread with a hard, flinty texture is undesirable. Flavor should be sweet, wheaty, and not too salty. After cooling, bread, when squeezed, should spring back to nearly its original shape (see fig. 12-1a). Aroma should be fresh and sweet, with no trace or sourness or off-odor.

TYPES OF YEAST BREADS

A high-gluten, white wheat flour is used to make white bread. The procedures discussed in this text are normally the ones used for making it; where variation is required in order to make other types, the changes are noted. Whole-wheat (graham) bread is made from 40 to 60 percent whole-wheat flour and 60 to 40 percent white flour. It is handled in the same way as white bread, except that it is mixed less. It may also be benched before reaching a full rise—a procedure frequently described as "taking it to the bench young." Its grain is slightly heavier and its volume is less than white bread's.

A combination of about 20 percent rye flour to 80 percent strong white flour is used for regular rye bread, but some rye breads contain 50 percent or more rye flour. Rye flour lacks good gluten, and so gives a heavy grain. When the ingredients for rye bread are mixed, less liquid is used and less mixing is done. Overmixing results in volume loss, holes in the crumb, and split sides. A loaf can burst in baking from overextension of the weak rye gluten. Some bakers increase the quantity of yeast 1 percent to give faster fermentation and keep shortening and sugar at minimal levels. Proofing time is reduced to between 30 and 35 minutes. *Docking*—making $\frac{1}{4}$-in.-deep slashes across the top before makeup—is common. Steam is used during the first 10 minutes of baking. Gas pressures may burst the bread if docking and steam are not used. If steam is not available, cold water may be brushed over the bread as it goes into the oven and again when it has completely risen in the oven, or a wash made by boiling 2 to $2\frac{1}{2}$ oz cornstarch to 1 qt water may be used in the same way.

Hard, French, Italian, and hearth breads require a crisp crust. To encourage this, bakers use a lean formula containing very little sugar and often no shortening. Docking is common, except on braided breads. Baking usually takes place on hearths or hot bricks; alternatively, cornmeal is sprinkled on pans to prevent them from sticking, and the bread is baked on them. Hard breads should not touch each other in baking.

Sweet doughs are used for rich dinner rolls, babas au rhum, breakfast breads, and coffee cakes. Some sweet doughs are as rich as cakes. Rich doughs retard (refrigerate) or freeze better than nonrich ones. A rolled-in sweet dough (Danish pastry) is taken to the bench young and given a short rest before the shortening is rolled in. It is then given a 45-minute rest before makeup. Between 2 and 4 oz margarine or butter is used for 1 lb of dough.

Soy flour is added to increase protein. If it is used, the bread has a deep creamy, almost yellow color. Corn flour, potato flour, raisins, nuts, and so forth are used for variety breads.

INGREDIENTS

Yeast dough is made from flour, liquid, salt, and yeast; richer yeast doughs contain fat, sugar, eggs, and flavoring. There are two main doughs: bread (or lean), and sweet (or rich). Each has many variations. Ingredient proportions usually match those given in table 12-1. Yeast bread should use a high-quality enriched hard wheat flour, or the bread in mixing should be enriched with a special nutrient pellet.

Salt contributes flavor, assists in developing a fine cellular structure, strengthens gluten, retards moisture absorption, and gives whiteness to the crumb. Graham and rye bread doughs and doughs high in milk and shortening need more salt. Salt controls yeast growth—especially wild yeast—and retards yeast action; if less salt is used, fermentation is faster. Use salt to control fermentation rates when temperatures are high. Do not mix salt and yeast together; add them separately. Add salt to sponges in the second mixing. Use calcium salt to make low-sodium bread.

Liquids assist in controlling fermentation and in establishing the correct temperature for fermentation. A slack dough ferments faster than a firm one. To obtain the correct temperature, carry out the following steps:

1. Add the flour temperature and room temperature, plus 10 to 15 Fahrenheit degrees for the expected rise in temperature from mixing friction; if these measurements are 65°F, 70°F, and 10 Fahrenheit degrees, the total is 145°F.
2. Multiply the desired dough temperature by 3, and subtract the sum in step 1 from this product. The result gives the proper fermentation temperature. Thus, if the dough should be at 75°F, the calculation is $3 \times 75 (= 225) - 145 = 80°F$. Occasionally, chipped ice or ice water may have to be used to bring the temperature to its required level.

TABLE 12-1. Relative percentages of ingredients in yeast breads

Ingredient	Lean (%)	Rich (%)
Flour, bread	100	65–100
Flour, cake		0–35
Sugar, granulated	2–3	6–25
Shortening	1–12	8–40
Eggs, whole		10–45
Yeast, compressed	2–3	2–8
Liquid	58–60	40–60
Milk, dry, nonfat	0–6	3–8
Salt	1–2½	1½–2½
Spices		¼–½
Flavoring		¼–½
Conditioner	¼–½	¼–½

* Use additional shortening—20–50% of the flour—for rolling in.

Hard-water minerals can strengthen gluten; an excess of them can toughen it so much that it does not ripen properly in fermentation. If the water is acidic, fermentation may occur too rapidly.

Conditioners (mineral yeast foods) promote good yeast growth, reduce fermentation time, and give a softer, drier dough with strong gluten—characteristics needed in machine production. Greater volume, better uniformity, improved keeping qualities, better oven spring, attractive color, and desirable grain and crumb smoothness result when conditioners are used. Crust bloom improves because diastase and maltase enzyme activity is favored. Conditioners also depress wild yeast action. They are added with liquids in straight doughs and with the second flour in sponges.

Product quality is affected by moisture. A lack of liquid prevents the dough from developing proper elasticity, tenacity, and viscosity. Insufficiently moist dough does not handle well in mixing, kneading, and shaping. Straight doughs take more liquid than do sponges. If the flour's absorption rate is not known, flour can be added to the liquid until the dough reaches proper consistency.

Usually, nonfat dry milk and water are used; fat can be replaced, if needed, at the rate of $4\frac{1}{2}$ oz per gallon of liquid whole milk. Milk improves flavor, nutrient value, keeping quality, and crust color. It softens cellular structure and depresses bread volume but strengthens flour proteins. Fermentation is retarded and stabilized by milk's buffering action, and crumb color is made more creamy. Since milk gives a softer crust, it is not used for hard-crusted breads. Up to 6 percent milk solids are used in lean doughs; rich ones may contain up to 8 percent milk solids. Excess milk solids may yield a sticky dough during mixing, but the stickiness disappears in fermentation. Flour and dry milk are sifted in together.

Sugar gives flavor and improves crust color. Yeast can feed on most sugars. Lean doughs contain between 2 and 10 percent sugar, and rich ones up to 25 percent; since sugar in a concentration above 10 percent slows yeast growth, more yeast must be used to counteract this. Milk sugar (lactose) cannot be used by yeast, but it browns well and thus gives good crust color.

Emulsifiers such as lecithin, monoglycerides, and diglycerides increase shortening's tenderizing action. Emulsifiers retain softness, retard staling, and reduce moisture loss. An excessive quantity harms bread quality.

Yeast is discussed in chapter 11.

Mold inhibitors hinder the growth of molds and keep bread moist and soft. Poor sanitation or improper cooling favors mold contamination. Mold develops rapidly at temperatures above 80°F; refrigeration or freezing inhibits it. Proper handling of bread, thorough baking, and the use of a mold inhibitor such as sodium or calcium propionate reduces mold danger. *Rope* is caused by *Bacillus mesentericus* bacteria. These bacteria digest bread and convert it into a sticky, dark-colored yellowish pasty mass with an odor similar to that of an overripe cantaloupe. Pressing the crumb together and pulling it apart reveals silky threads. Rope grows best at temperatures between 90° and 95°F. It is inhibited by good sanitation, by the addition of some acid to the dough, or by mold inhibitors. Once infected, all bakeshop floors and equipment must be thoroughly cleaned with steam and rinsed with a mild solution of vinegar. A pH of 4.6 kills *Bacillus mesentericus*; bread usually has a pH of from 5 to 5.5. Using 1 pt vinegar (40 to 45 grain) for every 100 lb of flour in a dough helps control rope; more vinegar may be used in dark flour breads.

One of the problems with using mold inhibitors is that they increase moisture; this produces heavier bread, which bakers like to sell, but the bread is of poor quality for use in sandwiches because they easily soak. French toast made from such bread is gummy inside, and a hot beef sandwich is soggy, pasty, and slippery. Good bread should have some chewing resistance, and some operations find that they must make their own bread to get the product they want.

Prepared bread or roll mixes containing all ingredients except water are on the market; they are handled in the same way as regular breads.

Bread can be thin-sliced, regular or thick-sliced; the thicknesses of these types, respectively, are $\frac{1}{4}$ to $\frac{1}{2}$ in., $\frac{1}{2}$ to $\frac{5}{8}$ in., and over $\frac{5}{8}$ in. Loaves can be obtained in 1-, $1\frac{1}{4}$-, $1\frac{1}{2}$-, 2-, and 3-lb sizes. Quick breads are often sold in $1\frac{3}{4}$ lb loaves. Rolls are 1 to 2 oz each; at one time one and a half rolls were calculated as a portion, but the standard portion is now nearer to one roll because people eat less bread.

PRODUCTION PROCEDURES

Three types of dough are made: straight, sponge and no-time. Most bread in foodservices is made by the straight dough method. The steps involved (and the time required for each) are as follows:

1. Weighing and mixing (12 min)
2. Fermentation (45 to 60 min)
3. Punching (3 min)
4. Benching and resting (10 to 15 min)
5. Makeup (20 min)
6. Proofing (15 to 30 min)
7. Baking (20 min for rolls, 60 min for loaves)
8. Cooling
9. Storing

These steps are discussed in detail in the subsections that follow. Total time for the straight method is 2 to 4 hours; for production by hand methods, about 45 minutes is required for 100 portions or 11 lb of dough.

Sponges are popular for mass production (see fig. 12-2). Horizontal high-speed mixers are used to produce them. About 60 percent of the flour and all of the liquid and yeast are mixed together, making a thick batter. This is fermented at from 77° to 80°F until it has doubled in bulk and is wavy and ripply. At a slight touch it collapses. After a punch, the remaining flour, the salt, the sugar, the shortening, the milk solids, the

(a)   (b)

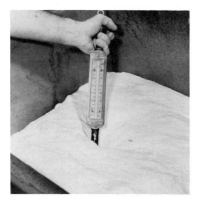

(c)   (d)

Figure 12-2. The sponge method is often used when a large quantity of bread is made. (a) Dough coming from the mixer is dumped into a dough trough. (b) Moving the sponge in a dough trough to the fermentation room. Notice the rough quality of the dough. (c) The temperature and humidity of the fermentation room must be carefully controlled. (d) The sponge, after undergoing the first fermentation, is moved back to the mixer. Notice the smoother quality of the dough at this stage. (*Courtesy American Baking Institute*)

nutrient enricheners, and the conditioners are added, and a second fermentation is begun; this usually lasts 1 minute for every percent of the flour added in the second mixing. Thus, if 40 percent is added, the second fermentation should last 40 minutes. Often the breakdown of flour use is 70–30 or 80–20.

A no-time dough is used when production time must be reduced. Maximum levels of conditioner, sugar, and yeast are used. Mixing is the same as for straight doughs. The dough comes from the mixer at about 90°F and is fermented at this temperature. No-time dough is taken to the bench young, about three-quarters fermented. Breads made from this dough usually lack the quality of straight dough breads. Big commercial bakeries use a no-time method in which the dough moves continuously through mechanical equipment until it is out of the oven and dumped.

Weighing and Mixing

Use standardized recipes, and weigh accurately. Assemble all of the ingredients. Small operations use an upright mixer equipped with a dough hook to do the mixing; large batches must be made in horizontal, high-speed mixers. Batches may also be made by hand. Mixing is done in three steps:

1. Rehydrate the yeast. (If instant yeast is used, mix it with the dry ingredients.)
2. Add the yeast-filled liquid to the remaining liquid and fat.
3. Add in the dry ingredients, and mix until a firm, solid dough that leaves the bowl sides is formed.

During mixing, the dough relaxes and becomes elastic and smooth. If strong flour is used, do not undermix it. The dough should stretch out into a thin sheet that is of uniform consistency and has no dense areas (see fig. 12-3). A flat hand pushed down on the dough should leave an impression, and points of dough pulled up should quickly subside. After 5 minutes of rest, a few bubbles about the size of silver dollars may show on the surface. The presence of too many bubbles indicates overmixing. Vary mixing time to suit flour strength. Undermix weak flours and use slightly less water to produce a firmer dough. A sweet dough should be developed less than lean ones. Dough should come from the mixer at between 74° and 84°F. It is then fermented.

Fermentation

Carbon dioxide gas is developed when yeast feeds on glucose. Diastase converts starches and dextrins into maltose, and other enzymes change maltose into glucose. Invertase, a yeast enzyme, converts refined sugar into glucose. Too strong a diastatic action gives a slack and sticky dough. Diastase malt or other special syrups may be added. The action of protein enzymes can inhibit strong gluten formation. Fresh or dried milk may be scalded to destroy these enzymes; usually, dry milk is treated during processing to reduce their quantity. Protease activity is reduced when aged flour or conditioners are used. The presence of some protease improves bread quality by tenderizing the gluten.

The dough ripens during fermentation; the gluten completely hydrates, becoming pliable, elastic, and less tenacious, with a soft, smooth, almost silky quality. Extended or too rapid fermentation or fermentation at too high a temperature leads to excessive acidity and a sour dough. Observe proper times and temperatures. Fermentation should end when the dough has approximately doubled in volume or when the fingers, inserted about 3 in. into the dough, meet little resistance and the dough recedes or puckers away from the fingers. A 2 percent loss in weight

(a)

 (b)

(c)

(d)

Figure 12-3. A dough after mixing. (b) A dough about three-fourths fermented. It can be taken to the bench if it is a rich dough, graham bread or rye bread. Finger indentations made at this point leave quickly. (c) Finger indentations after further rising leave less quickly. (d) Fully fermented dough puckers away from a hand thrust into it. (e) To punch, lift the dough up and turn it completely over.

occurs in fermenting. Doughs made from a poor gluten flour, graham and rye flour doughs, no-time doughs, sweet doughs, and doughs requiring considerable handling in makeup should be taken to the bench young. After fermenting, the dough is punched.

Punching and Resting

Knocking or pushing a dough down is not punching. Punching is folding a dough over from its sides into the middle until most of the gas is expelled. The dough is then flipped upside down. Punching puts the yeast near new food and relaxes gluten. If bucky, weak, or pastry flour is used, punching may be omitted and the dough brought directly to the bench to rest. Some straight doughs may be fermented again after punching. After punching, doughs are rested for from 10 to 15 minutes to become pliable for makeup; the resting time may be less for rich doughs than for lean ones.

Makeup

Makeup is the stage during which items are shaped. Bread is divided into proper sizes, rounded (molded), and usually given an intermediate proof, after which it is panned (see fig. 12-4). Baking loss is about 12 percent, so for each 1 lb of finished bread there must be 18 oz of uncooked dough. Scale dinner rolls at 1 oz each and breakfast rolls at 2 oz each.

To roll in shortening, first roll the dough to about $\frac{3}{4}$ to 1 in. thick in a rectangle that is three times longer than it is wide. Then dot margarine, butter, or special roll-in shortening over two-thirds of the surface. Fold the uncovered third over half of the covered part and fold the remaining covered third over the top, giving three layers of dough and two layers of shortening. Rest under refrigeration for 35 to 45 minutes (for Danish) or 10 to 15 minutes (for sweet doughs). Roll out the dough, fold it in thirds again, and rest. The dough is then ready for makeup. Figure 12-5 illustrates some of these steps.

Rounding shapes the divided pieces into smooth, round shapes. The dough should be soft and elastic; as it is rounded and as gas escapes, it may squeak like a mouse. The rounded surface should be smooth when done, since a rough surface allows gas to escape in proofing. After rounding, an intermediate proofing of 8 to 12 minutes is given, to allow the item to recover from the effects of makeup. If this proofing is not given, the dough will be tight and bucky and will shape poorly in the pan. Adept, rapid motion is needed. Figures 12-6 through 12-8 illustrate the makeup of various yeast breads; figures 12-9 through 12-12 show techniques for producing various types of dinner rolls and sweet rolls.

For retarded or frozen doughs, the quantities of sugar and yeast are increased. Richer doughs lend themselves to this handling. Take them to the bench young, perform the makeup, and then retard or freeze. An alternative approach is to divide the dough into 10-lb pieces, flatten them on baking sheets, cover, and retard or freeze. A retarding temperature of 40°F and a relative humidity of 85 percent holds dough for up to 72 hours. Table 12-2 describes the handling and flow of sweet dough.

Proofing

Proofing gives dough its final conditioning. The gluten becomes tender and extended, and the outer surface becomes smooth and light. During proofing the product approximately doubles in volume. Proofing temperatures should be between 90° and 100°F, and relative humidity should be

(a)

(b)

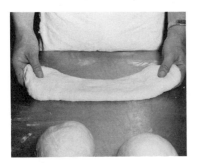

(c)

(d)

(e)

(f)

Figure 12-4. To make a loaf of bread, divide the dough and allow it to rest. (a) Shape the loaf. (b) Make a three-fold, and fold. (c) Stretch into a length double the pan size. (d) Fold again into three. (e) Pat the dough out and fold, sealing the edge. (f) The finished loaf should be panned with the seam side down.

(a)

(b)

(c)

(d)

Figure 12-5. (a) For a rolled-in dough, the dough is rolled to about ¾ in. thick; then two-thirds of it is dotted with a plastic shortening. (b) The uncovered third is folded over half of the covered dough and then the remaining third is folded over. (c) The dough is rested and then turned so that the length of the roll is parallel to the worker and rolled to about ¾ in. thick. (d) It is placed into a pan to rest in the refrigerator. Two fingers pressed into the dough indicate that this dough is at its second turn or rolling.

80 to 85 percent. The time required varies from 14 to 45 minutes, with 30 to 45 minutes the standard for bread loaves. No-time doughs have a shorter proofing period and are usually put into the oven slightly underproofed. Overproofing gives an open grain, gray color, a loss of flavor, and lower volume.

Baking

Baking firms the bread, preserving texture and shape. Load pans into the oven carefully, since proofed dough is fragile. Overloaded ovens may not regain baking temperatures rapidly enough to bake bread properly. Preheating ovens to a slightly higher temperature than needed, loading, and then setting the temperature at the desired level gives good results.

A 1-lb loaf should be baked at 425°F for 15 minutes and then at 375°F for 45 minutes. If the dough is slightly underproofed, bake it for 1 hour at from 375° to 400°F. Large loaves may require slightly lower temperatures and longer baking. Rolls spaced apart need to bake for 15 to 30 minutes at

(a)

(b)

(c)

(d)

Figure 12-6. Making a sweet dough into cinnamon rolls. (a) The dough is rolled into a long rectangular strip, which is liberally buttered and then spread with cinnamon and sugar (10 sugar to 1 cinnamon). (b) The dough is rolled lengthwise. (c) The dough is cut and panned on a greased baking sheet. (d) For variety, slices may be cut thicker than cinnamon rolls and then creased.

425°F, while pan rolls and others that touch need nearly as long to bake as loaves do. Bake rich doughs at slightly lower temperatures than are used for lean ones. Oven dampers may have to be open or closed, depending on the type of bread and the product size.

During early baking, the loaf's rise is quite rapid. Not only does carbon dioxide gas expand, but yeast activity proceeds at a very rapid rate until the bread reaches a temperature of 140°F, at which point the yeast is killed. This rapid rise is called *oven spring*. When heat completely swells the starch and coagulates the protein, the structure becomes firm. A shred or break on the side occurs because the rise inside the load continues after the exterior is set. Small products bake uniformly and do not show this shred. Docking (making a shallow slice on the top) is performed to allow for this final expansion and to prevent bursting. Color or bloom is developed on the outside through a caramelization of sugars

(a)

(b)

(c)

(d)

Figure 12-7. (a) To make pan rolls, cut the dough and roll it with both hands. (b) Place the round rolls into a muffin pan, and divide each with a wooden cutter dipped into butter. (c) A quick and easy way to make cloverleaf rolls. (d) To make fan tans or butter rolls, roll the dough and then fold it, making sure that the area between folds of the dough is liberally buttered; then cut the dough and place the pieces into muffin pans.

and dextrins. Low temperatures result in a pale, rubbery crust, poor oven spring, and poor texture. Excessive heat or sugar leads to an overbrown crust. Steam is used to retard crust formation and to develop thick, crisp crusts. A well-baked loaf of bread gives a hollow sound when tapped.

Cooling

Loaves, large rolls, and rolls that touch are dumped from their pans onto cooling racks after baking. This procedure allows steam and alcohol to escape. Drafts or too-cool air may cause cracking. Rolls that are to be served soon after baking should be completely baked, but rolls that are cooled and then reheated may be slightly underbaked. Brush breads with shortening to prevent their crusts from drying out during cooling.

(a)   (b)

(c)   (d)

Figure 12-8. Makeup of (a) Parker House rolls; (b) hamburger buns; (c) finger or wiener buns. (d) Bowknots and rosettes ready for proofing.

Storing

After cooling, wrap bread in moisture- and vapor-proof bags for storage periods of longer than 8 to 10 hours. Otherwise, store the bread on racks. Breads need protection; store them in dry, clean containers in a cool place. Use hard, crisp breads soon. Bake these daily, and store them in open boxes or paper bags.

Bread staling is a deterioration characterized by loss of aroma, increased firmness and crumbliness, and the development of a harsh crumb texture. Bread holds best when frozen in wraps. Store at 0°F or lower. To use frozen bread, unwrap and thaw it, preferably at 115°F or at room temperature. Microwave thawing may also be used. Frozen rolls may be heated uncovered at between 375° and 400°F for 5 to 10 minutes and then served immediately. Slightly stale bread may be used for French toast, toast, or grilled sandwiches. Overly stale bread can be used for dressings or crumbs. Breads stale more rapidly under refrigeration than they do at room temperature.

Table 12-3 presents a trouble-shooting guide to bread failures.

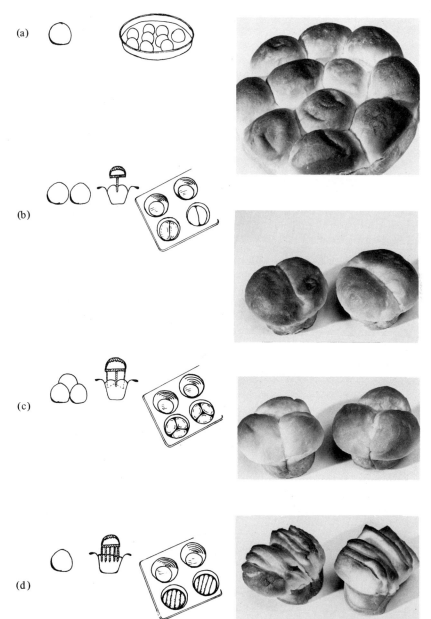

Figure 12-9. Techniques for making different rolls: (a) pan rolls; (b) twin rolls; (c) cloverleaf rolls; (d) fan tans or butter rolls.

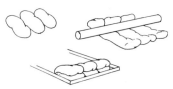

(a)

(b)

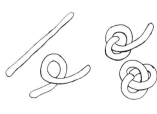

(c)

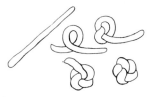

(d)

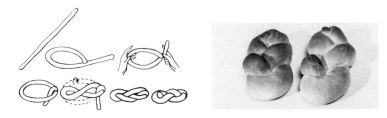

(e)

Figure 12-10. Techniques for making different rolls: (a) Parker House rolls; (b) single or bowknot rolls; (c) double or rosette rolls; (d) kaiser knot rolls; (e) triple or braided rolls. (*Courtesy Wheat Flour Institute*)

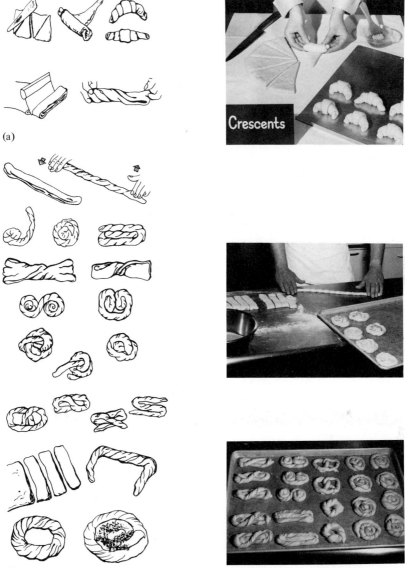

(a)

(b)

Figure 12-11. (a) Crescents may be made by several methods. When the roll is not made into a crescent shape, it is called a napkin roll. (*Courtesy Wheat Flour Institute*) (b) To make twists, proceed as for cinnamon rolls, but fold the dough over after covering only half of it with sugar, cinnamon, and butter. Twist as shown, using a reverse roll between the left and right hands. Many different products can be made during makeup from the twist-type product.

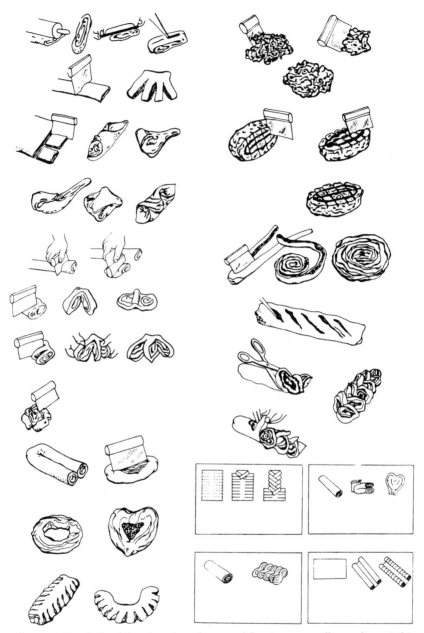

Figure 12-12. Rolls of dough such as those used for cinnamon rolls may be varied in size and made into diverse shapes. Different fillings and styles of cutting allow an almost endless variety of products to be offered on any menu.

TABLE 12-2. Handling and flow of sweet doughs

Mix from mixer at 74°–84°F

Normal fermentation			Retarding			
Sweet dough	Rolled-in dough	Danish	Danish	Sweet dough*	Sweet dough**	Rolled-in dough
Give ¾ to 1 full rise.	Give ¾ to 1 full rise.	Let loosen; roll in 2 to 4 oz of butter, margarine, or shortening per pound of dough. Rest 45 minutes; make up.	Let loosen; roll in 2 to 4 oz of butter, margarine, or shortening per pound of dough.	Flatten to fit sheet pan; refrigerate	Give ¾ normal fermentation.	Give ¾ normal fermentation.
Makeup.	Roll in 2 to 4 oz of butter, margarine, or shortening per pound of dough. Let dough loosen; make up	Make up.	Make up.	Bring to room temperature.	Make up.	Roll in 2 to 4 oz of butter, margarine, or shortening per pound of dough. Make up. Bring to room temperature.
			Refrigerate. Bring to room temperature.	Make up.	Refrigerate. Bring to room temperature.	
Proof. Bake.			Proof. Bake.			

NOTE: Use the retarding method only for richer sweet doughs; refrigerate at from 35° to 40°F, with relative humidity at 85 percent. Do not retard for more than 72 hours.
* This method has makeup after retarding.
** This method has makeup before retarding.

TABLE 12-3. Trouble-shooting bread failures

Fault	Possible causes	Possible remedies
Excessive volume	Too much yeast	Reduce yeast to 2 to 3%; check weighing procedures.
	Too little salt	Maintain from 2 to 2½%; check weighing procedures.
	Excess dough	Reduce scaling weights.
	Overproofed	Reduce proofing time; keep between 70–30 and 80–20 fermentation time for sponges.
	Oven too cool	Increase temperature.
Poor volume	Weak flour	Blend strong flour into flour, or use a stronger flour; give less mixing, shorter fermentation, and less proofing time.
	Flour too old or too new	Use aged flour; check age of flour.
	Water too soft or too alkaline	Use a conditioner; additional salt improves too-soft water.
	Lack of leavening	Use good yeast and handle it properly; have dough at proper temperature; reduce quantity of salt.
	Undermixing	Increase mixing times until gluten in dough is properly developed; check for proper volume of dough to mixer.
	Overfermented dough	Reduce fermentation time.
	Overmixing	Reduce mixing.
	Improper proofing	Proof between 90° and 100°F at 80 to 85% relative humidity; watch proofing time and maintain proper ratio between fermentation and proofing procedures.
	Too much or too little steam in oven	Open or close oven dampers; if steam is introduced into oven, establish better controls.
	Oven too hot	Reduce temperature.
Too dark crust	Excess sugar or milk	Reduce; check diastatic action of flour; it may be breaking too much starch down into sugars.
	Overmixing	Reduce mixing.
	Dough too young	Increase fermentation and proof periods.
	Oven too hot	Correct oven temperatures.
	Too long baking.	Reduce baking time.
	Oven too dry	Close oven damper during part of baking, or use steam.
Too pale or dull color on crust	Wrong proportions or ingredients	Check ratios of sugar, salt, or milk, and diastatic action of flour; increase ingredients to proper ratios; add diastase syrup.
	Soft water	Increase salt or add conditioner.
	Overfermentation	Reduce temperature or time of fermentation.
	Excessive dusting flour	Cover bench with bare minimum of flour.
	Proof temperature too high	Reduce temperature.
	Oven too cool	Increase temperature.
	Improper use of steam	Avoid excessive steam; open dampers to increase oven moisture.
Spotted crust	Improper mixing	Follow correct mixing procedures and sequence of adding ingredients.
	Excessive dusting flour	Reduce dusting flour.

continued

TABLE 12-3. Trouble-shooting bread failures (*continued*)

Fault	Possible causes	Possible remedies
	Excess humidity in proofing	Reduce relative humidity to between 80 and 85%.
	Water in oven or excessive moisture in steam	Check steam pipes and ovens; open dampers.
Hard crust or blisters	Lack of sugar or diastatic action	Increase sugars or check diastatic action of flour; check weighing of ingredients.
	Slack dough.	Reduce liquid; check mixing.
	Improper mixing	Check mixing procedures and sequence of ingredient addition.
	Old or young dough	Correct fermentation time.
	Improper molding or makeup	Correct procedures.
	Cool oven or too much top heat	Check damper-handling procedures and oven temperatures; check heating elements and heat source for proper functioning; check oven circulation.
	Cooling too rapidly	Cool more slowly; keep out of drafts.
	Too much fat on product	Reduce brushing of fat after makeup.
Poor shape	Improper makeup or planning	Correct procedures.
	Overproofing	Reduce.
Flat top or sharp corners	New flour	Age flour six to eight months under proper conditions.
	Low salt	Increase; check weighing procedures.
	Slack dough	Reduce liquid; check mixing.
	Young dough	Increase fermentation time.
	Excessive humidity in proofing	Reduce humidity.
Excessive break on side	Overmixing	Reduce mixing.
	Improper molding	Check molding, especially seam folds; place seam folds down on bottom of pan.
	Young dough	Correct; check proofing time.
	Oven too hot	Reduce temperatures.
Thick crust	Low shortening, sugar, or milk	Increase; check scaling procedures.
	Low diastase	Check diastatic action of flour; add malt syrup or diastase compound.
	Mixing improper	Correct mixing procedures.
	Improper proofing	Correct temperature, relative humidity, or time of proofing; check for wet crusts after proofing.
	Old dough.	Correct fermentation and/or proofing time.
	Improper baking	Correct temperatures and times; reduce steam and check for excessive or insufficient moisture in ovens.
Tough crust	Old or young dough	Check fermentation times.
	Improper mixing	Correct.
	Excess proof or wrong proof conditions	Correct.
	Oven cold or excess steam	Correct.

continued

TABLE 12-3. Trouble-shooting bread failures (*continued*)

Fault	Possible causes	Possible remedies
Lack of break or shred	Excess diastase	Decrease amount; use nondiastatic malt; check diastatic action of flour.
	Soft water	Increase salt or use conditioner.
	Slack dough	Reduce water substantially; check mixing.
	Improper fermentation or proof time	Correct.
	Oven too hot or too dry	Correct temperatures by damper control; introduce steam.
Ragged scaling or shelling on top	Green or old flour	Use properly aged flour.
	Old or young dough	Check fermentation or proof times and conditions.
	Stiff dough	Reduce flour or increase liquid.
	Crusting during proofing	Increase relative humidity; brush lightly with shortening.
	Excess salt	Reduce.
	Underproofing	Increase proofing time.
	Excessive top heat in oven	Check heat circulation and heat source in oven; check damper control.
	Cold dough	Add warmer liquid; check mixing, fermentation, and proofing temperatures.
	Excessive dough in pan	Check scaling.
	Lack of salt or milk	Check recipe and weighing procedures.
Too close grain	Low yeast	Increase; check weighing procedures.
	Underproofing	Correct.
	Excess dough in pan	Check scaling procedures.
Too coarse or open grain	Hard or alkaline water	Add vinegar or conditioner.
	Old dough	Use excess yeast; reduce fermentation time.
	Slack dough	Reduce liquid; check mixing times.
	Improper molding	Correct.
	Overproofing	Reduce time or check temperatures.
	Improper pan size	Check.
	Cold oven	Increase oven temperature.
	Excessive greasing	Check oiling or greasing of dough.
Gray crumb	High diastatic action	Reduce.
	High dough temperature or overfermentation	Check mixing, fermentation, and proof temperatures and times.
	Cold oven	Check temperatures and conditions of baking.
	Pans greasy	Check greasing.
Streaked crumb	Improper mixing	Check ingredient sequence of adding in mixing.
	Too slack or stiff dough	Check liquid or flour quantities; check to see if proper mixing times given.
	Excessive oil, grease, or dusting flour used.	Correct.
	High relative humidity	Reduce relative humidity in fermentation or proofing.
	Crusting of dough in fermentation	Increase relative humidity or brush with fat; cover to prevent moisture loss.
Poor texture	Alkaline or very hard water	Use conditioner or vinegar.
	Too slack or too stiff dough	Reduce or increase ingredients to correct ratios; check mixing.

continued

TABLE 12-3. Trouble-shooting bread failures (*continued*)

Fault	Possible causes	Possible remedies
	High sugar or excess yeast	Check ingredient ratios; check diastase, and decrease or increase as required.
	Lack of shortening	Increase.
	High dough temperature	Reduce liquid temperature or temperatures during fermentation or proofing.
	Overfermentation or proofing	Reduce.
	Excessive dusting of flour	Reduce.
	Oven too cool	Increase.
Off- and/or cheesy flavor	Inferior milk, rancid shortening; paint, gasoline, etc.	Check ingredients used; check flour, other ingredients for off-flavors; check storage areas where ingredients are held; check pans and other equipment for rancidity; check sanitation.
	Improper mixing or method	Check procedures.
Flat flavor	Low salt	Increase salt.

CRUMPETS AND ENGLISH MUFFINS

Crumpets and English muffins are special yeast-leavened products that are made in a way that is much the same as for bread products (see fig. 12-13). Their doughs usually have a higher liquid content. Crumpets leavened with baking powder are sometimes made, but they do not have the chewy texture of yeast-leavened crumpets. After fermentation, crumpet batter is poured into greased rings that are $2\frac{1}{2}$ to 3 in. in diameter and about $\frac{3}{4}$ to 1 in. deep, on a hot griddle. They are cooked until the bubbles on top are firm; then the ring is turned over, and the crumpet is cooked on the other side. The product is a honeycombed or web-structured moist muffin with a somewhat chewy texture.

English muffins are rich yeast doughs, soft almost to the point of being tacky. They are cut into round shapes, heavily proofed for about 15 minutes, and then carefully placed on a griddle—often in rings—and baked. When browned and partially done on one side, they are turned and baked on the other side. The griddle temperature should be about 350°F for both crumpets and English muffins.

QUICK BREADS

Quick breads belong to the batter and dough family. Leavening is usually done by a chemical leavener, but steam, air, or yeast may be used. Table 12-4 indicates how quick breads vary in ingredients. Mixes are marketed that need only liquid and perhaps egg added to produce high-quality

Figure 12-13. Crumpets in their metal shells (left) and English muffins (right) being baked.

products. They save labor and require less skill to make. Many such mixes can produce a wide variety of items. They have good tolerance in handling and lend themselves well to quantity work. Some operations make their own dry mixes. Frozen batters, frozen doughs, and some frozen baked products are also available. Table 12-5 presents scaling

TABLE 12-4. Relative percentages of ingredients in quick breads (flour = 100%)

Ingredient	Biscuits (%)	Muffins (%)	Cornbread (%)	Griddlecakes (%)	Waffles (%)	Popovers (%)	Éclair paste (%)
Flour, bread	0–50					100	100
Flour, pastry	50–100	100	100	100	100		
Sugar	0–2	10–65	5–25	2–10	15–30		
Shortening	20–30	20–40	6–20	5–15	40–50		100
Eggs	0–10	20–25	20–25	15–35	20–65	100	175
Liquid	60–70	70–80	80–90	125–200	130–180	200	200
Milk, dry, nonfat	7	8	8	10–15	10–15	20	
Baking powder, double-acting	6	6	8½	6–10	6–8		
Salt	1–2	1–2	1–2	1–2	1–2	1–2	1–2

NOTES: For greater tenderness, cake flour may be used in place of pastry flour for muffins and waffles. In cornbread, about 50% of the flour is cornmeal. For shortcakes, reduce the liquid to 50–60% and increase sugar to 15–20%.

TABLE 12-5. Scaling weights and baking temperatures and times for breads

Product	Pan size	Units per pan	Scaling weight	Baking temperature (°F)	Baking time (min)
		Yeast Breads			
Rolls, small	8 in.	12	1–1⅓ oz	400–425	15–20
	17 × 25 in.	72–100			
Rolls, medium	8 in.	8–12	1½–1¾ oz	400–425	15–20
	17 × 25 in.	60–85			
Rolls, large	8 in.	8	2–2⅓ oz	390–420	20–25
Cinnamon rolls	8 in.	8–12	1–2 oz	375–385	25
	17 × 25 in.	72–100		375	30
Sweet rolls	17 × 25 in.	24	2 oz	380–400	25
Tea rings	8 in.	1	10–12 oz each	375	30
	17 × 25 in.	4	with 2 oz filling		
Topped coffee cakes	8 in.	1	10–12 oz each	375	30
	17 × 25 in.	8	with 2 oz topping		
Fancy coffee cakes	8 in.	1	10–12 oz each	375	30
	17 × 25 in.	3–5	with 2 oz filling		
Bread, white	1¼	1	26½ oz	400	60
Bread, rye	1 lb	1	18 oz	400	45
		Quick Breads			
Brown, steamed	4 × 9 × 4 in.	1	1½ lb	Steam	60–90
Biscuit, 2¼ in.	17 × 25 in.	88	1¼ oz	425	15–20
Dumplings	8 in.	12	1½ oz	Steam	20–30
Cornbread	17 × 25 in.	1	6 lb	425	30
Griddlecakes			4 oz	350–375	3–5
Muffins, plain			1⅓–1½ oz	425	15–20
Muffins, bran			1½ oz	425	20–25
Breads, quick	7½ × 3½ × 2¼ in.	1	18 oz	350	60
Breads, date and nut	7½ × 3½ × 2¼ in.	1	22 oz	350	60
Breads, quick	4 × 9 × 4	1	1¾ lb	350	60–75
Cream puffs			1½ oz each with 2½ oz filling	450, then 375	15
Éclairs or popovers			2 oz each with 2 oz filling and ¾ oz topping	450, then 375	30–40

NOTES: A round or square pan 8 in. across may be used for any of the items that calls for an 8-in. pan. Fill cream puffs 2½ oz, eclairs 2 oz, using ¾ oz topping for eclairs.

weights and baking temperatures and times for both yeast and quick breads.

STANDARDS

A high-quality muffin is large for its weight. The crust is crisp, shiny, pebbly, and golden brown. A smooth crust of pale color can indicate toughness. Tops should be well-rounded and free of knobs. The interior crumb should be moist, light, and tender, with no tunneling (see fig. 12-14a). Plain muffins should have a creamy-white crumb with an even

(a) (b)

Figure 12-14. (a) This muffin sells by its appearance. (*Courtesy Processed Apple Institute*) (b) High-quality popovers show good expansion and crisp brown exteriors. (*Courtesy Wheat Flour Institute*)

grain and a delicate flavor that is neither too bready nor too sweet. Loaf breads, coffee cakes, and variety breads are made from muffin batter. Except for shape, the standard in each case is the same.

A high-quality biscuit should be well-shaped and regular, with straight, even sides and a level top; volume should be substantial. Crusts should be tender but not crumbly and should have a smooth, golden-brown color. The inside texture should be fine, even-grained, and fluffy, with a creamy white color free from yellow or brown spots. The biscuit should break easily, and the moist soft crumb should pull away in thin flakes or layers. Dropped biscuits vary somewhat from this standard—being shorter, less perfect in shape, and having crust qualities similar to those of muffins.

A popover or éclair paste product should have a round, irregular top of a delicate tan color; it should be large for its weight, with good height (see fig. 12-14b). Low volume indicates improper baking, excessive moisture, or a failure to mix properly. Too dark a color may indicate too high a baking temperature or too long a baking period. Popovers may be popped over on their sides at the top. They do not have as deep or as even a color as éclair paste products have. The interior should be hollow and large; bottoms should be shiny and even, with no holes; and crusts should be crisp, brittle, and tender. Interiors should be slightly moist, but not pasty, damp, or excessively dry.

A good pancake (griddlecake or hotcake) has a clear, even, brown color and good round shape, with no pitting on the top or bottom. The texture may be moist and slightly heavy, in which case the cake has the name *flannel*. In others, the texture may be less moist: firmer, drier, light, porous, open, and about $\frac{1}{4}$-in. thick. All griddle cakes should be well-cooked and tender inside, with firm, slightly crisp exteriors. They should be hot. Flavor should be pleasing and only slightly bready.

Waffles should be a light, even, brown color, with distinct grid markings, an even shape, and no ragged edges. Crusts should be tender and crisp, but crispness may vary according to recipe and baking time. Interiors should be open, with a tender, cream-colored crumb. Flavors should be slightly sweet, nutty, and pleasant.

PRODUCTS

Muffins

Thick, lean muffin batters can easily suffer from overdevelopment of gluten; even relatively rich batters are toughened with overmixing. Increasing richness or using a weaker flour, such as cake flour, allows more mixing. Mix at about 60°F to retard gluten development. Sift dry ingredients into a mixing bowl, and dump the blended egg, liquid, and liquid shortening into the middle. Using a mixer paddle, mix at slow speed for 15 to 20 seconds. The flour should just disappear, and the batter should look rough and lumpy, breaking easily when dropped from a spoon. Dry ingredients can be mixed in a large batch, and small parts of it can be blended with liquid ingredients and baked, as required. Sometimes solid shortening is cut into dry ingredients, as for biscuits, and the liquid and eggs added. Alternatively, shortening may be creamed with the sugar and eggs, and liquid added alternately with sifted dry ingredients. If either of these two variations are used, more shortening is needed. Using fine sugar rather than coarse sugar speeds sugar dissolving.

Portion with a No. 16 scoop or by hand, dipping and squeezing portions into lightly greased pans. Take batter from the inside edge out, reducing movement and thus toughness. Gingerbread, cornbread, and other batters may be so thin that they can be poured. If the batter is too deep in muffin pans or if the muffins are baked at too high a temperature, the likelihood of tunneling is increased.

Regular muffin pans (aluminum or black iron) should be conditioned by heavy greasing and by heating in a 450°F oven for about 15 minutes; then they should be removed and wiped clean. This process should be repeated three or four times. Teflon pans do not need such conditioning. Before adding batter, lightly grease and dust with flour to reduce sticking. Regular pans should not be washed after use but instead should be thoroughly cleaned with a clean, soft, absorbent cloth. Teflon pans can be washed. Pan and bake muffins immediately after mixing; otherwise some quality is lost. After baking, to avoid a soggy or overmoist product, dump the muffins from the pans or set them on their sides in the muffin cups, allowing steam to escape. Overmixing, mixing too slowly, adding too much flour or liquid, not adding sufficient leavening, or maintaining too low an oven temperature produces heavy muffins. Overgreased pans, too long a baking time, or too hot an oven results in heavy crusts.

Normally, about 6 to 7 lb flour or 14 to 16 lb batter gives 100 portions at an average of $1\frac{1}{2}$ muffins per person. About $2\frac{1}{2}$ oz (a 3-in. square, 1 in. thick) of coffee cake, Sally Lunn, or cornbread is a portion. An 18×26-in. pan can be cut 5×10 or 6×8 for portion-size rectangles. A loaf from a $5\frac{1}{2} \times 10\frac{1}{2} \times 3$-in. pan cuts into about twenty-five $\frac{3}{8}$-in. slices (two slices per portion); about 8 lb flour or 20 lb batter is needed for 100 portions of this size.

Baking-powder Biscuits

Cut the shortening for baking-powder biscuits into the dry ingredients with a pastry blender or mixer paddle operating at low speed; stop when the mixture looks like loose, coarse cornmeal. Overmixing gives a fine bready texture, while too little mixing produces a coarse texture. Next, add the liquid, mixing with a paddle at low speed until a soft dough is formed. Some good mixing is needed to develop texture and rise, but overmixing can produce too much toughness (see fig. 12-15a). Knead on a lightly floured bench to aid in dough development. Use the finger tips to lift up the dough, and then press the dough down with the heel of the hand (see fig. 12-15b). Deft touch and light pressure are required. Give the dough a half turn after each kneading (about twenty half turns in all). At the end of kneading, the dough should be soft and springy and not sticky. If kneading is omitted, a shorter, crisper, lower-volume biscuit is obtained. Using slightly more shortening and cutting the mixture to the size of small peas, coupled with good kneading of the dough, gives a good flaky biscuit. Flakiness can also be achieved by making a dough that is as slack as or slightly slacker than the dough for a dropped biscuit, and then adding the remaining flour during kneading.

For cutting, roll the dough to half the height desired for the final biscuit. Cut evenly and straight down; twisting may give a poor shape. Many operations cut biscuits from the rolled dough into squares or triangles, using a cutter or a knife, so that all dough is used in one rolling (see fig. 12-16a). Additional reworking of cutting scraps may yield tough, compact biscuits. Setting biscuits apart on the baking pan gives a crisper,

(a)   (b)

Figure 12-15. (a) Biscuit dough after liquid has been combined with a dry baking-powder biscuit mix. (b) Knead the dough on a floured surface, using the palms of the hands to develop gluten.

(a) (b)

Figure 12-16. (a) To save time and achieve more consistent quality, cut biscuits into squares with a lightly oiled bench knife. (b) Buttering scones after scoring them.

more highly colored biscuit, especially if the cut biscuit is washed with or dipped into melted butter, margarine, or shortening. Tops may be washed with milk, evaporated milk, or egg wash before baking. Short-cakes are rich biscuit doughs that contain extra sugar and shortening. Dumplings are made from variations on biscuit dough and may contain eggs.

A dropped biscuit is not kneaded. The dough is slightly moister and leaner than regular biscuit dough. Dropped biscuits are dropped onto greased baking sheets from a spoon, resulting in a product with less volume, a rougher appearance, a crisper crust, and a tenderer crumb. Bake all biscuit items at 425°F for 15 to 20 minutes.

Scones are made from rich biscuit dough containing egg. Raisins, nuts, currants, and other items may be added. Mix, knead, and roll as for biscuits; then pat out to cover the baking sheet. Cut the dough into rectangular shapes 1 in. wide and 2 in. long, using a scraper dipped into margarine or shortening to permit easy separation later after baking. The tops may be washed with egg wash or brushed with butter (see fig. 12-16b). Sometimes scones are cut and then panned. Some cooks score each scone in the center with a cutter dipped into margarine or butter, so a break appears here after baking.

A beaten biscuit is a Southern quick bread not typical of biscuits since no leavening is used. The flour usually contains phosphates to assist in giving a lightened product. The soft dough is pounded with a stick "twenty-four times for family, and forty-eight times for company." During pounding, it is folded to blend air into the dough.

Poor biscuit quality may result from one or more of the factors identified in table 12-6.

TABLE 12-6. Causes of poor-quality biscuits

Defect	Possible causes
Heavy or compact crumb	Overmixed or overkneaded dough
	Insufficient baking powder or shortening
	Too much liquid or flour
	Oven not hot enough
Pale crust	Oven not hot enough
	Too-deep pan used for baking
	Too much flour
Poor volume	Oven not hot enough
	Insufficient baking powder
Light but not flaky	Shortening cut into flour too finely
	Insufficient kneading
Poor shape	Too-slack dough
	Uneven rolling
	Twisting of the cutter
	Careless cutting or panning

Griddlecakes and Waffles

In density, waffle batter falls between griddlecake and muffin batters. Overmixing toughens waffles. As with muffins, richness or the use of cake flour permits more mixing. Griddlecakes have a thinner batter and—since the liquid disperses the gluten—can be mixed more. Occasionally, beaten egg whites are carefully folded into the batter at the end of mixing. This gives a lighter product and may reduce the amount of baking powder required. If the ratio (by weight) of fat to liquid in a hotcake or waffle batter is 1:4, the griddle or waffle grid need not be greased. Swedish pancakes, French pancakes, and blintzes usually contain no leavening agent. They are thin batters, high in egg and giving a slightly less tender product than the flannel cake.

Griddlecakes are baked on a lightly greased griddle at around 350°F. About 2 oz batter is placed on the griddle for a small cake, and 4 oz for a large one. For 100 portions of two large cakes each 17 lb flour or 50 lb batter (6 gal) is needed. As the heat strikes the batter, volume increases and bubbles rise to the top. When the edge shows a slight drying, the cake should be deftly turned (see fig. 12-17). Complete the baking in one turn, since additional turning lowers quality. The cake rises slightly in the center after the turn. When this recedes and the top becomes even, the cake is done. Even griddle heat is necessary. Too low a temperature gives a cake with poor color and texture. If the temperature is too high, the color is dark, and the cake is apt to be undercooked in the center. A pitted top indicates too high a heat or too long a time lapse before turning.

Waffles should be baked in a conditioned waffle baker. The batter is placed in the center to within about 1 to 1½ in. from the edge; baking spreads it out to the edge (see fig. 12-18). About 4 oz batter is needed per portion—30 lb for 100 waffles. Waffle batters contain more sugar, fat, and

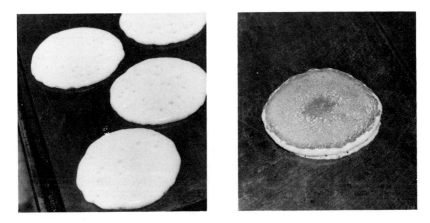

(a)   (b)

Figure 12-17. (a) These griddlecakes are ready to be turned. Notice the bubbles on the uncooked surface and the puffy quality of the batter. (b) A griddlecake that has been turned and is ready to be served.

eggs than griddlecake batters do, and some may be so rich that they are cake waffles and can be served topped with ice cream and a syrup as a dessert. Increasing baking time gives a crisper waffle. Crispness also depends on batter richness. Table 12-7 gives the yields from 30-lb lots of various dry mixes.

Éclair (Choux) Pastes and Popovers

An éclair or choux paste is made by cooking flour, shortening, and water into a smooth paste. This is cooled to about 150°F, and eggs are added in about four to five additions. After each addition, the batter is mixed well to obtain a smooth, velvety, shiny paste. Batter thickness should be sufficient to retain shape in panning. Often the batter is shaped with

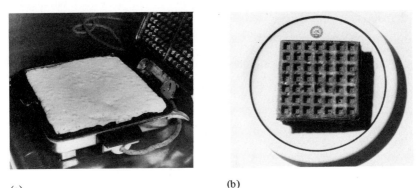

(a)   (b)

Figure 12-18. (a) This waffle iron has been filled too full. It will overflow when the lid is lowered. (b) A well-baked waffle.

TABLE 12-7. Yields from 30-lb lots of dry mixes

Mix	Yield	Mix	Yield
Griddlecakes	725 (4 oz each)	Bran muffins	720 (1 oz)
Waffles	300	Cornbread	375 (2 × 3-in.)
Biscuits	720 (2 in.)	Cornbread	520 (sticks)
Plain muffins	800 (1 oz)	Coffee cake or gingerbread	40 (8-in. layer)
			300 (2 × 3-in.)

pastry tubes. A medium-size cream puff or eclair requires about 2 oz batter. Using insufficient water or overcooking the batter may cause a broken emulsion; using excess water gives too soft a paste and a product with low volume.

A popover batter is a pour batter, like hotcake batter. It should be beaten well to develop gluten strength and a firm structure. The batter is panned into deep, heavy cups or well-conditioned muffin pans. Heavy iron preheated pans filled half full and placed into a hot oven immediately after panning give good volume. Failure to achieve volume may be caused by improper mixing, insufficient eggs, excess liquid, or too low heat.

The popover structure or éclair paste product is important to quality. Leavening is provided by steam, which forms rapidly inside the base of the batter early in baking. As it expands, it pushes upward, developing a large hole inside. Once full expansion is obtained, baking must firm the structure to prevent the product from collapsing after the steam condenses. To achieve these results, the baking temperature should be kept at 450°F for 15 minutes (to develop steam) and then dropped to 375°F, and the baking continued for 30 to 40 minutes. During this last period, the structural walls of the popover or éclair paste are dried out. Browning is not always an indicator of doneness. A rapid cold shock after oven removal may still collapse these products. To avert this, pull them to the oven front and allow to stand a few moments with the door open to reduce the heat gradually. About 5 minutes before the end of baking, the items may be lightly prickled at the top to allow steam to escape. Cream puffs, éclairs, French crullers, and other choux pastes are made from éclair pastes. Yorkshire pudding is made from popover batter.

A recipe for a choux paste may call for $\frac{1}{4}$ percent baking ammonia to 100 percent flour. This helps give rapid expansion. The amount of eggs used may be reduced slightly when baking ammonia is added. The ammonia quickly escapes through the thin walls. Ammonia is not used for popovers because these are usually served hot, and the ammonia flavor would still be present at that time.

Chapter Review

1. List the different steps in yeast bread making, and indicate what happens during each.

2. What are the different kinds of yeast breads, and what ingredients and techniques are needed to make them?
3. What is a sponge dough? a straight dough? a no-time dough?
4. What would be a good standard for a baking-powder biscuit?
5. How do griddle cakes differ in ingredient proportions from waffles and plain muffins?
6. How are choux pastes and popovers leavened?
7. Why is the baking temperature set high when choux pastes and popovers are first put into the oven?

CHAPTER 13

Cakes, Cookies, and Decorations

Outline

Goals

1. To identify the standards, principles, and techniques needed to make good cakes.
2. To name the types of cakes, list their ingredients, and explain how to make them.
3. To describe how recipes should be checked to see if they are in balance.
4. To show how to adjust recipes for different altitudes.
5. To describe the different mixing methods used in making different cakes.

6. To cover the panning, baking, cooling, and storage procedures for cakes.
7. To discuss the making and use of different frostings, icings, and fillings, and to indicate how to do simple decorative work.
8. To explain how to make different cookies.

CAKES

Cakes are a popular dessert well-suited to quantity food production. They cost relatively little, are easy to prepare, and have a good shelf life. A wide variety can be made by slightly varying a few ingredients, making it possible to carry only a modest number of ingredients and simplifying work (see table 13-1). Variety is also achieved by using different-shaped pans and different fillings and frostings. Years ago, maximum skill was needed to overcome the limitations of ingredients in making *gâteaux* (cakes) and tortes. At that time, cakes were leavened by air captured in egg foam (sponges) or through creaming (pound cakes) or by gas developed by yeast (babas au rhum); today, however, chemical leavening agents, improved shortenings, and high-stability cake flour simplify production. The introduction of cake mixes has simplified cake and cookie making, too.

High-quality ingredients, exact measurement, and efficient equipment are needed to produce good cakes. Recipes should be tested and balanced to suit operational conditions. Layouts should allow work to flow smoothly and efficiently from scaling to mixing to panning to baking to cooling to makeup. Poor tools, pans, or equipment can increase labor costs and diminish quality. Poor temperature control, excessive oven vibration, warped or sagging oven shelves, and uneven baking decks produce poor cakes. Reel ovens should be equipped with stabilized shelves. Vibration makes cakes separate in the center and gives them poor volume and crumb. Uneven heat results in low volume, dark and thick crusts, tunnels, uneven surface, shrinkage, and pulling away from pan sides. Even the best baker cannot overcome deficiencies in materials, equipment, or operating conditions.

TYPES OF CAKES

The ingredients and leavening agents used in cakes serve as a basis for classifying them into three groups: butter cakes, pound cakes, and foam cakes. Butter cakes are produced more frequently than the others, although *butter* may be a misnomer because hydrogenated shortening is usually used in its place. Some bakers claim butter makes a better-flavored cake than shortening or margarine.

The ingredients used in a butter cake are shortening, eggs, flour, salt, baking powder, liquid, and flavoring. Pound cake batters are used for fruit cakes, nut cakes, steam puddings, and the like. Pound cakes are made from equal weights of sugar, shortening, eggs, and flour, plus a bit of salt and flavoring; leavening is supplied by air incorporated during creaming. Pound cakes can be modified by adding liquid and baking powder. To keep them in balance, shortening and eggs must be de-

TABLE 13-1. Variations possible from three basic cake batters

Cake	Icing	Filling	Basic batters		
			White	Gold	Chocolate
Almond fudge	Almond toffee	Almond toffee			*
Almond gold	Almond toffee	Almond toffee		*	
Banana	Banana	Banana	*	*	
Bittersweet fudge	Bittersweet chocolate	Marshmallow			*
Butterscotch walnut	Butterscotch fondant and walnuts	Butterscotch	*	*	*
Carmel fudge	Caramel fudge	Caramel fudge	*	*	*
Cherry	Cherry cream	Cherry cream	*	*	
Chocolate	Chocolate fudge	Fudge	*	*	*
Chocolate chip	Vanilla fondant and Chocolate shavings	Vanilla fondant	*	*	*
Double dip caramel	Caramel fudge and marshmallow	Butterscotch	*	*	*
Double dip chocolate	Chocolate fondant and marshmallow	Marshmallow	*	*	*
Double fudge	Chocolate fudge	Fudge			*
Frosty silver	Coconut cream	Coconut cream	*		
Golden gate	Orange cream	Orange		*	
Lady Baltimore	Marshmallow or nut and fruit	Fruit and nut cream	*		
Lemonade	Lemon fondant	Lemon fondant	*	*	
Malted milk	Chocolate malted milk	Chocolate malted milk	*	*	*
Maple cream and nut	Maple fondant, walnuts	Maple cream or nut cream	*	*	*
Maple nut	Maple	Nut cream	*	*	*
Marshmallow macaroon	Marshmallow topped with macaroon coconut	Chocolate cream or marshmallow	*	*	*
Marshmallow pecan	Marshmallow topped with pecans	Marshmallow	*	*	*
Orange coconut	Orange fondant topped with orange coconut	Orange	*	*	
Pineapple sundae	Pineapple fondant	Pineapple fondant	*	*	
Spumoni	Chocolate fudge with chopped cherries	Fruit cream	*	*	*
Strawberry sundae	Strawberry fondant	Strawberry cream	*	*	

Source: Adapted from Procter & Gamble materials.

creased, while sugar is increased. Typical foam cakes are angel, sponge, and chiffon. Air in egg foam is the major leavening agent. Some contain a bit of baking powder to aid in leavening. In chiffon cakes, oil is an ingredient. A sponge cake may have shortening, but an angel cake does not. Liquid is frequently used in sponge or chiffon cakes. The light, delicate quality of foams requires a high-quality cake flour, eggs, and fine-grained sugar. Foam cakes are usually not prepared in more than 100-portion batches because their delicate structure is destroyed by a heavier batch weight.

STANDARDS

Good butter cake should be even on all sides, perfectly shaped, and slightly rounded on top. Rounding is less on large sheet cakes. Crusts should be shiny, golden, tender, thin, daintily crisp, and smooth, not blistered; it may have a slight puffy quality. The crumb should show a fine, even grain that is soft, moist, light, tender, and velvety. The crumb should show no signs of dullness, cloudiness, or streakiness. Color varies with the type. Chocolate color varies—an alkaline batter having a rich, reddish brown color that is not excessively dark, but a nonalkaline batter having a rich chocolate color. Butter cakes have a mild, sweet, rich, delicate, and buttery flavor. Chocolate cakes have a similar flavor, modified by the smooth chocolate flavor, with no trace of bitterness or soapiness from excess alkalinity.

A pound cake has an even shape, a slightly rounded top and a thin, soft, delicately brown crust that is slightly split on top. The crumb is smooth and rich, with no oiliness; the texture is firm, with fine, compact cells; and the flavor is sweet, delicately rich, and substantial.

The grain of angel cake is even, fine, light, feathery, and moist—more delicate and tender than a sponge or chiffon cake. The crumb should not be hard, brittle, or excessively moist. Cell walls should be clear and white, reflecting a delicate sheen. Sides should be even, and the top slightly rounded. A delicately browned crust, neither moist nor sticky, is desirable. The cake should stand high for its weight. Sponge or chiffon cake textures should be delicate, springy, and light, with a moist and soft crumb of delicate flavor and even grain; the crumb should not be coarse or excessively feathery. Fine, thin cells with a soft sheen indicate lightness and delicacy. The shape should be high and even, and the crust lightly browned. Crumb color is a light lemon-gold in sponges and slightly lighter in chiffons, unless other ingredients modify it. Figure 13-1 illustrates various cake standards.

CAKE BALANCE

Butter cakes are in balance if three requirements are satisfied: the weight of the sugar exceeds the flour weight; the shortening weight does not exceed the egg weight; and the liquid (milk and eggs) weight is about $1\frac{1}{2}$ times the sugar weight (see fig. 13-2). Whole eggs, whites, and yolks consist of approximately 65, 75, and 50 percent moisture, respectively. If yolks replace whole eggs, liquid is increased proportionately; if whites replace whole eggs, liquid is reduced proportionately. Before high-ratio shortenings and high-stability cake flours were developed, sugar could not exceed flour, but now the ratio of sugar to flour may go as high as $1\frac{1}{2}:1$. Higher ratios of shortening and sugar are used in chocolate and cocoa cakes because the starch in these extra ingredients allows this. Blended cakes contain more sugar than regular ones. A common rule in cake balancing is that, as liquid is increased, eggs and shortening are reduced; we can see this rule being put into effect as recipes are modified from a pound cake to a butter cake. The quantity and type of shortening

(a)

(b)

(c)   (d)

Figure 13-1. High product standards: (a) butter cake; (b) foam cake; (c) pound cake; (d) decoration.

and sugar control the sugar and liquid balance. If syrups are used in place of crystallized sugar, the syrup's liquid necessitates a reduction in other liquids.

Pound cake balance varies from proportions of 1 lb each of flour, shortening, eggs, and sugar to proportions that closely resemble those of a butter cake (see fig. 13-3).

Angel cake is in balance if two conditions are met: the sugar weight equals the egg white weight; and the flour weight is one-half to one-third the sugar weight *or* the egg white weight (see fig. 13-4). Variations are

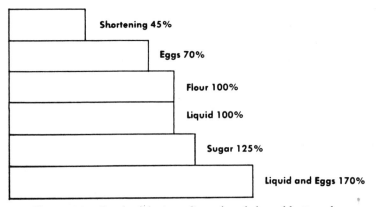

Shortening 45%

Eggs 70%

Flour 100%

Liquid 100%

Sugar 125%

Liquid and Eggs 170%

Figure 13-2. Graph of the ingredients for a balanced butter cake.

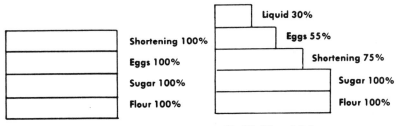

Typical Pound Cake   Modified Pound Cake

Figure 13-3. Balanced ingredients for a typical pound cake and for a modified pound cake. Leavening may be an additional ingredient in the modified cake. Notice that, as the pound cake is modified, its balance tends more and more toward that of a properly made butter cake.

(a)

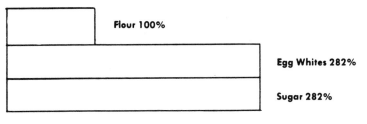

(b)

Figure 13-4. Ingredients for an angel cake. Cream of tartar, unlabeled, is in the front dish. (b) Graph of the ingredients for a balanced angel cake.

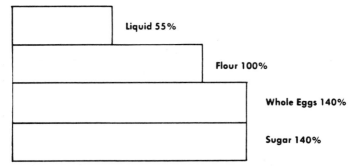

Figure 13-5.   Graph of the ingredients for a balanced sponge cake.

possible. For example, a successful cake results from 13 oz flour (100 percent), 32 oz egg whites (245 percent) and 26 oz sugar (200 percent). Sponge cakes balance if four points are in order: the sugar weight equals or slightly exceeds the egg weight; the combined liquid and egg weight is $1\frac{1}{4}$ times the sugar weight; the whole egg weight *or* the sugar weight exceeds the flour weight; and the whole egg *and* flour weights combined exceed the sugar *and* liquid weights combined (see fig. 13-5). Chiffon cake rules include five points: the sugar weight is $1\frac{1}{3}$ to $1\frac{1}{2}$ times the flour weight; the yolk weight is one-half that of the whites; the oil weight is one-half that of the flour; the liquid weight is three-quarters that of the flour; and the combined weight of the liquid *and* the eggs is about equal to that of the sugar *and* the flour (see fig. 13-6).

ALTITUDE ADJUSTMENT

Cake recipes are adjusted as elevation increases, to take into account the lighter atmospheric pressure. The adjustment varies for different cakes— less being needed in conventionally mixed butter cakes than in those made by the blending method. A rich butter cake or one high in mois- ture, such as applesauce cake, requires a different leavening adjustment

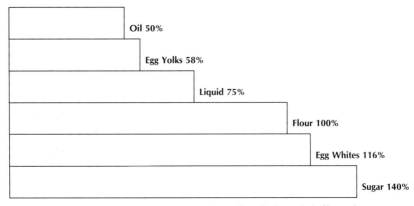

Figure 13-6.   Graph of the ingredients for a balanced chiffon cake.

from a common butter cake. At elevations of 3,000 ft or more, the sugar in angel cakes is reduced by 10 to 12 percent, and the cream of tartar is doubled. In sponge cakes, lemon juice is omitted and cream of tartar substituted for it, and eggs are beaten slightly less at altitudes above 3,000 ft. At 7,000 ft, the sugar in sponge cakes is reduced by 10 to 12 percent. Flour and eggs may be increased in butter and pound cakes at elevations of 1,000 ft or more, to give a firmer structure. Above 5,000 ft, the shortening in butter and pound cakes may have to be reduced to lessen its tenderizing effect. Butter cake pans may be greased more heavily, since there is a greater tendency for them to stick. Above 4,500 ft, some bakers increase their oven temperatures by 25 Fahrenheit degrees while maintaining the same baking time. Oven dampers may be closed to reduce moisture loss during the last part of the baking. Figure 13-7 and table 13-2 indicate recommended changes in leavening and other ingredients at different altitudes.

MIXING METHODS

Butter Cakes

The conventional (creaming) method and the blending method are the methods most commonly used for mixing butter cakes—the conventional sponge and muffin mixing methods being used less often. The blending approach is simpler than conventional mixing and produces a richer, sweeter cake with better texture and longer shelf life. Cake quality

TABLE 13-2. Approximate changes in butter cake recipe as elevation changes

| Altitude | Reduction (%) | | Increase % |
	Baking powder	Sugar	Moisture
1,500	5	0	0
2,000	10	2	0.01
2,500	14.4	3	0.015
3,000	19.8	4	0.02
3,500	22.8	4.9	0.025
4,000	26.8	5.9	0.03
4,500	30.4	6.8	0.035
5,000	34	7.8	0.04
5,500	37.2	8.7	0.045
6,000	40.5	9.6	0.05
6,500	43.3	10.5	0.056
7,000	46.4	11.5	0.06
7,500	49	12.4	0.067
8,000	52.7	13.3	0.072
8,500	54.1	14.6	0.077
9,000	56.5	16	0.083
9,500	58.7	16.8	0.088
10,000	60.8	17.7	0.093

Adapted from General Mills, Inc., materials.

Table 16-2. Percentage Reduction in Leavening as Altitude Increases

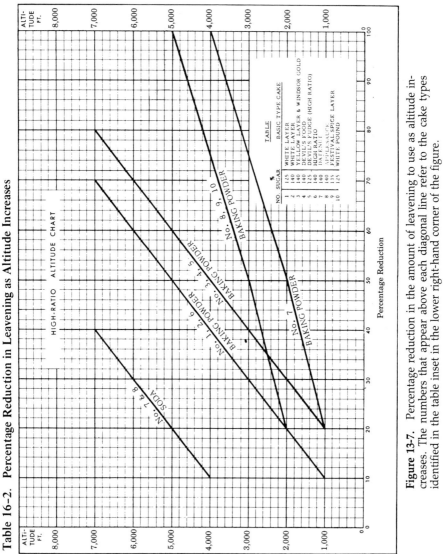

Figure 13-7. Percentage reduction in the amount of leavening to use as altitude increases. The numbers that appear above each diagonal line refer to the cake types identified in the table inset in the lower right-hand corner of the figure.

is usually rated as (from first to last) blended, cake mix, conventional, conventional sponge, and muffin.

Use bowl adapters to suit batch volume; batters should rise just above the mixing paddle when mixing is complete. Ingredients mix best at 75° to 80°F. Condition shortening 24 hours in advance. Use waxy, workable shortening to incorporate air and give spread; hard or excessively soft fats cream poorly. Adjust shortening temperatures to get the right consistency. Shortening emulsifiers give improved creaming action. In the conventional method, shortening is creamed to a waxy stage, and sugar is then added; creaming continues until a light color and fluffy texture are obtained, signaling maximum air incorporation. Sugar helps pull air in and also absorbs shortening, improving its spread in the batter. Scrape the bowl down frequently, moving ingredients from the bottom and sides into mixer action. (Mixing times in recipes do not include time spent scraping down the bowl.) Add eggs in three equal parts, creaming well at medium speed after each addition. A smooth, fluffy mixture free of sugar graininess should be evident at the end of mixing (see fig. 13-8). If all shortening, sugar, and eggs are added together and the mixture is creamed at medium speed, time and labor are reduced but the quality of the cake suffers.

After creaming at low speed, add one-quarter of the sifted dry ingredients and one-third of the liquid. Usually there are four additions of dry ingredients and three of liquid. Overmixing after the addition of flour may result in excessive gluten development and leavening loss, produc-

Figure 13-8.   Well-creamed shortening, sugar, and eggs just before the addition of dry ingredients and milk in the making of a conventional cake.

ing a heavy, compact cake with tunneling. Undermixing gives a coarse, poor crumb. The resulting batter is thick and smooth and must be spread in panning (see fig. 13-9). Give the pan several sharp raps after filling it, to free air bubbles.

In some conventional mixing, only yolks are added during creaming. Whites are beaten separately to a soft, glossy peak or are made into a soft meringue with part of the sugar, and this is carefully folded in just before panning. Use a whip, spoon, or hand to fold, making a down-and-under motion. Machine-blending may be carefully done at low speed until all egg foam is incorporated. Underblending leaves flecks of egg, which rise to the surface and cause an uneven, blistered crust; overbeating leads to a loss in volume. When beaten egg whites are added last, the amount of baking powder may be reduced.

Curdling may occur when eggs are added, especially if they are cold. Fine curds may eventually become part of a fine cake texture, but most bakers prefer no curdling. Warming the eggs or adding a bit of flour during the latter stages of creaming reduces the mixture's tendency to curdle. Dry eggs—if they are not added with the sifted ingredients—may be mixed with part of the liquid that is needed to refresh them, and the remaining liquid can be added later; this reduces curdling. Chocolate should be added during creaming, and cocoa should be sifted in with the flour.

The blending method mixes flour and shortening together with a mixer paddle for 3 to 5 minutes so that the flour is coated with shortening, promoting tenderness and evenness of grain and reducing moisture loss for improved keeping qualities (see fig. 13-10). The batter has a high tolerance to overmixing or undermixing. High-stability flour and emulsified shortening are best. The time and speed of mixing stated in recipes should be followed. Undermixing results in a coarse grain and lack of tenderness, while overmixing toughens and yields a compact grain. Batters mixed by the blending method are thin and pour.

(a)   (b)

Figure 13-9. (a) A conventional cake batter is so thick that it does not spread by itself in pans. (b) Instead it must be spread with a spatula.

(a)

(b)

(c)

(d)

Figure 13-10. The blending method. (a) The shortening is placed on top of the flour, salt, and leavening. (b) The mixture is mixed at slow speed for 3 to 5 minutes. (c) One-third of the liquid and the dry milk blended with the sugar are added, and the mixture is again mixed for 3 to 5 minutes, after which the eggs and remaining liquid are added. (d) The resulting batter pours easily.

Scrape down the bowl frequently. Add chocolate in melted form after blending the flour and shortening. Sugar, salt, baking powder, and dry milk solids are sifted and added with one-third to one-quarter of the liquid. Cocoa, spices, and other dry ingredients may be sifted in at this time. Adding liquid in two stages gives a smoother, lump-free batter. After mixing for 3 to 5 minutes, the eggs, remaining liquid, and flavoring are added and mixed for 3 to 5 minutes. Batter thinness is not an indicator of poor quality or low cake volume.

A variation of this method is to sift flour, salt, dry milk solids, and sugar into the mixing bowl, and then add the shortening and mix these ingredients at medium or slow speed for 2 minutes, adding one-half to two-thirds of the liquid early. Scrape down frequently. Next, add the eggs, the remaining liquid, and the leavening agent, and continue mixing for another 2 minutes. Some bakers vary the time to 3 minutes for the first mix and 1 minute for the second.

Another variation is the dump method. Flour, leavening agent, milk solids, salt, and sugar are sifted into the mixer. Shortening, eggs, and one-half of the liquid are added and mixed for 1 minute at low or medium speed. Next, the remaining liquid is added and mixed for 2 minutes. Quality is lower unless emulsified liquid shortening is used; then it becomes excellent.

Muffin-method cakes stale quickly and should be served soon after baking. Use the muffin method for nonrich cakes. The method involves mixing eggs, liquid, and melted shortening or oil together. This mixture is then poured into sifted dry ingredients, and everything is mixed together.

Use the conventional sponge method when soft shortenings must be used or when high mixing temperatures are encountered. Cream one-half of the sugar into the shortening; then sift the dry ingredients into this mixture and blend them, followed by the liquids. Beat warm eggs into a fluffy sponge with the remaining sugar, and carefully fold this into the batter. Another approach is to dissolve the sugar into one-half to two-thirds of the liquid and add the soft shortening, the sifted flour, and leavening agent to this, mixing for 3 to 4 minutes. Then add the eggs, flavoring, and remaining liquid, and mix the entire batter for 1 minute at medium speed.

Pound Cakes

Cream the shortening and sugar thoroughly; then add eggs, creaming until the mixture is light and fluffy. Add flour immediately if necessary to prevent curdling. Blend in the flour; bread flour can be used for half the total flour, giving structural strength. Use flour with high absorptive power. Strong structure is needed in fruit cakes, in order to carry fruit and nuts that may weigh 1 to $1\frac{1}{2}$ times as much as the batter. A variation is to beat warm eggs into a sponge with the sugar, fold in the flour, and blend the melted shortening in carefully; however, quality is lower. If only egg whites are used (giving a higher liquid content), 3 percent baking powder to 100 percent flour is used. Use fine or berry sugar, so it dissolves quickly. Pound cakes that are high in sugar and liquid have increased volume, but the grain is more open and the top crust breaks away more easily.

Foam Cakes

The use of eggs as foams is covered in chapter 7. The point at which egg foam is stiff enough to hold ingredients and yet soft enough to allow blending easily is critical in making foam cakes. Recognizing this point is a matter of experience and judgment.

Salt and cream of tartar make egg whites more extensible. Cream of tartar, being acidic, whitens the flavones of flour, but it is not a leavener. Beat whites at 110° to 125°F until they make soft peaks that bend over slightly at the top (stage 2, upper level). Underbeating or overbeating gives poor quality and volume. Fold one-third to one-half of the sugar into the beaten whites; the finer the sugar is, the finer the grain will be. Some recipes use part powdered and part granulated sugar, and some call for rolling the sugar with a rolling pin to break it down. Fold in the flour—sifted thoroughly with the remaining sugar—until it just disappears. This is a critical point: too much mixing yields a poor cake. Mixing part of the sugar with the flour makes the flour easier to incorporate. Machine blending at slow speed is possible for flour and sugar, but most bakers prefer to fold the flour in with a wire whip, spoon, or spatula, or by hand. Figure 13-11 illustrates key steps in the process of mixing angel

(a)

(b)

(c)

Figure 13-11. Making an angel cake. (a) Warm egg whites, salt, and cream of tartar are beaten to the upper foam stage. (b) Sugar is added and is blended in just until the mixture is smooth and peaks softly. (c) The remaining sugar, blended thoroughly with the sifted flour, is then carefully folded in by hand. Notice the spread of the fingers to encourage more rapid incorporation of the flour–sugar mixture.

cake batter. Angel cake mixes produce excellent results; they have a high tolerance to overbeating and underbeating. The cost is about the same, taking into account the labor involved in separating the eggs.

For sponge cakes, warm whole eggs or yolks are beaten into a stable foam with salt, lemon juice, or cream of tartar. Adding some sugar during beating gives a more stable foam that develops more rapidly. Eggs beat best at from 120° to 125°F; beating the eggs over 150°F water helps, or the sugar may be heated. Beat at high speed until the eggs form a thick, lemon-colored foam (about 10 to 15 minutes); underbeating yields a tough streak on the cake bottom, producing low volume and a heavy, compact grain. If egg yolks replace whole eggs, a liquid such as hot water, milk, or lemon juice makes up the difference. After beating is completed, carefully fold in the sifted flour—by hand or using a machine at low speed. If baking powder or other dry ingredients are used, sift them with the flour. Sponges may be made by beating yolks separately from whites, using half the sugar. Add liquid to the yolk–sugar mixture, and fold in the flour. Make the whites, cream of tartar, and salt into a soft meringue with the remaining sugar, and fold this into the batter carefully. Overmixing here results in a cake with a dry, heavy, close grain and a tough, rubbery texture. Undermixing leads to a coarse texture and uneven grain.

Delicate sponges may have hot milk or butter added after the dry ingredients are folded in; butter should be melted, and milk heated to 140°F. Final batter temperature should be 110°F. Some recipes call for adding hot milk alternately with the flour, but this takes much skill to do correctly without loss of foam. If the butter solidifies, the cake collapses in the oven. Fat breaks down egg foam, so the melted butter must be blended skillfully (preferably by hand-mixing). In place of warm milk or butter, hot water may be added to the beaten eggs just before the sifted dry ingredients are folded in; this gives a moist, soft, velvety sponge.

Chiffon cakes resemble sponges and are mixed in much the same way. They are slightly more stable and not so sensitive to overmixing and undermixing. Eggs are beaten warm, and all blending is done carefully. The cakes have good keeping quality.

Mixes

Most mixes contain all ingredients except water and eggs. Cakes made from mixes used to stale rapidly, but today stabilizers included in mixes produce cakes with a longer shelf life than regular-made cakes have. Many varieties are available, and relatively little skill, equipment, or inventory is needed to produce the cakes an operation requires. Operations may also prepare their own mixes. They start by blending flour, shortening, dry emulsifier, and sugar together—using emulsifier in the amount of 0.75 to 1 percent of total mix weight or 3 to 6 percent of shortening weight. (If emulsified shortening is used, less emulsifier is called for.) Monoglycerides, diglycerides, and polyoxyethylenes are used as emulsifiers. After the first mixture is blended, nonfat dry milk, salt, sodium acid pyrophosphate baking powder, and dried eggs are added. Cocoa is used for chocolate cakes. The mixture is then stored and treated as a regular mix. For batter, a ratio of 40 : 60 water to mix is used. About two-thirds of the liquid is added to the dry mix and blended at low speed for 1 minute. The bowl is scraped down, and the batter is mixed for 4 minutes at medium speed. Then the remaining water is added, and everything is mixed for 1 minute at low speed. The bowl is again scraped down, and the batter is mixed for 4 minutes at medium speed.

PANNING

Panning affects cake quality. Fill pans one-half to two-thirds full with butter cake or pound cake batter. Overfilled pans spill, diminishing quality or even collapsing; underfilled pans give low volume. Pans with sloping sides accommodate less volume than straight-sided pans. Greased sides of pans reduce volume by lessening cling. Pan-greasing mixtures may be composed of 7 lb shortening, 1 lb margarine, and 1 pt salad oil to 4 lb flour; salt and butter flavoring can be added to improve flavor. Paper liners are desirable for lining pan bottoms; they are removed after baking. Teflon, silicon, and other pan coatings reduce the need for greasing. If bottom crusts dry in baking, they should be moistened—especially for jelly rolls. Cupcakes or muffins are often baked in paper cups. Moist products such as applesauce cupcakes are removed from the paper cups after baking, but drier products are removed after being served. Overbrowning and turning-in of rims at a cake's edges indicate overgreasing. Black pans give more volume and bake more rapidly because they absorb more heat. Handle pans with care; do not bang them around or treat them in ways that cause them to lose their shape.

Protect thick cakes from outside heat on the sides and bottoms by using $\frac{1}{2}$-in.-thick wooden liners covered with $\frac{1}{4}$-in.-thick insulating material. Baking temperatures for these cakes are lower than those for thinner cakes. Well-controlled ovens may eliminate the need for protective mats.

Observe panning weights. Machine depositing is used in large bakeshops. For butter cakes, use 0.2 oz per square inch of pan. A round pan takes 75 percent of this weight. Thus, an 8-in. square pan takes $12\frac{3}{4}$ oz of batter ($8 \times 8 \times 0.2$) and an 8-in.-diameter round pan $9\frac{1}{2}$ oz ($8 \times 8 \times 0.2 \times 0.75$). Cakes with large surface areas should be panned thicker than cakes with smaller surface areas. Foam cake pans should be well-filled to build structure in baking. Standardized scaling weights ensure good portioning (see fig. 13-12 and table 13-3).

BAKING

Baking is critical to the quality of the finished product. A cake enters the oven as a viscous, aerated, semifluid batter and leaves it as a firm, tender, solid product. Batter movement occurs in baking; warm parts rise, while the cold batter sinks. Slip contributed by shortening and liquid is needed for such movement. Leavening makes the batter rise, and firming takes

(a)

(b)

(c)

(d)

Figure 13-12. Pound cake (a) and angel cake (b) being scaled. Professional bakers scoop and dump rapidly using this hand method. On the right-hand balance, an empty pan is set to tare the other. A 1-lb weight ensures that 1 lb of ingredients is added to the pan. (c) Thin batters are poured into containers by weight. (d) After being weighed once, the container can be filled to the mark and poured without weighing.

TABLE 13-3. Butter cake production scaling weights, by variety

	Variety cake			
Size cake	Yellow	Chocolate	White	Wedding
4-in. layer	4 oz	4 oz	4 oz	$7\frac{1}{4}$ oz
6-in. layer	$7\frac{1}{4}$ oz	8 oz	8 oz	12 oz
7-in. layer	10 oz	12 oz	12 oz	1 lb
8-in. layer	13 oz	1 lb	1 lb	1 lb 4 oz
9-in. layer	1 lb 1 oz	1 lb 4 oz	1 lb 4 oz	1 lb 8 oz
10-in. layer	1 lb 8 oz	1 lb 12 oz	1 lb 12 oz	2 lb
12-in. layer	2 lb 8 oz	2 lb 12 oz	2 lb 12 oz	3 lb
14-in. layer	3 lb 8 oz	3 lb 12 oz	3 lb 12 oz	4 lb
16-in. layer	4 lb 12 oz	5 lb	5 lb	5 lb
18 × 26-in. sheet	7 lb 8 oz	8 lb 8 oz	9 lb	

NOTE: Increase amounts by approximately 25 percent for square wedding cakes greater than 8-in. layer size. Scale an 18-in. square wedding cake to 8 lb.

place when the starch gelatinizes and the proteins coagulate. The result is a baked cake of stable volume.

A cake goes through four baking stages (see fig. 13-13). The first is a rapid rising of the quite fluid batter. Rising continues in the second stage, with the center higher than the sides; bubbles and a slight surface tan appear, and some batter firmness shows on the sides. In the third stage, rising is completed, the structure sets, and top browning increases and spreads over the surface; a slight aroma of baked cake is evident. In the fourth stage, browning is completed, the structure separates slightly from the pan, and a full aroma indicates that the cake is done. When done, most types of cake are firm to the touch, springing back and leaving no imprint, although some foam and rich butter cakes may lack this spring. If a toothpick or wire tester is inserted, it comes out clean.

Temperature is a critical factor (see fig. 13-14). Improved ovens and ingredients allow bakers to increase baking temperatures. Batters mixed by the blending method can be baked at higher temperatures than conventional cakes. Table 13-4 lists production scaling weights, baking tem-

(a)

(b)

(c)

(d)

Figure 13-13. Stages in cake baking. (a) The batter is quite fluid, and rapid rising occurs. (b) Rising continues, bubbles appear, and a slight surface tan forms. (c) The rising is complete, and the cake begins to set. (d) Baking is complete, color is deep, and a distinct aroma of baked cake and some separation from the sides of the pan are evident.

Figure 13-14. Cakes produced by oven temperatures that were (left to right) just right, too low, and too high.

TABLE 13-4. Production scaling weights, baking temperatures, and baking times for cakes

Type cake	Scaling weight	Baking temperature (°F)	Baking time (min)
LAYER			
Butter or Pound (1½ to 2 in. deep)			
6-in. diameter	6–8 oz	375	18
7-in. diameter	9–11 oz	375	20
8-in. diameter	12–14 oz	375	25
10-in. diameter	20 oz	360	35
12-in. diameter	1½–2 lb	360	
14-in. diameter	2¼–3 lb	360	
Foam cakes			
6-in. diameter	4–5 oz	375	20
8-in. diameter	9–10 oz	375	
10-in. diameter	16–18 oz	360	
12-in. diameter	1½–1¾ lb	360	
LOAF			
Pound, 3¼ × 3½ × 8 in.	1 lb	355	50
Pound, 3¼ × 6 × 11 in.	3 lb	325	100
Fruit, 3¼ × 3½ × 8 in.	1½ lb	315	90
Angel, 3¼ × 3½ × 8 in.	7–10 oz	365	
Angel, tube, small	8–10 oz		
Angel, tube, 10 in.	1½–2 lb	360	50
SHEET			
Butter, 1 × 18 × 26 in.	6–7 lb	360	35
Butter, 3 × 18 × 26 in.	8–10 lb	350	
Sponge, 1 × 18 × 26 in.	3 lb		
MISCELLANEOUS			
Ring, 6½-in. diameter	10–14 oz	375	
Oval loaf, 6¾ in.	8 oz	375	
Cupcakes, butter, per doz	14–16 oz	385	
Cupcakes, foam, per doz	7–8 oz	375	
Mary Ann shells, butter, per doz	1⅛–2¼ lb	385	

NOTE: Weights, times, and temperatures are average only; and must be adjusted for each cake. Butter cakes made by the blended method can be baked at slightly higher temperatures than can conventionally made cakes; temperatures given here are for blended type.

peratures and baking times for various types of cake. Small cakes are baked at higher temperatures than large ones, and thin ones are baked at higher temperatures than thick ones. Too high a temperature retards flavor and volume development. Crusts become dark, and the tops may split because inside areas are still rising after the outer area has set. Overbaking chocolate or cocoa cake impairs its flavor.

Setting cakes into preheated ovens improves their flavor. Even heat distribution is essential, and ovens must be level. Pans that touch in the oven reduce batter movement and hinder proper cake development. Do not place pans close to oven sides, where uneven heat occurs. Good thermostat control is needed, and oven heat should come mostly from the bottom—except in the case of jelly rolls and the like, where more top heat is needed to give a soft bottom for rolling.

Too hot an oven bakes the outside before the interior, and the resulting cake may be compact and tough, may have humps, and may show tunneling. Too cool an oven gives a crust that forms too late and cell walls that overexpand, producing a coarse, uneven grain and a pale, sticky crust. If the batter is underbaked or baked too slowly, the structure may not set sufficiently and the cake may collapse. A foam cake baked at too high a temperature becomes firm before complete expansion occurs, resulting in a heavy, tough texture, poor cell structure, low volume, and a hard crust. Baking at too low a temperature overexpands air cells, resulting in a coarse-grained cake and a pale, sticky crust. Fruit cakes and other heavy cakes may be steamed.

COOLING

Cool cakes for 15 minutes or longer, depending on their size and shape; then free the edges from the pan sides and dump the cakes onto racks. Turning a cake right-side-up is done by reversing the cake onto another rack. Removing the cake from the pan while warm dissipates bottom moisture and avoids sogginess. Handle gently. Cool sponge cakes for jelly rolls, and similar uses to about 110°F; then roll them into slightly moistened cloths to cool in this shape. When cool, unroll the sponge, spread with jelly, and reroll (see fig. 13-15).

Cooling too quickly causes excessive shrinkage. Some thin cakes can be cooled in their pans; while some moisture develops on the pan bottoms, sogginess does not occur. Butter cakes are usually loosened around the pan sides and then inverted. Allowing them to overcool before removal may cause sticking. Let loaf or pound cakes cool for 30 minutes; then free the edges, and invert the cake. Large wedding or pound cakes should be removed from their frames but not cut when warm. Invert foam cakes upon removal, resting the sides on supports to reduce pressure on the cake. Remove them when only slightly warm; the cooling they undergo prior to this point gives them structural firmness. Do not handle foam cakes while still quite warm. Loosen foam cakes from the sides and tube with a spatula or knife; then tilt and draw out gently. Figure 13-16 illustrates methods of removing sheet and layer cakes from their pans.

(a)   (b)

Figure 13-15.   (a) Roll a warm sponge cake into a slightly moistened cloth, and let it cool. (b) Unroll the cool sponge, and fill it.

STORAGE

Store cakes in a clean, cool place where they will not dry out. While staling is faster under refrigeration, cakes may be stored there anyway—especially in warm climates—to reduce mold. Mold often develops in places where cut surfaces are contaminated by a worker's fingers. Freezing cakes in moisture- and vapor-proof wraps holds their quality for a long time.

MAKEUP

Makeup is the final preparation for serving; included in makeup are shaping, filling, frosting, and decorating. Appearance and flavor are enhanced by these procedures.

Frostings and Icings

Icings are widely used to enhance appearance and flavor and to give moistness. Some cakes are served plain or are merely filled, but most are iced.

Frosting types include foams (meringue or marshmallow), butter creams, fondants (fudge), plain water icings, and glazes. Use high-quality ingredients, and keep colors and flavors moderate; too much of either detracts from, rather than enhancing, the product's quality. Fillings or frostings are spread liberally on cakes—but not so freely as to give an oversweetened, overmoist product. Fillings and frostings should complement the cake. Fondant frostings are more durable than others and may be used in localities where the humidity is high. Stabilizers purchased from a bakery supply outlet can assist in problems of stickiness, lack of stability, and failure to set up; agar, gelatin, gums, and cereals such as wheat, cornstarch, and tapioca flour are used. Using simple or corn syrup rather than water for moisture may lead to curdling or separation of these ingredients from some thin frostings.

Use $1\frac{1}{2}$ to $1\frac{3}{4}$ c (5 to 6 oz) of fluffy frosting for a two-tier 8-in. layer cake, and use 2 to 3 pt (10 to 15 oz) for an 18×26-in. cake; use $1\frac{1}{2}$ c (10 oz) and

(a)

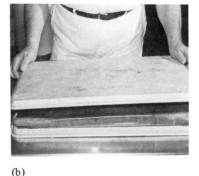

(b)

(c)

(d)

(e)

Figure 13-16. (a) To remove a sheet cake from the pan, first sprinkle the top lightly with granulated sugar. (b) Set an empty pan of the same size (bottom-down) on top of the cake; then invert and remove the top sheet pan. (c) Loosen the paper carefully on the farther side of the pan, and lift up. (d) Layer cakes can be dumped onto the hand and set on top of a pan. (e) Brush crumbs from the cake with a bench brush or with the hand.

about $1\frac{1}{4}$ qt (20 oz), respectively, of filling for cakes of these sizes (see table 13-5). To coat the sides of 8-, 9-, and 10-in. layer cakes with chopped nuts, coconut, or other coating, allow $1\frac{1}{2}$, $1\frac{3}{4}$, and $2\frac{1}{8}$ oz, respectively, of material (see table 13-6).

Fondant. Fondant is a mixture of water and sugar that is cooked to 240°F, cooled to 104°F, and mixed to form crystals. Cream of tartar or corn syrup is used to produce invert sugar. Plain fondant is a simple, creamy

TABLE 13-5. Variations obtained from plain butter cream icing

Variation	To 10 lb plain butter cream icing add:
Nut	Chopped nuts, 1 lb
Raisin	Ground raisins, 1 lb
Cherry	Candied cherries, 1 lb
Candied fruit	Candied fruit, 1 lb
Jam or Marmalade	Jam or marmalade, 1 lb
Almond*	Almond paste, 1 lb, and almond flavoring
Coconut	Macaroon coconut bits, 1 lb
Fondant	Plain fondant, 5 lb
Chocolate (Cocoa)	Cocoa, 10 oz, and water, 5 oz
Peppermint candy	Peppermint candy bits, 8 oz
Lady Baltimore	Chopped candied cherries, nuts, and raisins, mixed, 1 lb
Fresh fruit	Chopped drained fresh fruit, 4 oz

* Thin the almond paste first with a bit of egg white, so it goes into the butter cream without lumping.

white, smooth, crystalline mass that may be purchased in moist or dry form. Dry fondant mixes needing only water are on the market. A fudge icing is a rich fondant; the term *fudge* may be applied to chocolate, penuche, maple, and other creamy cooked fondants. Fondants can be used to make a butter cream, but powdered sugar works more satisfactorily. To thin fondants, use simple syrup. Do not heat fondants above 100°F.

Powdered Sugar Icings. Butter cream is a rich, smooth icing with a mellow flavor. Confectioners' sugar (6X to 10X), butter (or margarine or shortening), eggs, flavoring, and other ingredients are used. Eggs, usually whites, give lightness, moisture, and fluffiness. Thorough creaming

TABLE 13-6. Quantities of frosting to use per cake

Cake size	Type frosting	Filling weight	Weight to frost sides and tops
4-in. layer	Butter cream		2 oz
6-in. layer	Butter cream		5 oz
7-in. layer	Butter cream	3 oz	6½–8 oz
8-in. layer	Butter cream	4 oz	8–8½ oz
9-in. layer	Butter cream		11½ oz
10-in. layer	Butter cream		1 lb
12-in. layer	Butter cream		1 lb 7 oz
14-in. layer	Butter cream		2 lb
16-in. layer	Butter cream		2 lb 9 oz
18 × 26-in. sheet	Butter cream		3–4 lb (top only)
Cupcakes, per doz	Butter cream		5 oz (tops only)
7-in. layer	Boiled type	2 oz	4 oz
8-in. layer	Boiled type	2¼ oz	5 oz
7-in. layer	Fudge or fondant	3½ oz	9 oz
8-in. layer	Fudge or fondant	4½ oz	10 oz

NOTE: All layer cakes are two-layer.

increases lightness. The ratio of fat to sugar is usually $1:2$, and the ratio of eggs to sugar is usually $1:10$, but variations are possible. French butter cream is made by carefully folding $\frac{1}{4}$ lb softened butter or margarine into 2 qt boiled or marshmallow icing at about 70°F, with no stirring or beating. Simple or flat icings made from powdered sugar, called *plain water icings*, are composed of water or milk, flavoring, and confectioners' sugar. These ingredients are mixed to form a smooth, thick paste, which is warmed to 100°F and used to coat Danish pastry and sweet breakfast rolls. Plain water icings are also used as a plain fondant for coating cakes. They usually do not contain fat.

Boiled or Cooked Icings. Boiled icings are made by boiling sugar, water, and glucose or cream of tartar to a temperature of between 240° and 250°F. This mixture is poured over egg whites that have been beaten to a soft but firm peak (upper stage 2). As the hot syrup is added, the ingredients are beaten vigorously, and beating continues until a crystalline mass forms. Stiffness depends on the quantity of egg white to syrup, the temperature to which the syrup is cooked, and the frosting temperature. If confectioners' sugar and gelatin are added, a marshmallow frosting is made. Commercial meringue icings are often used.

Glazes. Glazes are heavy syrups of sugar and water that do not contain eggs but may contain gelatin. They are brushed onto items—or items are dipped into them—to give shine (see fig. 13-17). A glaze may be made from fruits such as apricot pulp or from waxy maize starch.

Decorator's or Royal Icings. Royal or decorator's icings are stiff icings used for ornamental work. They are made from egg whites, confectioners' sugar, cornstarch, flavorings, and cream of tartar or lemon juice; starch gives extra stiffness. Meringue powder with a bit of water may be used instead of egg whites. The icing can be used to make hard decorations by rolling it out thinly so that designs can be cut from it. The decorations are then colored or decorated. Some are made plastic for molding. After drying, the decorations are put on the cake, although sometimes they are made directly on cakes. Store them in tightly covered containers under refrigeration. If the icing is too stiff, thin it with simple syrup or a bit of egg white. A lighter decorator's icing is made with 1 T water to 1 lb confectioners sugar, beaten well. Decorate cakes with this icing directly, while still moist; air in the mass makes the icing fragile, so items will crumble if they are handled after drying.

Procedures

Before icing, remove the crust of the cake, if desired. Placing a damp cloth over the cake, allows the crust to be rolled away more easily. Trim ragged edges, and shape as required. Edges should be sharp. Do not attempt too intricate a design; broad outlines are easier to do. Brush away all crumbs before icing.

Have the icing at a proper consistency—not so thin as to be runny, nor so thick as to pull away. Select icings for stability, lack of bleeding or breakdown, absence of stickiness, and clear, glossy color. If the frosting

(a)

(b)

Figure 13-17. (a) Liquid form of a glaze made from waxy maize starch. (b) Fruit given gloss by this glaze.

is too stiff, warm it slightly or add a bit of simple syrup. Use paste colors. Blend any coloring with a small part of the icing first, and use this to produce the desired shade in the larger mass. Good color sense is required; so is a knowledge of how to obtain colors. Amateur bakers are identifiable by an excess of color in their icings, as well as by an excess of flavor. Moderation is a sign of craftsmanship.

For a layer cake, invert the first layer top-down on a turntable or decorator's wheel. Place the thickest layer on the bottom. If no wheel is available, invert the layer on wax paper. Spread the filling evenly on the first layer, and place the second layer on top of this. Deposit plenty of thin icing on the top center of the second layer, and work with a spatula to the sides, guiding the icing down the sides and spreading out the excess over the sides. Start on the sides with thick frosting, spreading with a spatula from the bottom upward and turning the cake while holding the spatula in a nearly vertical position to give a smooth side. Next spread the top, using a motion that spreads icing out toward the edges. Make a smooth surface by dipping the spatula into warm water, drying it and then smoothing out—or leave the surface irregular. An iced cake should convey a feeling of height, with sides even and top straight. Pile icing liberally on top to avoid a tight, peeled appearance. Allow iced cakes to dry before decorating them (see fig. 13-18a). For thin icings, place the cake on an open rack and frost as for petits fours (see fig. 13-18b).

Free small cakes of crumbs after making them into proper shapes. Pour a thin fondant or plain water icing over their tops as they sit on a wire rack over a sheet pan; direct the icing flow down the sides (see fig. 13-19). Remove the rack, and use a spatula to pick up the surplus icing for reuse. Repeat until all sides are covered.

A canvas, rubber, or plastic pastry bag is commonly used for decorating, but many bakers prefer to use cones made from parchment paper; such cones are simple to make, easily discarded, and flexible, so that each color can have its own cone (see fig. 13-20). Use heavy wax paper or brown wrapping paper if parchment paper is not available; regular wax paper is fragile, and wrapping paper soaks and splits easily. Many simple yet attractive designs can be made without adding special decorative icing or using a pastry bag (see fig. 13-21).

If only writing is to be done with the icing, do not cut the cone tip and do not use a metal tip; suit the tip to the desired writing size. Fill the bag or cone one-half to three-quarters full, placing the icing down toward the

(a)   (b)

Figure 13-18. (a) To ice a layer cake with heavy frosting, frost the sides first and then the top. Finish by holding the spatula perpendicular to the top, to give a smooth edge. (b) When the frosting is thin, pour the frosting onto the top and work it down the sides.

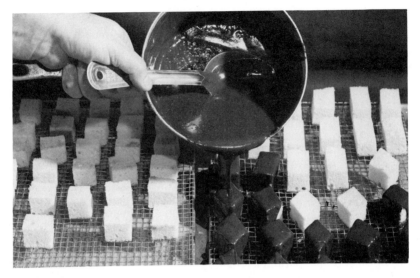

(a)

(b)

Figure 13-19.   To frost small cakes, such as petits fours, cut the cake into the desired shapes and then cover completely with fondant frosting. Finish with decoration.

(a)

(b)

(c)

(d)

Figure 13-20. (a) To make a paper cone, cut the paper into a rectangle and grasp it with two hands, rolling with the right hand. (b) Finish the cone, keeping the right hand inside to control the shape. (c) Cut about $\frac{1}{2}$ in. from the cone tip, and insert the metal tip. (d) After filling—using care to get the filling deep into the bag—fold the top with a double fold.

tip and away from the sides. Avoid capturing air, which may ruin a decoration by bursting out during work. Have the icing at the correct consistency. For writing and for other continuous-line work, icing should flow or string out (see fig. 13-22). If it is too thick, it will break as the tip is moved over the surface. A medium consistency is needed for border work, stiffer flowers, leaves, and other objects, to allow the petals and other forms to stand up. After filling the cone or bag, fold over the top, making a double (apothecary's) turn to prevent the icing from coming out the top. About ten tips are needed for usual decorating. Bakers must learn which tips are needed for which specific forms (see figs. 13-23, 13-24, and 13-25).

Apply icing at the correct pressure and angle. Right-handed decorators apply pressure with the right hand and use the left hand to guide and support the cone or to hold items while the right hand both directs the tip and applies pressure; icing seeping out the top indicates that left-hand

(a)

(b)

(c)

(d)

(e)

(f)

Figure 13-21. (a)–(e) Simple designs can be made without using a pastry bag. (f) This three-dimensional design is obtained by heavily dusting powdered sugar over a cake top that has been covered by a grid, and then removing the grid. (*Courtesy Standard Brands*)

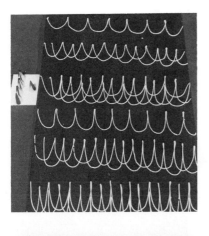

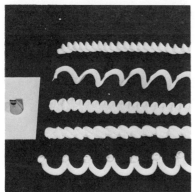

Figure 13-22. Some simple string designs. For this work, the frosting must be slightly thinner than that used for decorating objects. Many different borders can be made using one tube. Types of borders may also be combined.

Figure 13-23. To make plain drop flowers, use the star tube. Hold the bag so that the tube is perpendicular above the object to be decorated or over wax paper (where the flowers will be placed to dry). Force out the frosting, pushing down and breaking off abruptly with a pull up. A slight twist may be given to vary the shape slightly.

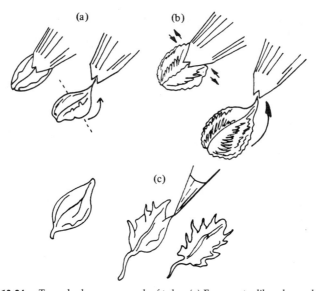

Figure 13-24. To make leaves, use a leaf tube. (a) Force out a liberal supply of frosting and, at approximately the leaf center, release pressure by lifting up to form the tip. (b) To obtain a jagged edge, follow the same procedure but move the tip rapidly back and forth while the other motions are being made as before. (c) Alternatively, leaves made as indicated in (a) can be given points by switching to a fine tip and using the same color.

pressure is being applied. Apply even pressure through the fingertips and thumb for fine work (see fig. 13-26a). Use the four fingers and palm for less delicate work (see fig. 13-26b). Relaxing pressure in moving the tip causes a break. Exerting heavy pressure causes a blob to come from the tip. Hold the cone vertically above the cake for drop flowers and similar items. Hold the tip at a 45° angle for writing and for making borders, leaves, flowers, stems, and other objects. Hold the bag at a right angle to the cake when decorating a side. To set preformed decorations into place, put a bit of fresh icing at the designated spot and set the decoration on top of it.

COOKIES

Cookie ingredients are much the same as cake ingredients. Some cookies come from what are virtually cake batters; most, however, are made from doughs that have a higher proportion of shortening and lower proportions of sugar and liquid. The conventional creaming method is often used. Foam cookies are made by methods similar to those used for foam cakes. Crisp cookies result from high ratios of fat and sugar to liquid. Soft cookies are produced when the liquid content is sizable or when hydroscopic sugar draws moisture into the dough. Chewy cookies are usually high in sugar and liquid and low in fat; eggs are responsible

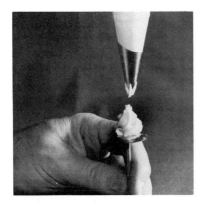

(a)

(b)

(c)

(d)

Figure 13-25. Making a rose. (a) Using a star tube, set a rosette on top of a decorator's nail. (b) Now with a petal tip, make petals around the rosette. (c) Continue until the rose is fully petaled. (d) Remove the rose with scissors and place it on wax paper to dry; then position it on the cake as desired.

for the chewiness. Soft cookies are usually baked a shorter time than crisp ones are. Thickness and size are other factors affecting crispness and softness. Many cookies are tight-grained, but some may be as open as cakes. Baking soda or ammonia is used to give spread. Ammonia is preferred, in the amount of $\frac{1}{4}$ to $\frac{1}{2}$% of the flour, because it gives better spread than soda; however, it should be used to leaven only thin and dry cookies, because ammonia flavor may be evident in thick, heavy, or moist products. Cookies with high sugar content spread more than those made from leaner dough. The coarser the sugar, the more the spread; thus, using powdered sugar reduces spread. Large bakeshops usually deposit cookies onto pans by machine.

(a)

(b)

Figure 13-26. (a) When light pressure is needed, force the frosting from the tip, using light pressure from the fingertips of the right hand. (b) When a large quantity of frosting is required, use the top hand, exerting pressure with the full hand. The bottom hand guides. Notice that the cone is held at a 45° angle to decorate the border.

PRODUCTION

A sugar or icebox cookie is usually in balance if the proportions are flour 100 percent, shortening 100 percent, sugar 50 percent, and eggs 10 percent, making a rich, sugary pastry dough. Most of these cookies are made by the conventional method. Alternatively, a one-stage or dump method may be used, in which all ingredients are combined at one time and mixed at slow speed for about 2 minutes at 70°F. Basic doughs may be altered to make many variations.

Some cookies are made with techniques and ingredients that resemble those used for foam cakes. For example, lady fingers are made from sponge cake batter; and many other cookies are only modifications of foam cake batter. In quantity work, macaroons are composed of almond paste, sugar, flour, and unbeaten egg whites, mixed at 85°F. Because of the batter's delicacy, only small batches of foam cookies are made. Meringue cookies are made from a hard meringue. Kisses, meringue bars, and macaroons can be made from egg whites beaten to a stage 2 foam. Underbeating yields a weak foam and leads to a tough, gummy cookie; overbeating extends air cells too much, so the product collapses in baking. Kisses are midway between soft and hard meringues in texture, taking less sugar than hard meringues. Flour and other ingredients are folded in carefully, in the same manner as for foam cakes. Baking temperatures are usually from 325° to 350°F. Adding glucose or invert sugar increases the product's chewiness. Adding glucose, invert sugar, or glycerine reduces the tendency of the sugar to crystallize. Weeping of egg foam is lessened by sifting $\frac{1}{2}$ oz cornstarch into each 1 lb egg whites. Foam cookies are glazed while they are still hot with a syrup–gelatin glaze called a *gelatin shine.*

Stiff doughs to be cut are wrapped in moisture-retarding wraps and chilled; they store well for several days. The time and labor involved make it expensive to roll and cut cookies. If it must be done, a canvas cloth should be used for an underliner, and the dough should be rolled about $\frac{1}{8}$-in. thick. Cut the cookies out as economically as possible, leaving only bits of unused dough; reworking toughens the cookie.

Semisoft batters are used for drop cookies. About 1 or $1\frac{1}{2}$ oz of batter is dropped, using a No. 30 or No. 20 ice cream scoop. In some operations, hand or pastry-bag depositing is done; macaroons, kisses, and meringues may be deposited in these ways. Deposit them approximately 2 in. apart. After depositing nonmeringue macaroons, allow them to stand for some time before baking. Holland or split macaroons are held refrigerated overnight and cut in the morning in the center so that the split appears. Kisses, meringues, and paste macaroons may be placed on greased paper, silicon-coated pans, greased and flour-dusted pans, or thin sheets of rice paper. Remove them while still warm, using a wet spatula or pancake turner. If they are cold, hold the baking sheet over heat for a moment. Rice paper can be broken away and left on the cookie bottom, since it is edible. Lady fingers may be deposited by making small sponge-batter fingers (about 3 in. long and $\frac{1}{2}$ in. wide) with a pastry tube. Allow at least 1 in. of space between these. Many foam-type or semisoft batters are machine-deposited. Batters or doughs containing nuts or chopped fruits, however, may not deposit well by machine, and some must be hand-dropped. Some semisoft or soft batters, such as nut squares and brownies, are spread evenly onto baking sheets about $\frac{1}{2}$ in. thick. After baking (and while still warm) they are cut into desired sizes. If the cookies are to be frosted, cutting may be done when they are cold.

Quite stiff doughs are made into rolls for icebox cookies. For large cookies, scale off 3 lb dough and make this into 2-in.-diameter rolls. Wrap the rolls in wax paper or plastic and refrigerate or partially freeze them. Each roll makes approximately fifty cookies. Small rolls—about 1$\frac{1}{2}$ lb and $\frac{3}{4}$ in. in diameter—produce tea-size cookies. A sharp knife or kitchen slicing machine may be used to cut the cookies about $\frac{1}{8}$ in. thick. Space the sliced dough on baking pans, about 1 in. apart. If the dough contains ammonia, slice it thicker, and space the slices a greater distance apart. Remove the cookies from the pan while hot.

Some stiff doughs are made into long rolls measuring about 1 to 1$\frac{1}{2}$ in. in diameter, and pieces weighing about 1 oz each are cut, using a pastry knife, and panned approximately 2 in. apart. Flatten these pieces into thin disks, and bake. Peanut butter cookies and others can be flattened with a fork; alternatively, a small can is put into a moistened cloth, the cloth-covered end is dipped into granulated sugar, and then it is pressed down to flatten the dough. The cloth must be redipped into sugar before another cookie is flattened. Fruit bars, hermits, and other thick doughs are made into 1$\frac{3}{4}$-lb rolls, which flatten into 3- to 4-in.-wide strips. Some of these doughs are glazed with a wash. After baking, each strip is cut into 1$\frac{3}{4}$-in. bars, yielding about twelve or thirteen bars per strip.

Use level, clean baking sheets. Some need no greasing; others may need liberal greasing and flour dusting. Make sure that pans are cool before cookies are placed on them for baking. Liberal greasing encourages spread, while dusting with flour reduces spread. When pans are too lightly greased, cookies with a high egg or sugar content may color excessively on the edges and may be difficult to remove. A small cookie is

TABLE 13-7. Scaling weights, baking temperatures, and baking times for cookies

Cookie type	Scaling weight	Baking temperature (°F)	Baking time (min)
Brownies	7$\frac{1}{2}$–8 lb	350–360	20–45
Butter, tea	$\frac{1}{3}$–$\frac{1}{2}$ oz	375	8–10
Drop, medium	$\frac{3}{4}$ oz*	350–400	8–15
Icebox, medium	1 oz	375	8–10
Rolled, small	$\frac{1}{2}$ oz	375	7–10
Rolled, large	1$\frac{1}{2}$ oz	375	9–12

* Use No. 40 scoop.

about the size of a 50¢ piece after baking; a medium one is the size of a silver dollar; and a large one is over 3 in. in diameter. Bar or fruit cookies are usually scaled at ¾ to 1 oz and sugar cookies at ½ oz or less. A normal yield is thirty-two to thirty-four cookies from each pound of dough. A dozen 3½-in.-diameter sugar cookies weigh between 11 and 12 oz before baking and about 10 oz after baking. Small cookies are scaled at three to four cookies per ounce, while meringue and other foam-type cookies are scaled at ½ to ¾ oz each, or 6 to 10 oz per dozen. Table 13-7 identifies scaling weights, baking temperatures, and baking times for various types of cookies.

BAKING

Cookies are usually baked at higher temperatures than cakes are. During baking, cookies must be watched carefully; too much baking overcolors them and ruins their flavor. Chocolate cookies burn easily. When cookies are done, they are of proper color and spring back slightly to the touch. Low oven temperatures result in tight-grained cookies that have poor color; high oven temperatures make the cookies too dark and restrict spread too much. Closing oven dampers in the first baking holds steam inside, encouraging spread. Crisp cookies may be soft while warm, but crisp upon cooling. After baking, protect such cookies from drafts and from too-rapid cooling. Many cookies should be removed from their pans while still warm.

STORING

Most cookie batters or doughs freeze well (except foam types). Stiff doughs are thawed under refrigeration, but softer mixes are thawed at room temperature. Frozen cookies thaw in opened packages in about 15 to 20 minutes. Do not pack cookies while they are still warm. Store cooled cookies in airtight containers or drawers. Include a piece of apple with soft cookies to keep them moist. Do not stack soft cookies. Foam-type cookies dry out easily; make them in batches that can be used quickly, and store them in airtight containers.

Chapter Review

1. What techniques are used in making a creamed (conventional) cake? a cake by the blended method? and a cake made by the muffin method?
2. If a butter cake recipe calls for 125 percent sugar by weight to 100 percent flour, is it out of balance?
3. What are the rules for adjusting cakes to differences in altitude?
4. Describe the steps in making an angel cake.
5. What are the four stages cakes go through in baking?
6. What kinds of frostings (icings) are most often used on cakes?
7. What is the correct procedure to use in frosting the top and sides of a cake?
8. What is a balanced recipe for sugar cookies? Give this in ingredient percentages.
9. What leavening agents are used to give cookies spread? Which one is best?

CHAPTER 14

Pies and Pastries

Outline

Goals

1. To identify the standards, principles, and techniques needed to make good pies and pastries.
2. To discuss the ratios of ingredients and the techniques needed to make different kinds of pie doughs.
3. To detail the making of puff paste.
4. To list the steps involved in rolling out pie dough and in baking single- and double-crust pies.
5. To indicate the kinds of preparation required to produce satisfactory pie fillings.

INTRODUCTION

Pies and pastries are popular, but they require an inordinate amount of labor unless the types and ingredients are wisely selected, a convenient layout is set up for production, and good techniques are used. Appropriate production standards should be established, such as hand-rolling eighty pie dough pieces in an hour. Assembly-line methods are desirable whenever possible. Three workers using precut dough disks, a prepared pumpkin filling, and a mechanical rolling machine produced 160 pumpkin pies ready for baking in 171 worker minutes. Pies may be single- or double-crust and may be filled with fruit, cream filling, egg custard, gelatin, and other sweetened and thickened mixtures. Ice cream, mousse, and other frozen desserts may be placed into baked pie shells. Many pastries, including tarts and dumplings, are closely related to pies.

STANDARDS

Regular pie crust is crisp and tender, with a short, easy break. It may be flaky, semiflaky, or mealy (see fig. 14-1). The surface is golden or cream-colored, darkening to a golden brown at the edge. The appearance typically is rough and blistery on the surface, although this varies with crust flakiness. The crust should cut easily without crumbling. Oiliness is tested by rubbing the crust between the fingers. The filling varies in consistency and type. A starch-thickened filling is delicate, smooth, and soft, sagging only slightly at the cut edge. Each piece of fruit should be clear and distinct. The filling's color should be clear and bright, and its texture should be neither gummy nor pasty. Flavor should be moderately sweet, pleasant, and characteristic of the product. Custard fillings should be sweet and mellow, not eggy. Figure 14-2 shows high standards for various types of pie.

PIE DOUGHS

Regular pie dough is made from flour, shortening, salt, and water. The flour and liquid form a paste, with shortening serving as a lubricant to separate the flour and give a tender product. Salt is added for flavor; since it strengthens gluten, its amount is carefully controlled and it is added with the water. Milk powder or liquid milk may be used to improve color and flavor, but the crust becomes less crisp as a result. If dry milk is to be used, add it with the flour. Adding glucose or corn syrup (2:100 to flour) to the water improves the dough's color and flavor. Some specialty pie or tart doughs are almost as rich as cookie dough. For example, eggs may be included to improve color, richness, and flavor; again, however, crispness is reduced and cost is raised. More fat must be used. Baking powder does not improve crust quality, but vinegar or

Figure 14-1. From left to right, flaky, semiflaky, and mealy pie crusts.

(a)

(b)

(c)

(d)

Figure 14-2. High standards for pies: (a) milk chocolate cream pie; (b) apple pie; (c) glazed fried pies; (d) prune tarts. The prune tarts are made from prefabricated tart shells that are simply filled.

cream of tartar reduces water hardness, increases gluten tenderness, and makes a whiter dough. Table 14-1 identifies the relative weight (in percentages) of pie dough ingredients. Pastry flour containing about 10 percent gluten is often used, providing good strength for a pliable dough that holds up well in rolling; it does not result in a tough dough unless handled improperly. Bread flour, which is used for puff paste doughs and flaky doughs, makes a paste that spreads out into thin sheets be-

TABLE 14-1. Percentages (by weight) of ingredients for different pie doughs

Ingredient	Mealy	Semiflaky	Flaky
Flour, pastry	100%	100%	100%
Shortening	50–60%	75%	100%
Salt	2–3%	2–3%	2–3%
Water	25–30%	30–35%	35–40%

tween layers of shortening. During baking, steam formed between these sheets in the pools of shortening lifts the sheets up developing flakiness.

Tenderness is an important quality factor. The amount of shortening, and the extent of mixing, and the method of blending in the shortening are key factors affecting tenderness. Flours with a low gluten content or with weak gluten need less shortening and can be mixed more. A strong bread flour needs a ratio of shortening as high as 80 to 100 percent (by weight) to 100 percent flour. Hard wheat flour mixes less easily into shortening. Bread flour yields a chewy crust, which may be desirable. Adding soy flour gives a shorter and mealier crust; it is also creamier in color. Graham cracker crusts have proportions of 100 percent graham cracker crumbs to 30 percent sugar to 55 percent butter or margarine. Cinnamon, almond flour, powdered sugar, and other ingredients may be added. Crumbled or ground ginger snaps, vanilla wafers, chocolate wafers, nuts, and other dried fine items may also be used. About 2 oz of the crumb mixture spread evenly and packed on the bottom and sides of a pan produces sufficient crust for a 9-in. pie. Another pan is then firmly pressed onto the crumbs, and the crust is baked 10 minutes in a 350°F oven or is left in a refrigerator overnight. Some crumb mixtures may also be sprinkled over meringues or whipped cream toppings.

For proper tenderness, a fat with good shortening power is needed. Plasticity should be good at 50° to 70°F. Soft or emulsified shortenings do not develop flaky doughs because they work too easily into the flour. Lard works well: it gives good tenderness and flavor and has the correct plasticity. Butter or margarine is sometimes used for flavoring, but the amount of shortening must then be increased—unless the curd and moisture are first removed by kneading and washing. Edible oils can be used, but the resulting dough is oily and hard to handle. This is because oils permeate the flour, making it difficult for the dough to produce a flaky crust. Hot-water pie crusts can be made, using oil or shortening with ingredient proportions identical to those for a regular pie crust.

Only the amount of water needed to yield a soft, pliable dough is used. Besides making the dough workable, water is converted into steam inside the dough layers, causing flaking. If the crust is too dry, the steam generated is insufficient, and a less flaky crust results. Excess water encourages toughness—possibly because it allows more complete hydration of the gluten. A sticky dough is difficult to roll and handle. As shortening increases, water is increased.

PRODUCTION METHODS

Precise scaling, good ingredients, and skillful techniques are required to produce good pies. A horizontal-cylinder slow-speed mixer may be used for large quantities of dough. Most bakers, however, use a vertical mixer at low speed, employing a pie crust blade to cut the shortening into the flour and a flat paddle to blend these with the water; others use only the flat paddle for both operations. Some prefer to hand-mix small quantities because they can work the shortening in better and can feel the dough development more surely. Good rollers, pastry boards (or canvas tops), cutters, and other equipment are essential. Mechanical rollers reduce the amounts of time and labor required. A cool dough rolls and handles better than a warm one. Puff paste and other doughs may be purchased commercially. Some may be panned for single-crust pies.

MIXING

The short and flaky qualities of a pie crust depend not only on the ingredients used, their quantity, and their quality, but also on the mixing method that is followed. Blending the shortening well into the flour gives a mealy crust. Restricting the amount of mixing, in order to leave fat in large pieces, gives a flaky or semiflaky crust. The crust flakiness comes from rolling and rerolling sheets of dough and shortening to make many finely separated layers of fat and dough.

The amount and vigor of mixing are critical to quality—especially after water is added, giving gluten the moisture it needs for development. Excessive speed or longevity of mixing favors gluten development, as does warmth; consequently, doughs should be kept cold. At 60°F, shortening blends well into flour while still retaining the firmness necessary to give large particles. Mixing friction and water absorption by flour develop heat. Water at a temperature of around 40°F or colder should be used. Hard, cold fat toughens crust; if too soft, however, flakiness is retarded. Overdevelopment of gluten gives a tough dough that shrinks. A 15-minute rest after mixing decreases baking shrinkage and makes a dough easier to roll. Some bakers refrigerate their pie dough for 12 to 24 hours, but others say that the resulting improvement in quality is small.

An upright mixer running at slow speed and using the pastry knife attachment blends flour and shortening in about 15 to 90 seconds—the time depending on the particle size desired. Mixing for about 40 seconds at slow speed using the standard paddle suffices to blend in the water. Add all the water, with the salt already dissolved in it, at one time, and spread it well over the blended shortening and flour. Mix only until the water is blended and the dough just leaves the bowl sides. In hand-mixing, water may be sprinkled over the flour–shortening mixture.

A short, tender (mealy) crust is made by blending the shortening into the flour until the mixture looks like coarse cornmeal. Alternatively, half the shortening may be blended well with the flour, and the remainder then added and mixed only until the shortening is no longer sticky. A ratio of 50 to 60 percent shortening to 100 percent flour is used. Mealy crusts are short and quite tender, and they soak less than do flaky ones. A mealy crust bakes with low shrinkage and colors well; it is used for the undercrust of double-crust pies and for the crusts of custard pies and others where soaking is a problem. A batter method can be followed in making a mealy crust. Mixing is the same as for regular crust, but 20 percent of the flour is withheld to be mixed later with the water and blended in this way. Another approach is to cream about 50 percent of the flour with the shortening until a smooth paste is formed, and then to blend in the rest of the flour. After this, water (with the salt) is added. The same ratios of ingredients can be used for a hot-water pie crust as for a normal mealy crust. Boiling water is added to the shortening and beaten until the mixture is smooth and fluffy. The salt and flour are mixed only until all wet spots have disappeared. In all of these crusts, overmixing toughens the crust ultimately produced.

Semiflaky dough has good tenderness and crispness and is considered the most adaptable dough for all purposes. It colors well in baking. For a semiflaky crust, proportions of 60 to 75 percent shortening to 100 percent flour is required. Good shortening plasticity is needed to enable the shortening to flatten out between sheets of dough paste. The shortening is cut into the flour until the mixture forms granules the size of large peas. Alternatively, one-third to one-half of the shortening can be well-blended into the flour, after which the remainder is cut in until the mixture forms units about the size of hazelnuts.

A flaky crust resembles puff paste in texture and, to some extent, in appearance. It makes excellent baked single crusts, but it soaks quickly after filling. Many bakers add fillings to flaky crusts just before service. Such crusts are good for top crusts of fruit pies, for tarts, for small pastry shells, and for top crusts of deep-dish pies, meat pies and poultry pies. Since it soaks easily, it is not used for undercrusts. Semiflaky or flaky dough trimmings may be rerolled with mealy dough and used for bottom crusts; reworking reduces flakiness.

STORAGE

Pie doughs can be stored for about a week under refrigeration. Some bakers shape batches of about 6 lb dough into 3-in.-diameter cylinders, from 15 to 18 in. long. These are put into moisture- and vapor-proof wraps or slightly moistened cloths. After they are chilled, a dough cutter is used to cut 1-in.-thick round pieces from them—5 to 6 oz each. These discs are then rolled out. Pie dough mix may also be refrigerated dry and kept until needed; storage in this case should be ten days or less, since rancidity develops quickly in such a mix.

MAKEUP

Regular pie crusts are usually rolled out to a thickness of about $\frac{1}{8}$ in., although some may be thicker. Bottoms should weigh about 6 oz and tops about 5 oz for 9-in. pies; crust thickness governs this amount. Experienced bakers may require less dough, since they waste little dough in rolling. For machine-rolling, pieces for top and bottom are 8 oz.

To hand-roll, use a pin or roller that is approximately $1\frac{1}{2}$ in. in diameter, 18 in. long, and slightly tapered at either end. Work on a smooth surface or board that has only a little dusting flour on it. Dough is toughened by the addition of too much dusting flour. Keep the rolling pin and the top of the dough only lightly dusted with flour. Rolling on a canvas requires

(a) (b)

Figure 14-3. (a) Roll crusts with a deft, light stroke, working the dough to all sides so that a good round about ⅛ in. thick is obtained. (b) Trim excess dough by rotating and cutting with the palms of the hands at the same time.

less dusting flour. Using quick, deft strokes, starting from the center, roll the dough into an oval shape; then turn the dough, and make the circle (see fig. 14-3a). Lift and turn the dough as frequently as necessary. The dough should be cold but not too stiff for rolling. When it reaches the desired shape, fold it once in the center, and place it into the pan without stretching. It can then be unfolded easily and shaped to fit the pan. Some bakers pick the dough up deftly with the rolling pin, lift it into the pan, and unfold it with the pin. Docking (making holes in the crust) is used for single crusts to prevent blistering in baking. Docking is not needed if crusts are double-panned (baked between two pans). Some bakers like to bake double-panned crusts upside down, to reduce shrinkage.

Time is saved if excess dough from the bottom and top crusts is removed at the same time; remove excess by means of a quick, deft turning motion between the hands (see fig. 14-3b). Edges can be made attractive by pinching the dough lightly with the thumb and index finger, pressing in with the index finger of the other hand. Using a pie crimper, a roller-docker, a pastry cutter, a bench brush, and a scrape facilitates work. The bottom and top crusts of double pies should be carefully sealed around the edges to lessen boil-out in the oven. If a hole is made in the top center of the crust and temperature is controlled, boil-out is not a problem. Moistening the edge of the bottom crust before putting the top on assists in giving a tighter seal. Washing the top with milk, cream, evaporated milk, a mixture of milk and eggs, butter, or margarine results in extra crust color. The type of wash governs the finished appearance of the crust. Usually, well-made crusts need no wash. Butter and margarine are best for giving products a home-made appearance.

PUFF PASTE PRODUCTION

Puff paste products are attractive because of their puffy, light quality. The French call puff paste *pâté de feuilletée*—"paste of many leaves."

Good puff pastes can be purchased that need only rolling and shaping. If they are to be made from scratch, use butter or a special puff paste shortening. Wash slightly softened butter in cold water to remove curd; then knead until plastic and waxy.

Puff pastes are made from bread flour. With the proportion of flour 100 percent, use 100 percent shortening, 1 percent salt and 35 to 50 percent water; 3 to 12 percent eggs and 0.75 percent cream of tartar may also be added. Sift the cream of tartar in with the flour to tenderize gluten and give a whiter dough. Eggs contribute color, strength, and nutritional value. Mix the flour, salt, and water until the mass forms a smooth, soft, pliable dough. This gives sufficient gluten strength to produce a tenuous sheeting dough that is neither stringy nor ropy. Water and flour may be mixed at 60°F for approximately 2 minutes, using a flat paddle at slow speed. Some bakers add 15 to 20 percent of the shortening at this mixing. After mixing, allow the paste to rest for about 10 to 15 minutes; then roll it into a ½-in. thick rectangle that is twice as long as it is wide. Always brush away excess flour. Next spot the shortening evenly over two-thirds of the rectangle, leaving a ½-in. margin at the edges, and fold the unspotted third of the rectangle over half of the spotted portion. Fold the remaining third of the rectangle over this folded portion to produce a three-fold dough. A four-fold dough is sometimes made; to do this, first mark the dough into fourths, dot shortening on the two inside fourths, and fold. Each outside fourth is folded over one of these. Brush the new tops free of flour, dot one of them with shortening and make another fold. This forms a mass with three layers of shortening and four of dough. Punch one finger into the dough to indicate the first turn. Allow the dough to rest for 20 to 25 minutes under refrigeration. Then give it a half turn so that the former length is now the width—thus crisscrossing the folds of each turn. Roll the dough into a rectangle of the same size as before, using smooth, even rolling to distribute layers of paste and shortening evenly without rupturing paste walls because of shortening slippage. Give the dough three or four folds, put two fingers into the dough to indicate the second turn, and refrigerate for 20 to 25 minutes. Remove the dough and turn it so that the former length is now the width. Roll, fold, and mark with three fingers to indicate the third turn. This folding and rolling produces thinner and thinner layers of paste and shortening. The maximum number of turns for a three-fold dough is six, and the maximum number for a four-fold dough is four. Excessive folding and rolling toughen the dough and give too thin a sheet of paste to yield good flaking. Puff paste trimmings are usually pressed together, rolled out, given a three-fold, and reused; however, the quality is not as good. Figure 14-4 illustrates various steps in the production of three- and four-fold puff paste dough.

Puff paste can also be made with hard wheat flour at 100 percent, puff paste shortening at 100 percent, water at 35 percent, salt at 1 percent, and cream of tartar at 0.75 percent. From 70 to 75 percent of the flour is mixed with 25 percent of the shortening and all of the water, salt, and cream of

(a)

(b)

(c)

(d)

(e)

(f)

Figure 14-4. Making puff paste. (a) The dough paste is rolled out until it is about three times longer than it is wide; it should be about $\frac{1}{2}$ in. thick, and two-thirds of the surface should be covered with a $\frac{1}{2}$-in.-thick layer of puff paste shortening. (b) The uncovered third is folded over. (c) It is then folded again to seal the shortening between layers of dough. This is called a *three-fold*. (d) The corresponding technique for making a four-fold. (e) The dough here has been given a four-fold. (f) After resting for 15 to 20 minutes, the dough is given a turn and rolled out to its original shape. Notice that, when a turn is made, the dough is parallel—not perpendicular—to the worker.

tartar. The mixture is rested for 30 minutes under refrigeration; then the remaining flour and 75 percent of the fat are mixed together thoroughly and rested for 20 minutes under refrigeration. Now, instead of being arranged with the paste outside and the shortening inside, the shortening–flour mixture is put outside and the paste is put inside, with the shortening–flour mixture folded over the paste. The dough is then given a three-fold, and from that point the procedure for regular puff paste is followed.

PASTRY MAKEUP

Pie doughs or puff pastes may be used to make pastries such as small pies, tarts, tartlets, turnovers, and dumplings (see fig. 14-5). To hold the

(a)

(b)

(c)

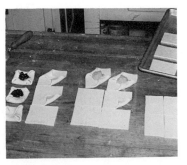

(d)

Figure 14-5. Some techniques for making items from puff paste. (a) Cream horns are made from strips of dough $\frac{1}{8}$ in. thick, $1\frac{1}{4}$ in. wide, and about 15 in. long. Roll the completed horn in sugar, and bake after a 30-minute rest. (b) Cut rounds with a plain cutter from dough $\frac{1}{16}$ in. thick. Cut $\frac{3}{8}$-in.-thick dough with the same cutter, and cut out the centers with a smaller cutter. Use the pastry brush to wash first rounds with a bit of water around the edges, and then place the rings upside down on top of the disks. (c) Cut $\frac{1}{8}$-in.-thick dough about 5 × 5 in. square, and wash the water. Using a pastry wheel or scraper, cut into the center as shown, leaving about 1 in. in the center uncut. Press every other corner into the center, and fill with washed or glazed fruit. (d) Many variations in shapes are possible. (*Courtesy Swift & Company*)

dough in place, dry beans or rice may be used to fill the inside of the shell. Docking and double panning are not needed when this is done. The beans or rice are then removed and stored in jars for reuse. Baked pastry dumplings and turnovers may be filled with meat, fruit, or other items. For these, the dough is usually rolled to a $\frac{1}{8}$-in. thickness; a No. 12 scoop of filling is then put in the center, and the dough is folded over. A leaner dough is needed for deep-fried items such as fried pies. If tartlet tins are not available, muffin pans may be used. In such cases, rounds of dough are cut to the proper size to fit over the outside of each cup; then they are docked and baked over the cup. Frequently a rich pastry dough resembling cookie dough is used for tartlets. For large tarts, pastry rings or tin hoops are placed on greased baking sheets and lined with dough. The tarts are then pinched to give a border at the edge, docked, and baked. Small tart shells are purchased already baked.

BAKING

Single-crust pies and small pastry shells are baked at temperatures of from 425° to 450°F for about 15 minutes; double-crust pies and filled pastries are baked at 425°F for 10 minutes, before dropping to 350° or 375°F for the remainder of the baking time. Too low a temperature toughens the crust, while too much heat causes overbrowning and a poorly cooked filling (see fig. 14-6). Baking time is reduced if double-crust pies are filled with hot filling. Brushing bottom crusts with eggs or flour does not reduce their tendency to soak.

PIE FILLINGS

The filling for a pie should be made with the same care as the crust, since both are essential to the quality of the finished pie. Single-crust pies and tarts are filled with many items, including blancmanges, cream puddings, bavarians, layers of cream pudding over which thickened layers of fruit filling are poured, marzipan, gelatin chiffons, and frozen fillings. Toppings of meringue, whipped cream, toasted coconut, crumbs, and

Figure 14-6. Crusts baked in (left to right) too slow an oven, an oven whose temperature was just right, and too hot an oven.

nuts may be added after baking. Unbaked single crusts may be filled with custards, chiffons, soufflés, or other uncooked fillings, and then baked. Double-crust pies usually have fruit fillings. Latticed tops are sometimes used for such pies. Alternatively, a streusel topping, called *French* or *Dutch* and made of flour, shortening, and spices, may be used to top pies.

About $1\frac{1}{2}$ pt to 1 qt (or $1\frac{1}{4}$ to 2 lb) of filling is needed per 9-in. pie. When pies are topped with meringues or whipped cream, the smaller quantity is used. Many fillings used for single-crust pies are similar to the desserts discussed in chapters 7 and 15.

The quality of fruit fillings is affected by the type of fruit, the thickening agent, the proportions of thickening agents and sweetening agents, and the method of preparation. Low-quality fruits should be avoided; the fruit may be broken, however, since appearance is not critical between crusts. Fresh fruit should be kept under refrigeration. Before it is used, the fruit should be picked over, and moldy or overripe pieces should be discarded; then the fruit should be washed and drained. Sugar, thickeners, and other ingredients are added next, and the fruit mixture is allowed to stand for 1 hour or so. Canned fruits should be opened just before use; standing for too long causes a decline in quality. Frozen fruits should be drained, and the juice should be thickened by itself and then reblended with the fruits. Instant or cold-setting starches can be used to avoid cooking the juice and to give a fresher flavor. It is often best to allow thickened fillings to stand for 1 to 2 hours before using them. Carry-over pie fillings should not be held for long periods; store them under refrigeration. Stored fillings are sometimes blended with fresh ones and used immediately. Canned prepared fillings are available, some of which are of good quality and contain a high enough ratio of fruit to paste (2:1 to 3:1) to make a presentable pie. The appropriate quantity of fruit to liquid depends on the type of fruit being used.

Cornstarch and flour are common thickeners. The best thickener for fruit pie fillings is a waxy maize starch, which gives clarity and brilliance to the fruit and forms a soft paste when cold. Waxy maize and converted starches are especially made to be used in such fillings; however, they should not be used for cream pie fillings (see fig.14-7). They set up with the same consistency when hot as when cold, have good tolerance, and give a more precisely thickened product than do other starches (see table 14-2).

TABLE 14-2. Variation in thickener quantities required for fruit fillings

Thickener	Quantity
Waxy maize or converted starch	$10-10\frac{1}{2}$ oz (8% solution)
Cornstarch, arrowroot, tapioca	$13-15\frac{1}{2}$ oz (10 to 12% solution)
Flour	20–30 oz (16 to 20% solution)

NOTE: Quantities listed are average amounts per gallon of liquid for fruit fillings.

Figure 14-7. Waxy maize starch runs from the cream pie filling at left, while the cornstarch-thickened filling at right remains stable.

Some bakers add gums such as carboxymethylcellulose (CMC), gum tragacanth, locust bean gum, or low-methyoxyl pectin to thicken certain fillings and to provide high clarity and brilliance to fruit and juice. Bakery supply firms are helpful in suggesting new products to improve fillings.

Usually the thickener is mixed with sugar and blended into hot liquid. Thickeners may also be blended with some liquid and added as a slurry. Cooking should continue until thickening is complete. The proper temperature for this is 203°F or higher for cornstarch and flour and 195°F for waxy maize. Rapid cooking and cooling are desirable to prevent acids from breaking down the starch.

If the quantity of sugar to fruit is high, withhold some of the sugar and add it to the mixture after thickening, thus preventing the excess sugar from retarding starch gelatinization. If 7 lb sugar is mixed with 1¼ gal water and 1 lb corn starch, swelling of the starch is prevented, and a dull, thin, watery, weak-flavored filling results. Including about 3 to 4 lb sugar with the water and starch is recommended, with the remainder to be added after thickening.

To make a lemon cream pie filling, blend the cornstarch, grated lemon peel, sugar, and salt together. Pour this mixture into the water and thicken, giving good agitation. When thickening is complete, stir a small amount of the hot mixture into lightly beaten egg yolks (stage 1). Next blend the yolk mixture into the hot thickened mixture, using good agitation; cook for 3 to 5 minutes, stirring constantly. Add the lemon juice and butter to the hot mixture immediately after removing it from the heat. Cool the filling quickly.

Custard pies are usually made with 2½ lb whole eggs to 1 gal milk or liquid. If yolks are used, the quantity of eggs may be reduced, in which case a finer custard results. Egg proportions should be higher for pies than for dessert custards, to ensure a firmer custard and to keep the crust drier. The techniques for mixing and baking are much the same as those for dessert custards.

Chiffon pie fillings closely resemble dessert soufflés, except that some are made from beaten egg whites in a starch- or gelatin-thickened mixture. These fillings are not baked; instead they are poured into baked pie shells and allowed to set. Gelatin desserts can be used to make chiffon pie fillings. These are actually snows, sponges, bavarians, or whips and are discussed in chapter 15. They may be combined with fruits and used in pie fillings. (Enzymes in raw pineapple, papaya, mango, figs, and some other fruits destroy gelatin, so these fruits must be cooked first). A parfait pie filling is a gelatin mixture into which soft ice cream and fresh or frozen drained fruits are folded just before the gelatin sets.

FINAL MAKEUP AND SERVICE

In many operations, single-crust cream pies are not filled until needed, to avoid crust soaking. The filling is cold and of a consistency to hold its shape when cut. Meringues and other toppings may be added shortly before service. Use pie markers for cutting, and do not cut too far ahead of service. Some fruit pies are best if slightly warm at service.

CHAPTER REVIEW

1. How do the proportions of ingredients and the techniques differ in the making of flaky, semiflaky, and mealy pie crusts? For what purpose is each type of crust the best suited?
2. Describe how a pie crust is made using an upright mixer. What blades or paddles are used?
3. What are the ingredient proportions for a puff paste? How is the shortening added? What is a *turn*? What is *three-fold dough*? What is *docking*?
4. How can inserting a thin layer of shortening between two layers of dough produce a flaky crust?
5. What is the proper technique for rolling out a pie dough to prevent shrinkage?
6. Why is a waxy maize or converted starch the best thickener for fruit pies?
7. Why is cornstarch or arrowroot used as the thickening agent for cream pies?
8. How should eggs be worked into a cream pie filling when cooking the filling?

CHAPTER 15

Desserts

Outline

Goals

1. To identify the standards, principles, and techniques needed to produce good desserts.
2. To discuss the use of fruits in various kinds of desserts.
3. To explain how egg-thickened desserts are made.
4. To cover the preparation and handling of junket and gelatin desserts.
5. To describe the kinds of frozen desserts and their ingredients, as well as the attendant equipment, sanitary procedures, quality standards, makeup, and service of these desserts.
6. To explain how crêpes (pancakes), fritters, and doughnuts are made.

414

INTRODUCTION

A dessert is a food (usually sweet) such as cake, pastry, pie, pudding, or fruit that completes a meal. Desserts should blend with and complement the meal they end, giving a sense of pleasant fullness and "topping off" the meal. They should be selected carefully for flavor, richness, color, variety, texture, form, appearance, and quantity. Plan desserts to balance the meal: if the meal needs buildup, serve a heavy dessert; and if the meal is fairly heavy, serve a light one. People are interested in nutrition more than in calories, but people dining out sometimes want a rich dessert because they are "off their diet." Desserts provide an opportunity to add decoration and color. Paying attention to desserts improves overall food acceptance and increases check averages. Offering desserts of distinction and excellence can do much to distinguish a food service from its competition.

For a time, desserts were omitted from many diners' meals (and still are for some), but desserts are making a comeback and patrons once again are receptive to them. In any case, it is still wise to plan light but good desserts. Some operations simplify dessert offerings to ice cream and sherbets, while others broaden the list but keep production simple by using mixes that are easy to transform into fairly acceptable desserts. Frozen desserts are also available.

STANDARDS

Dessert standards vary depending on type. In general, they should not be cloyingly sweet or bitingly tart. Good form and attractive shape are essential. Texture can vary—soft for some puddings, crisp for meringues, and in between for frozen desserts. Untrue, insipid or overabundant flavor, pasty texture, and excessive color are undesirable. Hot desserts should be hot, and cold ones cold. Form and shape should suit the particular dessert (see fig. 15-1).

FRUIT DESSERTS

PLAIN FRUIT

One of the simplest and finest desserts is fruit; it should be tart, sweet, and flavorful and (usually) served cold. Berries may be served plain, dipped in powdered sugar, or with cream and sugar. At times, a slightly sweetened crushed fruit is served over custard, pudding, or cake. Fresh berries may be cleaned by washing 1 or 2 qt of them at once under cold running water in a colander then examining and sorting. About 3 oz ($\frac{1}{2}$ c) is a portion. Fresh fruit such as apples, apricots, bananas, cherries, or peaches may be served whole, in halves, or in pieces. Many are served plain, but others may be served with cream and sugar.

Grapefruit and oranges may be halved, the seeds removed, and the sections loosened for service, or they may be peeled and thinly sliced.

Figure 15-1. High quality is indicated in this French apple dessert. (*Courtesy Processed Apple Institute*)

Grapefruit is excellent lightly broiled and served with a tablespoon of grenadine or crème de menthe. Oranges and grapefruit peel best when dropped into quite hot water for 3 to 5 minutes. The bitter white pith should be completely removed.

Fruits that tarnish can be dipped into a solution containing ascorbic acid, lemon juice, pineapple juice, or a commercial antioxidant (*not* sodium sulfite). Salt is not very effective as an antitarnishing agent. Sugar added to some fruits retards discoloration. Using stainless steel, glass, or silver knives avoids discoloration of fruit from iron salts.

Frozen fruit is best served while there is still some ice in it to give a better texture. About 3 to 4 oz ($\frac{1}{2}$ c) makes a portion. A 5-lb carton at 0°F takes 2 to 3 hours to thaw at room temperature and 4 to 5 hours to thaw under refrigeration. For best quality, use soon after thawing. Frozen fruit is often sweetened; the ratio of berries to sugar, for example, is typically 4:1.

Fruit cooked in light or medium syrup is called *stewed fruit* or *sauce*. If cooked in heavy syrup, it is called *compote*; and if cooked in extremely heavy syrup, it is called *preserves*. Table 15-1 gives proportions for making light, medium, and heavy syrups. About 15 lb EP fruit cooked in $1\frac{1}{2}$ gal light or medium syrup yields 100 $\frac{1}{2}$-c portions; 4 No. 10 cans of fruit usually serve 100 but the count of fruit per can is often a controlling factor. A 22-count (per No. 10 can) peach is a large serving; a 35- to 45-count peach is a medium serving.

TABLE 15-1. Densities of syrups for cooking fruit

Type of syrup	To make 1 gal of syrup, add:				Brix reading
	Sugar		Water		
	(lb)	(qt)	(lb)	(qt)	(degrees)
Light	3	$1\frac{3}{4}$	$7\frac{1}{2}$	$3\frac{3}{4}$	11–13.9
Medium	4–5	$2\frac{1}{2}$–$2\frac{3}{4}$	7–$7\frac{1}{4}$	$3\frac{1}{2}$	14–19.9
Heavy	7–8	4–$4\frac{1}{2}$	$6\frac{1}{2}$–7	3	20–23.9

To prepare dried fruits for use in compotes or for other purposes, first wash the dried fruits in cold water, drain them, and then cover them with boiling water. Some, after soaking for 24 hours, are ready to use without cooking. Cook by slowly simmering. Rapid cooking results in tough fruit that lack plumpness. About 100 $\frac{1}{2}$-c portions are obtained from 10 lb dried apricots or figs or 12 lb dried peaches, pears, or prunes. Some helpful conversions in calculating yields are as follows: 1 lb dried prunes yields 10 oz (2 c) pitted prunes; $1\frac{1}{2}$ lb (4 c) cooked prunes yields 1 lb (3 c) pitted prunes and $1\frac{1}{4}$ lb pitted prunes equals 1 qt pitted prunes. Table 15-2 provides other low-moisture fruit equivalents.

Low-moisture or vacuum dried fruits contain about 5 percent or less moisture. They occupy little storage space, give good-quality products, are low in cost, and do not require refrigerated storage to prevent insect infestation in warm climates. They are usually either soaked and then cooked slowly or started in cold water, brought to a simmer, and cooked until plump and tender. Sugar may be added at the start or after cooking, depending on the fruit and on the firmness desired (see fig. 15-2). The yield of 1 lb of low-moisture prunes, for example, is about $2\frac{1}{4}$ lb, giving about twelve portions.

Crisps and Betties

Crisps and betties are best served warm, with a light sweet-tart fruit sauce, whipped cream, or hard sauce. Carry-over fruits or small quanti-

TABLE 15-2. Low-moisture fruit equivalents

Item	Equivalent per pound of low-moisture fruit			
	Fresh AP (lb)	Canned regular pack no. 10 can	Canned solid pack no. 10 can	Evaporated or dried (lb)
Apple nuggets (sauce)	10	3	$1\frac{1}{4}$	3
Apple nuggets (sauce)	10	3		3
Apple pie slices	10	3	$1\frac{1}{4}$	
Apricot slices			1	3
Peach slices			1	$2\frac{1}{2}$
Pitted prunes				$2\frac{1}{2}$

Figure 15-2. The apple slices above were cooked gently in heavy syrup, while the mass below was produced when the same number of slices from the same apple were boiled in plain water. This shows how sugar firms up cellulose in fruits and vegetables.

ties of odds and ends of fruit can be used in these dishes. Crisps are composed of fruit, topped with a mixture of flour, sugar, and fat. The ingredients are assembled and baked; oatmeal may replace flour. The top is crisp, with soft fruit underneath. Betties are layers of cake crumbs between layers of fruit, butter, and sugar, baked so that the interior and bottom consist of soft fruit and crumbs while the top is crisp.

Biscuit-and-Fruit Desserts

Shortcakes are popular biscuit-based fruit desserts made from a rich baking-powder biscuit dough that may contain eggs. The dough is baked in two layers, with butter or margarine in between. Serve shortcakes warm with chilled crushed fruit between layers and over the top; crown with whipped or unwhipped cream. A Dutch cake is composed of rich biscuit dough in which a heavy layer of fruit is laid, covered with sugar, spices, and melted butter, and then baked. It is served hot with a warm, sweet-tart sauce. Cobblers consist of fruit topped with a layer of biscuit dough; cobblers are baked and usually served hot. Some may be topped with pie crust.

Fruit rolls are made by placing fruit over biscuit dough, and then rolling and cutting the dough as for cinnamon rolls. A roly-poly results when the whole roll is baked and slices are cut afterward. Fruit dumplings are pieces of fruit wrapped in a rich biscuit dough, placed into pans, covered with a fruit sauce or with slightly sweetened water or with plain water to about half their height, and then baked or steamed (see fig. 15-3). After cooking, a sauce surrounds the dumplings, and this is spooned over them at service. Steamed dumplings are browned under a broiler to improve their color; some are deep-fried. Fruit rolls, roly-polies, dumplings, and other biscuit-and-fruit desserts are usually served warm with a fruit sauce, hard sauce, brandy sauce, or foamy sauce.

PUDDINGS

Most puddings are easily made in quantity, are low in cost, and require little labor. There are many types; all are popular. Some puddings, such as cottage pudding, resemble cakes. A date pudding or other cakelike product high in fruit may be served hot or cold, with or without a hot or cold sauce; such puddings are easy to make for large groups.

Steamed (Boiled) Puddings

Steamed or boiled puddings are served warm and normally come with a sauce. They are usually made with suet as the shortening. Bread crumbs,

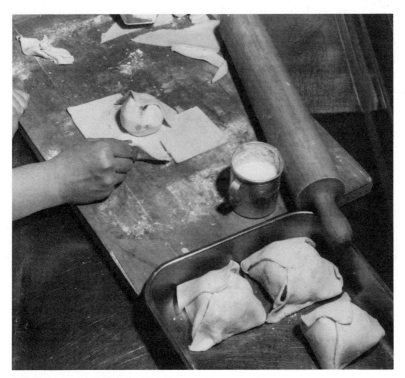

Figure 15-3. Procedure for making apple dumplings. When the pan is filled, a light sweet syrup is poured over the dumplings to about two-thirds their height, and the dumplings are baked.

strong flour, and eggs act as binders for large proportions of fruits and nuts. Only a small amount of moisture is added if the fruit is moist. The ratio of batter to fruit and nuts may vary from 1 : 1 to 1 : 2½. Many steamed puddings approximate pound cakes in their proportions of flour, shortening, and sugar. The leavening agent is usually soda, which promotes a porous texture and darkens the ingredients. Steamed puddings are heavier in texture than baked ones; the grain is usually tight and waxy, not pasty. Lighter puddings may resemble rich muffin batters, with their open grain and more delicate texture.

Containers in which puddings are cooked may be large or individual-size. Grease and flour the containers well and fill to two-thirds full to allow for expansion during cooking. Provide covers or tops to keep out condensate. Steam the pudding for 2½ to 3 hours and bake for about the same amount of time in a 325°F oven in pans of shallow water. To boil puddings in a bag, dip a strong muslin cloth into cold water, wring it out, turn it inside out, and dip it into flour. Turn the floured side in and drop in the batter. Tie the cloth loosely to allow for expansion, and lower the bag into water that is just boiling. The bag can also be suspended in a steam bath. When the pudding is cooked, remove the bag, dip it into cold water, and free the cloth. Let the pudding cool under cover or in water so that it does not form a tough skin. Puddings may be stored and later reheated in their containers, or they may be removed, wrapped in foil, and reheated in the foil wrap in steam or in a 325°F oven for about 45 minutes. Use very sharp or serrated knives for cutting. Reheat individual puddings in a roll or bun warmer. Select a sauce that complements the flavor and texture of the pudding.

Starch-thickened Puddings

Blancmanges and cream puddings serve as the base for many desserts. Blancmange is another name for cornstarch pudding made from hot milk, sugar, vanilla, a bit of salt and a thickener (cornstarch, arrowroot, or some other starch). Use 6 to 12 oz cornstarch per gallon of liquid. If the blancmange is to be served molded, use 12 oz per gallon of thickener to liquid. Adding eggs to a cornstarch pudding makes it a cream pudding. Starch is for such desserts reduced because of the thickening power of the eggs. A chiffon or light, fluffy texture may be imparted to a cream pudding by first adding only the yolks to the pudding mixture, beating the whites into a meringue with part of the sugar, and then folding the meringue in while the mixture is hot. The hotter the mixture is when blended with the meringue, the firmer the chiffon will be.

To make a blancmange, heat the milk after reserving some for blending with the sugar and cornstarch or with the cornstarch only. Add a bit of hot milk to the cold milk, and blend this with the cornstarch. With good agitation, stir this into the hot milk and cook for about 10 minutes or until the temperature exceeds 200°F. An alternative method is to mix the sugar and cornstarch together and stir these ingredients in with good agitation.

For a cream pudding, beat the eggs (or yolks only) well, and add some of the hot thickened blancmange to them, blending well. Return this blended egg mixture to the hot blancmange, giving good agitation so that the eggs blend before cooking (see fig. 15-4). Keep stirring until the temperature of the mixture exceeds 195°F. If either a blancmange or a cream pudding contains a lot of sugar, withhold part of it until the starch and eggs are cooked; adding it afterward prevents the sugar from interfering with the thickening of the starch and eggs.

Tapioca pudding is made by adding tapioca to sweetened milk or fruit juice and cooking to thicken. Either pearl or granular (quick-cooking) tapioca is used. Granular tapioca gives a less ropy pudding; pearl tapioca needs soaking before cooking. Overmixing causes ropiness and lowers quality. Tapioca cream puddings contain eggs. The egg yolks are cooked with the tapioca, the milk, part of the sugar, and the flavorings. This hot,

Figure 15-4. A cream pudding is a cornstarch pudding (blancmange) with eggs added. To blend in the eggs, mix them well, add a bit of the hot pudding, and blend well. Then, using good stirring, blend this egg mixture into the hot pudding mixture as shown.

Figure 15-5. A tapioca cream pudding is being prepared. The hot tapioca mixture is being folded into an egg white meringue. The hotter the pudding mixture is when it is stirred into the meringue, the stiffer the final pudding will be.

thickened mixture (at a temperature above 190°F) is carefully folded into a meringue composed of egg whites and the remaining sugar, to give a chiffon texture (see fig. 15-5). Sago, farina, and cornmeal are also used in starch-thickened puddings. Indian pudding contains molasses and is thickened with cornmeal. Arrowroot gives a soft, delicate pudding and is used for high-quality products. Serve $\frac{1}{2}$ c pudding as a portion; $3\frac{1}{4}$ gal pudding makes 100 portions.

EGG-THICKENED DESSERTS

Custards

A conventional baked custard is made with $1\frac{1}{2}$ to 2 lb whole eggs per gallon of liquid. Egg proportions are less if only egg yolks are used or if cereals such as bread, rice or cake crumbs are included; reduce eggs 2 oz for every 8 oz cereal. Some recipes may specify a small quantity of flour or other starch. Poor-quality eggs make a weak custard. Baking temperatures should be between 325° and 340°F. Too low a temperature leads to a weak custard, and too high a temperature produces a broken one with a watery, open texture (syneresis) instead of a firm, smooth, solid clabber. The cut surface of a good custard is even and sharp; it possesses a soft sheen tinted a slight creamy tan. The top should be delicately browned. The container holding the custard should be put into a pan of water so that direct heat does not cause syneresis. Because custards bake after coming from the oven, they should be removed just before they are completely done. A custard is completely cooked when the tip of a knife inserted near the edge comes out clean (see fig. 15-6). Experienced bakers can judge doneness by moving the pan and observing the custard's firmness. If desired, custards may be steamed, but cover to keep condensate out.

For best results, have the milk hot and the mixture close to 140°F when it is placed into the oven. To stop the custard from cooking after oven removal, set it in a well-aerated spot or into a pan of cold water.

Stirred or soft custards are similar to baked ones in composition, but they are stirred instead of baked. When cool, they have the consistency of a thin to medium white sauce. Syneresis is a problem, and constant stirring is required to prevent curdling. Coagulation is an endothermic action and 185°F is roughly the temperature at which coagulation begins. As soon as the temperature exceeds 185°F, coagulation is complete. Disappearance of foam is also an indicator of doneness. Soft custards can be made in 1 to 2 gal batches in a trunnion kettle or over hot water; good

Figure 15-6. One of the best ways to test for doneness of a custard. The knife tip should come out clean.

Figure 15-7. A fruit soufflé. (*Courtesy Poultry and Egg National Board*)

stirring is essential. If hand-stirred, quantities of up to 3 qt can be made. Again, preheating the milk so that the mixture is at 140°F gives better results. Soft custards are often poured over fruit or slices of cake. Floating island is a dessert made by pouring soft custard over soft meringues, which then float on top of the custard.

SOUFFLÉS

Some soufflé desserts are gelatin products that include beaten eggs to give lightness (see fig. 15-7). Baked soufflé is a dessert thickened and leavened by eggs. It is delicate and usually must be prepared to order. It is made by beating yolks separately with sugar, blending in flavoring, and then folding in stiffly beaten egg whites—a procedure similar to the method used to make foamy omelets. It is baked in a slow or moderate oven. Service must be immediate, since the soufflé may collapse.

MERINGUES

A meringue is an emulsion of air cells dispersed in heavy egg-and-sugar syrup. Hard meringues are often used as a base for desserts, while soft ones are used as toppings for pies, puddings, and other desserts (see fig. 15-8).

Hard meringues may have 1 oz water added for each 1 lb whites to aid in bringing the sugar into solution, and they may have 1 oz vinegar or lemon juice or $\frac{1}{4}$ oz cream of tartar to tenderize the whites and give the meringue a stable foam. If vinegar or lemon juice is used, omit the water. Between $1\frac{3}{4}$ and $2\frac{1}{4}$ lb sugar is used for each 1 lb whites. Meringues are

(a)   (b)

(c)   (d)

Figure 15-8. (a) The ingredients for and the making of a soft meringue for topping pies. (b) The ingredients for a hard meringue. (c) Putting hard meringues on a baking sheet prior to baking them. Afterward, the center is usually filled with fruit, ice cream, or pudding. (d) A small individual shell and a pie shell made from hard meringue, plus soft meringue on a piece of lemon pie.

baked for 1½ hours at 275°F or for 50 minutes at 325°F. They should dry out rather than bake, but they should not be dry enough to shatter when handled. Heavy ovens may be preheated to 325°F, the heat turned off, and the meringues placed into the oven to dry overnight. Baking is done on lightly greased pans, on ungreased paper, or on nonresinous wooden boards that are 1 in. or more thick.

A 1 : 1 weight ratio of sugar to egg whites is used for soft meringues; for a sweeter, tenderer, and more flavorful product, this ratio can go to 3 : 2; ¾ t cream of tartar is used for each 1 lb egg white. A bit of salt adds flavor to both hard and soft meringues. Soft meringues made from fresh, dried, or frozen egg whites are good culture media for bacteria; to make them less inviting to bacteria, they should be baked well for 12 to 18 minutes at 350°F. Meringues from mixes or processed whites can be baked at 475°F for 5 minutes or at 425°F for 6 minutes; alternatively, can be browned with a torch or a hot, flat, iron instrument, since they have been pasteurized. Scale meringue shells at 1¼ oz each or 15 to 18 oz per dozen.

In order for whites intended for meringues to whip to a good foam (stage 3), they should be at 110° to 125°F; using fine sugar speeds dissolving time and prevents graininess. Add salt and acid at the start of beating and add sugar in small increments, beating well to blend and dissolve it. Failure to whip sufficiently results in a thin meringue that lacks volume, weeps, and slips. Overbeating before adding sugar can cause a meringue failure.

Meringues, especially soft ones, tend to develop weeping or leakage (moisture that separates out as tiny droplets or gathers under the meringue). Possible causes include excess moisture, high sugar content, improper beating, and placing an unbaked meringue on a cold filling before baking. To avoid slippage, put meringues on warm fillings; or, use stabilizers such as locust bean gum, gum arabic, gum tragacanth, powdered carageenin gum or agar. Stir the last two into a small quantity of boiling water before adding them to the meringue. Some bakers use $\frac{1}{2}$ oz cornstarch or tapioca flour for each 1 lb whites, dusting this over the meringue during the last stage of beating. Prepared stabilizers may be obtained from bakery supply houses. When spreading meringues on pies or other desserts, attach the edges firmly to the crust or sides. A quantity of from 3 to 5 oz meringue provides a liberal topping for a 9-in. pie.

Two other meringues are used for dessert topping. Italian meringue is a boiled frosting whose ratio of sugar to egg whites is 1 : 1. Cook the sugar in half its weight of water until it reaches a temperature of 244°F; then beat this into whites that have been whipped to stage 3 foam (lower level). Swiss meringue is made with a sugar-to-whites ratio of between 1 : 1 and 3 : 2. The mixture is beaten over boiling water at medium or high speed until the meringue is quite stiff; use $\frac{1}{4}$ oz cream of tartar for each 1 lb whites. A 7-minute frosting is also used as a topping.

Manufacturers' directions for meringue powders should be followed. These fine and stable products are widely used today. Normally 1 qt lukewarm water and 1 lb sugar are used with each 6 oz meringue powder.

JUNKET DESSERTS

A dessert resembling custard is prepared from sugar, flavoring, milk, and rennet (an enzyme that sets milk into a clabber). The milk and sugar are warmed to 98°F, at which point flavoring and a junket tablet are added. The mixture sets after being poured into containers and chilled. Jarring or stirring breaks the curd. A portion is usually $\frac{1}{2}$ to $\frac{3}{4}$ cup. Junkets are often used as desserts for people on diets.

GELATIN DESSERTS

Gelatin desserts are easy to make, have low labor and material costs, and lend themselves to presentation and merchandising. They are well-adapted to blending with fruits, foods, or fruit juices. They also store well and are not highly perishable.

For good gelling, $1\frac{1}{2}$ lb gelatin dessert or $2\frac{1}{2}$ oz pure gelatin is needed per gallon of liquid. Sugar, flavoring, and coloring are usually added to a pure gelatin mixture. After setting, the gelatin may be riced, cubed, or mixed with other items for service. Gelatin can also be beaten to a light foam before setting. Gelatins poured over cake cubes or crumbs make attractive desserts; use them in this manner at the syrupy stage to prevent soaking. Whipped egg whites, whipped cream, blancmanges, cream puddings, and melted ice cream may be blended with gelatin mixtures to produce different desserts. A snow or sponge is made by chilling a gelatin mixture until its volume doubles. Shredded cooked pineapple or applesauce is used for pineapple or apple snows. Beaten egg whites are often folded in to give a light texture. Apricot, prune, peach, or other fruit sponges are also popular. Serve these with a stirred custard.

A bavarian consists of whipped cream folded into a sweetened gelatin mixture. The best bavarians rely on milk instead of water for their liquid. Cooked rice or cake crumbs, ground nuts or diced fruits may be added. Bavarians are also made by blending a blancmange or cream pudding into a syrupy gelatin mixture along with stiffly beaten egg whites, whipped cream, or a soft ice cream (see fig. 15-9). Some bavarians are whipped to a foam before the other ingredients are added.

A Spanish cream is a thin, stirred custard to which gelatin or a flavored gelatin dessert is added in sufficient quantity to make it set. Just before setting, whipped cream or stiffly beaten egg whites are folded in; the product is not as rich as a typical bavarian. Many variations exist.

(a)

(b)

Figure 15-9. (a) Folding beaten dry milk and gelatin into a chocolate cream pudding mixture to make a low-calorie bavarian cream. (b) An orange marmalade bavarian. (*Courtesy General Foods*)

FROZEN DESSERTS

Frozen desserts are extremely popular, and considerable variety can be gained not only by using different kinds of frozen desserts but by changing the way in which they are served. These desserts are low in cost and—if purchased already prepared—take little production labor before being available for service.

TYPES

Ice cream, sherbet, and ices are mixtures that are frozen by mechanical freezers, which whip air into them as they freeze. Desserts such as mousses, parfaits, frozen puddings, and frozen fruits are not whipped during freezing: they are either whipped before freezing or not at all. Slushes or granites are only partially frozen and are coarse and granular. Philadelphia ice cream consists of milk, cream, sugar, flavoring, and perhaps a stabilizer. Adding eggs produces French ice cream. Often ground vanilla bean is added, showing up as slight dark specks. Ice cream is also combined with fruits, nuts, cake crumbs, macaroons, and many other desserts. Vanilla ice cream must be at least 10 percent milkfat, but if fruit, nuts, chocolate, or other products are added, to an ice cream, the amount of milkfat can be as low as 8 percent. Mixtures used for milkshakes and malts are often lower in milkfat.

INGREDIENTS

A good ice cream contains between 9 and $12\frac{1}{4}$ percent milk solids, 14 percent sugar, 10 percent or more milkfat, and about $\frac{1}{2}$ percent stabilizer, and the rest flavorings and water. Milkfat can account for up to 22 percent of the ice cream; and sugar, 18 percent. Corn syrup may replace 30 percent of the total sugar. To obtain an ice cream that is $14\frac{1}{2}$ percent sugar, 12 percent milkfat, 11 percent nonfat milk solids, and $\frac{1}{2}$ percent gelatin, use the following proportions:

20 percent heavy whipping cream (40 percent milkfat)
46 percent whole milk (4 percent milkfat)
28 percent condensed milk (8 percent milkfat, 45 percent sugar)
$\frac{1}{2}$ percent vanilla
2 percent sugar
$\frac{1}{2}$ percent gelatin
3 percent water gel

Some dessert-makers substitute nonfat milk solids and butter for cream. During pasteurization and homogenization, the melted butter is easily put into a stabile solution. It is not uncommon to use milk and cream for ice cream that cannot be used as fresh products. If these are used, an alkaline neutralizer such as sodium bicarbonate, sodium carbonate, or sodium hydroxide may be added to obtain a desirable pH. Mixes should be aged for at least 4 hours at 30° to 40°F to increase the mix's viscosity and to improve its stability and colloidal properties. Aging mixes for 24 hours gives a better foam (overrun) and body. Allowing a mix made of dry milk to age improves the product's flavor by allowing the milk sugar (lactose) to go into solution. Colorings and flavorings must be federally approved. Only the highest-quality flavorings, spices, fruits, and nuts should be used. Normally, only vanilla mix is made, since it is the base for all other ice creams. Chocolate and a few other items may be added at the start of freezing, but nuts, fruits, and most other special ingredients are added just before the product is withdrawn from the freezer.

Milkfat tends to make a harder dessert, while fillers such as nonfat milk solids and eggs counteract hardness. Excessive milkfat may also cause graininess—especially when rapid agitation churns the fat into small butter globules. Consequently, an ice cream high in fat must not be overbeaten.

EQUIPMENT

To make its own mix, an operation needs mixing vats, a pasteurizer, a homogenizer, a filter, a cooler, a freezer, and a hardening cabinet. A batch freezer is used for small quantities, and a continuous freezer is used for large ones. If an operation buys its own liquid or dry mix, it only needs to have a freezer and a hardening cabinet. The simplest procedure, of course, is to purchase frozen desserts ready to use. It is important that equipment be sized properly for the quantities to be made and that no bottlenecks occur because some equipment is too small or is otherwise unsuitable for the rest of the equipment. Smooth flow is extremely important. Hardening cabinets should be conveniently located so that minimum time passes between withdrawal from the freezer and entry into the cabinet. Sanitizing equipment, sinks, work tables, storage spaces, and other accessories should be placed in such a way as to speed work and minimize labor requirements.

PRODUCTION PROCEDURES

Frozen desserts begin to freeze at about 27° to 28°F; at around 24°F, the mixtures harden considerably and freezing terminates, in order not to overburden the freezer's motor. Freezing should occur within 5 to 8 minutes. Most desserts are whipped as well as frozen; a dasher inside the freezer removes frozen bits from the sides of the chamber and also acts as a whip. During freezing, the dasher moves slowly; but when the machine is switched from *freeze* to *whip*, it moves at from 175 to 250 rpm, developing a foam that increases volume considerably. This process is called *overrun*. Ice cream should have an overrun of 80 to 100 percent. At overruns of under 80 percent, the flavor is flat and the texture is compact, heavy, and pasty. Excessive overrun gives a frothy, foamy product that is lacking in flavor. Overrun for an iced dessert containing no milk but some egg whites should be from 25 to 30 percent, and for sherbet it should be 20 to 50 percent. Thus, if 50 gal ice cream mix is whipped until an overrun of 100 percent is achieved, the final volume of ice cream produced is 100 gal—1 gal weighing $4\frac{1}{2}$ lb. A pint of 100 percent overrun ice cream should weigh 9 oz. Scooping packs ice cream, reducing its overrun. Mixtures containing over 18 percent sugar develop poor overrun. Gelatin increases overrun but also increases whipping time. Egg yolks speed and increase overrun development. Citrates and phosphates increase it, too, while calcium salts decrease it. Butterfat decreases overrun, but nonfat milk solids increase it. Freezing an ice cream too much before whipping it reduces overrun.

When the dessert in the freezer is ribbony and appears slightly dry and dull, the amounts of freezing and overrun are correct. It should now flow from the freezer slowly when the dispensing mechanism is operated at slow speed. Use prechilled cups or cans to catch the mixture as it comes from the machine.

Freezing should be rapid enough to enable the product to develop fine crystals, and the beating should be sufficiently hard to retain this fineness. Rapid hardening is also essential for developing a fine, smooth texture. The lowest temperature for most hardening cabinets is $-25°F$. Hardening should occur in 6 to 12 hours; if it takes longer than this, the product may become coarse in texture. Stabilizers and emulsifiers help retain fine crystal development in storage, as do milkfat, eggs, and nonfat milk solids.

SANITATION

After pasteurization, a mix's bacterial count should not be more than 35,000 to 50,000 per gram or cubic centimeter. Nuts, spices, fruits, and other products added later can introduce bacteria, so they should be purchased as sterilized or low-bacterial-count products. After opening these products, use care to ensure that they are not contaminated. Moldy or spoiled fruit should not be used. The work area, storage spaces, and equipment must be kept clean and sanitary. Steam-clean, boil, or use special solutions for sterilizing. Equipment is usually given a preliminary rinse, dismantled, given a thorough wash, rinsed, and sanitized. Mechanical equipment is reassembled and filled to about half of capacity with a sanitizing solution, and the machine is operated for about 1 minute. The solution is then drawn off, but the equipment instead of being rinsed is left open for free air circulation. Before being reused, this equipment is rinsed, sterilized, and rinsed again. Only air-drying is recommended.

QUALITY STANDARDS

Ice cream may be scored on the following scales: flavor, 45; body and texture, 30; appearance, 15; color and packaging, 5; and melting quality, 5. The flavor should be pleasant and true with proper acidity and sweetness. Texture should be smooth with a fine grain or creaminess evident. Defective texture is described as fluffy, weak, crumbly, watery, icy, soggy, or gummy. Body is associated with the ice cream's feel in the mouth. It should not be too heavy or pasty nor too open or frothy. Some slight firmness is desirable. Appearance should be bright and smooth with a good bloom. Some brilliance is desirable in products that are low in milk. Some desserts contain excessive amounts of starch paste, gums, or other fillers to build body and texture and otherwise mask inferior quality. When the product is thawed, this shows up in its retained shape: very little liquid appears. The best products thaw completely into a liquid.

SERVICE

Store frozen desserts at 0°F or lower, but for service have it at from 8 to 15°F (see fig. 15-10). Below or above these service temperatures, a packed and less flavorful product results. Avoid holding excess stocks. Obtain quantities in sizes that are used quickly, and rotate stocks as rapidly as possible. Vanilla, strawberry, and chocolate ice cream are usually stocked as standard items, as are orange and pineapple sherbets. Move items from frozen storage to service cabinets at least 24 hours before service, in order to condition them.

Scooping incorrectly destroys texture. Normal scooping shrinkage is between 40 and 45 percent; 5 gal ice cream usually yields 100 No. 10 scoops or 130 No. 12 scoops. To estimate dipping efficiency, weigh 6 portions on a scale and calculate their average weight. Divide this amount into the net weight (in pounds) of a full container. Thus, if 6 dips weigh 18 oz (an average of 3 oz per dip), a 5-gal container holding 22 lb 6 oz (or 358 oz) net, gives 119 scoops. Often 62, 51, 42, 35, 26, and 20 dips, respectively, are obtained per gallon from No. 30, 24, 20, 16, 12, and 10 scoops (see fig. 15-11). Too soft or too hard a product yields fewer dips. Portioning or cupping desserts as they are withdrawn from the freezer and then hardening them so they can be served without scooping avoids scooping loss. Typical fountain portions are listed in table 15-3.

Figure 15-10.   Have ice cream chilled to between 8° and 12°F for best results in dishing. (The angle used in taking the picture distorts the reading, which shows 8°F.

(a)

(b)

Figure 15-11. (a) The proper type and size of scoop must be used to obtain best results in serving frozen desserts. (*Courtesy Ice Cream Merchandising Institute*) (b) The size scoop indicates the number of scoops that *should* be obtained per quart (but never is)—from left to right, No. 40, No. 30, No. 24, No. 20, No. 16, No. 12, and No. 10. Normally about half as many scoops are obtained per quart of frozen dessert as the number indicated on the scoop; this is a result of packing.

TABLE 15-3. Fountain portions

Fountain item	Size scoop	Number of scoops per portion
Banana split	No. 30	3
Bowl of ice cream	No. 30	4
Parfait	No. 30	3
Ice cream soda, malt, or milkshake	No. 24	2
Pie, cake, or pudding à la mode	No. 20	1
Sundae	No. 20	2
Table d'hôte, plain	No. 16	1
Sundae, meal portion	No. 12	1
À la carte portion	No. 10	1

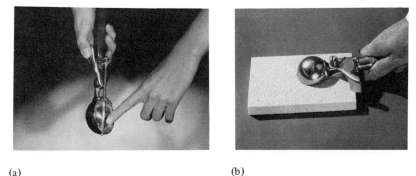

(a)   (b)

Figure 15-12. (a) Use a good sharp-edged scoop, and make sure that it is in good working order. (b) To scoop, dip into cool water, drain for a moment on a pad, and use.

Scoops should be clean and smooth, with a sharp edge free of nicks (see fig. 15-12a). Before scooping, dip the utensil into clear water, and drain it for a moment on a clean pad (see fig. 15-12b). If the scoop is cold, the dessert sticks and packs. Scooping is illustrated in figure 15-13.

Among the most familiar forms of service for ice cream are the sundae,

(a)   (b)

(c)   (d)

Figure 15-13. Scooping frozen desserts with either the mechanical or the nonmechanical scoop is much the same. Shown here is the use of the nonmechanical scoop. (a) Insert the scoop about $\frac{1}{2}$ in. deep into the frozen dessert, starting at the outer edge or where the last scoop left off. (b) Draw lightly and evenly across the surface, rolling the dessert into a ball. (c) When the scoop is filled, turn it upward with a twist of the wrist, breaking off the ice cream. (d) Keep the surface smooth, working evenly across the top.

the parfait, the ice cream soda, the frappé, the freeze, the float, the milkshake, and the banana split. Figures 15-14 through 15-17 illustrate standard methods for producing these. Frozen desserts are served in many other ways, as well. Meringue shells filled with ice cream may be covered with fruit and topped with whipped cream. A baked Alaska is made by placing a No. 24 scoop of ice cream on a 2-in. square of cake, covering this with soft meringue, and baking until the meringue is delicately browned. Frozen log rolls, cupcakes, éclairs filled with frozen desserts, bombes, and coupes bring variety without high cost. Combining flavors of ice creams, sherbets, and ices, offering interesting accompani-

Figure 15-14. The standard sundae begins with about ½ oz of syrup, followed by two dips of No. 24–scoop ice cream dropped *lightly*, followed by 1 oz of syrup, and topped with whipped cream, nuts, and a cherry. (*Courtesy Ice Cream Merchandising Institute*)

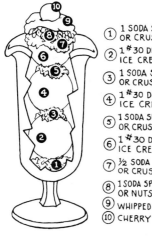

1. 1 SODA SPOON SYRUP OR CRUSHED FRUIT
2. 1 #30 DIP ICE CREAM
3. 1 SODA SPOON SYRUP OR CRUSHED FRUIT
4. 1 #30 DIP ICE CREAM
5. 1 SODA SPOON SYRUP OR CRUSHED FRUIT
6. 1 #30 DIP ICE CREAM
7. ½ SODA SPOON SYRUP OR CRUSHED FRUIT
8. 1 SODA SPOON OF NUTS OR NUTS IN SYRUP
9. WHIPPED CREAM
10. CHERRY

Figure 15-15. Method for making the standard parfait. (*Courtesy Ice Cream Merchandising Institute*)

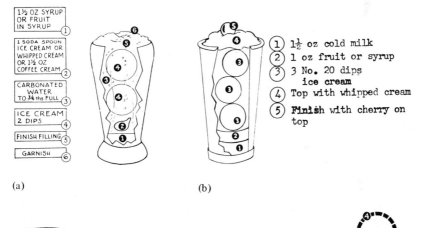

(a)

1½ OZ SYRUP OR FRUIT IN SYRUP (1)

1 SODA SPOON ICE CREAM OR WHIPPED CREAM OR 1½ OZ COFFEE CREAM (2)

CARBONATED WATER TO ¾ths FULL (3)

ICE CREAM 2 DIPS (4)

FINISH FILLING (5)

GARNISH (6)

(b)

1. 1½ oz cold milk
2. 1 oz fruit or syrup
3. 3 No. 20 dips ice cream
4. Top with whipped cream
5. Finish with cherry on top

(c)

1. JUICE OF ORANGE LEMON OR LIME
2. SIMPLE SYRUP ¾ OZ FOR ORANGE 1½ OZ FOR LEMON OR LIME
3. 1 SCOOP CRACKED ICE
4. 2 #24 DIPS OF FRUIT ICE OR SHERBET (SAME FLAVOR AS DRINK)
5. 5 OZ CARBONATED WATER
6. 1 SLICE FRESH FRUIT
7. CHERRY

(d)

1. 6 OZ COLD PASTEURIZED MILK
2. 2 #24 DIPS ICE CREAM
3. 1½ OZ SYRUP
4. POUR INTO A WHIPPED CREAM DOTTED THIN SHELL GLASS

Figure 15-16. Methods for making standard fountain drinks: (a) ice cream soda; (b) frappé; (c) freeze or float; (d) old-fashioned milkshake. If malt is added to the milkshake after step 1, a malted milk can be made by following the remainder of the milkshake method. (*Courtesy of Ice Cream Merchandising Institute*)

① MEDIUM RIPE BANANA   ④ WHIPPED CREAM
② 3 #24 DIPS ICE CREAM   ⑤ GROUND NUTS
   ASSORTED FLAVORS
③ ½ OZ EACH OF 3 TOPPINGS   ⑥ CHERRY OR GARNISH

Figure 15-17. Method for making the standard banana split. Drop the banana into the dish gently—even when not making the dessert in front of customers. (*Courtesy Ice Cream Merchandising Institute*)

ments, and using different and unusual toppings enhance menu interest, as do *à la modes*.

FRIED DESSERTS

FRITTERS

Fritters are usually deep-fried, but they may instead be pan-fried in a liberal quantity of fat (see fig. 15-18). Many consist of fruit dipped into a batter and fried. Others are muffin mixtures containing fruits, or other items. The batter is scooped with a No. 30 scoop and deep-fried. Many variations are served, frequently with syrup.

PANCAKES AND CRÊPES

Thin batters that resemble plain omelets slightly thickened with flour are used in place of pancake batter to make dessert pancakes or crêpes. No leavening agent is used. The cakes, which are very thin, are made by

Figure 15-18. Two types of fritters. The apple fritters on the left have been dipped in batter and fried. The items on the right are banana fritters made by mixing diced bananas into a fairly stiff fritter batter and deep-frying fritter-sized portions of the batter.

pouring only enough batter into a hot buttered pan to cover the bottom with a thin coating. Cooking is rapid. When the bottom of the crêpe is nicely browned, turn it and brown the other side. The second side is the interior side of the crêpe at service. Pancakes and crêpes may be made ahead of time and rewarmed. They also freeze well. To serve, warm the cakes, place them on a clean surface, fill them as desired, fold, and serve. Small cakes, 4 to 5 in. in diameter, are served two to three to a portion; one large cake usually constitutes a portion. Roll the cake after filling, or fold it in four (see fig. 15-19). Butter creams, applesauce, marmalades, red currant jelly, *Bar-le-Duc* jelly, sour cream, and other fillings are used. Serve quite warm. Many crêpes are flamed, while some are dusted with powdered sugar or burned in the same manner as French omelets are. Granulated sugar sprinkled over the top aids in drawing liquor up for burning. Warming the liquor or using one that has a high proof aids in burning.

DOUGHNUTS

The three primary varieties of doughnuts are cake, yeast, and French. The first type is made from a lean cake or rich muffin dough, the second from a sweet yeast dough, and the third from a rich éclair paste (choux paste); all are deep-fried. French doughnuts (crullers) are also called twisted cake doughnuts. Cake doughnuts may be made into balls, fingers, or other shapes (see fig. 15-20). Yeast doughnuts may be made into bismarcks, long johns, and others. The quality of the finished product depends on recipe balance, ingredients, and techniques of dough mixing, handling, and frying. Normally, a doughnut recipe is in balance if it falls within the ratios listed in table 15-4. Significant departures from these proportions in any major ingredient make it necessary to adjust others in order to obtain a desirable product. Do not store mixes for longer than three months.

a   b

Figure 15-19. (a) Rolled crêpes or French pancakes. These are filled with strawberry preserves and dusted with powdered sugar. (b) Crêpes suzette should be filled with an orange butter cream filling, folded in four, and then flamed with rum, brandy, or a mixture of liqueurs.

Figure 15-20. Doughnuts made from a single cake doughnut recipe. (*Courtesy Procter & Gamble*)

TABLE 15-4. Ratios for doughnut recipes (flour = 100%)

Ingredient	Type doughnut		
	Cake	Yeast	French (cruller)
Flour, bread		65–100%	50–100%
Flour, pastry or cake	100%	0–35%	0–50%
Sugar	10–50%	8–20%	
Eggs, whole	5–25%	3–15%	125–155%
Liquid (water)	50–60%	50–70%	155%
Shortening	2–8%	8–20%	30–65%
Baking powder, double-acting	2–4%		
Salt	½–1%	½–2%	1–2%
Mace, nutmeg, or other spice	¼–½%	¼–½%	
Vanilla, lemon, or other flavoring	¼–½%		
Milk, nonfat dry	5–11%	5–7%	0–3½%
Egg yolks	0–16%	2–8%	
Yeast		2–6%	
Baking ammonia			0–¼%

NOTE: Pastry flour may be used in place of blends of bread and cake flour; overly tender cake doughnuts would result from 100% cake flour, unless a very lean dough were used. It is best to omit baking ammonia from doughnut recipes since it breaks down the frying fat.

Only operations that make huge quantities of cake doughnuts face the hazards of making them from basic ingredients (see fig. 15-21). Most operations today use mixes prepared from ingredients specifically designed to give high quality. Quality still can be lost, however, through improper measuring or mixing techniques. Follow the manufacturer's directions. Do not overmix or undermix. Hold ingredient temperatures at 50° to 60°F during mixing, to reduce gluten development and avoid a tough product. Hand-cut doughnuts should be slightly stiffer than those dropped by mechanical droppers. Scale cake doughnuts at 1 oz each.

The sweet dough used for yeast doughnuts should be slightly more slack than the dough used for regular sweet-dough products. A dough containing 4 percent yeast to 100 percent flour should receive a punch in $1\frac{1}{4}$ to $1\frac{1}{2}$ hours and should go to the bench 15 to 20 minutes later. Proof the dough a maximum amount of time—from 10 to 20 minutes. About 10 dozen doughnuts are made from 6 lb flour, which makes 13 lb dough. Scale yeast doughnuts at $1\frac{1}{2}$ oz each. Machine-cutting or hand-cutting may be performed. Make holes as shown in figure 15-22. Handle the shaped dough carefully when adding it to the frying fat.

French doughnuts are made from éclair (choux) paste, whose ingredients are described in Chapter 11. The batter—preferably warm—is put into a large pastry bag equipped with a large star tube. About 2-in.-diameter circles weighing slightly under 1 oz are deposited either on greased, heavy paper or on a light metal plate (see fig. 15-23a). The holder is lowered easily into hot fat and, when the doughnuts free themselves, removed (see fig. 15-23b). Often four turns are required to cook them properly, since they must be crisped thoroughly before removal (for the same reason that cream puffs must be thoroughly baked before oven removal). The serrated edges left by the star tube on top should remain visible after frying. French doughnuts may be machine-shaped if quantities are large.

When a doughnut, fritter, or other product is dropped into hot fat and fried, it expands. This development is called *break*. Doughnuts need a good break to reduce grease soaking and to develop a good texture and grain. The method of cutting and dropping, the temperature of the frying fat, and the frying conditions can all affect break. Fry cake doughnuts for $1\frac{1}{2}$ to 2 minutes at 385° to 395°F; 390°F is considered ideal (see fig. 15-24). Fry yeast doughnuts for 2 to $2\frac{1}{4}$ minutes at 360° to 365°F. Fry French doughnuts for 2 to $2\frac{1}{4}$ minutes at 365°F. Adjust temperatures so that the interior is completely cooked when it reaches the desired color. Excessive heat gives a dark doughnut that has a raw interior, a tight, compact grain, and low volume. Surface appearance is also poor. Too low a temperature results in excessive expansion with attendant poor color, break, and texture and a high level of fat absorption. Slide hand-cut doughnuts carefully into the frying fat. Keep a mechanical dropper not farther than 2 in. above the fat. Do not overcrowd doughnuts in the fryer: allow for expansion in cooking and for turning space. Desirable fat absorption is about 3 oz per dozen; 4 oz or more is considered excessive.

(a) (b)

(c)

Figure 15-21. The quality of a cake doughnut is affected by a number of factors including (a) whether the dough is too rich or too lean, (b) whether the dough is too slack or contains too much flour, and (c) whether the dough is poorly cut or dropped.

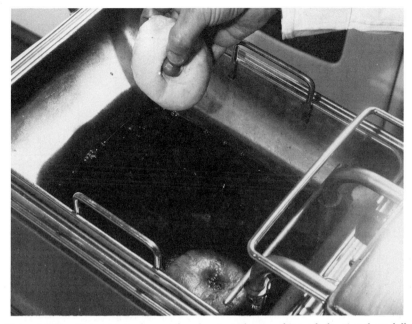

Figure 15-22. Cut out raised yeast doughnuts without making a hole; give them full proof and then, when dropping the doughnut into the fat, gently make a hole.

After drying, doughnuts may be dipped into different coatings. First, cool to 80°F; if doughnuts are dipped while still warm, escaping steam soaks the coating. Greasy doughnuts make the coating appear soaked. Improper storage also destroys coatings. Powdered sugar coatings may be stabilized by adding from 5 to 10 percent starch or nonfat dry milk. A

(a)   (b)

Figure 15-23. (a) To make French doughnuts, first make an éclair (choux) paste, and deposit it in rings on greased paper or on metal plates sized to fit the fryer. Then lower the paper or metal plate into the fat. (b) When the doughnuts begin to swell, they free themselves from the plate and rise to the top. At this time, remove the paper or metal plate and allow the doughnuts to continue frying.

FAT ABSORPTION IN RELATION TO FRYING
TEMPERATURE AND DOUGH RICHNESS

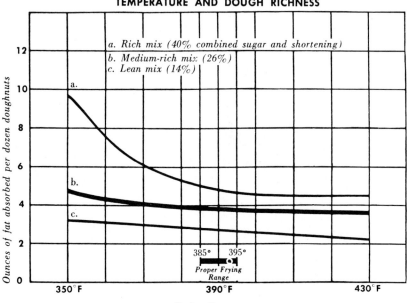

Frying Temperature

Figure 15-24. Fat absorption by cake doughnuts in relation to frying temperature and dough richness. Fat at a temperature from 385° to 395°F fries a cake doughnut rapidly and seals the surface from fat penetration. Lower temperatures do not seal the surface as rapidly, and as a result the doughnut absorbs more fat. At temperatures above 395°F, absorption is less but the danger of scorching or breaking down the fat is increased.

fondant or plain powdered sugar icing soaks less if some fat (10 to 15 percent) of the total icing weight, is creamed into it. Yeast doughnuts are best when dipped into fine sugar or into sugar and cinnamon or when glazed; the glaze consists of 40 percent water, 10 percent glucose or 5 percent invert sugar, and 0.1 percent cream of tartar or 3 percent glycerine, brought to a boil with 100 percent 4X to 6X sugar. After the glaze is removed from the heat, 1 percent hydrated gelatin is stirred in. The doughnuts are dipped into this glaze and then set on a wire rack over a pan to catch the excess as it drips off. Have the glaze warmed to about 110°F for dipping. Doughnuts may be iced or decorated. Yeast doughnuts, long johns, or bismarcks may be filled with jelly or jam, custard, marshmallow filling, butter cream, whipped cream, or a fruit filling. The consistency of the cooked doughnut is important. If the consistency is too soft, the doughnut soaks; and if too firm, it fills poorly and has a pasty texture. Most doughnuts are filled with a cream puff filler or similar device. Occasionally, French doughnuts are filled, but more often they are merely dusted with powdered sugar or brushed with plain fondant or buttercream icing.

Chapter Review

1. Many desserts are made from fruits. Match the fruit or other dessert name given below with its description.

Fruit dumpling	Dutch cake	Baked custard	Roly-poly
Blancmange	Shortcake	Soufflé	Bavarian
Cobbler	Meringue	Betty	Junket
Compote			

_____ Fruit over and between a rich biscuit—usually topped with whipped cream.

_____ Dough-wrapped fruit baked in a light syrup.

_____ Fruit put between layers of a rich biscuit dough, sliced in the manner of a cinnamon roll, and baked—usually served with some sauce.

_____ Eggs whipped to a foam and made into a light, delicate, baked dessert.

_____ Whipped cream folded into a gelatin mixture.

_____ Egg whites beaten stiff with sugar and baked.

_____ Dessert prepared from milk, sugar, flavoring, and rennet.

_____ A mixture of different fruits; sometimes the fruit is cooked.

_____ A rich biscuit dough on top of which fruit (usually sliced apple) is placed, with sugar and perhaps cinnamon over this; the product is then baked.

_____ Milk, sugar, and flavoring thickened with cornstarch.

_____ Eggs, milk, sugar, and flavoring that are mixed and baked.

_____ Fruit in layers between which are rich crumbs, butter, and sugar; the whole is then baked.

_____ An underlayer of fruit, with a topping of flour, sugar, and butter or shortening over it; the whole is then baked.

2. What is the difference between Philadelphia ice cream and French ice cream?
3. What is the best way to scoop ice cream?
4. How is a crêpe made? What are crêpes Suzette?
5. To what group of desserts do bismarcks, crullers, and long johns belong? How are they made?
6. What are fruits dipped into batter and deep-fried called?
7. How is baked Alaska made?

Appendix A Tables

TABLE A-1. Equivalents between fresh and frozen foods

Food item	Frozen (lb)	Fresh (lb)	Waste eliminated (%)
FISH AND SEAFOOD			
Cod and haddock fillets	5	15	67
Flounder fillets	5	20	75
Halibut fillets and steaks	5	10	57
Lobster meat	1	32	62
Mackerel fillets	5	9	42
Red perch fillets	5	25	80
Swordfish steaks	5	$6\frac{1}{4}$	20
VEGETABLES			
Asparagus	$2\frac{1}{2}$	5.4	54
Broccoli	$2\frac{1}{2}$	5.5	55
Cauliflower	$2\frac{1}{2}$	10.0	75
Brussels sprouts	$2\frac{1}{2}$	7.0	64
Corn, cut	$2\frac{1}{2}$	2 doz ears	
Green beans	$2\frac{1}{2}$	4.0	48
Wax beans	$2\frac{1}{2}$	4.0	48
Beans: lima, fordhook, or baby	$2\frac{1}{2}$	$7\frac{1}{2}$–9	63
Peas	$2\frac{1}{2}$	$7\frac{1}{2}$–9	67
Peas and carrots	$2\frac{1}{2}$	6–$6\frac{3}{4}$	63
Pumpkin	$2\frac{1}{2}$	4.0	48
Spinach	$2\frac{1}{2}$	3.9	63
Squash	$2\frac{1}{2}$	6.9	37
Succotash	$2\frac{1}{2}$	4.0	63
Mixed vegetables	$2\frac{1}{2}$	4.0	63
POULTRY			
Broilers, 12–24 oz	1	$1\frac{1}{2}$	33
Fryers, $1\frac{1}{2}$–$2\frac{1}{2}$ lb	2	3	33
Fowl, 2–$3\frac{1}{2}$ lb	$2\frac{1}{2}$	$3\frac{3}{4}$	33
Ducks, $3\frac{1}{2}$–5 lb	4	$4\frac{3}{4}$	30
Turkeys, 9–30 lb	$22\frac{1}{2}$	30	25
Geese	7	10	30
FRUITS			
Apples	30 (7:1)	35:4	24
Apricots	30 (5:1)	$26\frac{2}{3}$:5	6
Berries	30 (4:1)	25:6	4
Cherries	30 (5:1)	27:5	8
Cantaloupe	30 (7:1)	52:4	50

continued

TABLE A-1. Equivalents between fresh and frozen foods (*continued*)

Food item	Frozen (lb)	Fresh (lb)	Waste eliminated (%)
FRUITS			
Peaches	30 (4:1)	$31\frac{1}{2}$:6	24
Pineapple	30 (4:1)	47:6	48
Rhubarb	30 (3:1)	$25\frac{2}{3}$:8	14

NOTE: Most frozen fruit is packed in some sugar; in this table, the ratio of fruit to sugar normally packed is shown in parenthesis after the 30-lb container size. In the column for fresh fruit, the quantity of fruit plus the proportionate amount of sugar necessary to equal the 30-lb is given. Waste is the excess over 30 pounds.

TABLE A-2. Ounces and their decimal equivalents of a pound

Ounces	Decimal part of a pound	Ounces	Decimal part of a pound	Ounces	Decimal part of a pound	Ounces	Decimal part of a pound
$\frac{1}{4}$	0.016	$4\frac{1}{4}$	0.266	$8\frac{1}{4}$	0.516	$12\frac{1}{4}$	0.766
$\frac{1}{2}$	0.031	$4\frac{1}{2}$	0.281	$8\frac{1}{2}$	0.531	$12\frac{1}{2}$	0.781
$\frac{3}{4}$	0.047	$4\frac{3}{4}$	0.297	$8\frac{3}{4}$	0.547	$12\frac{3}{4}$	0.797
1	0.063	5	0.313	9	0.563	13	0.813
$1\frac{1}{4}$	0.078	$5\frac{1}{4}$	0.328	$9\frac{1}{4}$	0.578	$13\frac{1}{4}$	0.828
$1\frac{1}{2}$	0.094	$5\frac{1}{2}$	0.344	$9\frac{1}{2}$	0.594	$13\frac{1}{2}$	0.844
$1\frac{3}{4}$	0.109	$5\frac{3}{4}$	0.359	$9\frac{3}{4}$	0.609	$13\frac{3}{4}$	0.859
2	0.125	6	0.375	10	0.625	14	0.875
$2\frac{1}{4}$	0.141	$6\frac{1}{4}$	0.391	$10\frac{1}{4}$	0.641	$14\frac{1}{4}$	0.891
$2\frac{1}{2}$	0.156	$6\frac{1}{2}$	0.406	$10\frac{1}{2}$	0.656	$14\frac{1}{2}$	0.906
$2\frac{3}{4}$	0.172	$6\frac{3}{4}$	0.422	$10\frac{3}{4}$	0.672	$14\frac{3}{4}$	0.922
3	0.188	7	0.438	11	0.688	15	0.938
$3\frac{1}{4}$	0.203	$7\frac{1}{4}$	0.453	$11\frac{1}{4}$	0.703	$15\frac{1}{4}$	0.953
$3\frac{1}{2}$	0.219	$7\frac{1}{2}$	0.469	$11\frac{1}{2}$	0.719	$15\frac{1}{2}$	0.969
$3\frac{3}{4}$	0.234	$7\frac{3}{4}$	0.484	$11\frac{3}{4}$	0.734	$15\frac{3}{4}$	0.983
4	0.250	8	0.500	12	0.750	16	1.000

SOURCE: *Standardizing Recipes for Institutional Use*, Circular 233, Agr. Ex. Station, Michigan State University.

TABLE A-3. Approximate substitution equivalents in quantity food production

Ingredient	Substitute	Measure	Weight
Flour (2 c, 8 oz)	Cornstarch	1 c	
Cake flour (1 qt, 1 lb)	Hard or all-purpose flour	$3\frac{3}{4}$ c + $\frac{1}{4}$ c cornstarch	$13\frac{1}{2}$ oz + $2\frac{1}{2}$ oz cornstarch
Syrups, honey, etc. (1 pt, 1 lb 6 oz)	Sugar	$2\frac{1}{2}$ c + $\frac{1}{2}$ c water + $\frac{1}{8}$ t cream of tartar	$1\frac{1}{4}$ lb sugar + 4 oz water + $\frac{1}{8}$ t cream of tartar
Chocolate, bitter (2 c, 1 lb)	Cocoa	$3\frac{1}{2}$ c + $\frac{3}{4}$ c shortening	$12\frac{1}{2}$ oz + $3\frac{1}{2}$ oz shortening
Milk, whole (1 qt, 2 lb)	Dry milk, whole*	$\frac{7}{8}$ c + $3\frac{5}{8}$ c water	$3\frac{3}{4}$ oz + $1\frac{7}{8}$ lb water
Milk, whole (1 qt, 2 lb)	Dry milk, nonfat*	$\frac{3}{4}$ c + $3\frac{1}{2}$ c water + 2 T shortening	$3\frac{1}{2}$ oz + $1\frac{3}{4}$ lb water + 1 oz shortening
Milk, nonfat (1 qt, 2 lb)	Dry milk, nonfat*	$\frac{3}{4}$ c + $3\frac{5}{8}$ c water	$3\frac{1}{2}$ oz + $1\frac{7}{8}$ lb water
Milk, whole (1 qt, 2 lb)	Evaporated milk	No. 1 tall can + water to equal 1 qt	$14\frac{1}{2}$ oz + water to equal 1 qt
Eggs, whole (1 pt, 1 lb)	Dried whole eggs	$1\frac{1}{4}$ c + $1\frac{3}{4}$ c water	5 oz + $12\frac{1}{2}$ oz water
Eggs, whites (1 pt, 1 lb)	Dried whites	$1\frac{1}{4}$ c + $1\frac{3}{4}$ c water	3 oz + 14 oz water
Eggs, yolks (1 pt, 1 lb)	Dried yolks	$1\frac{1}{4}$ c + $1\frac{3}{4}$ c water	6 oz + 11 oz water
Eggs, whole (1 pt, 1 lb)	Frozen whole	1 pt (10 eggs)	1 lb
Eggs, whites (1 pt, 1 lb)	Frozen whites	1 pt (18 whites)	1 lb
Eggs, yolks (1 pt, 1 lb)	Frozen yolks	1 pt (24 yolks)	1 lb
Butter (1 pt, 1 lb)	Margarine	1 pt	1 lb
Butter or margarine (1 pt, 1 lb)	Fat or oil	$1\frac{5}{8}$ c + $\frac{1}{2}$ t salt + 2 T water	14 oz + $\frac{1}{2}$ t salt + 1 oz water
Cream, coffee, 18% (1 qt, 2 lb)	Milk, nonfat, and butter	$3\frac{1}{2}$ c milk + $\frac{3}{4}$ c butter	26 oz milk + 6 oz butter
Cream, whipping, 40% (1 qt, 2 lb)	Butter	$1\frac{3}{4}$ c + $2\frac{1}{4}$ c milk	40% of cream weight
	Milk, nonfat, and butter	3 c milk + $1\frac{1}{3}$ c butter	20 oz milk + $12\frac{1}{2}$ oz butter
Leavening agents			
Tartrate baking powder ($\frac{3}{4}$ c, 4 oz)	SAS/baking powder	$\frac{3}{8}$ c	2 oz
Tartrate baking powder ($\frac{3}{4}$ c, 4 oz)	Soda and cream of tartar	3 T soda + $\frac{2}{3}$ c cream of tartar	1 oz + 3 oz
SAS Phosphate baking powder ($\frac{3}{8}$ c, 2 oz)	Phosphate baking powder	$\frac{1}{2}$ c + 1 T	3 oz
SAS Phosphate baking powder ($\frac{3}{8}$ c, 2 oz)	Soda + liquid	3 T + (1 c sour milk or 1 c buttermilk or [1 c milk + 1 T vinegar or lemon juice] or $\frac{1}{2}$ to 1 c molasses)	

* Measure equivalent is for regular dry milk; for instant, use $1\frac{1}{3}$ c for every $\frac{3}{4}$ c of regular.

TABLE A-4. Equivalent weights and measures of foods

Food	Weight	Approximate measure
BEVERAGES		
Cocoa	1 lb	$4\frac{1}{2}$ c
Coffee, urn grind	1 lb	$4\frac{1}{2}$ c
Coffee, instant	1 oz	$\frac{1}{2}$ c
Tea	1 lb	$1\frac{1}{2}$ qt
CEREALS AND CEREAL PRODUCTS		
Barley, pearl	1 lb	$2\frac{1}{2}$ c
Bran, all-bran	1 lb	2 qt
Bran flakes	1 lb	3 qt
Bread crumbs, dry	1 lb	$1\frac{1}{4}$ qt
Bread crumbs, fresh	1 lb	$2\frac{1}{2}$ qt
Bread crumbs, dry sifted	1 lb	1 qt
Bread, soft, broken, $\frac{3}{4}$-in. cubes	1 lb	$2\frac{1}{4}$ qt (packed 2 qt)
Bread slices, $\frac{5}{8}$ in.	1 lb	16 slices
Cake crumbs, soft	1 lb	$1\frac{1}{4}$ qt
Cornflakes	1 lb	$1\frac{1}{4}$ gal
Cornmeal	1 lb	$3\frac{1}{2}$ c (3 qt cooked)
Cornstarch, stirred	1 lb	$3\frac{1}{2}$ c (1 c = $4\frac{3}{4}$ oz, 1 oz $3\frac{1}{2}$ T)
Crackers, crumbled	1 lb	$2-2\frac{1}{2}$ qt
Cracker crumbs	1 lb	$1\frac{1}{4}$ qt
Crackers, graham	1 lb	40 crackers
Crackers, small, square saltine	1 lb	108 crackers
Crackers, large, soda	1 lb	56 crackers
Cracked wheat	1 lb	$3\frac{1}{2}$ c (5 to 6 c cooked)
Farina	1 lb	$2\frac{2}{3}$ c
Flour, graham or whole-wheat	1 lb	$3\frac{1}{2}$ c
Flour, cake, unsifted	1 lb	$3\frac{3}{4}$ c
Flour, cake, sifted	1 lb	1 qt
Flour, rye, straight-grade, sifted	1 lb	$1\frac{1}{4}$ qt
Flour, white, bread, sifted	1 lb	1 qt
Flour, white, bread, unsifted	1 lb	$3\frac{3}{4}$ c
Hominy grits	1 lb	$2\frac{1}{2}-3$ c ($6\frac{1}{2}$ lb or $3\frac{1}{4}$ qt cooked)
Macaroni, 1-in. pieces	1 lb	$3\frac{1}{2}-4$ c ($3\frac{3}{4}$ lb or $2\frac{1}{2}$ qt cooked)
Noodles	1 lb	$6-8\frac{1}{2}$ c ($3\frac{3}{4}$ lb or $2\frac{1}{4}$ qt cooked)
Oats, rolled	1 lb	$4\frac{3}{4}$ c ($2\frac{1}{4}$ qt cooked)
Rice	1 lb	$2\frac{1}{8}$ c ($2\frac{1}{2}$ lb or $2\frac{1}{2}$ qt cooked)
Soya flour	1 lb	$1\frac{1}{4}-1\frac{1}{2}$ qt
Spaghetti, 2-in. pieces	1 lb	$1\frac{1}{4}$ qt (4 lb or $2\frac{1}{2}$ qt cooked)
Tapioca, quick-cooking	1 lb	$2\frac{2}{3}$ c ($7\frac{1}{2}$ c cooked)
Tapioca, pearl	1 lb	$2\frac{3}{4}$ c ($7\frac{1}{2}$ c soaked and cooked)
Wheat cereals	1 lb	$2\frac{7}{8}$ c (6 c cooked)
Wheat, shredded	1 lb	20 small biscuits
DAIRY PRODUCTS		
Butter or margarine	1 lb	2 c
Cheese, grated or ground	1 lb	$2\frac{1}{4}$ c light pack, $3\frac{3}{4}$ c loose pack
Cheese, cubed	1 lb 1 oz	1 qt
Cheese, cottage	1 lb	$2\frac{1}{4}$ c

continued

TABLE A-4. Equivalent weights and measures of foods (*continued*)

Food	Weight	Approximate measure
DAIRY PRODUCTS		
Cheese, Philadelphia cream	1 lb 9 oz	3 c
Cream, 18%	$8\frac{3}{4}$ oz	1 c
Cream, 30–40%, whipping	1 lb	1 pt (doubles volume in whipping)
Milk, condensed, sweetened	11 oz	1 c
Milk, dry, instant	1 lb	$5\frac{3}{4}$ c
Milk, dry, nonfat, regular	1 lb	1 qt
Milk, dry, whole, regular	1 lb	$3\frac{3}{4}$ c
Milk, evaporated	1 lb	$1\frac{7}{8}$ c
Milk, fresh, liquid	$8\frac{1}{2}$ oz	1 c
EGGS, LARGE		
Eggs in shell	$1\frac{1}{2}$ lb	1 doz
Eggs, whole	1 lb	1 pt (9–11)
Eggs, whites	1 lb	1 pt (17–20)
Eggs, yolks	1 lb	1 pt (19–23)
Eggs, hardcooked, chopped	1 lb	$2\frac{1}{2}$ c (1 doz = $3\frac{1}{2}$ c)
Eggs, dry, whole, packed	1 oz	$\frac{1}{4}$ c
Eggs, whole, dry	1 lb	$1\frac{1}{4}$ qt ($1\frac{1}{2}$ c (6 oz) + $1\frac{7}{8}$ c water = 1 doz eggs)
Eggs, whites, dry	1 lb	2 qt ($\frac{3}{4}$ c (2 doz) + $1\frac{1}{2}$ c water = 1 doz whites)
Eggs, yolks, dry	1 lb	$4\frac{1}{4}$ c ($1\frac{1}{8}$ c (4 doz) + $\frac{3}{8}$ c water = 1 doz yolks)
Meringue	6 oz	1 c
FATS AND OILS		
Bacon fat	15 oz	1 lb (1 lb = $2\frac{1}{8}$ c)
Butter or margarine	14 oz	1 pt
Creamed fat	1 lb	$2\frac{1}{2}$ c
Hydrogenated shortening	$14\frac{1}{2}$ oz	1 pt
Oil	1 lb	$2\frac{1}{4}$ c
Suet, chopped	1 lb	$3\frac{3}{4}$ c
FRUITS		
Apples	1 lb	3 size 113 (3 c pared, diced, or sliced)
Apples, sliced	1 lb	$4–4\frac{1}{2}$ c
Apples, diced $\frac{1}{2}$ in.	1 lb	1 qt
Applesauce	1 lb	$1\frac{7}{8}$ c
Apples, canned, solid pack	1 lb	1 pt
Apple nuggets	1 lb	$6\frac{2}{3}$ c
Apricots, dried	1 lb	$3\frac{1}{4}$ c ($1\frac{3}{4}$ lb or 5 c cooked)
Apricots, canned, heavy pack	1 lb	1 pt
Apricots, canned, halves, no juice	1 lb	1 pt (21 halves)
Apricots, fresh	1 lb	8 medium
Avocados, Calavos, medium size	1 lb	2–3
Bananas, AP, medium size	1 lb	3 (peeled 10 oz)
Bananas, peeled	1 lb	$2\frac{1}{2}$ c diced (1 medium banana = 30 $\frac{1}{8}$ in. slices or $\frac{3}{4}$ c or $\frac{1}{3}–\frac{1}{2}$ c mashed)
Blackberries, fresh	1 lb	1 qt
Blackberries, water pack, drained	1 lb	3 c
Blueberries, fresh	1 lb	3 c

continued

TABLE A-4. Equivalent weights and measures of foods (*continued*)

Food	Weight	Approximate measure
Cantaloupe	1 lb	1 melon 4 in. in diameter
Cherries, red, heavy pack, drained	1 lb	3 c
Cherries, Royal Anne, drained	1 lb	3 c
Cherries, candied	1 lb	3 c or 120 cherries
Cherries, Maraschino	1 qt	60–70 cherries
Citron, chopped	1 lb	$2\frac{1}{2}$ c
Cranberries, fresh	1 lb	1 qt (1 lb AP = $3\frac{1}{4}$ c sauce)
Cranberries, dehydrated	1 lb	$8\frac{1}{2}$ c
Cranberries, whole	$2\frac{1}{2}$ lb raw	1 qt cooked
Currants	1 lb	$3\frac{1}{2}$ c (1 c = $4\frac{1}{2}$ oz)
Dates, pitted	1 lb	$2\frac{3}{4}$ c (1 c = 6 oz; 1 c = $8\frac{1}{4}$ oz if packed)
Dates, unpitted	1 lb	$2\frac{1}{2}$ c ($1\frac{3}{4}$ c pitted)
Figs, dry	1 lb	3 c (1 c = 5 oz)
Grapefruit, 32s	1 lb	12 sections, $1\frac{1}{4}$ c juice
Grapes, whole, stemmed	1 lb	1 qt
Grapes, cut	1 lb	$2\frac{2}{3}$ c
Oranges, 88s, diced with juice	1 lb	$2\frac{1}{4}$ c (1 orange = $\frac{1}{2}$ c diced or $\frac{1}{3}$ c juice)
Oranges, 88s, Florida	1 doz	1 qt juice
Oranges, rind, grated (also lemon)	$1\frac{2}{3}$ oz	$\frac{1}{4}$ c (1 t = $\frac{1}{8}$ oz)
Oranges, rind, grated (also lemon)	$6\frac{1}{2}$ oz	1 c
Peaches, canned, sliced with juice	1 lb	$\frac{7}{8}$ c
Peaches, fresh	1 lb	3–5 peaches
Peaches, dry, loose pack	1 lb	1 qt
Pears, canned, drained, diced	1 lb	$2\frac{1}{2}$ c
Pineapple, slices	1 lb	8–12 slices ($2\frac{1}{2}$ c)
Prunes, dried, sizes 30–40, uncooked	1 lb	3 c ($2\frac{1}{2}$ lb or 5–6 c cooked)
Prunes, cooked, pitted, with juice	1 lb	$2\frac{1}{4}$ c
Pumpkin	1 lb	$2\frac{1}{2}$ c
Raisins	1 lb	3 c (1 c = $5\frac{1}{4}$ oz; 1 lb cooked = 1 lb $9\frac{1}{2}$ oz or 1 qt)
Raspberries	1 lb	$3\frac{1}{2}$ c ($2\frac{1}{4}$ c cooked)
Rhubarb, raw, 1-in. pieces	1 lb	1 qt (cooked $1\frac{3}{8}$ lb or $2\frac{1}{2}$ c)
Strawberries, fresh	1 lb	$3\frac{1}{4}$ c
MEATS		
Bacon, diced, packed	1 lb	$2\frac{1}{4}$ c
Bacon, raw, sliced	1 lb	15–25 slices
Bacon, cooked	1 lb	85–95 slices
Beef, dried, solid pack	1 lb	1 qt, scant
Beef, ground, raw	1 lb	1 pt
Beef, cooked, diced	1 lb	3 c
Chicken, ready-to-cook	5 lb	5 c cooked, diced meat (40% yield)
Chicken, cooked, cubed	1 lb	$2\frac{1}{2}$ c
Crabmeat, flaked	1 lb	3 c
Ham, cooked, diced	1 lb	$3\frac{1}{4}$ c
Ham, cooked, ground, packed	1 lb	1 pt
Ham, raw, AP	1 lb	1 c fine-diced, cooked
Meats, chopped, cooked, moist, packed	1 lb	1 pt (loose pack = 1 qt)
Oysters, 1 qt, eastern	2 lb	40 large, 60 small
Salmon, canned	1 lb	1 pt

continued

TABLE A-4. Equivalent weights and measures of foods (*continued*)

Food	Weight	Approximate measure
Sardines, canned	1 lb	48, 3 in. long
Sausage, link	1 lb	16
Sausage meat	1 lb	1 pt
Shrimp, 2 lb AP	1 lb EP	$3\frac{1}{4}$ c (5 lb in shell = gal)
Tuna	1 lb	1 pt
Turkey, ready-to-cook	30 lb	15 lb clear meat
Wieners	1 lb	10 (6–7 frankfurters)
MISCELLANEOUS		
Compressed yeast	$\frac{1}{2}$ oz	1 cake ($8\frac{1}{2}$ oz = 1 c)
Dry active yeast	1 lb	$2\frac{1}{2}$ lb compressed
Gelatin, granulated, unflavored	1 lb	$3\frac{1}{2}$ c (1 oz = $3\frac{1}{2}$ T)
Gelatin, prepared, flavored	1 lb	$2\frac{1}{3}$ c (1 oz = $\frac{1}{4}$ c)
Marshmallows ($1\frac{1}{4}$ in.)	1 lb	80
NUTS		
Almonds, shelled	1 lb	$3\frac{1}{2}$ c ($\frac{1}{4}$ lb shelled)
Almonds, blanched	1 lb	3 c
Coconut, shredded	1 lb	$4\frac{1}{2}$–7 c (depends on shred type and pack tightness)
Coconut, ground or fine shread	$2\frac{3}{8}$ oz	1 c
Coconut, shredded, medium	1 oz	7 T
Filberts	1 lb	$3\frac{1}{3}$ c ($\frac{1}{2}$ lb shelled)
Peanut butter	1 lb	$1\frac{7}{8}$ c
Peanuts, chopped	1 lb	1 qt ($\frac{2}{3}$ lb shelled)
Pecans	1 lb	$4\frac{1}{4}$ c ($\frac{1}{3}$ lb shelled)
Walnut meats	1 lb	$4\frac{3}{4}$ c ($\frac{1}{2}$ lb shelled)
Walnut meats, chopped	1 lb	1 qt
Nut meats, ground	$4\frac{1}{4}$ oz	1 c
SALAD DRESSINGS AND CONDIMENTS		
Catsup or chili sauce	9 oz	1 c
Cooked salad dressing	1 lb	1 pt
French dressing	1 lb	$2\frac{1}{8}$ c
Horseradish, ground	1 lb	$2\frac{1}{4}$ c
Mayonnaise	1 lb	$2\frac{1}{8}$ c
Olives, small	1 lb	$3\frac{1}{2}$ c or 135 olives (1 No. 10 = $4\frac{1}{2}$ lb drained weight or 350 large olives)
Pickles, chopped	1 lb	$2\frac{1}{2}$ c
Pickles, small	1 gal	80 (about 225 gherkins or 25 large per gal)
SPICES, SEASONINGS, LEAVENINGS		
Allspice, ground	1 lb	$4\frac{1}{2}$ c (1 oz − $4\frac{1}{2}$ T)
Baking powder	1 lb	$2\frac{1}{2}$ c (1 T = $\frac{7}{16}$ oz; 1 oz = $2\frac{1}{2}$ T)
Celery seed	1 lb	1 qt (1 oz = $\frac{1}{4}$ c)
Chili or curry powder	1 oz	3 T
Chocolate, grated	1 oz	5 T (1 c = $3\frac{3}{4}$ oz; 1 lb = 1 qt or 16 squares)
Chocolate, melted	1 lb	$1\frac{7}{8}$ c (1 oz = 2 T)
Cinnamon, ground	1 lb	1 qt (1 oz = $\frac{1}{4}$ c)
Cloves, ground	1 lb	$3\frac{3}{4}$ c (1 oz = $3\frac{3}{4}$ T)

continued

TABLE A-4. Equivalent weights and measures of foods (*continued*)

Food	Weight	Approximate measure
Cloves, whole	1 oz	5 T
Cream of tartar	1 lb	3 c (1 oz = 3 T)
Flavoring extracts	$\frac{3}{8}$ oz	1 T ($\frac{1}{8}$ oz = 1 t)
Ginger, ground	1 lb	$4\frac{3}{4}$ c (1 oz = $4\frac{3}{4}$ T)
Mustard, ground	1 lb	5 c (1 oz = 5 T)
Nutmeg, ground	1 lb	$3\frac{1}{2}$ oz (1 oz = $3\frac{1}{2}$ T)
Paprika	$3\frac{1}{4}$ oz	1 c (1 T = $\frac{3}{8}$ oz)
Pepper	1 oz	$\frac{1}{4}$ c
Sage, ground	1 oz	$\frac{1}{2}$ c
Salt	1 lb	$1\frac{2}{3}$ c (1 oz = $1\frac{2}{3}$ T)
Soda	1 lb	$2\frac{1}{2}$ c (1 oz = 2 T; $6\frac{1}{2}$ t = 1 oz)
Vinegar	1 lb	2 c (1 oz = 2 T)
Worcestershire sauce	$9\frac{1}{2}$ oz	1 c

SUGARS AND SYRUPS

Food	Weight	Approximate measure
Corn syrup	11 oz	1 c
Honey	12 oz	1 c
Jam or jelly	$1\frac{1}{2}$ lb	1 pt
Molasses	11 oz	1 c
Sugar, cocktail cube	1 cublet ($\frac{1}{6}$ oz)	$\frac{1}{2}$ t (small cube = 1 t; tablet = $1\frac{1}{2}$ t; 96 cubes, medium, per lb)
Sugar, granulated	1 lb	$2\frac{1}{4}$ c (super-fine 2 c)
Sugar, confectioners', stirred	1 lb	$3\frac{1}{2}$ c
Sugar, confectioners', 4X, sifted	1 lb	$4\frac{1}{2}$ c (unsifted $2\frac{3}{4}$ c)
Sugar, brown	1 lb	3 c (packed $2\frac{1}{4}$ c)

VEGETABLES

Food	Weight	Approximate measure
Asparagus, fresh	1 lb	20 stalks
Asparagus, canned tips, drained	1 lb	19 stalks
Asparagus, canned cuts, drained	1 lb	$2\frac{1}{2}$ c
Beans, baked	1 lb	$1\frac{7}{8}$ c
Beans, lima, dried, small, AP	1 lb	$2\frac{1}{3}$ c ($2\frac{1}{2}$ lb or $1\frac{1}{2}$ qt cooked)
Beans, lima, fresh, unshelled	1 lb	$\frac{2}{3}$ c shelled
Beans, lima, fresh, shelled	1 lb	$2\frac{1}{4}$ c
Beans, lima, drained, cooked fresh or canned	1 lb	$2\frac{2}{3}$ c ($1\frac{1}{2}$ lb = 1 qt)
Beans, kidney, dry, AP	1 lb	$2\frac{1}{3}$ c ($2\frac{1}{4}$ lb or $1\frac{1}{2}$ qt cooked)
Beans, string, cut, uncooked, EP	12 oz	1 qt
Beans, navy, dry, AP	1 lb	$2\frac{1}{3}$ c ($2\frac{1}{2}$ lb or $1\frac{3}{4}$ c cooked)
Bean sprouts	1 lb	1 qt
Beets, cooked, diced, drained	1 lb	$2\frac{1}{4}$ c (3–4 medium whole)
Beets, cooked, sliced, drained	$1\frac{1}{2}$ lb	1 qt (1 lb = $2\frac{3}{4}$ c)
Brussels sprouts, AP	1 lb	1 qt
Cabbage, shredded, EP	12 oz	1 qt (1 lb = $5\frac{1}{2}$ c; 1 lb = 7 c loose pack)
Cabbage, AP, shredded, cooked, drained	1 lb	$3\frac{1}{2}$ c
Carrots, $\frac{1}{2}$-in. cube, raw	1 lb	$3\frac{1}{4}$ c
Carrots, diced, cooked, drained	1 lb	$2\frac{1}{2}$ to 3 c
Carrots, ground, raw, EP	1 lb	$3\frac{1}{4}$ c
Carrots, AP	1 lb	4 medium; 6 small
Cauliflower, 1 crate	$12\frac{1}{2}$ lb, net, EP	10 qt
Cauliflower, head, medium	12 oz	4–5 portions
Celery, diced, EP	$1\frac{1}{4}$ lb	1 qt (1 lb = $3\frac{1}{4}$ c)

continued

TABLE A-4. Equivalent weights and measures of foods (*continued*)

Food	Weight	Approximate measure
Celery, dehydrated	1 lb	$9\frac{1}{2}$ c
Corn, cream-style	1 lb	$1\frac{7}{8}$ c
Corn, whole-kernel, drained	1 lb	$2\frac{1}{3}$ c
Cucumbers, diced	1 lb	$2\frac{1}{2}$ c
Eggplant, diced, $\frac{1}{2}$-in. cubes	1 lb	$4\frac{1}{2}$ c
Eggplant, sliced, 4-in.-diameter, $\frac{1}{2}$-in. thick	1 lb	8 slices
Garlic, crushed	1 oz	6–9 cloves
Lettuce, average head	1 lb	10–12 leaf cups
Lettuce, shredded	1 lb	8 c (packed 5 c)
Lettuce, leaf	1 lb	30 salad garnishes
Mushrooms, fresh	1 lb AP	$1\frac{1}{3}$ c cooked
Onions, AP	1 lb	4–5 medium
Onions, chopped	1 lb	$2\frac{1}{2}$–3 c
Onions, grated or minced	5 oz	1 c
Onions, dehydrated	1 lb	$9\frac{1}{2}$ c
Parsley	1 lb	3 bunches (6 c chopped)
Parsnips, AP	1 lb	3–4 medium
Parsnips, diced, raw	1 lb	$2\frac{1}{2}$–3 c
Parsnips, diced, cooked	1 lb	$2\frac{1}{2}$ c
Parsnips, mashed	1 lb	1 pt
Peas, fresh, $2\frac{1}{2}$ lb AP	1 lb EP	1 pt scant, 5 portions
Peas, canned, dried	1 lb	$2\frac{1}{4}$ c
Peas, dried, split	1 lb	$2\frac{1}{3}$ c ($2\frac{1}{2}$ lb or $5\frac{1}{2}$ c cooked)
Peppers, green	1 lb	5–6 medium
Peppers, green, chopped	1 lb	$3\frac{1}{2}$ c
Pimientos, chopped	8 oz	1 c
Potatoes, white, medium, AP	1 lb	3–4 ($\frac{3}{4}$ lb pared; 1 pt mashed)
Potatoes, dehydrated, cube	1 lb	$4\frac{3}{4}$ c
Potatoes, dehydrated, flake	$3\frac{1}{2}$ oz	1 c
Potatoes, dehydrated, granule	7 oz	1 c
Potatoes, cooked, diced $\frac{1}{2}$-in. cube	1 lb	3 c
Potatoes, sweet	1 lb	3 medium
Potato chips	1 lb	5 qt (20 1-c portions $\frac{3}{4}$ oz)
Pumpkin, cooked	1 lb	1 pt
Radishes, whole, topped and cleaned	1 lb	1 qt
Rutabagas, cubed, cooked	1 lb	3 c
Rutabagas, raw, cubed, EP	1 lb	$3\frac{1}{3}$ c
Sauerkraut, uncooked	1 lb	3 c
Spinach, raw	1 lb	5 qt, loose pack
Spinach, 1 lb raw, AP, cooked	13 oz (EP)	$1\frac{1}{2}$ c cooked, 3 portions
Spinach, canned, drained	1 lb	1 pt
Squash, summer, AP	$1\frac{1}{2}$ lb	1 3-in.-diameter
Squash, Hubbard, cooked, mashed	1 lb	$2\frac{1}{8}$ c
Tomatoes, canned	1 lb	1 pt
Tomatoes, dried	1 lb	$3\frac{1}{2}$ c
Tomatoes, fresh	1 lb	3–4 medium
Tomatoes, fresh, diced	1 lb	$2\frac{1}{4}$–$2\frac{3}{4}$ c
Turnips, AP	1 lb	4–5 medium
Turnips, raw, diced	1 lb	$3\frac{1}{2}$ c
Watercress	1 lb	5 bunches

TABLE A-5. Standard portions for entrées and accompaniments

Food	Portion and serving method
MEATS	
American chop suey	4-oz ladle, rounded
with corn soya	2 T, No. 32 scoop
with rice	No. 16 scoop
Baked hash, beef or corned beef	No. 10 scoop or heaped serving spoon, 5–6 oz
Beef or other meat and noodles	No. 8 scoop rounded or 6-oz ladle rounded, about 7 oz ($\frac{3}{4}$ c)
Beef patty	No. 8 scoop before cooking; use tongs
Beef or other meat stew	6-oz ($\frac{3}{4}$-c) ladle
Chili con carne	6-oz ladle rounded to give 8 oz
Corned beef and cabbage	3 or 4 oz sliced beef (tongs); 3 to 4 oz cabbage (spoon)
Cold cuts	3 oz., tongs or spatula
Cabbage rolls	2 rolls, 3 oz each (use 2 oz meat filling); use spoon
Creamed meats	4-oz ($\frac{1}{2}$-c) ladle; use 8 to 10 lb cooked meat per 100; serve over toast, biscuits, or No. 16 scoop rice
Croquettes	No. 10 or 12 scoop for 1; No. 20 scoop for 2; $1\frac{1}{2}$ oz sauce
Frankfurters, 6 to 7 lb	2 (tongs)
with sauerkraut	1 rounded serving spoon, 3 oz
Fritters	2 (tongs); portion with No. 20 scoop; 2 strips bacon
Ham a la king	4-oz ladle rounded
Ham, baked, boned	5–6 oz before cooking (tongs)
Ham, baked, slices	3–4 oz after cooking (tongs)
Ham, fried	6 oz before cooking (tongs)
Hamburgers	2 (tongs); portion with No. 20 dipper
Liver, braised	3 to 4 oz before cooking, 2 strips bacon (tongs)
Meatballs and spaghetti	No. 20 scoop, 2 meatballs, 2 serving spoons spaghetti and sauce
Meat sandwich, hot	2 oz meat, 1 or 2 slices bread (tongs); 2-oz ladle gravy
Meatloaf	4–5 oz cooked; slice and use spatula or tongs
Meat pie	2 serving spoons, rounded, 8 oz
with pie crust	Cut 17 × 25 baking pans 5 × 9, 45 portions
with biscuit	$2\frac{1}{2}$-in. diameter; serve 1 with 6 oz stew
Meat turnover	2 oz meat, No. 16 scoop; serve with 2-oz ladle gravy
Mock drumsticks	5 oz before cooking, serve 1
New England boiled dinner	6 oz before cooking, 3–4 oz after (tongs); 5 oz vegetables and 5 oz potatoes
Pork chop	3 per lb before cooking, serve 1; 6 per lb, serve 2
with dressing	2–3 oz; use serving spoon or No. 16 scoop
Pork chop with pocket	3 per lb, $1\frac{1}{2}$ oz stuffing (tongs)
Roasts, meat or poultry	3 oz cooked (tongs)
with dressing	2–3 oz meat cooked; 4 oz ($\frac{1}{2}$ c), No. 10 scoop, rounded, of dressing
Sausage, bulk	3 oz before cooking (tongs)
Sausages, link, 14 to 16 per lb.	2 (tongs)
Spareribs	8–12 oz before cooking (tongs)
Steak, braised, Swiss, etc.	6–7 oz raw, 4 to 5 oz cooked (spoon)
Steak, dinner, dry-heat type	8 oz AP, no bone (tongs); size may vary with institution
Steak, ground	3 per lb, No. 8 scoop rounded; 4 oz cooked (tongs)
Steak, stuffed	5–6 oz before cooking; $1\frac{1}{2}$ oz dressing (tongs)
Stew	No. 8 scoop rounded or 6-oz ($\frac{3}{4}$-c) ladle, rounded
Veal birds	5 oz before cooking; $1\frac{1}{2}$ oz dressing (spoon)
Veal cutlet	4 oz before breading; 5 oz breaded
Veal chop	5 oz
Wieners, 10 to lb	2 (tongs)

continued

TABLE A-5. Standard portions for entrées and accompaniments (*continued*)

Food	Portion and serving method
FISH	
Fillet, baked or fried	3 per lb before cooking; 4 oz if breaded
Steak	3 per lb
Creamed fish dishes	4-oz ladle, rounded; 1 slice toast, 1 biscuit or No. 16 scoop of rice
Shrimp wiggle	4-oz ladle, rounded; slice of toast or biscuit or No. 16 scoop of rice
Shrimp, deep fried, fantail	4–5 (tongs)
Strips, breaded, deep-fried	1 oz each, serve 3 (tongs); about 35% breading
Croquettes	No. 10 scoop for 1; No. 20 scoop for two; 1½ oz sauce
Loaf	4-oz slice; in 17 × 25 pan, cut 5 × 9, in 12 × 20 pan, cut 4 × 6; bake 1 in. deep in these
Scalloped salmon, tuna, etc.	1 4-oz ladle, rounded, 5–6 oz; if thick, use rounded serving spoon
Fish and noodles	Serving spoon, rounded, 5–6 oz
Tuna, potato chip dish	Serving spoon, rounded, 5–6 oz
Souffle	Cut 17 × 25 pan, 5 × 9; 12 × 20 pan, 4 × 6
POULTRY	
Chicken fricassée, unboned	12 oz raw meat (spoon)
Chicken, creamed	6 oz (¾ c); about 2 oz cooked chicken per portion
Chicken, fried	2 pieces or 1 half (12 oz before cooking)
Chicken or turkey, roast	2–3 oz with dressing, 4 oz without, 2 oz gravy
Duck or goose	12–16 oz before cooking
LUNCHEON ENTRÉES*	
American noodles	5 oz, 1 well-rounded serving spoon
Baked beans	6-oz ladle or 2 serving spoons or 1 heaped serving spoon
Baked lima beans	6 oz, 1 heaped serving spoon
Baked eggs, creole	4-oz ladle, rounded
Baked rice and cheese	5 oz (⅔ c), 1 well-rounded serving spoon
Beef biscuit roll	1 4-in.-diameter; 2-oz ladle gravy
Buttered apples with sausage	3 apple halves, 2 sausages
Cheeseburgers	1 No. 16 scoop, 2 each; slice cheese ¾–1 oz each
Cheese fondue	4 oz, 1 oz sauce; cut 12 × 20 pan 4 × 6; use spoon and ladle
Creole spaghetti	1 well-rounded serving spoon (6 oz)
Eggs à la king or creamed eggs	2 halves egg on half slice of toast; 2 oz sauce
Omelet	4 oz (spoon); if cut, use spatula
Goulash	6-oz ladle
Italian delight	4-oz ladle
Italian spaghetti	1 heaped serving spoon spaghetti, 4 oz ladle sauce
Macaroni and cheese	1 heaped serving spoon, 5–6 oz
Macaroni hoe	1 heaped serving spoon, 5–6 oz
Meat soufflé	1 heaped serving spoon, 1½ oz sauce
Pizza pie	Cut 18 × 20-in. baking sheet 4 × 5; use spatula
Scalloped ham and potatoes	1 heaped serving spoon, 5–6 oz
Scalloped meat dishes	1 heaped serving spoon, 5–6 oz
Scrapple	4 oz, 2 slices
Spanish rice	1 well-rounded serving spoon, 5 oz
Stuffed cabbage	1 or 2
Swedish meatballs	2 2-oz meatballs after cooking; portion with rounded No. 20 scoop

continued

TABLE A-5. Standard portions for entrées and accompaniments (*continued*)

Food	Portion and serving method
Tamale pie	1 heaped serving spoon, 5–6 oz
Welsh rarebit	4-oz (½-c) ladle, on toast, biscuit, or No. 16 scoop rice

VEGETABLES

Food	Portion and serving method
Most canned vegetables	3 oz (½ c), 1 rounded serving spoon
Apples, buttered, cooked	½ c, 3–4 pieces (serving spoon)
Asparagus tips	3–5 canned, 4 to 6 fresh
Beans, navy, lima or other	4–5 oz (serving spoon)
Beets, Harvard	½ c, 1 rounded serving spoon
Beet greens, other greens	3 oz (½ c) (tongs or serving spoon)
Broccoli, buttered	2–3 pieces, 3 to 4 oz (tongs)
Cabbage, steamed, fried, etc.	3 oz (½ c) (serving spoon)
Onions, creamed	2–3 small onions (serving spoon)
Potato puff	5 oz, ⅔ c (spoon)
Potato, browned, steamed, etc.	5 oz (serving spoon)
Potato, au gratin, creamed, etc.	4–5 oz (serving spoon)
Potato, baked	5–6 oz (tongs)
Potato, hash brown, etc.	4–5 oz (serving spoon)
Potato, mashed	1 No. 10 scoop or serving spoon, 4 oz
Potato, French fried	4 oz, 8–10 pieces (tongs or spoon)
Potato cakes	4 oz (serving spoon)
Rice, steamed	No. 10 scoop, rounded (⅔ c)
Squash, acorn, baked or steamed	⅓ or ½ squash
Squash, hubbard	6–7 oz piece before baking
Squash, mashed	4 oz; 1 rounded serving spoon
Sweet potatoes, baked	5–6 oz (tongs)
Sweet potatoes, candied or glazed	2 slices, 4 oz
Scalloped sweet potatoes and apples	4 oz (serving spoon)
Tomatoes, escalloped or stewed	4-oz ladle
Vegetable pie	5 oz, 1 well-rounded serving spoon
Vegetables, creamed	3–4 oz

SALADS

Food	Portion and serving method
Coleslaw	3 oz (serving spoon)
Cottage cheese	No. 20 scoop
Deviled egg	2 halves
Gelatin	12 × 20 pan, 1 in. deep, cut 5 × 10; 50 portions
Mixed fruit	1 rounded serving spoon, No. 12 scoop
Mixed vegetable	1 rounded serving spoon
Sliced tomato	2 large or 3 medium slices
Head lettuce, 1 lb average	⅛ head, 2 oz serving
Potato, cold or hot	1 No. 10 or No. 12 scoop (4–5 oz)
Waldorf	1 rounded serving spoon, 3 oz
Fish or meat salad, entrée type	5–6 oz, 1 c
Brown bean	4–5 oz

continued

TABLE A-5. Standard portions for entrées and accompaniments
(continued)

Food	Portion and serving method
DRESSINGS AND SAUCES	
Mayonnaise, boiled, etc.	1–2 T; portion depends upon salad size
French or other liquid	1–2 T; portion depends upon salad size
Cranberry sauce, apple-sauce, etc.	1–2 T (2–2½ oz), 1 scant serving spoon or No. 16 scoop
SOUP	
Cup	6 oz, ¾ c
Bowl	8 oz, 1 c
Tureen	10–12 oz, 1¼–1½ c
BREADS	
Biscuits	2–3, 1 oz each (raw weight)
Bran rolls	2, 1 oz each (raw weight)
Cinnamon rolls	2, 1½ oz each (raw weight)
Cornbread, coffee cake, etc.	1 piece, 2 oz; cut 18 × 26 in. baking sheet 6 × 8
Muffins	2, 2½ oz each (raw weight)
Griddlecakes	3, 3–4 oz each (raw weight)
Potato doughnuts	2, 2 oz each (raw weight)
Hot rolls	2, 1 oz each (raw weight)
Sweet-dough items, breakfast	1, 3 oz each (raw weight)
White or other bread, sliced	1–2 slices, 1 oz each

* A 12 × 20-in. baking pan filled 4 in. deep with food (16–18 lb of food) may be cut 5 × 8 to give 40 6–7 oz portions. (Use 6-in.-deep pan)

TABLE A-6. Standard portions for desserts

Food	Pan size	Portion
BUTTER CAKES		
Sheet, 1-layer	18 × 26 in.	Cut 6 × 8 (48 portions)
	13½ × 22⅞ in.	Cut 5 × 9 or 6 × 8 (45 or 48 portions)
	12¾ × 23 in.	Cut 5 × 9 or 6 × 8 (45 or 48 portions)
Sheet, 2-layer	18 × 26 in.	Cut 12 × 5 (60 portions)
	13½ × 22⅞ in.	Cut 3 × 20 (60 portions)
	12¾ × 23 in.	Cut 3 × 20 (60 portions)
Square, 1-layer	9½ × 9½ in.	Cut 3 × 4 (12 portions)
Square, 2-layer	9½ × 9½ in.	Cut 3 × 7 (21 portions)
Round, 2-layer	8-in. diameter	Cut into 12 portions
Angel food	16 oz	Cut into 16 portions
Chocolate roll, jelly roll, etc	18 × 26 in., rolled	34–36 portions
Cupcakes	1 No. 16 scoop	1 each
Doughnuts, cake	1 oz	2
COOKIES		
Brownies, date bars, etc	18 × 26 in.	Cut 54; serve 1 each
	13½ × 22⅞ in.	Cut 5 × 9 (45 portions)

continued

TABLE A-6. Standard portions for desserts (*continued*)

Food	Pan size	Portion
PIES		
One- or two-crust	10 in.	Cut into 8 portions
(use marker)	9 in.	Cut into 7 portions
	8 in.	Cut into 6 portions
Crust, double	9 in.	12 oz
Crust, single	9 in.	$6\frac{1}{2}$ oz
Filling, cream	9 in.	$1\frac{1}{2}$–2 pt ($1\frac{1}{2}$–2 lb)
Filling, custard	9 in.	$1\frac{1}{2}$ pt ($1\frac{1}{2}$ lb)
Filling, fruit	9 in.	$1\frac{1}{2}$ pt ($1\frac{1}{2}$ lb)
PUDDINGS		
Apple crisp, brown betty, etc		4 oz
Apricot whip		$\frac{3}{4}$ c
Bread pudding	$13\frac{1}{2} \times 22\frac{7}{8}$ in.	$\frac{1}{2}$ c; cut 5 × 9
Cobblers, etc	$13\frac{1}{2} \times 22\frac{7}{8}$ in.	$\frac{1}{2}$ c; cut 5 × 9
	12 × 20 in.	$\frac{1}{2}$ c; cut 6 × 8
Cream, rice, tapioca, etc		$\frac{1}{2}$ c; No. 10 scoop
Cream puff or éclair batter		1 oz (small), 2 oz (large)
Cream puff or éclair filling		$1\frac{1}{2}$ oz; No. 20 scoop
Icebox cake	$12\frac{3}{4} \times 23$ in.	Cut 5 × 10
Icebox pudding		No. 20 scoop
Jello	$12\frac{3}{4} \times 23$ in.	Cut 5 × 9
	12 × 20 in.	Cut 6 × 8
Whipped cream topping		2 T (2 qt = 100 portions)
ICE CREAM		
Brick (1 qt)		Cut into 8 portions
Bulk		No. 12 scoop
Sundae		No. 16 scoop; 2 oz sauce
MISCELLANEOUS		
Graham cracker roll, etc	$9\frac{5}{8} \times 5\frac{1}{2} \times 3\frac{1}{4}$-in. loaf	Cut into 16 portions
Pineapple delicious		$\frac{1}{2}$ c; No. 10 scoop rounded
Shortcake		$2\frac{1}{2}$-in. diameter biscuit; $\frac{1}{3}$ c fruit; 2 T whipped cream
Steamed pudding	1-qt mold	Cut into 12 $3\frac{1}{2}$-oz portions; 2 oz sauce
	12 × 20 in.	Cut 6 × 10
Meringues		2-oz ($\frac{1}{3}$-c) ladle syrup or sauce; 2 T whipped cream
Sauces for topping		3 T (vary with richness)

NOTE: The following batch amounts are generally valid: 8 8-in. round 2-layer cakes serve 96; 6 9 × 13-in. 1-layer sheet cakes serve 96; 1 9 × 13-in. 2-layer sheet cake serves 30; 4 12-in. round 2-layer cakes serve 120; and 3 14-in. round 2-layer cakes serve 120.

TABLE A-7. Canned foods: servings per can or jar

Product	Content—can or jar (approx.)			Size of each serving (approx.)
	Net weight or volume	Cups or pieces	Servings	
FRUITS				
Apples; applesauce; berries; cherries; grapes; grapefruit and orange sections; fruit cocktail; fruits for salad; sliced peaches; pears; pineapple, chunks, crushed, tidbits	8¼–8¾ oz	1 c	2	½ c
	16–17 oz	1¾–2 c	4	½ c
	1 lb 4 oz	2¼–2½ c	5	½ c
	1 lb 13 oz	3¼–3½ c	7	½ c
	6 lb 2 oz–6 lb 12 oz	12–13 c	25	½ c
Apricots, whole (medium size)	16–17 oz	8–14	4	2–3 apricots
	1 lb 13 oz	15–18	7	2–3 apricots
	6 lb 10 oz	50–60	25	2–3 apricots
Apricots, halves (medium size)	8¾ oz	6–12	2	3–5 halves
	16 to 17 oz	12–20	4	3–5 halves
	1 lb 13 oz	26–35	7	3–5 halves
	6 lb 10 oz	95–130	25	3–5 halves
Peaches or pears, halves	16–17 oz	6–10	3	2 medium halves
	1 lb 13 oz	7–12	7	1 large half
	6 lb 10 oz	45–65	25	2 medium halves
Pineapple, sliced	9 oz	4	2	2 slices
	1 lb 4 oz	10	5	2 slices
	1 lb 14 oz	8	8	1 large slice
	6 lb 12 oz	28–50	25	1 large or 2 small slices
Plums or prunes	8¾ oz	7–9	2	2–3 plums
	16–17 oz	10–14	4	2–3 plums
	1 lb 14 oz	12–20	7	2–3 plums
	6 lb 10 oz	40–60	25	2–3 plums
Figs	8–9 oz	6–12	2	3–4 figs
	16–17 oz	12–20	4	3–4 figs
	1 lb 14 oz	18–24	7	3–4 figs
	7 lb	70–90	25	3–4 figs

Cranberry sauce	6–8 oz	¾–1 c	4	¼ c
	1 lb	2 c	8	¼ c
	7 lb 5 oz	12–13 c	50	¼ c
Olives, ripe, drained	4½ oz	varies	varies	3 olives
	9 oz	varies	varies	3 olives
	1 lb 2 oz	varies	varies	3 olives
	4 lb 2 oz	varies	varies	3 olives
VEGETABLES				
Asparagus cuts; beans, green, wax, kidney, lima; beets; carrots; corn; hominy; okra; onions; peas; peas and carrots; black-eyed peas; pumpkin; sauerkraut; spinach and other greens; squash; succotash; sweet potatoes; tomatoes; mixed vegetables; potatoes; white, cut, sliced	8–8½ oz	1 c	2	½ c
	12 oz	¾–1½ c	4	½ c
	16–17 oz	2 c	4	½ c
	1 lb 4 oz	2¼–2½ c	5	½ c
	1 lb 13 oz	3¼–3½ c	7	½ c
	6 lb 2 oz–6 lb 12 oz	12–13 c	25	½ c
Asparagus spears (medium size)	10½ oz	9–12	2	4–6 spears
	14¼–16 oz	16–28	3	4–6 spears
	1 lb 3 oz	20–30	5	4–6 spears
	4 lb 4 oz	115–145	25	4–6 spears
Potatoes, white, peeled, whole, small	16–17 oz	8–12	4	2–3 potatoes
	6 lb 6 oz	55–65	25	2–3 potatoes
Beans, baked, with pork, in sauce	8¾ oz	1 c	1–2	½–¾ c
	1 lb	1¾ c	3–4	½–¾ c
	1 lb 10 oz	3 c	4–6	½–¾ c
	6 lb 14 oz	12–13 c	16–25	½–¾ c
Mushrooms	2 oz	⅓ c	1	⅓ c
	4 oz	⅔ c	2	⅓ c
	8 oz	1½ c	4	⅓ c
	6 lb 7 oz	12–13 c	36	⅓ c
Pimientos; peppers, red, sweet	2 oz	¼ c	—	—
	4 oz	½ c	—	—
	7 oz	1 c	—	—
	6 lb 13 oz	12–13 c	—	—

continued

TABLE A-7. Canned foods: servings per can or jar (*continued*)

Product	Content—can or jar (approx.)			Size of each serving (approx.)
	Net weight or volume	Cups or pieces	Servings	
JUICES				
Apple; cherry; cranberry; grape; grapefruit; grapefruit-orange; loganberry; nectars; orange; pineapple; prune; tangerine; carrot; sauerkraut; tomato; vegetable cocktail; vegetable	6–8 oz	¾–1 c	1–2	4–6 oz
	12 fl oz	1½ c	3	4 oz
			2	6 oz
	1 pt	2 c	4	4 oz
			3	6 oz
	1 pt 2 fl oz	2¼–2½ c	5	4 oz
			3	6 oz
	1 pt 7 fl oz	3 c	6	4 oz
			4	6 oz
	1 qt	4 c	8	4 oz
			5	6 oz
	1 qt 14 fl oz	5¾ c	12	4 oz
			8	6 oz
	3 qt	12 c	24	4 oz
			16	6 oz
Lemon; lime	5½–6 oz	¾ c	—	—
SOUPS				
Condensed	10½–12 oz	1¼ c (2½ c prepared soup)	3	¾ c
	3 lb 2 oz	5¾ c (11½ c prepared soup)	12–16	¾ c
Ready-to-serve	8 fl oz indiv.	1 c	1	1 c
	12 fl oz	1½ c	2	¾ c
	15 fl oz	2 c	3	¾ c
	1 pt 5 fl oz–1 pt 9 fl oz	2½–3 c	4	¾ c
	3 qt	12 c	20	¾ c

MEATS AND POULTRY

Chili con carne, with or without beans	15–16 oz	2 c	3–4	$\frac{1}{2}$–$\frac{2}{3}$ c
	1½ lb	3 c	4–5	$\frac{1}{2}$–$\frac{2}{3}$ c
	6 lb 12 oz	12–13 c	18–24	$\frac{1}{2}$–$\frac{2}{3}$ c
Corned beef	12 oz	—	4	3 oz
	6 lb		30	3 oz
Corned beef hash	8 oz	1 c	1–2	$\frac{1}{2}$–$\frac{2}{3}$ c
	1 lb	2 c	3–4	$\frac{1}{2}$–$\frac{2}{3}$ c
	1½ lb	3 c	5–6	$\frac{1}{2}$–$\frac{2}{3}$ c
	5 lb 8 oz–5 lb 14 oz	12–13 c	18–24	$\frac{1}{2}$–$\frac{2}{3}$ c
Deviled ham	2¼–3 oz	$\frac{1}{3}$ c	3–4	1½ T
	4½ oz	$\frac{1}{2}$ c	5–6	1½ T
Deviled meat; potted meat; meat spreads	2–3¼ oz	$\frac{1}{3}$ c	3–4	1½ T
	5½ oz	$\frac{3}{4}$ c	8	1½ T
Luncheon meat	12 oz	—	4	2 slices (3½ × 1¼ × $\frac{3}{16}$ in.)
	6 lb	—	32	
Tongue, beef, lamb, pork	6 oz	—	2	3 oz
	12 oz	—	4	3 oz
Hams, whole (small)	1–2 lb	—	5–10	3 oz
(medium)	1½–4 lb			2 slices (4 × 3 × $\frac{1}{8}$ in.)
(large)	6–8 lb			
	9–14 lb		3–4/lb	
Poultry, boned, chicken or turkey	5–6 oz	—	2	3 oz
	12 oz		4	3 oz
	1 lb 14 oz		10	3 oz
	2 lb 3 oz		12	3 oz
Sausage, pork, frankfurters	8 oz	11–12	3–4	3 sausages
	12 oz	8–9 large	4	2 sausages
Stew, beef or lamb	1 lb	2 c	2	$\frac{3}{4}$ c
	1 lb 4 oz	2½ c	3	$\frac{3}{4}$ c
	1½ lb	3 c	4	$\frac{3}{4}$ c
Vienna sausage	4 oz	8–10	2	4–5 sausages
	9 oz	16–20	4	4–5 sausages

continued

TABLE A-7. Canned foods: servings per can or jar (continued)

| Product | Content—can or jar (approx.) | | | Size of each serving (approx.) |
	Net weight or volume	Cups or pieces	Servings	
FISH AND SEAFOOD				
Clams	$7\frac{1}{2}$ oz	1 c	2	$\frac{1}{2}$ c
Crab meat	$5\frac{1}{2}$–$7\frac{1}{2}$ oz	$\frac{3}{4}$–1 c	2–3	$\frac{1}{3}$–$\frac{1}{2}$ c
Mackerel	1 lb	2 c	4	$\frac{1}{2}$ c
Oysters	8 oz	1 c	2	$\frac{1}{2}$ c
Salmon	$7\frac{3}{4}$ oz	1 c	2	$\frac{1}{2}$ c
	1 lb	2 c	4	$\frac{1}{2}$ c
Sardines	$3\frac{1}{4}$–4 oz	6–10	$1\frac{1}{2}$	5–7 sardines
Sardines, pilchards	15 oz	6–7 large	4	$1\frac{1}{2}$ sardines
Shrimp, drained	$4\frac{1}{2}$–$6\frac{1}{2}$ oz	25–35	3–4	10–12 medium size; 6–8 jumbo size
Tuna in oil	6–7 oz	1 c	2	$\frac{1}{2}$ c
	13 oz	$1\frac{3}{4}$ c	4	$\frac{1}{2}$ c
INFANT FOODS				
Vegetables and Fruits				
Infant: strained; homogenized	$4\frac{3}{4}$ oz	$\frac{1}{2}$ c	—	—
Junior: chopped	$6\frac{1}{2}$ oz	$\frac{3}{4}$ c	—	—
	8 oz	$\frac{7}{8}$ c	—	—
Meats				
Infant: strained	$3\frac{1}{2}$ oz	7 T	—	—
Junior: chopped	$3\frac{1}{2}$ oz	7 T	—	—
Soups				
Infant	$4\frac{3}{4}$ oz	$\frac{1}{2}$ c	—	—
Junior	8 oz	$\frac{7}{8}$ oz	—	—

Notes: The net weight of various foods in the same size can or glass jar varies with the density of the food; for the most part, only minimum weights are shown in the table. Cups or pieces and servings are approximated in the table, and sizes of servings are given in rounded numbers.

TABLE A-8. Can sizes

| Size can | Approximate quantity | | Products contained |
	Net weight	Cups	
8 oz	8 oz	1	
Picnic	10½–12 oz	1¼	Fruits, vegetables, specialties
12 oz (vacuum)	12 oz	1½	Soups, fruits, vegetables, meat and fish specialties
No. 300	14–16 oz	1¾	Pork and beans, baked beans, meat products, cranberry sauce, blueberries, specialties
No. 303	16–17 oz	2	Fruits, vegetables, meats, ready-to-serve soups, specialties
No. 2	1 lb 4 oz or 1 pt 2 fl oz	2½	Juices, ready-to-serve soups, fruits, vegetables, specialties
No. 2½	1 lb 13 oz	3½	Fruits, pumpkin, sauerkraut, pork and beans, greens, tomatoes
No. 3 cylinder or 46 oz	3 lb 3 oz or 1 qt 14 fl oz	5¾	Fruit juices, vegetable juices, pork and beans, condensed soup, some vegetables
No. 10	6 lb 8 oz–7 lb 5 oz*	12–13	Fruits and vegetables for institutional use

* Jellies, jams, and other heavy items will weigh more than this.

TABLE A-9. Can substitutions for no. 10 size

Net weight of no. 10	Cans to substitute	Net weight substituted
6 lb 10 oz	7 No. 303's	7 lb
6 lb 10 oz	5 No. 2's	6 lb 2 oz
6 lb 10 oz	4 No. 2½'s	7 lb 2 oz
6 lb 10 oz	2 No. 46 oz or 2 No. 3 cylinder	5 lb 12 oz–6 lb 4 oz

**TABLE A-10. Fiber content of some foods
(g per 100 g EP—slightly less than 4 oz)**

Item	Fiber	Item	Fiber	Item	Fiber
Almonds	2.6	Corn, puffed	0.4	Pears, raw, with	
Apple, raw	1.0	Cornbread	0.2–0.5	skin	1.4
Applesauce, sweet	0.6	Cornmeal, cooked	0.1	Peas	2.0
Artichoke	2.4	Crackers, white	0.1–0.4	Pecans	2.3
Asparagus	0.7	Crackers, graham	1.1	Peppers, sweet	1.4
Avocado	1.6	Cranberries	1.4	Pickles, cucumber	0.5
Bamboo shoots	0.7	Cucumber, raw	0.3	Pimientos, canned	0.6.
Bananas	0.5	Dandelion greens	1.3	Pineapple, raw	0.4
Barley, pearl	0.5	Eggplant	0.9	Pizza	0.3–0.4
Beans, dry, cooked	1.5	Endive or escarole,		Plums	0.4–0.6
Beans, lima, cooked	1.8	raw	0.9	Popcorn, popped	1.7
Beans, snap	0.6	Figs, raw	1.2	Potatoes, boiled	0.5
Beets	0.7	Figs, canned	0.7	Potato chips	1.6
Beet greens	1.1	Filberts (hazelnuts)	3.0	Peas	2.0
Blueberries, raw	1.5	Fruit cocktail or		Prunes, cooked	0.8
Bran, wheat	7.8	fruit salad	0.4	Pumpkin, canned	1.9
Bran flakes (40%)	6.5	Gooseberries, raw	1.9	Radishes, raw	0.7
Brazil nuts	3.1	Grapefruit, pulp	0.2	Raisins, dry	0.9
Bread, white	0.2	Grapes, raw	0.6	Raspberries, raw	0.3–0.5
Bread, whole-wheat	1.6	Guava	5.6	Rhubarb, cooked	0.6
Bulgar	1.7	Jam	0.1	Rice, white, cooked	0.1
Cabbage	0.8	Kale	1.1	Rice, brown, cooked	0.3
Cakes, plain	0.1–0.3	Kohlrabi	1.0	Rutabagas	1.1
Carrots	1.0	Kumquats, raw	3.7	Salsify	1.8
Cashews	2.6	Lentils, cooked	1.2	Sauerkraut	0.7
Cauliflower	0.6	Lettuce, raw	0.5–0.7	Soybean sprouts	1.4
Celery	0.7	Loganberries, raw	2.0	Spinach	0.6
Chard, Swiss	0.7	Macadamia nuts	2.5	Squash, summer	0.6
Chayote, raw	0.7	Macaroni products,		Squash, winter	1.5
Cherries, sweet	0.6	cooked	0.1	Strawberries, raw	0.6
Chestnuts	1.1	Melons, raw	0.3–0.6	Succotash	0.9
Cocoa powder	4.3	Mushrooms,		Sweet potatoes or	
Coconut, dried	4.0	cooked	0.8	yams	0.6
Coleslaw	0.7	Mustard greens	0.9	Tomatoes, raw	0.5
Collards	0.7	Noodles	0.1	Tomatoes, cooked	0.6
Cookies, plain	0.1–0.4	Oatmeal, cooked	0.2	Tomatoes, canned	0.4
Cookies, fig bars	1.7	Okra	1.0	Turnips	0.9
Cookies, macaroons	2.1	Olives	1.4	Turnip greens	0.7
Cookies, oatmeal	0.8	Onions, dry	0.6	Walnut meats	2.1
Corn, sweet, cob	0.7	Onions, green, raw	1.0	Wheat flour, white	0.3
Corn, cream style	0.5	Oranges, pulp	0.4–0.5	Whole-wheat flour	2.3
Corn, kernel	0.8	Papaya, raw	0.9	Wheat, rolled,	
Cornflakes	0.7	Parsnips	2.0	cooked	0.5
		Peaches, raw	0.5	Wheat flakes	1.6
		Peanuts, roasted,		Wheat, puffed	2.0
		no skins	2.4	Wheat, shredded	2.3

NOTES: Fiber quantities listed for all vegetables are cooked and drained-weight values, unless otherwise noted. The source of these data (USDA, *Composition of Foods*, Agricultural Handbook No. 8, U.S. Government Printing Office, Washington, D.C., 1963) does not indicate whether crude or dietary fiber is being identified, but the date of printing would suggest that the values stated are for crude fiber.

Appendix B
Converting to the
Metric System

The metric system originated in France, following the French Revolution. For a long time, the French had used a very cumbersome system of weights and measures, but at this point they decided to introduce a new system based on decimal units. They also wanted to make the translation of weights into measures and vice versa as simple as possible.

The basic unit they selected for weight was the gram, defined as the weight of 1 cubic millimeter of water at 20°C; thus, 1,000 cubic millimeters of water at this temperature weighed 1 kilogram (1,000 grams). Various terms and prefixes taken from the Greek language were used to indicate values. Among these are the following:

Liter: Basic unit of volume; is equal to the volume of 1,000 grams of water; slightly more than our quart.
Gram: Basic unit of weight; 1,000 grams is the weight of 1 liter of water and is equivalent to about 2.2 pounds.
Meter: Basic unit of length; slightly longer than our yard.
Deca-: Means 10 times; thus, 1 decameter is 10 meters.
Hecto-: Means 100 times; thus, 1 hectoliter is 100 liters.
Kilo-: Means 1,000 times; thus, 1 kilogram is 1,000 grams.
Mega-: Means 1,000,000 times; thus, 1 megacycle is 1 million cycles.
Giga-: Means 1 billion times; thus, 1 gigameter is 1 billion meters.
Tera-: Means 1 trillion times; thus, 1 teragram is 1 trillion grams.
Deci-: Means 1 tenth of; such as 1 decimeter.
Centi-: Means 1 hundredth of; such as 1 centigram.
Milli-: Means 1 thousandth of; such as 1 milliliter.
Micro-: Means 1 millionth of; such as 1 micrometer.
Nano-: Means 1 billionth of; such as 1 nanoliter.
Pico-: Means 1 trillionth of; such as 1 picometer.

Thus, a hectometer is 100 meters. To indicate 100 square meters, the term *hectare* is used; 1 hectare is approximately 2.5 acres.

To translate one of our units of weight or measure into metric units, we need to know how much or how many units we have; then we can multiply this value by the value given in table 3-3 on page 91. For instance, if we have 6 feet and wish to change this to meters, the table indicates that we multiply the number of feet by 30 to get centimeters; this gives a value of 180, and since there are 100 centimeters

465

**TABLE B-1. British imperial fluid
measure conversion to metric values**

When you know:	You can find:	If you multiply by:
British Ounces	Milliliters	28.400
British Pints	Liters	0.568
British Quarts	Liters	1.136
British Gallons	Liters	4.544
Milliliters	British Ounces	0.035
Liters	British Pints	1.760
Liters	British Quarts	0.883
Liters	British Gallons	0.220

to the meter, we have 1.8 meters. If we wish to move from metric to our own system, table 3-3 also lists factors by which to multiply the metric value. For instance, if we have a value of 700 grams and want to change this value into ounces, we consult the table and find that the metric value should be multiplied by 0.035, giving a result of 24½ ounces.

There are other ways to translate metric quantities into our values or our values into metric. For instance, there are slightly more than 28 grams in 1 ounce, or 454 in 1 pound. Thus, if we have 10 ounces and want to change this into grams, we could estimate the amount as 10 × 28 = 280 grams. Or if we have 1½ pounds in a recipe, the translation would be 1½ × 454 = 681 grams. Various precisely equivalent values between our system and the metric system are given in tables 3-7 through 3-11 on pages 101–103. These values are slightly more accurate than those computable from table 3-3; however, table 3-3 is much simpler to use.

Table 3-3 is suitable for translating all Canadian and English values except Imperial or British liquid volumes. This is because the Imperial gallon (used in British Commonwealth countries) is 277.42 cubic inches, while ours is only 231 cubic inches. This makes all British units of volume 1.20 times larger than the American, including the British pint, quart, and other standard liquid units based on the gallon. If we wish to translate American units into British, we must multiply by 1.2; to translate British units back into American, we must multiply by 0.833. Table 3-8 on page 102 gives equivalents of many such values, already worked out. Thus, we see in this table that an Imperial pint equals 0.15 American gallons, 0.6 American quarts, 1.2 American pints, and 4.8 American gills. The metric measure and weight values are also given for the Imperial units.

The difference in the fluid ounce between the American and British ounces is not the same as the other fluid measures. In the United States a fluid ounce is $\frac{1}{16}$ pint or 29.6 cc (cubic centimeters) or 455.1 grains.* The British ounce is $\frac{1}{20}$ pint, which is therefore 28.4 cc or 437.5 grains. (The British pint is 568 cc or 568 grams.) Table B-1 gives a multiplying factor similar to those in table 3-3 and converts the British liquid volume into metric values and vice versa.

Our American cup used in measuring ingredients is about ¼ liter—but not quite, since it contains in fluid measure 236 milliliters. There are 16 tablespoons in 1 cup, which makes 1 tablespoon in our measure equal to 15 milliliters. There are 3 teaspoons in 1 tablespoon, so 1 teaspoon holds 5 milliliters. (In British values, 1 cup equals 284 ml (milliliters), 1 tablespoon equals 18 ml, and 1 teaspoon equals 6 ml.)

An American cup of molasses or honey weighs about 300 grams, and a British cup of such material weighs about 360 grams. An American cup of flour, on the

* A grain was set long ago as the weight of a grain of wheat.

other hand, weighs about 110 grams (British, about 132 grams). It is much wiser in working with most foods not to measure but to weigh; and recipes should call for weights rather than measures whenever possible, because this gives far more accuracy and more standard products.

Using such equivalents as given in this appendix, the recipe for béchamel sauce on page 22 would translate into metric values as follows:

1. 1 gallon = 3.8 liters, so 2 × 3.8 = 7.6 liters is the total yield.
2. A $\frac{1}{4}$-c portion is calculated as 236 × 0.25 = 60 ml.
3. The $1\frac{1}{2}$ gal white stock would be $1\frac{1}{2}$ × 3.8 = 5.7 liters.
4. 2 oz sliced onions or $\frac{1}{4}$ cup would be respectively 55 grams or 60 ml.
5. The carrots would be 225 grams or about 350 ml.
6. Since the bay leaves are by count, there is no change in values.
7. 1 lb butter is 450 grams or 2 c or about 470 ml.
8. 1 lb flour is 450 grams or 4 c or about 940 ml—almost 1 liter.
9. 1 gal milk is 3.8 liters.
10. $\frac{1}{2}$ oz salt is about 15 grams, and 1 T equals 15 ml.
11. 1 t pepper equals 5 ml.

Undoubtedly, as we move into the metric system, many recipes will be retested; and some slightly different amounts of ingredients may eventually be specified to round off values in metric units—such differences not causing an appreciable difference in the product. Many of the tables we use will also have to be revised. For instance, the beginning of table A-4 (page 447) can easily be revised to express metric amounts:

BEVERAGES

Cocoa	100 g	235 ml (1 c)
Coffee, urn grind	100 g	235 ml (1 c)
Coffee, instant	25 g	120 ml ($\frac{1}{2}$ c)
Tea	100 g	330 ml ($1\frac{1}{3}$ c)

CEREALS AND CEREAL PRODUCTS

Barley, pearl	100 g	130 ml (0.55 c)

We will also change our kitchen measures. Our 2-oz ladle for portioning gravy will become a 60-ml ladle, although the size of the portion will remain about the same. Similarly, a No. 12 ice cream scoop (used as a tool to dish a rounded portion of about 3 oz) will become perhaps a 90-ml scoop. A basting spoon for holding a rounded 3 oz might be renamed a 90-ml spoon. Since potatoes are usually portioned at 5 oz, the standard portion will become perhaps 150 grams, but the same dishing tool will be used.

Gradually, the names and labeling will be changed to metric terms. We might have a bit of difficulty at first, but soon we will become accustomed to the change and see that it is much simpler and easy to use than our present one. We are working today with a terribly complex and cumbersome system, and it is high time we got rid of it.

Glossary

A la, à le (au, aux). *To the, with, at,* or *in;* in the mode of style; *à la Colbert,* with Colbert sauce; *au jus,* with natural juice; *à la moutarde,* in mustard.

Abaisse. Thin bottom crust or undercrust.

Abalone. Tenderized, thin muscle of a large sea mollusk; the portion looks much like a veal cutlet in shape and is like a scallop in texture, flavor, and color.

Abatis. Giblets; *abatis,* heads, liver, kidneys, giblets, and so forth.

Absinthe. A liqueur that has a licoricelike flavor.

Acids. Acidulated liquids used in cooking, such as plain or seasoned vinegar, lemon juice, tomato juice, and other tart liquids.

Agar. Seaweed product with gelatinous properties, used to make permanent emulsions.

Aide. Kitchen or dining room helper.

Aiguillettes. Small strips of cooked meat; stuffed puff pastes served as hors d'oeuvres.

Ail. Garlic; *aillade* or *aïoli,* mayonnaise garlic sauce that may also contain mustard.

A la king. With cream or béchamel sauce containing mushrooms, green peppers, and pimientos.

A la mode. In the usual fashion; *boeuf à la mode,* braised larded beef; *cake* or *pie à la mode,* topped with ice cream.

Alimentary pastes. Macaroni products, rice, and so forth.

Allemande. Velouté sauce thickened with egg yolks, *à l'allemande,* German style.

Almond. *Amande* (Fr.); *à l'amande,* slivered almonds sautéed lightly in butter and served over fish; *amandine,* served with almonds.

Almond paste. Ground almonds, sugar, and egg whites; also called *marzipan.*

Ambrosia. A mixture of fruit and coconut used as a dessert; *ambroisie* (Fr.).

Amontillado. A semidry sherry.

Anchovy. A small salted fish used for appetizers and seasoning; *anchois* (Fr.).

Andalouse. Spanish style; mayonnaise mixed with heavy red tomato purée and perhaps chopped peppers and pimientos; not to be confused with our Spanish sauce made of whole tomatoes, onion, peppers, and garlic, which is more heavily seasoned.

Angel food. A white cake leavened with egg whites.

Angels on horseback. Oysters broiled with strips of bacon around them and served on toast.

Anisette. A cordial heavily flavored with anise seed, giving it a licorice flavor.

Annatto. A yellow food coloring frequently used to color cheese and butter.

Antipasto. Italian hors d'oeuvres, relishes, and other foods used as a first course or as snacks.

Arroz con pollo. A Spanish dish of chicken and rice; the sauce usually has tomatoes in it.

Artichoke. *Artichaut* (Fr.); bud of a plant belonging to the thistle family and usually called *globe* or *French artichoke*, in contrast to the *Jerusalem* or *girasol artichoke*, which is a tuber resembling a potato.

Aspic. Gelatin-set mixture; may be clear or seasoned with meat stock, spices, tomato purée, or other foods; may be used as a glaze or as a body in which to set other foods.

Attereaux. Skewers; attereaux style is to alternate pieces of food on a skewer and then bake, broil, or cook.

Au beurre. Cooked in butter.

Au bleu. Live fish stunned with a sharp blow on the head, cleaned quickly, and plunged into a boiling, acidulated liquid or court bouillon; the flesh turns slightly blue.

Au four. Baked in an oven.

Au gras. Cooked in fat or covered with a rich meat gravy.

Au gratin. Escalloped and covered with cheese; food covered with a sauce (usually cream or béchamel), sprinkled with crumbs and cheese, and baked; cheese may be omitted.

Au lait. With milk.

Au jus. With natural gravy.

Au maigre. With no meat; a Lenten dish.

Au naturel. According to nature; cooked simply, or uncooked.

Baba. A light yeast-raised cake or rich sweetened bread; usually served soaked with rum and called *baba au rhum* (see *brioche*).

Bagels. Crisp hard rolls in the shape of a ring, frequently served with lox (salmon) during the Jewish holidays.

Bagration. Fish-base soup, made from a thin velouté, cooked macaroni, sole, fish quenelles, crayfish, and so forth; the macaroni and velouté base are the characteristic features.

Bain-marie. A hot-water bath for holding foods for service; a double boiler in which foods are cooked.

Bake. To cook by dry heat; now usually done in an oven, but occasionally done in ashes, under coals, or on heated stones or metals; when applied to meats it is called *roasting*.

Baked Alaska. Ice cream on cake covered with meringue and baked in a quick oven.

Banbury. A small tart filled with spiced citrus peels and raisins; also a small round English cheese.

Bannock. Scottish cake usually made of oatmeal or ground barley.

Barbecue. To roast slowly on a gridiron or spit over coals, or on hot stones in a covered pit or trench; while cooking, the food is usually basted with a highly seasoned sauce, or it may be cooked in the sauce, which is made of tomato catsup or purée, chili sauce, mustard, vinegar, spices, chopped vegetables, and perhaps some sweetening.

Bard. Bacon or salt pork slices used to cover poultry or fish in roasting.

Bar-le-Duc. A preserve of white currants; the term may also be applied to red currant jelly or to gooseberry, strawberry, or other fruit preserve; seeds should be removed.

Baron. Double sirloin of beef; saddle and leg of lamb or mutton.

Barquettes. Small pastry shells that are filled for hors d'oeuvres or desserts.

Baste. To moisten food while cooking, for added flavor or to prevent drying out; the liquid is usually melted fat, meat drippings, stock, water, water and fat, or a sauce.

Batter-dip. To dip into a batter consisting of egg, milk, flour, salt, leavening, and perhaps sugar; performed before deep-frying.

Bavarian. A fruit gelatin mixture into which whipped cream has been folded before setting; also called *bavarian cream; bavarois* (Fr.).

Béarnaise. Hollandaise sauce seasoned with tarragon; *à la béarnaise,* Swiss style; means from Bern, Switzerland.

Beat. To mix vigorously to incorporate air.

Beaten biscuit. A Southern unleavened bread made light by pounding and folding; phosphates have usually been added to the flour.

Béchamel. One of the basic sauces; made of chicken or veal stock, thickened with roux, and finished with rich milk or cream.

Beefsteak pie. A meat pie, two-thirds beef and one-third kidney, cooked with vegetables in a gravy and baked with a biscuit crust.

Beignets. Fritters.

Bel Paese. A soft, rich Italian cheese.

Benedictine. Orange-flavored liqueur originated by Benedictine monks.

Bercy. A sauce of white wine or lemon juice, onions, meat marrow, demiglaze, and melted butter; a fish sauce.

Beurre. See *butter.*

Bifsteck. A steak cut from the butt or large end of the beef tenderloin, usually weighing 5 to 6 ounces.

Bigarade. Brown sauce seasoned with orange peel and juice; may be slightly sweet and used with roast duck; the sour and bitter Seville orange is the best orange to use.

Bill of fare. The menu.

Biscuit. A small roll, either yeast or quick bread; a rusk, toast, and so forth; in French, *biscotte* usually means a rusk.

Bisque. A thick cream soup made of shellfish; also indicates a frozen dessert—ice cream with finely chopped nuts added.

Blanc. White; white sauce.

Blanch. To precook or cook in boiling water or steam (1) to inactivate enzymes and shrink food for canning, freezing, or drying (vegetables are blanched in boiling water or steam, fruits in boiling fruit juice, syrup, water, or steam); or (2) to aid in removal of skins from nuts and fruits; many items after blanching are then dipped into cold water.

Blancmange. Cold pudding made of cornstarch, milk, sugar, and flavoring; usually molded.

Blanquette. Stew or ragoût in white cream or velouté sauce; the meat is white, such as veal or chicken breast; a light fricassée.

Blend. To mix thoroughly two or more ingredients; a creaming paddle, wire whip, or pastry cutter may be used on a mechanical mixer; see *beat, cut, knead,* and *mix.*

Bluepoints. Small oysters, usually from Chesapeake Bay.

Boil. To cook in water or a liquid largely water at a boiling temperature (212°F at sea level).

Boitelle, à la. Cooked with mushrooms.

Bombe. Molded dessert of two or more ice creams; may also be called *bombe glacé.*

Bonbons. Candies or sweets.

Bonne femme. Term used for soups, stews, and so forth; simple home-style.

Bordelaise. Brown sauce seasoned with red wine, garlic, shallots, and diced or sliced poached marrow; onions are reduced in white wine, added to a velouté sauce, and finished with butter, after which tarragon is added for a white *bordelaise* or a *bonnefoy* sauce.

Border. (Fr.) *bordure (en);* to surround with a border, such as a planked item circled with duchess potatoes.

Borscht. Russian or Polish soup containing beets and cabbage and garnished with sour cream.

Boston cream pie. Two layers of cake filled between with cream pudding or custard sauce and topped with powdered sugar or whipped cream.

Bouchée. Small cake or small patty shell or choux paste with cream filling; literally, *mouthful*; may also be a small hors d'oeuvre made from puff paste.

Boucher. Butcher.

Bouillabaisse. Thick fish soup or stew; served in large soup plates or dishes, with toast, may be seasoned with saffron and should contain five or six different fish and shellfish, including mussels, clams, and lobsters; also called *soupe marseillaise.*

Bouillon. Soup; stock is richer than a broth and usually comes from beef; *bouilli* (Fr.), boiled beef.

Boulanger. Baker.

Boulettes. Forcemeat balls.

Bouquet garni. Parsley, bay leaves, thyme, onions, and other herbs finely chopped; usually tied in a small cloth and cooked with the food but removed when proper seasoning is attained; also called *sachet* or *fagot.*

Bourgeois. Natural; plain, family-style; *à la bourgeoise,* served with vegetables.

Bourguignonne. A brown sauce for fish, meat, and eggs, reduced with red wine and small cooked onions, with mussels added; for snails, a basic butter seasoned with chopped thyme, tarragon, garlic, chervil, marjoram, parsley, and lemon juice; cleaned, drained snails are returned to the shells and baked with this sauce.

Braise. To brown meat or vegetables in a small amount of fat, and then cook slowly in a covered utensil in a small quantity of liquid; the liquid may be juices from meat, water, milk, cream, stock, tomato juice, and so on.

Bread. (1) To coat with bread crumbs alone. (2) To coat with egg or liquid and then crumbs. (3) To coat with flour, egg, and/or liquid and then crumbs. To *egg* usually means to bread.

Bread sauce. Milk flavored with onions, bay leaf, and cloves, thickened with fresh white bread crumbs.

Bretonne. Brown sauce with tomatoes, chopped onions, and garlic; or cold tart sauce with mustard and horseradish, slightly sweetened.

Brie. A soft, rich French cheese.

Brioche. Baked yeast bread, frequently sweetened and almost rich enough to be called a cake; may be somewhat like sweet-dough products.

Brochet. A skewer; *en brochette,* meat and food roasted or broiled on a skewer; the term *à la broche* is also used.

Broil. To cook by radiant or direct heat.

Brouillé. Scrambled.

Brown betty. Rich cake or bread-crumb pudding, heavy with apples or other fruit.

Brown bread. Steamed bread served with baked beans; the bread usually is distinguished by the ingredients of white and rye flour, cornmeal, molasses, and raisins.

Brown sauce. One of the four basic sauces; see *espagnole.*

Brunoise. Vegetables or meat diced in ⅛-inch squares.

Brunswick stew. Southern dish of chicken, rabbit, or ground meat with corn, onions, okra, salt pork, tomatoes, and lima beans; the true stew is made of squirrel meat.

Brush. To clean with a stiff brush; to brush on ingredients such as butter and fondant frosting.

Bubble and squeak. Corned beef and cabbage.

Buffet. A large table displaying foods that are served from it; see *russe.*

Burn. To burn sugar on top of food with a hot poker, as for an omelet.

Butter. *Beurre* (Fr.); *au maître d'hôtel,* with soft butter spread over or with butter melted until it froths; *au meunière,* with browned butter; *au beurre noir,* with black butter; each is butter with a bit of lemon juice, a bit of cayenne, and parsley added. *Beurre fondu,* melted butter; *beurre d'anchois,* softened butter seasoned with anchovy paste. Many basic butters are used as spreads for canapes or in cooking as seasonings.

Café. Coffee; *café noir,* black coffee; *café au lait,* coffee with milk; also used to indicate a coffee house or restaurant.

Camambert. A rich, soft, French cheese.

Canapé. A small open-faced sandwich used as an appetizer; may be served on a fried or toasted piece of bread or crisp cereal product; the spread is tangy.

Canard. Duck; *canardeau* or *caneton,* young or female duck, respectively.

Candy. (1) When applied to fruit, fruit peel, or ginger, it means to cook in a heavy syrup until plump and transparent, and then to drain and dry; can also be called *crystallize.* (2) When applied to sweet potatoes and carrots, it means to cook in sugar or syrup.

Cannelloni. Thin strips of Italian paste stuffed with meat and cooked.

Capers. Small pickled buds used for garnish or seasoning; *câpre* (Fr.).

Capon. Desexed male chicken weighing usually from 5 to 6 lb.

Caramel. Sugar heavily browned; to *caramelize* is to heat sugar or foods containing sugar until a brown color and a characteristic flavor develops.

Carne. Spanish for meat; *chili con carne,* beans with meat.

Carré. Back and shoulders; the rack.

Casserole. A hollow mold of rice or potatoes or other products; a dish in which foods are braised or baked; a *cassolette* is an individual casserole.

Caviar. Salted roe of the sturgeon; see *roe.*

Cèpe. A wild mushroom.

Cervelat. A smoked bologna sausage.

Chablis. A white, good-bodied wine; sometimes called *white Burgundy.*

Champignon. Mushroom.

Chantilly. Sweetened and flavored whipped cream.

Chapon. *Capon* (Fr.); a crust of bread boiled or soaked in the soup; a crust of bread rubbed with garlic and placed in a salad for flavoring.

Charlotte russe. A mold lined with bread, cake, lady fingers, or sponge cake and filled with a bavarian; may also be bread or cake soaked with fruit sauce and served cold with whipped cream.

Chartreuse. A famous liqueur; a dish consisting of vegetables and no meat, after the custom of the monks who founded the Carthusian order.

Chasseur. A sauce consisting of equal parts brown and tomato sauce, with chopped onions or shallots, parsley, and a bit of lemon juice; often called *hunter sauce* on American menus.

Château, au. Specialty of the house; see *maison.*

Chateaubriand. A steak weighing about 12 oz or more, cut from the center of a beef tenderloin; may be cooked variously; also the name given to a cold or hot sauce served with this steak.

Chaud. Hot.

Chaudfroid. Cooked meat prepared for service cold; frequently highly decorated; a sauce used to cover cold decorated meats; called *mayonnaise collée* if from mayonnaise, *chaudfroid brun* if from brown sauce, and *chaudfroid blanc* if from velouté sauce.

Chausson. Fruit jam in a pastry puff; a covered tart.

Chef de cuisine. Head chef; *chef de nuit,* night chef; *sous chef,* assistant chef.

Chef's salad. Tossed greens and chopped vegetables garnished with strips of tongue, ham, cheese, or chicken and served with French dressing.

Chemise (en). Cooked with the skins on (usually potatoes); *chemiser* (Fr.), to line or coat a mold.

Cherries jubilee. Dark cherries in syrup slightly thickened with starch, covered with kirsch, and ignited; sometimes served with a garnish of ice cream or whipped cream.

Chevalier. Food dipped in batter, fried, and served with cream sauce.

Chicken cacciatore. Chicken sautéed in olive oil, and then braised with diced onions, green peppers, whole tomatoes, and a bit of consommé and white wine, until tender. Mushrooms may be added.

Chiffonnade. Shredded or minced vegetables; shredded or minced onions, beets, parsley, green peppers, and chopped egg in French dressing.

Chili con carne. Beans with meat.

Chinoise. China cup; a strainer.

Chipolata. Brown sauce with onions, mushrooms, little veal sausages, bacon, and carrots, seasoned with Madeira or sherry wine; can also be tiny sausages served as hors d'oeuvres.

Chitterling. Fried or pickled sausages made from hog intestines.

Chop. To cut into small pieces with a knife or other sharp tool.

Chop suey. Chinese mixed vegetables seasoned with meat and soy sauce and served with rice.

Choux. Cabbage.

Choux paste. An éclair or cream puff batter.

Chowder. A thick soup containing diced potatoes, sautéed onions, and bacon or salt pork.

Chow mein. Chinese chicken or pork and vegetable dish, with fried noodles and soy sauce.

Chutney. A sweet East Indian relish made of mangoes and other ingredients; the usual accompaniment for curry.

Civet. Rabbit stew or ragoût; see *jugged.*

Clairet. Claret wine, a light red wine.

Clam bake. Ears of corn, lobsters, fish, clams, and potatoes, rolled in wet seaweed, then in wet cloths, and baked in a barbecue pit or 350°F oven; typical procedure is to bake on hot stones in a pit dug in the sand.

Cloche. Glass bell for covering a dish; *sous cloche,* under cover or bell.

Cochon. Pig; *cochon de lait,* suckling pig.

Cockie-leekie or **Cocky-leeky.** A Scottish soup; chicken broth with celery and leeks; cooked prunes may be served separately, and many recipes call for the stock to be made from a rooster or cock.

Coddled egg. Boiling water is poured over an egg; as it stands in the water, the egg is allowed to cook to desired firmness; in quantity cookery, eggs are placed in cold water, brought to a boil, and removed from heat to cook until done.

Colbert. Brown sauce seasoned with onions previously reduced in white wine; sauce is finished with maître d'hôtel butter; consommé with spring vegetables and poached egg.

Coleslaw. Shredded cabbage with boiled dressing or mayonnaise; hot slaw is served after heating in a hot dressing.

Collops. Cutlets; may also be called *escalopes.*

Compote. Stewed fruit; occasionally poultry stew.

Confit. Preserve or jam; may also be called *confiture.*

Conserve. A preserve; fruit or vegetables in heavy syrup.

Consommé. A strong, clear, clarified soup made from two or three kinds of meat.

Coq-au-vin-rouge. Chicken sautéed in red wine and brown sauce, with mushrooms and onions.

Coquille. Shell of shellfish used for au gratin fish dishes; coral of lobster.

Corned beef. Pickled beef.

Côte. Rib, cutlet, or chop; *côtes de boeuf,* ribs of beef.

Côtelette. Cutlet or cutlet-shaped.

Cottage potatoes. Thinly sliced raw potatoes sautéed in shallow fat.

Cottage pudding. Warm cake served with hot fruit sauce over it; baked pudding served with a warm dessert sauce.

Coulis. Rich meat juice; frequently, jellied strained gravy.

Country style. Served with salt pork or fat bacon.

Coupe. Cup, goblet, or bowl; diced fruit served in a coupe glass topped with a frozen dessert or whipped cream.

Court bouillon. Water, vinegar, or wine, herbs, and seasonings in which fish is cooked or over which it is steamed; fish bones and trimmings may be used to enrich the stock.

Couvert. Setting; cover; place setting.

Cover charge. Fixed charge added to a meal or food prices for entertainment.

Cream. To work one or more foods to a soft and creamy mass, using a spoon, mixer, or other tool; applied to thorough mixing of fat and sugar to incorporate a large quantity of air, which gives a light, fluffy mixture; on a mechanical mixer, a creaming paddle is used for this purpose.

Cream sauce. A white sauce to which cream or rich milk has been added; a term sometimes incorrectly applied to béchamel sauce.

Crécy. With carrots.

Crème de menthe. A liqueur flavored with mint; there are white and green varieties.

Creole. Louisiana-type cookery using ingredients such as green peppers, rice, filé seasoning, okra, and saffron in dishes.

Crêpe. Pancake; *crêpes suzette,* thin pancakes rolled with orange butter, filled with a cream center, covered with warm brandy or rum, and served flaming; the Russians call crêpes *blini* or *piroshki,* depending upon the type of filling used.

Crevette. Shrimp; *crevette rose,* prawn about 1½ to 2 inches long.

Crimp. To make deep gashes on salmon, cod, haddock, or skate as it leaves the water; soak in cold water for an hour or so, boil in salted water, and cook only to doneness.

Crisp. To moisten and refrigerate until crisp; to cook until the outer surface is crisp.

Croissants. Crescent-shaped rolls or croutons; also crescent-shaped confectionery.

Croquette. Cone-shaped chopped meat, breaded, and deep-fried; the binder of the meat is usually heavy white sauce; sometimes the term is applied to sweet deep-fried pastries.

Croustade. Hollow, fried bread square into which food in a sauce is placed; may also be any starch product shaped to contain other foods.

Croûte (en). Placed under crust.

Crouton. Toasted or fried bread; frequently used as a soup garnish; *croûtes* (Fr.).

Cuisinier. A cook.

Cuisson. Meats braised or cooked in their own juices.

Cullis. A purée soup made of pulped flesh of game, meat, poultry, or fish.

Cumberland. A sauce made of currant jelly, lemon juice, port wine, lemon and orange rind, mustard, onions, and ginger; may be hot or cold.

Curaçao. An orange-flavored liqueur.

Curry. East Indian stew containing curry seasoning; frequently, cooked meat added to a béchamel sauce that has been seasoned with curry; served with chopped nuts, shredded coconut, chutney, and other dishes.

Cut. (1) To chop. (2) To incorporate fat into dry ingredients with the least amount of blending; on a mechanical mixer, the pastry blender paddle is used.

Dagout. Drippings; see *fond.*

Danish pastry. Yeast, sweet dough, and shortening rolled out similar to puff paste to give a flaky soft bread; used for breakfast rolls and other rich rolls.

Dariole. A mold lined with thin paste, filled with custard, and topped with whipped cream.

Dauber. To braise in wine.

Dauphinoise. Braised dish in sauce topped with buttered crumbs.

Découper. To cut up.

Déguster. To cook; to reduce or get rid of.

Déjeuner. Breakfast; *déjeuner à la fourchette,* luncheon.

Délayer. To soak; see *soak.*

Delicatessen. Place where cold buffet foods are sold.

Dènte (al). Means *to the tooth;* a slight firmness remaining in foods after cooking, as in vegetables or macaroni products, giving some chew.

Denver sandwich: Filling of chopped cooked ham added to lightly beaten egg; frequently served on toasted bread.

Devil. *Diable* (Fr.); usually tangy sauce with meat-stock base, seasoned with mustard, cayenne, and onions, reduced in white wine; pimientos, green peppers, and other minced items may be added; sometimes a tangy tomato sauce is used; deviled crab or deviled eggs are tangy preparations.

Devonshire cream. Cream clotted by scalding the cream and removing clots as they form on the surface; served chilled.

Dice. To cut into cubes of about $\frac{1}{2}$ to $\frac{1}{4}$ in. in size.

Dinde. Female turkey; *dindon,* male turkey; *dindonneau,* young turkey.

Diplomate. Normandy sauce seasoned with lobster.

Dobostorte. Thin layers of sponge cake filled with rich chocolate cream.

Dock. To piece, prick, gash, or cut.

Dolma. Turkish forcemeat; ground meat mixture cooked in cabbage leaves.

Dredge. To coat lightly; see *flour.*

Dresser. To garnish.

Duchesse. Usually applied to mashed potatoes that contain egg yolk; the mixture is frequently used for potato puff; used also as a topping for baked meat pies; can be forced from a pastry tube into forms, piped around planked items, or used otherwise and baked.

Dugléré. With tomatoes.

Du jour. Food ready to be served; means *of the day.*

Eau. Water.

Eau de vie. Brandy; literally, *water of life.*

Éclair. Fingerlike choux paste filled with cream or pastry cream; frequently chocolate-frosted.

Écarlate. Any sauce containing red food, such as lobster coral, beets, or red tongue.

Écrevisse. Crayfish.

Egg. See *bread.*

Émincé. Finely minced; mincemeat; sometimes used to indicate thin slices.

Empanadas. See *pasty.*

En bellevue. In aspic; literally, *in good sight.*

Enchiladas. Mexican tortillas filled with a chicken, cheese, and tomato mixture, with grated cheese on top; usually some raw chopped lettuce is added at the last minute.

En cocotte. In small individual casserole.

En coquille. In shell.

English monkey. See *monkey.*

English muffin. Round yeast bread baked on a griddle.

En papillote. To cook in paper bag.

Entrecôte. Literally, *between the ribs:* frequently used to indicate a steak.

Entrée. Main dish.

Entremets. Desserts served either cold (*froid*) or hot (*chaud*); *entremets de danseur,* desserts served at the end of a course meal; may also be applied to buttered vegetables or large salads.

Épaule de mouton. Shoulder of mutton.

Épigramme. Small cutlet of tender meat.

Espagnole. Brown sauce; one of the basic sauces made from brown stock and browned roux; a small quantity of tomatoes may be added.

Essence. Rich stock of meat or vegetable flavors; an extract of meat flavors; finely divided or pulped foods used to give predominant flavor to a food; dessert flavorings may also be called this.

Éstouffade (étuver or étouffer). Smothered and braised; frequently a term used to indicate chicken cooked in this manner.

Étuvée. Type of stew.

Fagot. Celery, bay leaf, peppercorn, thyme, and garlic wrapped together and used as a *bouquet garni.*

Faisan. Cock pheasant; *faisane,* hen pheasant; *faisandeau,* young pheasant.

Fanchonette. Small pie or tart topped with meringue.

Farce. Forcement stuffing; *farci,* stuffed, filled with forcemeat.

Farina. *Farine* (Fr.); coarsely ground endosperm of wheat; the French tend to call all finely ground flours *farine.*

Fariner. To dredge with flour; see *flour.*

Fausse tortue. Mock turtle; usually a soup made of green peas in imitation of real turtle soup; seasoned with sherry or Madeira wine; stock is usually rich veal, and diced meat from cooked calves' head may be added.

Fermière. Farmer's wife style; baked in earthen dish with minced green onions, chives, parsley, butter, and a bit of white wine.

Feuilletée (pâte). Puff paste; means *many leaves;* reworked scraps are called *demi-feuilletée.*

Filet. Boneless piece of meat, usually the tenderloin; *fillet,* boneless piece of fish.

Financière. Banker's style; brown sauce containing diced ham, usually seasoned with mushrooms, truffles, and white or Madeira wine.

Fines herbes. Finely cut green herbs used for seasoning or garnish.

Finnan haddie. Lightly smoked salted haddock.

Flamande. Velouté sauce seasoned with rich fish stock, mustard, lemon juice, and chopped parsley; carrots, pickles, and grated horseradish are sometimes added.

Flamed. *Flambé* (Fr.); set afire with brandy, liqueur, or other product, and usually served flaming.

Flan. Custard; open tart.

Florentine. With spinach; frequently means an item served over creamed spinach; *Florentine soup* is cream of spinach soup.

Flour. To coat with flour; to dredge in flour; usually salt, pepper, and other seasonings are added to the flour, and paprika may be added for color.

Foie. Liver; *foie de veau,* calf's liver; *foie gras,* goose liver.

Fold. To combine by using two motions, cutting vertically through the mixture and turning over and over by sliding the implement across the bottom of the mixing bowl with each turn; usually done with a spatula or whip; can be done with care with a whip in an automatic mixer; with very delicate products, such as a butter sponge, the hands should be used.

Fond. Drippings in a pan; *fond brun,* brown drippings; also a rich stock of meat and vegetables.

Fondue. Melted or blended; a light custardlike entrée that resembles a soufflé; hot melted cheese entrée; *Swiss fondue,* melted Swiss cheese in white wine seasoned delicately with kirsch and dipped up with French bread; custard of eggs and milk poured over bread, to which diced meat or fish is added, and the product baked.

Forcemeat. Pulped meat bound together with soft crumbs and egg yolks and poached in tiny balls or pieces; used as a garnish.

Four. Oven.

Fourré. Coated with sugar, cream, or other preparations.

Franconia. Browned; potatoes browned with the roast.

Frappé. Partly forzen; coarsely frozen.

French dressing. Oil and vinegar or lemon in the ratio of 2:1; diverse seasonings may be added to give many variations.

French ice cream. Rich ice cream containing eggs; may also be seasoned with ground vanilla bean.

French onion soup. A bouillon soup thick with sautéed, thinly sliced onions and served in a *petite marmite* dish, topped with a slice of French bread covered with grated parmesan cheese; the whole dish is richly toasted under a broiler before serving.

French toast. Bread dipped in egg and sautéed.

Friandines. Small patties or croquettes.

Fricandeau. Larded and braised leg of veal; can also be a large larded slice from the rump.

Fricassée. Cooked by braising; usually applied to fowl, rabbit, or veal; for white fricassée, no browning occurs.

Fricot. Stew or ragoût.

Frit. Fried.

Froid. Cold.

Fromage. Cheese; *fromage glacé*, ice cream molded in shape of cheese.

Fruit. Fruit; *fruit divers*, mixed fruit; *fruit glacé*, candied fruit; *fruit sec*, dried fruit.

Fry. To cook in fat; (1) cooking in a small amount of fat, also called *sautéing* or *pan-frying*; (2) cooking in deep fat, called *deep-frying*.

Fumet. Stock from fish, game, or meats, reduced with wine and slightly more concentrated than an essence; a rich stock over which foods are steamed.

Galantine. Decorated boneless meat, game, or poultry piece; frequently has a crust around the meat and decoration in the meat; boned meat or poultry cooked in a casing and served cold.

Garbure. Baked stew or thick soup containing much cabbage and salt pork.

Garde manger. Cold-meat cook.

Garnish. An edible food used to decorate another; *garniture* (Fr.).

Gâteau. Cake; *gâteaux assortis*, assorted cakes.

Gaufre. Waffle; a crisp ice cream wafer.

Gelée. Jelly; any type of gel.

Genevoise. Rich fish essence reduced with red wine; sauce contains no meat; Geneva style, not Genoa style.

Genoise. Genoa style; rich in butter and eggs.

Glacé. Iced, frosted, frozen, glassy, glazed, candied, crystallized; some desserts are said to be *glacé* when covered with a thick sauce; a glaze; coated with a thin syrup cooked to the crack stage, or covered with a starch- or pectin-thickened gel; in the latter sense, pies, tarts, and bread may be glazed with apricot or strawberry glaze, a jam, a jelly, or the like; *glacé de viand*, meat glaze; *glacé de boeuf*, beef glaze; *glacé de veau*, veal glaze.

Glacé royale. An icing; a sauce made of mousseline sauce and Mornay sauce or cream sauce blended in equal amounts.

Glaze. A rich stock reduced one-fourth in volume, used to heighten flavor in stocks, sauces, or meat dishes; a *demiglaze* is rich stock reduced one-half; to coat meat, poultry, or fish with a meat essence containing a high amount of gelatin; to give a glossy, shiny coat; to place vegetables in a mixture of butter or margarine and sugar or syrup and coat with a glaze by sautéing or ovenizing.

Gnocchi. Italian pastry or cracker seasoned with Parmesan cheese; Italian dumpling.

Godiveau. Forcemeat made of veal kidney.

Golden buck. Welsh rarebit over poached egg.

Gorgonzola. Italian cheese resembling Roquefort cheese.

Goulash. Hungarian stew heavily seasoned with paprika.

Gras. Fat.

Gras-double. Tripe.

Gratin. Browned.

Greek. *Greque* (Fr.); Greek style; usually seasoned with olive oil and garlic.

Grid. The part of a broiler on which foods are placed for broiling.

Grill. To fry on a griddle; sauté or toast; *grille* (Fr.), broiler; the term is no longer used to indicate broiling.

Grind. To reduce to small particles by cutting, crushing, or grinding.

Grits. Coarsely ground hominy cooked as a porridge and served for breakfast; *gruau* (Fr.), oatmeal, grits, groats, gruel.

Groseille à maquereau. Gooseberry; *groseille rouge,* red currant; *groseille noire,* black currant.

Gruyère. Cheese resembling Swiss cheese.

Guava. An applelike fruit that makes a tart, deep pink (almost red) jelly.

Gumbo. Also indicated by the term *okra;* a Creole-type dish; usually contains okra, tomatoes, and rice.

Hachis. Hash; minced meat, sometimes spelled *hachée.*

Haggis. Scotch sausage cooked in sheep's stomach.

Ham. Cured, smoked leg of pork. *Smithfield,* Virginia ham from pigs that have been fed a heavy diet of peanuts; a drier, more heavily cured ham. *Westphalia, Prague, Polish,* and *Bayonne* hams are similar to the Smithfield and require slow and extended cooking to tenderize.

Hard sauce. Creamed butter and powdered sugar, flavored variously; used as a dessert sauce.

Haricot. Kidney or navy bean; stewed meat with turnips; *haricot vert,* green bean; *haricot d'Espagne,* red bean.

Harlequin. See *Neapolitane.*

Hasenpfeffer. Rabbit stew cooked with tart wine; may be finished with sour cream.

Hash-browned potatoes. Boiled potatoes, sliced, chopped, or diced, and sautéed until they have a crisp outer crust.

Hashed potatoes in cream. Boiled, sliced, or diced potatoes in rich béchamel or cream sauce.

Hâtelet. Small skewer; silver skewer.

High tea. A formal tea more elaborate than an ordinary tea.

Hodgepodge (hotchpotch). A mixture; a stew; *hochepot* is a mixture of meat and vegetables served with broth in a soup dish.

Hollandaise. Sauce made of egg yolks, butter, lemon juice or vinegar, and seasonings.

Homard. Lobster.

Hors d'oeuvre. Appetizer; side dish after the soup in a very formal meal; means a dish served outside of the ordinary dishes.

Huître. Oyster.

Hungarian goulash. See *goulash.*

Hush puppies. Cornmeal paste deep-fried; a Southern dish, and very delicious.

Ice. Sweetened fruit juice and water; frozen.

Impératrice. Rich supreme sauce; also name of a consommé.

Indian pudding. A New England dessert of baked cornmeal, milk, brown sugar, eggs, raisins, and flavoring.

Indienne. Generally used to indicate dishes flavored with curry.

Irish stew. A stew made of lamb or mutton with dumplings.

Italienne. Dishes distinguished by the use of Italian pastes and grated Parmesan cheese; may also be used to indicate use of tomato sauce; ground meat sauce with vegetables and oregano used with spaghetti.

Jackson (à la). A cream of potato soup; vegetables and macaroni may be added.

Jambalaya. Creole rich dish containing tomatoes, onions, saffron, other season-ings, and fish, shellfish, poultry, or meat.

Jambe. Leg; *jambon*, ham.

Jardinière. Mixed garden vegetables with carrots and turnips usually included; usually cut in strips ⅛ in. thick by 1 in. long, or diced.

Jolie fille. Dishes fair to look upon; usually decorated pieces.

Jugged. Braised and usually served in a casserole, as in *jugged hare.*

Julienne. Vegetables or meats cut into matchlike strips; used for garnishing and seasoning.

Junket. A dessert of sweetened and flavored milk set to a clabber with rennet.

Jus. Juice of fruit, vegetable, or meat; see *au jus.*

Kebabs. Marinated pieces of lamb or mutton cooked on skewers; may also have vegetables or other foods between pieces of meat.

Kiev. Stuffed with seasoned butter.

King. See *à la king.*

Kippered. Lightly salted and smoked fish; *kippers,* smoked herring.

Kirschwasser. Liqueur made from cherries.

Kisses. Meringue-type dessert.

Knead. To work a thick product with a pressing motion by folding and stretch-ing; to knead with a mechanical mixer is to use the dough hook.

Knöpfli. Tiny Swiss dumplings; made much like *spätzle,* except that the dough is thicker; *klösse* (Ger.).

Kosher. Food handled according to Jewish religious customs.

Kuchen. German cakes, not necessarily sweet; see *lebkuchen* below.

Kummel. Caraway; liqueur seasoned with caraway seed.

Lachs. Smoked salmon; *lox* or *locks,* a Jewish dish of thinly sliced smoked salmon, served with bagels.

Lait. Milk.

Langouste. Spiny lobsters with no claws; only the tails are used.

Langues de chat. Small cakes called *cat's tongues.*

Lard. Bacon, salt pork, pig's fat; to *lard* is to pull strips of salt pork, bacon, or fat through meat prior to cooking it; *lardoon,* larding needle; *lardon,* strips of fat used for larding.

Lasagne. Broad, ribbonlike Italian noodle.

Lebkuchen. German cakes that are quite sweet; usually honey is a part of the sweetener used.

Legumes. Group of vegetables comprising beans, peas, and lentils.

Liaison. A thickening agent such as starch, or the yolk of eggs.

Limburger. A soft, strongly flavored German cheese aged in much the same way that camembert is.

Limpa. A Swedish bread.

Locks. See *lachs.*

Loin. Area from last rib to rump, except on pork, where it is the area from shoulder blade tip to rump; *longe* (Fr.); *longe de porc,* loin of pork; *shortloin,* area from last rib to edge of hip bone.

London. *London mixed grill* is an English (double, or two sides of loin) chop with kidney, bacon, small sausage, and mushrooms; a London broil is tender flank steak cooked rare and sliced thin.

Lox. See *lachs.*

Lucullus. Rich brown sauce garnished with truffles, cocks' combs, quenelles, foie gras, chicken kidneys, and mushrooms; seasoned with sherry; applied to costly dishes.

Lyonnaise. Heavily seasoned with onions and perhaps some parsley.

Macaroon. Small cake or cookie made of beaten egg whites, sugar, and almond paste or fine coconut.

Macédoine. Mixture of vegetables, either raw or cooked, for salad or vegetable; can also refer to a mixed fruit sauce or mixture of fruit.

Madeira. A wine much like sherry; brown sauce reduced with Madeira wine; some make a Madeira sauce with half brown sauce and half tomato sauce, seasoning with Madeira wine or sherry; *Madère* (Fr.).

Maggi. A flavoring essence, largely monosodium glutamate (MSG), used to add flavor to stocks, sauces, and gravies.

Maigre. See *au maigre*.

Mais. Corn; sometimes used to refer to wheat or other cereals.

Maison (à la). Specialty of the house.

Maître d'hôtel. Person in charge of the dining room; head waiter.

Manhattan. A cocktail made from bourbon or rye whiskey and sweet (French) vermouth.

Marasquin. A liqueur made from maraschino cherries.

Marengo. Chicken fried in oil and braised in white wine and mushrooms; garlic and tomatoes are frequently added.

Marinade. A combination of oil and vinegar or wine used to give added flavor to meats; marinate, *marinate*, to tenderize in a marinade; sometimes the marinade may be a pickling or brine solution.

Marmite. Small soup dish in shape of pot (see *petite marmite*); *grande marmite*, soup in which large pieces of meat cooked in the soup are sliced and served with the soup.

Marseillaise. Chopped onions, fines herbs, and garlic fried in oil, reduced in red wine and, with chopped anchovies, added to tomato sauce; *soupe à la Marseillaise* is a bouillabaise.

Martini. A cocktail made of gin and dry (Italian) vermouth.

Maryland. Meat or poultry dredged with flour, egg, and crumbs, and fried; served with cream gravy and corn fritters.

Marzipan. Almond, egg white, and sugar paste confections in the shape and color of fruit or vegetables; see *almond paste*.

Mask. To cover completely; usually applied to a cover of mayonnaise or other thick sauce, but may refer to a cover of forcemeat or jelly.

Matelote. Sailor fashion; onions and mushrooms sautéed, and then reduced in red wine, with rich essence of fish added, and brown sauce; a dish of different sorts of fish (eel, carp, perch, and so forth) braised with vegetables and red or white wine.

Matignon. Minced raw or cooked mashed vegetables, used for seasoning foods.

Mayonnaise. Oil, eggs, and vinegar or lemon juice in emulsified form for use as a salad dressing or as a preparation for other sauces; *mayonnaise collée* see *chaudfroid*.

Meatloaf. Ground meat with diced or minced vegetables, shaped into loaf form and baked; loaf may be made of ground beef, ground veal, ground ham, mixed ground meats, or fish mixtures.

Meat pie. Diced meat with vegetables in gravy, usually cooked under a biscuit or pastry crust; see also *pasty, pirog, piroshki, ruff, shortcake, tourtière, turnover*.

Médaillon. A cake shaped like a large medal; beef tenderloin tips or small pieces of *foie gras* or other items.

Melba. Usually a dessert consisting of half a peach on ice cream, covered with Melba sauce (puréed raspberries or strawberries, seasoned with Curaçao).

Mêlé. Mixed.

Melt. To liquefy.

Mère poularde. A flat, unfolded plain or French omelet.

Meringue. Egg whites beaten stiff with sugar, used to top pies or desserts; adding more sugar makes a stiff meringue that can be used as a base for many desserts.

Meunière. Dredged with flour and sautéed in butter; see *butter*.

Mexican. Usually a dish containing refried beans, onions, tomatoes, hot chili peppers, mild peppers, and kernel corn.

Mignon. A delicate morsel; *filet mignon*, the butt of the tenderloin cut as a steak and frequently wrapped in bacon; the French use the small end of the tenderloin for the filet mignon.

Milanaise. A dish containing tomato sauce combined with *allemande* or *béchamel* sauce, together with some Italian pastas; some add parmesan cheese.

Mince. *Emincer* (Fr.); to cut or chop into small pieces.

Minestrone. Thick Italian vegetable soup distinguished by a leafy vegetable, red kidney beans, and an Italian pasta, among other products; usually served with parmesan cheese; there are at least four distinct types of minestrone soup originating in various districts of Italy.

Mint. *Menthe* (Fr.); a mint sauce may be served hot or cold and is made of mint, vinegar, water, and sugar combined with the drippings of meat (usually lamb or mutton); some chefs add a bit of orange marmalade; *crème de menthe*, a mint-flavored after-dinner liqueur; *menthe poivrée*, peppermint.

Minute steak. Steak (usually sirloin) $\frac{1}{2}$ in. thick, cooked only a short time.

Mirabeau. A velouté sauce from rich chicken stock, with crushed garlic added; may also be applied to an egg, steak, or garnish that may vary considerably in ingredients used.

Mirepoix. Diced vegetables used for imparting flavor to dishes.

Miroton. Cold meats warmed up.

Mix. To combine ingredients so as to blend them together.

Mixed grill. A Frenched chop, kidney, bacon, sausage, broiled or grilled tomato, and mushroom.

Mock turtle soup. See *fausse tortue*.

Mold. To obtain a desired form by placing in a mold or device (see *shape*).

Monkey. Very similar to rarebit, except that the thickening agent is soft bread crumbs soaked in milk, instead of flour or some other starch thickener; normally served over toasted English muffins, and usually called *English monkey*; burned sugar dissolved in water to give a brown color to foods.

Montmorency. Dark or pie cherries used in a product; a sweet-sour cherry sauce sometimes served over baked ham.

Mornay. A béchamel, white, or cream sauce seasoned with grated parmesan cheese.

Mousse. A froth or foam; used to describe a delicate, aerated, smooth mixture; a frozen dessert made from a base of whipped cream.

Mousseline. A custardlike forcemeat made of egg whites and cream; a very smooth mixture; *mousseline sauce*, one part whipped cream to two parts mayonnaise or hollandaise sauce; see *glacé royal*.

Mulligatawny. Chicken broth, rice, corn, raw apples, and curry combined to make a soup; vegetables, meats, and chutney may be added.

Muscat. The large muscat raisin; *muscatel*, a sweet (dessert) wine.

Nantaise. Normandy sauce with shrimp, chervil, and tarragon added; also called *Nantua sauce*.

Napoleon. Pastry consisting of sheets of puff paste filled with custard, frosted, and cut into finger shapes.

Neapolitan (napolitaine). A dish containing spaghetti; a brown sauce containing some currant jelly, diced ham, nutmeg, thyme, and a bit of malaga wine; some chefs add a bit of horseradish; the name also refers to two or more layers of ice cream, ice, or sherbet in brick form; also applies to gelatin layers in different colors; *harlequin* is used synonymously; see *panache*.

Neutral sauces. Sauces that contain no meat stock, such as hollandaise, mayonnaise, and bread sauce.

Newburg (Newberg or Newburgh). Béchamel or cream sauce flavored with sherry; may be thickened by a liaison of egg yolks.

New England boiled dinner. Boiled beef, boiled ham, or both with boiled cabbage, carrots, rutabagas, turnips, onions, parsnips, and potatoes.

New Orleans. Same as *Creole.*

Nivernaise. Shredded vegetables in poulette sauce; glazed carrots.

Noisette. Nuts, hazel nuts; the kernel or eye of the main loin muscle (*longissimus dorsi*) or fish fillets; pieces from small end of beef tenderloin (see *tournedos*), about 1½ in. in diameter, of which usually two or three are served as a portion; a *noisette* of lamb may be a piece from the loin; *noisette sauce,* a hollandaise or supreme sauce to which a small amount of hazelnut butter or paste is added just before service with salmon, trout, or other boiled fish.

Noix. Nut or walnut; *noix de coco,* coconut; *noix de pistache,* pistachio nut; *noix de veau,* veal cutlet taken from the muscle called the *kernel* on the leg.

Normandy. Rich fish velouté and cream reduced; a bit of cayenne may be added; for desserts, *à la Normandy* means a delicate, smooth mixture that often contains whipped cream.

Nougat. Almond cake; an amorphous confection containing chopped or whole almonds.

Nouilles. Noodles or shredded egg paste; see *knöpfli, spätzles,* and so forth.

O'Brien. Chopped green pepper, onion, and pimiento added; usually applied to cooked potatoes diced and sautéed with these items added.

Oeuf. Egg: *oeufs brouillés,* scrambled eggs.

Oka. A cheese; see *port salut.*

Onion Soup. See *French onion soup.*

Orly. A dough using beer for a liquid.

Ovenize. To place in an oven to sauté or fry; to oven-roast.

Pailles. Straws; *pailles au fromage,* cheese straws; *pailles pommes de terre,* shoestring potatoes.

Pain. Bread.

Pain de boeuf. Meat loaf.

Panache. Two or more kinds of an item in a single dish; panache ice cream may also be called *neapolitan* or *harlequin* ice cream.

Panade. Bread soaked, squeezed dry, and used for stuffings, dressings, or forcemeats; *empanadas,* a pasty.

Panard. Thick white sauce used as binding for croquettes.

Pan-broil. To cook on a hot frying pan or grill without adding fat or liquid; fat is poured off as it accumulates.

Paner. To cover with bread crumbs; the crumbs are at times called *panure.*

Pan-fry. To sauté or cook in a small quantity of fat in a sauté pan.

Panier. Basket.

Papillote (en). In paper; to bake in paper; *côtellette en papillote,* cutlet baked in paper; the term is also used to indicate paper frills on chops and other items.

Parboil. To cook partially by boiling.

Pare. To trim or cut off the outside covering; see *peel.*

Parfait. Variegated foods; a frozen dessert served in a parfait glass, with layers of ice cream interspersed with layers of fruit or syrup and topped with whipped cream; a smooth mousselike frozen dessert.

Parfumer. To flavor or season.

Parisienne. Paris style; cut into small, round ball shapes; *parisienne potatoes,* small round potato balls, deep-fried.

Parker House rolls. A rich yeast dinner roll folded in half like a pocket book and baked.

Parmentier. Name of the man who introduced potatoes into French cookery; *à la Parmentier,* with potatoes.

Parmesan. A hard Italian cheese, usually grated and used as a seasoning with macaroni products.

Passer. To strain.

Pastrami. A highly spiced corned beef brisket.

Pastry. A baked good made of pie or puff paste dough, such as a pie or a tart; *pâtisserie* (Fr.).

Pasty. Flaky pie dough filled with diced meat, potatoes, and gravy and baked.

Pâté or **paste.** May mean a fine paste mixture, a pie, or thick dough; a shell of puff paste, a small circular flat cake, or a hamburger, potato, or vegetable patty.

Paupiette. Thin slices of meat spread with forcemeat, rolled, dipped in batter, and fried; a *roulade* or *rouleau.*

Paysanne. In peasant style; usually a dish served with shredded or diced cooked vegetables; also the name of a fairly thick country-type soup; a diced product.

Peel. To remove outside skin or rind by mechanical means or heat; *peler* (Fr.).

Pêle-mêle. Mixed up; tossed.

Pepperpot. Soup popularized in Philadelphia; diced salt pork, onions, green peppers, potatoes, and other vegetables with julienne tripe in a rich stock, usually beef.

Périgeux. Truffles; Périgord is a district in France known for its fine truffles.

Persillade. With parsley; *persillées,* new potatoes boiled, buttered, and dusted with chopped parsley.

Petit. Small, little, tiny, dainty.

Petit déjeuner. Breakfast.

Petite marmite. A vegetable or pot-au-feu soup containing sliced beef or chicken, served in a small individual pot and topped with a cheese-toasted crouton; see *marmite.*

Petits fours. Small cakes; *pâté de petit four,* pastry of the little oven.

Petit lait. Buttermilk.

Petits pois. Green peas.

Pfeffernüsse. Hard German cookies that contain a small amount of ground black pepper; literally, pepper nuts.

Philadelphia ice cream. Simplest type of ice cream, consisting of thin cream, sugar, and flavoring.

Pièce de résistance. Main dish; the most important dish.

Pièce Montée. A display piece.

Pilaf. Turkish rice dish; *pilau* (Fr.).

Pipe. To place a border around an item; see *border.*

Piquant. *Piquante* (Fr.); tangy sauce containing vinegar, white wine, and sautéed onions, with chopped capers and fine herbs added; some chefs add brown sauce; served with hot or cold pork, mutton, or fatty meats.

Piqué. Larded with strips of salt pork or bacon.

Pirog. Minced or finely diced meat baked in yeast, pastry, or biscuit dough; *calzone* (It.).

Piroshki. Baked biscuit dough filled with a meat, cheese, vegetable, or fish mixture; sometimes means rolled pancakes with a filling of this type.

Pizza. Italian pie with a crisp yeast bottom, baked with a seasoned tomato mixture, cheese, and other items on top.

Plank. To broil fish or meat on a plank, surrounded with vegetables and edged with a border of duchess potatoes.

Plat. Plate or platter; *plateau,* tray.

Plombière. A mixture of candied fruits with ice cream.

Pluck. Lights (lungs), heart, and liver.

Poach. To simmer in a small quantity of water that barely covers the item; *pocher* (Fr.).

Poêler. To brown in a saucepan in butter and then cover and braise; the cooking is fast, and excess moisture is avoided in braising; a process between braising and roasting; sometimes a white mirepoix is called a *poêle*.

Pois.   Peas.

Poisson.   Fish; *poissonier,* fish cook.

Poivrade.   A tangy, tart brown sauce used on game meats, especially venison; a part of the marinade in which meat is soaked.

Polenta.   Dish made of cornmeal or farina; grated parmesan cheese is usually sprinkled over it.

Pollo.   Chicken (It. or Sp.).

Polonaise.   Polish style; velouté sauce made slightly tart with lemon juice and a bit of horseradish; may also signify a preparation of beet, horseradish, cabbage, and sour cream.

Pomme.   Apple; *pomme de terre,* potato; *pomme d'amour,* tomato.

Pompano.   A fine fish caught in Florida or Caribbean waters.

Popover.   A bread made of a mixture of flour, milk, and eggs that is leavened by steam.

Port (du) Salut.   A soft, richly flavored cheese also called *oka* or *trappist* after the Trappist monks, who originated it.

Potage.   Soup, usually thick; *potagier,* soup cook.

Potato chips.   Thinly sliced rounds of potato cooked to a crisp stage in deep fat.

Pot-au-feu.   Literally, *pot on the fire;* a soup made from rich stock of somewhat anonymous character because the ingredients are waste items obtained in other food production; usually a flavorful vegetable soup; may also refer to a stock pot cooking on a range or in a steam-jacketed kettle.

Poulet.   Young fowl; *poularde,* a fat pullet; *poulette sauce,* egg yolks added to supreme sauce for thickening; may contain chopped mushrooms; normally a chicken stock is used for the basic velouté sauce, but some poulette sauces used for fish are made from a fish stock.

Praline.   A confection made of brown or maple sugar and pecans; mixed broken pecans carmelized; brown sugar or maple sugar nougat; sometimes refers to burnt almond flavoring.

Prawn.   A large shrimp.

Printanière.   Spring vegetables diced small with peas and asparagus; the name of a consommé containing these vegetables.

Profiterolès.   Tiny choux (éclair) pastes filled with vegetables, meats, or tangy fillings; sometimes used as a garnish for soup; may also be filled with sweetened mixtures and used as a dessert.

Prosciutto.   An Italian ham, usually thinly sliced.

Provençale.   Brown sauce heavily diluted with tomato purée and seasoned with garlic; the true sauce is made by cooking tomatoes with minced garlic, a few onions, salt, pepper, and a bit of oil, and then sieving.

Provolone.   A smoked Italian cheese with a rich, mellow flavor.

Puff paste.   Mixture of strong flour and water that is layered with shortening between folds and rolled out many times until thin sheets of dough and shortening are produced; baked and used as a pie dough.

Pumpernickel.   Bread made from whole rye flour.

Purée.   Foods rubbed through a sieve; slightly coarser than pulped foods; a soup made from puréed food.

Quadrillé.   Checkered by layering.

Quenelles.   Oval or other fancy-shaped forcemeats.

Quiche Lorraine.   A pie dough overlaid with bacon and Swiss cheese in a custard and baked; nutmeg may be sprinkled on top; often used as an hors d'oeuvre.

Rabbit.   See *rarebit.*

Ragoût.   A stew of meats and vegetables, usually quite thick and savory; a thick concentrate of an item such as tomato purée, often called *tomato ragoût.*

Ramekin. Small individual baking dish or pastry shell, or the item baked in it; small cheesecake served as an hors d'oeuvre.

Rare. Underdone.

Rarebit. Also called *rabbit* or *Welsh rarebit*; melted cheese dish made with white sauce or stale beer or ale thickened with an egg yolk liaison; seasoned rather heavily; see also *fondue, golden buck, monkey,* and *Yorkshire buck*; when seasoned with anchovy and served with oysters, the dish is called *Capetown Rarebit.*

Rasping. Crumbs; grated cereal particles; *râpé* (Fr.).

Ratafia. Name of a liqueur.

Ravigote. Cold sauce, quite tart, containing chopped eggs, fine herbs, and capers; usually made of oil and vinegar but sometimes made with mayonnaise; also may be a tart sauce with fine herbs served hot; the term means to give appetite or vigor.

Ravioli. Small Italian pastes filled with meat, cheese, or vegetables, served in a rich tomato sauce and sprinkled over with parmesan cheese.

Réchauffé. Warmed over.

Recherché. The best; the most refined.

Reduce. To evaporate part of a liquid by simmering or boiling. The recipe should state the amount of reduction to be obtained.

Réforme. Dishes named after the famous Reform Club of London; a poivrade sauce made quite tart with gherkins, capers, cooked egg white, and tongue, all cut julienne.

Refroidir. To cool or chill.

Regency (régence). Allemande sauce with mushrooms and truffles diluted with rich stock from the item it is to accompany.

Reine (regina). Chicken soup; creamed chicken or sweetbreads in patty shell; means also a young or fat chicken.

Releves (removes). Roasts and boiled meats on the menu; entrées, but in larger quantity than just a serving; *relever,* to improve.

Rémoulade. Mayonnaise seasoned with mustard, chopped dill pickles, anchovy, capers, and fine herbs, usually highly seasoned with ground pepper; may mean in cookery to reduce to a paste or grind.

Render. To free fat from a connective tissue by means of heat.

Rhin. Rhine; *Rhin du vin,* Rhine wine.

Riblette. Thin slices; a rasher.

Riced. Put through a ricer; frequently done with hot boiled potatoes.

Richelieu. Sauce, usually over a tenderloin steak, consisting of brown sauce seasoned with Madeira sauce and tomato paste; also a consommé or a garnish.

Ris. Sweetbread; *ris de veau,* veal sweetbreads.

Risotto (rizotto). A rice dish.

Rissolé. Browned or seared; with a brown or toasted coat; oven-browned potato.

Roast. To bake; applied to certain foods, such as meats and chestnuts; see *bake*.

Robert. Rich brown sauce with minced onions, mustard, and white wine.

Rockefeller. Creamed spinach and fine herbs; usually spread over raw oysters, topped with bread crumbs and parmesan cheese, and baked; worcestershire, tabasco, anchovy paste, and absinthe or anisette may be added to the mixture for seasoning.

Rocks. Semihard dropped cookies or cakes containing raisins and nuts.

Roe. Fish eggs; beluga caviar is best quality; pressed sturgeon caviar is widely used for spreads, pastes, and so forth; codfish and whitefish roe (both hard and frequently colored gray or black) and herring and salmon roe (both soft, the latter tinted red), as well as other roe, are used as substitutes for caviar.

Roly-poly pudding. Rolled pastry or biscuit dough that is covered with fruit paste or jam and steamed or baked; served with a hot sauce.

Roquefort. Famous French blue cheese; *Roquefort dressing,* about 5 oz Roquefort cheese to 1 qt French dressing; chopped chives may be added.

Rothschild. See *angels on horseback.*

Rôtir. To roast; *rôti* or *rôt,* a roast; *rosbif,* roast beef; *rôtisseur,* roast cook; *rôtisserie,* equipment for roasting before an open fire, usually on a spit.

Rouennaise. A dish featuring duck; made famous in the city of Rouen, France.

Roulade. Roll; rolled meat; term rouleau is used synonymously.

Roux. A mixture of equal parts flour and fat, used to thicken sauces and other foods.

Royale. In the royal style; a custard, plain or combined with other foods, used as a soup garnish.

Ruff. A meat pie or fried meat turnover.

Rusk. A crisp twice-baked bread.

Russe. Russian style; *Russian buffet,* foods on a buffet distinguished by caviar and Russian fish in a large glass or ice bowl on a stand.

Sachet. See *bouquet garni.*

St. Florentin. Deep-fried mashed potato croquettes containing diced ham.

St. Germain. A split pea soup; a dish containing purée of peas.

St. Hubert. Hunter style.

Salamander. A small broiler used for browning dishes in the cook's section.

Salisbury. A steak made of ground beef, milk, bread crumbs, and seasonings.

Sally Lunn. A breakfast coffee cake with about the same richness as a muffin.

Salmagundi. An old English dish of fresh and salted meats, fish, onions, and various seasonings.

Salmi. A stew of roasted game or meat in a rich brown sauce.

Salpiçon. Finely diced or chopped meat and vegetables (sometimes mushrooms and truffles are included) for flavoring sauces and other dishes; a mixture use for croquettes.

Saratoga. Indicates fried potato chips; also a shoulder or neck lamb chop.

Sauce. A concentrated, flavored accompaniment to food, usually liquid; *saucer,* to cover with sauce; *saucier,* sauce cook; *saucière,* sauceboat; *sauce vin blanc,* a velouté made of rich fish stock.

Saucisse. Sausage.

Sauerbraten. Pot roast (German) marinated in wine or water, vinegar, and seasonings; *sauer,* sour.

Sauerkraut. Soured or pickled cabbage.

Sauté. To fry quickly with just enough fat or butter to prevent sticking; see *fry* and *pan-fry; sautoir,* a frying pan.

Scald. To heat liquid to just below it's boiling point or to dip an item into very hot or boiling water to facilitate removal of an outer surface, or for other reasons; see *blanch.*

Scallop. Also *escalope;* to bake food, usually cut in pieces, in a sauce or other liquid; the top is usually covered with crumbs; food and sauce may be mixed together or placed in alternate layers; *au gratin* may be used synonymously; to cut food on a bias.

Scallopini. Veal cutlet sautéed; *scallopine Bolognese* (Fr.), ham and potatoes served with cutlet or minced veal with sauce, seasoned with parmesan cheese.

Scallops. Meat or muscle of the sea or bay scallop, a shellfish.

Schnitzel. Breaded and sautéed; see *wiener schnitzel.*

Scone. A rich biscuit dough baked usually in triangular form; a Scottish tea cake made from wheat, rye, or barley flour.

Score. To cut lightly across an item; to mark lightly, as scoring an omelet by burning.

Scotch broth. Soup made from mutton stock and containing cooked barley and vegetables; often called *Scotch mutton broth.*

Scotch woodcock. Half of hard-cooked or chopped creamed eggs seasoned with anchovy paste.

Scrape. To remove in thin layers with a sharp or blunt instrument.

Scrapple. Diced or ground pork cooked in cornmeal and seasoned.

Scrod. Cod or haddock about $2\frac{1}{2}$ lb in weight.

Sear. To brown the surface by a short application of heavy heat; used to develop flavor and color.

Sec. Dry; *sauté sec*, braised in dry white wine.

Semolina paste. Macaroni products; semolina is the endosperm of durum wheat, which makes a high-quality macaroni product.

Shake. To toss vigorously up and down in a container.

Shape. To form into a desired pattern either with hands or with molds.

Shepherd's pie. A meat pie covered with mashed potatoes and then baked.

Sherbet. A frozen dessert consisting of fruit juices, milk, sugar, stabilizer, and coloring; *soret* (Fr.).

Shir. To bake.

Shore dinner. Combined seafoods and shellfish served with french-fried, shoe-string, or baked potatoes and coleslaw.

Shortbread. A rich Scottish cookie.

Shortcake. A rich, slightly sweet biscuit dough that is split, with fruit in between and on top, and served with whipped cream or plain cream over; a shortcake biscuit covered with meat in gravy.

Shred. To tear or cut into small pieces.

Simmer. To cook in a liquid at a temperature of around 185°F, so that bubbles form slowly and break at the surface.

Simple. A menu term meaning coffee, tea, or other light food served without another food.

Singe. To remove hair or feathers by fire.

Skewer. A wooden or metal pin for securing meat or on which to place meat for roasting or barbecuing; also used as a verb, as to *skewer* a roast; see *attereaux* and *hatelet*.

Slice. To cut with a knife or mechanical slicer into thin pieces of fairly substantial size; not cut or chopped; to carve.

Smorgasbord. A buffet of light foods acting as appetizers; herring, butter, and rye bread are traditional components.

Smothered. Covered; *calf's liver smothered*, grilled calf's liver covered with fried or sautéed onions.

Soak. To immerse for an extended period of time in a liquid to rehydrate, to prevent from drying out, to keep from tarnishing in the air, or to preliminary step in cleaning.

Soubise. A sauce made from cooked puréed onions added to a béchamel sauce.

Soufflé. Puffed; a dish made light, usually by folding in beaten egg whites and baking; a puffed-up french-fried potato, either Irish or sweet.

Sous chef. Assistant to the head chef.

Sous cloche. See *cloche*.

Southern fried chicken. Dredged in flour and deep-fried; see *Maryland*.

Spanish. A tomato sauce with chopped ham or bacon, celery, carrot, and onion sautéed in bacon or ham fat, with added brown or tomato sauce; *Spanish omelet*, filled with tomatoes, peppers, onions, mushrooms, olives, celery, parsley, and spices; *Spanish cream*, a custard mixture firmed with gelatin, with whipped cream usually folded in just before the mixture sets.

Spareribs. Rib sections of pork behind the area from which the bacon is taken; corresponds to the bone section behind the plate and brisket in beef.

Spätzle. Austrian noodle made by running heavy noodle batter through a colander into boiling stock; used with braised meats.

Spit. A skewer on which meat is turned before open heat.

Sponge.   A cake made light with beaten eggs; a soft bread batter considered the first stage in bread production; a soft, light, aerated mixture.

Spoonbread.   A Southern soft bread made of cornmeal paste, eggs, and milk; actually a soufflé.

Springerle.   A cookie pressed with a mold before baking.

Spumone.   A rich Italian ice cream; sometimes spelled *spomoni*.

Squab.   A young pigeon that has not left the nest.

Squid.   A cephalopod related to the octopus; usually deep-fried after batter-dipping for hors d'oeuvres, or cooked with tomato or other sauces.

Steak and kidney pie.   See *beef steak pie.*

Steam.   To cook in steam, with or without pressure; the steam may be applied directly to the food, as in a steamer or pressure cooker.

Steep.   To allow a substance to stand in liquid at a temperature below the boiling point in order to extract flavor, color, or other qualities.

Stew.   To simmer or boil in a small bit of liquid; for meat, temperature is around 185°F; a meat and vegetable dish in gravy.

Steward.   Person who is in charge of purchasing and ordering and who may plan menus with chef; largely responsible for food cost.

Stilton.   An English blue cheese with a brown outer crust.

Stir.   To mix foods with a circular motion in order to blend or obtain a uniform consistency.

Stock.   A liquid seasoned by meat or vegetable essence.

Stollen.   A German yeast-leavened cake containing milk, eggs, butter, sugar, fruits, and nuts in addition to basic bread ingredients.

Stroganoff.   Sautéed beef in sauce of sour cream, mushrooms, and onions.

Strudel.   Viennese dessert consisting of thin sheets of cooked paste, fruits, cheese, honey, and other items.

Succotash.   A vegetable mixture of fresh corn and lima beans; tomatoes are sometimes added.

Suèdoise.   Swedish, a whipped cream sauce containing horseradish and apple-sauce.

Sukiyaki.   A Japanese dish of mixed vegetables sautéed in a light oil and seasoned with beef or other meat and a bit of sugar.

Supreme.   Of finest quality; velouté sauce to which heavy cream is added.

Sweetbreads.   Thymus glands of animals.

Sweet dough.   A yeast-leavened dough rich with sugar and eggs.

Sweetmeats.   Candies.

Swiss fondue.   See *fondue.*

Swiss steak.   A braised steak.

Tamale.   Meat in a rolled cornmeal dough, flavored with chili and baked or boiled in corn husks.

Tartar sauce.   Chopped onions, dill pickles, celery, shallots, chives, and parsley in mayonnaise with capers; most chefs specify that it contains no sweet pickles.

Tart.   Small pie or pastry-filled item; *tartelette,* small tart.

Tasse.   Small cup.

Tea.   A beverage served with dessert items such as tarts, cookies, small cakes, sandwiches, or other foods; *high tea,* elaborate service with quite fancy foods; *thé* (Fr.).

Terrine.   A stew or ragoût; an earthenware pot resembling a casserole.

Thermidor.   Cream sauce seasoned with wine and herbs; cream added to *sauce vin blanc.*

Thicken.   To add eggs, flour, or other products to foods and then to cook them until more firm; gelatin, rennet, and other products may be added to foods to thicken while cold.

Thousand island dressing. Mayonnaise and chili sauce with chopped eggs, green peppers, chives, and other items.

Timbale. A chopped or puréed meat, vegetable, or other food bound with eggs and baked in a mold or pan; may also be a crust or case in which foods are served.

Toad-in-the-hole. Sausages or meat baked or fried in batter.

Tomato sauce. Fine herbs sautéed, usually in salt pork, seasoned with bay leaf, thyme, and other seasonings, next cooked with tomato purée or paste and white or brown stock, and, then thickened with roux. This sauce is considered one of the basic sauces; it may or may not contain meat stock.

Torte. Pie or cake; rich, cakelike product.

Tortillas. Mexican flat pancake-type items containing cornmeal, flour, eggs, and seasonings into which seasoned meat or other items are rolled.

Tortoni. A frozen dessert containing tortoni biscuit (ground dried macaroons and chopped blanched almonds); usually a very rich ice cream is the base.

Toss. To mix lightly.

Tournedos. Small steaks cut from the narrow part of beef tenderloin about $1\frac{1}{2}$ in. thick. They resemble kernels or noisettes, which are the eye of the meat taken from lamb loins, pork loins, or other animals; weight is about $2\frac{1}{2}$ oz each; cooked much like filets, chateaubriands, or other tenderloin steaks.

Tourner. To cut or shape vegetables; also an expression used to indicate curdling.

Tourtière. Canadian meat pie containing salt pork.

Tranche. Slice of meat or bread; *tranche de saumon,* slice of salmon; *trancher,* to slice or carve; see *slice.*

Trifle. Sponge cake soaked in wine and served with sauce or whipped cream.

Tripe. Stomach of cattle.

Truffle. *Truffe* (Fr.); fungi grown in France in clusters below ground under oaks; pigs are trained to root them out; they resemble mushrooms, are black in color, and are used to flavor and garnish meat dishes; see *Périgeux.*

Turbot. A delicately flavored, white-fleshed fish.

Turn. To carve or trim in some manner; a *turned oliver* is a pitted olive, and a *turned mushroom* is a mushroom carved or decorated on the top.

Turnover. A baked or fried food encased in pie or puff paste.

Turtle. Reptile used largely to make soup; tenderest parts may be used for steaks.

Tutti-frutti. A mixture of fruits.

Veal cutlet. Slice of calves' meat from the leg; *veal cutlet Holstein,* bread cutlet sautéed in butter and served with fried egg, anchovy, and potatoes; see *wiener schnitzel; côtelette du veau* (Fr.); *veal birds,* dressing or forcemeat rolled in thin slices of veal cutlet and braised.

Velouté. A basic sauce of white stock thickened with *roux;* means *velvet* or *smooth;* may also be used to indicate a white stock. A fish velouté is a white stock or sauce made from lean white fish flesh and bones; the sauce is seasoned with white wine and may be called *sauce vin blanc.*

Venison. Flesh of all antlered members of the deer family: deer, caribou, elk, moose, and so forth.

Verjuice. Juice of unripe fruit; usually tart juice of grapes or apple; *verjus* (Fr.).

Vichy. Famous springs in France; vegetables cooked in this water had excellent flavor; now used to indicate boiled and buttered vegetables, usually sprinkled with parsley; most often applied to carrots.

Vichyssoisse. Hot or cold cream of potato soup; when cold, it is served with a garnish of chopped chives on top.

Villeroi. Allemande sauce seasoned with the article it accompanies; may be seasoned with mushroom and ham stock, with onions, or with tomatoes.

Vin. Wine; *vin de xérès,* sherry or Madeira-type wine.

Vinaigrette. Tart sauce; see *ravigote.*

Vin blanc sauce. See *velouté.*

Vol-au-vent. Puff paste shells to be filled with sauce mixtures, such as creamed chicken, braised lamb kidneys and mushrooms, or crab Newburg.

Waldorf. An apple salad containing celery and walnuts with a boiled or mayonnaise dressing.

Welsh rarebit. See *rarebit.*

Western sandwich. Chopped ham, green peppers, onions, and beaten egg, fried and served as a sandwich.

White sauce. Seasoned milk thickened with a starch paste; one of the basic neutral sauces; if cream is added, it is called *cream sauce.*

Wiener schnitzel. Breaded veal cutlet braised until tender and served with slice of lemon and anchovy fillet; some cooks bake the cutlet in sour cream or tomato sauce.

Woodcock. Small game bird; see *Scotch woodcock.*

Yankee pot roast. Braised pot roast with vegetables; frequently accompanied by dumplings or corn fritters.

Yorkshire buck. Welsh rarebit on poached egg on toast; *Yorkshire rabbit,* bacon instead of egg is used.

Yorkshire pudding. Popover batter poured into roast beef drippings and baked; served with roast beef, with some *au jus* spooned over it.

Zeste. The colored part of the peel of citrus fruit.

Zwieback. Hard, crisp bread toasted and then baked again until thoroughly dry; a rusk.

Bibliography

Cameron, Allan. *The Science of Food and Cooking.* 3d ed. Philadelphia: Trans-Atlantic Publishers, 1973.

Ecstein, Eleanor. *Menu Planning.* 3d ed. New York: Van Nostrand Reinhold, 1983.

Eschback, Charles. *Foodservice Management.* New York: Van Nostrand Reinhold, 1974.

Fuller, John. *The Professional Chef's Guide to Kitchen Management.* New York: Van Nostrand Reinhold, 1985.

Gaman, P. M., and Sherrington, K. B. *The Science of Food.* 2d ed. Elmsford, N.Y.: Pergamon Press, 1981.

Gates, June. *Basic Foods.* New York: Holt, Rinehart and Winston, 1981.

Gisslen, Wayne. *Professional Cooking.* New York: John Wiley & Sons, 1983.

Khan, Mahmood A. *Foodservice Operations.* New York: Van Nostrand Reinhold, 1987.

Kinder, Faye, and Green, Nancy R. *Meal Management.* 6th ed. New York: Macmillan, 1983.

Knight, John, and Kotschevar, Lendal H. *Quantity Food Production, Planning, and Management.* 2d ed. New York: Van Nostrand Reinhold, 1989.

Kotschevar, Lendal H. *Management by Menu.* 2d ed. New York: John Wiley & Sons, 1986.

Kotschevar, Lendal H. *Quantity Food Purchasing.* 3d ed. New York: Macmillan, 1987.

Kotschevar, Lendal H., and Terrell, Margaret. *Foodservice Planning.* 2d ed. New York: Macmillan, 1985.

Longgree, Karla. *Quantity Food Sanitation.* 3d ed. New York: John Wiley & Sons, 1980.

McWilliams, Margaret. *Food Fundamentals.* 3d ed. New York: Macmillan, 1979.

Medved, Eva. *Food Preparation Principles and Theory.* New York: Prentice-Hall, 1986.

Miller, Jack. *Menu Pricing and Strategy.* 2d ed. New York: Van Nostrand Reinhold, 1987.

Mizer, David, et al. *Food Preparation for the Professional.* 2d ed. New York: John Wiley & Sons, 1987.

Morgan, William J. *Food Preparation Principles.* 3d ed. Berkeley, Calif.: McCutchan Publishing, 1976.

Newmark, Norma, et al. *Food Preparation Principles and Procedures.* 6th ed. Dubuque, Iowa: William C. Brown, 1973.

Paul, Pauline C., et al. eds. *Food Theory and Applications.* New York: Macmillan, 1972.

Potter, Norman N. *Food Science.* 4th ed. New York: Van Nostrand Reinhold, 1986.

Powers, Jo Marie. *Basics of Quantity Food Preparation.* New York: John Wiley & Sons, 1979.

Powers, Thomas. *Foodservice Operations: Planning and Control.* New York: John Wiley & Sons, 1980.

Scanlon, Nancy Loman. *Marketing by Menu*. New York: Van Nostrand Reinhold, 1985.

Still, Jean. *Food Selection and Preparation*. New York: Macmillan, 1981.

Terrell, Margaret E. *Professional Food Preparation*. 2d ed. New York: Macmillan, 1979.

Vail, Gladys, et al. *Foods*. 7th ed. Boston: Houghton Mifflin, 1979.

Van Duyn, K. A. *Successful Kitchen Operation and Staff Management Handbook*. Englewood Cliffs, N.J.: Prentice Hall, 1976.

Index